AMERICAN POLITICS AND SOCIETY

NINTH EDITION

DAVID McKAY

WILEY Blackwell

This edition first published 2018
© 2018 John Wiley & Sons Ltd

Edition History

Edition history: Martin Robertson (1e, 1983, and 2e, 1989), Blackwell Publishers (3e, 1993, 4e, 1997, and 5e, 2001), Blackwell Publishing Ltd (6e, 2005, and 7e, 2009), John Wiley & Sons Ltd (8e, 2013)

Registered Offices

John Wiley & Sons, Inc., 111 River Street, Hoboken, NJ 07030, USA
John Wiley & Sons Ltd, The Atrium, Southern Gate, Chichester, West Sussex, PO19 8SQ, UK

Editorial Office

9600 Garsington Road, Oxford, OX4 2DQ, UK

For details of our global editorial offices, customer services, and more information about Wiley products visit us at www.wiley.com.

Wiley also publishes its books in a variety of electronic formats and by print-on-demand. Some content that appears in standard print versions of this book may not be available in other formats.

Library of Congress Cataloging-in-Publication Data

Names: McKay, David H.
Title: American politics and society / David McKay.
Description: Ninth edition. | Hoboken, NJ : Wiley-Blackwell, 2017. | Includes
   bibliographical references and index.
Identifiers: LCCN 2017002327 (print) | LCCN 2017002996 (ebook) | ISBN
   9781119167532 (paperback) | ISBN 9781119167556 (Adobe PDF) | ISBN
   9781119167549 (ePub)
Subjects: LCSH: United States—Politics and government. | BISAC: POLITICAL
   SCIENCE / General.
Classification: LCC JK275 .M337 2017 (ebook) | LCC JK275 (print) | DDC
   320.473—dc23
LC record available at https://lccn.loc.gov/2017002996

Cover images: (Stars, USA Flag) © LuVo/Gettyimages; (Lincoln Statue) © Gary Morrow / EyeEm/Gettyimages; (Voters) © Blend Images – Hill Street Studios/Gettyimages; (The White House) © Richard Nowitz/Gettyimages; (The Statue of Liberty) © Marcel Germain/Gettyimages
Cover design by Wiley

Set in 10/13pt Minion Pro by Aptara

Printed in Singapore by C.O.S. Printers Pte Ltd

1   2018

BRIEF CONTENTS

CONTENTS

LIST OF PLATES

LIST OF FIGURES

LIST OF TABLES

PREFACE TO
THE NINTH EDITION

Donald Trump's surprising victory in the 2016 presidential elections was significant in a number of respects. It was, of course a victory only in the Electoral College – his rival Hillary Clinton actually polled almost 3 million more popular votes than her opponent. Nonetheless, it heralded a new period in American politics that was to be in stark contrast to the Obama years. With Republican control of both the presidency and Congress the stage was set for the implementation of a range of policies long proposed by the Republican right including deregulation, immigration and tax reform, the repeal of President Obama's health-care reforms, and a major change in the direction of American foreign and foreign economic policy. 2016 also brought into sharp relief the deep social and regional divisions in American politics. Ethnic and sexual minorities, educated women and the bulk of the population in the larger coastal cities continue to support the Democratic agenda, while working class whites and especially those in the South, the Midwest and rural areas were solid in their support for Republican candidates.

For eight years Barack Obama found it hard to achieve great legislative success or to project to the wider world the will of a unified nation. Instead, the polarization that had characterized American politics since the 1990s continued. While Donald Trump enjoys the advantages of unified government, the checks and balances in the American constitutional system, not to mentions divisions in the Republican Party, will continue to ensure that conflict over means and ends in both domestic policies such as government spending, health care and public morality, and over the American role abroad will persist. Democrats continue to favour multilateral solutions to international problems, while the Republicans support a more belligerently unilateral role on issues ranging from trade with China to climate change, to the Iranian nuclear programme and achieving peace in the Middle East. So, as the world looks to the US for leadership in economic and foreign policy, the pluralism and complexity that characterizes the American political system will continue to limit what presidents can do.

These problems are the unifying theme of the ninth edition of *American Politics and Society*. Both Americans and non-Americans continue to have high expectations of the world's most powerful government, but rarely are these expectations fulfilled. Instead, the system is increasingly characterized by adversarial politics, with one side constantly blaming the other for policy failures. As in earlier editions, these political conflicts are at all times both placed in careful institutional context and related to the broader historical environment – both domestic and international.

I would like to thank the Department of Government, University of Essex for their support over what is now 30 years since the first edition of this book appeared. I trust it is as fresh and stimulating now as it was then. Justin Vaughan and Liz Wingett of Wiley-Blackwell provided typically professional advice and direction throughout. Finally, thanks to my wife Sherri Singleton and to my daughter Isla Singleton-McKay for their always positive and encouraging support.

Mistley, Essex

February 2017

CHAPTER 1
GOVERNING IN A POLARIZED SOCIETY

Outline

- The Chapters to Come
- Note
- Glossary

A State divided into a small number of rich and a large number of poor will always develop a government manipulated by the rich to protect the amenities represented by their property.

– HAROLD LASKI, BRITISH POLITICAL THEORIST (1893–1950)

American Politics and Society, Ninth Edition. David McKay.
© 2018 John Wiley & Sons Ltd. Published 2018 by John Wiley & Sons Ltd.

The last edition of this book emphasized the political importance of growing income and wealth inequality in the United States. Since then this phenomenon has grown in importance. Nobel Laureate Paul Krugman has shown how this growing inequality is in stark contrast to the middle years of the twentieth century when America experienced what has been called a 'Great Compression' or incomes and wealth becoming more equally distributed. Since then, however, the rich have increased their share of income and wealth substantially, while the real incomes of poorer Americans have stagnated or even fallen.[1] In addition, beginning in the 1980s and accelerating since the late 1990s, American politics has been increasingly characterized by ideological polarization on a wide range of non-economic issues ranging from foreign policy, immigration and the environment to moral issues such as abortion, prayers in public schools and sexual minorities' rights. Today, the Republicans are consistently on the right on these issues while the Democrats are (slightly less consistently) on the left. The upshot has been the emergence of a much more confrontational and abrasive style of politics centred on the proper role of government in society. Interestingly these differences do not easily align with the 'traditional' position of Democrats and Republicans on the role of government. In particular, categorizing the Republican Party as the 'hands off' party is difficult to reconcile with the extraordinary appeal of Donald Trump in 2016, who argued for a greatly enhanced federal government role in foreign affairs, trade policy and immigration, as well calling for major reforms of federal taxation and health care. Meanwhile the Democrats remain active supporters of big government in social policy, the environment, many aspects of the economy and civil rights. There is, in fact, a deep paradox here, because for much of the history of the Republic, Americans have been suspicious of big government both in terms of its role in domestic affairs and in terms of its role in the wider world. Unlike the citizens of most West European states – and indeed of America's immediate neighbours, Mexico and Canada – Americans have always mistrusted the very *idea* of big government. Low taxes and limited public spending have been populist rallying cries since the beginning of the Republic. Today, however, the US has, in absolute terms, by far the largest government of any country on earth, which provides for a vast array of social and economic programmes as well as military forces and commitments with global reach.

At the inception of the Republic, no question aroused as much passion as did the proper scope of the federal government in society. What the Founding Fathers decided on was an institutional structure that required the assent of several diverse constituencies (those electing the House, Senate and president) before a bill was passed. The presidential power of veto provided an additional check on government, as did the institution of federalism, which served further to fragment government in the new republic. These institutional features were both a product of and reinforced by a public philosophy of limited government. From the very beginning Americans accepted that government was a necessary evil and that essential services such as law and order, sanitation and education should be provided by state and local rather than the federal government. The first 10 amendments to the Constitution (the Bill of Rights) provided citizens with legal protection from a potentially intrusive central government. In particular, the First Amendment rights of freedom of speech, assembly and religion were designed to act as bulwarks against the power of the state. Americans also mistrusted standing armies. Instead they placed their faith in a people's militia or, later, in armies and navies that would be largely disbanded once a national emergency had passed.

What is remarkable about the ensuing 150 years of American history is just how powerful an influence this public philosophy was. For it was not until the 1930s and the 1940s that the federal government assumed a permanent and extensive role in social policy and defence. But many Americans remain deeply ambivalent about these new functions. Support for the particular benefits provided by a range of social programmes such as Medicare and social security is high, but, as the battles over federally mandated health care show, antipathy to the general notion of the federal government supporting those in need remains. Politicians preach the virtues of less government and lower taxes while promising to defend existing programmes. A similar tension exists in a range of conscience issues. Those who want to protect 'family values' are usually opponents of big government, yet the advance of their agenda would require government action to curb individual choice in such areas as abortion, stem cell research and the rights of sexual minorities. Politicians known to be tough on crime support an extension of the powers of government, including those of federal agencies such as the Department of Homeland Security (DHS). But these very same politicians often preach the virtues of limited government.

Nowhere is this tension more obvious than in foreign and defence policy. Public support for a major world role waxes and wanes according to the historical circumstances. It was high during and immediately after the Second World War, but fell dramatically in the aftermath of defeat in Vietnam. Even so the need to balance the power of the Soviet Union required the Americans to retain large armed forces, including the nuclear deterrent, whether they liked it or not. With the demise of the old communist enemy most commentators expected the US to take on a different role aimed at least in part towards advancing a humanitarian agenda, as the interventions in Somalia, Bosnia and Kosovo showed. After 9/11 all this was to change. US interventions abroad became justified as part of the war on terrorism. By definition, this involved the sort of military role associated with big government and strong states. Following the difficulties involved in the interventions in Iraq and Afghanistan the tide turned once again, but, as far as those on the political right were concerned, not against a strong American role over such issues as nuclear weapons in Iran and North Korea, so much as against messy, expensive – and ultimately unwinnable – ground wars in distant lands fighting elusive enemies such the Islamic State (ISIS).

Of course, the balance between limited government and an expanded federal role ebbs and flows as historical events such as recessions and wars change values and interests, but never has it taken on the form it has today, with both Democrats and Republicans deeply divided on the role of government, and with Republicans in particular unable to reconcile their traditional antipathy to government with the need for decisive federal government intervention in such areas as immigration, health care, trade policy and tax reform.

For an introductory textbook, ideological conflict in the context of deep ambiguity on the proper role of government provides a useful theme. It helps international comparison. In comparable countries – Britain, France, Italy, Japan and Germany there have also been signs of polarization – although not in the form of a simple binary choice that now dominates many aspects of American politics. Instead, mainstream parties have persisted although often at the expense of allowing extremist parties of the right and left to increase their voter appeal. Nor do these countries display the same level of uncertainty about the role of government or the 'state' as do Americans. Most citizens of France and Germany are perfectly happy to see the government provide for a wide range of services in welfare, transport and economic development. Americans, by way of contrast, often seem to resent the role of the government in these areas while at the same time expecting the government to play a prominent role, especially during times of emergency or economic dislocation. *American Politics and Society* constantly makes comparisons of this sort, so educating students on the importance of a set of uniquely American beliefs and values.

These values are, of course, articulated in the context of the institutional structure of American politics. This structure has been the subject of much criticism in recent years. Critiques have been based in part on specific institutional arrangements, and in particular the separation of powers. With one party often controlling the presidency and another Congress, governing has, so the argument runs, become more difficult than in the past. Underpinning this critique is the simple fact that the American public has an unusually high degree of access to their political institutions – whether at the local, state or national levels. Access is facilitated not only by the sheer number and variety of democratically accountable political institutions, from local school boards through to the US Congress, but also by the fact that Americans take their First Amendment rights to express their views very seriously. Thus, the many points of access for the expression of the democratic will are combined with a high expectation on the part of the public that their demands will be translated into policy.

The great paradox of the American arrangements is, of course, that open and free access to decision-makers does *not* always translate into the satisfaction of public demands. Often the very institutional complexity of the system cancels out competing demands and leads to no change or incremental rather than radical change. It is this dynamic that explains many of the policy problems of recent years, such as continuing battles over reform of the health-care system and immigration. Institutional arrangements thus facilitate the airing of sometimes-strident public demands while often limiting what governments can actually do. Given the deepening ideological divide which has accentuated the intensity of public demands, it is perhaps unsurprising that public frustration with political institutions has increased markedly over the past three decades.

These problems were more than amply illustrated during the 2016 presidential election campaign. On the left the eventual Democratic nominee, Hillary Clinton had to fend off an often-close challenge from Senator Bernie Saunders, who as self-avowed socialist tapped into an unsatisfied demand among many Americans, and in particular the better educated young, for radical solutions to reduce wealth and income inequality. Meanwhile the Republican Party was in the midst of a political civil war between the far right represented by Ted Cruz, the moderate right represented by John Kasisch and the insurgent populism of Donald Trump, whose agenda included Draconian solutions to a wide range of issues, but in particular immigration, trade policy and tax reform. In the event Donald Trump's populism prevailed and in a dramatic upset his brand of populism won him a narrow victory over Hillary Clinton in the ensuing general election. His success will no doubt serve to sharpen further the ideological divide in American politics.

Chapters to Come

The main purpose of this book is to lead the student through the main institutions of American federal government while at all times placing these institutions in a broader economic, social and comparative context.

Chapter 2 is devoted to a discussion of the role of beliefs and values in American politics and how these link into the broader society and economy. As such it places a special emphasis on the remarkable way in which the tension in American political thought between the philosophy of limited government and high public expectations of the democratic process has been accommodated within a uniquely *American* ideology. Chapters 3 to 15 cover the main institutions and processes of American government, with each designed to provide basic information and to discuss the relevance of historical trends as well as the relevance of recent research findings in political science. Special attention is paid to the relationship between, on the one hand, the institutional structure of government and, on the other, the public's expectations of the performance of politicians and political processes. Chapters 16 to 20 are designed to add substance and perspective to earlier chapters by examining the policy process in five currently crucial areas: the regulation of public morality in such areas as civil rights; social policy; economic policy; the environment; and foreign policy. Chapter 21 attempts to assess the performance of American government over the past decade. Through the use of comparisons with other countries, the chapter makes an audit of the political system and provokes students critically to evaluate the government in terms of democratic responsiveness and public accountability. Particular attention is paid to the ways in which the US is now perceived from abroad, and whether or not we are entering a new era where American power and influence are on the wane.

The general orientation of this and earlier chapters reflects my conviction that the study of political institutions can be productive only when placed in the broader comparative and historical perspective. The alternative is to condemn the reader to an uninspired descriptive account, which is a fate I would not want to impose on any student of what is one of the most interesting subjects in social science.

Glossary

Great Depression   The economic dislocation during the 1929–38 period

Note

1   Paul Krugman, *The Conscience of a Liberal* (New York and London: Allen Lane/Penguin Books, 2007).

CHAPTER 2
BELIEFS, VALUES AND AMERICAN SOCIETY

It has been our fate as a nation, not to have ideologies but to be one.

– RICHARD HOFSTADTER

The American ideology can be described in five words: liberty, egalitarianism, individualism, populism and laissez faire.

– SEYMOUR MARTIN LIPSET

American Politics and Society, Ninth Edition. David McKay.
© 2018 John Wiley & Sons Ltd. Published 2018 by John Wiley & Sons Ltd.

The Nature of American Beliefs and Values

One of the most enduring debates in social science concerns the relationship between the mass public's beliefs and values and political authority. Liberal scholars label these beliefs 'political culture', or 'a historical system of widespread, fundamental, behavioural, political values actually held by system members (the public)'.[1] Political culture therefore embraces the dominant pattern of beliefs and values which are acquired and modify and change as a result of a complex process of socialization and feedback from the political system. In other words, individual citizens acquire attitudes towards politics through learning from parents and from their environment (socialization), and these adapt and change as political authorities produce particular responses or policies over time (feedback). Political culture is made up of the sum of individual beliefs and values and, crucially, it is essentially *independent* of political authority. In some systems it may be incompatible with prevailing political institutions – as in Spain during the 1970s when an authoritarian regime was replaced by democracy, or in Weimar Germany before the rise of Hitler – in which case regime change occurs. In other systems, ethnic, religious, racial, cultural or linguistic divisions may be so great that no single political culture and institutional structure can accommodate these differences. In such cases civil war may ensue or the country may break up. The break-up of the former Soviet Union, Yugoslavia and Czechoslovakia could be explained in this way, as can events in modern-day Iraq, Syria and Afghanistan. In other cases again, the political culture supports and succours the political system. Liberal scholars invariably label the modern American system thus. Politics and political culture may change in the USA, but they tend to be mutually supportive. Regime change is extremely unlikely in such a situation.

Radical critics of the political culture perspective argue that public beliefs and values are imposed from above by those in positions of power. Beliefs constitute an *ideology*, therefore, whose function is to legitimate the prevailing system of political authority and economic organization. This radical perspective identifies the United States as a country where a dominant ideology imposed by powerful elites is particularly influential:

> The dominant ideology is more powerful in the United States than in any other capitalist democracy. Most political debates in the United States take place within the framework of this ideology. … So powerful is the dominant ideology in this country that existing economic and political arrangements frequently appear not merely as the best possible arrangements but as the only possible ones.[2]

These two apparently incompatible positions are not as far apart as they may seem, for when American beliefs are examined, both liberals and radicals accept the importance of similar attitudes and values held by the mass of the population. Most scholars agree that the ideology is made up of liberty, egalitarianism, individualism, democracy, populism and the rule of law under a constitution.[3] As the following summary shows, within this system of beliefs and values there are a number of tensions, and especially those involving conflicts between equality and inequality and between freedom and security. Often these tensions concern ambiguity over the proper role of government in American society.

Liberty

Survey research starting in the 1950s and continuing to this day found a high level of support among Americans in favour of *general* statements of free speech and opinion (for example, 'People who hate our way of life should still have a chance to talk and be heard'), but much lower support for *specific* statements (for example, 'A book that contains wrong political views cannot be a good book and does not deserve to be published').[4] Moreover, the level of support for specific freedoms was much higher among elites (politically influential people) than among the mass public. This disjunction between general and specific support is not exclusively American; citizens of many countries would answer positively to general statements advocating freedom. Clearly, freedom of expression is not an absolute value, and there have been times in American history when public tolerance of 'un-American' values has been very low. The anti-communist hysteria following the First and Second World Wars demonstrated just how limited freedom could be in the United States.[5] And until the mid-1960s the attitude of white Americans in the South towards the African American population was the very opposite of libertarian, based as it was on systematic racial segregation and discrimination.

Since the 1960s, however, there has been evidence of some important changes. Racial tolerance has generally improved, and attitudes towards 'un-American' beliefs (communism, atheism) have become more liberal, as have attitudes towards sexual minorities. Note also, that increasingly libertarian attitudes towards people with racist views (see figures 2.1a–2.1d). In spite of these changes, antipathy to 'non-American' values, including today those associated with Islam, clearly remains, so it would be misleading to characterize the United States as a country where 'freedom of expression' or 'liberty' is assigned an inviolate

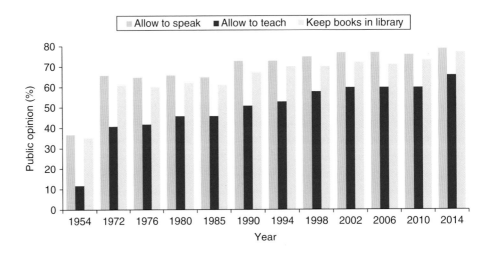

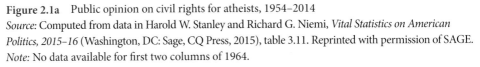

Figure 2.1a   Public opinion on civil rights for atheists, 1954–2014
Source: Computed from data in Harold W. Stanley and Richard G. Niemi, *Vital Statistics on American Politics, 2015–16* (Washington, DC: Sage, CQ Press, 2015), table 3.11. Reprinted with permission of SAGE.
Note: No data available for first two columns of 1964.

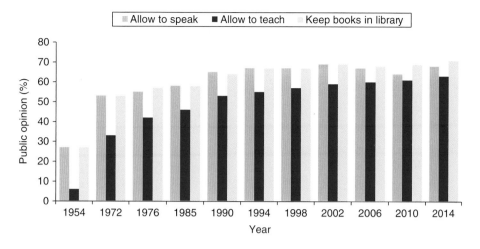

Figure 2.1b   Public opinion on civil rights for communists, 1954–2014
Source: Stanley and Niemi, *Vital Statistics on American Politics, 2015–16,* computed from table 3.11.
Reprinted with permission of SAGE.

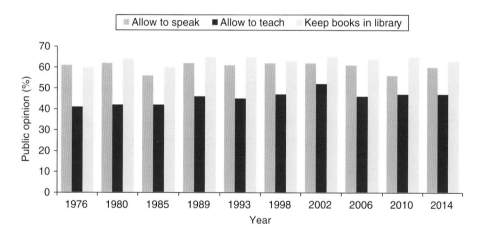

Figure 2.1c   Public opinion on civil liberties for racists, 1978–2014
Source: Stanley and Niemi, *Vital Statistics on American Politics, 2015–16,* computed from table 3.11.
Reprinted with permission of SAGE.

status. This is a question we will return to in chapter 13 when we discuss the implications of an increasingly intrusive security state for individual freedom.

Three final qualifications need to be added to this conclusion, which should serve as a warning against simple over-generalizations in this area. First, as later chapters show, there was a quite dramatic advance in the legal protection of all individual rights, and especially freedom of expression, from the 1960s through to 2001, although some evidence exists of a return to anti-libertarian values since then. Not all these advances have

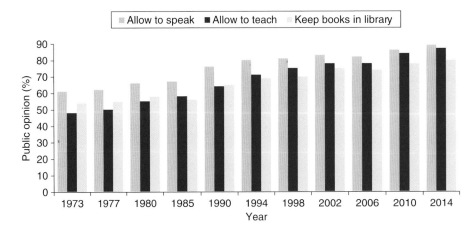

Figure 2.1d   Public opinion on civil liberties for homosexuals, 1973–2014
Source: Stanley and Niemi, *Vital Statistics on American Politics, 2015–16*, table 3.11. Reprinted with permission of SAGE.

been simply procedural. Objectively, American citizens, newspapers and other media now enjoy much more freedom than they used to. As this development can cause governments and officials serious difficulty and embarrassment, it seems to contradict claims that Americans are being manipulated by dominant elites.

Second, the American political system is uncommonly fragmented and devolved. Some of the worst examples of the infringement of individual freedom have occurred within *state* and *local* jurisdictions with the open acquiescence of local populations. This applies particularly to racial questions and criminal procedural rights. As society has become nationalized, so such activity has been exposed and has led to the spread of more uniform, federally imposed standards. Although far from being complete, the nationalization of standards has, of course, involved a more intrusive federal government. Many on the right argue that this expanded federal role represents an extension of governmental power beyond its proper limits. A very small minority on the extreme right goes further, and refuses to recognize the authority of the federal government. As we will see in later chapters, attempts to reduce the power of the federal government by returning power to states and localities may indeed limit the scope of government, but can also result in fewer freedoms for some.

Third, if we expand liberty or freedom to include economic individualism or the freedom to accumulate wealth and pass that wealth on to the next generation, then there is no doubting that the United States is a free country. Indeed, the US has very generous capital gains and – especially – inheritance tax laws, so much so in fact that very few of the beneficiaries of wills pay any tax at all.

Equality

Early foreign observers of the American scene, from de Tocqueville to Dickens and Bryce, noted the remarkable absence of deference to position or status in the United States.

'Equality of estimation' or esteem is what Bryce called it, or the tendency of Americans to treat each other as equals, whatever their education, occupation or social class. This remains broadly true – although, of course, other countries have been moving in the same direction. 'Equality' was one of the earliest rallying cries of revolutionary America, but from the very beginning it implied an equality of opportunity rather than equality of condition. The argument ran something like this: provide equal status for all citizens (except slaves, of course, and, in many contexts, women) under the law and every individual would be capable of achieving self-fulfillment. As the country developed, so it became accepted that the precondition for equality of opportunity was a certain standard of education. Consequently, education achieved – and retains – a very special status in American social policy. Almost alone among major social programmes, there is a broad consensus that education, at least at the elementary and secondary levels should be provided out of public rather than private funds.

Critics argue that the constant stress on equality of opportunity helps to legitimize what is a very unequal society. Originally the emphasis was on the frontier and unlimited land. More recently the appeal has shifted to education and all the benefits this can bring. By constantly reassuring the population that everyone can succeed given personal effort and a good educational base, the citizenry are, so the argument runs, being duped into accepting what are very considerable material inequalities in the society. No doubt there is something to this – certainly Americans have traditionally believed that their economic position (or the position of their children) would improve[6] – but such a perspective fails to distinguish between equality before the law and the material or economic benefits which equality of opportunity can bring. The former, which is close to equality of dignity or esteem, is highly developed in the United States and recognized as an important element in citizenship. Legislation designed to prevent unfair or unequal treatment by private bodies and authorities is far-reaching and, compared with similar laws in other countries, is quite rigidly enforced. In recent years discrimination against women and ethnic minorities has been the main focus of these laws, but the idea that all citizens, irrespective of background, should be treated equally is deeply entrenched, even if it is often not actually achieved.

Clearly such laws can be implemented in such a way that they conflict with those notions of individualism that underpin the philosophy of limited government. As the next section highlights, by placing the interests of the group above those of the individual's worth affirmative action can cause serious tensions between equality and individualism. The same is true of growing material inequality, which can only be redressed by public policies that single out the rich for increased taxation, the proceeds of which are redistributed to the less well off.

Individualism

Nothing more accurately seems to represent Americanism than a stress on individual rather than collective action. Trade-union membership is low in the USA, historically, collectivist political parties of the left (and also of the right) have failed to win mass support and the society is infused with a degree of self-reliance which is rarely found in other countries. This spirit of

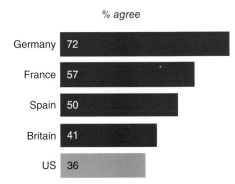

% agree

Germany	72
France	57
Spain	50
Britain	41
US	36

Figure 2.2a   Success in life is determined by forces outside our control, selected countries 2011
Source: Pew Research Center, Pew Global Attitudes Project, 'The American-West European Values Gap', 17 November 2011, question 15.a. Reprinted with permission of Pew Research Center Global Attitudes Project.

	Nobody in need	Freedom to pursue life's goals
US	35	58
Britain	55	38
Germany	62	36
France	64	36
Spain	67	30

Figure 2.2b   Which is more important: that nobody should be in need, or freedom to pursue life's goals? (%)
Source: Pew Global Attitudes Project, 17 November 2011, question 61. Reprinted with permission of Pew Research Center Global Attitudes Project.

self reliance has its roots in the Puritanism that flourished in both colonial and post-colonial America, and it remains a potent force, as public antipathy to welfare dependency and, in comparison with most European countries, a surprisingly wide acceptance of job insecurity show. For general indicators of American self-reliance in comparative context, see figures 2.2a and 2.2b.

So, as far as the distribution of resources is concerned, Americans prefer private to public institutions. Indeed, the 'state' as such is held in quite low esteem compared with its status in other countries. But we should be wary of inferring that Americans are always antipathetic to government-provided goods and services. The evidence suggests that when questions on government benefits are couched in general terms, Americans show antipathy to government provision, but when asked about specific programmes, such as social security, health care or education, they show a higher level of support.[7] More recently the growing inequality characteristic of the US economy has led many Americans to accept a more intrusive government role. Hence the popularity of socialist candidate Bernie Sanders in 2016, and the support for Donald Trump's Draconian policies on immigration and Muslim's freedom of movement during the same election campaign.

Notwithstanding these developments America's tradition of antipathy to government has a number of roots, and there is no space for an extensive discussion here. We should note, however, that this tradition has at least in part depended on the continuing success of capitalism. From beginnings where self-reliance and economic individualism were the very essence of the new society, capitalism flourished as in no other country, and not until the Great Depression of the 1930s did it need sustained support from government. Industrialization, infrastructure development and urbanization were provided by the private market, rather than, as in most European countries, by the central government. Of course government played a role, but mainly at the state level and in response to the needs of capitalism, not as a leader and director of investment and resources.

Moreover, as suggested, today, when government intrudes into almost every aspect of society, it continues to be treated with suspicion by many Americans. What is remarkable about this suspicion is just how deeply it is embedded in the American political culture – and even persists when, as during the 'Great Recession' of 2018–2012, capitalism falters badly. In comparable countries, including America's main economic competitors in Europe and Asia, and where governments have been dominant in economic development or in dictating the central – often elitist – values of the society, the citizenry are generally more accepting of a prominent central state.

Two further points on individualism. First, observers make the mistake of inferring a general *cultural* individualism when noting the undoubted prevalence of *economic* individualism in the United States. Yet as our discussion of freedom and references to religion suggests, collectivist thinking often influences Americans. Whether it is McCarthyism, fundamentalist Christianity or the recent incursions into civil liberties associated with the 'War on Terror', there is no short-age of examples of Americans moving, sometimes blindly, in masses. By this measure many Americans, especially at the local level, have often shown less respect for cultural variety than applies in more centralized 'cosmopolitan' countries such as Britain and France.

Second and related to this is the fact that laws designed to provide equality of opportu-nity often conflict with notions of individualism. Positive discrimination in favour of ethnic minorities, women or the disabled can mean the application of rules and standards intended to benefit whole social *groups*. In such instances, the merits of *individuals* are sometimes subordinated to those of the group. Hence racial or gender quotas applied to employment or admission to college give preference to particular groups at the expense of 'advantaged' indi-viduals who are not members of these groups (usually whites or Asians). This tension between equality and individualism has become an important issue in American politics.[8] Although it is very difficult to generalize in this area, many on the right and in the Republican Party favour laws that respect individual merit, while many on the left and in the Democratic Party favour laws which respect the collective interests of disadvantaged groups. In 1997 voters in California passed a law that outlawed the use of quotas in affirmative action, but the courts have yet to endorse a total ban on all positive discrimination programmes.

Another dimension to this debate concerns the periodic calls for government to play some role in reducing *material* inequalities. Hence during the 2010–16 period President Obama fought hard to preserve social programmes in such areas as welfare and health care even in the face of a huge budget deficit. The Republican-controlled House of Representatives and after 2014 the Senate, however, had quite different priorities and favoured tax reductions in tandem with budget cuts in the very social programmes that President Obama sought to preserve.

Democracy, populism and the rule of law

If democracy is defined in terms of a simple devotion to *majoritarianism* then there is no doubting that Americans believe in it. Majority opinion carries a weight and independent value in the USA that is unusual elsewhere. This does not only translate into a broad accep-tance of the legitimacy of elections and, at the state and local levels, initiatives and referen-dums. It also means that on occasion ill-judged policies and programmes have been adopted following a surge of (often populist) moral fervour. Such was the case with prohibition and, arguably, the search for 'quick fix' solutions to America's crime problems. Hence in the 1990s many states passed laws designed to ensure that repeat offenders were sent to prison for good. These 'three strikes and you're out' laws led to all sorts of anomalies, including the imposition of life sentences for minor offences and the release of long-term violent offenders to make room for such unfortunates. More recently, politicians have scrambled to demonstrate their resolve against terrorism with the 2001 Patriot Act passing through both houses of Congress with large majorities even although the new law allowed for a suspension of basic freedoms in some circumstances.

As far as general political arrangements are concerned, American attitudes present us with something of a paradox, for they combine strong *general* support for the Constitution and the system as such with considerable disillusionment with *particular* processes and institutions. One of the first and most impressive of the political culture studies discovered that Americans were overwhelmingly supportive of the political system and Constitution compared with other countries. True, this survey dates from the early 1960s when people were generally more optimistic about society, but there is still evidence that Americans believe their system to be basically sound (few want to emigrate; most greatly admire the constitutional framework).[9] However, since the mid-1970s increasing numbers of people have become disillusioned with the party system, the presidency, Congress and the federal bureaucracy.

One good surrogate measure of confidence in government is public satisfaction 'with the ways things are'. Public satisfaction declined during the recession of the early 1990s, but recovered during the prolonged economic boom years of the second Clinton administration. Malaise has set in again in the context of the long wars in Iraq and Afghanistan and continuing economic problems that persisted for the subsequent decade.

But too much can be read into these shifting sentiments. Citizens may often be disillusioned with particular institutions, governments or politicians, but they are not *alienated* from the system in a way that threatens the regime.[10] The institutions and processes that succour American democracy and the rule of law are highly respected. If anything, recent evidence of declining trust in government reflects an increasing sophistication among voters, who are now making more conscious connections between what parties and politicians promise and how they perform.

Claims that the system is essentially stable appear to be supported by the relative absence of regime-challenging parties and protest movements in American history. The Civil War apart, most protest activity has been inspired by single issues (civil rights, the Vietnam War), or has been accommodated within existing parties and institutions. Radical critics are quick to point out that this is because truly revolutionary movements have been nipped in the bud by an unholy alliance of corporations and government. But much more repressive tactics have been employed in other countries to no avail, which raises the question of why much less extensive measures should have been so successful in America.

More convincing perhaps is the claim that, unable to mobilize politically against the prevailing ideology, increasing numbers of Americans have turned to non-political violence and anti-social behaviour. There can be no doubting that America is a violent society (more than 13,000 people were murdered in 2015, although this figure has declined sharply since 1993, when more than 24,000 were murdered, and reached a low point in 2013), but it is extraordinarily difficult to make clear causal connections between this sort of pathology and political values and institutions. Violence and crime have always been a part of what was for many generations a frontier society. What we can conclude is that until the 1960s (and possibly beyond), violence and intimidation in the South were part of a southern social structure built on racism and exploitation. Obviously this was as much a political as a social or economic phenomenon. As significant are the continuing high (but falling) levels of random violence and serious crime among the racial and ethnic minorities of America's inner cities. There seems little doubt that these citizens are often politically excluded, isolated and socially alienated. For them, the optimism, materialism and egalitarianism that continue to dominate political discourse must either seem an irrelevance or serve as a diversion from their everyday lives.

We can conclude this section by noting what is undoubtedly the most important feature of the American political culture: its ability to accommodate apparently deep divisions over the role of government in society, without challenging the constitutional order or what many have defined as 'Americanism'. Such is the devotion to Americanism that it has been uniquely effective in overpowering other systems of beliefs and values. Samuel Huntington has made this point well:

> It is possible to speak of a body of political ideas that constitutes 'Americanism' in a sense which one can never speak of 'Britishism', 'Frenchism', 'Germanism' or 'Japanesism'. Americanism in this sense is comparable to other ideologies or religions. 'Americanism is to the American', Leon Samson has said, 'not a tradition or a territory, not what France is to a Frenchman or England to an Englishman, but a doctrine – what socialism is to a socialist'. To reject the central ideas of that doctrine is to be un-American. There is no British Creed or French Creed; the Académie Française worries about the purity of the French language, not about the purity of French political ideas. What indeed would be an 'un-French' political idea? But preoccupation with 'un-American' political ideas and behaviour has been a recurring theme in American life. 'It has been our fate as a nation', Richard Hofstadter succinctly observed, 'not to have ideologies but to be one.'[11]

Plate 2.1   Statue of Liberty
Source: Bruce Davidson/Magnum.

What is interesting about this ideological consensus is how it is supported by virtually all social and political groups – however antagonistic towards one another they may appear.

Plate 2.2   Registration day, 25 May 1918. Mrs Anne J. Curry, the first woman to sign her name on the registration sheets
Source: Corbis/Bettmann.

As Michael Foley notes, 'Americans fight each other in their efforts to expand the American creed'.[12] Even citizens from as close a country (geographically and culturally) as Canada find this phenomenon startling. What follows is a description of a Canadian's first encounter with the USA in the 1960s:

My first encounter with American consensus was in the late sixties, when I crossed the border into the United States and found myself inside the myth of America. Not of North America, for the myth stopped short of the Canadian and Mexican borders, but of a country that despite its arbitrary frontiers, despite its bewildering mix of race and creed, could believe in something called the True America, and could invest that patent fiction with all the moral and emotional appeal of a religious symbol…. Here was the Jewish anarchist Paul Goodman berating the Midwest for abandoning the promise; here the descendant of American slaves, Martin Luther King, denouncing injustice as a

violation of the American way; here an endless debate about national destiny ... conservatives scav-
enging for un-Americans, New left historians recalling the country to its sacred mission.

Nothing in my Canadian background had prepared me for this spectacle.... It gave me
something of an anthropologist's sense of wonder at the symbol of the tribe ... to a Canadian sceptic, a gentile in God's country [here was] a pluralistic, pragmatic people bound
together by an ideological consensus. Let me repeat that mundane phrase: *ideological consensus*. For it wasn't the idea of exceptionalism that I discovered in '68.... It was a hundred
sects and factions, each apparently different from the others, yet all celebrating the same
mission.[13]

In our discussion of the deep ambivalence which many Americans show towards the role
of the federal government in society and economy, it should always be remembered that,
no matter how fierce the ensuing ideological battles, almost all the protagonists believe that
their positions are true to essentially *American* political values. It is for this reason that what
so often look like deep and bitter political divisions, including the increased polarization
characteristic of the period since the late 1990s, almost never become the basis of challenges
to the constitutional order.

The remainder of this chapter is devoted to the ways in which these values interact with
the growth and present-day functioning of the American society and economy.

Values and American Society

Immigration and demographic change

Until the mid-nineteenth century the United States was an 'imperialist' continental power,
constantly expanding its territory by treaty, annexation and conquest. It was expansionist
both in the sense that it dominated the other continental powers – Mexico, Britain, France
and Spain – and in the sense that numerous Native American tribes were overwhelmed
by a technologically more advanced and populous society. It was, above all, America's
economic might that enabled it to swallow up huge tracts of territory during this period
(map 2.1). Population increases were also very considerable and did not fall below 20 per
cent per decade until 1920. Ever since then, the population has continued to grow rapidly:
there remains around a 10 per cent increase per decade – a remarkably high figure for
an advanced industrial country with a small agrarian population (figure 2.3). Both high
natural increases and immigration account for this population growth, although since 1971
there has been a small natural *decrease* for the white population.[14]

The United States was virtually built on an ideology of immigration, with successive
generations of Americans promoting the country as a land of freedom and opportunity.
The appeal was simple. Free from the corruption and oppression of Europe and rich in land
and natural resources, the United States could and did absorb vast numbers of immigrants,
first mainly from Britain, then from Germany, Ireland, southern and eastern Europe, and
most recently from Asia, Mexico, Cuba, Canada, the Caribbean and other American countries. As figure 2.4 shows, a high level of immigration continues even today, with more
than 1.3 million new Americans arriving in 2014 alone.

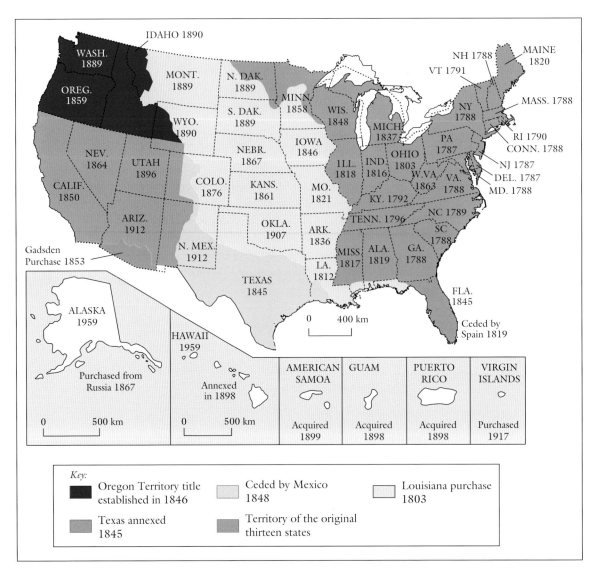

Map 2.1   US territorial expansion

Source: US Census, *Statistical Abstract of the USA 1981*, fig. 7.1 (p. 194).

Note: Dates under state names denote year of statehood.

In comparative context this is a high figure, for no other industrial country allows such an influx. During periods of labour shortage or political emergency, many European countries have encouraged some – often temporary – immigration, but none permits a continuing high level of immigration, which persists even during periods of high unemployment and low rates of economic growth. Not that mass immigration has gone unopposed. During and following the truly massive waves of immigration from southern and eastern Europe that occurred in the 1880–1910 period, opposition to what for many Americans represented an 'invasion' by alien cultures was fierce and finally culminated in the 1924 Immigration

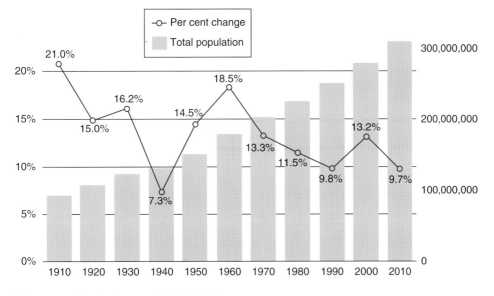

Figure 2.3   Population growth, 1910–2010
Source: US Census Bureau, population estimates, historical data, www.census.gov/popest/data/historical/index.html.

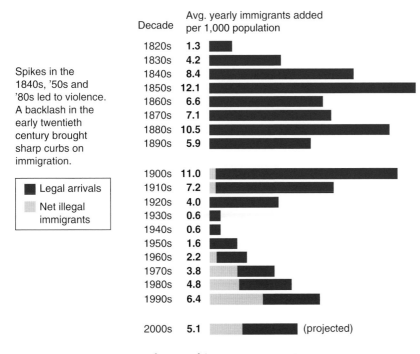

Figure 2.4   Immigration to the United States, 1820s to 2000s
Source: Pew Research Center at www.pewresearch.org/topics/immigration/.

Plate 2.3   Immigrants leaving Ellis Island, waiting for the ferry to New York c.1900
Source: Corbis/Bettmann.

Act. This law limited annual immigration to 150,000 and established preference quotas for the immediate family members of US citizens. The effect of this was to favour immigration from Canada and northern and western Europe. Immigration fell dramatically during the 1930s and 1940s as economic depression and war took their toll both on economic opportunity and on freedom of movement.

With immigration increasing once more after 1950, criticism of the patent biases in immigration law intensified, and in 1965 a new law was adopted with fairer, more balanced quotas. None the less, and following further amendments to the law in 1980, 1986 and 1996, immigration continued at between 2 and 4 per cent of the total population per decade and during the 1990s some 9.8 million immigrants arrived in the USA.[15]

Since about 1970 the immigration controversy has been fuelled anew by substantial illegal immigration, mainly from Mexico, and by the social tensions which large numbers of Cuban, Haitian and Central American newcomers have brought, especially to Florida and the southwestern states. Illegal immigration has accelerated as poorer Mexicans have sought employment across a long and poorly policed border. Estimates of the numbers involved vary widely, but are at least in the low millions (figure 2.4). In 2010 Arizona passed a particularly tough immigration law that empowered state officials to stop any individual suspected of being an illegal and demand proof of citizenship. The ensuing backlash from the state's Hispanic community helped to politicize the issue not only in Arizona but throughout the country. In 2012 the Supreme Court invalidated part of the law but the 'show your papers' provision remains. A number of states have since enacted similar laws. Very generally, Republican politicians take a harder line on illegal immigration, while Democrats, although they condemn it, are more prepared to accept that the government has some responsibility towards supporting the families of illegal immigrants, and especially the children of illegals who, they argue, are blameless and should be provided with educational and other benefits. During the 2016 presidential campaign the issue reached a new level of intensity with Republican candidate Donald Trump threatening mass deportation of illegal immigrants and the erection of a wall all the way across the US–Mexican border. We will return to this theme in later chapters.

As the country and economy have grown, so both the composition and spatial distribution of the population have changed. Obviously, with mass immigration during the nineteenth and early twentieth centuries the country became more ethnically diverse, and although these earlier immigrants are now generally assimilated into American society, many retain some national, ethnic or religious identity, which has its origins in Europe. More recently, immigration and high relative birth rates have led to substantial increases in the Asian and, in particular, the Hispanic populations. By 2015 18 per cent of the population was Hispanic in origin (mainly Mexican, Puerto Rican and Cuban) and 13.2 per cent black. For recent figures and projections see figure 2.5.

The most important manifestation of anti-immigrant sentiment occurred with the defeat of the comprehensive Immigration Reform Act 2007. This law would have granted a limited amnesty to millions of illegal immigrants, and although sponsored by President Bush it

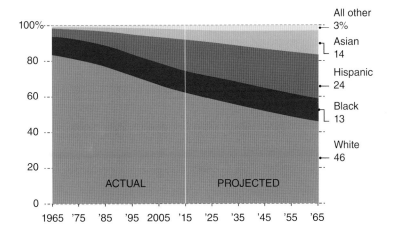

Figure 2.5   Projections: resident population by ethnic origin, 1965–2065
Source: US Census at www.pewresearch.org/fact-tank/2016/01/27/the-demographic-trends-shaping-american-politics-in-2016-and-beyond/.
Note: Whites, blacks and Asians include only single-race non-Hispanics; Asians include Pacific Islanders. Hispanics can be of any race.

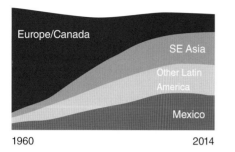

Figure 2.6   Statistical portrait of US foreign born population, 1960–2014
Source: Pew Research Center at www. pewhispanic.org/2016/04/19/statistical-portrait-of-the-foreign-born-population-in-the-united-states-key-charts/.

failed to win enough support in the Senate to ensure passage. Much of the opposition came from Republicans, who saw it as official approval for illegal immigration. Republicans also generally oppose the DREAM Act (acronym for Development, Relief, and Education for Alien Minors) that would grant young illegal immigrants a limited right to stay in the US – with the possibility of permanency later – should they achieve a certain educational standard or have served in the military. However, as of 2016, the law had failed to pass through Congress, although the Obama administration DACA programme (Deferred Action for Childhood Arrivals) effectively provided the protection of the DREAM proposal to alien minors.

In the case of the Hispanic population, a linguistic as well as an ethnic dimension is involved, for Spanish is the mother tongue for many, and in some areas, notably California and the southwest, demands have been made for an official bilingualism. However, no state has such a policy and in recent years state initiatives have been introduced to limit bilingualism in elementary and secondary education. The dramatic shift from European to Hispanic and other sources of immigration is shown vividly in Figure 2.6.

America today is a highly urban society, the number of people living in metropolitan areas reaching 81 per cent of the population in 2015. One interesting post-1970 trend has been an increase in the non-farming rural population. Agricultural employment has declined sharply over the past 30 years and most people actually living in the country are not, in the main, farmers, but people seeking a new lifestyle away from the crowded cities and suburbs. Indeed, the growth of smaller towns and rural areas is a general phenomenon in advanced industrial societies.

None the less, urban areas are still growing, although not in a uniform or even manner. The inner or central areas of many of the older industrial cities continue to decline, although since the 1980s a number of these cities have experienced a revival of their downtown areas. In addition there have been some quite dramatic changes in the distribution of population among the largest metropolitan areas. Two broad trends can be discerned. First is the very rapid growth of the southern and western cities and the relative decline of the northern cities. This is, of course, part of the 'Sunbelt–Snowbelt' divide much talked of in the 1970s. Second, since 1990 there have been clear signs of revival among some of the older metropolitan areas, with, for example, the Chicago, New York and Cleveland areas showing renewed growth. At the same time, some of the Sunbelt cities' growth rates has slowed – especially after the housing crash in 2008 that seriously affected employment and population growth. These figures should, however, be treated with some caution. The metropolitan census areas cover large urban agglomerations, which contain within them many variations. Within the Detroit region, for example, the central part of the city of Detroit continues to decline while many of the surrounding suburbs, towns and cities are still growing.

CONTROVERSY 1   IMMIGRATION: THE CHANGING NATURE OF THE DEBATE

Immigration has been a source of controversy in American politics since the first part of the nineteenth century. Throughout, critics of immigration have argued that mass immigration would 'flood' the country with people who were culturally alien and/or would fail to contribute economically. Hence, the Irish, southern and eastern European, Jews, East Asians (Chinese and Japanese) and, most recently, Southeast Asians and, in particular, Hispanics from Central and South America have successively been the target of anti-immigrant sentiment (for the changing ethnic mix of immigrants, see Figure 2.6).

Originally, opposition came from 'nativist' Americans, or those who believed that the 'purity' of the northern European Protestant stock would be corrupted by the new arrivals. Indeed, the 1924 Immigration Act was specifically designed to favour northwest Europeans. In the event, the southern and eastern Europeans against whom the law was directed became fully assimilated into American society. Today the debate is argued on what at first look like different grounds, although racist nativist sentiment persists in places. There are three main dimensions to the current debate. First, opponents of immigration argue that many Hispanics, and especially immigrants of Mexican origin, hold a greater allegiance to the mother country than to the USA. Unlike earlier waves of immigrants, they maintain their linguistic and cultural identity across generations. Second, illegal immigration is widespread across poorly policed borders. Third, they argue that during difficult economic times, the new immigrants – and especially their children – constitute a strain on hard-pressed education, welfare and social services. During the 2016 presidential campaign Donald Trump's call for a wall to be built across the US–Mexican border was reminiscent of some the more extreme nativist sentiments of the early part of the twentieth century.

While illegal immigration is a serious problem – although hardly a new one – the other criticisms have little foundation in fact. We simply do not know how the Mexican American community will develop over time. Precisely the same criticisms were directed at Italian, Jewish and Polish communities at the beginning of the twentieth century. As for constituting an economic burden on social services, in the longer run the opposite is likely, for immigrants play a large part in bringing down the average age of the American population. As such they or their progeny may be the very people who will pay the taxes to finance the pensions and medical care of older, longer-established Americans. None the less, anti-immigrant sentiment has been on the rise, as the debates in the 2016 presidential election campaign and the subsequent election and policies of Donald Trump show.

One of the most interesting features of American urbanization is that for the most part it has not resulted in what in some countries is identified as a dominant metropolitan culture focused on one or a few dominant cities. Unlike in Britain, France, Russia or Mexico, no American urban area has a monopoly on economic, social and political power. Instead it is spread among a number of centres. In addition, Americans have always mistrusted urban sophistication. They have instead idealized rural and small-town America, which many continue to see as the representation of traditional American values such as democracy and community.

Economic change

From very humble beginnings the American economy had grown to the world's largest by the end of the nineteenth century, and by 1945 the United States had established an effective global hegemony in economic affairs. America's per capita income was easily the highest in the world for a large country, and the economy had achieved a remarkable degree of self-sufficiency. By 2015 the economy had grown to a staggering $17.9 trillion and the median annual family income was around $53,000. As the economy has grown so there has been a shift, first out of agricultural employment into manufacturing and, most recently, out of manufacturing into service industries. By 2015 less than only 0.6 per cent of the labour force was employed in agriculture – even though the USA is the world's largest food producer. Of the non-agricultural labour force those employed in goods-related jobs (mining, construction, transportation and manufacturing) fell from 37.7 per cent in 1960 to around 11.5 per cent in 2015, while service sector jobs increased to over 75 per cent of the total. With most Americans working in the service sector (managerial, technical, office, sales, government, education, health, transport and distribution), talk of a post-industrial society is not entirely misplaced – although it is only through great productivity advances in agriculture and manufacturing that the economy is able to sustain such a diversity of service sector jobs.

In spite of these improvements, the American economy began to experience difficulties in the early 1970s, which led many to challenge the long-held notion that the USA was the land of economic opportunity and upward mobility. Some of these derived from world economic problems, but others were a result of peculiarly American circumstances. Very generally, US productivity increases did not keep pace with those of major competing countries. Concern at the apparent 'deindustrialization' of the USA increased perceptibly during the early 1980s as unemployment rose and industrial output fell. However, between 1982 and 1989 the economy recovered well, with both unemployment and inflation falling rapidly (figure 2.7), and US productivity rates improving in relation to other countries, with the notable exception of Japan. But much of this new growth was in the service sector, which generated mainly low-paid unskilled jobs.

By the early 1990s the economy had slowed once again, with unemployment rising to 7.4 per cent (figure 2.7). There was general acceptance that the recession of the early 1990s had resulted in part from excessive borrowing (by the government and individuals) during the 1980s. Indeed, by 1992 there was an emerging consensus that the boom of the 1980s had been built on very shaky foundations. US investment levels had remained

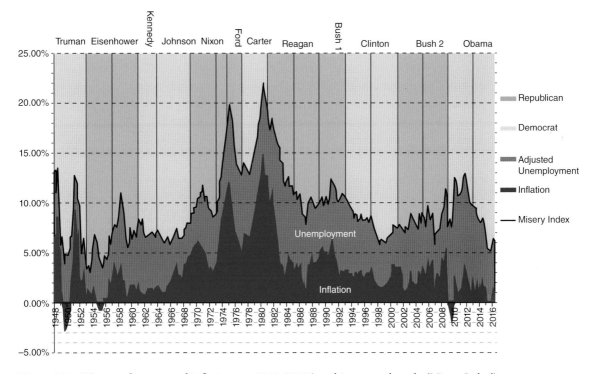

Figure 2.7   US unemployment and inflation rate, 1948–2016 (combine to produce the 'Misery Index')
Source: www.InflationData.com.

relatively low, and few American families had seen their real incomes rise during the decade. Indeed the poorest 20 per cent of families saw their incomes decline. This fact, above all, led to a major reappraisal of the role of government in the economy during the 1990s. A new consensus emerged on the need for a balanced budget – an imperative that happily coincided with a long and steady economic recovery after 1993. Unemployment fell (figure 2.7) and the long-term decline in real wages was arrested, if not reversed. The economic traumas of the 1970s and 1980s led many observers to claim that the American dream was over; that the ever-improving well being of the country which was the very foundation of equal opportunity and democracy had come to an end. Sustained recovery during the 1990s and early 2000s appeared to signal a return to affluence, with low infla- tion and unemployment. Even so, many American families manage to maintain their real incomes only by working long hours and/or generating two or more incomes from family members. This was brought into sharp relief during the recession of 2008–10 when unemployment rose rapidly and many Americans felt uneasy about their future and job security. When, after 2010, the economy began to recover, it was faltering in nature with unemployment staying stubbornly high through 2011 (figure 2.7). Some improvement occurred in the 2012–2016 period but real wages failed to keep pace with rising costs. As a result, some began to question whether the 'American dream' of ever greater affluence had come to an end.

CONTROVERSY 2   HOW CLASSLESS IS AMERICAN
SOCIETY?

The traditional view of American society is that it is less affected by class status and class divisions than many European societies – and in particular countries that retain their old aristocracies such as Britain. However, data on income and wealth equality consistently identify the US as very unequal – and getting more so. This is particularly true when the US is compared with such countries as Japan, Germany and the Scandinavian states. This contradiction can partly be explained by distinguishing between objective and subjective social class. Subjectively or in terms of how people feel about social class, America appears relatively classless. There are, in other words, few outward displays of deference or the assumption that certain people are not only born to privilege but have a right to be advantaged. This said, there is increasing evidence that in objective terms the more disadvantaged members of society are increasingly pessimistic about their chances for social improvement both for themselves and for their children. Add to this a high degree of physical separation in housing and education (at all levels), and it is not surprising that many commentators have noted increasing class divisions in the country. Indeed, in 2005, the *New York Times* devoted a special section to class spread over 11 days (see www.nytimes.com/2005/05/15/us/class/shadowy-lines-that-still-divide.html). The general conclusion was that, although an overwhelming majority of Americans continue to believe in the merits of equal opportunities in an open society, increasing numbers believed that a privileged few were benefiting at the expense of the majority. With the advent of what has been called the 'Great Recession' after 2008, more and more Americans became pessimistic about the future and, during the 2016 presidential election campaign, class became a major issue, with socialist Bernie Sanders challenging 'establishment' figure Hillary Clinton from the left and Donald Trump challenging the Republican establishment by moving the party to a more populist position on the right. Indeed, it is now commonplace to talk of the American 'working class' – a term that was used hardly at all until recently. Instead most Americans identified themselves as 'middle class' and referred to others as either 'upper middle class' or 'lower class'. Implicit in these categories was the assumption that the vast majority was middle class. Today, however, 'working class' is an accepted term for many if not a majority of Americans.

There is one aspect of the American economy that is relatively new, however, and that is the fact that government is now inextricably involved in managing economic change. By 2016 around 38 per cent of the gross national product (GNP) was accounted for by government spending. While this figure is not high in comparative perspective (see figure 18.1,

Controversy 3 Americans' Ambivalent View of Government and Taxes

Instead of accepting taxes with resignation, many Americans openly resent having to pay them. The basic assumption is that the government is taking their money and that, unless checked, governments will take more and more. As Ronald Reagan put it: 'The government's view of the economy could be summed up in a few short phrases: if it moves, tax it. If it keeps moving, regulate it. And if it stops moving, subsidize it.' Compared with most Europeans, Americans have an essentially hostile view of taxation. While these views are more common among Republicans than among Democrats, taxation and the size of government often take on a moral dimension in political debates. Taxes are usually portrayed at best as necessary evils and at worst as simply unacceptable. Europeans, on the other hand, see taxation in a more pragmatic light: 'We have to have them and if it is necessary for them to rise then so be it.'

The great paradox is, of course, that Americans' loathing of government taxing and spending is combined with a serious reluctance to see their pet programmes cut. So a typical senior (over 65) American may consistently vote for anti-government Republican candidates, but woe betide any politician who threatens his or her social security (old-age pension) or Medicare (health care for the old) benefits. Many seniors would riposte that they have paid for these benefits through payroll taxation over many years. But the fact is that there is no clear link between what people pay in payroll taxes and what they eventually get out. This accepted, Americans are very sensitive to the link between specific taxes and particular benefits. This helps explain why they are more hostile to federal spending than to state and local spending. With the latter a clear link between (say) school taxes and the operation of the local schools can be discerned. With federal taxes, their attitude is 'who knows where the money goes?'

chapter 18), it is dramatically higher than before the Great Depression, and the 1930s and the Second World War transformed the ways in which the federal government intervenes in society. As we have already established, Americans remain deeply ambivalent about this role. On the one hand they *expect* the federal government to provide a wide range of social benefits, to regulate the market and to ensure that growth and employment are kept on an ever upward curve. On the other hand, the public bemoans higher taxes and the media are constantly reminding the citizenry of waste and inefficiency in government programmes. This ambivalence extends to what have become the very complex ways in which the American economy interacts with the rest of the world economy. As is stressed in chapter 18, the economy is now undoubtedly more interdependent with those of other countries. As a result, further limits exist on the ability of politicians to deliver what they promise in economic policy.

Social Structure

One of the most fundamental questions in social science is the relationship between social structure and political activity. In most countries, social class, religion, language or region are important determinants of how people think and behave in relation to political authority. The purpose of this section is, therefore, to provide some background on American society as a prelude to our later analysis of political attitudes and behaviour.

Income and wealth

The pre-eminence of equality of opportunity as an underlying value in American society has undoubtedly limited the growth of an explicitly class-based politics in the USA. Americans are supposed to be essentially middle class, eschewing both the working class and aristocratic values associated with many European countries. By many objective indicators the United States should, indeed, have a predominantly middle-class culture. In 2015, more than 80 per cent of all workers were in service sector jobs. Within this category the largest groupings were 15 per cent in government, 12 per cent in business and professional services, 12 per cent in health care and 10 per cent in retail. Just 9 per cent worked in manufacturing and 1.5 per cent in agriculture. Of course within these categories a wide variety of skill and salary levels is represented. Health care, for example, would include everything from senior consultants to lowly catering workers. Americans are also highly educated and enjoy a very high level of home ownership, two indicators commonly employed to measure social class.

In 2015, more than 81 per cent of all 18 year olds had achieved a high school certificate, and of these approximately 30 per cent went on to complete a four-year undergraduate degree, a very high percentage in cross-national context. As notable are the housing figures, 65 per cent of all housing units being owner-occupied in 2015 although this represents a 1.5 per cent decline over an eight-year period in the wake of rapidly falling house prices down to 2012. Another measure of the middle-class nature of American society is the high level of stock (share) ownership in corporations. More than 60 per cent of American families own stock or hold stock in a variety of pension funds, dramatically more than in most developed countries, although most stockholders own less than $25,000 worth of equity.

Yet some sociologists have questioned these 'objective' indicators, arguing that the relationship between employed and employer is little different for white- and blue-collar workers. Moreover, these figures tell us nothing about the distribution of wealth and income, or about the continuing existence of many truly poor Americans. In fact most measures place the United States at or near the bottom end of income and wealth inequalities, when comparisons across countries are made. There has also been a trend towards increasing inequality of incomes in the USA over the past 20 years. As figures 2.8a and 2.8b graphically illustrate, the poorest 20 per cent of the population have suffered falls in income in the past 30 years, while the richest 5 per cent increased their incomes by more than 80 per cent. Tax cuts implemented by the Bush administration in 2004 and 2005 further increased the relative wealth of the rich (those with a family income in excess of $200,000 – see figure 2.8b). In fact these data show how the tax system actually increases rather than decreases income inequality, at least for high-income earners.

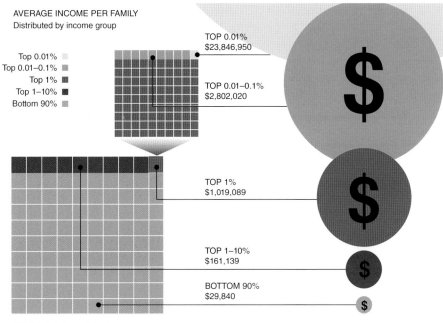

Figure 2.8a   Income inequality in the US, 2011

Source: Emmanuel Saez, University of California, Berkeley, http://emlab.berkeley.edu/~saez/TabFig2010.xls

Figure 2.8b   Wealth inequality in the US, 1913–2013

Source: Exploding wealth inequality in the United States, Emmanuel Saez, Gabriel Zucman, 28 October 2014, fig. 1, http://voxeu.org/article/exploding-wealth-inequality-united-states.

These figures do not always translate into increased levels of poverty. In fact, measuring the number of poor people in the USA is difficult. Poverty is a relative concept and it is extraordinarily hard to measure accurately. There is in fact an *official* poverty measure and there is a broad acceptance that families living below 125 per cent of this level are effectively living in poverty. This translates into an income of around $23,000 for a family of four in 2011, and the incidence of poverty has remained at around roughly 12 per cent of the population since 1990. Large variations exist by place of residence and ethnicity (Figures 2.9a and 2.9b). Note that in recent years the incidence of poverty has increased markedly among the young and blacks and Hispanics. Note also the dramatic improvements from the late 1960s when a number of new social programmes were introduced (see chapter 17). No matter which way it is measured one thing is certain: America does have a large population of poor people; not perhaps poor in the sense of living below subsistence level, but certainly poor in the sense of having little hope of full-time, secure employment and access to good housing and an acceptable living environment.

Of course poverty is not randomly scattered throughout the country. Its incidence is highest in the southern and southwestern states and in rural and inner-city areas (see Figure 2.9a). African American and other minorities (often in single parent families) are also greatly over-represented among the poor (Figure 2.9b).

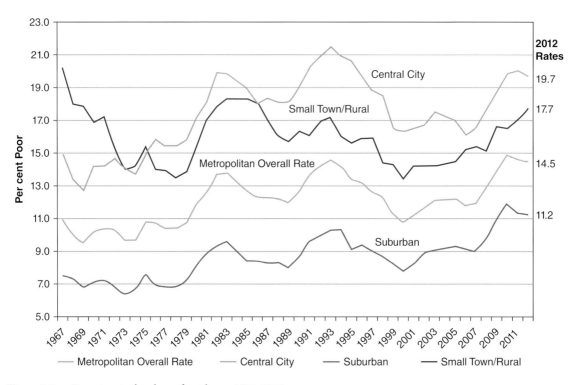

Figure 2.9a   Poverty rates by place of residence, 1967–2010
Source: United States Census Bureau.

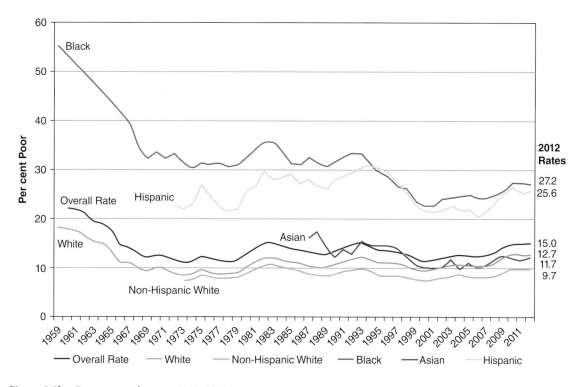

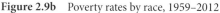

Figure 2.9b   Poverty rates by race, 1959–2012
Source: United States Census Bureau.
Note: Black poverty rate data from 1960 to 1965 is not available. The line shown connects the 1959 rate of 55.1 per cent to
the 1966 rate of 41.8 per cent and is included to represent the trend but not to imply specific numerical data.

In spite of these inequalities, most of which have been characteristics of American
society for many generations, class did not emerge as a major social cleavage in American
politics until recently. Most notably in 2016 it was the apparent neglect of white working
class interests by the Democrats that helped Donald Trump to victory. In addition Senator
Bernie Sanders made class central to his bid to capture the Democratic nomination that
year. In the event Hillary Clinton edged him out only to be narrowly beaten by Donald
Trump in the general election.

True, there have been occasions when at least the embryo of a national working-class
or populist movement could be identified, and in particular geographical areas class-based
parties have achieved some considerable success. But their impact has been limited. Compared with the effects of radical movements on the national politics of other countries,
it has been slight. Scholars have pondered long and hard as to why this should be so. As
later chapters show, institutional arrangements, particularly federalism and the electoral
system, militate against minority and radical political parties. Probably more important is
the absence of a feudal and aristocratic past, with all the deeply rooted social cleavages that
such arrangements imply. Related is what has been called a dominant ideology of equality

and liberty, with its promise of unlimited opportunity and social mobility. Certainly the United States has in the main been a remarkably successful country economically. Even by the mid-nineteenth century the American standard of living exceeded that of Britain, then one of the most affluent of the old European powers. Combined with bountiful and cheap land, this must constitute at least part of the explanation for the failure of socialism.

None the less, rapid urbanization and industrialization had their social costs, just as they did in other countries, and the economy has by no means always performed well. During the Great Depression, for example, the level of social distress among both working- and middle-class people was very high. Given this, many historians and social scientists are obliged to fall back on the explanations based on beliefs, values and ideology when accounting for the absence of a powerful socialist party.

Some scholars have argued that a repressive state (mainly at the state and local levels) in cooperation with repressive private (corporate) power prevented the emergence of a radical trade union and socialist movement during the late nineteenth and early twentieth centuries. But comparisons with equivalent events in Europe appear seriously to weaken this argument. There certainly was repression in the USA, but its character was essentially fragmented, erratic and uncoordinated compared with what were the often quite draconian and highly centralized measures employed by some European governments.

Race and ethnicity

As noted, the United States is highly diverse in its ethnic and racial make-up. Indeed during 2012 the number of births for non-white Americans exceeded the white figure for the first time in the country's history. Within the white population it is increasingly difficult to find distinctive characteristics based on ethnicity. To be sure, many Americans still describe themselves as Italian Americans or Irish Americans, but these labels have less meaning than they used to as groups are assimilated into the broader American culture. Not surprisingly, this is less true of more recently arrived immigrant groups, most of whom are Hispanic or Asian. 'Hispanic American' is a very broad category and embraces people of Mexican origin who have been in the USA for many generations (some in the southwestern states since before the founding of the Republic), as well as immigrants from Mexico, Central and South America and some parts of the Caribbean and Europe. Chinese, Vietnamese and Japanese make up the majority of the Asian population, although there are an increasing number of arrivals from other parts of Asia, including the Indian subcontinent. Finally, there are around 2.7 million Native American Indians living (often in abject poverty) mainly in the west and southwest.

As can be seen from figure 2.5, the numbers of Hispanic and Asian Americans have been increasing particularly rapidly in recent years, reflecting both high birth rates and immigration. This trend is set to continue into the foreseeable future. With the partial exception of some Asian groups, these minorities are generally poorer and less well educated than the white population. While some improvement in the status of African Americans and Hispanics has occurred over the past 30 years, by many relative measures the position of blacks in particular has actually deteriorated. There are good historical reasons for the disadvantaged status of African Americans. Until the 1960s they suffered from what was effectively an apartheid system in the southern states. Over the past 20 years, the continuing collapse of the black family unit is cited by many commentators as a major cause of the cycle of poverty and disadvantage that affects so many African Americans, especially those living in inner-city areas.

One particular problem for African Americans is that, as they are greatly over-represented among blue-collar and low-paid jobs, they are more vulnerable to fluctuations in the economy than are other social groups. This has become particularly serious as the labour market has become more flexible and unions weaker.[16] Better-educated and professional African Americans, by way of contrast, have continued to improve their position in society.

Although the political behaviour of the black population is distinctive (as chapter 6 shows), black separatist or nationalist movements have never achieved any significant success. Along with other ethnic minorities, African Americans have tended to mobilize politically within the context of established institutions and political parties. This is not to deny the importance of an ethnic dimension to politics; within the Democratic Party, for example, and at the level of local politics, ethnicity has been and continues to be a significant voting and organizational cue. But the United States has never nurtured an ethnic politics based on separatism or a complete rejection of the dominant 'American' values and political institutions. In marked contrast to the position in such countries as Canada, Belgium, Ireland and Spain, ethnic, religious or territorial divisions have not manifested themselves in ways that challenge the constitutional order.

In one key area blacks and other minorities have made considerable advances: they now hold more important political offices than at any time in their history. However, an inverse relationship between the status of the office and the number of African Americans represented exists. By 2016, 46 or 10.5 per cent of members of the House of Representatives were black (compared with 14 per cent represented in the population as a whole) and 2% of the more prestigious Senate. At the state and local levels their advance is equally patchy. In 2015, more than 10 of the nation's larger cities had black mayors. By that year most of the country's cities including Houston, Chicago, Los Angeles, Philadelphia, Detroit, Atlanta, Washington, DC and New Orleans had or had had black mayors. In the same year only 2.7 per cent of all elected officials in the USA were African Americans.

Gender

One of the most important developments in American society over the past 30 years has been the changing attitude towards the status of women. Until the late 1960s, although women enjoyed full legal and voting rights alongside men, few held important positions of political and economic power. By the 2000s, however, most objective indicators pointed to some improvement in the position of women. This said, women continue to earn less than men in comparison with many other countries (figure 2.10).

It is also the case that younger women have made less progress than older women. Few women occupy the very top positions in society, whether in the professions, government, or industry and commerce. In one crucial area, childcare, the USA lags behind comparable countries. Government-provided or subsidized pre-school places are few and far between,

Women's earnings as a percentage of men's for most recent available year

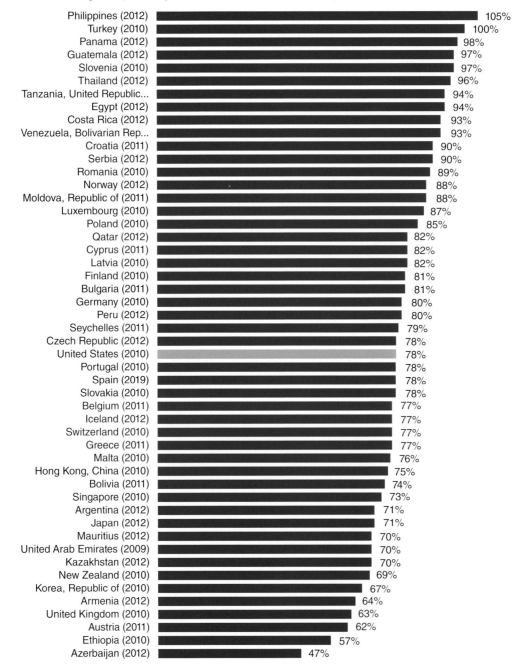

Philippines (2012)	105%
Turkey (2010)	100%
Panama (2012)	98%
Guatemala (2012)	97%
Slovenia (2010)	97%
Thailand (2012)	96%
Tanzania, United Republic...	94%
Egypt (2012)	94%
Costa Rica (2012)	93%
Venezuela, Bolivarian Rep...	93%
Croatia (2011)	90%
Serbia (2012)	90%
Romania (2010)	89%
Norway (2012)	88%
Moldova, Republic of (2011)	88%
Luxembourg (2010)	87%
Poland (2010)	85%
Qatar (2012)	82%
Cyprus (2011)	82%
Latvia (2010)	82%
Finland (2010)	81%
Bulgaria (2011)	81%
Germany (2010)	80%
Peru (2012)	80%
Seychelles (2011)	79%
Czech Republic (2012)	78%
United States (2010)	78%
Portugal (2010)	78%
Spain (2019)	78%
Slovakia (2010)	78%
Belgium (2011)	77%
Iceland (2012)	77%
Switzerland (2010)	77%
Greece (2011)	77%
Malta (2010)	76%
Hong Kong, China (2010)	75%
Bolivia (2011)	74%
Singapore (2010)	73%
Argentina (2012)	71%
Japan (2012)	71%
Mauritius (2012)	70%
United Arab Emirates (2009)	70%
Kazakhstan (2012)	70%
New Zealand (2010)	69%
Korea, Republic of (2010)	67%
Armenia (2012)	64%
United Kingdom (2010)	63%
Austria (2011)	62%
Ethiopia (2010)	57%
Azerbaijan (2012)	47%

Figure 2.10   Pay gaps around the world, latest year

Source: International Labour Organization and *Wall Street Journal*, http://blogs.wsj.com/economics/2014/04/11/is-the-gender-pay-gap-closing-or-has-progress-stalled/, Is the Gender Pay Gap Closing or Has Progress Stalled? Josh Zumbrun, 11 April 2014.

and childcare is now an important political issue. In 1993 the Clinton administration-sponsored Family Leave Bill was passed by Congress, which gave workers in all larger companies the right to take time off work for pregnancy and family emergencies.

One reason why the status of women has changed relates to the flat or declining real hourly earnings of many American workers. As average earnings have stagnated, so more women have entered the labour force in order to increase the real value of family incomes. They have often found lower paid jobs in the service sector, while the number of higher paid traditionally 'male' jobs in the manufacturing sector has declined. Indeed, by early 2012 the unemployment rate for men was identical to that for women (6.8 per cent of those over 20) – although women's rate of participation in the labour force was lower (59 per cent compared with 73.5 per cent).

Given these developments it is not surprising that women have mobilized politically to elevate a range of issues, from childcare to abortion and family leave, to the top of the political agenda.

Women have also become more active in politics generally and are increasingly regarded as politicians in their own right, irrespective of their positions on 'women's' issues. As can be seen from figure 2.11, however, they still have a long way to go.

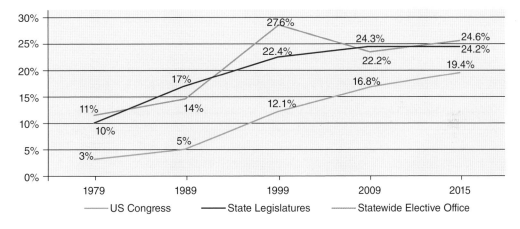

Figure 2.11   Women in elected office, selected years, 1979–2015 (%)
Source: Centre for American Women and Politics (CAWP), 2008. Eagleton Institute of Politics, Rutgers, the State University of New Jersey.

Religion

Americans are a highly religious people – more so than the populations of most comparable countries. There is also a multiplicity of religions, sects and denominations, and some commentators have argued that religion has been a prime source of the 'creedal passion' associated with various reform movements in American history.[17] Yet in spite of this and the clear links between religion and politics, religion has not constituted a major social division in American society equivalent to the role played by denomination in Ireland, the

Netherlands, Belgium or even Germany. Like ethnicity, religious differences are important in the United States but they have, more often than not, been subsumed under a dominant set of peculiarly *American* beliefs, values and institutions.

This accepted, the Christian right has asserted itself in national politics over the past 30 years as the Supreme Court and Congress have increasingly set national (and often liberal) standards on such issues as abortion, religious prayers in schools, gay rights and women's rights in employment. It would be wrong, however, to argue that Americans are becoming more religious. Although religious commitment – notably belief in God and the afterlife and church attendance – remained remarkably constant for most of the twentieth century, more recently religious beliefs have weakened. So between 2007 and 2014 those being absolutely certain that God exists declined from 71 to 63 per cent of the population.[18] And while Republican political candidates of the religious right have been in the ascendant during this period, their electoral success has been mixed. In Congress, most Republicans are now associated with the agenda of the religious right. This is a point that is developed in later chapters. In presidential politics, however, candidates supported by the religious right have had more mixed success. Some evidence indicates that such support may have hurt presidential candidates such as George Bush Senior in 1992 and

Plate 2.4   Evangelical meeting: mass congregation deep in prayer at the Christian Evangelical event Promise Keepers
Source: Dario Mitidieri/Getty Images.

Bob Dole in 1996. And while the religious right no doubt helped George W. Bush achieve victory in 2000 and 2004, Republican candidate John McCain took steps to distance himself from this part of the electorate in 2008. In 2012 Mitt Romney went to great pains to appease evangelical Christians on such issues as abortion and same-sex marriage – a stance that may have damaged him electorally among more centrist independent voters. Paradoxically, the thrice-married casino operating Donald Trump managed not only to win the 2016 Republican nomination but also won the general election. Once elected, however he quickly aligned with the moral conservatives in the party on such issues as abortion.

Region

Region has played a somewhat different role in American history. From the very beginning the South was culturally and economically separate from the rest of the United States, and although a rising sense of national identity strengthened North–South linkages during the 1820–40 period, this was shattered by the Civil War and its aftermath. Only very slowly between 1865 and 1960 was the South reincorporated into the mainstream of American society. The South's distinctiveness was, of course, based on its slave and later segregationist economy, which produced a system of social stratification with no parallel in the rest of the country. It was also a one-party region dominated by racist and often corrupt local and state Democratic parties. But the South was different in other ways. Until the post-1945 period it was predominantly rural and poor. Immigrants avoided the region; industrial and infrastructure investment was sparse; change came only slowly. Not until what had effectively become an economic and social backwater was jolted by the rapid economic growth of the 1950s and 1960s and by an increasingly strident civil rights movement did southern society begin to change. Since 1960, in fact, migration, urbanization and economic growth have transformed many southern states. To the casual visitor many parts of the South are today indistinguishable from the rest of the country. Democratic Party hegemony has broken down, although, the African American population apart, the region remains essentially conservative but Republican rather than Democratic. Old-style southern society has by no means disappeared, especially in the poorer, less developed states (notably Arkansas, Mississippi and Alabama). Racism still exists, as does a peculiarly 'un-American' resistance to change. But the South can no longer lay claim to the very special and separate status that for so long distinguished it from the rest of the country.

No other region has the distinctiveness of the South, but each is no less complex and diverse for that. The Pacific states (Washington, Oregon and California) and Hawaii tend to be more urban, liberal and internationalist than the rest of the country. The mountain and desert states (Utah, Montana, Idaho, Wyoming, Colorado, Arizona, New Mexico and Nevada) are more rural and conservative, although urbanization and immigration are changing Colorado, Arizona and Nevada very rapidly. The Midwest is generally conservative but also has a populist streak that can lead to more liberal policy initiatives in such states as Wisconsin and Minnesota. New England and some of the northeastern states, once the heartland of the Republican Party, are now predominantly Democratic, while parts of the Middle Atlantic states (Maryland, Delaware and northern Virginia) are now dominated by wealthy suburbs.

Perhaps the most remarkable feature of what are distinctive and diverse states and regions is that they have not been the springboard for successful separatist or even third-party movements – a fact which speaks volumes for the strength of universally held *American* values and beliefs.

Communications

Compared with comparable European countries and Japan, the United States is geographically vast. To put it in perspective, the USA has about five times the population of the United Kingdom, yet the US population per square mile in 2010 was 89 compared with 670 for the UK. From the very beginning of the Republic, communications have assumed a central place in American life. While today modern air transport has shrunk the size of the country considerably, intra-US business still has to be conducted in four time zones (six including Alaska and Hawaii).

Until the advent of radio in the 1920s and 1930s almost all news in America was locally generated. Even today virtually every one of the over 1,500 newspapers in the USA has a local base (the major exceptions being *USA Today* and the *Christian Science Monitor*) – although some, like the *New York Times* and the *Wall Street Journal*, do now publish national editions. The vast majority of the more than 3,000 television and radio stations are also locally based.

It would be misleading to claim that most *news* is local, however, or that Americans do not have a consciousness of national affairs and events. On the contrary, most Americans are reading, listening to or viewing the same national news most of the time. There are a number of reasons for this. First, most newspapers carry syndicated national columns put out by news services or the more prominent regional papers such as the *New York Times* and *Washington Post*. Second, and more important, most local stations subscribe to one of the three major national networks: CBS (Central Broadcasting System), ABC (American Broadcasting Corporation) and NBC (National Broadcasting Corporation). Each puts out daily news programmes, which receive very high viewing figures. In addition, Fox, CNN (Cable News Network) and CNBC broadcast national and international news around the clock.

Most radio stations broadcast music. 'Talk radio', as Americans call it, is limited mainly to news and religious programmes, many of them broadcast nationally. For all these reasons, information dissemination in the USA has a strong national dimension – stronger, for example, than in Canada. This is not to say that local news is unimportant or disregarded. It is, rather, to claim that Americans have a strong sense both of national and of local events. *International* events tend to come a distant third in terms of people's consciousness. Only international events with a clear American dimension – for example, the war in Iraq or the re-establishment of diplomatic and trading links with Cuba – receive extensive attention from the media.

It is difficult to judge the exact effect of internet usage on these trends. What we do know is that, as of 2015, more than 84 per cent of Americans were internet users – one of the highest figures in the world. The dissemination of information via the internet is much faster than through any other medium. This was amply shown in 2008 when Democratic candidate Barack Obama raised tens of millions of dollars through supporters sending $50 or $100 through their home computers. In 2016 both Hillary Clinton and Donald Trump made extensive use of the internet for fundraising and campaigning. The rise of social media also increasingly provides parties and candidates with means to send instant messages to millions of supporters at virtually no cost. Hence in 2016 Republican candidate Donald Trump made extensive – and often controversial – use of his Twitter feed to send instant messages relating to his and his opponents' candidacies.

All of the recent technological changes in communications have had or will have an important impact on American politics. Above all, they have served to increase the quantity and quality of citizens' *access* to politicians and political institutions. Thus, citizens are now able to make their views heard in a variety of novel and often immediate ways. How *effective* these communications are, is, of course, another matter which later chapters address.

Summary

This chapter has highlighted the most salient features both of the American ideology or belief system and of US demography, social structure and economy. We concluded that America is exceptional in having a set of beliefs and values that is uniquely American. These include liberty, equality of opportunity, individualism, democracy and the rule of law. Although these values change over time, the uniqueness of American beliefs persists through time. It was also noted that increasing wealth and income inequality is putting strains on Americans' belief that equality of opportunity will always ensure that each successive generation will be more successful than the last. This is a theme that we will return to in later chapters.

The second half of the chapter focused on the social structure of the US. Among the most important points noted was the changing nature of US immigration and the fact that this issue has become increasingly controversial in American politics as the number of illegal immigrants from Mexico and Central America has risen. Again we will return to this point in later chapters.

Questions for Discussion

1   What evidence is there that a distinctive American ideology is on the decline?
2   What is the role of religion in American politics? Answer with reference to the period since 1980.
3   Why is immigration such an important political issue in the United States?
4   Why are political alignments on the east and west coasts so different from the rest of the United States?

Glossary

African American   Americans of African (usually of slave) descent

alienation   The concept that citizens are alienated from, hostile to or distant from values in society

Americanism   A unique mix of characteristics that constitutes the American 'ideology'

Christian right   Those holding fundamentalist Christian views on the political right

collectivist   The notion that society is made of collective units such as class, religion or ethnicity

deindustrialization   The process of moving from an industrial or manufacturing economy to a knowledge-based service economy

hegemony   The idea that one country is powerful enough to dictate economic and military terms to other nations

Hispanic American   Americans with Spanish second names, mainly of Mexican origin but also from other parts of the Americas, the Caribbean and the Iberian peninsula

ideology   A coherently interrelated set of ideas guiding the organization of society

majoritarianism   The idea that what the majority wants has value in itself

objective/subjective social class   The difference between the actual economic/social condition of individuals and perceptions of their condition by themselves or others

political culture   The beliefs and values that make up society

prohibition   The constitutional amendment banning the production, sale and consumption of alcohol in the USA between 1919 and 1933

South, the   12 southern states of the Union made up of the 'Deep South' and the border states

Sunbelt–Snowbelt   The distinction between the high growth states of the South and Southwest and the slower growth states of the upper Midwest and the Northeast

talk radio   The label given to non-music radio stations

Notes

1   Donald J. Devine, *The Political Culture of the United States* (Boston: Little, Brown, 1972), p. 17. *Liberal* is used here to describe those who see society as made up of free, self-motivated individuals rather than as a description of where individuals stand on a liberal–conservative continuum.

2   Ira Katznelson and Mark Kesselman, *The Politics of Power*, 4th edn (New York: Harcourt, Brace, Jovanovitch, 1987), p. 29.

3   Samuel P. Huntington, *American Politics: The Promise of Disharmony* (Cambridge, MA: Harvard University Press, 1981), p. 14.

4   More than 80 per cent of respondents to a 1962 survey agreed with the first question, and just 50 per cent with the second. Herbert McLoskey, 'Consensus and ideology in American politics', *American Political Science Review*, 8 (1964), tables 2 and 3.

5   See Seymour Martin Lipset and Earl Raab, *The Politics of Unreason: Right Wing Extremism in America, 1790–1970* (Chicago: University of Chicago Press, 1978).

6   Although during the early and mid-1990s and again during the 2000s falling or flat real family incomes led many Americans to doubt that their living standards would continue to rise. This fact helped to secure Democrat Bill Clinton's victory in 1992 and Barack Obama's in 2008.

7   This is a consistent survey finding: see the *General Social Surveys, 1972–90*, Cumulative Codebook, National Research Center, University of Chicago, 1990.

8   For a discussion, see Aaron Wildavsky, 'Resolved, that individualism and egalitarianism be made compatible in America: Political-cultural roots of exceptionalism', in Byron E. Shafer (ed.), *Is America Different? A New Look at American Exceptionalism* (Oxford: Oxford University Press, 1991), pp. 116–37.

9   Eighty-two per cent of respondents said they were proud of their Constitution and governmental system,

compared with 46 per cent of the British, 7 per cent of West Germans and 3 per cent of Italians. Gabriel A. Almond and Sydney Verba, *The Civic Culture: Political Attitudes and Democracy in Five Nations* (Boston: Little, Brown, 1965), table 1.

10   See Jack Citrin, 'The political relevance of trust in government', *American Political Science Review*, 68 (1974), pp. 973–88, for a discussion of this point.

11   Huntington, *American Politics*, p. 25.

12   Michael Foley, *American Political Ideas: Traditions and Usages* (Manchester: Manchester University Press, 1993), p. 44.

13   Quoted ibid., p. 44.

14   Deaths and abortions have exceeded live births.

15   For a comprehensive discussion, see Louis DeSipio and Rodolfo O. de la Garza, *Making Americans, Remaking America: Immigration and Immigrant Policy* (Boulder: Westview Press, 1998).

16   *Economic Report of the President, 1995* (Washington, DC: US Government Printing Office, 1995), p. 179.

17   See Huntington, *American Politics*, chapters 1, 2, 5 and 6.

18   http://www.pewresearch.org/fact-tank/2015/11/04/americans-faith-in-god-may-be-eroding/

Further Reading

The classic statement on American individualism is Louis Hartz, *The Liberal Tradition in America* (New York: Harcourt Brace, 1955). On exceptionalism, see Byron E. Shafer (ed.), *Is America Different? A New Look at American Exceptionalism* (Oxford: Oxford University Press, 1991). For an overview of American political ideas see Michael Foley, *American Political Ideas: Traditions and Usages* (Manchester: Manchester University Press, 1991). Also see Everett Carll Ladd, *The American Ideology: An Exploration of the Origins, Meaning and Role of American Political Ideas* (Storrs: Roper Center for Public Opinion Research, 1994). For an account of exceptionalism, see Seymour Martin Lipset, *American Exceptionalism: A Double-Edged Sword* (New York: Norton, 1996), and also Andrew Bacevich, *The Limits of Power: The End of American Exceptionalism* (New York: Metropolitan Books, 2008). On immigration, see Desmond King, *The Liberty of Strangers: Making the America Nation* (Oxford, Oxford University Press, 2005). On the emerging white populism see Justin Gest, *The New Minority: White Working Class Politics in an Age of Immigration and Inequality* (Oxford: Oxford University Press, 2016). For comprehensive data on American society and economy, see the annual *Statistical Abstract of the United States* (Washington, DC: US Government Printing Office).

CHAPTER 3
CONSTITUTIONAL GOVERNMENT

The American Constitution is the most wonderful work ever struck off at a given time by the brain and purpose of man.

– W. E. GLADSTONE

Good government should be sufficiently neutral between the different interests and factions to control one part of the society from invading the rights of another, and at the same time sufficiently controlled itself, from setting up an interest adverse to that of the whole society.

– JAMES MADISON

American Politics and Society, Ninth Edition. David McKay.
© 2018 John Wiley & Sons Ltd. Published 2018 by John Wiley & Sons Ltd.

Almost all governments pay formal allegiance to a written or (more rarely) unwritten constitution, but in many countries constitutions represent only a limited constraint on the exercise of power. Even more rarely do constitutions survive political and social changes, invasions and wars. The American Constitution is unusual, both because it has remained almost unaltered since its ratification in 1789, and because it continues as a major source of authority in the political system. Indeed, even the most cursory examination of America's basic political institutions – Congress, presidency, federalism, the electoral system – instantly shows the influence of the Constitution. To most foreign observers, the apparent resilience of the Constitution and constitutionalism is one of the most remarkable features of American politics, and one that requires some explanation. Among the most important questions raised by this phenomenon are: Why has the Constitution been amended so little through history? What real influence does it have today? In particular, by limiting the power of central government, has it helped to aggravate the tension between the public's expectations of government and the ability of political institutions to satisfy those expectations? Before we tackle these questions it is necessary to approach the crucial issue of why the Constitution took the shape that it did.

Origins

Most dramatic regime changes following a revolution or war are quite easy to explain. France in 1789 was seething with discontent at a corrupt and insensitive monarchy. Russia in 1917 was long overdue for a revolution to sweep away an archaic, feudal order. And the numerous colonial wars of independence in the post-1945 period were predictable, given the rapid political and economic changes that the Second World War and its aftermath had brought. The American Revolution fails to fit any of these neat stereotypes, however. In fact, by some definitions it was not a revolution at all. Many of the citizens of the 13 colonies considered themselves 'true born Englishmen' who, being increasingly denied the rights that they thought all free citizens deserved to enjoy, were entitled to challenge the 'illegitimate' exercise of power by George III. They saw their task, therefore, as one of asserting independence from a regime that had betrayed its own principles. Moreover, unlike most revolutionary wars, the War of Independence and the eventual emergence of a new constitutional system had few immediate consequences for the distribution of wealth, power and status. If anything, it reinforced trends already underway. It was essentially a conservative revolution that, in marked contrast to parallel events in France, did not lead to new class divisions in society. This is not to say that radical or revolutionary elements were absent. They were very much present, but the real power remained in the hands of a solid middle class and professional property-owning elite.

The unusual nature of these events stems from the unique characteristics of American colonial society. From the very beginning, the British Americans had displayed a marked degree of independence and self-sufficiency. In the 13 colonies, and especially in New England, the local community became virtually the only meaningful level of government – and even then government is far too strong and modern a label to attach to what were remarkably successful self-governing entities. Sam Bass Warner has captured the spirit of these seventeenth-century communities very well:

> For a generation or two, medieval English village traditions fused with a religious ideology to create a consensus concerning the religious, social, economic and political framework for a good life. Each of several hundred villages repeated a basic pattern. No Royal statute, no master plan, no strong legislative controls, no central administrative officers, no sheriffs or justices of the peace, no synods or prelates, none of the apparatus typical of government then or now.[1]

Although such communities were partly transformed by economic development and population increases during the eighteenth century, the essential independence of the colonies continued to be expressed through local governments and, later, colonial assemblies whose activities were largely tolerated by Crown-appointed governors. Admittedly, considerable variation existed between different colonies – and particularly between the plantation and slave economy of the South and the more diverse agrarian and mercantilist economy of the North, but each colony respected the independence of the other. Meanwhile, the coercive forces available to the English – troops garrisoned on colonial soil – were tiny and scattered over a vast area. In this sense the whole enterprise depended on continued cooperation and consensus between colonized and colonizers.

This description implies a colonial rule which was essentially distant and benign, and such indeed was the case until the 1760s, when the English, acting under a monarch determined to assert his power over increasingly corrupt and strident Whig interests at home, decided to exercise much greater control over the colonists. All goods imported to the colonies had to pass through British ports, a tax (stamp duty) was imposed on all legal documents and newspapers, a revenue tax was levied and colonial assemblies were prohibited from issuing their own paper currency. These economic restrictions were viewed by the colonial elites as an outrageous infringement of basic rights. During the eighteenth century the idea that men possessed certain inalienable rights spread rapidly under the influence of the social contract theorists (Locke, Rousseau) and pamphleteers (Thomas Paine), and became particularly popular in a colonial America infused with a spirit of liberty and independence. Life, liberty and property were rights that governments were obliged to protect through the representation of the people in parliaments and assemblies. And should those assemblies fail to fulfil their contractual obligations to the people, then elections would ensure the incumbency of new representatives charged with carrying out the people's wishes. A monarch exercising executive power outside any representative mechanism was clearly not legitimate.

While this rather sophisticated view of events was probably held only by educated elites, the smallholders and artisans who made up the bulk of the population did have some notion of individual rights and were, by any European standard, highly independent and assertive. Indeed, for more than 100 years up to the revolution, acts of political (usually mob) violence were quite common, as they were in England. Most people with some stake in society – a farm or other property, or a valuable manual or intellectual skill – were quite used to resorting to extra-legal methods should their grievances be ignored by established political channels. Given this tradition, a growing sense of being independent colonists which economic growth and better communications had brought, and the change in English policy, outbreaks of armed resistance were almost to be expected. In fact, by the early 1770s the English had already repealed or greatly modified the most onerous tax and trade measures, but resentment at English interference with the colonists' freedom remained and in 1774 the colonial assemblies sent delegates to a national Continental Congress – the first real assertion of national independence by the colonists. By 1775 fighting had broken out in Massachusetts and in 1776 the Continental Congress adopted the Declaration of Independence that, with stirring rhetoric, marked the true beginnings of the United States:

> We hold these truths to be self-evident, that all men are created equal, that they are endowed by their Creator with certain unalienable rights, that among these are life, liberty, and the pursuit of happiness; that to secure these rights, governments are instituted among men, deriving their just powers from the consent of the governed; that whenever any form of government becomes destructive of these ends, it is the right of the people to alter or to abolish it, and to institute new government, laying its foundation on such principles, and organising its powers in such form, as to them shall seem most likely to effect their safety and happiness.

For the next seven years, the colonists successfully fought their revolutionary war against the British (and also against a significant minority of colonists who remained loyal to the Crown). In 1781 they established a new system of government under the Articles of Confederation. In effect, this – the first American Constitution – was little more than a formal recognition of the Continental Congress. A Congress was created, but no executive or judiciary. The new arrangements were very much like those of a confederation: individual states retained considerable autonomy, giving to the Congress only limited powers – namely to declare wars, establish treaties, regulate weights and measures, oversee Indian affairs, run a post office, and establish an army and navy. Crucially, no mandatory power to raise taxes was established. Instead, Congress had to rely on voluntary contributions from the state legislatures. Furthermore, each state could issue its own paper money and generally regulate commerce within its boundaries.

Such a weak, leaderless system of government could not last long, especially in the face of a number of very urgent problems confronting the new nation. Revenue needed to be raised nationally to provide for a common defence. Some central control of the currency and the enforcement of contracts needed to be created, and a common external tariff was needed to protect American goods from cheap British imports.

Moreover, the war had widened the gulf between the better-off, who had lent money to finance the fighting, and a growing debtor class who had mortgaged small farms and houses to raise income in the face of economic dislocation. In 1786 a small rebellion had broken out in Massachusetts, a state where the law on debtors was particularly harsh, when Daniel Shays led over 1,000 men to block the proceedings of the state's high court.

Although quickly put down, Shays's rebellion served to remind richer citizens that the new Congress was ill equipped to provide some degree of national economic security and uniformity. Prior to the rebellion a number of attempts had been made to strengthen Congress, and a convention to discuss trade problems had met at Annapolis, Maryland, in 1786. Although only five states attended, a resolution to meet in Philadelphia with the more ambitious aim of constitutional revision had been agreed at the convention. Shays made such a meeting that much more imperative, and during the summer of 1787, 55 delegates assembled in Philadelphia charged with the momentous task of producing new constitutional arrangements for the United States.

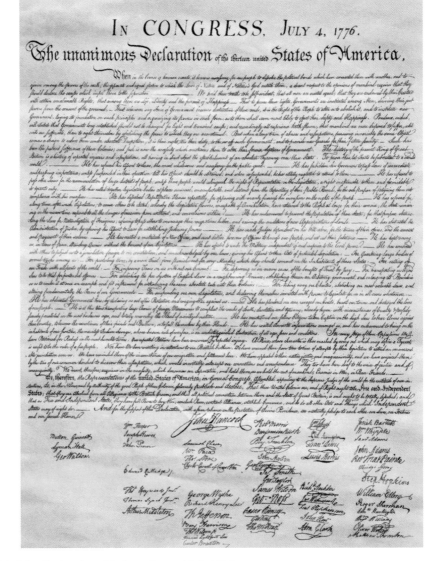

Plate 3.1   Declaration of Independence, 4 July 1776
Source: Dario Mitidieri/Getty Images.

The American Constitution

While the 55 delegates – the Founding Fathers – were obviously not operating in the absence of political and economic constraints, they were able genuinely to combine normative judgements on what best would make for a good system with provisions imposed on them by political necessity. They were not, in other words, engaged in the exercise of naked political power. Nor were they obsessed with retributive measures against past masters. And, unlike many twentieth-century harbingers of regime change, their actions were not informed by a single, closed ideology. Instead, they could afford to compromise, to show pragmatism and to draw on a number of political theories and constitutional arrangements at that time commonly discussed by the educated and liberal-minded.

The Founding Fathers were certainly educated, with about one-half having college degrees – a very high proportion for that time. They were also established (and comparatively young) men of property and status – merchants, lawyers, planters, doctors, intellectuals. George Washington presided over the meetings, although he played virtually no role in the proceedings. Inviting Washington – who came only reluctantly – was a clever ploy, as he was the one figure almost universally respected in the new nation. The real driving force behind the convention and its proceedings was James Madison of Virginia, a brilliant young politician who had helped to write Virginia's constitution and who eventually penned most of the Constitution, and Alexander Hamilton from New York, one-time aide to Washington during the war, who had helped to set up the Annapolis convention.

As delegates from the state legislatures, the Founding Fathers were not directly elected by the people – indeed, one state, Rhode Island, was not even represented, dominated as it was by a disgruntled debtor class. In one curious respect, this lack of a universal popular mandate gave them some extra freedom, for, meeting in secret, they could eventually produce a document as a *fait accompli* and then lobby hard for its acceptance by the states. As we will see, this in effect is precisely what they did.

What were the main influences on the framers? Four main ideas stand out: social contract theory, representation, the separation of powers and federalism. We have already mentioned the idea of the social contract, with its provision of obligation on both governed and governors. Although this was central to the thinking of Hobbes and Rousseau, it was Locke's vision of the social contract that most influenced the founders. To Hobbes, the contract was a very one-sided affair where the people traded their freedom for the security that a strong state would bring. Rousseau's contract was far more idealized, involving as it did the identification and implementation of the general will of the people. Locke, in contrast, made *representation* the central canon of his ideal society. Citizens, or those with a stake in society, men of property, were entitled to a government that would champion their natural rights. Through representative institutions – free elections and assemblies – the people could hold the rulers accountable for their actions. Obedience to the law (the people's side of the contract) was, therefore, conditional on the government fulfilling its side of the contract – the guarantee of life, liberty and the protection of property.

Representative government carries with it other notions, notably majority rule and the implication that there are clear limits to democracy. Both were accepted by the Founding Fathers, and their limits on democracy were, by modern standards, quite severe. Only the lower house of the legislature, the House of Representatives, was to be elected directly by the people (Article 1, Section 2).[2] Senators were to be nominated by the state legislatures (Article 1, Section 3), and the president was to be elected by an Electoral College, the members of which were to be appointed by the state legislatures (Article 2, Section 1). The framers' very limited acceptance of democracy reflected their fear of unbridled majority rule. If the people could vote for all the main officers directly, it raised the spectre of an insensitive – and possibly tyrannical – permanent majority capable of riding roughshod over the minority. As Thomas Jefferson had noted some years before the convention, 'an elective despotism was not the government we fought for'. Note also that the electoral qualifications of those who could vote for the House of Representatives were to be determined by the state legislatures (Article 1, Section 2). In most cases this meant a very limited suffrage consisting of white, property-owning males. None of this was incompatible with popular sovereignty or a republican form of government. Sovereignty resided in the people (albeit a minority of them), not in a monarch or emperor. And this, together with the majoritarian provisions in the Constitution, guaranteed a republican system – at least in terms of late eighteenth-century values.

The framers were not only worried about the possibility of tyranny by the majority, they were also aware of the dangers of concentrating too much power in any one institution. A powerful executive suggested monarchical or despotic leadership. A powerful legislature carried with it the possibility of rule by an insensitive majority. A device existed to overcome these dangers – the separation of powers. Borrowing in part from the ideas of the French philosopher Baron de Montesquieu, who greatly admired what he thought was a division of powers in the English system, the framers went about a deliberate separation of authority between legislature, executive and judiciary. Congress was accordingly given a separate power base (or constituency) from the presidency, and although the judiciary was not given the formidable power of judicial review it was later to assume, Supreme Court and other federal judges were to be appointed by the president with the consent of the upper house, the Senate. The precise jurisdiction of the courts, however, as well as the final say on the appointment of judges, was accorded to Congress (Article 3).

To ensure that no one branch could dominate the federal government, a system of *checks and balances* was introduced. So both houses of the legislature had to approve a bill, but the president could exercise a veto over it. The Senate and House of Representatives could, in turn, override a veto if two-thirds of the members present in both houses voted for it (Article 1, Section 7). Congress was also given some control over executive appointments, which had to be filled with the 'advice and consent' of the Senate (Article 2, Section 2). These checks and balances should not imply an *equality* of power and authority between the institutions. There is no doubt that the framers intended the Congress, and in particular the House of Representatives, to be the key *source* of policy. This is clear from Article 1, Section 8, which enumerates the powers of Congress. Because these included fiscal, monetary and regulatory powers, as well as the authority to raise armies and declare war, they were, in contemporary terms, quite comprehensive. Significantly, the directly elected chamber, the House of Representatives, was given special responsibility for revenue bills (Article 1, Section 7), thus reflecting the popular demand ('no taxation without representation') that the 'people's branch' should be directly accountable to the voters on taxation matters. (The basic constitutional arrangements are shown in figure 3.1.)

Executive and judicial branches were, in contrast, given few specific powers, although the dictum that the 'executive power shall be vested in a president' (Article 2, Section 1) leaves open the question of where executive power begins and ends. Congress was, then, expected to be the source of most legislation, but its power would be checked both internally (both houses have to pass a law before it becomes law) and by the president. These checks are essentially negative in nature, suggesting that the framers had a greater fear of the abuse of power than of an inability to exercise it. They therefore produced a document

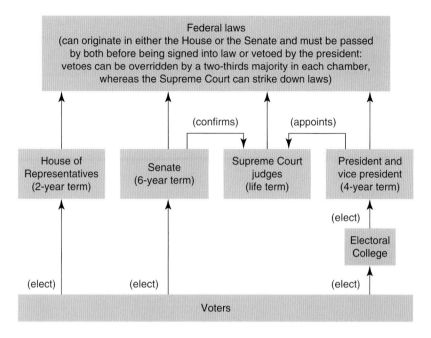

Figure 3.1   The separation of powers and the law-making process

that specifically attempted to limit governmental power. We have already mentioned the fear of democracy, majority rule and a despotic executive. In addition, some of the framers were deeply suspicious of the machinations of groups, parties or 'factions'. James Madison, in particular, feared that government might become the creature of some class or special interest. He eloquently outlined his position in *The Federalist*:[3]

> Among the numerous advantages promised by a well constructed Union, none deserves to be more accurately developed than its tendency to break and control the violence of faction.... By a faction, I understand a number of citizens, whether amounting to a majority or minority of the whole, who are united and actuated by some common impulse of passion, or of interest, adverse to the rights of other citizens, or to the permanent and aggregate interests of the community. There are two methods of curing the mischief of faction: the one, by removing its causes; the other by controlling its effects. There are again two methods of removing the causes of faction: the one, by destroying the liberty which is essential to its existence; the other by giving to every citizen the same opinions, the same passions and the same interests.[4]

Madison is in no doubt that the only solution is to control the effects of faction. Liberty is essential, and where it exists factions will exist, and giving an equal voice to every citizen can be achieved only in a pure democracy; pure democracy is impractical and dangerous except in very small communities. This leaves the control of faction to a republican form of government or the sort of representative system with a limited suffrage, some indirect elections, a separation of powers, and the operation of checks and balances that was eventually adopted.

The convention was by no means united on basic constitutional arrangements. Alexander Hamilton feared that, without a strong executive, few of the nation's pressing problems would be solved. Madison, in contrast, feared both a strong executive and an overbearing legislature. More serious was the division between the larger and the smaller states over the fundamentals of the representative system to be adopted. The smaller states favoured the ascendancy of state over federal power and a unicameral (one-house) legislature based on equal votes for each state. They also supported the idea of a multi-person executive that could be removed by a majority of the states. Proposed by William Paterson of New Jersey, these arrangements came to be known as the *New Jersey Plan*. In contrast, Governor Randolph of Virginia proposed a bicameral legislature in which both houses were elected on a population basis. However, the lower house would be directly elected, while the upper house would be elected by the lower house from nominees provided by the state legislatures and the executive would be elected by Congress for a minimum of one term (this was known as the *Virginia Plan*). After much debate, the convention eventually voted narrowly (five to four with one state delegation tied) for a compromise that contained elements of both plans. Called the *Connecticut Compromise* after being proposed by Robert Sherman of Connecticut, this established the House of Representatives on a population basis and the Senate on an equal representation of the states basis. In fact, debates on federalism and the delineation of powers between centre and periphery were among the most acrimonious at the convention. For, in addition to the small state–large state dichotomy, there was the thorny problem of the very different interests represented by the southern, as opposed to the northern, states.

The distinctive economy and culture of the South posed a potentially even greater problem and was eventually resolved only by the unsavoury expedient of counting slaves as three-fifths of a free person for the purpose of representation in the House and in distributing federal taxes. Of course, this did not mean that slaves could vote or play any part in the political process. They could not. It simply meant that slave owners were taxed on the number of slaves under their ownership on a three-fifths basis. Many northern delegates disliked this compromise, but accepted it knowing that the South would not tolerate any serious incursion into its slave-based economy. The South was also an exporter of cotton and other agricultural produce and had much less interest in the protectionist (barriers against free international trade) policies which northern politicians favoured. To safeguard their position, southerners demanded that a two-thirds majority be required to ratify treaties in the Senate. In this way, it was hoped that trade agreements favouring the North would be avoided.

These controversies over the status of the South and large versus small states should not obscure the fact that the framers were obliged to create some sort of federal system. After all, the convention was made up of representatives of the states, and the war had been waged against a strong central government. A centralized unitary system in the style of England was completely unacceptable to most delegates. What eventually transpired was a highly flexible federalism. Indeed, reading the Constitution it is not at all clear where federal power begins and ends, which gives at least great potential power to the centre (see the discussion in chapter 4).

The genius of the Constitution was that, although it was the first written constitution ever to be adopted by a country, and although it propounded the virtues of a republican form of government – a radical idea, indeed, in the late eighteenth century – it remained intrinsically *conservative* in content and implication. The founders, and particularly the most influential and able of them, were hardly social visionaries. Instead, their hopes for the new country were tinged with caution and not a little pessimism about human greed and selfishness. As Madison put it, 'As there is a degree of depravity in mankind which requires a certain degree of circumspection and distrust, so there are other qualities in human nature which justify a certain portion of esteem and confidence.'[5]

As with most educated eighteenth-century men, the essentially inegalitarian view that there are worthy and unworthy, talented and talentless, wise and stupid men in the populace prevailed. The president was to be elected by an electoral college made up, it was hoped, of wise, educated and established citizens, free from the rabble-rousing and instant judgements which democratic processes inspired. Senators, too, were expected to be elder statesmen elected by their peers for a leisurely six years and able, therefore, to hold in line a potentially capricious and unruly lower house. What the framers hoped for, therefore, was firm, cautious and responsible government.

The Constitution was designed to provide the basic framework for such a system of stable and, above all, *limited* political power. This applied to both the legislature and the executive. Indeed, the legislature could remove the president (and any other civil officer of the United States) only for 'treason, bribery or other high crimes and misdemeanors'. Even then the House of Representatives was charged with actually impeaching (formally accusing) the president, while the Senate was given the job of trying the president, conviction requiring a two-thirds majority. These complex impeachment arrangements were designed to prevent rash and politically motivated attempts to remove presidents and other officers. By and large they have worked. It is generally accepted that the two occasions on which presidents have been impeached – Andrew Johnson in 1866 and Bill Clinton in 1999 – occurred when a politically motivated House of Representatives was intent on removal. In neither case, however, was conviction secured. By way of contrast, Richard Nixon resigned in 1974 knowing that the constitutional case against him was sufficient to secure not only probable impeachment but also conviction (for a fuller discussion, see chapter 11).

The Constitution was also intended to stand the test of time – an objective that was greatly aided by a cumbersome amendment process. Amendments have to be proposed by a two-thirds vote in both houses of Congress and then ratified by three-quarters of the state legislatures or by a ratifying convention in two-thirds of the states. Alternatively, a national convention at the behest of two-thirds of the state legislatures can propose an amendment that in turn can be ratified by Congress or by a ratifying convention (Article 5). The first method (Congress proposing, the state legislatures ratifying) has become the normal amending mechanism, and it is testimony both to the flexibility of the Constitution and to the difficulties inherent in the amending process that, between 1791 and 1992, there have been only 17 amendments (see tables 3.1 and 3.2).

Reflecting on the personal interest which the framers had in a successful economy and on the pressing economic problems that the Articles of Confederation had patently failed to solve, some commentators have claimed that the whole exercise in Philadelphia was motivated by economic interest rather than by the higher ideals of liberty, republicanism and

Table 3.1   Amendments affecting elections and officeholders

Amendment	Purpose	Proposed	Adopted
12	Reform of Electoral College	1803	1804
15	Voting rights extended to all races	1869	1870
17	Direct election of senators	1912	1913
19	Voting rights extended to women	1919	1920
20	'Lame duck' session of Congress abolished[a]	1932	1933
22	Presidents limited to two terms	1947	1951
23	Voting rights extended to residents of District of Columbia	1960	1961
24	Voting rights democratized – abolition of poll tax	1962	1964
25	Reform of president succession in case of disability	1965	1967
26	Voting age lowered to 18	1971	1971
27	Prohibition on members of Congress to raise their salaries before the next election	1990	1992

[a]This changed the date of new congressional sessions from March to January to shorten the period during which the old Congress could act.

Table 3.2   Amendments affecting powers of the federal government

Amendment	Purpose	Proposed	Adopted
11	Limited federal courts' jurisdiction over suits involving the states	1794	1798
13	Abolished slavery	1865	1865
14	Extended due process of Bill of Rights to the states	1866	1868
16	Established power to introduce a national income tax	1909	1913

civic virtue.[6] While there is certainly something to this, it seems odd that the fundamental disagreements on major questions which did occur involved delegates with an equal stake in economic success. Virtually *all* the delegates were men of property, so the more simplistic of the economic theories of the Constitution should predict no real disagreement on basic principles. Yet those who voted against the Constitution had just as much of a stake in prosperity and stability as those who voted for it. A more persuasive way to characterize the framers' motivations is to accept that they were indeed troubled by economic dislocation and the ever-present threat of uncontrolled democracy, but differed markedly on which system would best overcome these problems. Crucially these differences were not only instrumental and pragmatic. Delegates also differed *intellectually* and represented more than one political philosophy and conception of human nature. What they all undoubtedly did agree on was the need for a stronger central government to ensure that the fragile new republic at least had a reasonable chance of survival.

Biographies   Hamilton and Madison

As the two main authors of the Federalist Papers who played such a role in securing the ratification of the Constitution, James Madison and Alexander Hamilton have come to be seen as the main influences on the institutional shape of the federal government. As personalities the two were very different. Hamilton was born in the West Indies and attended King's College (now Columbia University in New York) where he displayed a prodigious energy. After fighting in the Revolutionary War, he became a lawyer and eventually was one of New York's delegates to the Constitutional Convention – although he played only a small part in the writing of the document. He wrote 51 of the 85 Federalist Papers, however, where his belief in a strong federal government and in particular a powerful chief executive was articulated. After a period as Treasury Secretary in the 1790s he fell out with Thomas Jefferson over the role of the federal government. Eventually he died in a duel with Aaron Burr the defeated candidate for president in 1800. James Madison was born on a Virginia plantation, and, rather than being a man of action, he was small in stature and highly intellectual. As a Virginia delegate to the Constitutional Convention, he wrote large parts of the Constitution as (with John Jay) he did of the Federalist Papers. Like Hamilton, he believed in a strong federal government, but he was also convinced that federalism in a large and complex country would help guarantee democracy by isolating those factions or special interests that might otherwise take control of the centre. This perspective is known as Madison's 'Compound Republic'. Madison broke with Hamilton on this issue and, with Thomas Jefferson, formed the first Republican Party. Madison went on to pursue an illustrious career as Secretary of State (under Thomas Jefferson) and served for two terms as President of the United States (1809–17). Hamilton's fame among Americans was enhanced by the Broadway hit musical *Hamilton*, which opened to rave reviews in 2015.

Ratification

Fearful of failure, the framers wrote into the Constitution the requirement that ratification could be achieved by just nine of the 13 states – and then by special state conventions rather than by state legislatures, some of which were dominated by politicians who believed that direct democratic control by the people was the best form of political organization. The framers also labelled themselves Federalists, thus imposing on opposition groups the unattractive sobriquet 'Anti-Federalist'. Opposition was, in fact, fragmented, coming as it did mainly from the more remote rural areas. There was a geographical split, but not a North–South one. Instead, it was the commercial interests of the coastal areas, the larger towns and cities and the big landowners of the South who supported ratification. The Anti-Federalists were concentrated in 'the part most remote from commercial centers, with interests predominantly agricultural. It included the fractious Rhode Island, the Shays region of Massachusetts and the centre of a similar movement in New Hampshire'[7] (see 3.2).

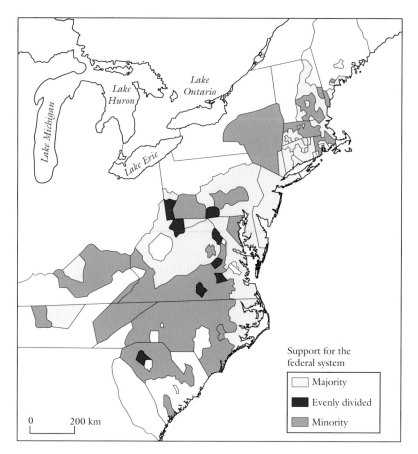

Map 3.1   The geography of ratification
Source: O. G. Libby, as reproduced in J. C. Clark Archer and P. J. Taylor, *Section and Party*
(New York: John Wiley, 1981), p. 50. Reprinted by permission of John Wiley & Sons Ltd.

Federalist lobbying in favour of the Constitution was intense and inspired the first truly national political debate in the United States. Very generally, the Anti-Federalists complained that the Constitution was insufficiently democratic and that it implied a strong and domineering central government. Complaints that individual rights were not specifically guaranteed by the Constitution were also common, and to ensure ratification in some states the Federalists accepted that a Bill of Rights would be added as soon as the first federal government was established. Between 1787 and 1789, state conventions, one after the other, voted for ratification. Success was assured when the New York convention eventually ratified by a margin of three votes. The Federalists won because they were better organized and had all the leading politicians and statesmen behind them, and because the Anti-Federalists were obliged to fight a negative campaign, the Articles of Confederation being their only immediate alternative to the Constitution. To appease the remaining Anti-Federalists the first Congress quickly voted for 10 amendments, which, once ratified by the states in 1791, became the Bill of Rights. Interestingly, a number of additional amendments failed in Congress or during ratification, almost all of which would have made the system more democratic. One proposed that the electorate should issue binding instructions to their members of Congress, thus turning them into delegates. Another suggested that there should never be less than one member of Congress for every 50,000 inhabitants. The mind boggles at the consequences for American politics if either or both of these proposals had been adopted.

The Adaptive Constitution

Change by amendment

No constitution can elaborate the precise relationship between institutions and political forces. If it attempts to do so it runs the danger of being ignored. Successful constitutions must, therefore, be flexible and open to varying interpretations. In some ways, the shorter and vaguer the document the better. Completely unambiguous statements lead to rigidity and can render a constitution unworkable. The US Constitution is free of all these faults. It does, of course, lay down certain guidelines and rules, but it says remarkably little about the precise powers of the main institutions, or about how authority should be shared between federal and state governments. When a comparison is made between the United States of 1789 (3.5 million people, agrarian, confined to the east coast) and the United States of 2017 (more than 325 million people, highly industrial, a continental and world power) the true success of the Constitution can be appreciated. For virtually the same document applies today as applied more than 225 years ago. Moreover, if we examine the 17 amendments (in addition to the first 10 amendments, the Bill of Rights) that have been accepted in this period, their significance is almost certainly not as great as the changes in interpretation to which the Constitution has been subjected.

Of the 17 amendments, some are relatively trivial, two were devoted to the adoption and subsequent rejection of prohibition, and the remainders are devoted either to electoral questions or to limiting and expanding the role of the federal government.

Amendments affecting elections and officeholders

The first important amendment here was the twelfth, adopted in 1804 to simplify the election of the Electoral College, which in turn elects the president. As mentioned above, the Founding Fathers hoped that a group of elder statesmen (the Electoral College) would choose the president but, with the emergence of competing political parties, it soon became obvious that the College had become highly partisan in nature. In 1800 the vote in the College was a tie between Thomas Jefferson and Aaron Burr. When the vote was referred to the House of Representatives it took numerous ballots to decide the eventual winner (Jefferson). The Twelfth Amendment ensured that any election in which a candidate received less than a majority of the Electoral College would then be decided in a run-off election in the House of Representatives. Votes for president and vice president were combined. Previously the College had elected the two officers separately. Gradually between

1800 and 1832 the state legislatures voted to provide for the direct popular election of members of the Electoral College. Surprisingly, this system persists. Americans still do not vote directly for a presidential candidate, but for members of the College. Moreover, it is (Maine and Nebraska apart) a *winner-takes-all* mechanism, so that the candidate who gets a majority of votes in a particular state wins *all* that state's Electoral College votes. What determines the number of Electoral College votes in a state? Each state simply has one vote for each representative and senator, which means that the votes are distributed roughly in proportion to population (the number of representatives in any state changes regularly in accordance with population shifts (see chapter 6), and because there are only two senators per state this introduces a very small bias in favour of low-population states). The major criticism of this system is that it is possible for a candidate to win the Electoral College vote but receive fewer popular votes than another candidate. Just this happened in 1824, 1876, 1888, 2000 and 2016. Another criticism focuses on the danger of Electoral College members failing to vote for the candidate mandated by the electorate. Again, this has happened on rare occasions, but it has never been critical.

Clearly the Electoral College system favours the larger states. If a candidate wins just seven states – New York, California, Texas, Pennsylvania, Illinois, Florida and Ohio – he or she amasses 209 votes (in 2016) even if he or she wins by only a narrow margin in each of these states. And only 270 Electoral College votes are needed for victory. Talk of reforming the system is never far from the surface in the United States, and the mechanism probably persists because there are only two main parties,[8] and some bias in favour of big population centres does compensate for other biases in the system in favour of smaller states and rural areas. The extraordinary contested 2000 result, where Florida's 27 Electoral College votes were eventually awarded to George W. Bush by a margin of just 1,725 votes, showed the operation of the Electoral College at its worst. Democratic candidate Al Gore won the popular vote and only the intervention of the US Supreme Court stopped the recount in some Florida counties that might have resulted in a victory for Gore. Bush eventually won the Electoral College by just one vote more than that needed for victory (271). Since then two states – Ohio and Florida – have emerged as pivotal swing states because in closely run elections such as 2000 and 2004 small swings to either party in these evenly balanced states can deliver a decisive number of Electoral College votes.

Almost all the other amendments affecting elections have been designed to expand the electorate or to hold elected officials more accountable or responsive to the public (table 3.1). These changes, together with the abolition of property qualifications for voting at the state level during the first part of the nineteenth century, have, in total, greatly increased the democratic element in the Constitution. None is controversial except the Twenty-second, limiting presidential terms to no more than two. Although never tested, it is conceivable that a popular and successful president may be denied a third term by the amendment.

Amendments affecting the powers of the federal government

In one sense, changes in electoral qualifications were to be expected as the democratizing trends of the nineteenth and twentieth centuries took hold. Given this, it would also be unsurprising if the Constitution had been frequently amended to expand the powers of the federal government. Yet as table 3.2 shows, only three amendments have had this purpose, the thirteenth, to assert federal power over those states where slavery was legal, the fourteenth, imposing the Bill of Rights on the states, and the sixteenth, establishing the power to introduce a national income tax. And of these three, the Fourteenth Amendment was not, in fact, applied to the states until the twentieth century.

Evidence of just how difficult it is to ratify an amendment is provided by the experience of the Equal Rights Amendment (ERA). This amendment, which read 'Equality of rights under the law shall not be denied or abridged by the United States or any state on account of sex,' has, in fact, been before Congress since 1923. In 1972 Congress voted for the amendment by large majorities and within a year 25 states had voted for it. It then ran into trouble, however, as some state legislators began to fear that in its implementation women might, for example, be required to take up combat positions in battle. Eventually, the amendment died three votes short of formal ratification.

The other major attempt to amend the Constitution in recent years also failed. By the late 1980s, 33 states had passed the Balanced Budget Amendment requiring the federal government to balance its annual budget. By the late 1990s, however, it was clear that the amendment would not win the necessary number of states, and the issue passed temporarily from the political agenda. (By 2012 many on the Republican right renewed calls for the amendment in the context of a ballooning budget deficit.) At any one time a number of amendments are being mooted or discussed by Congress and the state legislatures. The dice are clearly loaded against any one being ratified, however, given the super-majority rules required for passage.

Change by interpretation

Much more important have been changes in constitutional interpretation, which owe more to the development of American society and economy than to the wording of the Constitution as such. We can identify four such changes:

1 The assertion of federal over state power.
2 The assertion of executive over legislative power.
3 The emergence of the Supreme Court as the final arbiter of the Constitution.
4 The growing protection of individual rights under the federal government.

Each of these four is dealt with in detail in later chapters. For now it is enough to point out that the first two were certainly not intended or envisaged by the framers, the third probably was and the fourth has developed in a way which could not possibly have been predicted in 1787.

Although the Constitution is ambiguous on the question of federal–state relations, there can be no doubt that the relationship that had developed by the twenty-first century was light years away from anything the framers could have intended. Today the federal government intrudes into almost every facet of economic and social life, leaving to the states very little that *constitutionally* they can call their own except perhaps their territorial integrity and equal representation in the Senate. In 1791 it was broadly expected that the Tenth Amendment's dictum – 'The powers not delegated to the United States by the Constitution, nor prohibited by it to the States, are reserved to the States respectively, or to the people' – would leave the states unequivocally in charge of a number of governmental functions. As the next chapter demonstrates, this was not to be.

Similarly, Congress was expected to be the major source of legislative initiative, while the president implemented laws with prudence and efficiency. The reality in the twenty-first century is very different. For while Congress does play a greater role in policy initiation than almost any other national legislature, and is indisputably a powerful and independent institution, it has largely forfeited the lion's share of the legislative function to the president and to a vast and complex executive branch.

The reasons why government has become larger, more centralized and concentrated in executive rather than legislature is addressed in detail in later chapters. But these trends have occurred in almost all countries with rapid economic and social development, the mobilization of populations by parties and groups and the corresponding increase in demands placed on all governments, particularly those with the greatest potential for resource distribution and regulation by central governments.

In 1803 the Supreme Court asserted the power of judicial review, or the right to declare any Act of Congress or action by the executive branch as incompatible with the Constitution and therefore illegal. Actions by states can also be struck down by the Supreme Court. Although used sparingly at first, this power has been utilized with increasing frequency, and, as we will see in chapter 15, has had profound consequences for the working of the political system. Although some of the founders may have envisaged the Court playing the role of final arbiter of the Constitution, none could have foreseen the intimate involvement of the nation's highest court in such questions as abortion, electronic bugging and political party campaign finance.

Finally, citizens' rights to free speech, assembly, religion, privacy, 'due process' and the equal protection of the laws have slowly been extended to apply to the states. This is crucial, for slavery was an institution protected by state governments and constitutions. Following the Civil War, the Thirteenth and Fourteenth Amendments swept away slavery and, in theory, discrimination. The Supreme Court failed to enforce the Fourteenth Amendment in the South until after the Second World War, however, so allowing the perpetuation of segregation and the worst sort of racial discrimination. Deference to states' rights extended to other areas, such as standards of occupational safety, employment conditions and criminal justice. So for many Americans, civil rights and liberties were anything but 'God given rights'. Only under federal legislation did they exist, and, until the twentieth century, the federal government played only a small role in the lives of individual citizens. Beginning in the 1930s and accelerating between 1945 and 1970, this anomalous situation was slowly corrected, with the Supreme Court insisting in case after case that the Bill of Rights and Fourteenth Amendment apply to all American governments, whatever their status. So in cases involving national security, privacy, racial, religious and sex discrimination, and the administration of justice, the Supreme Court has insisted that all authorities have an obligation to heed constitutionally defined rights. Of course, this does not mean to say that the Court has always favoured a liberal position, or that it has come down on the side of individuals rather than governments – although until the 1990s it generally did so. Since then, the re-emergence of national security as an overriding interest has led to the passage of laws including the 2001 Patriot Act, which many liberal commentators believe to be unconstitutional. The Supreme Court has yet to make a definitive judgement on this law, however.

Changes in official attitudes to civil rights and liberties parallel the growth of government noted above. As governments at all levels have increasingly intruded into the lives of individuals, so the need for protection from arbitrary governmental authority has grown. As we will discover in chapter 12, governments – and especially federal governments – have also been active in controlling the abuse of individual rights by *private* bodies, in particular by corporations. It seems highly unlikely that the framers could have foreseen that the question of individual rights would have become part of a complex web of interaction between myriad private and public institutions and individuals.

Assessing the Constitution

Some of the most dramatic changes in American government and society over the past 230 years have involved institutions and political processes not even referred to in the Constitution. Parties emerged during the early years of the nineteenth century as the major agents of political mobilization. Interest groups have grown in number and influence until today some commentators seriously argue that they are the true sources of political power and influence. Similarly, the nationally organized media equipped with formidable electronic resources can play a crucial role in swaying political opinion. Does this mean that the Constitution is of relatively little importance? Not at all, for all these changes have had to be accommodated within certain institutional limits which the Constitution imposes. Political and economic changes have indisputably altered the relationships between institutions and the broader society, but they have not been transformed in such a way that the document has ceased to have meaning. Congress remains separated from the presidency. Interest groups, presidents, individual citizens, the media – even foreign governments – have to accept that the independent power of Congress can and frequently does thwart presidents. The courts are also independent and have shown, especially in the 1960 to 1990 period, that president and Congress must sometimes tread warily when exercising their powers. States, too, remain important political units – although, as we will discover in the next chapter, their relationship with the federal government is now more one of interdependence than autonomy. Taken together, the two central pillars of the Constitution – the separation of powers and federalism – have undoubtedly served to limit the exercise of centralized political power.

Criticisms of the modern Constitution usually concentrate either on the continuing political hiatus between executive and legislature or on the progressive weakening of the states in relation to the federal government. American presidents are, in comparison with chief executives in most industrial countries, uncommonly constrained by the essentially negative power of Congress. But as we will see, American government is not only constrained by the separation of powers. Getting policy efficiently formulated and implemented is also affected by the complexity of the executive branch and, simply, by the many competing interests in American society which have created and nurtured so many access points to those with political power. Again the separation of powers has served to increase the number of access points and thus has made it easier for determined minorities to block central control and regulation. Put another way, the Constitution has helped limit the exercise of centralized power, while at the same time providing citizens with a multiplicity of access points for the voicing of grievances. Only rarely do the two institutions speak with one voice, as was the case in the two years following 9/11 when a dominant president and pliant Republican Congress came together to fight the 'War on Terror' at home and abroad.

Federalism also fragments power. By definition, the institution of federalism limits central political power. Arguments suggesting that the decline of the states' legal autonomy is in part attributable to the Constitution's failure to define precisely where state sovereignty begins and ends are less persuasive. Such a strict delineation of powers would have been inflexible and ultimately unworkable, and in any case the states were admirably independent until this century. The gradual erosion of their legal powers was not, therefore, a matter so much of constitutional failure as it was a consequence of the states' inability to deal with the pressing social and economic problems that industrialization and other changes brought. As the next chapter shows, however, federalism is far from dead. Indeed, in recent years the states have, in some areas, regained power. And often they have done so following popular opposition to the imposition of national standards in such areas as capital punishment and abortion.

Any assessment of the Constitution has to recognize that, as with any constitution, its continuing influence is ultimately dependent on those in positions of political power accepting its legitimacy. Had its provisions proved a major threat to power-holders, it would have been ignored or radically amended. No doubt the Founding Fathers recognized this and, anticipating problems, deliberately opted for a short and rather vague document that would stand the test of time. But this would hardly have been enough had America been torn by fundamental divisions based on class, ethnicity, language or religion. The framers knew that good government was all about the business of reconciling differences between competing groups and interests in society, and no doubt they were aware that the United States would experience social and political conflict of varying intensity. But the conflict between North and South apart – and this very nearly put paid to the Union – the United States has been remarkably unaffected by fundamental political divisions. Free from a feudal past and lacking deeply rooted religious, ethnic, linguistic and, at least in recent decades, regional divides, the country was able to accommodate quite extraordinary economic and demographic changes within a single, almost unchanging, constitutional structure. While it is impossible to measure the contribution of the Constitution to this relative consensus on political fundamentals amid rapid change – no doubt the causal lines run in many directions – it seems reasonable to conclude that by limiting the exercise of central power, the Constitution has made some important contributions in this area.

This does not mean to say that the Constitution will continue unchanged for ever, of course. And there are more than enough critics who claim that the basic division of power between legislature and executive is inappropriate for the sort of efficient policy-making needed to run a world power with vast and complex responsibilities at home and abroad. Whether this is true, later chapters reveal. But whatever the charges, the Constitution is under no imminent threat either from domestic political conflict or from radical amendment. According to the simple measure of its ability to survive, therefore, it must be deemed a success.

Summary

This chapter has discussed the origins of the American Revolution and the reasons why the Founding Fathers chose to create a new Constitution in Philadelphia in 1787. They were influenced by social contract theory or the idea that governments must be held accountable for their actions through periodic elections, the separation of powers to control central authority and federalism or the idea that power should be shared between the federal government and the states. The chapter has outlined the main provisions of the Constitution as well as the ratification process, which eventually included a Bill of Rights enumerating the basic freedoms of the American people.

The ways in which the Constitution has changed through time, both in terms of formal amendments and through interpretation, are also covered, and the chapter concluded with an assessment of US constitutional arrangements.

Questions for Discussion

1 What were the main points of disagreement among the authors of the US Constitution?' How were they resolved?
2 How democratic is the US Constitution? Answer with respect to which institutions of the federal government are today subject to popular control.
3 Why have there been so few amendments to the Constitution since it was ratified? Which of the amendments has had the greatest impact on American politics?
4 'The separation of powers has made it almost impossible for presidents to govern successfully.' Discuss.

Glossary

Articles of Confederation   The first US Constitution drawn up after the War of Independence

Balanced Budget Amendment   The (failed) amendment introduced in the 1980s banning the federal government from running a deficit

bicameralism   Rule by two legislative chambers such as the House and the Senate

Bill of Rights   The first 10 amendments to the Constitution enumerating basic rights ratified in 1791

Compound Republic   The Madisonian notion that the US was made of numerous interests and factions that could be accommodated by federalism and the separation of powers

Connecticut Compromise   The constitutional compromise that established the House of Representatives elected on a population basis and the Senate on a territorial basis

due process   The idea that all citizens should be subject to clear and fair processes under law

Electoral College   Election of the chief executive by a college of electors rather than directly by the people

Equal Rights Amendment (ERA)   The failed amendment guaranteeing rights to women proposed in the 1970s

federalism   The division of sovereignty between national state governments

judicial review   Review of legislation and executive actions by the Supreme Court to determine compatibility with the constitution

majority rule   Rule by a plurality of the voters

New Jersey Plan   The defeated constitutional proposal that the US should be governed by a single house based on equal votes for each state

separation of powers   The separation of governmental powers into legislative, executive and judicial

social contract theory   The idea that the people enter into a contract with the government with both sides accountable for their actions

unitary system   A system of government where the central government is sovereign and local units subordinate to the centre

Virginia Plan   The defeated constitutional proposal involving an elected lower house and an upper house elected by the lower house with nominees from the states

winner-takes-all   The arrangement whereby a majority or plurality in a constituency wins all the representation

Notes

1   Sam Bass Warner, *The Urban Wilderness: A History of the American City* (New York: Harper & Row, 1972), p. 8.

2   The full text of the Constitution is given in the Appendix.

3   The *Federalist Papers*, written mainly by Madison and Hamilton, were published after the convention to persuade some of the states to accept the Constitution. They comprise a remarkable collection of essays which reflect some of the most crucial debates of the convention.

4   *The Federalist*, no. 10, in *The Federalist Papers* (New York: Mentor Books, 1961), pp. 77–8.

5   *The Federalist*, no. 55, ibid., p. 346.

6   The classic statement of this view is Charles Beard's *Economic Interpretation of the Constitution of the United States* (New York: Macmillan, 1913).

7   O. J. Libby, quoted in J. C. Clark Archer and Peter J. Tay-
     lor, *Section and Party* (New York: Wiley, 1981), p. 49.
8   Should no candidate receive a majority in the College
     – a likelihood if the USA had a multi-party system –
     then the House of Representatives chooses the presi-
     dent on the basis of one vote per state delegation. This

massive bias in favour of the smaller states would not
be tolerated for long were the system put to the test –
although it did occur twice in the nineteenth century.
In recent years the USA has only rarely produced serious third-party candidates, and few have accumulated
Electoral College votes.

Further Reading

On the revolutionary period, see Nick Bunker, *An Empire on the Edge: How Britain Came to Fight America* (London: Bodley Head, 2015). See also Bernard Bailyn, *The Ideological Origins of the American Revolution* (Cambridge, MA: Harvard University Press, 1992). Two classic accounts of the making of the Constitution and the early years of the Republic are Samuel H. Beer, *To Make a Nation: The Rediscovery of American Federalism* (Cambridge, MA: Harvard University Press, 1994), and Stanley Elkins and Eric McKitrick, *The Age of Federalism: The Early American Republic, 1788–1800* (Oxford: Oxford University Press, 1994). A recent critique of the ways in which constitutional arrangements affect modern American politics is Anthony King, *The Founding Fathers v. the People: Paradoxes of American Democracy* (Cambridge, MA: Harvard University Press, 2012).

CHAPTER 4
FEDERALISM AND INTERGOVERNMENTAL RELATIONS

The problem which all federalised nations have to solve is how to secure an efficient central government and preserve national unity, while allowing free scope for the diversities, and free play to the members of the federation. It is … to keep the centrifugal and centripetal forces in equilibrium, so that neither the planet States shall fly off into space nor the sun of the Central government draw them into its consuming fires.

– LORD JAMES BRYCE, *AMERICAN COMMONWEALTH*

American Politics and Society, Ninth Edition. David McKay.
© 2018 John Wiley & Sons Ltd. Published 2018 by John Wiley & Sons Ltd.

*This Nation has never fully debated the fact that over the past 40 years, federalism –
one of the most essential and underlying principles of our Constitution – has nearly
disappeared as a guiding force in American politics and government.*
– RONALD REAGAN, 1981

*'No, it'll go back to the states', Trump said. 'They'll perhaps have to go – they'll have
to go to another state [to get an abortion].' President elect Donald Trump's response
when asked what would happen if his plan to achieve a reversal of the Supreme Court's
position on abortion came to fruition.*
– DONALD TRUMP, *CBS SIXTY MINUTES*, 2016

To many foreign observers, the practice of American federalism presents itself as something
of a conundrum. On the one hand is the extraordinary variety of contrasting public policies
displayed by the states. Most states levy an income tax, but some do not; most have capital punishment, but, as of 2016, 19 do not; state-mandated land-use planning is light years away from
the policy agenda in Texas – a state which prides itself on its free market in land – but in Hawaii
state planning is a fact of life. In Louisiana laws governing the sale of intoxicating liquors are lax,
while Utah has very restrictive laws on the sale of alcohol. On the other hand, American observers repeatedly tell us that federalism is dying, or is even dead; that the federal government has
effectively usurped the powers of the states and now plays the dominant role in American government. Federalism, so we are told, has been transformed from a system of shared sovereignty
with each level of government supreme in its own sphere and converted into a complex web
of intergovernmental relations where political and economic forces, not constitutional imperatives, are the key variables. A major purpose of this chapter is to explain the apparent paradox of
continuing state variety and increasing federal power. To achieve this, attention is paid to what
has been called 'fiscal federalism', or the financial relations between different levels of government, and to recent attempts to revive the institution of federalism. In addition the chapter will
focus on the role that the states play as policy innovators in areas as diverse as health care and
environmental protection – a role that has taken on a new significance in the past 20 years.

Federalism in Theory and Practice

As outlined in figure 4.1, there are three basic forms of government operating in the modern
world. Under unitary government sovereignty is vested in the central authorities, which can
in turn decide on the shape of regional and local governments. This is the case in such countries as Britain, France and Japan. Under confederal arrangements sovereignty is vested in the
state or regional governments, whose agreement is required in order to sanction action by
the central government. The US Articles of Confederation and the Confederacy during the
Civil War operated roughly in this way, and such organizations as the United Nations and the
North Atlantic Treaty Organization (NATO) approximate to confederal systems. The defining feature of federalism is that of *dual sovereignty* or a *sharing* of powers between state and
central governments. Under federalism each level of government is assumed to be supreme
in at least one policy area. Typically the federal government would have responsibility for

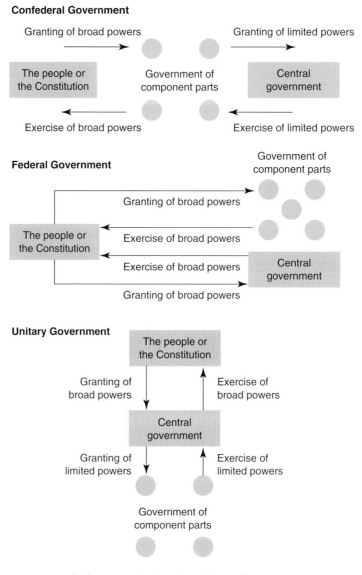

Figure 4.1   Constitutional relations in the three basic forms of government

defence and foreign affairs, while the states would control such things as education and law and order. The three models represented in figure 4.1 are, of course, idealized types. In reality most political systems, while labelled unitary or federal, actually share features of both.

American federal arrangements are among the world's oldest, and the US example is often held up as a model of what federalism should look like. At the same time, it was not so long ago that many Europeans viewed US federalism with a combination of distant interest and condescension. A constitutional division of powers between centre and periphery might, so the argument ran, suit such large and diverse countries as the United States, but they were clearly inappropriate for relatively homogeneous countries like Britain and

France, with their centralized metropolitan political cultures based on dominant capital cities. For social reformers, federalism was viewed with particular scepticism. How, after all, could resources be distributed from rich to poor areas and from the haves to have-nots of society in the absence of a powerful central government operating unhindered by 'regressive' state governments? Critics pointed to the stark inequalities of American society, which seemed so often to correlate with state boundaries – widespread poverty in Mississippi and Alabama, an easy affluence in Connecticut and Minnesota.

In recent years, however, the institution of federalism has experienced something of a revival. Centralized governments have been criticized as spendthrift and insensitive, and federalism has been cited as a compromise solution to the claims by increasing numbers of regions and ethnic minorities in a variety of countries for more autonomy. To the critic of the over-centralized state, federalism's advantages seem obvious. Local and regional cultural, political and economic characteristics can be preserved; government can be brought 'closer to the people'; and central power can be limited by ensuring that the administration of a whole range of domestic policies is conducted at the state and local level. Federalism is, of course, much more than the mere devolution of powers that, to a greater or lesser extent, exists in all states, unitary and federal. As indicated, *dual sovereignty* is the central theoretical condition for federalism. This involves not just the sharing of policy responsibilities between different levels of government; it additionally *guarantees* constitutional integrity to state governments. No federal government can abolish its constituent states as a British government can, theoretically at least, abolish all its local governments. Naturally the crucial question is: which powers should reside in the state governments and which in the federal government? Historically, under 'classic' or 'dual' federalism,[1] defence and foreign affairs together with some aspects of financial or macroeconomic management have been considered federal government responsibilities, while most domestic policies – education, roads, welfare, the administration of justice – have been allocated to state and local governments.

Few constitutions, however, specify precisely which policy areas should be the responsibility of different levels of government. Article 1, Section 8 of the US Constitution, for example, does enumerate the powers of Congress, but it does not do so in a way that unambiguously defines the federal role. Congress is given the power to regulate interstate commerce, but what does this mean? The regulation of interstate transport? The movement of manufactured goods across state boundaries? The regulation of banking across state lines? The regulation of those aspects of *intrastate* commerce that are affected by *interstate* transactions? Or what? Clearly what Congress does here and what remains a *state* responsibility is left undefined by the Constitution.

In reality, the delineation of the federal and state roles has been left to judicial interpretation and to the ways in which the courts have reacted to shifting political and economic environments. As was pointed out in chapter 3, workable constitutions have to be flexible and open to new interpretation, and any attempt to lay down in a permanent fashion the limits to federal or state powers would be doomed to failure. As we shall see, for federalism the cost of flexibility has been the gradual and steady erosion of the states' powers by the federal government.

In strict constitutional terms, the states are guaranteed just four things: equal representation in the Senate (Article 1, Section 3); the right to jurisdictional integrity (Article 4, Section 3); the right to a republican form of government (Article 4, Section 4); and protection against invasion and domestic violence (Article 4, Section 4). What in reality they

Table 4.1   Types of government in the United States, 1977, 1992, 2002, 2012

Type of government	2012	2002	1992	1977
Total	90,056	85,576	85,006	79,913
US government	1	1	1	1
State governments	50	50	50	50
Local governments	90,005	87,525	84,955	79,862
County	3,031	3,034	3,043	3,042
Municipal	19,519	19,429	19,279	18,862
Township	16,360	16,504	16,656	16,822
School district	12,880	13,506	14,422	15,174
Special district	38,266	35,052	31,550	25,962

Source: Statistical Abstracts of the United States, most recently 2012, https://www.census.gov/govs/cog/2013.

have retained in addition to this has varied with the historical period and a whole range of economic, social and political forces. They remain an important level of government, not just for constitutional reasons, but also because they are a convenient jurisdictional base for a range of powerful actors and interests in contemporary America. Political parties, for example, are organized on a state rather than a national basis – a fact that gives the states a key role in nominating presidents and in electing members of Congress and senators. We elaborate on this point below, but for now it is important to stress that local as well as state governments are important power bases in the American system. Localism is as strong in the USA as in any country, and this is in spite of the weak constitutional position of local governments (in theory, they are constitutionally subordinate to state governments, although some state constitutions guarantee them some autonomy or 'Home Rule'). The power of local governments is reflected in their resilience. In spite of the many pressures to consolidate into larger units – pressures which exist in all industrial countries – the number of local units in the USA remains high (table 4.1).

Note also the variety of local units, which derives from variations in state law. Twenty states, for example, have townships, which generally have the powers of municipalities but which, unlike municipalities, usually cover areas irrespective of population concentrations. Special districts, which continue to increase in number, have been created to perform a specific local function, such as fire protection, soil conservation, water supply or sewerage. They are legally separate from, although almost always linked politically to, municipal and county governments. In recognition of the weakness of classic or dual federalism, and of the strength of local governments, some commentators have argued that, rather than become involved in arcane discussions on the constitutional status of federalism, it is now more appropriate to talk of *intergovernmental relations* (IGR).[2] Such a focus obliges the student to examine the political and economic relationships between different levels of government – a focus largely adopted by this chapter.

To understand why, as a constitutional concept, federalism has changed so much over time, it is necessary to examine the historical evolution of IGR in the USA.

The Evolution of American Federalism

Opting for a federal rather than a unitary or confederal system of government in 1787 was understandable. Government under the Articles of Confederation had been minimal. A weak Congress (there was no executive branch) was obliged to rely on the cooperation of 13 near-independent states. In economic affairs this proved almost impossible, and internal tariff barriers, together with the absence of a common currency, rendered the new republic almost impotent against the economic might of Britain. If a confederal system relying on the cooperation of constituent states was unworkable, the other most tried alternative, unitary government, was inappropriate for historical and political reasons. It was, after all, the centralized and highly insensitive power of England that had prompted the revolt of the colonies. Each colony had in addition its own traditions and history, which might have been threatened by a centralized system. Finally, unitary government was associated with a strong executive – not a feature likely to endear the system either to the artisans and small-holders who made up the bulk of the American population or to those sections of the elite who supported Madison's notion of the Compound Republic (see chapter 3).

A federal system involving the sharing of authority between central authority and con-stituent states was a natural compromise. Hence the Constitution gave to the federal gov-ernment authority to raise armies, to tax and to regulate interstate commerce – powers that were notably absent under the Articles of Confederation – while the individual traditions of the states were protected both by the checks and balances imposed on the central institu-tions of Congress and presidency and by the Tenth Amendment ('The powers not delegated to the United States by the Constitution, nor prohibited by it to the States, are reserved to the States respectively, or to the people'). The fundamental problem which federalism attempts to solve – the tension between central authority and local autonomy – is still very much with us today. In the late eighteenth century, however, this tension took on a very different form from that presently at work in the United States. Then, a strong federal government was needed for two purposes: to defend the young republic against a hostile outside world, and to provide an open and orderly market for the free exchange of goods and services within the borders of the new nation-state. At all levels governments' role was limited and, although some conflict between state and federal governments existed, it rarely reached the point where it intruded greatly into citizens' lives. In an agrarian and small-town soci-ety characterized by poor communications and a strong tradition of localism, the federal government was a remote and, in terms of people's everyday dealings, a relatively minor authority. Today, in contrast, federal, state and local governments intrude into almost all areas of social life through a bewildering array of policies and programmes. It is not surpris-ing, therefore, that federal–state–local relations today are very different from those of late eighteenth-century America. Initially, debate was concentrated on the *regulatory* powers of the federal government – and especially the extent to which federal law in the area of inter-state commerce could take precedence over state law. By the mid-nineteenth century, with the emergence of slavery as a national issue, the role of the federal government in protecting the rights of citizens was added to the policy agenda. These issues remain an important part of current debate on federalism, but they have been transformed by the vastly enhanced spending power of the federal government.

An examination of the more celebrated Supreme Court cases on federal–state relations confirms these shifts in emphasis. Prior to the Civil War, the most significant cases concerned such things as the right of the federal government to establish a national bank free from state taxation (*McCulloch* v. *Maryland*, 1819) and to regulate interstate commerce – in this case the operation of ferries between New York and New Jersey (*Gibbons* v. *Ogden*, 1824). Later the Court, led by Chief Justice Taney, resolutely defended the right of the southern states to permit slavery – a right promptly removed by the war and the subsequent Thirteenth and Fourteenth Amendments. Between 1870 and 1938, the Court resisted attempts by the federal government to regulate industrial and commercial life – although anti-monopoly laws were upheld and a graduated federal income tax (one where the more you earn the more tax you pay) was eventually approved through constitutional amendment (Sixteenth Amendment, 1913). With the exception of the income tax question, which did inspire a vociferous debate on the role of the federal government, the period up to 1933 was characterized by a general agreement that the states were the proper level of government for most domestic policy formulation and implementation. Federal government power was on the increase, but presidents and Congresses generally accepted that *direct* intervention by the government in the economic and social life of the nation was undesirable.

All changed with the Depression of the 1930s and the advent of the New Deal. From 1933 the federal government began to legislate in a variety of new areas, from social security to public works. In reaction to what it saw as an unlawful interpretation of the Commerce Clause and Necessary and Proper Clause,[3] the Supreme Court struck down much of this new legislation in the name of the states' rights. Had these decisions prevailed, Roosevelt's New Deal would have been in serious trouble, and only a last-minute change in Court opinion prevented a constitutional crisis (see chapter 15).

Since this famous turnabout, the executive and judicial branches have been in approximate agreement over the *economic* role of the federal government in American society, although as we shall see this role has once again become a matter of controversy since the 1990s. Conflict has not disappeared from debate on federalism, however. The civil rights issue, in particular, inspired intense dispute between the states and all branches of the federal government during the 1950s and the 1960s. While state (and more recently local) resistance to federal civil rights laws and judicial decisions should not be underestimated, scholars have probably been right in emphasizing that conflict as such is not now the main characteristic of American federalism.

Morton Grodzins was the first to recognize the cooperative nature of federalism in the 1940s and 1950s. Using the metaphors of layer cake and marble cake to characterize conflictual and cooperative federalism, Grodzins identified the crucial transition of federalism from the intergovernmental antagonisms of the nineteenth century to the mutual interest and collaboration typical of the period from the late 1930s to the late 1950s.[4] Economic distress and external threat combined to transform the role of the federal government during this period. Lower-level governments responded to national emergency not with antagonism but in a spirit of cooperation and consensus. Since the 1960s, however, federalism has developed further, and cooperation is certainly not the main characteristic of intergovernmental relations today. Now, with the proliferation of programmes and policies at all levels of government, a much more confused and fragmented situation exists.

There are two main aspects to the complex picture which makes up federalism today: the changing federal role, especially in fiscal federalism, and the continuing debate over whether national standards in public policy should prevail, as opposed to standards set by state governments. As we will see, these two areas have been the source of intense passions in modern America.

The Changing Federal Role

The transformation of the federal role, 1930–1970

The reasons why the federal role increased over time are complex. Most relate to the close connection between administrative and political centralization and what might be called the nationalization of economic and social life. It is easy to be over-deterministic in this area – certainly the causal lines run in many directions. The evolution of mass-based political parties nominating presidents with national appeals was no doubt both an effect and a cause of the increasingly nationalized nature of economic life during the late nineteenth and early twentieth centuries. As corporations began to organize on national lines, so the need for national standards and regulations grew. Demands for minimum standards of (say) food processing or for fair competition required the sort of political mobilization that could come only from mass-based political parties. As these strengthened, so the need for better and more centralized organization on the part of commerce and industry to combat (or cooperate with) the federal government emerged. The growth of news dissemination inevitably aided this process, especially after the introduction of radio and television.

While all these forces were important, the main impetus to the growth of federal power came from two rather different sources – economic depression and war. As we noted earlier, it was the programmes of the New Deal and the massive military spending on the Second World War that transformed the federal role. Public spending as a percentage of Gross Domestic Product (GDP) increased from just 10 per cent in 1929 to 23 per cent in 1949, and the federal share of this expenditure increased from 2.6 to 16 per cent – much of it after 1939 as a result of increased defence spending.

A major spur both to increased federal spending and to producing qualitative changes in intergovernmental relations was the growth of federal grants in aid to state and local governments. There are two distinctions within any intergovernmental transfer system that must be drawn if the system is to be understood. First, it is necessary to distinguish between grants and payments that are paid *directly* to the population by the federal government and those that are paid to lower-level governments. The former – in the USA such things as social security, Medicare, agricultural subsidies – constitute a major part of federal spending. Grants to states and localities include both aid which goes directly to individuals through state and local governments – welfare used to be the most important item here – and aid for programmes such as highways and law enforcement where the state or local government constitutes the final stage in the transfer transaction. Figure 4.2 shows federal budget grants to state and localities for the 1960–2015 period. Note the rapid rise in grants to state and local government between 1960 and 1980, and their subsequent decline between 1980 and 1990. The initial rise is accounted for by the increased spending during Lyndon Johnson's Great Society, and the decline in

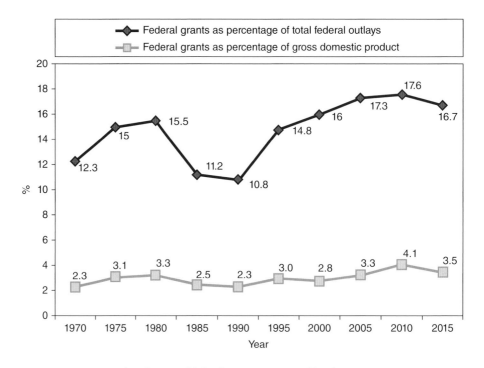

Figure 4.2   Percentage distribution of federal grants to state and local governments, 1960–2015
Source: Data from Robert J Dilger, Federal Grants to State and Local Governments as a Percentage of GDP and as a Percentage of Total Outlays, 1970–2015, source computed from data at https://www.fas.org/sgp/crs/misc/R40638.pdf, 2015.

the 1980s by the cuts in welfare by the Reagan administration. Finally, note the recovery of federal grants in the 1990s that has been maintained ever since. Note also the increase after 2009 when much of the federal economic stimulus spending to overcome recession came in the form of grants to lower-level governments. A clue to the rapid rise in grants in aid to lower-level governments during the 1960–80 period is the increase in general-purpose block grants after 1972. Indeed, the second crucial distinction in IGR is between block grants, which are general appropriations given to states and localities, and *categorical* grants, which are given for specific programmes and policies and which often have strings attached. For example, the Urban Renewal Program introduced in 1949 was categorical: it allocated monies to local governments specifically for the financing of downtown renewal. From 1954 until 1974, this money was available only if recipient governments abided by a 'workable programme' or general plan of how new development would fit in with existing housing and other facilities. In 1974, however, Urban Renewal, along with a number of related programmes, was replaced by Community Development Block Grants that carried considerably fewer restricting regulations. The Community Development Block Grant was just one of a series of block grants introduced by the Nixon and Ford administrations between 1970 and 1976. President Nixon was the architect of the main block grant scheme, General Revenue Sharing, introduced in 1972 and eventually abolished during the 1980s.

The Reagan administration: federalism revived?

CONTROVERSY 4 FEDERAL VERSUS STATE POWER

The proper balance between federal and state power has shifted dramatically through American history, and during two periods the issue dominated American political discourse. This was true in the 50 years up to the outbreak of the Civil War, when the most important domestic issues were the creation of a national bank, the tariff (to what extent American goods should be protected against foreign competition) and slavery. The southern states opposed the tariff and supported slavery, and considered federal interference in these areas unconstitutional. From 1933 to the 1950s public sentiment shifted dramatically towards the federal government, which was seen as the only possible salvation from the ravages of economic depression. States, on the other hand, were regarded as conservative and corrupt. It was during this period that most Americans accepted the need for federal action in welfare, social security, labour relations and support for industry and agriculture. Federal rather than state action was also deemed necessary to regulate banks, the stock market and mortgage credit.

More recent years have seen a resurgence of state in relation to federal power, with supporters of the states arguing that the states are the proper level of government for deciding a range of policy issues including penal and criminal procedural questions, abortion, gay marriage, employment practices and welfare. Indeed, the 1996 welfare reforms which devolved most welfare provision to the states (see chapter 17) were in part based on the experience of such states as Wisconsin and Minnesota. Generally, Republican administrations and the Supreme Court have favoured state over federal power, while the Democrats have for the most part favoured federal power. The resurgence of the states has, however, been tempered by their increasing fiscal problems (see figure 4.3). Most state constitutions require balanced budgets, so as economic recession took hold after 2008 the only way for the states to achieve this was through cutting state programmes (and raising taxes). To compensate for this, federal grants in aid have increased (figure 4.2).

In the twentieth century the federal versus state power debate was conflated with debate on the proper size and scope of government in society. Those favouring the states are usually also critics of government generally. Conversely, supporters of federal power also argue for a general extension of the role of government. But the issue is more complex than this, for even conservatives reluctantly accept the need for an enhanced federal role in some circumstances. Twenty-first-century Americans may distrust federal power, but they still need it not only to regulate the economy, but also during periods of serious economic dislocation and when natural disasters strike. Few would argue against emergency federal aid in such situations.

On the contrary, the public – and even conservative state governments – are usually unhappy because the aid is inadequate. And such demands are made even when the same people bemoan what they see as the domineering power of the federal government. Moreover conservatives' position on federalism is often determined by the nature of the issue rather than by a consistent commitment to states rights. Hence on moral issues such as abortion, gun control and gay rights they favour the often more conservative stance of state law, but on other issues such as immigration and prevention of terrorism laws they favour the more draconian action that only federal legislation can ensure. This paradox came into sharp relief with the election of Donald Trump in 2016. Trump's controls on immigration required a concentration of power in the federal government at the expense of state and local laws on immigration.

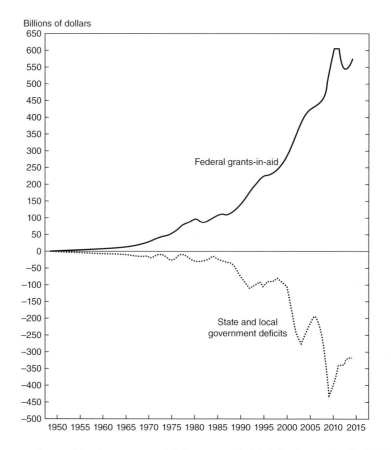

Figure 4.3   State and local government deficits compared with federal grant-in-aid, 1948–2015
Source: Stanley and Niemi, *Vital Statistics on American Politics, 2015–16*, figure 8.4. Reprinted with permission of SAGE.
Note: Amount in current dollars.

The 1960s as well as the 1970s were a period of rapidly rising federal expenditure. Many of the programmes through which this money was spent were associated with Lyndon Johnson's Great Society: Model Cities (1966) to reinvigorate inner-city areas; mass transit (1966) to provide cities with more efficient public transport; subsidized housing for 'moderate' and lower-income families (1968); Medicaid or medical aid for the poor (1965); and a whole host of smaller social welfare and other policies. In addition, the Great Society period witnessed an expansion of *existing* programmes – Urban Renewal, welfare and education. Many of these programmes – and especially the newer ones – had two features that, although not new, became much more pronounced during the 1960s. There was, first, the tendency for them to bypass the states and transfer funds directly to local governments. The states had long been identified as 'regressive' or 'backward' participants in the social reform process. Dominated by rural conservatives, state legislatures tended not to favour social reform measures. Given this, the Great Society's focus on aid to local governments was understandable. Second, it was within the jurisdictions of local, not state, governments that the social problems which inspired increased federal aid existed. Urban problems – racial conflict, inner-city decay, crime, poor housing, poverty – began to dominate the policy agenda during these years.

By the mid-1970s, therefore, through a broad range of categorical and block grant programmes, the federal government was providing help for most local governments as well as increasing numbers of individuals. A slightly more analytical way of putting this is that the federal government was increasingly perceived as a provider for both *redistributive* and *developmental* policies. The former redistributes income, usually through individuals, from better-off to poorer citizens. Developmental policies are those designed to improve the infrastructure – water and utility supplies, roads, mass transit, education and law enforcement. Redistributive policy had, since its inception in the 1930s, always been viewed as a federal responsibility, although welfare benefits were channelled through the states. Developmental policy had traditionally been considered a state and local government function.[5]

Small wonder that these new emphases, together with burgeoning civil rights legislation, bothered both fiscal conservatives and defenders of classic federalism. Bypassing the states was bad enough, but when this was combined with huge increases in government expenditure in areas where the federal government had traditionally played little or no role it appeared to many that not only federalism but America's free enterprise tradition was withering away.

The 1970s: Nixon and Ford as reluctant providers

Both Nixon and Ford faced a solidly Democratic House of Representatives throughout their tenure in office, and federal aid to state and local governments increased rapidly during these years. Although, during the second term of the Nixon administration, efforts were made to cut many of these programmes, they came to little. Not only was Congress deeply hostile to this project, the administration was itself weakened by the unfolding drama of the Watergate scandal. President Ford was even more hemmed in than was his predecessor, for in 1974 the Democrats won a landslide victory in the mid-term elections. The so-called 'Watergate Congress' was intent on a further expansion of the federal role, and federal aid to state and local government increased more rapidly during the mid-1970s than at any time since the Second World War. As a percentage of GDP grants increased from 1.5 per cent in 1965 to 3.1 per cent in 1975 (figure 4.2)

The election of Jimmy Carter led many commentators to conclude that the federal role would receive a further impetus. Carter was, of course, a Democrat and at that time the influence of the 'urban lobby' – supporters of grants, affirmative action, housing subsidies and welfare – in the Democratic Party remained strong. Paradoxically, however, it was during the Carter years that federal aid to state and local governments peaked. Carter believed in fiscal rectitude or the idea that the first responsibility of the national government was to balance the budget. What this meant in practice was holding back that part of federal spending that was considered 'controllable'. In practice this translated into attempts to limit aid to state and local governments. Other items on the budget were much less easy to cut. Defence spending had been reduced during the 1970s but the latter half of the decade saw increased east–west tensions that required greater defence expenditures. The other major budget item – social security – involved the distribution of *automatic* payments to old-age pensioners, widows and the disabled, so could not be touched. Carter did attempt to reform the federal welfare role and he even tried to forge a 'national urban policy', but lacking a clear commitment to specific reforms in these areas, his plans came to nothing.

A further reason for the decline in support for federal aid in the late 1970s was an increasing awareness that many of the new programmes of the Johnson/Nixon era were inefficient, corrupt or both. In many instances state and local governments, strapped for cash, simply diverted money from programmes designed for particular purposes into general funds which were used to pay salaries and the like. This was an especially serious problem when federal money went directly to local governments or to the private sector. Housing and urban development programmes were particularly prone to this sort of abuse. Intellectual and political opinion was turning against the view that big government was the answer to all of society's problems. For in spite of all the new programmes and policies, no improvement in crime levels, education and urban conditions generally was discernible. At the same time, the economic dislocations of the 1970s led many to believe that excessive government spending was a cause of inflation and recession. An obvious step towards correcting these problems would be a reduction in federal government aid to state and local governments. As we will see, it was left to the Reagan administration to implement these changes.

The Reagan administration: federalism revived?

In his campaign speeches and his 1981 inaugural address, Ronald Reagan made the revival of federalism a central part of his programme to rekindle traditional American values. The federal government had become inefficient, insensitive and cumbersome and, so the argument ran, should be reduced radically in size. One way to achieve this was to revive Richard Nixon's original idea and consolidate myriad categorical grant-in-aid programmes into a number of block grants. In this way, the states would be returned to their 'rightful' position as the main source of domestic policies and programmes. Accordingly, during 1981 the administration proposed consolidating 83 categorical programmes into six human services block grants (health services, preventive health services, social services, energy and emergency assistance, local education services and state education services). The total amount of federal money involved here was $11 billion. At the same time the 1981 Budget Reconciliation Act reduced federal spending in a wide range of programmes. Some intergovernmental programmes were eliminated altogether, while others were subject to substantial real cuts.

Briefing   US Federalism in Comparative Perspective

Students of federalism typically measure the strength of states in relation to the federal government by looking at four key features:

1. How well the states are protected constitutionally. In some systems such as the Swiss, state powers are carefully enumerated and protected in the constitution. In the US, they are not. As this chapter has shown, in the American system this has been a matter for interpretation, with the courts gradually ceding more and more power to the federal government.

2. The extent to which the upper house acts as a 'chamber of the states'. In Switzerland and Germany upper houses perform this role and protect the states from incursions from the federal government. In the US, although the Senate initially played this role, it ceased to do so in the first part of the nineteenth century. Today, US senators, although they may defend their own state's interest, do not act collectively for all the states. Instead party and ideology influence how they stand on particular issues.

3. The fiscal independence of the states. By some criteria, the American states have more autonomy than Australian states or the German Länder. They can levy their own taxes and spend them as they wish. However, federal spending is dominant in some areas, and the American states increasingly depend on grants in aid from the federal government.

4. The nature of the party system. If parties are mainly or solely state-based – as with the Belgian parties or the Parti Quebecois in Canada – it suggests strong states in relation to the federal government. American parties are national rather than state-focused however. They may be decentralized, but there is no 'Texas' party for example, although until the 1970s the Democrats in the South did have a distinctive and exclusive base.

By most measures the US has a relatively weak federal system, therefore, and is clearly more centralized than the Swiss or the Canadian system. Of other major federal systems only the Australian is more centralized.

Later, in 1982, the administration presented an even more radical plan for a 'New Federalism' involving a 'swap' of the three main welfare programmes funded by the states and federal government on a matching basis. Welfare and food stamps would be taken over by the states, while the federal government assumed responsibility for Medicaid (medical care for the poor). This plan was combined with a massive 'turnback' to the states of most other grant-in-aid programmes, which, initially at least, would be funded by a special trust fund.

In just five years, however, the fund would be wound up, leaving the states in glorious isolation. In the meantime, an immediate 25 per cent cut in funding would be imposed.

The plan was greeted with almost unanimous opposition from the states, Congress and even from within the Office of Management and Budget – Medicaid was the most rapidly growing item in the federal budget. Within months the 'swap' plan was dropped, as was the grandiose scheme for a near-complete devolution of programmes to the states. In the event, Congress accepted some of the consolidations into block grants and some of the cuts. During the rest of the Reagan years this became the general pattern. Generally, transport, education and capital spending programmes suffered most. These 'developmental' programmes had been reduced considerably by 1990.

Although the grand strategy of the New Federalism had to be abandoned, Ronald Reagan had succeeded in reversing the historical trend towards ever-increasing federal aid for developmental purposes. Indeed, federal grants declined from 3.3 per cent of GDP in 1980 to 2.3 per cent in 1990 (figure 4.2).

George H. W. Bush and Clinton: an adapting federal role?

In his 1989 inaugural address, George Bush mentioned federalism and the states not once. And although the president did later pledge that he would continue the Reagan agenda of devolving power to the states, he lacked political and emotional commitment to the idea.

During the Bush years a Democratic Congress found itself under increasing pressure to resume higher levels of intergovernmental aid. By 1989–90 a number of states and cities were beginning to experience fiscal stress as economic recession eroded tax bases, but politicians were unwilling or unable to increase taxes. Federal programmes were, once again, viewed by states and localities as possible saviours. In 1992 first the Los Angeles riots and then the Miami hurricane demonstrated that, like it or not, federal governments are expected to come up with major aid programmes following local or regional disasters. In both cases the Bush administration produced emergency aid packages. In spite of these events, the Bush years saw no major reversal of the trends established during the Reagan years.

During his first campaign for president, Bill Clinton gave the strong impression that he would resume the old-style fiscal federalism of the 1960s and 1970s. He proposed an immediate $19.5 billion economic development package to stimulate the economy. He was politically close to a group of economists who believed that the federal government should play an enhanced role in the provision of infrastructure and in particular transport and communications in order to facilitate faster economic growth. What this would mean in practice would be greatly increased developmental aid to state and local governments. Once elected he appointed one of these economists, Robert Reich, as his Secretary of Labor, and during the first two months of his administration a revival of fiscal federalism looked imminent.

By the end of Clinton's first term, however, the political agenda had changed to such an extent that the administration's position on federalism looked more like that of President Reagan than President Johnson. What accounts for this transformation? For one thing, President Clinton's ambitious economic stimulus programme immediately ran into trouble in Congress. Republican senators managed to block the legislation, and by the summer of 1993 many

Democrats had become sceptical of the need for such an ambitious programme. For another thing, the economy recovered fast and any new federal expenditure looked incompatible with the need to reduce the budget deficit. Within the administration, the influence of the fiscal conservatives increased, while that of the proponents of an enhanced federal role declined. In the event, the only important measure passed that enhanced the federal role was a crime bill, which provided new federal resources for local police enforcement.

The agenda changed again after the election of the Republican 104th Congress in 1994. Thereafter, proposed changes involved a *reduction* rather than an increase in federal aid to state and local governments. In particular, the new Congress wanted to change the *redistributive* as well as the *developmental* role of the federal government. Federal welfare programmes, in particular, were seen to encourage dependency and discourage work. 'Workfare' rather than welfare became the slogan of the 1990s, and the states were to be allocated a major role in a reformed welfare system. In 1996 Congress enacted welfare reform, which effectively delegated the responsibility for welfare provision to the states. We will return to this subject in chapter 17.

George W. Bush: a 'fair weather' federalist?

In spite of his tenure as governor of Texas, and statements during his 2000 election campaign in support of the states, George W. Bush did not share Ronald Reagan's enthusiasm for state sovereignty. Instead he tended to support devolution to the states when it was politically expedient and to reject it when it was not. Hence his administration consistently challenged state laws that pursued a liberal agenda in such areas as the medical use of marijuana, stem cell research, same-sex marriages and environmental protection. In some instances, the administration actually supported legislation that directly challenged state courts. Such was the case with Terry Schiavo, a brain-dead patient whom the Florida courts had decided should be allowed to die. The Bush administration, however, pushed through a federal law overturning the decision. What is interesting about this new 'centralization' is that in many instances the states were painted as the 'progressive' or liberal influences while the federal government was portrayed as conservative – an exact reversal of the traditional roles.

The same was true of the administration's response to Hurricane Katrina, which devastated New Orleans in 2005. Initially, at least, it was left to state and local governments to deal with the crisis, and only after a public outcry was the federal government forced to take action.

This said, when it suited the president's ideological agenda he supported state prerogatives, as was the case in such areas as prayers in public schools, gun control and capital punishment. As far as fiscal federalism is concerned, the Bush administration was equally unconcerned with philosophical niceties. As figure 4.2 shows, federal grants increased from 2.9 per cent of GDP during the late 1990s to a peak of 3.6 per cent in 2003. Indeed as a percentage of federal outlays grants have increased to historically high levels. This is partly the result of a (Republican) Congress increasingly intent on 'earmarking' pork-barrel benefits for constituents in such areas as transportation, agriculture and public works.[6] (The initial fiscal prudence of the 104th Congress was soon to evaporate; for a discussion, see chapter 8.) In addition, the administration supported expansionist federal programmes in education, agriculture, homeland security, energy and health. While these have involved increased federal spending, sometimes federal initiatives have included 'unfunded mandates' or federal directives in such areas as education that require state and localities to comply with federal law in the absence of federal funds to finance the full implementation of the law. Such was the case with the No Child Left Behind Act, which mandated universal testing of elementary and secondary schoolchildren with the threat of the withdrawal of federal aid should the schools not comply (for further discussion, see chapter 17). In the event almost all schools did comply.

In effect, the Bush administration held no consistent view of federalism. It certainly paid lip service to the *idea* of devolving power to the states, but when this clashed with political priorities – as it often did – then these invariably trumped any traditional Republican notion that the states were in some way sovereign in certain policy areas.

Barack Obama: back to the 1960s?

Barack Obama's relations with the states were dominated by the economic problems that beset his first term. What this meant in practice was greatly increased aid to the states combined with more strings attached to federal largesse. Of the $787 billion in the fiscal stimulus package, one-third went to the states through a number of programmes ranging from Medicaid to infrastructure to education. At the same time much of this new money was given on the provision that it should be spent quickly and not 'vired' or transferred into other programmes. The rules included the careful monitoring of expenditure to ensure that it went where intended. As Obama's first term was also a period of state fiscal crisis (see figure 4.3), the federal government was in a strong position to tighten its grip on the states.

Paradoxically, however, Obama invoked federalism to defend his position on some moral issues, and in particular same-sex marriage. In 2012 he bravely stated his support for this institution, but also expressed his belief that it was up to the states to decide whether to legislate for same-sex unions or not. This was, of course, quite different from his position on abortion – he was a strong supporter of the *Roe* v. *Wade* ruling that allowed women to opt for abortion irrespective of where they lived (see chapter 16, pp. 362). Later in 2016 he supported the right of transgender citizens to use the public bathrooms of their choice rather than be forced by some state laws that insist that such peoples' birth certificate status should determine which public toilets they use. Note also that by 2017 the lion's share of federal grant money was channelled to individuals through the states and that payments to individuals constitute by far the largest component (figure 4.4). This reflects the rapid expansion of Medicaid (medical care for the poor), which was greatly enhanced under the 2010 Affordable Care Act (also known as Obamacare) but which was only implemented some years later. We will return to this subject in chapter 16.

A Changing Court Role?

As indicated above, as far as the economic and social dimension of federalism is concerned, the Supreme Court deferred to the other branches from the late 1930s onwards. In other

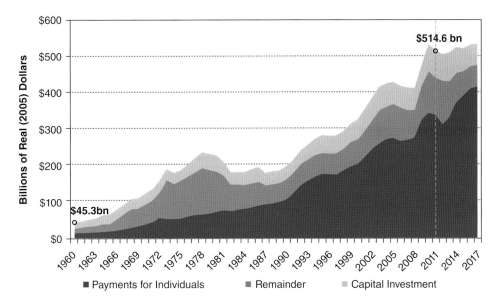

Figure 4.4   Outlays for federal grants to state and local governments by function, 1960–2017
Source: Mercatus Centre, George Mason University, http://mercatus.org/sites/default/files/Federal-grant-aid-state-and-local-data-chart-1.jpg.

words, where the federal government's powers over the economic and social affairs of the states began and ended would be decided by president and Congress rather than by judicial interpretation of the Constitution. Indeed, in 1985, in what looked like a landmark decision (*Garcia* v. *San Antonio Metropolitan Transit Authority*), the Court argued that the federal government could regulate the wages of San Antonio bus workers because the limits to federal power 'inhered principally in the workings of the national government itself'. Most commentators took this to mean a complete abdication of the role of the Supreme Court in arbitrating between state and federal law. However, just seven years later the Supreme Court appeared to reverse itself with two dramatic decisions, which seemed to put strict constitutional limits on what the federal government could do. In the first, *New York* v. *United States*, the Court struck down a 1985 law requiring states to dispose of radioactive waste. In the majority decision, Justice Sandra Day O'Connor invoked the Tenth Amendment and reasoned that 'The Constitution … [does not] authorize Congress simply to direct the States to provide for the disposal of radioactive waste generated within their borders.' Later in *US* v. *Lopez* (1995), the Court appeared to go further by striking down a federal law which would have established gunfree zones within 1,000 yards of schools. In passing this law Congress had invoked the interstate commerce clause by arguing that high crime levels around schools could increase the cost of insurance and travel. What the Court was doing here was arguing that there *were* limits to the interpretation of the Commerce Clause. As Chief Justice Rehnquist put it:

We pause to consider the implications of the Government's arguments. The Government admits, under its 'costs of crime' reasoning, that Congress could regulate not only all violent crime, but all activities that might lead to violent crime, regardless of how tenuously they relate to interstate commerce. Similarly, under the Government's 'national productivity' reasoning, Congress could regulate any activity that it found was related to the economic productivity of individual citizens: family law (including marriage, divorce, and child custody), for example. Under the theories that the Government presents … it is difficult to perceive any limitation on federal power, even in areas such as criminal law enforcement or education where States historically have been sovereign. Thus, if we were to accept the Government's arguments, we are hard pressed to posit any activity by an individual that Congress is without power to regulate.

These decisions were followed by others in a similar vein, including a 1997 case (*Printz* v. *United States*) that invalidated parts of the 1997 Brady gun control, which required background checks on would-be purchasers.

While these decisions are of obvious importance, they do not necessarily represent unambiguous limits on the ways in which the federal government can control the powers of the states. Much depends on the circumstances of individual laws and individual cases. What is clear, however, is that, for the first time since the 1930s, the Supreme Court does recognize limits to what can be done in the name of the Commerce Clause. In so doing it has begun to recognize that the Tenth Amendment does have some validity and application. Another way of viewing this is to argue that a conservative Supreme Court, such as the present one, will actively limit attempts by Congress to apply national standards in a range of social policy and criminal justice areas.

With the re-election of Barack Obama in 2012 and the Republicans continuing to control the House, many commentators believed that the stage was set for the Court to strike down liberalizing legislation under the Commerce Clause, just as it did in the 1920s and 1930s. This would bring into sharp relief the polarized nature of American politics, with a conservative Supreme Court aligned not only against the other branches of the government, but also against the more liberal states. However, this did not come to pass. In the landmark 2012 decision *National Federation of Independent Business* v. *Sebelius* the Court upheld Obama's Affordable Health Care Act that greatly increased federal control over health care (but it did strike down the provision that obliged the states to greatly expand Medicaid funds).

And in *United States* v. *Windsor* (2013), the Court ruled that Congress could not define marriage to exclude same-sex marriages regardless of state law. A further victory for the administration was scored in *Arizona* v. *United States* (2012), which held that most of the provisions of the strict Arizona immigration statute were pre-empted by federal law because the 'state may not pursue policies that violate federal law'. In effect the Supreme Court could only count on three consistently conservative members – Justices Thomas, Scalia and Alito, with Chief Justice Roberts and Justice Kennedy sometimes siding with the liberals on the question of federal versus state power. We will return to this point in chapter 15.

The Future of American Federalism

Most observers would agree that classical federalism, with state and federal governments each sovereign and separate in their own designated area, is effectively dead – indeed, there is serious doubt that it ever applied in the United States. Cooperative federalism, which dominated intergovernmental relations from the 1930s to the 1970s, is also inappropriate as a description of the 2000s. Competitive interdependence is a much more accurate label, but it describes federal, state and local relations, not just federal–state interactions. If this is so, what is left of federalism? A lot more than would have been expected just 15 or 20 years ago. For, as argued, since the late 1980s not only has there been a top-down attempt to devolve power by Congress, but also the Supreme Court has made serious attempts to revive federalism by strengthening the Tenth Amendment and by reinterpreting the Commerce Clause. While this is not the equivalent to a return to the pre-1937 era, it does show the general trend towards the devolution of power in the USA. And, of course, the states do remain very important administrative and political units. As we noted at the beginning of the chapter, the states preserve variety – each continues to have its own separate legal and political system, and travelling from state to state the observer is aware of distinctive political cultures. Certainly, the states preserve a degree of local or regional political autonomy that is quite unfamiliar in more centralized political systems. The states are now also much more *efficient* and professional as policy-makers than ever before. As state government has increased in size and status it has attracted more able personnel. Governors are of higher quality, and corruption, although still a part of some states' political culture, is less prevalent than it used to be. Finally, states now do a great deal more than they used to, not only in administering federal programmes but also in running their own. But this resilience and growth derive not so much from constitutional imperatives as from traditions, custom and the fact that the states remain *politically convenient* jurisdictions for the representation of a variety of interests. State law remains pre-eminent in many areas of economic and social life, including industrial relations, insurance and almost all aspects of family law. At the same time, state and local taxes are the main source of revenue for a range of distinctive state and locally provided services, including transport, education and law enforcement. As noted, the role of the states has increased as federal governments have required them to participate in the implementation of federally funded or partly funded programmes. In addition, the states have now become policy leaders in a number of crucial areas, including environmental protection and health care. The constitutional position of the states may also be weak, but in many respects they remain *politically* independent.

Put another way, many voters expect state rather than federal authorities to be responsible for a wide range of public policies. Indeed, the states are at the very heart of some of the most important issues in American politics. Federal law, for example, mandates the right to abortion. Anti-abortion or pro-life activists want to return decisions on the subject to state legislatures, many of which would abolish the right to abortion. Under pressure from voters, whether directly via initiatives or through state legislatures, the states have taken important decisions in a range of other areas, including affirmative action, same-sex marriage, penal policy, health care, environmental protection and education. And in contrast to the 1960s and 1970s, Congress and the federal courts have been reluctant to challenge these decisions and reassert federal power. Often, the contrast between federal and state policy reflects the growing polarization in American politics, with liberal states such as Massachusetts and California advancing a progressive agenda in health care, moral issues and environmental protection in contrast to the conservative federal policies of the 2001–2009 period. The election of a liberal Democratic president in 2008 and again in 2012, caused this dynamic to change, and the potential for conflict shifted to a

Plate 4.1   Rick Scott, Governor of Florida, addressing crowd
Source: Joe Raedle/Getty, www.gettyimages.co.uk/license/458291896.

battle between the Republican House of Representatives (and also the Senate after 2014) together with the more conservative states in the south and the west and the federal government.

Although after 2016 the Republicans controlled both the presidency and Congress it did not herald an end to conflicts over federalism. Many of those states still controlled by the Democrats opposed Trump administration policies that conflicted with state and local preferences in such areas as immigration, environmental protection and abortion.

Summary

While the US has a federal system of government or a division of powers and popular sovereignty between the federal and the 50 state governments, the exact relationship has changed considerably over time. The main changes since the beginning of the twentieth century have been the rise of the power of the federal government that, following the Great Depression and the Second World War, became the dominant partner in the American system. From the 1930s to the 1970s federal intervention in the affairs of the states occurred because only the federal government could play a redistributive and developmental role in such areas as welfare, transportation and housing given the limited financial and political sources of most states. Since the 1970s, the federal government role has changed again. Starting with the Reagan administration, a roll-back of federal aid occurred with the intention of reducing expenditure and returning power to the states. Most recently, the Obama administration was more active in its use of federal power, using it as a lever to help states stimulate the economy. At the same time, like George W. Bush, Obama was sometimes selective in his attitude towards federal power, leaving, for example, the matter of same-sex marriages to state rather than federal law. However, against all expectations, in 2012 and 2013 the Supreme Court handed down important decisions that strengthened the federal government in relation to the states. In *Arizona* v. *US*, much of Arizona's law giving police the power to stop those suspected of illegal immigration was invalidated, and in the same year Obama's Affordable Care Act was upheld having been challenged by 26 states as unconstitutional. Finally, in 2013 the Court ruled that Congress had no tight to define marriage as exclusively heterosexual irrespective of state laws.

Questions for Discussion

1   How has federalism changed since the 1980s? Answer with respect to the moral issues that are often at the heart of federal/state conflict.
2   Why do the states increasingly depend on federal grants in aid that end up being channelled to individual citizens? How has the composition of such grants changed over recent years?
3   How strong is the US federal system compared with federalism in other countries?
4   To what extent have the states become conservative in public policy while the federal government has often been viewed as liberal? Answer with respect to the 1981–2017 period.

Glossary

block grants   Grants from the federal government to the states not allocated to specific purposes

categorical grants   Grants from the federal government to the states allocated to specific purposes

centralization   The act of centralizing authority and power

classical federalism   Federal arrangements where the division of power between the centre and the states is clear and unambiguous

Commerce Clause   The power in the US Constitution giving the federal government the power to regulate interstate commerce

competitive interdependence   The modern condition of US federalism where the states and the federal government are competitive and interdependent

conflictual federalism   The condition where conflict between the states and federal government exists

cooperative federalism   The condition where the relationship between the states and the federal government is essentially cooperative

developmental policies   Those policies that involve economic and social development, such as transportation and urban renewal

dual sovereignty   The division of power and sovereignty between different levels of government

earmarking   Guaranteeing funding for specific constituency projects or benefits as attachments to bills

fiscal federalism   Those aspects of federalism involving taxing and spending

Gross Domestic Product (GDP)   The financial total of all activity in the economy

intergovernmental relations   The political relationship between federal, state and local government

localism   The devotion of citizens to a local territory or jurisdiction

New Federalism   The label attached to Ronald Reagan's attempts to devolve power to the states

No Child Left Behind Act (NCLB)   The institution of universal testing of school-children's performance by the federal government

pork-barrel politics   Legislation designed to benefit individual constituencies

redistributive policies   Policies designed to redistribute resources across social classes, age cohorts or jurisdictions

regulatory powers   Powers designed to regulate economic, social or political activity

unfunded mandates   Federal policies requiring states to implement policies but not funded by the federal government

workable programme   Policies with provisions designed to assess the social and economic impact of programmes

Notes

1   The classic statement on the nature of dual federalism is by Morton Grodzins, *The American System* (Chicago: Rand McNally, 1966).

2   This abbreviation is taken from Deil S. Wright, *Understanding Intergovernmental Relations* (North Scituate: Duxbury, 1978).

3   Section 8, Clause 18, which empowers Congress to make laws which are necessary and proper to implement its enumerated powers, including the regulation of interstate commerce.

4   Grodzins, *The American System*

5   These distinctions are taken from Paul E. Peterson, *The Price of Federalism* (Washington, DC: Brookings Institution, 1995).

6   See Thomas E. Mann and Norman J. Ornstein, *The Broken Branch: How Congress is Failing America and How to Get It Back on Track* (New York: Oxford University Press, 2006), chapter 5.

Further Reading

For a good account of the ways presidents increasingly use federal grants to advance their agenda, see John Hudak, *Presidential Pork: White House Influence over the Distribution of Federal Grants* (Washington, DC: Brookings, 2014). For the traditional view of the transition from conflictual to cooperative federalism, see Morton Grodzins, *The American System* (Chicago: Rand McNally, 1966). For a general introduction, see Joseph Zimmerman, *Contemporary American Federalism* (New York: State University of New York Press, 2009). For a comparative perspective, see David McKay, *Designing Europe: Comparative Lessons for the European Union* (Oxford: Oxford University Press, 2001).

CHAPTER 5
AMERICAN POLITICAL PARTIES
POLARIZED AND DISUNITED

A democratic society has to provide a mode of consistent representation of relatively stable alignments or modes of compromise in its polity. The mechanism of the American polity has been the two party system. If the party system, with its enforced mode of compromise, gives way, and 'issue politics' begin to polarize groups, then we have the

American Politics and Society, Ninth Edition. David McKay.
© 2018 John Wiley & Sons Ltd. Published 2018 by John Wiley & Sons Ltd.

classic recipe for what political scientists call 'a crisis of the regime', if not a crisis of disintegration and revolution.

– DANIEL BELL, *THE PUBLIC INTEREST*, 1977

Disloyal R's are far more difficult than Crooked Hillary. They come at you from all sides. They don't know how to win – I will teach them!

TWEET BY DONALD TRUMP, 11 OCTOBER 2016

To the outside observer, the American party system can be very difficult to understand. Parties appear to be coalitions of many interests. They are organizationally weak and in a constant state of crisis. In contrast, most European political parties have quite vivid public images based on class, regional, religious, linguistic, ethnic or ideological divisions.

While this is an oversimplified characterization of the two types of party system, it remains broadly true that American parties cover a narrower band of the ideological spectrum than do their European counterparts. Historically they have also been much less *programmatic*, offering their supporters very general and diffuse policy options rather than the more structured and specific policy programmes associated with European parties – although there have been signs of the emergence of more programmatic parties in the US in recent years. What is true of almost all party systems is that they are constantly developing and adapting to rapid social and economic changes – a fact which leads so many commentators to attach the label 'crisis' to the most recent development or electoral event. The remarkable thing about the American system is that it has always had just two major parties – although not always the same two parties – competing for major offices at any one time. Moreover, until recently these parties have been largely non-ideological and inclusive in style and policy substance, and this in a country constantly being buffeted by the very major social changes that immigration, industrialization and urbanization have brought. So a defining characteristic of both the Democrats and the Republicans is that they have constantly sought to appeal to as wide a spectrum of voters as possible. As such they have been obliged to promise *general* rather than *specific* benefits to voters. Once in office, however, party politicians have been obliged to focus on the provision of specific benefits. Honouring specific promises to one group often means penalizing another group. With the increasing polarization characteristic of American politics, this problem has become more acute over the past 20 years. We will return to this point later.

A large part of this chapter is devoted to explaining why the American party system has taken the particular shape it has. As we shall see, however, although this system retained its two-party, largely non-ideological status through most of history, it has by no means been static or unchanging. In organization and function the parties have changed quite dramatically over the past 240 years – and indeed have changed considerably over the past 20 years. To understand these changes it is first necessary to discuss the functions that political parties normally perform in political systems.

The Functions of Parties

Although often abused by politicians and publics alike, political parties do perform vital functions in every political system, and in countries with democratic traditions they are an indisputably necessary part of the democratic process. In the American context parties perform at least five major functions.[1]

Aggregation of demands

In any society, social groups with particular interests to promote or defend need some means whereby their demands can be aggregated and articulated in government. Traditionally, political parties have performed this function – hence the association of party with particular social groups, regions or religions. In the USA parties have acquired just such associations, although, as noted, to a lesser extent than in some other countries. Hence, the Democrats became the party of southern interests quite early in history, although by the 1930s the Democrats had also become the party of northern industrial workers. The Republicans were originally the anti-slavery party of the North but eventually developed into the party of national unity and later became identified as the party most interested in defending free enterprise and corporate power, an identification that remains to this day.

But generally parties in the United States have not been exclusively associated with one social group or class or one geographical region. Instead they tend to be coalitions of interests, aggregating demands on behalf of a number of social groups and regional interests. Even in today's more heated ideological climate this remains true, although the Republicans have come to resemble a more partisan and ideologically committed party than in the past.

Conciliation of groups in society

Even in the most divided society some conciliation between competing or conflicting interests has to occur if government is to operate efficiently. Political parties often help this conciliation process by providing united platforms for the articulation of diverse interests. Indeed, in the USA, there has hardly been a major political party that has not performed this function. In recent history, the Democrats have attempted (and until 1964 largely succeeded) in reconciling a rural segregationist South with the interests of the urban industrial North. In specific elections, the particular coalition of support established is uniquely determined by contemporary issues and candidates. So in 1960 Democratic presidential candidate John F. Kennedy managed to appeal to both the Catholic voters of the North (Kennedy was himself a Catholic) and southern Protestants. In 1968 and 1972, the law-and-order issue cut across regions and classes and helped bring victory to Richard M. Nixon, the Republican candidate. By 1980 the Republicans had forged a new coalition consisting of a regional component (the West and the South), a religious/moral component (the Christian right) and an economic/ideological component (the middle classes and supporters of a 'return' to free enterprise). By conciliating such diverse groups and offering a common programme, Republican candidate Ronald Reagan was assured victory. In 1988 George Bush managed to retain the loyalty of sufficient numbers of these same groups to win. In 1992 Bill Clinton was successful in reviving at least parts of the old New Deal coalition by appealing to industrial workers, minorities, women and many middle-class voters on the issue of economic revival. His appeal in 1996 was slightly different, based as it was on a vote for the status quo. As in 1992, however, Clinton managed to form a complex coalition of support based on gender, ethnicity and region (the West and the industrial North).

In 2000, Al Gore almost managed to re-create this winning coalition. He won most of the northeastern and Pacific states and won large majorities among women and ethnic minorities. In contrast to Clinton, however, his overall popular majority did not translate into a victory in the Electoral College. And, in contrast to Bob Dole in 1996, George W. Bush managed to win some key industrial states, such as Ohio, and, of course, the hotly disputed Florida vote – a feat he managed to repeat in 2004. In 2008 Barack Obama created what looked like a more long-lasting coalition consisting of younger voters, minorities and women, with geographical strength spread almost everywhere except the deep South, Texas and the more conservative mountain and plains states. Indeed, the 2012 results demonstrated the resilience of this coalition, with the Democrats winning every state they had won in 2008 with the exception of North Carolina and Indiana. Obama's showing was particularly strong among Hispanic and Asian voters – two groups that are growing rapidly in numbers and influence. While the same was true of Hillary Clinton's support in 2016 it was not enough to overcome the surge in white working class support for Donald Trump in the key 'battleground' states of Ohio, Pennsylvania, Michigan and Wisconsin. By losing narrowly in most of these states and also winning Florida Trump was able to secure an Electoral College majority – although not a majority of the national popular vote.

Clearly, political parties have to appeal to a number of competing and potentially conflicting interests if they are to succeed in a country as diverse and complex as the United States. As a result, parties have tended to move towards the middle of the ideological spectrum, avoiding those more extreme positions likely to alienate potential supporters. Noting this tendency towards moderation, political theorists have produced a more general model of party behaviour that assumes that if parties are rational and really want to win elections they will *always* move towards the median voter or the centre ground in politics. Only in this way can they ensure majority electoral support.[2] Whatever its merits in other countries, this theory seems particularly apt in the United States, where with rather few exceptions (of which more below) parties have remained generally moderate.

Staffing the government

In a modern, complex society parties are a necessary link in the relationship between government and people. According to social contract theory, governments must be held accountable for their actions. If they are perceived to be failing, then the people can always replace them at election time. Unfortunately, accountability and responsiveness can never be continuous or complete except in very small societies or communities. Given this, parties provide the public with a focus for accountability. Once elected, a president appoints government officials to fill the major posts in the new administration. Not only departmental chiefs (members of the cabinet) but also the top civil service positions are filled in the main through party linkages (see chapter 10). When judging the performance of the government, therefore, the public can look to the record of an administration united by a common party label and, presumably, a common set of policies. As the party is rooted in society via party organizations, staffing the government through party helps to ensure an intimate link between the implementation of policies and public preference. This at least is the theory of how party should operate in government. As we will discover below, the practice is rather different. One serious practical problem occurs when party organization, rather than reflecting the interests of social groups or regions, is instead merely the vehicle for the promotion and election of a particular *candidate*. Another problem, to which we now turn, occurs when different branches of government have different constituencies and therefore distinct party organizations.

Coordination of government institutions

As has already been noted several times, American government is uncommonly fragmented. National legislature is separated from executive. Federalism adds a further fragmenting influence by giving state (and through the states, local) governments considerable independence from the federal authorities. In centralized systems with cabinet government, parties actually dominate institutions. In Britain, for example, powerful political party organizations nominate candidates, fight elections and, if successful, form the government out of a majority in the House of Commons. By exercising control over the party organization and in particular over nominations for office, governments (or oppositions) can usually ensure the obedience of individual Members of Parliament. In this sense party is hardly needed as a coordinating influence, because a system of *party government* prevails. In marked contrast, America's separated powers and federal arrangements greatly aggravate problems of coordination, and as numerous American political scientists have pointed out, party is the main means whereby disparate institutions can coordinate the formulation and implementation of policy.[3]

So, even if state and local government, Congress and president have different constituencies, a common party label can provide a means of communication and coordination. In fact, Democratic governors, mayors and members of Congress usually do have more in common with Democratic presidents than with Republican presidents – although we will discover below that they often do not. Certainly there have been periods in American history when relations between Congress and president have been greatly aided by political party ties. During the Jeffersonian period, for example, something approaching party government prevailed. More recently, Presidents Franklin Roosevelt and Lyndon Johnson (both Democrats) used party ties greatly to enhance their relations with Congress and thus erect major new social programmes. During the 1969–77 and 1981–93 periods Republican presidents faced a Congress dominated by Democrats, although the Republicans held the Senate between 1981 and 1987. Divided government of a very different sort prevailed after 1994 when the Republicans controlled Congress and the Democrats the presidency. George W. Bush enjoyed unified government from 2002 to 2004 – which together with the national solidarity resulting from 9/11 attacks on New York and Pentagon helped him to make a significant impact on the legislative agenda. Most recently Barack Obama enjoyed unified government after 2008 with the Democrats winning not only the presidency but also increased majorities in both houses of Congress. However, this unity was short-lived for in 2010 the Republicans regained the House of Representatives (although not the Senate), thus making the last two years very difficult in legislative terms. In 2012 this pattern prevailed, although the Republicans lost seats in both the House and the Senate. Full divided government returned in 2014 when the Republicans made dramatic gains to capture the Senate and make large advances in the House. As a result, the last two years of the Obama presidency were marked by hostile relations between the two branches. Against all expectations, the Democrats lost the presidency in 2016 and also failed to make anything but minor inroads into the Republican majorities in the House and the Senate. From 2017, therefore, the US enjoyed a period of unified government.

At the state and local levels, the coordinating function of party has taken a rather different form. In the decades immediately following the Civil War, municipal, and to a lesser extent state, governments proved less than adequate in dealing with successive waves of immigrants from Europe. Hopelessly divided, and fragmented institutionally and politically, local governments could do little to improve transport, housing and other urban facilities, or even to ensure a reasonable degree of public order. Political parties filled this void through the creation of the political machine – an informal 'government' based on patronage, bribery and corruption.[4] Machines depended on tightly knit grassroots organization, with the party providing ordinary citizens with direct access to the political authorities. Officials in the legitimate government gained through patronage and bribes, and the party was given a guarantee of political power in return. Although hardly welfare organizations, the urban machines of the late nineteenth and early twentieth centuries did at least keep government going in the great cities by providing an essential buffer between the immigrant masses and a hostile economic and political environment.

Promotion of political stability

Parties do not always promote political stability. In many countries parties mobilize movements against existing regimes and are a major force in bringing regime change. Moreover, if *governmental* (as opposed to regime) stability is the measure, it is clear that the multiparty systems of western Europe do anything but promote stability, as the Italian, Belgian and other systems testify (although recent changes in the Italian electoral system have led to more stability). In 'mature' democracies, however, parties do help to socialize citizens into an acceptance of the regime, if only by legitimizing national parliaments and assemblies and facilitating the peaceful transfer of power from one government to another.

For reasons to be discussed below, America's two-party system has proved remarkably resilient, with the result that the country has never suffered the problems associated with a proliferation of organized parties. Although the causal lines are blurred, it does seem reasonable to argue that American political parties have helped to promote political stability. Quite frequently, for example, political movements outside the mainstream of American political life have had their policies pre-empted by one of the leading parties. This happened to the Populists during the 1890s when much of their programme was adopted by the Democrats, and to a number of left-wing parties and movements during the early New Deal period. Moreover, the two most significant third parties of the twentieth century, the Progressives and the American Independent Party, grew out of existing parties and were eventually reincorporated into them. In both cases the breakaway was led by a single charismatic figure – Theodore Roosevelt in the case of the Progressives in 1912 and George Wallace in the case of the American Independent Party in 1968. In fact George Wallace effectively *was* the party, and without him it simply disappeared. But the crucial point is that the issues which inspired both movements – dispute over the federal government's role in economy and society and the racial integration of the South – and which the existing parties could not accommodate, did *not* lead to a permanent shift in party alignments. Instead, either the Democrats and Republicans adapted to the new demands, or the movements themselves were reincorporated into the mainstream once the protest had been made. In a rather different context, Ross Perot's strong showing as a third candidate in 1992 (19 per cent of the vote) showed disillusionment among voters with the Republican and Democratic Party candidates. Significantly, however, it did not lead in any way to the emergence of a third party. Indeed, Perot's second challenge to the two-party system in 1996 proved much less effective, when he managed just 8 per cent of the vote. Since then third parties have played a minor role, although Ralph Nader's candidacy as an Independent in 2000 may well have had the effect of denying Al Gore victory (Nader won just 406,000 votes but almost all of these would have gone to Gore had Nader not stood).

Sometimes factions within existing parties can have an impact on policy. Such was the case with the Tea Party movement after 2009, which by operating within the Republican Party managed to shift the political agenda further to the right. More famously in 2016 Donald Trump won the Republican nomination by appealing to a broad section of the electorate including many voters who found his demagogic, populist appeal irresistible. At the same time the Republican 'establishment' who favoured more moderate candidates such Marco Rubio of Florida and John Kasich of Ohio were outraged that such an unpredictable candidate could capture the nomination. In the event Trump went on narrowly to win the presidency although, once elected, it was not always clear which faction he represented within the Republican Party. While he was clearly on the political right some of his policies, and in particular those relating to enhanced federal spending, sat uncomfortably with the fiscal conservative wing of the party.

Briefing   Why Only Two Parties in the US?

Given the extraordinary geographic, ethnic, religious and social diversity of the United States, it is something of a puzzle that the country has only ever had two main political parties. Scholars usually identify two sets of explanations – institutional and ideological. US electoral arrangements undoubtedly inhibit the growth of third parties. Because of the Electoral College system, in order to win the presidency it is necessary to have strength in a majority of states. Social movements with regional bases, such as the Populists, were at a marked disadvantage, therefore, and no exclusively regional party has ever come remotely close to winning a majority of Electoral College votes. Third parties are also disadvantaged in Congress, where party cues are the pathway to power and influence. In addition all national elections in the US are organized on a simple plurality basis (the first past the post wins). Winning a large proportion but less than a plurality of the vote yields nothing in the way of seats. To gain power it is necessary to win more votes than the next person.

Plurality voting can produce third parties, however, as the Canadian example shows. This has led some commentators to argue that third parties in America are further disadvantaged by other factors, and in particular the pervasive influence of American 'ideology' and the absence of a feudal past. The argument runs something like this: an ideology of equality of opportunity and democracy trumps social movements based on region, class, ethnicity or religion, all of which assume some advantage in exclusivity. If there is no obviously dominant social, regional or ethnic group why mobilize except in the context of 'broad church' parties? Even southern blacks, the most oppressed group in US history, failed to create their own party, preferring instead first to ally with the Republicans and more recently with the Democrats.

These factors do not totally explain the absence of third parties. It could be that political oppression has played a part, especially with regard to socialist parties in the 1900–1950 period, and more obviously in the case of African Americans prior to 1970.

The constantly impressive ability of American political parties to absorb potentially destabilizing social movements has no doubt contributed to the stability of the system, although the more enquiring mind could note that the two major parties have been able to perform this function only because there have been so few deep divisions in American society. A more divided society could not possibly sustain such a monopoly of power shared by two such amorphous and adaptable parties. This is clear when the US is compared with divided societies such as those of Canada or Belgium. In both cases linguistic and religious cleavages are such that they are faithfully reflected in the party system.

Crisis and Change in the American Party System

At least since the early 1950s political scientists have bemoaned the decline of American political parties. The 'crisis' has been identified mainly in terms of a constant erosion of the five functions listed above. In what is already a highly fragmented political system, the decline of these functions has, so the argument runs, led to inefficient government and an erosion of the legitimacy of institutions.

In order to understand this critique it is necessary to be familiar with the development of American political parties. Table 5.1 provides a schematic outline of their history by identifying five distinct stages of development. Such a brief summary of the parties' growth must oversimplify somewhat. In particular, the outline implies that the parties have mobilized different regions and social groups in a coherent way throughout history. But this has never been the case. With the notable exception of the Civil War period, the parties have always represented broad coalitions, and they have almost always eschewed appeals to those class-based ideologies that exploit social divisions in society.

Table 5.1   The development of American political parties

	Majority party	**Minority party**
1789–1800	*Federalist* A coalition of mercantile and northern land-owning interests led by Alexander Hamilton, George Washington and John Adams.	*Republican* (the first Republican party) A coalition of farmers and planters based in the central and southern states and led by Thomas Jefferson.
1800–56	*Democratic-Republican* The original Republican coalition was consolidated in this period under James Madison. Later, under the leadership of Andrew Jackson and Martin Van Buren, the party broadened its mass appeal and was renamed the Democratic Party.	*Federalist* then *Whig* Federalists, Whigs and a number of smaller parties failed to challenge the Democratic-Republican ascendancy. Victories by the conservative Whigs in 1840 and 1848 were temporary exceptions and led to the rather inauspicious presidencies of William Harrison and Zachary Taylor, both of whom died in office.
1856–1932	*Republican* The slavery issue produced a second Republican Party championing the anti-slavery unionist cause under Abraham Lincoln. Following the Civil War, a coalition of industrialists, bankers, northern and western farmers and some industrial workers proved formidable. Apart from Abraham Lincoln, only Theodore Roosevelt (1901–9) proved a memorable president. The era of strong local and state party organizations and machine politics.	*Democratic* Democratic strength remained firmly rooted in the South where poor whites and larger landowners supported the party (those blacks briefly enfranchised after the war supported the Republicans). The four Democratic victories of 1884, 1892, 1912 and 1916 were greatly aided by splits in the Republican ranks.
1932–64	*Democratic* The era of the New Deal coalition, with the South, the unions, the big cities, ethnic groups and intellectuals providing a near-permanent majority in the House and the Senate. Franklin Roosevelt, Harry Truman, John Kennedy and Lyndon Johnson were notable presidents.	*Republican* Republican victories in 1952 and 1956 were attributable to the charismatic appeal of Dwight Eisenhower. Main Republican support came from rural areas, big business, middle-class suburbanites, the West and New England.
1964–80	*Democratic* Period of the breakdown of the New Deal coalition. The South first voted for segregationist candidate George Wallace and then increasingly for Republican candidates. Vietnam and social issues split the traditional blue-collar, industrial-worker Democratic vote, some of which defected to the Republicans. The Democrats remained the majority party in Congress and in state and local government but managed only one presidential election victory, in 1976.	*Republican* With victories by Richard Nixon in 1968 and 1972, the Republicans exploited divisions in the Democratic Party. They also made major inroads into the South. Their association with the Watergate scandal (1973–7), however, led to an overwhelmingly Democratic Congress in 1974 and indirectly helped the defeat of President Ford in 1976.

(Continued)

Table 5.1   (*Cont'd*)

	Majority party	Minority party
	No clear majority party	
	Democratic	*Republican*
1980–	Although the Democrats won the 1992 and 1996 presidential elections, their support was gradually eroded during these years. They lost the Senate 1981 to 1987 and both houses of Congress after 1994. Generally their support collapsed in the South, and they were no longer the dominant party at the state and local levels. Their appeal remained high among women, minorities, and in the northeast and Pacific West of the country, however. By 2000, popular opinion was almost exactly divided between the two parties – a fact vividly shown in the 2000 election result. The Republicans continued to dominate Congress and presidency until 2006 when they lost Congress to the Democrats. In 2008 they also lost the presidency and the House to the Republicans in 2010. Divided government continued in 2015 and 2016 with the Democrats in control of the White House and the Republicans controlling Congress but was replaced in 2017 by Republican control – albeit a tenuous one – of both branches.	With three presidential election victories and success in Congress after 1994, there was much talk of a Republican realignment. Although this was true of the South and the mountain states, the West and the North and East remained highly competitive at the state, local and national levels. The Republicans did, however, redefine themselves as the party of low taxes, strong moral or family values, security at home and strength abroad. Ideological polarization greatly increased the electorate's interest in politics, which showed itself in increased turnout and a much more confrontational and abrasive style of politics. In spite of congressional defeats in 2006 and 2008 and impressive wins by Barack Obama in 2008 and 2012, the Republicans regained control of the House in 2010 and the Senate in 2014. However in 2016, the emergence of Donald Trump as candidate for president revealed a deep division in the party between a populist wing and a more traditional or establishment conservative wing.

Until the early years of the nineteenth century, parties were considered useful only as temporary expedients, or as 'factions' necessary to mobilize political power in response to particular crises. As was emphasized in chapter 3, the Constitution and the political culture generally in the new republic were deeply suspicious of political parties and their implied threat of government by factions, tyrannical majorities and mass political action. Significantly, when, under the guidance of Andrew Jackson and Martin Van Buren, mass parties did develop, they did so in a way which largely avoided the dangers foreseen by the Founding Fathers. The new Democratic Party appealed to broad principles of political equality (at least for white males) rather than to narrow class and sectional interests. It also transformed the party into a highly *instrumental* organization. For the first time the idea that working for the party could bring specific rewards for the individual became influential. So party membership and loyalty brought with them rewards or political 'spoils', of which patronage was the most important. Clearly, delivering the vote and distributing patronage required organization, and it was during this period that local and state parties acquired permanent organizations. What united these new party organizations was a simple belief in equal opportunity for white males (and a concomitant opposition to aristocratic political values) and in the party as a distributor of spoils. Beyond this the party represented little that was tangible. Great local and regional variety was encouraged rather than tolerated.

A party based on equality and democracy (achieved mainly through the extension of the franchise) and which adopted a new instrumentalism in organization was hardly likely to undermine the republicanism and constitutionalism that the Founding Fathers so feared would be threatened by mass parties. From the very beginning, therefore, mass political parties in the United States built their electoral competition not on appeals to class, ethnic or religious division, but by adapting their programmes to what was always a broad base of support for individualism and democracy. In this context the parties were also able to aid the presidential nomination process by limiting competition and providing truly national constituencies.

As we know, this new party system was far from being completely successful. Southern Democrats were determined to champion their exclusive sectional interests, and inspired the creation of a new party (the Republicans) devoted to the abolition of slavery. The Civil War effectively destroyed the first mass party system. As table 5.1 shows, what emerged after the war was a dominant Republican Party, again depending on a broad coalition of support – although not, notably, including the South. It was also during the latter half of the nineteenth century that parties became associated with corruption and the growth of the large urban political machine. Much has been written about the machine, although no one quite captured the spirit of the period like George Washington Plunkitt, the notorious boss of New York's Tammany Hall. His comment that 'you can't keep an organization together without patronage. Men ain't in politics for nothin'. They want to get somethin' out of it' gives some of the flavour of the time.[5] Milton Rakove has characterized the machine in slightly more academic terms: 'An effective political party needs five things: offices, jobs, money, workers, and votes. Offices beget jobs and money; jobs and money beget workers; workers beget votes; and votes beget offices.'[6] It follows that if one party controls all the offices it effectively controls the politics in that jurisdiction. Just such a pattern emerged in numerous nineteenth-century towns and cities (and in a modified form in some states). Scholars have cited a number of reasons for the spread of machine politics, the most important being the growing need for an institution capable of integrating a diverse and ever-increasing number of urban immigrants into American society. With state and local authorities unwilling or unable to provide immigrants with good government, political machines stepped in to fill the gap.

The new Americans, confused, intimidated or exploited by employers, landlords or the police, could turn to party precinct captains or ward bosses for help. In return, the machine demanded electoral loyalty.

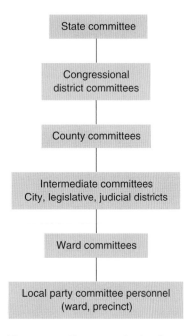

Figure 5.1   Party organizational structure

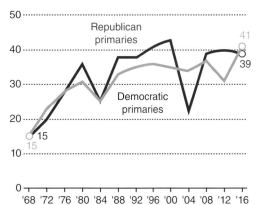

Figure 5.2   The rise of primaries, 1968–2016
Source: Pew Research Center, www.pewresearch. org/fact-tank/2016/02/17/near-record-number-of-primaries-this-year-but-not-quite-as-early/ft_16-02-12_primariesgrowth/
Note: Data do not include so-called 'beauty contest' primaries, which play no role in delegate selection. Data for 2016 are for scheduled primaries.

Machine politics permeated party systems from the lowest ward and precinct level up to city and in some cases state committees. Figure 5.1 shows the basic party organizational structure which emerged during this period and which still holds true in most states today. As is developed below, this structure used to be very much a 'bottom-up' affair, with the committees at county level and below as the key organizational units.

In spite of the emergence of a largely middle-class reform movement intent on cleansing the cities of machine politics, the machine remained an important part of the American scene until well after the Second World War. But some of the reforms introduced in the late nineteenth and early twentieth centuries did have a significant and lasting effect on American politics. A major concern of the reformers was to remove the partisan element from the electoral process. Accordingly, most of the proposed changes involved weakening the link between parties and electors. Party labels were removed from voting lists; elected mayors were sometimes replaced by city managers appointed by the local assembly; candidates were elected 'at large' or from a list covering the whole city, rather than on a ward-by-ward basis; and, most significantly, *primaries* were introduced in order to deny the party machines control over nominations for office. Instead, voters were given a direct say in who was to be nominated through an intra-party primary election.

These and other reforms hardly transformed the American party system. At best they had a limited effect in certain areas and regions, particularly in the more populist mountain and western states. *Local* party machines were, in any case, the main target of the reformers, for it was in the burgeoning industrial cities that the most corrupt regimes had developed.

Primary elections, however, soon affected national parties as an increasing number of states adopted them for presidential elections. By 1916 no fewer than 20 states required the parties to go direct to the voters to decide the selection of delegates to the national nominating convention rather than relying on party machines with party bosses deciding among themselves who should go to the convention pledged to a particular candidate.

In fact, between the 1920s and the 1960s this democratizing trend in American political parties received little fresh impetus. On the contrary, this period witnessed something of a return to old-fashioned party politics. Presidential primaries declined (to a mere 16 or 17 in 1968), as the nominating power reverted to the state party caucuses. And at the local level parties often found ways of bypassing the institutional obstacles to party hegemony (see figure 5.2).[7]

However, it would be misleading to characterize these trends simply as a return to the old model. In many ways they were profoundly different from those of the late nineteenth century. Above all, after 1932 the Democratic Party emerged as the 'majority' party, constructed around a seemingly invincible coalition consisting of the South, northern industrial workers, ethnic minorities and an increasingly insecure middle class. Local, state and even national Democratic Party organizations were greatly strengthened by this enduring coalition, which scored victory after victory at every level of politics. But unlike in the nineteenth century, these party organizations did not primarily function as intermediaries between the authorities and urban masses. By the 1930s welfare and social security reforms reduced the dependence of the poor on party workers, and government officials themselves became increasingly professional and less susceptible to bribery and corruption.

Instead, parties developed into modern organizations performing, albeit imperfectly, many of the functions described above. The parties also became markedly more ideological, with the Democrats clearly emerging as the party of the left and the Republicans as the party of the right. Indeed, almost all the major social and economic reforms in the 1933–68 period were initiated by Democratic administrations. While hardly socialist in conception or outcome, these have resulted in a greatly increased role for the federal government in society.

"WHAT ARE YOU DOING HERE?"

Plate 5.1   The Democratic donkey faces the power of money represented by the Republican elephant on Wall Street, where out-of-control business trusts feed coins into their respective campaign funds, 1904
Source: Stock Montage/Getty Images.

But even by the 1940s there were signs that the New Deal coalition was not completely secure. The South, in particular, found what were very hesitant steps taken by the Truman administration on civil rights unpalatable, and by the 1968 election the Democratic-led integration of the South resulted in open revolt, with George Wallace leading a breakaway southern party intent on preserving racial segregation. As importantly, the considerable – and in historical terms very untypical – ideological cohesion of the Democratic Party began to crumble as suburbanization, affluence and a changing occupational structure slowly transformed the political agenda. We discuss the relationship between these changes and voting in some detail in chapter 6, but for now it is important to explain their effects on political parties.

It is obvious that if parties are to perform their functions competently they must have some internal cohesion. Within Congress a party label must mean something more than mere nomenclature. If a common party is the major means whereby Congress and president can cooperate, then president and legislators must have at least some shared policies and perspectives. When a president staffs the executive branch, he must assume that his appointees broadly share his philosophy of government. Such party cohesion must have roots in the broader society; in effect some form of party organization must exist to facilitate the exchange of ideas, and to mobilize electoral support and nominate candidates. It was the apparent erosion of cohesion and party organization from the mid-1960s that worried so many commentators. Three major questions are raised here. What was the nature of party decline? What explains it? And, more controversially, does it really matter – especially given recent evidence of revival in the state and national parties?

The Decline and Rise of Political Parties

In *The Party's Over*, first published in 1971, the journalist David Broder argued that American parties were in a process of disintegration, with their main functions being replaced by special-interest groups and media images.[8] Between then and the end of the century claims that the parties were declining were never far from the surface and by some measures parties did become much less influential than they had been in earlier eras. There are a number of ways of measuring party decline, the most common of which are membership, party identification, organization and control over candidate nominations, ideological cohesion, the role of party in government and, of course, voting patterns, including electoral turnout. Party membership is not a meaningful measure in the USA, as it is equivalent to the simple act of registering (usually as a Democrat or Republican) to vote in most states. In other words, people do not *join* and pay dues in the European manner. Party identification, or the psychological attachment which individual voters have to particular parties, weakened steadily until the 1990s, with the number of independents clearly on the rise (see figure 6.2, chapter 6).

Weaker party identification (ID) produces a more fickle electorate prone to sudden shifts in loyalty, to ticket-splitting and to voting for individual candidates or issues rather than according to traditional party ties. Party ID did decline during the 1970s and 1980s, but since the 1990s it has stabilized or even strengthened. We will return to this point in chapter 6. Measuring changes in party organization is rather more difficult. Certainly the party machine model no longer applies. Research has shown that even in what used to be archetypal machine cities such as Chicago or Philadelphia, elected officials no longer expect party loyalty and service in return for the patronage they dispense.[9] But the typical party organization described above still applies, even if individual activists' motivations have changed.

Party organization has always been loose in the United States, and it used to be the case that the higher the level of committee, the looser it became. Much of the essential work of fundraising and campaigning occurs at the precinct level, with the counties also playing a major role in some states. State parties vary in organizational strength. In some states (mainly in the West) state parties are quite powerful in such areas as fundraising and slating statewide candidates. Unfortunately, there is no consistent pattern; much depends on the history and tradition of individual states.

Until the 1970s it was normal to characterize the national party committees as little more than very loose *ad hoc* organizations that emerged every four years to help to arrange the national conventions. They are very much more than this today, however. The Republican National Committee (RNC), in particular, has acquired a range of new resources and powers since the 1970s, including a capacity to run direct mailing campaigns on behalf of candidates at the national and the state levels. The RNC also provides staff and technical services (polling, breakdowns of local and regional voting patterns) for candidates. Much of the impetus for this new role came from RNC chairmen William E. (Bill) Brock (1977–81) and his successor Frank Fahrenkopf (1981–8), both of whom realized the potential for a national role in what had become a much more ideologically unified Republican Party. Perhaps the greatest change in the role of the national committees concerned the growth of 'soft money' contributions to the various national committees. 'Soft money', or donations not tied to any particular candidate's campaign, was essentially unregulated by national campaign finance law. It could be used for generic advertising and issue advocacy and could be transferred to state parties, which in turn could use it to boost the election chances of state and local candidates. The rising strength of the national committees has, therefore, also helped to revive state party committees. Such was the concern at the distortions in information that soft money could produce, a campaign began to ban the practice. Congress seemed reluctant to act, however, until the Enron corporate scandal spurred it into action (for a discussion of the Enron affair, see chapter 14). The result was the 2002 Bipartisan Campaign Reform Act of 2002, which eliminated all soft money donations but also doubled the contribution limit of 'hard' money from individuals from $1,000 to $2,000. These reforms were substantially undermined by the *Citizen's United* v. *Federal Election Committee* 2010 Supreme Court decision that effectively removed the amount that organizations (including corporations) could donate indirectly to campaigns. This gave rise to *SuperPACs* capable of raising very large sums to promote or defeat candidates (see chapter 14, pp. 312–13).

Until the 1990s one of the most important functions performed by the Democratic national committees was the initiation of a series of inquiries into the presidential nominating process, including how the party chooses delegates to the national convention. The first of these, the McGovern–Fraser Commission (1969), recommended that state parties change their rules so as to allow greater participation by minorities, women and the young at the convention. Two subsequent inquiries, the Mikulski Commission (1972–3) and the Winograd Commission (1975–8), further refined these rule changes. Most recently the Hunt Commission (1981–2) and the Fairness Commission (1984–5) moved the party in a quite different direction, requiring as they did increased representation of party regulars and elected officials (the so-called superdelegates who were to play a supporting role in nominating Hillary Clinton in 2016). In addition the new populism in party organization greatly increased the number of primaries in presidential elections in both the Democratic and Republican parties (figure 5.2).

What of the party activists themselves? Only about 2 per cent of the adult population are active participants in party organizations, almost all of which are locally based. Generally, over the past few years these activists have become more candidate- and issue-oriented, one of their main motivations being to promote a particular candidate or to fight for just one special issue. Initially, critics argue that these trends weakened party organization and coherence further, but with deepening ideological polarization after the 1990s candidates became increasingly identified with broader positions corresponding to general party positions. Hence in the 2004, 2008 and 2012 presidential elections and in recent state and congressional elections, Republican candidates have tended to be aligned in favour of a strong military, lower taxes and stricter codes of moral behaviour. Democrats have been aligned on the opposite side.

Candidate-centred parties have been quick to exploit new technologies to advance their positions. So, since the 2000 presidential elections, national, state and local parties have worked assiduously to raise money for candidates, often using internet-based campaigns during what in 2008 was a very long and expensive primary season for the Democrats. In this way Barack Obama was able to accumulate a campaign war chest of over $250 million.

Biographies   Lee Atwater and Karl Rove – Republican Party 'Heavies'

Between the 1980s and 2006, national Republican electoral strategy was dominated by two powerful individuals, Lee Atwater and Karl Rove. Atwater was adviser to Nixon, Reagan and George H. W. Bush, and one of the first exponents of 'smash mouth politics', or the deliberate destruction of opponents' reputations and careers. Atwater was also chair of the Republican National Committee between 1989 until his death from a brain tumour in 1991. His most famous ploy was the creation of a TV advert in 1988 claiming that Michael Dukakis, the Democratic candidate that year, had, as governor of Massachusetts, released Willie Horton, a convicted murderer who subsequently committed rape while on parole. The story is credited, at least in part, with the defeat of Dukakis. Karl Rove was a protégé of Atwater's who worked first for George H. W. Bush and then masterminded the victory of the president's son as governor of Texas in 1994. Rove subsequently became chief electoral strategist for Bush in the 2000 and 2004 campaigns. Widely dubbed George Bush's 'brain', Rove was also skilful at trashing the opposition. He eventually left his official position as domestic policy adviser in 2006, following claims that he was involved in leaking the identity of CIA agent Valerie Plame – although he was never officially charged with any crime. Both Atwater and Rove were typical of a new breed of media-savvy political consultant who saw their role as serving their political masters in ways that elevate winning above all other considerations. In this sense they are often viewed as amoral – and possibly corrupt – manipulators of the media rather than political aides whose job is to inform and educate officeholders on policy matters. By 2016, however, the role of campaign strategists seemed to have diminished in the wake of Donald Trump's successful nomination where he at least claimed to depend not on manipulative campaign advisers but on his own judgement and 'feel' for what the electorate wanted boosted by his extensive use of social media. Whether this becomes the model for future campaigns, however, remains to be seen.

Changing Party Ideology: 1970–2017

A host of surveys has shown how, since the mid-1960s, the issues which bound the New Deal coalition together – and which provided a convenient target for the Republicans – have either receded in importance or been diluted by the emergence of other, less class-based, issues. Until the mid-1970s, the major change involved the decline of economic issues in relation to 'social' issues. In 1975 Walter Dean Burnham characterized this shift in the terms of what social scientists call 'cross-cutting cleavages' or the fact that individuals and social groups often lack ideological coherence across all issues. Hence, in the late 1960s many industrial workers and labour union members remained on the left on economic and class issues while finding themselves on the right of the political spectrum over racial questions and the Vietnam War. Figure 5.3 shows these cross-cutting divisions in the 1990s and figure 5.4 attempts to characterize the divisions of the 2008–17 period. Although not shown by these figures, which give no indication of the *distribution* of support for these issues, the major shift from the earlier period was the emergence of a more ideologically coherent right, which first emerged with the Reagan presidency. In the 1970s and through the 1990s the majority party,

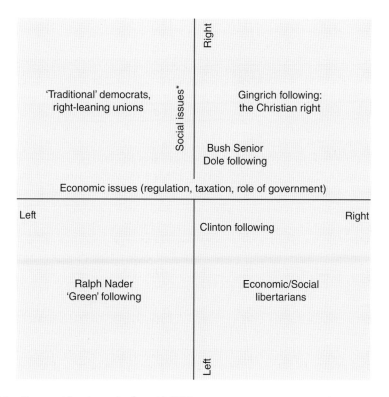

Figure 5.3   Cross-cutting issues in the mid-1990s
Note:*'Social issues' include affirmative action, abortion, civil liberties and the environment.

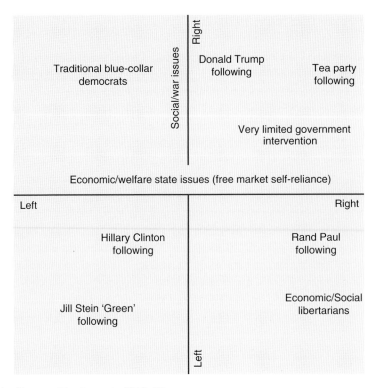

Figure 5.4   Cross-cutting issues in 2015–17
Note:*Social/war issues: includes affirmative action, abortion, same-sex marriage, immigration, civil liberties, environment and US role abroad.

the Democrats, was in disarray, its support being split between the two left-hand segments of figure 5.3. This ideological polarization was to continue into 2004, 2008 and 2012, when the two candidates were deeply divided on most issues, but in particular social issues and the role of the federal government in health care and managing the economy. This polarization is shown in figure 5.4, which provides a slightly different definition of the two issue dimensions. 'Economic/welfare state issues' refers to such questions as job security (providing a minimum notice of dismissal for laid-off workers), education, training, the role of the federal government in the economy, health care and equity in the federal taxation system. The social/war dimension refers to the conscience and gender issues (abortion, civil liberties, same-sex marriage), affirmative action (civil rights enforcement), the environment, consumer protection, childcare and, for the first time since the 1970s, public and candidates' position on America's role abroad. Very generally, the Republicans supported a more interventionist and unilateral foreign policy, while the Democrats favoured a more cautious and multilateral approach.

Indeed, by the early 2000s the Republican Party had acquired a much more ideologically cohesive profile, with most supporters locating themselves quite close to the president's position (the upper-right-hand quadrant of figure 5.4). And while the Democrats remain a much broader coalition than the Republicans, they too have become more cohesive, especially on social, civil liberties and foreign policy issues. During 2016 the victory of Donald Trump over his more establishment Republican opponents in the nomination contest revealed for the first time a serious split in Republican support between a populist wing and a more traditionally conservative wing (figure 5.4). This was particularly true of economic issues, with Donald Trump's stance on free trade and government spending being further to the centre than the typical Republican member of Congress. A further and related development of note is that the influence of parties *in government* has by some measures increased since the 1980s. Following the election of Ronald Reagan in 1980, the Republicans managed to forge a new unity organized around reform of the economy and conservatism on moral issues. By the mid-1990s this new agenda was the centrepiece of the Republican electoral victories in Congress, which were followed by an unusual degree of ideological cohesion among House (and, to a lesser extent, Senate) Republicans. Later, the Bush administration was also to display an unusual degree of ideological cohesion in government. We examine these developments in greater detail in later chapters, but for now it is important to note that this new ideological cohesion was not part of a dominant social movement rooted in the electorate in the manner of the New Deal of the 1930s. Democrats continued as a major if not always majority party among the electorate, and the dramatic Republican congressional advances in 1994 proved short lived at least until the second Obama term when they recaptured both the House and (in 2014) the Senate. Instead, the electorate remained remarkably evenly divided between the two, as the 2016 results showed. For in that election the Democrats made some inroads into the Congressional Republican majorities and did, of course, win the popular (if not the Electoral College) vote in the presidential contest.

Explaining Party Change

Reference has already been made to the social and economic changes usually invoked to explain party change. From the 1950s through the 1980s, affluence, increasing levels of education and suburbanization produced less 'solidaristic' communities, as the sociologists put it. In other words, a political life based on an individual's place of work or neighbourhood became increasingly irrelevant as the mobile service sector worker living in a sprawling suburb or semi-rural area replaced the blue-collar inner-city industrial worker as the 'norm' in American society. This new, essentially middle-class, citizen acquired a political life defined not just in terms of occupation or geographical location, but also in terms of his or her individual characteristics, preferences, prejudices and particular interests. In response to this much more complex and less categorizable voter, the parties themselves changed, becoming even less programmatic and ideological.

While appealing, this sociological analysis seems less relevant in the twenty-first century than it once was. On the left many Americans, including African Americans, many Hispanics and working women, show considerable ideological consistency across many issues.

They tend to be anti-war, supportive of social programmes and childcare, and are generally critical of what they see as a white male-dominated agenda that tolerates high levels of income and wealth inequality. At the other end of the political spectrum, the Republican right, while showing some ideological cohesion on a range of issues, were increasingly divided between a populist and a more traditionally conservative wing. More importantly, this analysis suggests some simple past when American political parties represented 'left' and 'right' in society with reasonable coherence. But, as has been repeatedly pointed out in this chapter, this has never been the case. Parties have historically tended towards the non-ideological, and even the New Deal Democratic Party was marked by a degree of internal dissension and compromise over policies that would be unusual in European class-based parties. By 2016 the modern Republican Party had also grown into a much broader coalition than existed just a few years earlier with the Trump candidacy representing a significant shift towards a populist, rather than traditionally conservative stance (see Briefing on Populism and American Political Parties).

Briefing   Populism and American Political Parties

Populism is the idea that the largely homogeneous mass of ordinary people are intrinsically honest and hard working while a small privileged elite manipulate political institutions to their personal advantage at the expense of the masses. It is distinct from socialism because no grand theory of class exploitation is involved. Indeed small business owners and farmers who are essentially conservative may be influenced by populist ideas because they believe that big government and big banks treat them unfairly by imposing penal terms and expensive regulations on their operations. In fact the first major populist movement was driven by disgruntled farmers in the second half of the nineteenth century, and their Populist Party amassed more than 1 million votes in the 1896 election. Later, Theodore Roosevelt's Progressive Party split the Republican vote in 1912. By then the populist appeal had extended to many industrial workers unhappy at the ways in which giant corporations failed to heed their interests. Populist solutions to societal problems usually involve regulation of the big corporations and unions as well as (often ill-defined) attempts to devolve power away from Washington and the elite media and towards ordinary voters. While populist sentiment has always been present in both the Democratic and Republican Parties it was not until 2016 that populist candidates came dramatically to the fore. In the Democratic Party Bernie Sanders advanced a radical agenda designed to return power and resources to the mass of middle and lower income voters, while the Republican nominee, Donald Trump railed against Washington, the national media and foreign multinationals. In the event Donald Trump's brand of populism prevailed and especially so among white working class voters, who believed that their interests would be served by immigration controls, protectionist trade polices, lower taxes and enhanced federal government investment in infrastructure.

A related explanation for the changing role of parties concentrates less on societal changes and more on the performance of government itself. Hence the 'overload' thesis argues that the increasing democratization of American society has placed an excessive load on what is in any case a complex decision-making system. Unable to cope with the array of competing demands placed on them, institutions have increasingly come under fire from a disenchanted public. Indeed, during the early 1970s a burgeoning literature on declining trust in government hinted that public disillusionment with political institutions posed a threat to democracy itself.[10] Although this particular argument is now largely discredited, it remains the case that parties continue to take much of the blame for public disenchantment with politics. To repeat the point, it has been the failure of parties to provide coherent programmes, to staff the government, to help smooth relations between Congress and president which, so the criticism goes, accounts for the apparently growing gap between public expectations of government and the ability of political institutions to satisfy them. Hence the rise of more populist candidates of the right and left as was dramatically illustrated in the 2016 election (see Briefing on Populism and American Political Parties).

Unravelling cause and effect when explaining party change is difficult. The rise in the importance of social issues from the 1960s and through the 2000s resulted in large part from changes in American society. Parties and political institutions were profoundly affected by these changes and, once affected, in turn influenced the public's perception of the performance of government. This complex interaction of institutions and society is, of course, a continuous process and it may well be that, not only in the USA but also in other mature democracies, the age of the highly organized political party rooted in socially stable communities is over. A crucial question is raised by this prospect: can liberal democracy function properly with a different sort of political party that is rooted not in community but in personalities and issues that cut across community and region?

Stronger but more Polarized Parties

Pointing to the indicators discussed above, the more pessimistic observers reluctantly accept the demise of traditional parties, warn of the deleterious consequences and plead, somewhat forlornly, for party revival, or more 'consensual' institutions.[11] In essence, they claim that modern parties tend to erode the vital five functions discussed earlier.

Presidential–congressional liaison becomes difficult; presidents have few cues to guide them when appointing officials; a presidential nominating process outside the control of party boosts 'media-created' candidates who may be skilful at campaigning and winning primaries but rarely make good presidents. Above all, loose, amorphous parties are obliged to make general promises to the electorate rather than offer to satisfy specific demands. As a result, the public's regard for parties has declined, and the gap between public expectations of government and the ability of politicians to meet these expectations has declined.

Before we accept the critique in full, however, we should note the following. First, amid all the criticism of the parties, not a single third party has emerged with even the semblance of electoral strength. Third-party *candidates* have sometimes done well, but they represent more of a protest vote than some discernible social movement. Such was certainly the case with John Anderson in 1980 and Ross Perot in 1992 and 1996. The institutional obstacles in the way of third parties in the USA are well known and continue to apply (see Briefing on Why Only Two Parties in the US?).[12] But a much more significant obstacle is the continuing distaste among the American electorate for parties based on class, region, religion and ethnicity. Second, it is important to stress again that the parties continue to be important *in government* as indicators of electoral behaviour. Certainly they have *changed*, and today perform rather different functions or perform traditional functions in a different manner. As already noted, state and national party organizations have been strengthened in recent years, and the influence of party in Congress has undoubtedly increased since the 1980s.

The very same forces that precipitated the reforms of the early 1970s also set in motion a period of soul-searching that is still very much with us. Disquiet with the ways in which candidates are selected remains. National parties are now stronger, but their authority in part depends on the support of incumbent presidents. This is one reason why the Republican National Committee was able to achieve so much during the 1980s compared with its Democratic counterpart. With Bill Clinton as president, the Democratic National Committee experienced a revival during the 1990s.

Briefing   The Rise (and Fall?) of the Tea Party Movement

The Tea Party movement (named after the famous Boston Tea Party that jettisoned tea into Boston harbour in protest against British taxes) has its origins in outrage among some Republicans against the Obama administration's fiscal stimulus package, which pumped $787 billion into the economy in 2009. Not one Republican member of the House signed the law and, to ensure passage, three Republican senators voted with the Democrats in the upper house. Tea Party supporters are what might be called constitutional conservatives – they believe that the federal government has seriously overstepped its role as laid down in the Constitution. They are particularly incensed at what they see as irresponsible and uncontrolled increases in federal taxes and spending. Their positions are often described as extreme because ideally they would dismantle all federal programmes save those devoted to defence and internal security. It would be wrong to describe them as libertarians, however, partly because they hold authoritarian views on such things as drug use, and partly because their anger is directed at federal as opposed to state

government spending. The movement has no formal organization but mobilizes on an ad hoc basis in support of or against particular candidates. It has managed to deliver some notable scalps, including Democrat Martha Coakley of Massachusetts, who was ousted by Republican Scott Brown in what is known as a liberal Democratic state. Thanks partly to the efforts of Michele Bachmann (R-Minnesota) it also now has an official caucus in the Congress with (in 2016) 48 House members and three Senate members. All of them are Republicans and share membership with the more vocal and coherent Republican Congressional grouping known as the Freedom Caucus. Although the movement lost some impetus after 2012 – indeed the House caucus is now largely inactive – their agenda undoubtedly overlapped with the populist appeal of 2016 Republican nominee Donald Trump. For while Trump is far from being a committed fiscal conservative his disdain for the 'Washington elite' resonated with many Tea Party supporters, many of whom voted for him in both the primaries and the general election.

Recent party revival is not equivalent to the party strength associated with smoke-filled rooms and party machines, but more, not fewer, people are now actively involved in party organizations – witness Bernie Sanders' impressive mobilization of tens of thousand of left-wing activists in his bid for the Democratic 2016 nomination.

Party activists may be motivated more by issues or candidates than by party loyalty, which in any case is nothing new in American politics, but the label 'Democrat' or 'Republican' continues to mean a great deal to most Americans. That this is so is amply demonstrated by the continuing importance of party labels in congressional elections – very few candidates dare to call themselves Independent. Moreover, the emergence of a more ideologically committed Republican Party with unusually strong links between party supporters at the state, congressional and presidential levels surely represented the best evidence yet of party revival. In response, the Democratic Party too has become more cohesive – even if only as an oppositional force against the Republicans.

Indeed, not since the 1960s – or possibly even the 1930s – has American politics been so ideologically charged. This may not be an ideology rooted in cohesive and stable communities as it was in earlier eras, but it is palpable nonetheless. Above all it is a divide on what this chapter has called the social issue that links as much to values and lifestyles as it does to simple economic issues. Today, the two political parties are deeply divided over such questions as civil liberties, abortion, the US role abroad, the role of the family in society and the redistributive role of federal taxation. As the next chapter will show, this new divide has had profound implications for how Americans vote in national elections.

Summary

The US is unusual in having had just two dominant parties throughout its history. Initially, the main differences between the parties were based on region and economic interest, a division that was aggravated by the Civil War and its aftermath when the Democrats became the party of the South and the Republicans the party of the North. Throughout, however, electoral arrangements have ensured that to win the presidency parties have to build broad national support. As a result the parties have almost always been broad coalitions rather than narrowly sectional. The parties have also always been highly decentralized, with state and local organizations dominating. In recent years both parties have become more ideological and less pragmatic. This is particularly true of the Republican Party, which has evolved into a party almost exclusively of the right.

Questions for Discussion

1 Why did Donald Trump win the 2016 Republican nomination? What are the implications for the future of the Republican Party?
2 What is the regional distribution of support for the parties? How has it changed over the past 70 years?
3 Compare the ways in which the two candidates for presidency in 2016 used their respective parties during the campaign. To what extent was party important for them compared with personal organizations?
4 What has been the role of populist sentiment in the history of American political parties?

Glossary

affirmative action   Policies designed to redress patterns of discrimination based on race, ethnicity, gender, age or disability

candidates at large   Two or more party candidates elected across constituencies rather than on the basis of exclusive constituencies

cross-cutting cleavages   Issues that elicit support patterns across ideological, class, ethnic, gender or territorial lines

Freedom Caucus   A grouping of 30 plus House Republicans devoted to the advance of far right public policies

governmental stability   Continuity of government incumbency over time

legitimacy   Moral acceptance of political or constitutional arrangements among voters

median voter   The typical voter, or that which approximates to the statistical median

New Deal coalition   The coalition of industrial workers, farmers, intellectuals and the South that underpinned Democratic Party success from 1933 to 1969

overload thesis   The idea that excessive demands on governments undermine their ability to govern

party government   Rule based on the dominance of parties in government

party identification   The psychological attachment to parties held by voters over time

plurality   The party or political unit that wins the most votes in an election, which may not be a majority

political machine   A structured political party organization that monopolizes power in a jurisdiction

primaries   Intra-party elections to decide nominated candidates for the general election

programmatic parties   Parties presenting clear programmes for change to the electorate

regime stability   Constitutional systems that persist through time

segregationist   Social systems based on the segregation of society on racial or ethnic grounds

social contract theory   The idea that the people enter into a contract with the government with both sides accountable for their actions

soft money   Political advertising funded not by political parties but by other interests

solidaristic communities   Homogeneous communities that share values and political views

superdelegates   Delegates to the Democratic National Convention chosen on the basis of their position or political service

Tammany Hall   A general term to describe big-city political machines

Tea Party   A movement within the Republican Party started in 2009 to promote candidates adhering to a right-wing minimal federal government agenda

Notes

1   This list of functions – although not the discussion of them – is taken from Gerald M. Pomper, 'Party functions and party failures', in Gerald M. Pomper et al., *The Performance of American Government: Checks and Minuses* (New York: Free Press, 1972), pp. 46–63.

2   Anthony Downs, *An Economic Theory of Democracy* (New York: Harper & Row, 1957).

3   This has been a recurring theme among critics of the separation of powers at least since the time of Woodrow Wilson (president, 1913–19), who wrote on this subject as a political scientist before becoming president.

4   The classic account of the machine is by Harold F. Gosnell, *Machine Politics: Chicago Model* (Chicago: University of Chicago Press, 1937).

5   William Riordan, *Plunkitt of Tammany Hall* (New York: E. P. Dutton, 1963), p. 63.

6   Milton Rakove, *Don't Make No Waves, Don't Back No Losers* (Bloomington: Indiana University Press, 1975), p. 42.

7   The city of Chicago, for example, was 'reformed', but the mayor retained his position as 'boss' through control of the Cook County Democratic Party, which contains the city.

8   David Broder, *The Party's Over* (New York: Harper & Row, 1971).

9   For a general discussion of party decline, see Martin P. Wattenberg, *The Decline of American Political Parties, 1952–1994* (Cambridge, MA: Harvard University Press, 1996).

10   See, in particular, the tenth anniversary edition of *The Public Interest*, essays by Daniel Bell and Samuel P. Huntington, no. 41 (Fall 1975).

11   An eloquent essay on this theme is Samuel P. Huntington, *American Politics: The Promise of Disharmony* (Cambridge, MA: Harvard University Press, 1981).

12   The American electoral system puts additional burdens on third parties, for all states require a minimum number of registered voters to sign a petition before a party can field a candidate. Furthermore, acquiring strength in one state or region – the usual pattern for American third parties – is rarely enough to ensure national impact. Victory in a presidential election is achievable only via mass national support, and without at least the prospect of winning at this level third parties cannot hope to be taken seriously.

Further Reading

An excellent account of changes in the party system is provided by Robert Harmel, Matthew Giebert and Kenneth Janda, *American Parties in Context; Comparative and Historical Analysis* (Abingdon: Taylor and Francis, 2016). The best historical (but analytical) account of American parties is William Nisbet Chambers and Walter Dean Burnham (eds), *The American Party Systems: Stages of Political Development* (New York: Oxford University Press, 1975). One of the better textbook treatments of parties is Jeffrey M. Stonecash, *Understanding American Political Parties: Democratic Ideals, Political Uncertainty, and Strategic Positioning* (London: Routledge, 2012). See also Sandy Maisel, *American Political Parties and Elections: A Very Short Introduction* (New York: Oxford University Press, 2007).

CHAPTER 6
ELECTIONS AND POLITICAL PARTICIPATION

Elections commit the people to a sense of responsibility for their own betterment. It seems clear that they are essential to us as props of the sentiment of legitimacy and the sentiment of participation.

– W. J. M. MACKENZIE, POLITICAL STUDIES

There is currently a widespread sense, shown by public opinion surveys and complaints by informed observers that the American electoral system is in trouble. Some believe

American Politics and Society, Ninth Edition. David McKay.
© 2018 John Wiley & Sons Ltd. Published 2018 by John Wiley & Sons Ltd.

that this trouble is minor and can be dealt with through moderate reforms; others think it goes deep and requires extensive political surgery, perhaps accompanied by sweeping changes in the larger social order.

– A. JAMES REICHLEY, *ELECTIONS, AMERICAN STYLE*

America's claim to status as a democratic country depends almost entirely on the nature and extent of public participation in political life, and from the earliest years of the republic there has been dispute and controversy over what, precisely, participation means. To the educated eighteenth-century citizen, 'democracy' was equivalent to a republican form of government that limited electoral participation to those with an established stake in society – white men of property. Any further extension of participation raised the spectre of rule by the mob and the eventual breakdown of civil society. In contrast, a much wider electorate imbued many artisans and small farmers, especially in New England, with a more egalitarian brand of democracy that implied participation. Slowly, during the nineteenth and twentieth centuries, this egalitarian spirit gained ascendancy over the more elitist views of the Founding Fathers.

Today, the degree of electoral participation would truly shock eighteenth-century man. Measured in terms of the number of public offices open to electoral choice, the United States is the most democratic of countries; in total approximately 530,000 posts are elected, from the humblest local officials, through local and state judges, mayors, councillors, governors and legislators, to the vice president, president and members of the US Congress. In addition, many Americans vote in primary elections to nominate the party candidates who will stand in the election proper. Many states and localities have also introduced a number of devices associated with populism or direct democracy. Hence, some citizens vote in referendums or in initiative and recall elections, all of which are designed to give the voter a direct say in policy-making.[1] Further, there are no formal barriers to the participation of any particular social group. Property and taxpaying restrictions were abolished by the 1840s, effectively enfranchising all adult white males. Women won the right to vote in national elections following the adoption of the Nineteenth Amendment in 1920. Formal restrictions on southern blacks' electoral participation were swept away by the 1965 Voting Rights Act and by a number of Supreme Court decisions. Finally, the Twenty-Sixth Amendment, ratified in 1971, reduced the minimum voting age to 18.

By the simple measure of electoral access, therefore, there is no doubting the democratic nature of the American system. Yet, as our discussion of political parties revealed, there is very much more to participation than mere access to elections. More important are questions of *choice* and *control* over government policy. Many people ask whether the United States can be 'truly' democratic when electoral turnout is low and when the choice offered by elections has, at least historically, often been so narrow. More recently, criticism has been directed at the enormous expense involved in US elections and at the exaggerated rhetoric of election campaigns that may have increased the social and political divisions in American society. The remainder of this chapter is devoted to these and related questions. The first section concentrates on electoral behaviour – why Americans vote as they do, what sort of choice they are offered by the electoral process, and how patterns of behaviour have changed over time. The second section looks at the increasing polarization of the electorate and how this has affected voting patterns. The third section introduces a discussion of non-electoral participation, which is continued in later chapters.

Patterns of American Electoral Behaviour

Basic questions

Observers of voting behaviour usually first ask the simplest and most obvious question: 'Who has voted for which party?' So we are used to reading opinion poll findings, which indicate that support for a particular party has risen or fallen, or that some region, or ethnic or social group has shifted its allegiance away from or towards a party. Survey or poll data can be an invaluable aid when answering these questions, and have helped to establish some very general norms or expectations about people's voting behaviour. So table 6.1, showing the distribution of votes by social group since 1972 in presidential elections, confirms tendencies which apply in most democratic countries: higher socio-economic status, white voters tend to be more conservative (i.e. vote Republican) than younger, lower-status, ethnic minority voters. Table 6.1 also reveals patterns which may be peculiarly American: the South of the USA appears markedly more conservative than the East; women are much more prone to vote Democrat than are men. But even these general trends provoke a number of deeper questions. What, precisely, is meant by 'conservative' and 'liberal' in the American context? To what extent does the *party* as opposed to candidates and issues determine voting behaviour? It must be that the balance of influence shifts quite markedly between the three, for some candidates manage to overcome party ties and attract voters from the other party. Hence we saw the phenomenon of the 'Reagan Democrats' during the 1980s, when many traditional Democratic voters switched their allegiance to the Republicans. The same phenomenon was evident in some parts of the country in 2016 when many working-class white voters voted for Donald Trump. Other questions arise. Why are African Americans so overwhelmingly Democratic in their loyalties? What accounts for the regional variations in voting behaviour? We return to these questions in detail below, but for now it should be noted that American voting behaviour seems considerably more complex than electoral participation in other countries. In many European countries, for example, class, regional, ethnic or religious divisions are quite clearly defined and can act as accurate predictors of voting intentions. In the USA, however, the political parties are loose coalitions, and ideological and other social cleavages are relatively weak, so analysing who votes for whom and why can be that much more difficult.

We can broadly categorize the Democrats as the liberal or even 'left' party and Republicans as the conservative or 'right' party, but when the whole range of candidates in each of these parties is examined there are numerous exceptions even to this generalization. To complicate matters further, federalism and the separation of powers have spawned myriad elections and distinctive levels of government, each with a different constituency. At the national level this shows itself most graphically in the relationship between presidential and congressional elections. Individual members of Congress are beholden to their own constituents, whose interests may be quite separate from those of the national electorate responsible for electing the president. It used to be the case that the successful party at the presidential election would also at least be partly successful at the congressional level, but in recent years voters have increasingly split their tickets and voted for one party at the congressional level and the other at the presidential level. In 1972, for example, the near-landslide victory of a Republican president, Richard Nixon, was not accompanied by any

Table 6.1 Distribution of the 1976–2016 presidential vote by social group and issues (%)

		1976	1980	1984	1988	1992	1996	2000	2004	2008	2012	2016
100% of the electorate[a]	Total vote											
	Democrat	50	41	40	45	43	49	48	48	53	51	48
	Republican	48	51	59	53	38	41	48	51	46	48	46
	Independent	–	7	–	–	19	8	2	–	–	–	–
Men	Democrat	50	36	37	41	41	43	42	44	49	45	41
	Republican	48	55	62	57	38	44	53	55	48	42	54
	Independent	–	7	–	–	21	10	3	–	–	–	–
Women	Democrat	50	45	44	49	45	54	54	51	56	55	53
	Republican	48	47	56	50	37	38	43	48	43	44	42
	Independent	–	7	–	–	17	7	2	–	–	–	–
White	Democrat	47	36	35	40	39	43	42	41	43	39	37
	Republican	52	56	64	59	40	46	54	58	55	59	58
	Independent	–	7	–	–	20	9	3	–	–	–	–
Black	Democrat	83	85	90	86	83	84	90	88	95	93	88
	Republican	16	11	9	12	10	12	8	11	4	6	8
	Independent	–	3	–	–	7	4	1	–	–	–	–
Hispanic	Democrat	–	56	62	69	61	72	62	53	67	71	65
	Republican	–	35	37	30	25	21	35	44	31	27	29
	Independent	–	8	–	–	14	6	2	–	–	–	–
Asian	Democrat	–	–	–	–	31	43	54	56	62	73	65
	Republican	–	–	–	–	55	48	41	44	35	26	29
	Independent	–	–	–	–	15	8	4	–	–	–	–
18–29 years old	Democrat	51	44	40	47	43	53	48	54	66	60	55
	Republican	47	43	59	52	34	34	46	45	32	37	37
	Independent	–	11	–	–	22	10	5	–	–	–	–
30–44 years old	Democrat	49	36	42	45	41	48	48	46	52	52	50
	Republican	49	55	57	54	38	41	49	53	46	45	42
	Independent	–	8	–	–	21	9	2	–	–	–	–
45–59 years old	Democrat	47	39	40	42	41	48	48	48	49	47	47
	Republican	52	55	60	57	40	41	49	51	49	51	48
	Independent	–	5	–	–	19	9	2	–	–	–	–

(Continued)

Table 6.1 (*Cont'd*)

		1976	1980	1984	1988	1992	1996	2000	2004	2008	2012	2016
60 and older	Democrat	47	41	39	49	50	48	51	46	47	44	45
	Republican	52	54	60	50	38	44	47	54	51	56	53
	Independent	–	4	–	–	12	7	2	–	–	–	–
Liberals	Democrat	71	60	70	81	68	78	80	85	89	86	84
	Republican	26	25	28	18	14	11	13	13	10	11	10
	Independent	–	11	–	–	18	7	6	–	–	–	–
Moderates	Democrat	51	42	47	50	47	57	52	54	60	56	52
	Republican	48	49	53	49	31	33	44	45	39	41	41
	Independent	–	8	–	–	21	9	2	–	–	–	–
Conservatives	Democrat	29	23	17	19	18	20	17	15	20	17	15
	Republican	70	73	82	80	64	71	81	84	78	82	81
	Independent	–	4	–	–	18	8	1	–	–	–	–
Not a high-school graduate	Democrat	–	51	50	56	54	59	59	50	63	64	–
	Republican	–	46	50	43	28	28	39	49	35	35	–
	Independent	–	2	–	–	18	11	1	–	–	–	45
High-school graduate	Democrat	–	43	39	49	43	51	48	47	52	51	–
	Republican	–	51	60	50	36	35	49	52	46	48	51
	Independent	–	4	–	–	21	13	1	–	–	–	–
Some college education	Democrat	–	35	38	42	41	48	45	46	51	49	43
	Republican	–	55	61	57	37	40	51	54	47	48	52
	Independent	–	8	–	–	21	10	3	–	–	–	–
College graduate	Democrat	–	–	–	37	39	44	45	46	50	47	49
	Republican	–	–	–	62	41	46	51	52	48	51	45
	Independent	–	–	–	–	20	8	3	–	–	–	–
Postgraduate education	Democrat	–	–	–	48	50	52	52	55	58	55	58
	Republican	–	–	–	50	36	40	44	44	40	42	37
	Independent	–	–	–	–	14	5	3	–	–	–	–
White Protestants	Democrat	41	31	27	33	33	36	34	32	34	30	37[b]
	Republican	58	63	72	66	47	53	63	67	65	69	60[b]
	Independent	–	6	–	–	21	10	2	–	–	–	–

White Catholics	Democrat	52	40	42	43	42	48	45	43	47	40	45[b]
	Republican	46	51	57	56	37	41	52	56	52	59	52[b]
	Independent	–	7	–	–	22	10	2	–	–	–	–
Jewish	Democrat	64	45	67	64	80	78	79	74	78	71	71
	Republican	34	39	31	35	11	16	19	25	21	29	24
	Independent	–	15	–	–	9	3	1	–	–	–	–
Born-again or evangelical Christians	Democrat	–	40	30	24	31	–	–	34	41	21	18
	Republican	–	56	69	74	56	–	–	65	57	78	81
	Independent	–	3	–	–	14	–	–	–	–	–	–
Attend religious services at least once a week	Democrat	–	–	–	–	36	–	39	38	43	36	40
	Republican	–	–	–	–	48	–	59	60	55	63	56
	Independent	–	–	–	–	15	–	2	–	–	–	–
Under $15,000	Democrat	–	49	–	–	58	59	57	63	73	63	53
	Republican	–	43	–	–	23	28	37	36	25	–	–
	Independent	–	7	–	–	19	11	4	–	–	35	41
$15,000–$29,999	Democrat	–	–	–	–	45	53	54	57	60	–	–
	Republican	–	–	–	–	35	36	41	42	37	–	–
	Independent	–	–	–	–	20	9	3	–	–	–	–
$30,000–$49,999	Democrat	–	–	–	–	41	48	49	50	55	57	51
	Republican	–	–	–	–	38	40	48	49	43	42	12
	Independent	–	–	–	–	21	10	2	–	–	–	–
$50,000–$74,999	Democrat	–	–	–	–	40	47	46	43	48	44	46
	Republican	–	–	–	–	41	45	51	56	49	–	–
	Independent	–	–	–	–	18	7	2	–	–	52	50
$75,000–$99,999	Democrat	–	–	–	–	–	44	45	45	51	–	–
	Republican	–	–	–	–	–	48	52	55	48	–	–
	Independent	–	–	–	–	–	7	2	–	–	–	–
$100,000 and over	Democrat	–	–	32	–	–	38	43	41	49	54	47
	Republican	–	–	65	–	–	54	54	58	49	–	–
	Independent	–	–	–	–	–	6	2	–	–	45	48
$200,000 and over	Democrat	–	–	–	–	–	–	–	35	52	–	–
	Republican	–	–	–	–	–	–	–	63	46	–	–
	Independent	–	–	–	–	–	–	–	–	–	–	–

(Continued)

Table 6.1 (Cont'd)

		1976	1980	1984	1988	1992	1996	2000	2004	2008	2012	2016
Better today	Democrat	30	–	–	–	24	66	61	19	37	84	72
	Republican	70	–	–	–	61	26	36	80	60	15	24
	Independent	–	–	–	–	14	6	2	–	–	–	–
Same today	Democrat	51	–	–	–	41	46	35	50	45	18	46
	Republican	49	–	–	–	42	45	60	49	53	80	46
	Independent	–	–	–	–	17	8	3	–	–	–	–
Worse today	Democrat	77	–	–	–	60	27	33	79	71	58	19
	Republican	23	–	–	–	14	57	63	20	28	40	78
	Independent	–	–	–	–	25	13	4	–	–	–	–
Population over 500,000	Democrat	–	–	63	62	58	68	71	60	70	69	–
	Republican	–	–	35	37	28	25	26	39	28	29	–
	Independent	–	–	–	–	13	6	3	–	–	–	59
Population 50,000 to 500,000	Democrat	–	–	46	52	50	50	57	49	59	58	–
	Republican	–	–	53	47	33	39	40	49	39	40	35
	Independent	–	–	–	–	16	8	2	–	–	–	–
Suburbs	Democrat	–	35	38	42	41	47	47	47	50	48	45
	Republican	–	55	61	57	39	42	49	52	48	50	50
	Independent	–	9	–	–	21	8	3	–	–	–	–
Population 10,000 to 50,000	Democrat	–	–	–	38	39	48	38	48	45	42	–
	Republican	–	–	–	61	42	41	59	50	53	56	34
	Independent	–	–	–	–	20	9	2	–	–	–	–
Rural areas	Democrat	–	39	–	44	39	44	37	39	45	37	–
	Republican	–	55	–	55	40	46	59	59	53	61	62
	Independent	–	5	–	–	20	10	2	–	–	–	–
First-time voters	Democrat	–	–	38	47	46	54	52	53	69	70	56
	Republican	–	–	61	51	32	34	43	45	30	30	47
	Independent	–	–	–	–	22	11	4	–	–	–	–

Source: 2008 and earlier *New York Times* CBS polls; 2012 www.cbsnews.com/election-results-2012/exit.shtml?state=US&race=P&jurisdiction=0&party=G.

[a]Percentage of electorate data are from 2008.

[b]2016 data refer to all Protestants and Catholics irrespective of race.

significant inroads by his party into the Democratic majorities in both houses of Congress. The pattern was similar in 1984, 1988, 1992 and 1996. In 1996 Bill Clinton won the presidency for the Democrats but the Republicans retained control of both houses of Congress.

The result in 2000 was one of the most unusual in American history but confirmed what appeared to be the end of presidential 'coattails' in Congress. George W. Bush won the election with a minority of the popular vote and a majority of just one in the Electoral College. Meanwhile the drift back to the Democrats continued at the congressional level, where the Senate was split 50/50 and the Republican advantage in the House was just seven seats. After 2006 divided government returned with the triumph of the Democrats in both the House and the Senate. While in 2008 unified government returned, with the Democrats increasing their majorities in the House and the Senate and winning the presidency by a comfortable margin. By 2012, however, the Republicans had re-captured the House, and they regained control of the Senate in the 2014 midterm elections. 2016 did, of course, produce one of the greatest upsets in US electoral history. Few expected Donald Trump to win but he secured a comfortable Electoral College margin of victory even if he did lose the popular vote by more than 2.8 million. The Democrats also underperformed in Congress leaving the Republicans with control of both houses.

A second question raised in any simple description of voting behaviour is: who actually votes? A wealth of social science and professional opinion poll research enables us to make quite accurate assessments of electoral participation patterns. Very generally, people of higher socio-economic status (a combination of income, occupation and education) vote and participate in other political activities to a much greater extent than people of lower socio-economic status.[2] The relationship between voting and age is a little more complex, with participation rising from a low at 18 to a peak during middle age and then declining gently in later middle and old age. Until the late 1960s one of the most dramatic differences in participation was between black and white Americans. Until the civil rights legislation of the mid-1960s, very few southern blacks were able to register to vote (for example, in 1964 a mere 7 per cent in Mississippi) and among those registered actual turnout was low. Since the 1965 Voting Rights Act, however, registration has steadily increased, and by 1990 the percentage of African Americans registered to vote was only 8 per cent below the figure for whites. Black turnout remains generally lower than that of whites, but mainly because a disproportionate number of blacks are of low socio-economic status. In 2008, with an African American candidate running for president, turnout among blacks actually matched that of whites at around 60 per cent – and in 2012 the two groups also had a similar turnout rate of approximately 60 per cent. However, in 2016 black turnout declined slightly and the number voting Democrat fell from 93 per cent in 2012 to 88 per cent (Table 6.1).

Finally, turnout among women is slightly higher than for men. However, the gap is small (around 2 per cent in 2016) and, compared with differences based on socio-economic status and age, voter participation rates between men and women are comparatively close.

A third basic question is: how many of the people actually vote? In the USA turnout is notoriously low for all elections. Even the contest perceived by most people as the most significant – electing the president – hardly inspires a high level of mass participation. Since 1960 turnout has been declining, and now rarely exceeds 55–60 per cent for presidential elections and 50 per cent for congressional contests (figure 6.1).

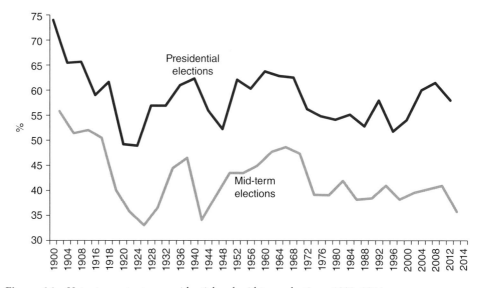

Figure 6.1   Voter turnout rates, presidential and mid-term elections, 1900–2014
Source: Michael P. McDonald, Associate Professor, University of Florida, Department of Political Science, United States Elections Project, http://electproject.org/.

In 1996 turnout sank to 48.4 per cent – the lowest for a presidential election since 1924, although it did recover to 51 per cent in 2000 and to an impressive 64 per cent in 2008, only to slump again in 2012 to 60 per cent and fall further to 58 per cent in 2016.

At the state and local levels turnout is even lower and can fall as low as 20 per cent. This seeming political apathy has long puzzled and disturbed American political scientists. Explanations usually fall into one of two categories – institutional and non-institutional. The institutional barriers to voting are, in fact, considerable, although claims that the formidable *number* of elections reduces turnout are probably erroneous. After all, turnout at presidential elections has remained generally low in spite of their relative infrequency and the disproportionate amount of publicity and attention paid to them by political parties and the media. More significant are America's voter registration laws. Under the laws of individual states, voters must themselves make the decision to register, and most states apply minimum residency requirements. Although for presidential elections Congress has reduced this requirement to only 30 days, the fact remains that in a mobile, open society many people fail to register or to register in time. Unlike in most European countries, there is no automatic nationally organized compulsory registration system, and recent studies have shown that, were such a system introduced, turnout might increase by between 10 and 12 per cent. In 1993 Congress passed the so-called 'motor voter' law, which encouraged states to allow people to register to vote whenever they applied to renew their driving licence. Although by some estimates this increased the number of citizens registered to vote by 9 million by 1996, there is little evidence that these new registrees actually voted. Indeed, 1996 exit polls showed that the percentage of first-time voters (of all those voting) dropped from 11 to 9 per cent.[3]

Non-voting may also be linked to the fact that the USA has a first past the post, single-member, district electoral system rather than one based on proportional representation (PR).

Table 6.2   Voter turnout by registered voters and voting-age population, selected countries (major national elections 1968–2014)

Vote as a % of registered voters		Vote as a % of voting age population	
Australia	91	Sweden	82
Denmark	85	Denmark	80
Sweden	85	Australia	78
France	80	France	71
Italy	75	Netherlands	71
Netherlands	74	Italy	68
Germany	71	Germany	66
Canada	68	Canada	62
United Kingdom	66	United Kingdom	60
United States	66	United States	53
Japan	52	Japan	51
Switzerland	48	Switzerland	38

Source: Data from Institute for Democracy and Electoral Assistance, www.idea.int/vt.

By closely relating votes cast to representation in legislatures, PR 'wastes' few votes. Under a single-member district system, however, voters know that in many constituencies their vote will make no difference because of the large majority enjoyed by one party. Their incentive to vote is, therefore, reduced. In fact, if turnout is measured in terms of the *number of people who are registered*, then the picture looks very different (table 6.2). Nonetheless, Americans remain concerned with their rate of voter participation. The American data in table 6.2 are for presidential elections. Turnout for House and Senate elections, which are, after all, for national offices, is low by international standards. Moreover, an increasingly educated population should lead to an improvement in turnout. Very broadly, two schools of thought have attempted to explain this: the sociological and public choice. Public choice theorists argue that it is simply not rational to vote when the choice offered by parties is so limited.

Certainly, the relative absence of well-defined and deep-rooted social cleavages articulated by class-based or ethnically or regionally based parties reduces the direct and immediate interest the voter has in ensuring that 'his' or 'her' party is represented in government. American parties and candidates rarely promise social revolution; nor do they often promise to defend well-defined sectional, class, religious or ethnic interests. And this applies even in ideologically charged elections such as those in 2008 and 2016. Moreover, research has shown that citizens often vote *retrospectively*; or they decide to vote for party A rather than party B by judging an incumbent's past performance – usually in terms of whether the party's period in office has increased the voter's real income. As Morris Fiorina and others have shown, it is difficult to make this calculation when party programmes are so diffuse and when the appeal to voters is by individual *candidates* rather than parties.[4] This more atomized, individualized politics may account for the decline of voting among all social groups between 1960 and 1996. Interestingly, voter turnout went up in 2000, 2004 and 2008 when the differences between the parties were perceived by voters to be large. On a range of issues, therefore, voters felt that they had more to lose should 'their' party lose the election. This was particularly true in 2008 when, in the context of serious economic dislocation and unpopular foreign wars, voters turned out in record numbers to vote for Barack Obama, whose policy positions were starkly different from those of the incumbent Bush administration. A similar pattern was repeated in 2012 when, in spite of continuing economic woes, Barack Obama's base constituency of women, city dwellers and ethnic minorities remained loyal. Turnout declined slightly in 2016 perhaps reflecting the lowered expectations that black and other minority voters had in the Hillary Clinton candidacy. Turnout was also down in the more liberal areas (mainly larger cities) in the 'swing states' such as Pennsylvania and Michigan that proved so crucial in determining the outcome of the election.

The sociological school argues, simply, that poorer, less well-educated citizens vote less than richer, better-educated citizens. The data certainly confirm this, with around 50 per cent of manual workers apparently excluded from voting altogether.[5] Again this is a mainly American phenomenon. In other democracies the (usually much smaller) number of non-voters is drawn from all social groups, with few citizens caught in a pattern of permanent non-voting. Non-voting among lower-status groups can also be linked to rational expectations. Their sense of political effectiveness tends to be lower because they are poorer and, as importantly, they find it difficult to identify with a party that fails to appeal to voters on class lines. Significantly, between 1968 and around 2000 the party that used to project such an appeal, the Democratic Party, moved further and further away from class-based politics and towards issue- and candidate-based politics. Since then, however, the Democrats have renewed their class appeal as income and wealth inequalities have risen and economic dislocation has intensified. Indeed, at least some of the increased turnout in 2008 can be explained in terms of large numbers of voters supporting a Democratic candidate who promised a redistribution of incomes through the tax system and hefty increases in federal spending to boost the economy. In 2012 the same issues dominated the election, with Republican candidate Mitt Romney associated with a privileged elite and Barack Obama with the middle class and less well off. Paradoxically, in 2016 it was the Republican candidate, Donald Trump, who made a class-based appeal to poorer white voters by promising them jobs and tax reductions. Meanwhile Hillary Clinton was increasingly associated with the politics not of class but of identity based on race, ethnicity and gender.

Concern about non-voting in the United States is compounded by the fact that an increasingly educated and sophisticated population should have led to increased rather than decreased electoral participation. This phenomenon, above all, confirms political scientists' claims that voters cannot easily make rational decisions when faced by inchoate parties and a politics based on individual officeholders unable to offer effective programmes of social and economic change.

The 'American Voter' Model and the New Deal Coalition

During the 1950s and early 1960s a number of studies were published whose findings established a 'model' of American voting behaviour (the seminal work was *The American Voter*, published in 1960[6]). The unique contribution of this work was to explain the voting of individual citizens in terms of *psychological* orientation. By asking survey respondents how they felt about parties, candidates and issues, and then relating these sentiments to actual political behaviour, it was possible to build up a cognitive picture of how individuals thought about politics. The results were surprising, to say the least. In a more recent study, Nie, Verba and Petrocik summarized the findings thus:

> The American public had a remarkably unsophisticated view of political matters characterised by an inability to consider such matters in broad abstract terms.… Citizens had inconsistent views when one looked across a range of issues.… Most Americans had strong, long term commitments to one of the major political parties and this commitment served as a guide to their political behaviour.… Citizens felt relatively satisfied with the political system and relatively efficacious.[7]

Very few – a mere 2.5 per cent of *The American Voter*'s sample – were categorized as ideologues, or people who thought about politics in abstract terms. Most evaluated candidates and parties in terms of the benefits they brought to social groups (42 per cent) or in terms of the 'nature of the times' (24 per cent). In other words, most voters had little sense of 'left' and 'right' or the role that parties and candidates might play in moving society in a particular direction. Instead, immediate or recent events or simple promises by politicians to lower taxation, say, or to increase social spending influenced voters. Reinforcement of this analysis was provided by studies showing that voters were often inconsistent in their views across issues. Some citizens favouring increased social spending also wanted a reduced role for government in society; anti-communists were not always in favour of an increased role for the United States as international policeman. Most importantly of all, when attitudes on all issues were examined it was not possible to find any pattern consistent with a coherently thought-out ideology, whether liberal, conservative, socialist or whatever.[8]

The image projected, therefore, is one of a rather ill-informed voter who thinks rather little about politics. However, in one important respect American voters were found to be consistent – in their attachment to political parties, voters displayed enduring loyalties. Labelling this phenomenon *party identification*, voting analysts discovered that people acquired a positive or negative psychological attachment to a party early in childhood which remained with them throughout their lives.

In essence citizens were *socialized* by family and other social cues into thinking of themselves as Democrats or Republicans, a phenomenon which may account for the fact that 78 per cent of respondents to a 1958 survey had the same party identification as their parents. Not all voters were found to be strong party identifiers. Some identified less clearly with a party, while others considered themselves either independent or independently supportive of one or other of the parties (see figure 6.2).

We discuss this changing pattern of party identification below, but for now note the consistency of Democratic support, which constitutes a clear majority for most of the period. As these figures are for voting in presidential elections they raise an interesting question: how is it that the Republicans managed to win most presidential elections between 1968 and 2016 given the inbuilt Democrat majority implied by the preponderance of Democratic identifiers?

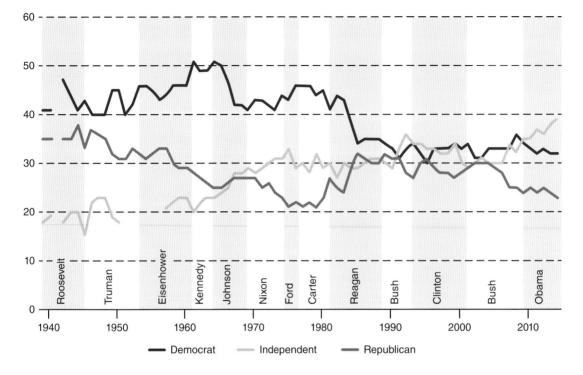

Figure 6.2   Trends in party identification, 1952–2014
Source: Pew Research Center, www.people-press.org/interactives/party-id-trend/.
Note: 1939–1989 yearly averages from the Gallup Organization interactive website. 1990–2014 yearly totals from Pew Research Center.

In answering this question, political scientists at first stressed that party identification was very much a psychological orientation to politics. There may be elections when voters deviate from their normal identification because of the particular appeal of the candidate (as was the case in the 1950s with Dwight Eisenhower) or because of the importance of certain issues (for example, law and order in 1968). Obviously, however, the Democratic majority must come from somewhere; it cannot be purely psychological. The answer is that there have been certain periods in American history when rapid social and economic changes have forged new political coalitions. During these periods orientations towards parties change as the parties themselves come to represent an emergent social group or region. By implication, during these years of turbulence, the voter is guided by the issues and by objective economic and social circumstances. Political scientists have called such transitions periods of *realignment*, when new electoral majorities are built. Between 1896 and 1928 the Republican Party reigned supreme. Urbanization, economic depression, the naturalization and integration of new immigrant groups and the emergence of an organized working class transformed party politics during the 1920s and early 1930s, however, and culminated in the resounding Democratic victory of 1932 (table 6.3). From the late 1920s the Democrats became the party associated with the urban working class, trade unions and the underprivileged. The near invincibility of what was to be called the New Deal Coalition

Table 6.3 Presidential election results, 1928–2016

	Candidates	Party	Electoral College vote	Popular vote	Percentage share	Number of states won[a]
1928	Herbert Hoover	Republican	444	21,392,190	58.2	42
	Alfred E. Smith	Democratic	87	15,016,443	40.8	6 (all southern)
	Norman Thomas	Socialist	0	267,420	1.0	0
1932	Franklin D. Roosevelt	Democratic	472	22,821,857	57.3	42
	Herbert Hoover	Republican	59	15,761,841	39.6	6 (all northeastern)
	Norman Thomas	Socialist	0	884,781	2.2	0
1936	Franklin D. Roosevelt	Democratic	523	27,751,597	60.7	46
	Alfred M. Landon	Republican	8	16,679,583	36.4	2 (Maine and Vermont)
	Norman Thomas	Socialist	0	187,720	0.5	0
1940	Franklin D. Roosevelt	Democratic	449	27,244,160	54.7	38
	Wendell L. Wilkie	Republican	82	22,305,198	44.8	10
	Norman Thomas	Socialist	0	99,557	0.2	0
1944	Franklin D. Roosevelt	Democratic	432	25,602,504	52.8	36
	Thomas E. Dewey	Republican	99	22,006,285	44.5	12
	Norman Thomas	Socialist	0	80,518	0.2	0
1948	Harry S. Truman	Democratic	303	24,179,345	49.5	32
	Thomas E. Dewey	Republican	189	21,991,291	45.1	12
	J. Strom Thurmond	States' Rights Dem.	39	1,176,125	2.4	4 (all southern)
	Henry A. Wallace	Progressive	0	1,157,326	2.4	0
	Norman Thomas	Socialist	0	139,572	0.2	0
1952	Dwight D. Eisenhower	Republican	442	33,936,234	55.2	40
	Adlai E. Stevenson	Democratic	89	27,314,992	44.5	8 (all southern)
1956	Dwight D. Eisenhower	Republican	457	35,590,472	57.4	41
	Adlai E. Stevenson	Democratic	73	26,022,752	42.0	7 (all southern)
1960	John F. Kennedy	Democratic	303	34,226,731	49.9	23[b]
	Richard M. Nixon	Republican	219	34,108,157	49.6	26
1964	Lyndon B. Johnson	Democratic	486	43,129,484	61.1	46
	Barry M. Goldwater	Republican	52	27,178,188	38.5	5 (Southern and Arizona)
1968	Richard M. Nixon	Republican	301	31,785,480	43.3	32
	Hubert H. Humphrey	Democratic	191	31,275,166	42.7	14
	George C. Wallace	American Independent	46	9,906,473	13.5	5 (all southern)

(Continued)

Table 6.2 (*Cont'd*)

	Candidates	Party	Electoral College vote	Popular vote	Percentage share	Number of states won[a]
1972	Richard M. Nixon	Republican	520	47,169,911	61.3	49
	George McGovern	Democratic	17	29,170,383	37.3	2 (DC and Massachusetts)
	John G. Schmitz	American	0	1,099,482	1.4	0
1976	Jimmy Carter	Democratic	297	40,830,763	50.1	24
	Gerald R. Ford	Republican	240	39,147,973	48.0	27
	Eugene J. McCarthy	Independent	0	756,631	1.0	0
1980	Ronald Reagan	Republican	489	42,951,145	51.0	46
	Jimmy Carter	Democratic	49	34,663,037	41.0	5
	John B. Anderson	Independent	0	5,551,551	7.0	0
1984	Ronald Reagan	Republican	525	54,450,603	59.2	49
	Walter Mondale	Democratic	13	37,573,671	40.8	2 (DC and Minnesota)
1988	George Bush	Republican	426	47,917,341	54.0	40
	Michael Dukakis	Democratic	112	41,013,030	46.0	11
1992	Bill Clinton	Democratic	370	44,908,233	43.0	32
	George Bush	Republican	168	39,102,282	37.4	18
	Ross Perot	Independent	0	19,741,048	18.9	0
1996	Bill Clinton	Democratic	379	47,401,504	49.2	31
	Bob Dole	Republican	159	39,197,350	40.7	19
	Ross Perot	Independent	0	8,085,285	8.4	0
2000	George W. Bush	Republican	271	50,456,002	47.9	30
	Al Gore	Democratic	266	50,999,897	48.4	21
	Ralph Nader	Green	0	2,882,995	2.7	0
2004	George W. Bush	Republican	286	62,025,554	50.7	31
	John Kerry	Democratic	251	59,026,013	47.3	20
	Ralph Nader	Independent	0	406,940	0	0
2008	Barack Obama	Democrat	365	69,445,229	52.9	29
	John McCain	Republican	173	59,923,677	45.7	22
2012	Barack Obama	Democrat	332	65,915,795	51.1	27
	Mitt Romney	Republican	206	60,933,504	47.2	24
2016[c]	Donald Trump	Republican	306	62,625,928	46.2	30
	Hillary Clinton	Democrat	232	65,152,112	48.2	21

[a]From 1960 includes Alaska and Hawaii. From 1964 includes Washington, DC.

[b]Fifteen Electoral College votes were cast for segregationist candidate Harry F. Byrd, including eight in Mississippi, which he effectively 'won'.

[c]Preliminary figures.

Plate 6.1   Republican 2016 candidates at one of the Republican debates
Source: Getty.

was assured because of the support guaranteed by the traditionally Democratic South. By the mid-1930s the intellectual establishment and many members of an insecure middle class had joined the coalition, resulting in the *maintaining* elections of 1936, 1940, 1944 and 1948. Not until incumbent Democrats (most notably Harry Truman) began to support civil rights for Southern blacks did the first cracks in the majority appear (in 1948).

The Republican victories of 1952 and 1956 were, according to the scholars, *deviating* elections. In other words, the Democrats remained the 'natural' majority party, but the specific circumstances of these elections allowed the Republicans to triumph. Eisenhower was an avuncular, charismatic war hero; in contrast, Adlai Stevenson, the Democratic candidate, projected an aloof, intellectual and narrowly eastern establishment image. This personality contrast was, above all, responsible for the Republican victories. Significantly, these successes were only partly repeated at the congressional level. Following Republican victories in 1946 and 1952, after 1954 Congress was firmly controlled by the Democrats.

The Decline of the New Deal Coalition and the Rise of a Divided Electorate

This neat and appealing theory of electoral behaviour seemed to be reinforced by the 1960 and 1964 presidential elections. Democratic victories returned, with the Republicans reverting to their normal status as the minority party. However, from the late 1960s a number of developments appear which in total present a rather serious challenge to the accepted theory. In particular we note the following.

Partisanship declines

A popular interpretation of Richard Nixon's victory in 1968 was that it heralded a new Republican majority.[9] More citizens were suburban, middle class and conservative, so the Republicans should find themselves ascendant. Moreover, the South, so long solidly Democratic, could no longer tolerate the integrationist policies of Democratic presidents. They famously won back Congress in 1994,[10] and the presidency in 2000 and, more convincingly, in 2004.

Superficially, the 1972 election seemed to reinforce these trends (table 6.3). Yet 1968 and 1972 were not classic *realigning elections* like 1932. The number of Republican Party identifiers, far from increasing, decreased slightly during these years (see figure 6.2), and the Democrats retained their dominance of Congress. Similarly, at the state level there was little evidence of an unstoppable Republican surge. Note, however, that Democratic Party identification also declined during the 1960s. This fact, together with the rise of independent identifiers, has led some commentators to speculate that what was occurring was party *dealignment*, or the slow demise of party identification as a key indicator of political preference.

By 1976, this process of dealignment seemed to have stabilized (figure 6.2), but at the same time neither party had recaptured the centre stage in the way in which the Republicans did after 1896 or the Democrats did after 1932.

Another indicator of declining partisanship is 'ticket splitting' or the tendency for voters to divide their loyalties between candidates of different parties. Ticket splitting rose sharply from 1952 to 1980. By that year some 34 per cent of the voters split their tickets between presidential and house candidates. A similar picture emerged for state-wide offices (elections for senators, governors, state legislatures) in a number of states and regions.

In spite of the Republican victories in 1980, 1984 and 1992, the Democrats continued to control the House of Representatives and (bar the 1981–7 period) the Senate. The Republicans also failed to build a permanent majority among the 50 states – although their control of the South strengthened. By the early 2000s some signs that, at last, the Republicans had become the majority party were evident. They famously won the presidency in 2000 and more convincingly in 2004. Moreover, by 2004 they controlled 28 of the Governors' mansions. However, their success was short-lived. They lost both houses of Congress in 2006 and only managed to hold on to 22 of the Governors' mansions. By 2008 it was the Republicans that looked like the minority party, for after the elections of that year they controlled neither Congress nor presidency nor a majority of the states. In terms of party identification, the Democrats enjoyed a dramatic surge in support in 2007 and 2008 (figure 6.3) as the Republicans became increasingly associated with a failing economy and a deeply unpopular president fighting an unpopular war in Iraq. The Democratic surge proved to be short-lived, however. Recession plagued Obama's first term and the Democrats were trounced by the Republicans in the 2010 mid-term elections. By 2010 the Republicans had also narrowed the party identification gap (figure 6.3). However, Barack Obama famously won a second term for the Democrats in 2012, although the Republicans retained control of the House, thus putting paid to any claims that a re-alignment to Democratic dominance was occurring. 2016 also failed to settle the question of which was the dominant party. For although Donald Trump won the

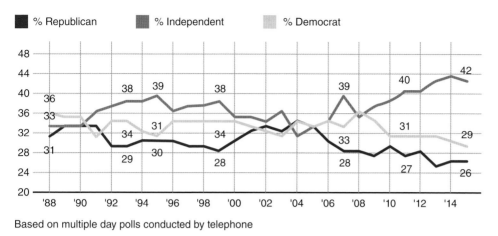

Based on multiple day polls conducted by telephone

Figure 6.3   Trends in party identification, 1988–2015
Source: 11 January 2016, Democratic, Republican Identification Near Historical Lows by Jeffrey M. Jones, Gallup at www.gallup.com/poll/188096/democratic-republican-identification-near-historical-lows.aspx.

Electoral College, he lost the popular vote by more than 2 million and the Democrats made small inroads into the Republican congressional majorities in both the House and the Senate.

A natural corollary to changing patterns of partisanship is that citizens (or at least those of them who vote) are using some other criterion when making a decision on whom to vote for. Candidates and issues had always played some part in the voting calculus, of course, but from the 1970s they began to play a much more prominent role. It also follows that if people are voting for individual candidates or for particular issues, the electorate is much more sophisticated than implied by the 'American Voter' model. Indeed, in their 1976 work, *The Changing American Voter*, Nie, Verba and Petrocik discovered that from about 1964 voters showed a significantly increased consistency in their views on domestic and foreign policy issues. Unlike the rather unthinking citizen portrayed by *The American Voter*, the public appeared more able to see the connections between issues, parties and candidates and to view the world in terms of broad ideological categories such as 'liberal' or 'conservative'. Certainly, presidential elections took on a more ideological stance after the 1970s. In 1980 there was a clear-cut choice, with the conservative Ronald Reagan facing an incumbent president, Jimmy Carter, identified – albeit reluctantly on his part – with the liberal cause. There was also a clear-cut choice in 1984, with Ronald Reagan appealing directly to the right and Walter Mondale to liberals and the left. In 1988, however, the two candidates were much closer together on basic issues. So much so, in fact, that George Bush worked hard to label Michael Dukakis a 'liberal' so as to secure the conservative vote. George Bush found his identification with conservative policies a liability in 1992, however, when the electorate called for new economic policies following a period of recession. Bob Dole tried to learn this lesson four years later in 1996, when he worked hard to capture the middle ground. Incumbent Bill Clinton also moved to the centre, and in the context of a healthy economy this was sufficient for him to win re-election.

Plate 6.2   US President Barack Obama speaks during a campaign rally at Virginia Commonwealth University, 5 May 2012 in Richmond, Virginia
Source: Sara D. Davis/Getty Images.

CONTROVERSY 5   NON-VOTING: DOES IT MATTER?

According to rational choice theory – the school of social behaviour arguing that all an individual's political actions are motivated by self-interest – rational citizens rarely have an incentive to vote. In other words, the costs of voting, including actually registering and travelling to the polling station, are usually greater than the benefits – the chance that an individual vote will make a difference to the outcome. In the vast majority of cases the individual vote makes not the slightest difference. (The major exceptions are elections with very small electorates; for example, committee or small-town meetings.) Indeed, most of us know perfectly well when we go to the polling booth that our one vote will not, on its own, count. Instead we reason collectively rather than individually and assume that the total of votes for a particular candidate is what matters. It could be argued that in the United States, where turnout is low, a more individualistic political culture has deterred 'rational' citizens from voting. Moreover, American political parties are made up of broad coalitions of interests rather than particular groups and interests. It is therefore more difficult for citizens to see a close identity between their own interests and those of a party. Compare this with Northern Ireland, for example, where it would be almost inconceivable for a Protestant to vote for Sinn Fein or for a Catholic to vote Unionist. Perhaps not surprisingly, turnout in Northern

Ireland is high. This analysis implies that, by some measures and notably voter rationality, it does not matter that election turnout is low in the United States. However, there is a further dimension to US turnout, which is simply the fact that, as in all other countries, low turnout is closely correlated with social class. Low-income Americans vote the least; higher-income better-educated Americans vote the most. Moreover, unlike in some other countries, non-voters often permanently exclude themselves from participation in the electoral process and fail to vote throughout their lifetimes. This phenomenon has led some commentators to conclude that political alienation among the disadvantaged is greater in the US than elsewhere. The fact that so many poor and disadvantaged people do not vote also helps to skew the electoral agenda towards the middle class and the rich. As a result, the claim is that political parties are reluctant to pursue redistributive policies in such areas as taxation, health and education for fear of offending the majority of middle-class voters.

Interestingly, there are occasions in American history when poorer voters do turn out to vote in numbers greater than might be expected. Usually this is when economic dislocation adds a class dimension to politics that is usually absent. Just such an event occurred in 2008 when Barack Obama promised income redistribution and job-creation programmes to speed recovery. Turnout among the poor and minorities increased correspondingly. A similar pattern occurred in 2012 when, in spite of continuing economic dislocation, Barack Obama managed to appeal to poorer voters by contrasting his support for a social agenda favouring the disadvantaged with that of his Republican opponent, Mitt Romney. The Democrats failed to maintain this pattern in 2016, however when Donald Trump famously succeeded in winning over disgruntled white working class voters. Meanwhile the 'Obama coalition' showed some signs of weakening as turnout among poorer urban minorities failed to match the 2008 and 2012 figures.

It was not until the elections of after 2000, however, that ideology and issue voting returned resolutely to the centre of the stage. In all four elections since then elections the distance between the candidates was large, with the Democrats identified as liberal and the Republicans as conservative. In 2000 the electorate was remarkably evenly divided between the two parties as it was in 2004. However in 2008 the balance shifted to the Democrats as more voters aligned themselves with a candidate intent on policies designed to stimulate the economy. What is interesting about these developments is the increasing coincidence of party identification with issue and candidate alignments. In other words to most Americans the label 'Democrat' means being liberal in domestic and social policy, and unlike earlier periods this applies across a whole range of issues – to foreign policy, the environment, the economy, immigration and the social issues (abortion, family values). Republicans are associated with precisely the opposite positions. These trends were reinforced in 2012: Mitt Romney was identified as a champion of the rich and privileged, while Barack Obama deliberately pitched his campaign to appeal to the broad mass of working Americans. And, as noted, Donald Trump turned class alignments upside down by winning the support of many white working-class voters and especially those living in smaller towns and rural areas.

CONTROVERSY 6   ARE AMERICAN ELECTIONS CORRUPT?

The 2000 presidential election brought to the attention of the world the sometimes erratic and possibly corrupt nature of American elections. In some states 'convicted felons' are ineligible to vote, which means that in Florida, for example, more than 10 per cent of male African American voters are disenfranchised. Worse still, the official list of felons has been shown to be wildly inaccurate, containing as it does a large number of non-felons. These and other problems associated with voting in the US derive from the simple fact it is the state legislatures that decide the technical details of voter eligibility as well as how votes are counted and the size and shape of constituencies. While some overt corruption undoubtedly occurs, the most cited problems are usually technical in nature, such as insufficient voting places, inefficient vote counting and out-of-date or improperly drawn up electoral rolls. But the most serious distortion of elections is in fact perfectly legal – the manipulation of constituency boundaries to favour the party that controls the state legislature. Known as 'gerrymandering', this practice has become more widespread in recent years, and with the Republicans on the ascendant in state elections until 2004 and again after 2010, this meant a system that favoured Republican incumbents. Hence both state and national electoral boundaries (for the House of Representatives) were drawn up in such a way that concentrated Democratic votes and dispersed Republican votes to ensure a Republican majority. The resulting constituencies are often bizarrely shaped and look like doughnuts, embryos, lobsters and other odd constructions. This practice (which is of course indulged in by both Republican and Democratic states) has resulted in a remarkably uncompetitive House with, in 2004, no more than about 25 competitive seats. Only Iowa has had the temerity to assign redistricting to an independent bureau. In the rest of the states, voters have little real choice, except in state-wide elections (for senators and governors), where redistricting is, of course, irrelevant. The Democratic House victories in 2006 and 2008 are all the more remarkable because they were achieved in spite of the considerable advantage enjoyed by most Republican incumbents in the House of Representatives. Perversely, in 2016 Donald Trump claimed that the system was biased against the Republicans by alleging that over 3 million votes for the Democrats were fraudulent (votes cast by dead people, non-residents and aliens). However, there was no evidence whatsoever that this was true.

Partisanship revives

In an important book published in 1992, a group of scholars based at the University of California, Berkeley, and at Brigham Young University argue that the decline of party voting in the USA had been greatly exaggerated.[11] Most people who may, in answer to survey questions, call themselves independents, do in fact have some allegiance to one of the major parties. The number of pure independents has changed little in the 50 years up to 2012. But,

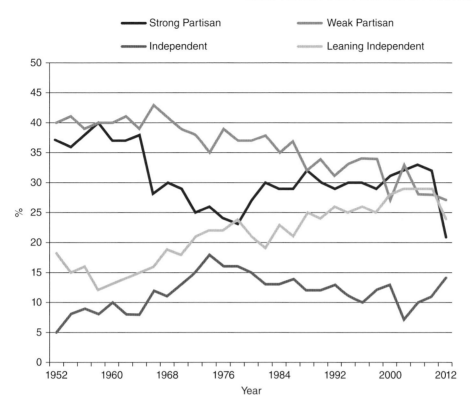

Figure 6.4   Strength of partisanship, 1952–2012
Source: Computed from American National Election Studies (ANES) data at Party Identification
7-Point Scale (revised in 2008) 1952–2012, www.electionstudies.org/nesguide/toptable/tab 2a_1.htm.

as can be seen from figure 6.4, the number of voters with some party affiliation who lean independent has steadily increased and, as a group, these voters are now as numerous as strong party identifiers, whose numbers have dropped considerably since 2000.

In addition, there has been a discernible ideological polarization of the electorate, with more people calling themselves liberal in the period since about 1990 (figure 6.5). It would also appear that many of these voters are more certain in their ideological commitment than was the case in the past, and are thus less likely to be persuaded by candidate appeal.

The crucial importance of gender

The 'gender gap' among voters has been increasingly pronounced for at least the last seven presidential elections, with more women voting Democrat than should have been expected from national trends. In 1996, women split their vote 54 versus 37 per cent between Clinton and Dole, compared with a 44 versus 44 per cent margin for men. In 1992 only 46 per cent of women voted for Clinton, compared with 41 per cent of men. Younger, educated and single women are especially prone to vote Democrat, reflecting, perhaps, an antipathy towards the tendency for Republican candidates to be conservative on a range of issues which resonate

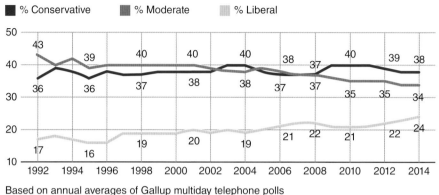

How would you describe your political views -- [very conservative, conservative, moderate, liberal or very liberal]?

Based on annual averages of Gallup multiday telephone polls

Figure 6.5   Liberal–conservative self-identification, 1972–2014
Source: 9 January 2015, U.S. Liberals at Record 24%, but Still Trail Conservatives, by Lydia Saad, Gallup at www.gallup.com/poll/180452/liberals-record-trail-conservatives.aspx.

with women (abortion, childcare, gun control, education, affirmative action, aggressive foreign policy). There are a number of other interesting aspects to this phenomenon. For one thing, the personal behaviour of candidates seems to be less important than their stand on the issues. The scandals surrounding Bill Clinton, for example, including his admitted dishonesty over his sexual affairs, seemed to do him little electoral harm among women.

In 2000 the gender gap between the two candidates remained substantial (54 per cent of women voted for Gore and only 43 per cent for Bush). As in the past, the gap was especially large among younger working women and minority women, who increasingly see the Republican Party as dominated by sexist, older white males. The gender gap persisted in 2004, although it narrowed to around 7 per cent (table 6.1). This may have been because 'security' or protection from terrorism was an important issue in the election, and many women assign security a very high value. However in 2008 the gap returned with a vengeance, with no fewer than 56 per cent of women voting Democrat, compared with 49 per cent of men – a trend that continued in 2012 when 55 per cent of women voted for Barack Obama compared with only 45 per cent of men. Perhaps surprisingly given Donald Trump's 2016 campaign comments on women, that which were widely seen as sexist, Hillary Clinton actually won the support of slightly fewer women than did Barack Obama in 2012. This may be explained by the number of working class white women who, along with their male equivalents, supported Donald Trump that year.

Voters and foreign policy
Although 'strength abroad' was a dividing issue in the 1980s, with Reagan supporters being decidedly more hawkish than Mondale voters, the issue all but disappeared from the political landscape after the end of the Cold War. All this changed with 9/11, which had the effect

of rallying almost all Americans behind the flag in the 'War on Terror'. However, the Bush administration's conduct of the war, and especially the invasion of Iraq in 2003, led to a deepening divide on the question, so that by the 2004 election campaign foreign policy had once again become an important issue. Republican voters were very much more supportive of an aggressive foreign policy than were Democrats. In fact by 2003 the gap was a yawning 25 percentage points. It should be stressed that most of those who opposed the Bush administration's policy in Iraq did support a vigorous anti-terrorist strategy. It is just that they viewed the Bush strategy as heavy-handed and ineffective. They were also highly critical of the threat that they saw the policy posed for civil liberties at home. After 2010 the foreign policy issue declined in importance, partly because neither of the conflicts in Iraq and Afghanistan was resolved satisfactorily and partly because the economy continued to trump other policy areas as an election issue. However the triumph of Donald Trump over Hillary Clinton in 2016 promised to return foreign affairs to the centre of the stage.

Region

Major changes in the regional pattern of voting have occurred since the 1960s. During the first half of the twentieth century the South was solidly Democratic, and until the 1930s New England was solidly Republican. Today the South is markedly more Republican than Democratic, not just at the presidential but increasingly at the state and local levels as well. The region is far from being as solidly Republican as it used to be Democratic, however, even if it is conservative. In 1996 Bill Clinton, himself very much a southerner, won five of the South and border states to the seven secured by Bob Dole. And while, in the two subsequent presidential elections, the Republicans swept the board by winning *all* the southern states in 2008, the Democrats won Virginia, North Carolina and Florida. Even in 2012 Barack Obama managed to win Florida and Virginia and in 2016 Hillary Clinton won Virginia, although the Republican vote in the Deep South states remained solid.

The mountain, plains and western states are also mainly Republican, with the notable exception of the Pacific states (Washington, Hawaii, Oregon and California), and especially California, which is now unambiguously Democratic at the presidential level. Northern and northeastern states are more Democratic and liberal – as should be expected from their industrial past. Bill Clinton managed a near-sweep of these regions in both 1992 and 1996, as did Al Gore in 2000, John Kerry in 2004 and Barack Obama in 2008 and in 2012. In 2016, however, Donald Trump easily won Ohio and narrowly won Michigan and Pennsylvania mainly thanks to his appeal among white working class voters. So we should be wary of assuming that the North and East can always be labelled Democratic. At the congressional, state and local levels the Republicans remain quite strong in many of the northern states, and voter preference at the presidential level is often as much dictated by the attractiveness of individual candidates as it is by party label.

None the less, at the presidential level by 2012 the geographic distribution of votes seemed to have settled into a pattern – most of the South, mountain and plains states voting Republican, and the Pacific and northeastern states voting Democratic. The so-called 'battleground states' – Florida, Ohio, North Carolina, Pennsylvania and Michigan –are also now consistently competitive. In effect, therefore, the vagaries of the Electoral College concentrate presidential election outcomes in a relatively small number of states.

Race and ethnicity

Finally, we should note the very high and consistent support for the Democrats among African American and some other minority voters. In 1984, a staggering 90 per cent of blacks voted Democrat, 4 per cent up on 1980 and against the national trend. In 2000, 90 per cent voted for Gore and a mere 9 per cent for Bush. And in 2016 just 12 per cent voted for Donald Trump. Two conclusions can be drawn from these figures. Either the vast majority of blacks perceive themselves to be the direct beneficiaries of Democratic policies or they display a remarkable sense of group solidarity. On the former point, Democrats are more supportive of the civil rights and welfare policies from which many African Americans benefit. But by no means all blacks are direct beneficiaries of these policies, and the high support for the Democrats implies that the party is always unambiguously in favour of welfare and civil rights, which is certainly not the case. Indeed, the Clinton administrations supported quite draconian reforms to the welfare system, involving reductions in welfare benefits for mothers with dependent children (see chapter 17). More feasibly, most African Americans feel a strong sense of racial solidarity and vote Democrat because they know that many of their number are more likely to benefit from Democratic policies than from Republican measures. No other social group of significant size shows such solidarity, which speaks volumes for the very special and troubled status of blacks in American history and present-day society. Of course, in 2008 and again in 2012, with a black candidate for president even more voted Democrat than is 'usual', with the figure reaching over 90 per cent. The bias towards the Democrats is also evident among other ethnic minority groups, including Hispanics, Asians and Jews. The Hispanic vote is of particular import given the rapid increase in the Hispanic population and their concentration in key election states such as Florida, New Mexico and Colorado. Indeed in 2012, 71 per cent of Hispanics voted Democrat, up from 56 per cent in 2004. Perhaps surprisingly given Donald Trump's characterization of illegal Mexican immigrants as 'criminals and rapists' during the 2016 campaign this figure fell to 65 per cent in the election of that year, although turnout among minorities in general was down on 2012.

Class

While there has always been some degree of class voting in the US, it took on a new meaning in 2008 and especially in 2012. With steady and falling real incomes being experienced by many Americans, rising fuel and food costs and continuing job insecurity, increased evidence of class voting emerged during the 1990s and 2000s. In particular, white males tended to align themselves on the left on economic issues (job security, health-care reform, taxation) but were towards the centre or the right on many of the social issues, and especially the war issue. Paradoxically this very same group swung decisively towards Donald Trump in 2016, almost certainly because during the campaign he spoke directly to their interests, while Hillary Clinton campaigned on broader, general issues.

We can conclude, then, that the volatility that characterized the electorate in the period from the 1970s to the late 1990s has been replaced by a rather different pattern. The electorate is now much more polarized on what might broadly be called social/war and economic issues. These include civil rights and liberties, the environment, family issues including same-sex marriage and abortion, job security, taxation and the role of the US abroad. Although the welfare/economic issues looked less important in the aftermath of 9/11 and

CONTROVERSY 7   DOES THE DECLINE IN SOCIAL
CAPITAL MATTER?

Since the publication of Robert Putnam's *Bowling Alone: The Collapse and Revival of American Community,* concern has been expressed at the decline of social capital in the US. Social capital refers to networks of reciprocal social relations, or the glue that holds society together. According to Putnam, the main indicators of social capital have been moving in the wrong direction – declining trust in government, falling voter turnout, less direct participation in political meetings and such things as direct action campaigns. Putnam sees this as part of a general decline in civic community in the US that extends into the non-political. Hence people now join fewer clubs (such as bowling leagues, thus the title Bowling Alone), entertain less at home and are generally more isolated from one another. This phenomenon is general but is most serious in larger, rapidly growing cities and in ethnically and linguistically mixed communities. Putnam believes that this development could have dire consequences. In essence, if citizens are not engaged in society and politics they are less likely to acquire a commitment to the polity. They are also less likely to trust not just political authority but also authority in general, and even each other. The result could be a partial breakdown of civil society and the undermining of political legitimacy. Putnam and others offer a number of solutions, and in particular support official efforts to engender 'deliberative democracy' at the community level. Critics point out that although Putnam's data may be sound, they do not relate to more serious indicators of political stability and strife in the US and elsewhere. So such indicators as political violence, demonstrations, strikes, boycotts, regime-threatening political parties and movements, and even general crime levels all show rapid falls over the past 30 years just as 'social capital' has been declining. It may be, therefore, that a more individualized (and isolated) society is what people want, and the political implications of this are relatively minor. Whatever the consequences of declining social capital, the debate is likely to rage on for some years to come.

during most of the presidency of George W. Bush, they returned to centre stage with the serious economic dislocation and fuel and food price rises after 2008. As suggested above, there is a strong gender/region/race/class dimension to this cleavage, with the electorate roughly evenly divided between the liberal and conservative positions. And while the 2008 and 2012 results showed that the demographic trends favoured the Democrats in 2016 these were overcome (in the Electoral College balance of votes, at least), partly because Donald Trump honed in directly on the grievances of white working-class voters. Younger voters as well as Hispanics, Asians and African Americans are all strongly Democratic (see table 6.1). Stanley Greenberg has characterized this divide in the following way:

There is no doubt that this represents a new and important development in American politics. In essence, the volatility and unpredictability that characterized American politics for much of the post-1970 period has been replaced by a much more confrontational and abrasive style of politics. How long this new divide will last is difficult to predict, but the strength of feeling is such that it is likely to have implications for the nature of political debate in America for some years to come.[12]

Non-Electoral Political Participation

As implied above, elections must by their very nature represent limited means of control over those forming and implementing policy. A considerable degree of centralized political power is necessary even for a relatively low level of economic efficiency, national security and social justice. With centralized power, individual citizens casting their votes in periodic elections can only hope to exercise an occasional veto influence over those at the apex of the constitutional system. This applies even in state and local elections, where voters, although closer to the officeholders, are still several steps removed from day-to-day decision-making.

But elections are just one of a number of means whereby citizens can influence the decision-makers. Participation extends to a number of other activities, particularly those associated with the local community. Historically, the local community was the primary focus of political life, with both formal and informal access to local officials being the very essence of American democracy. For most Americans, then, non-electoral participation involves contact with local officials or community leaders over such questions as school management, zoning, public works projects and law enforcement. This is a continuing, constantly changing activity. It is also perceived by all parties to be highly legitimate, and local policies *are* created, modified and vetoed through citizen involvement. Of course, this process is not equivalent to direct or pure democracy. The earlier noted biases against participation by lower income groups, women and ethnic minorities remain, and virtually no apparently local policy issue is entirely local today. Federal and state funding of local programmes ensures that local political activity is but one of a number of influences at work. None the less, the importance of local community activity should not be underestimated, especially in the light of the very high percentage of citizens (17 per cent in 1987) who had directly helped to *form* a group or organization to solve a local community problem.[13] The same study shows the continuing strong relationship between income and education, on the one hand, and participation on the other. It should come as no surprise, then, that ethnic and racial minorities, who tend to be poorer than better-off whites, participate much less in politics. It is noteworthy, however, that Latino Americans and in particular non-citizens have the lowest participation rates. This reflects the fact that many among these groups are recent arrivals in the USA and therefore have had less opportunity to become involved in community affairs. Figure 6.6 shows how participation levels have changed since the 1950s. Interestingly, all types of activity have increased in this period, thus confounding some of the more pessimistic of the declining 'social capital' claims (see Controversy 7). These figures do not show the level or intensity of citizen involvement, however.

So, recent research has dwelt on the wider question of 'social capital', or the extent to which citizens are engaged in the broader political and social community. In particular, Robert Putnam, in his book *Bowling Alone*, shows that in the mid- and late 1990s, irrespective of the trends shown in figure 6.6, Americans were becoming less involved in other

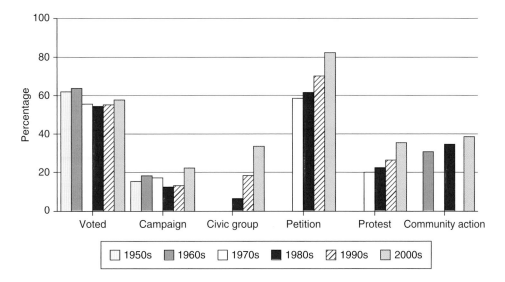

Figure 6.6   Trends in American political participation, 1950s to 2000s
Source: Citizenship Norms and the Expansion of Political Participation (pages 76–98), Russell J.
Dalton, Version of Record online: 1 February 2008, DOI: 10.1111/j.1467-9248.2007.00718.x,
figure 2. John Wiley & Sons Ltd. © 2008 The Author.

forms of civic and social activity. Their levels of political knowledge and grassroots activism
had declined, as had their membership and participation in local clubs and organizations.
Even informal social ties such as entertaining at home had declined. And all of this was
particularly true of younger rather than older voters and of those living in the West and
large cities rather than smaller rural communities.[14] Putnam and others bemoan this development and argue that this much more selfish and less trusting society holds dangers for
democracy.

This said, in comparative context, American levels of non-electoral political participation are very high. As can be seen from figure 6.7, while Americans may not be inclined
to vote in elections, they are much more involved in community work and contact officials
more frequently than the citizens of comparable countries – although they now tend to do
this in isolation from one another by mail or email. Again, this relates to dissatisfaction with
electoral politics, where the public's demands are often left unfulfilled.

There are two further varieties of political participation that are important for the political process. The first involves the activities of national interest groups. As chapter 14 shows,
there is hardly an area of economic or social life that is not influenced by interest groups.
How representative or democratic groups are is a point we cover below, but, as implied
above, interest-group membership and loyalties do cut across party allegiances, so their
activities must be considered an additional part of the representative process. As will be
discussed in the next chapter, the internet has had an important effect on electoral political
participation, but it has also made it much easier for like-minded people to access information and communicate with one another on particular issues. This has almost certainly
made it easier to organize non-electoral campaigns on such issues as the environment,

abortion and opposition to Wall Street and all it represents. As a result large numbers of small financial contributions can be amassed much more easily than in the past – a phenomenon that helps redress, at least in part, the great financial and organizational advantage that large corporations have in advancing their interests.

Second, there are all those political actions usually viewed as external to the established channels of political access: demonstrations, marches, boycotts and, more rarely, acts of political violence and terror. Clearly, the last are evidence of the breakdown of democratic processes, and at the national level, at least, have been remarkably rare in the US. In recent history they have largely been confined to the actions of isolated individuals (assassinations, hijacks) or have been precipitated by a single, sometimes ephemeral, issue (the Vietnam War, civil rights). At the local level the picture is somewhat different. Until the 1960s political violence was a relatively common feature of some parts of southern society, with the black population being the victims of systematic intimidation and random violence. Rarely, however, has local political violence been motivated by a desire for regime change. More often the motivation has been the assertion of authority over a politically and socially subordinate minority group. Often, these illegal acts were implicitly endorsed by the legitimate authorities.

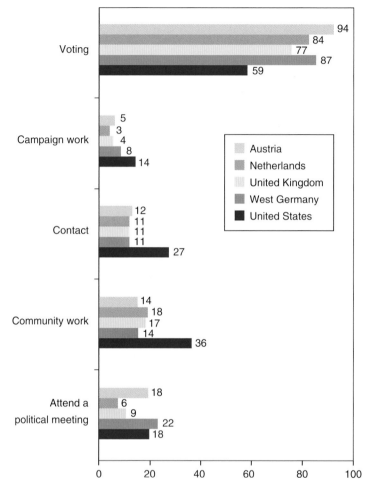

Figure 6.7   Comparative political activity rates in five countries (%)

One partial exception to this generalization is the 'survivalist' and militia movements that emerged in the late 1980s and 1990s. Although for the most part these fiercely antigovernment groups are non-violent, there have been some notable exceptions. The bombing of the federal building in Oklahoma City in 1996, which killed 164 people, is generally attributed to one of the more extreme of these groups. It is easy to exaggerate the size and importance of such organizations, however. They represent a tiny fraction of Americans, and they lack ideological and organizational coherence.

More difficult to evaluate are acts of political protest – demonstrations, marches, boycotts, political strikes. These are very much a part of American life and at certain times have played a crucial role in politics. Starting in the 1940s and reaching a crescendo in

Table 6.4   Political activities by race (% active)

Activity	Anglo-whites	African Americans	Latinos	Latino citizens
Vote	73	65	41	52
Campaign work	8	12	7	8
Campaign contributions	25	22	11	12
Contact	37	24	14	17
Protest	5	9	4	4
Informal community activity	17	19	12	14
Board membership	4	2	4	5
Affiliated with a political organization	52	38	24	27

Source: Sidney Verba, Kay Lehman Schlozman and Henry E. Brady, *Voice and Equality: Civil Voluntarism in American Politics* (Cambridge, MA: Harvard University Press, 1995), table 7.9. Copyright © 1995 by the President and Fellows of Harvard College. Reprinted by permission of the publisher.

the early 1960s, these were precisely the methods successfully employed by the civil rights movement – a fact that must help to explain the greater proclivity for the African American community to partake in this type of political activity today (table 6.4).

Other than civil rights, however, it is difficult to find an issue where protest is successful and broadly accepted as legitimate, and even the civil rights movement helped to inspire the urban riots of the 1960s, which aroused bitter controversy and, eventually, a 'backlash' from many whites. This is not to deny that protest has been influential. In many instances – over unemployment in the 1930s and the Vietnam War in the 1960s – clearly it has. But it is almost impossible to *measure* its influence, or in some cases to judge whether it actually helped or hindered the cause in question.

What we can conclude is that protest is very much a last resort. Only when the unambiguously legitimate means of access are either unavailable or exhausted do individuals and social groups have recourse to protest. In some cases, such as southern blacks in the 1950s and early 1960s, they had no choice, because within southern states normal channels of access were closed. But even in this example, the movement needed and received vital support from established political actors and institutions in the North. In other cases – protest over the Vietnam War, nuclear energy, the use of abortion, for example – some argue that direct political action was illegitimate because normal channels of access were available and the democratic process took its course. This last point demonstrates nicely the problems involved in discussing political participation. As emphasized, 'the democratic process' – whether electoral or through interest-group activity – must always be an imperfect representative mechanism. Some individuals and social groups will win or lose more than others; some have disproportionately greater access and hence greater political power than others. What is perhaps remarkable about the American system is that, in spite of the obvious biases in the system in favour of certain interests and classes, there is a broad acceptance of basic constitutional arrangements. Protest and political violence are comparatively rare. Most Americans accept the legitimacy of the established channels of political access – elections and the activities of interest groups.

Plate 6.3   Peace march, Washington, DC, 1967
Source: Marc Riboud/Magnum.

While this is true, evidence of increasing cynicism about political institutions suggests that, for many voters, the electoral system is far from being a perfect mechanism for the translation of public demands into public policy. As chapters 8 to 11 show, this helps explain the disenchantment often shown towards Congress and incumbent presidents.

Summary

American citizens have numerous opportunities to decide on their representatives at the national, state and local levels. Generally the Republicans are the party of the right and the Democrats of the left, with lower-income groups and ethnic minorities tending to vote Democrat and the better-off Republican. There are many exceptions to this pattern, however, especially if voting is broken down by regions. Turnout in the US is generally low – although increasing markedly in recent national elections, in part because some of the institutional barriers to voting have been reduced. Many Americans vote according to their party identification, or the psychological attachment they have to parties. Since the 1980s, however, there has been increasing evidence of voting based on ideology, issues and candidates, with the ideological divide being especially pronounced since 2000. Indeed, the 2008, 2012 and 2016 elections showed a marked polarization of the electorate into liberal and conservative camps. Non-electoral political participation is also important in the US, where citizens engage in political campaigns and movements rather more than in comparable countries. Extreme regime-threatening politics rarely occur in the US, however.

Questions for Discussion

1   Why are women more likely to vote Democrat than men? Answer with respect to changes in voting patterns from 1980 to 2016.
2   Account for the rise in the number of Americans calling themselves Independents since 1980? What is the significance of this development?
3   Why do Americans vote as they do? Answer with specific reference to the 2016 presidential election.
4   Discuss the changes in non-electoral political behaviour that have occurred since the 1950s. How important is this means of political expression today?

Glossary

'American Voter' model   The model of voting behaviour based on party identification

coattails   The secondary political effects of victory in a presidential election that spills over into victory for the president's party in Congress

Cold War   The ideological conflict between the West and the Soviet Union and China between 1949 and 1991

dealignment   The weakening of party identification in elections to the point where voters abandon traditional voting cues

deviating elections   Elections, such as those of 1952 and 1956, where voters temporarily vote out of line with their party identification

gerrymandering   The manipulation of electoral boundaries for political advantage

initiative   Voters placing an item on the ballot sheet through the presentation of a minimum number of signatures

maintaining elections   Elections, such as those of 1960 and 1964, that maintain the majority party in power

'motor voter' law   Voter registration laws that allow voters to register to vote when renewing their driving licences

New Deal Coalition   The coalition of industrial workers, farmers, intellectuals and the South that underpinned Democratic Party success from 1933 to 1969

party identification   The psychological attachment to parties held by voters over time

realignment   A major shift in party identification from one party to another, as happened in 1932

recall (elections)   Citizen-inspired elections to recall an official from office. Used at the state level only

referendums   Votes directly on state ballot sheets on a particular aspect of public policy

retrospective voting   Voting in support of or against candidates based on their record in office

social capital   The accumulated networks of social interaction based on trust and community identity

survivalist movement   Extremist militia groups who prepare for complete social breakdown and possible violent conflict with the federal government

voter registration laws   Laws governing the conditions under which citizens can register to vote

Notes

1 'Recalls' enable the electorate, following the presentation of a minimum number of signatures, to hold a special election to recall an official from office. Initiatives are similar devices, enabling the electorate by petition to vote directly on a proposition (such as a tax change), thus bypassing the state or local legislature. Referendums are proposed by legislatures and present to the electorate the opportunity to vote directly on an issue. Referendums – but not recalls and initiatives – are increasingly common in Europe to legitimize constitutional changes, such as the peace agreement in Northern Ireland or membership of the European Union.

2 See, in particular, Sidney Verba and Norman H. Nie, *Participation in America: Political Democracy and Social Equality* (New York: Harper & Row, 1987).

3 Quoted in *USA Today*, 8 November 1996, p. 3A.

4 Morris P. Fiorina, *Retrospective Voting in American National Elections* (New Haven: Yale University Press, 1981).

5 See Walter Dean Burnham, 'The turnout problem', in A. James Reichley (ed.), *Elections, American Style* (Washington, DC: Brookings Institution, 1987), table A4.

6 Angus Campbell et al., *The American Voter* (New York: Wiley, 1960).

7 Norman H. Nie, Sidney Verba and John R. Petrocik, *The Changing American Voter*, enlarged edn (Cambridge, MA: Harvard University Press, 1979), p. 42.

8 Philip Converse, 'The nature of belief systems in mass publics', in David E. Apter (ed.), *Ideology and Discontent* (New York: Free Press, 1964), p. 543.

9 Kevin Phillips, *The Emerging Republican Majority* (New York: Doubleday Anchor, 1970).

10 Walter Dean Burnham, 'Realignment lives: The 1994 earthquake and its implications', in Colin Campbell and Bert A. Rockman (eds), *The Clinton Presidency: First Appraisals* (Chatham: Chatham House, 1996).

11 Bruce E. Keith et al., *The Myth of the Independent Voter* (Berkeley and Los Angeles: University of California Press, 1992).

12 Stanley Greenberg, *The Two Americas: The Current Political Deadlock and How to Break It* (New York: Thomas Dunne Books, 2004), p. 1.

13 Sidney Verba, Kay Lehman Schlozman and Henry E. Brady, *Voice and Equality: Civic Voluntarism in American Politics* (Cambridge, MA: Harvard University Press, 1995), table 3.6.

14 Robert D. Putnam, *Bowling Alone: The Collapse and Revival of American Community* (New York: Simon & Schuster, 2000).

Further Reading

The best analysis of political participation in the US is Sidney Verba, Kay Lehman Schlozman and Henry E. Brady, *Voice and Equality: Civic Voluntarism in American Politics* (Cambridge, MA: Harvard University Press, 1995). For a discussion of changes in electoral behaviour, see Bruce Keith et al., *The Myth of the Independent Voter* (Berkeley and Los Angeles: University of California Press, 1992). The classic statement of the voter as rational actor is Morris P. Fiorina's *Retrospective Voting in American National Elections* (New Haven: Yale University Press, 1981). Presidential elections are fully covered by Nelson W. Polsby, Steven E. Schier, David A. Hopkins and Aaron Wildavsky, *Presidential Elections: Strategies and Structures of American Politics* (New York: Rowman & Littlefield, 2011). On the 2008 election, see Robert G. Boatright, Janet M. Box-Steffensmeier, David E. Campbell and Roger H. Davidson, *The American Elections of 2008* (New York: Rowman & Littlefield, 2009). On the 2016 contest, see Stephen J. Wayne, *The Road to the White House 2016: The Politics of Presidential Elections*, 10th edn (New York: Wadsworth, 2016) and Thomas Lake and Jodi Enda, *Unprecedented: The Election That Changed Everything* (New York: Melcher Media, 2016).

CHAPTER 7
THE MEDIA AND AMERICAN POLITICS

Fox News is so biased it is disgusting. They do not want Trump to win. All negative!
                                                    – DONALD TRUMP, FACEBOOK POSTING, 2016

Why don't other countries see the world the way we do? News coverage is a large part of the answer. Eric Alterman's new book, What Liberal Media?, doesn't stress international comparisons, but the difference between the news reports Americans and Europeans see

American Politics and Society, Ninth Edition. David McKay.
© 2018 John Wiley & Sons Ltd. Published 2018 by John Wiley & Sons Ltd.

*is a stark demonstration of his point. At least compared with their foreign counterparts,
the 'liberal' US media are strikingly conservative.*

– PAUL KRUGMAN, LIBERAL COLUMNIST, 2004

The mass media are sometimes called the fourth estate or even the fourth branch of government because of the widespread perception that they are politically powerful. This is hardly surprising, because it is only through the media that presidents can build support, candidates win approval and incumbent politicians bolster their public image. Television, radio, the print media and the internet are therefore virtually the only communications channels for politicians, parties and organized interests. Moreover, there is a further perception that the increasingly public nature of American politics has elevated the media to new heights of influence. The purpose of this chapter is to analyse the political role of the different media outlets, and in particular to examine any political bias that they hold. We will also look at the question of censorship and control of the media by governments. First, how have the American media evolved over time, and how are the different media outlets organized?

Media Structure and Organization

The growth of the mass media

The print media have always played an important part in American politics. As the US is the first mass-participation democracy with fully developed political parties, local newspapers have long played a role in supporting particular candidates and causes. By the end of the nineteenth century almost all cities boasted at least two newspapers, often competing for stories and news scoops of a political nature. In the 1920s the Ben Hecht play *The Front Page* (made into successful movies in 1931 and 1974) was as much truth as parody in its portrayal of newspapermen as desperate to execute a news scoop by raking the muck on local political leaders. Until well into the twentieth century most of this news was *local* and produced exclusively by *local* papers. Given the size of the country and limited communications this was understandable, for distributing a paper more than a few dozen miles (or, with railways, a few hundred miles) on a daily basis was impossible. As we will see, this localism persists in one form or another even today.

Media information did not become nationalized until the coming of radio and television during the twentieth century, and initially almost all radio news was local. Franklin Roosevelt's radio fireside chats of the 1930s represented the first example of a national politician communicating directly with the voters via the mass media, but it was not until the coming of television that the media took on a truly national political role. Television ownership increased from 9 per cent of households in 1950 to nearly 80 per cent by 1960. The latter was also the year of the first live debate between presidential candidates Richard Nixon and John F. Kennedy, and these debates have become an established feature of presidential elections ever since. It was also at about this time that television political advertising took hold. At first this was almost completely unregulated. The candidates with the most money, raised from any source, could do the most advertising. As will be developed in chapter 8, campaign finance reform legislation, notably in 1974 and 2002, placed limits on paid political advertising –

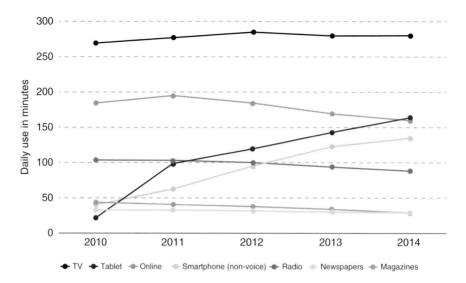

Figure 7.1   Daily media usage, 2010–2014
Source: emarketer, Statistica, 2015.

although these were greatly diluted by the 2010 Supreme Court decision, *Citizens United v. FEC* (see p. 346). From the very beginning radio and television did, of course, broadcast national news bulletins, and, as in other modern societies, national news dissemination in the US plays a particularly important role during wars and national emergencies such as the Second World War and the aftermath of 9/11. However, in recent years television stations have devoted less and less time to news in general and to international news in particular. This is a point we will return to later. Newspaper circulation rose rapidly until the middle of the twentieth century, since when both circulation and readership have declined. The internet is a recent phenomenon, but one that is growing very rapidly. By 2014 around 86 per cent of North American households (USA and Canada) had access to the internet, by far the highest of the world's major regions. As can be seen from figure 7.1, although TV usage remains high (mainly among older Americans), more time is now spent on the internet (online, tablets and smart phones combined), while newspaper and magazine usage is relatively unimportant.

Organization and Ownership

Television and radio

Almost all of the more than 3,000 television and radio stations in the US are locally based, but most are affiliated to one of the three national networks, the Central Broadcasting Company (CBC), the National Broadcasting Company (NBC) and the American Broadcasting Company (ABC). These were originally radio networks that sold programmes to local stations, and the same principle was adopted with the advent of television. Thus, local affiliates will broadcast the national news from their network, which is a half-hour slot going out in the early evening. The three national networks are available to all television viewers, but nearly 70 per cent of the population subscribes to cable or satellite television, which provides access to dozens of additional channels. There are also now a number of 24-hour news channels, including CNN, CNBC and the Fox News service owned by Rupert Murdoch. In fact Fox is now a fourth network, as it has its own programming and around 200 affiliated stations, almost a quarter of which it owns. Most radio stations broadcast music. 'Talk radio', as Americans call it, is limited mainly to news and religious programmes, many of them broadcast nationally.

Finally, a Public Broadcasting System (PBS) exists which is free of advertising and is funded by private charitable donations and some government funding. PBS radio produces its own shows, which are a mixture of current affairs and music. PBS television undertakes limited programme production, but buys in programmes from other public broadcasting networks, notably the British Broadcasting Corporation (BBC).

All broadcasting has been regulated by the Federal Communications Commission, which has been operating since 1934. Its main purpose is to issue broadcasting licences but also to keep ownership diverse and thus prevent the concentration of media power in one person or one company. However, this policy has often resulted in local monopolies. In 1996 Congress passed the Telecommunications Act, which opened up both broadcasting and telephone services to more competition. The number of television stations that a single company could own was greatly increased so long as no one company controlled more than 35 per cent of the total viewing market. The upshot has been a spate of takeovers and mergers, with two networks, CBS Corporation and News Corporation (Fox), now owning enough stations to exceed the 35 per cent limit. Of course exceeding 35 per cent does not mean that viewers in those areas only have access to (say) Fox programmes, because viewers are still able to choose from numerous other stations and channels. It simply means that CBS and Fox have managed to buy stations that broadcast to more than 35 per cent of the public. The degree of concentration in ownership is even higher for cable broadcasters, where just a handful of companies control about 80 per cent of the market.

Critics of the 1996 Act argue that increased concentration of ownership has hurt the smaller, community-based stations, especially those serving ethnic and other minorities. They also claim that increased concentration has led to more standardized (and not necessarily higher-quality) programmes. As will be discussed below, concentration of ownership extends to all media outlets including the press, film production and some aspects of the internet.

A further recent development is the rise of streaming channels such as those provided by Netflix and Amazon. Netflix had more than 45 million subscribers in the US as of 2016 and has led to a small but significant drop in the market share held by traditionally broadcast channels.

Newsprint

Almost all newspapers in the United States are locally organized. Even today virtually every one of the over 1,500 newspapers in the USA has a local base (the major exceptions being *USA Today* and the *Christian Science Monitor*) – although some, like the *New York Times* and the *Wall Street Journal*, do now publish national editions. It would be misleading to claim that most *news* is local, however, or that Americans do not have a consciousness of national affairs and events. On the contrary, most Americans are reading the same national news most of the time. There are a number of reasons for this. First, most smaller newspapers carry syndicated national columns put out by news services or the more prominent regional papers, such as the *New York Times*, *Chicago Tribune* and *Washington Post*. Second, as with television, ownership is increasingly concentrated in a few hands. Indeed it is often the same companies that own television and other media, such as corporate giants Gannet Company and News Corp. These chains tend to have similar editorial policies or to buy the same syndicated columns, so there is much less regional and local variation than would otherwise be expected. Finally, weekly and monthly magazines (*Time*, *Newsweek*, *US News and World Reports*, *The Economist*, *Harpers*, *The Atlantic*) are genuinely national in scope, and command a much higher (although declining) readership than in countries such as Britain.

No discussion of the news media would be complete without reference to the serious decline in readership and revenues they have suffered since the dawn of the internet age. Many newspapers have closed and even major titles such as the *Los Angeles Times* and the *New York Times* are in serious financial difficulties. Not only has the internet taken readers away from the print versions of papers, it has also stripped them of the very profitable classified and display advertising that once constituted their staple income (see figure 7.2). As elsewhere in the world, advertising of jobs, houses, cars and other items has migrated almost lock, stock and barrel to the internet. And efforts to replace print with digital editions available online have made little difference to overall income (figure 7.2).

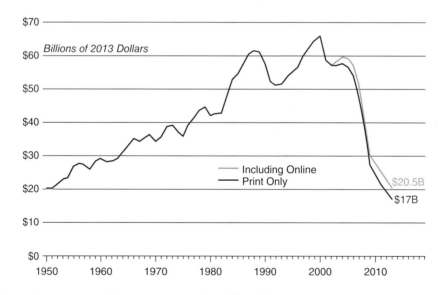

Figure 7.2   Newspaper advertising revenue adjusted for inflation, 1950–2012
Source: AEIdeas, Mark J. Perry, 7 October 2013, Chart of the day: Newspaper advertising revenue will likely continue its decade-long free fall to below 1950 levels, https://www.aei.org/publication/chart-of-the-day-newspaper-advertising-revenue-will-likely-continue-its-decade-long-free-fall-to-below-1950-levels/.

How Biased? The Media and the Political Agenda

Television and radio

Most television stations and certainly the three main networks (NBC, CBS, ABC) strive to achieve impartiality in their news and current affairs programme dissemination. They will, in other words, try to give equal time to both Republican and Democratic perspectives. However, local stations tend to reflect the biases and prejudices of local communities, so a local station in Utah or Mississippi will have a very different editorial line from stations in New York or San Francisco. Fox stations, and in particular the Fox national network news, are clearly on the right politically. Indeed the Fox 24-hour news channel has been lavishly praised by Republicans and condemned by Democrats. In contradiction of its on-air slogan of 'fair and balanced', the main device used by the network is to hire articulate and forceful right-wing pundits to comment on the news, but to choose ineffective liberal spokespersons (see Biography, below). No doubt responding to Fox's growing market share, some of the CNN (the American network, not those based abroad) news coverage also moved to the right, although since about 2008 its stance has moved back towards the political centre or even the left.

Fox maintains that it is merely redressing what it and many on the right see as a general 'liberal bias' in the main networks created by big-city (New York and Los Angeles) intellectuals and snobs. This accusation became more vociferous during the 1998–2008 period and reached a crescendo with the publication in 2002 of Ann Coulter's *Slander: Liberal Lies about the American Right*.[1] This heavily referenced polemic claimed that bias against the right was systematic and deliberate. In response, liberal journalist Joe Conason produced a refutation of these claims in his book *Big Lies: The Right Wing Propaganda Machine and How It Distorts the Truth*.[2]

But this debate aside, the main academic criticism aimed at the networks is not that they are politically biased but that they trivialize and distort the news. With increasing commercialization, networks compete furiously for what is a declining market. As a result they opt for soundbite, market-driven journalism and have reduced the time devoted to the analysis of news. Indeed the definition of what constitutes news has changed as the networks seek to serve their core viewing audience. Hence on the evening news, which is watched mainly by older Americans, there is almost always a news item devoted to health care or ageing problems. Other news, and especially news from abroad, is consequently squeezed out. As Kathleen Jamieson notes, generally TV news trivializes by reporting in one of five modes:

- *Appearance versus reality*. So a news item might show that a new 'miracle drug' can have serious side-effects.
- *Little guys versus big guys*. This is, of course, a common populist theme in American politics, and it is constantly stressed by the networks, whether it be corporate chiefs' remuneration or a housing foreclosure brought on by sharp bank lending policies.
- *Good versus evil*. This theme might stress heroics by an individual police officer against a criminal, or children saved from abuse by vigilant neighbours.

- *Efficient versus the inefficient.* This often takes on inefficient spending by the federal government, such as 'Navy orders $2,000 lavatory seat', and then contrasts this with the $20.00 seat available in the local store.
- *Unique or bizarre events versus the routine.* These are frequently reported at the end of a bulletin, and may cover freak events involving animals or unusual weather. Much of the reporting from abroad covers such 'news' stories.[3]

All of these points beg the question of the political influence of television. Unfortunately this is very difficult to measure, but studies agree that television and other media rarely change people's political views but, rather, tend to reinforce them. This is, of course, particularly true when a station or programme pursues a clear political line. So Fox viewers will tend to watch the channel because its political line reassures them. One thing is for sure: the public are much less trusting of news reporting than they used to be. As can be seen from figure 7.3, there has been a marked decline in public confidence in the media since the 1970s. These figures are for all media, but as most Americans receive their news information from television it is a direct commentary on the deteriorating state of television news reportage.

Moreover, as can be seen from figure 7.4 trust is lowest among Republican voters rather then among Democrats, whose level of trust declined only slightly over recent years while trust among Republicans fell by 20 percentage points. Disdain for the media helps explain the appeal of Donald Trump in 2016, who constantly challenged media spokespersons during the election campaign, including, famously, the Republican-leaning Fox News network (see Biography, p. 155).

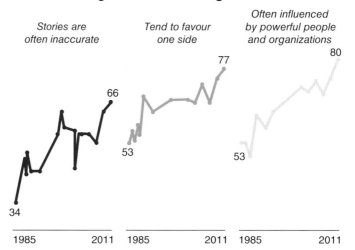

Evaluations of overall press performance grow even more negative

Figure 7.3   Public confidence in the media, 1985–2011
Source: Pew Research Centre, 'Press Widely Criticized, But Trust More than Other Information Sources: Views of the News Media: 1985–2011', 22 September 2011. The Pew Research Center for the People and the Press, a project of the Pew Research Center.

% Great deal/Fair amount of trust

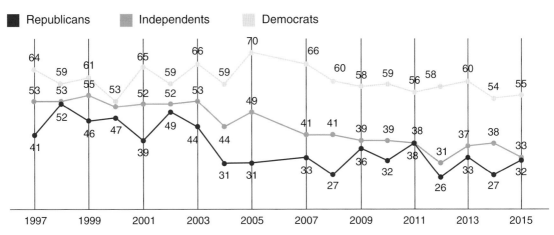

Figure 7.4   Trust in the media by party, 1997–2015
Source: 28 September 2015, Americans' Trust in Media Remains at Historical Low, by Rebecca Riffkin, Gallup at
www.gallup.com/poll/185927/americans-trust-media-remains-historical-low.aspx.

None of this is to deny that politicians and political parties sometimes use the television to manipulate voters. There are two ways in which this can happen. First and most obviously, paid political advertising can make or break candidates. In 2012, for example, incumbent Republican governor Scott Walker narrowly won an attempt to be recalled by popular vote at least in part because he was able to raise seven times more for his campaign than his Democratic rival Tom Barret. Most famously Barack Obama massively outspent both Democratic opponent Hillary Clinton and Republican John McCain on media advertisements in 2008. The 2016 pattern was somewhat different for although Hillary Clinton outspent Donald Trump by a considerable margin, Donald Trump received extensive free coverage in part because his rallies were covered by national news outlets because of their theatricality and unpredictability and in part because he made constant use of (free) social media and in particular Twitter.

Second, politicians, and especially presidents, can manipulate the media to their advantage in a number of ways. If bad news is to be announced, its release can be delayed until after the early evening news has been broadcast. By the following day it will already be in the newspapers and early morning TV shows. As 'old' news, it is less likely, therefore, to be the lead item on the forthcoming evening news. Presidents can also time high-publicity camera events to hit the news at the optimum moment, as when, following the invasion of Iraq in 2003, George W. Bush landed on an aircraft carrier off San Diego accompanied by a banner reading 'mission accomplished'.

Much of the above analysis can also be applied to radio, but there are differences. As noted earlier, there is in fact very little news on American radio, but over the past 20 years right-wing commentary shows put out by such polemicists as Rush Limbaugh and Laura Schlesinger have grown hugely in popularity.[4] These shows are syndicated to hundreds of local stations, and at his peak Limbaugh, who lambasts liberals and panders to people's prejudices, had a listening audience of over 20 million. These 'talk radio' shows have been much criticized for the damage they may do to the rights of the poor, minorities, women and other disadvantaged groups.

Newsprint

Most daily newspapers in the United States tend towards the Republicans or the right of the political spectrum, although in terms of readership this tendency is partly corrected by the broadly liberal large-circulation papers on the two coasts, and notably the *New York Times*, *Los Angeles Times* and *Washington Post*. The Republican bias in smaller towns and cities is easily explained by the fact that these papers are often owned by local businesspeople whose main political interest is to protect and improve local economies. This tendency is particularly marked in the South, the Midwest and the mountain states. Any Republican or Democratic bias is not, however, always immediately obvious because of the long-established convention in American journalism of making a distinction between editorial and opinion. So, unlike the vast majority of British papers, US papers make a serious effort to report the news in news columns and to reflect editorial opinion in opinion columns. Typically, the front page of a newspaper will reveal little or nothing of the paper's political position, which will only be apparent from reading the opinion columns in the centre pages. In the UK even quality broadsheets now fail to make this distinction, and often state controversial opinions as banner headlines.

A further feature of the American press is its generally conservative editorial and presentational style. This is not to be confused with *political* conservatism, but refers rather to the fact that tabloid papers and sensational headlines are generally the exception rather than the rule. Instead, most American papers appear staid and serious – even in comparison with the British quality press. They also carry little in the way of foreign news, and in the case of the smaller local papers, little national news. The major exceptions are the aforementioned big-city papers, which have a readership well beyond their urban bases. Typically they will lead with national or international stories.

As with television, it is very difficult to measure the political influence of the press. Endorsements of presidential candidates may have some effect – and Republican candidates almost always receive more endorsements than Democrats – but again, as with TV, newspapers almost certainly reinforce existing political views rather than change them. Two other features of the press are noteworthy. First, ownership concentration has produced a much more standardized press than prevailed a few years ago. With newspaper sales declining it is now rare for smaller cities to have more than one daily paper, which typically will carry the same syndicated columns as all the other papers in the group. Editorial policies are accordingly more risk-averse and often more conservative. What keeps these papers alive is advertising, and in particular classified advertising. Serving local business and especially real estate and property developer interests is often paramount.

Second, the US boasts a large and varied weekly and monthly news and opinion press that (*Time* and *Newsweek* apart) increasingly reflects the political polarization of American society. Hence on the right the *National Review*, the *American Conservative, Commentary* and other conservative publications are in direct conflict with liberal and left publications such as *The New Republic, The American Prospect* and the *Atlantic*. Needless to say these magazines generally only preach to the converted.

Biography   The Rise and Fall of Roger Ailes – Creator of the Fox News Network

Born in Warren, Ohio, into a blue-collar background Ailes rose rapidly as a political consultant after graduating from the University of Ohio. He advised Richard Nixon in 1968 and 1972, Ronald Reagan in 1984 and George H. W. Bush in 1988. After working for the cable news channel CNBC he was hired by Rupert Murdoch of News Corporation to create the Fox News channel in 1996. Ailes had a very clear vision of what Fox News should be. In spite of its slogan 'Fair and Balanced' it quickly established itself as an unashamedly right-wing news outlet and champion of the conservative Republican movement that emerged at about the same time. Fox News was heavy on opinion, and elevated right-wing commentators such as Sean Hannity, Greta Van Susteren and Bill O'Reilly to national fame. It very quickly eclipsed CNN as the leading cable news channel, and by the mid-2000s had won more than 2 million regular viewers. It was also extremely profitable and generated revenues of over $2 billion in 2015. Ailes also wanted Fox News to project a particular image using leggy, heavily made up blondes as its key news anchors. By 2016 one presenter, Megyn Kelly, achieved particular fame in part because she was an accomplished television performer and in part because she became the butt of Donald Trump's anger when he accused her of being biased against him in one of that year's Republican candidate debates. She later reconciled with Trump thus generating more publicity both for Fox and for Trump. Ailes resigned in 2016 following accusations from a large number of Fox employees and others of sexual harassment spread over several decades. Measuring the political effects of the Ailes creation is difficult, but research has shown that it appeals to less well-educated rural and suburban whites. In this sense it projects a populist image championing the 'little guy' against the venality of big government and the 'stupidity' of liberal elites. One thing is for sure – Fox News gave to the conservative movement a national platform that it lacked before and may well have contributed to Donald Trump's 2016 victory in the presidential election.

The internet

As noted, more Americans have access to the internet than do the citizens of any other region of the world, and with access figures exceeding 85 per cent (in 2014) and rising, the medium is used by most Americans. The specifically political use of the internet is apparent from the fact that email and social media have replaced the postal service as the main means whereby constituents communicate with elected representatives. Given the ease of use and minimal cost of this medium, the number of communications going both ways has increased very substantially. This can have important consequences. Most notably, the meteoric rise in support for Democratic candidate Barack Obama in the 2008 presidential race was due in part to his highly organized internet fundraising campaign. Obama had the advantage of a youthful base of support accustomed to and eager to use the internet. So far the internet has been used mainly as a means of reinforcing conventional campaigning. Some internet fundraising is used to pay for TV advertisements and direct mailing. Eventually, however, it is possible that the medium could become the means of direct communication between politicians and voters. One obvious problem with the internet is that politicians cannot control the message. Social media in particular, can be used to embarrass politicians by revealing scandals or exaggerating stories or events. Sometimes these are picked up by the mainstream media and become major news stories, as with revelations about Barack Obama's pastor, Jeremiah Wright, in 2008. Widely available on the net was a video of Wright pronouncing 'God damn America', which damaged Obama during the primary campaign. In 2012 the candidates used the internet both to raise money and to mobilize people to vote, but the Obama campaign's use of a highly trained 'tech team' proved to be more effective. It is estimated that Obama had around 50 million followers on Facebook and Twitter – 10 times the number he had in 2008. In 2016 Donald Trump amassed over 9 million Twitter followers and responded to events with timely tweets that were widely cited in the print media and on TV. Significantly the use of Twitter and Facebook is free, and both media strive to stay free of political bias – a position that Mark Zuckerberg, the creator of Facebook, found increasingly difficult to maintain given his clear distaste for many of Trump's policies.

The internet also gives to those supporting or opposing a cause unprecedented access to a range of relevant information and intelligence. So much so, in fact, that the internet will almost certainly become the main source of political information for informed and active citizens. More than this, the net may facilitate a new form of deliberative democracy where voters can directly engage in debate with candidates and incumbent politicians.

CONTROVERSY 8   HOW BIASED ARE TELEVISION AND RADIO?

In many countries and universally in autocratic non-democratic regimes, news is controlled by governments so citizens hear or see only the 'government' line in news and other programmes. In the absence of a state communications medium (barring government websites), the US is free of such strictures, but debate on media bias continues unabated. On the right the accusation is that the 'elite' press and TV networks are biased against the religious right, the armed forces and Republicans. So the claim is that the liberal media adopt a condescending stance towards 'ordinary God-fearing' Americans while advancing a hidden agenda that supports the interests of social liberals in such areas as environmental protection and family values. On the left the accusation is that the media are reluctant to challenge the primacy of corporate America or of America's belligerent policies towards the rest of the world and especially poorer countries.

This debate has taken on new meaning since the advent of Fox News and radio 'shock jocks' such as Rush Limbaugh, who unashamedly advance a right-wing position. Given that there is no real equivalent on the left – the mainstream news networks (CBS, NBC and ABC) at least strive towards objectivity – it could be concluded that there is a right-wing bias to TV and radio news coverage in the US. During the 2012 campaign much of the ideological conflict centred on interpretation of the facts. Repeatedly, Fox News and other right-wing media questioned the veracity of opinion polls and refused to believe that Obama was in the lead. This almost assumed the status of parody when, on election night, Fox News Republican contributor Karl Rove refused to accept that CBS News had called Ohio for Obama. In the event, Obama won Ohio with relative ease. By way of contrast the right-wing media's optimism over the Trump candidacy in 2016 proved to be justified, although their coverage of the campaign was every bit as biased as it had been in previous election years. As President Trump went on to excoriate what he called the 'mainstream media' (the big city broadsheets, CNN, CBS, NBC and ABC) as biased and dishonest. Most commentators agreed that these attacks were politically motivated rather than bearing any resemblance to the truth.

Controlling the Media

Under the First Amendment, Americans are guaranteed freedom of speech, and there has in fact been very little direct censorship of the media through American history. Noted exceptions include Abraham Lincoln's order closing down newspapers for printing pro-southern stories in 1861, and the censorship of anarchist and communist publications during the 'red scare' periods following the First World War and in 1947–57. More recently the attempt by the Nixon administration to ban the *New York Times* from publishing the *Pentagon Papers* revealing details on the government's conduct of the Vietnam War was blocked by the Supreme Court in the famous 1971 case *New York Times* v. *United States*.

While in comparison with restrictions on the press and television in other countries, including Britain, the United States has been remarkably free from direct government censorship, this is not to say that the media always feel free to publish and broadcast everything they want to. On the contrary, commercial considerations often place limits on what can be written or aired, and this is particularly true at the local level. So local TV stations or newspapers cannot easily offend their core subscribers, and therefore will support (say) local property development plans, or restrictions on the sale of alcohol. More serious are those instances where commercial or political pressures prevent free expression. Just this happened during the McCarthyite 'witch hunts' of the early 1950s, when not even noted liberal papers and broadcasting channels dared to speak out against the dismissal of employees who failed to sign loyalty oaths or who were jailed for alleged communist sympathies.

Some have argued that a similar climate of fear prevailed after 9/11, at least in the sense that voicing open opposition to the way in which the 'War on Terror' was being conducted was often branded by the administration as 'unpatriotic'. In addition the FBI can intercept anyone's email if they are believed to be connected with terrorism.

While this sort of self-censorship undoubtedly occurs, it is not as important as the limits on the expression of a variety of opinions and perspectives that the increasing concentration of ownership media produces. Until the 1980s and 1990s the sheer number of media outlets and the limits on concentrated ownership that the 1934 Communications Act imposed, did guarantee a wide variety of opinions. This has undoubtedly been reduced in recent years.

The Media and American Democracy

It is often assumed outside the United States that the American media are so commercialized and concerned with ratings (audience and readership figures) that they are among the most commercial in the world. Public broadcasting, which is designed to serve the public interest, is very undeveloped and represents a tiny proportion of media output. This accepted, this brief review has emphasized the complex nature of the media in America, and, notwithstanding recent concentrations, media remain essentially local in nature. As in other democracies, television, radio and now the internet serve as crucial intermediaries between politicians, officials and the public. Also as elsewhere, the particular media prism through which the public receives information by necessity distorts and slants news and information. In the American case the main distortions are:

- Placing high priority on American news to the detriment of foreign news – and when the US is engaged in military action abroad, this 'foreign news' crowds out other foreign news.
- Seeking a lowest-common-denominator consensus position that is least likely to damage ratings or offend advertisers. If something mildly offensive occurs, such as singer Janet Jackson's baring of a nipple at the half-time Super Bowl (American football) show in 2004, the network (in this case CBS) issues an abject apology. More serious has been the reluctance of the networks to take a clear editorial line on national political issues, including the war in Iraq.
- Trivializing the news by simplifying stories and airing 'soundbite' clips that often distort complex political and public policy issues.
- In the case of Fox News the American right now enjoys a national television platform for its views that has no equivalent on the left. This may have increased the sense of political polarization in the United States.

Most of these criticisms can be more accurately directed at television rather than the press. Indeed, many of the larger regional newspapers such as the *New York Times* and the *Washington Post* have very high editorial standards and cover some stories to a depth unheard of among equivalent European papers. And even network television can and does produce programmes that advance the public interest. This was amply demonstrated in 2004 when the CBS news magazine *60 Minutes* was the first to expose the abuse of prisoners by American soldiers in Iraqi jails. Ultimately, the test of a free press is whether it can indeed act not only as a channel of communication between politicians and the public, but also as an additional check on the abuse of governmental power. Sometimes it has performed this function well (as with Watergate), but often it has failed to (as with McCarthyism).

More recently the reaction of the media to the draconian measures adopted by the government in reaction to the events of 9/11, although at first muted, eventually represented an often critical assessment of the Patriot Act and associated legislation. And with the rise of the internet, the sort of media conformism typical of the McCarthyite period is very unlikely to recur.

Summary

This chapter has described the general structure and organization of the US media, noting that, in spite of their essentially local roots, recent changes have led to increasing concentration of ownership and control and to the standardization of news and information. Television news generally tries to be objective, although this is less true of some of the cable networks. Newspapers are almost all locally based (although not locally owned) and tend to reflect the political cultures of local communities. They also strive to separate news reporting from editorial opinion. While there are almost no political controls on the media, a high degree of self-censorship occurs, and given the importance of advertising television news in particular shies away from the controversial and tends to trivialize the news. Access to information via the internet is increasing very rapidly and is now a major means of raising money in political campaigns. While a 'free press' is highly prized in the US, self-censorship has led many to question the media's contribution to American democracy.

Questions for Discussion

1   Describe the main ways in which Americans access political news. Do they receive fair and balanced information?
2   How did media coverage affect the outcome of the 2016 presidential election?
3   What are the likely consequences of the decline of print and television news and the rise of internet news for American democracy?

Glossary

conservative editorial style   The staid and traditional presentational style of most American newspapers

editorial and opinion distinction   The distinction in US papers and television between reporting facts and expressing opinions

Federal Communications Commission (FCC)   The authority responsible for regulating the electronic media

market-driven journalism   News, programmes or editorial content designed to maximize commercial revenue

mass media   The general term governing mass communication via television, radio, the press and the internet

national networks   The three main television and radio networks – CBS, NBC and ABC – that sell programmes to franchised local stations

ratings   Viewing, listening and readership figures widely used to inform programme content and design

shock jocks   Radio journalists with sensationalist and/or extreme political views

soundbite   A brief extract from a television or radio interview designed to attract viewers' or listeners' attention

talk radio   The label given to non-music radio stations

Notes

1   Anne Coulter, *Slander: Liberal Lies about the American Right* (New York: Crown Books, 2002).

2   Joe Conason, *Big Lies: The Right Wing Propaganda Machine and How It Distorts the Truth* (New York: Thomas Dunne Books/St Martin's, 2003).

3   Kathleen Hall Jamieson, *The Interplay of Influence: News, Advertising, Politics, and the Mass Media*, 5th edn (Belmont, CA: Wadsworth, 2000).

4   In 2004 Rush Limbaugh was prosecuted for illegal use of prescription drugs. As a result many stations dropped his show, but his listening figures recovered later in the decade.

Further Reading

Good academic accounts of the impact of the media on politics include Kathleen H. Jamieson, *The Interplay of Influence: News, Advertising, Politics and the Mass Media*, 6th edn (Belmont, CA: Wadsworth, 2008), and Doris Graber, *On Media: Making Sense of Politics* (New York: Oxford University Press, 2012). A right-wing critique of the liberal media is Ann Coulter, *Slander: Liberal Lies about the American Right* (New York: Crown Books, 2002). A more academic response is provided by Joe Conason, *Big Lies: The Right Wing Propaganda Machine and How It Distorts the Truth* (New York: Thomas Dunne Books/St Martin's, 2003). For a critique of the ways in which the media sensationalizes the news, see David Murray, Joel Schwartz and S. Robert Lichter, *It Ain't Necessarily So: How the Media Remake our Picture of Reality* (New York: Penguin, 2002), and Lance W. Bennett, *News: Politics of Illusion*, 6th edn (New York: Longman, 2005). On the media and the 2008 election, see Kate Kenski, Bruce W. Hardy and Kathleen Hall Jamieson, *The Obama Victory: How Media, Money, and Message Shaped the 2008 Election* (New York: Oxford University Press, 2010).

CHAPTER 8
CONGRESS I
THE PEOPLE'S BRANCH?

Outline

- Representation and Congress
- Briefing: Forms of Representation
- Congressional Elections
- Legislators as Rational Actors
- The Work of Members of Congress
- Conclusions

- Summary
- Questions for Discussion
- Glossary
- Notes
- Further Reading

About half the population thinks that every person in Congress, including their own representative, should be thrown out. That's the center not holding.

– NOAM CHOMSKY, 2013

The US Congress is usually – and accurately – referred to as the most powerful legislature in the world. While a common trend in other democratic countries has been the rise of powerful executives and the relative decline of assemblies and parliaments, Congress has been remarkably successful in maintaining its independence from executive influence. This is not to deny that the powers and functions of Congress have changed over time. Clearly they have, and the particular way in which the institution operates today is very different

American Politics and Society, Ninth Edition. David McKay.
© 2018 John Wiley & Sons Ltd. Published 2018 by John Wiley & Sons Ltd.

even from 20 years ago. But throughout its history, Congress has remained an essentially autonomous institution. Even during periods of executive ascendancy – most recently during the Johnson and Nixon years and in the post-9/11 Bush years – Congress never became the mere instrument of presidents.

The independence of Congress derives in part from its constitutionally defined powers and in part from the particular way in which the American party system has evolved. Constitutionally, Congress was given three main powers, all of which remain important today. First, all legislative power is vested in the House of Representatives and the Senate, and within this broad function Congress is given special powers to appropriate monies, raise armies and regulate interstate commerce. Second, the House of Representatives has a constitutionally established right to declare war. Finally, the Senate is specifically empowered to ratify treaties and approve appointments by the president to the judiciary and executive branch. The House can impeach executive judicial officers for wrongdoing and the Senate is charged with the responsibility for trying impeached officers. In addition, from very early in its history, Congress established the right to oversee and investigate the behaviour of the executive. In total these powers are impressive, especially when it is remembered that originally Congress was expected to be the major initiator as well as approver of legislation. As with other legislatures around the world, Congress has partly (although by no means entirely) forfeited the responsibility for initiating legislation to the president. Unlike most other assemblies, however, Congress retains an

Plate 8.1   Senate majority leader Mitch McConnell addressing Congress
Source: Alex Wong/Getty, www.gettyimages.co.uk/license/546532964.

independent power to approve legislation, appropriate monies and generally oversee the executive branch.

The simplest explanation of this autonomy is the distinctive constituency base which individual members of Congress enjoy. In contrast to parliamentary systems, the electoral fortunes of presidents and legislators are not directly linked. Presidents can, and often do, face a legislature dominated by a party other than their own. But this constitutional arrangement has been reinforced by the nature of the American party system. It is certainly possible to imagine a system characterized by bicameralism and the separation of powers where political party ties are strong and the electoral fortunes of legislators are interdependent with those of the executive. Only rarely has this been the case in the history of the United States. Much more common is a very loose party relationship between the president and members of Congress, with the legislators remaining essentially independent.

Representation and Congress

The sort of party government associated with parliamentary systems greatly restricts the representative function of individual legislators. In Britain, for example, the individual Member of Parliament (MP) is largely tied, through party discipline in the House of Commons, to the policies of either government or opposition. Crucially, his or her electoral survival depends on an official party nomination or endorsement.[1] So, while MPs may exercise some independent pressure on party leaders or governments, it is limited. Clearly, this close organic link between executive and legislator limits the representative function of MPs. The electorate may benefit, at least in theory, from the coherent programmes and policies which party government produces, but the interests of individual constituencies do tend to become subordinated to national policy objectives. Curiously, British MPs are quick to insist that they come closest to what is called 'trustee' representatives; that is, they are elected by the people on trust to exercise their own judgement. They are not delegated to carry out a specific programme, to the letter and without discretion. In reality they are closer to being party delegates than trustees are. Members of Congress are patently not delegates either in the sense of being slaves to a party programme or in the sense that they are mandated by their constituents to carry out specific policies. Indeed, the idea of a representative being a direct delegate of the people has relatively few applications in modern industrial societies. In small communities – for example, in early New England town meetings – such a concept has meaning. But no member of Congress can accurately and continuously carry out the wishes of diverse and volatile electorates. Even if he or she knew what the electorate wanted, the individual member of Congress has but limited powers to influence what is a complex national policy process.

In truth, members are much closer to being trustees of their electorates. They are elected on the promise that they will exercise their judgement on behalf of their constituents' interests. And should they fail in the opinion of the electorate to defend and promote these interests, they are punished in subsequent elections. If members of Congress are not delegates, neither are they representative in the microcosmic sense (representative of the general

Table 8.1   Characteristics of the 104th, 106th and 114th Congresses, 1995–2017

	104th	106th	114th
House			
Democrats	197	211	189
Republicans	235	223	246
Independents/vacant	3	1	0
Women	48	56	78
Men	385	379	357
Blacks	38	35	46
Hispanics	17	19	33
Asian/Pacific Islander/Native American	3	3	14
Senate			
Democrats	47	45	44
Republicans	53	55	54
Independents	0	0	2
Women	8	9	20
Men	92	91	80
Blacks	1	0	2
Hispanics	0	0	4
Asian/Pacific Islander/Native American	3	3	1

Source: Computed from data available from the Congressional Research Service at Membership of the 114th Congress: A Profile, Jennifer E. Manning, Senior Research Librarian, 1 July 2016, https://www.fas.org/sgp/crs/misc/R43869.pdf.

population in ethnic and socio-economic terms). In fact by this measure they could hardly be less representative. An overwhelming majority of senators and representatives are white, college-educated, middle-aged, middle class and male. In the 114th Congress (2015–17) only 78 women were elected out of the total 435 members of the House, and only 20 senators were women. Just two African American senators and just 46 black representatives were elected (table 8.1). Lawyers and businesspeople are greatly over-represented among the members in both houses, although there has been a dramatic decline in the number of lawyers in the House over the past 40 years (figure 8.1). Among the 'other' professions, educators and representatives with government backgrounds predominate.[2]

To claim that members approximate most closely to a trustee form of representation is accurate, but tells us very little about the precise linkages between legislators, constituency and party, and how these have changed over time. Until recently, for example, it was commonly asserted that party had weakened its influence on members, with constituency pressures in the ascendant. At the same time, many voters have grown disillusioned with what they see as members who put their self-interest first and the public interest second. The remainder of this chapter is devoted to the ways in which the representative system raises public expectations of what members of Congress can do for them. The chapter concludes with a preliminary discussion of the links between constituency influences on members of Congress and their work within the House and the Senate.

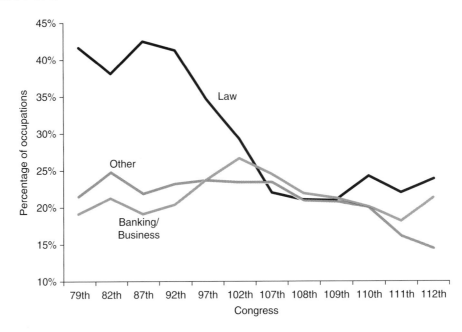

Figure 8.1   Occupations of members of Congress, 1945–2015
Source: Computed from data at Representatives and Senators: Trends in Member
Characteristics Since 1945, Congressional Research Service, R. Eric Petersen, Coordinator,
Specialist in American National Government, 17 February 2012.

Briefing   Forms of Representation

Direct Representation. Assumes that the electorate (or the citizens) directly instruct representatives to implement policies. Such instructions can only work in small communities such as in eighteenth-century New England, when town hall meetings made direct orders to the officers responsible for community affairs.

Delegate Representation. Applies when a larger electorate takes a majority decision to instruct delegates to vote on their behalf in a legislature or other decision-making body. This happens in American primary elections, where pledged delegates are chosen to vote for a particular candidate at the convention. In the UK the trade union 'bloc vote' also used to operate in this fashion, with union

delegates instructed to follow a particular line at the party conference. Such arrangements cannot easily work in modern legislatures where decisions are taken on varied and complex issues which cannot easily be foreseen when voters make their choice for a particular candidate. Also, should the representative fail to carry out the voters' wishes they have no sanction to apply except at a possibly distant periodic election.

Microcosmic Representation. Assumes that the representatives should be a microcosm of the electorate. So in the US, the House and the Senate should be 50 per cent female, 13 per cent black, 17 per cent Hispanic and so on. Quite apart from the technical problems involved in

CONGRESS I: THE PEOPLE'S BRANCH? 167

such arrangements there is, of course, no guarantee that (say) black or female politicians will always loyally represent 'black' or 'female' issues, especially when many issues (for example, in foreign policy or environmental protection) have no consistently black or female dimension.

Party Representation. Assumes that political parties produce programmes of change in manifestos that elected representatives loyally adhere to once in office. Voters, therefore, have clear cues available to them when choosing between parties. In countries where there are deep religious, ethnic, regional, linguistic or ideological divides such as in Belgium, Northern Ireland, or Scotland in the UK, parties operate in much this manner. In many countries, however, including the US, the parties are broad coalitions of interests that rarely produce clear programmes of change – a fact that is complicated by the American separation of powers. This said, after 1994 the US Republican Party became much more programmatic than historically had been the case, and since then party lines have become more important as cues informing voter choice.

Trustee Representation. Recognizes the difficulties involved in more direct forms and assumes that representatives can be trusted to carry out the wishes of the electorate. Generally this form of representation assumes that there is a broad coincidence of values between the majority and the elected official. So in the US context, a senator from Utah would be expected to follow a broadly conservative, family-values line in harmony with the Mormon values prevalent in the state of Utah. Similarly a San Francisco representative would be expected to vote a liberal line. Problems occur, however, when constituencies are large and varied and when the values of either the electorate or the representative change once in office. A variation on this type is virtual representation, where the elected official is assumed to know 'what is best' for constituents without them actually voting. Edmund Burke championed this view when arguing that wise and experienced men could represent the disenfranchised masses in the eighteenth English parliament. Disenfranchised African Americans in the South were also patronized in this way until they won the vote after the 1960s.

Congressional Elections

Representatives are elected every two years, senators every six (with one-third elected for their six-year term every two years). This simple fact helps to account for what are some starkly contrasting trends in the electoral dynamics of the two houses, but there are also some common trends. Let us examine the latter first.

The spread of direct primaries

As with presidential elections, primaries are now the major means whereby members of Congress win their party's nomination for office. One major consequence of the demise of party conventions (the standard nineteenth-century and early twentieth-century form of nomination) has been to weaken the role of political parties in the nomination process. By being able to appeal directly to the electorate, the senator or representative now owes much less allegiance to local and national party figures.

Changing partisan control

Until 1994 it was widely believed that Democratic dominance of the House of Representatives was a near-permanent feature of American politics. As can be seen from table 8.2, the Democrats managed to maintain a large majority in the House for many years. They

Table 8.2   Composition of Congress, by political party, 1965–2019

	Party and president	Congress	House			Senate		
			Majority party	Minority party	Other	Majority party	Minority party	Other
1965	D (Johnson)	89th	D-295	R-140	–	D-68	R-32	–
1967	D (Johnson)	90th	D-247	R-187	–	D-64	R-36	–
1969	R (Nixon)	91st	D-243	R-192	–	D-57	R-43	–
1971[a]	R (Nixon)	92nd	D-254	R-180	–	D-54	R-44	2
1973[a,b]	R (Nixon)	93rd	D-239	R-192	1	D-56	R-42	2
1975[c]	R (Ford)	94th	D-291	R-144	–	D-60	R-37	2
1977[d]	D (Carter)	95th	D-292	R-143	–	D-61	R-38	1
1979[d]	D (Carter)	96th	D-276	R-157	–	D-58	R-41	1
1981[d]	R (Reagan)	97th	D-243	R-192	–	R-53	D-46	1
1983	R (Reagan)	98th	D-269	R-165	–	R-54	D-46	–
1985	R (Reagan)	99th	D-252	R-182	–	R-53	D-47	–
1987	R (Reagan)	100th	D-258	R-177	–	D-55	R-45	–
1989[e]	R (Bush)	101st	D-259	R-174	–	D-55	R-45	–
1991[e]	R (Bush)	102nd	D-267	R-167	1	D-56	R-43	–
1993[e]	D (Clinton)	103rd	D-259	R-175	1	D-57	R-43	–
1995[e]	D (Clinton)	104th	R-235	D-197	1	R-53	D-47	–
1997[e]	D (Clinton)	105th	R-227	D-207	1	R-55	D-45	–
1999[e]	D (Clinton)	106th	R-223	D-211	1	R-55	D-45	–
2001	R (Bush)	107th	R-221	D-212	2	R-50[f]	D-50	–
2003	R (Bush)	108th	R-229	D-205	1	R-51	D-48	1
2005	R (Bush)	109th	R-232	D-202	1	R-55	D-44	1
2007	R (Bush)	110th	D-233	R-202	–	D-50	R-49	1
2009	D (Obama)	111th	D-257	R-178	–	D-58	R-42	2[g]
2011	D (Obama)	112th	D-193	R-242	–	D-51	R-47	2[g]
2013	D (Obama)	113th	D-201	R-234	–	D-53	R-45	2[g]
2015	D (Obama)	114th	D-189	R-246	–	D-44	R-54	2[g]
2017	R (Trump)	115th	D-194	R-239	–	D-46	R-52	2[g]

Source: US Congress, Joint Committee on Printing, Congressional Directory annual; beginning 1977, biennial.

Note: D = Democratic, R = Republican. Data for beginning of first session of each Congress. Excludes vacancies at beginning of sessions.

'–' represents zero.

[a]Senate had one independent and one conservative Republican.

[b]House had one independent Democrat.

[c]Senate had one independent, one conservative Republican and one undecided (New Hampshire).

[d]Senate had one independent.

[e]House had one independent.

[f]By virtue of casting vote of vice-president. Committee assignments distributed on a 50/50 basis.

[g]Two independents caucus with the Democrats.

were also strong in the Senate and controlled that house for all but six years in the 1965–95 period. In the mid-term election of 1994, however, the Republicans swept the board, winning back both the House and the Senate, leading many commentators to conclude that an era of Republican dominance was about to begin. However, in the 1996 presidential election the Republicans' majority was reduced, and in 1998 they suffered a further small loss in the House. This last result is highly significant because the party in control of the presidency almost always loses seats at mid-term. The 1998 result (a four-seat loss in the House and no change in the Senate) was the worst result for the non-presidential party at mid-term since 1934.

In 2000 the very narrow Electoral College victory by George W. Bush actually carried negative 'coattails'. The Democrats gained four seats in the Senate, producing a 50/50 split, and two seats in the House, reducing the Republicans' working majority to seven. Again very unusually, the 2002 mid-term elections actually produced small net gains for the party controlling the presidency, with the Republicans gaining eight seats in the House and one seat in the Senate. In the 2004 elections Bush did achieve small gains both in the House (the Republicans won three extra seats) and in the Senate (four extra seats). All was to change again in 2006 when in a truly startling result the Democrats regained the House with 32 extra seats and even more impressively the Senate with six additional seats. In 2008 the Democrats made further gains in both houses only to lose them in very dramatic fashion in 2010 when they lost control to a Republican landslide (table 8.2). There was little change in 2012, although the Democrats made small gains in both houses. However in the 2014 mid-term elections the Democrats lost control of the Senate and in spite of having many fewer seats up for election in 2016 they made only a net gain of two in that year. They also failed to make significant inroads into the Republican House majority.

So in spite of faltering by the Republicans in the late 1990s, the 1994 turnaround and the subsequent Democratic revival after 2006 followed by a return to Republican dominance after 2010 does represent a major change in American politics, and it raises two important questions. Why did the Democrats manage to maintain their grip on Congress for so long – especially as the Republicans actually won most of the *presidential* elections during this period? Second, what accounts for the Republican victories after 1994, the subsequent Democratic revival after 2006 and the startling Republican triumphs in 2010 and 2014? As far as the first question is concerned, undoubtedly the Democrats benefited from being the majority party – more Americans identified with the Democrats than with the Republicans. The Democrats also benefited from being the majority party in another sense, for in single-member-district, first past the post electoral systems majority parties usually score more constituency victories than would be expected from their aggregate popular vote. Democrats also dominated state legislatures, which are responsible for drawing up the boundaries of congressional districts. Although the courts have been active on the question of malapportionment (see chapter 15), a considerable amount of discretion remains – especially over the shape of constituencies rather than the balance of population between districts. As Gary Jacobson has pointed out, at least as far as the House is concerned, Democrats were actually better campaigners and politicians than their Republican counterparts. They were used to winning and to delivering the goods. As a result they continued to win.[3]

By the mid-1990s most of these advantages had been eroded. The number of people identifying with the Democrats declined and the number of Republican identifiers increased (see figure 6.2). Their hold on the state legislatures also weakened. By the mid-1990s the two parties controlled roughly the same number of state legislatures and the Republicans actually held a handsome majority of the state governorships. As we established in chapter 6, these changes were greeted by many as evidence of a Republican realignment. What seems more likely is that a changing political agenda worked to the Republicans' advantage, but not to the extent that they became in any sense the dominant or majority party. As far as congressional elections are concerned, the Republicans benefited from public support for lower taxes, a balanced budget, an enhanced role for state governments, welfare reform, and tougher law and order policies. But many issues on which the Democrats have the advantage – education, gender- and race-based questions, the environment, gun control, and the protection of Medicare and social security – remained very important to many voters. Add to this the economic woes after 2006 and the deep unpopularity of the war in Iraq, and the Democratic successes of 2006 and 2008 are not so surprising. This was hardly a long-term development, however. Amid continuing economic gloom, the Republicans won back the House in 2010 in quite spectacular fashion, although they were unable to win the Senate. In 2012 they were unable to consolidate their advantage and lost small numbers of seats in both houses. As was discussed in chapter 6, although Democratic Party identifiers increased substantially after 2006, so did the number of independents, many of whom switched their allegiance to the Republicans at the 2010 mid-term elections. However, as noted the Republicans lost ground in the 2012 House elections – indeed, more House votes were cast for Democrats than for Republicans in that year. In the 2014 mid-term elections, however, the Republicans made sweeping gains in both houses and captured the Senate for the first time since 2006. Most commentators agree that this election was a referendum on the performance of the Obama administration whose popularity waned amid continuing economic troubles and deep ambiguity about the US world role. Together with the surprise election of Donald Trump in 2016, the Republicans held on to their congressional majorities in that year, albeit with slightly reduced majorities.

Regional change

While at the congressional level the Democrats continue to show strength in the North the East and the Pacific states, they have lost what was the solid support of the southern states. The South is now effectively a Republican region, as are the mountain and prairie states. The old industrial northeast remains primarily Democratic, as do the Pacific states. In Florida, Virginia and much of the Midwest and in selected industrial states, notably Ohio, the parties are quite finely balanced. Even these generalizations can be misleading. At any time a Democrat can win many southern districts and a Republican many northeastern districts. Much depends not only on the socio-economic and ethnic make-up of the district in question, but also on the popularity of the incumbent president and personal appeal and financial resources of the candidate running for office.

The importance of money

For both senators and representatives, money has become a crucial resource in congressional elections. With voters acting in response to the appeal of individual candidates rather than to parties, both incumbents and challengers must ensure that the voters know who they are and what their record is. This translates into buying television time for advertisements as well as spending money on mailings, meetings and other attention-seeking devices.

Campaign finance has been through three distinct phases over the past forty years. Prior to the 1970s the personal efforts of candidates in raising money were less important than winning the party endorsement or the endorsement of the big corporations and labour unions. Large donations from such sources could help clinch the election of a particular candidate. However, in the second stage, declining partisanship and the passage of the Federal Election Campaign Act (FECA) in 1974 meant that candidates were forced to rely more and more on their own capacity to raise funds or to persuade others to contribute to their campaigns. FECA was designed to reduce candidate dependence on money, but in fact the very opposite has happened – campaign spending actually increased following the passage of the act. What accounts for this? In part it is because the Supreme Court struck down a central provision in the Act that limited contributions from candidates' own fortunes, and in part because the law encouraged the growth of political action committees (PACs). Although PACs are limited to giving $5,000 per candidate per campaign, they account for a high proportion of campaign financing. Individuals are limited to $2,000 per candidate, but there are no limits on what candidates themselves can spend on their campaigns. As can be seen from table 8.3, the latest legislation (the Bipartisan Campaign Reform Act of 2002, partly sponsored by John McCain) has produced a complex set of rules for contributions to both individuals and party committees. The new law actually increased the amount that individuals and PACs can contribute – in part to compensate for the fact that the limits had hardly changed in 28 years – but it effectively outlawed the use of 'soft-money' advertising. 'Soft money' refers to contributions not to official campaign committees but on behalf of interest groups that support or oppose the policy positions of candidates. For example, a pro-life (anti-abortion) group could advertise the fact that a candidate 'endorsed' the 'killing' of unborn children. One of the effects of such advertisements was to implant in the minds of voters much more extreme candidate policy positions than actually existed. After much debate and legislative wrangling, Congress eventually outlawed most soft-money advertising in 2002. The Supreme Court upheld the new law in 2003 (*McConnell* v. *Federal Election Commission*). However, the third stage in campaign finance law and the one that still prevails today was a result of the dramatic 2010 decision, *Citizens' United* v. *FEC*, when the Supreme Court effectively abolished all controls on campaign spending by corporations, unions and other organizations provided the money was not channelled through official campaign organizations. This has encouraged the growth of 'SuperPACs' able to raise unlimited funds that can be used to help or hinder the election chances of candidates (see chapter 14, pp. 312–13) and the explosion of money channelled not through official party campaigns but through non-party sources (figure 8.2).

Until quite recently it was common to contrast the advantages of incumbency in the House and the Senate. Of those seeking re-election to the House, a remarkably high and generally rising percentage were re-elected up until 1990 (90 per cent in that year).[4] The

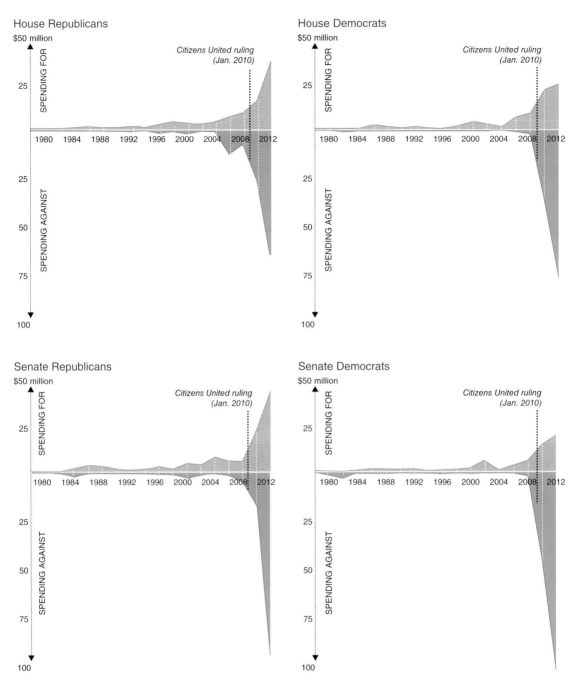

Figure 8.2   Non-party independent expenditures in House and Senate elections, 1978–2012 (all values in millions of US dollars)
Source: Brookings Institution at www.brookings.edu/research/interactives/2013/non-party-spending-house-and-senate.
These data were compiled from Table 3-14 of Vital Statistics on Congress Source: Campaign Finance Institute analysis of Federal Election Commission data.

Table 8.3 Contribution limits under the Bipartisan Campaign Reform Act of 2002

Donors	Candidate committees	PAC[a]	Recipients — State, district, and local party committees[b]	National party committees[c]	Special limits
Individual	$2,000 per election[d,e]	$5,000 per year	$10,000 per year combined limit	$25,000 per year[d]	Biennial limit of $95,000 ($37,500 to all candidates and $57,500 to all PACs and parties[f])[d]
State, district, and local party committees[b]	$5,000 per year combined limit	$5,000 per year combined limit	Unlimited transfers to other party committees	Unlimited transfers to other party committees	
National party committees[c]	$5,000 per election	$5,000 per year	Unlimited transfers to other party committees	Unlimited transfers to other party committees	$35,000 to Senate candidate per campaign[d,g]
PAC multicandidate[h]	$5,000 per election	$5,000 per year	$5,000 per year combined limit	$15,000 per year	
PAC not multicandidate[h]	$2,000 per election[d]	$5,000 per year	$10,000 per year combined limit	$25,000 per year	

Source: Federal Election Commission, *January 2003 Record*, vol. 29, 11; reproduced in Harold W. Stanley and Richard G. Niemi, *Vital Statistics on American Politics, 2003–4* (Washington, DC: Congressional Quarterly Press, 2003), table 2.1. Reprinted with permission of SAGE.

[a]These limits apply to both separate segregated funds (SSFs) and political action committees (PACs). Affiliated committees share the same set of limits on contributions made and received.

[b]A state party committee shares its limits with local and district party committees in that state unless a local or district committee's independence can be demonstrated. These limits apply to multicandidate committees only.

[c]A party's national committee, Senate campaign committee, and House campaign committee are each considered national party committees, and each has separate limits, except with respect to Senate candidates – see special limits column.

[d]These limits will be indexed for inflation.

[e]Each of the following is considered a separate election with a separate limit: primary election, caucus or convention with the authority to nominate, general election, runoff election, and special election.

[f]No more than $37,500 of this amount may be contributed to state and local parties and PACs.

[g]This limit is shared by the national committee and the Senate campaign committee.

[h]A multicandidate committee is a political action committee that has been registered for at least six months, has received contributions from more than 50 contributors and – with the exception of a state party committee – has made contributions to at least five federal candidates.

contrast with the Senate used to be considerable, where in 1980 only 73 per cent of those seeking re-election were successful. In the last several elections, however, the incumbency advantage has diminished, as results since 2006 have shown.

In spite of the fact that incumbents have a clear advantage over challengers, they *believe* that unless they raise a large amount of money and organize and campaign well, they are in danger of losing. Indeed, as far as the House is concerned, incumbents virtually never cease to campaign. With elections every two years and the ever-present threat of an aggressive challenger, they cannot afford to let their guard slip. One consequence of this fraught environment is that vacant seats are at a premium. When representatives decide to quit after a few terms and to seek alternative careers, the 'out' party is likely to build an impressive campaign organization in order to win the seat. As Burdett Loomis has noted:

> Only open seat candidates build organizations that resemble an incumbent's enterprise (with no accounting for congressional staff, district offices, communications capacities, and travel expenses). In the end, that is what much of the struggle for open seats is all about – to obtain the resources of incumbency for the future. One measure of the Republicans' 1994 success is that they won twenty-one open seats previously held by House Democrats and six such seats in the Senate.[5]

Senators are, of course, more secure by virtue of their six-year term. Challengers will rarely manage to amass the money and staff to match incumbents – although there are celebrated exceptions to this rule. In 1996, for example, incumbent John Kerry of Massachusetts narrowly held off a challenge by Republican governor William Weld. In the same election conservative Republican incumbent Larry Pressler of South Dakota was defeated by Democrat Tim Johnson. Even more dramatic was the 2004 defeat of Democratic Minority Leader Tom Daschle of South Dakota, who lost to Republican challenger Tom Thune in a bruising $26 million battle. And in 2012 Democrat Elizabeth Warren defeated Republican Scott Brown who had famously won Ted Kennedy's long-held Massachusetts Senate seat in a 2010 special election. More than $70 million were spent on this contest, much of it by Brown's corporate backers. There were more surprises in 2016 and in particular in Wisconsin where Ron Johnson won an unexpected victory over challenger Russ Feingold. National Republican leaders had just about given up on Johnson. But in the event he won 50.2 per cent of the vote.

Given the personalized nature of congressional electoral politics, how do members reconcile their commitment to campaigning and winning re-election on the one hand and their obligations to public policy-making on the other? To answer this question we have to look more carefully at the work of members, and in particular at the sort of strategic choices they face when seeking election or re-election.

Legislators as Rational Actors

Senators' and representatives' determined efforts to get elected or re-elected essentially involve an interaction between the candidate and the constituency. Party is important – indeed it has become more important in recent years – but it is often trumped by the personalities and performance of the politicians themselves. This electoral interaction is not simply one of candidate projection and media promotion. Members are also required to tend to the needs and interests of their constituencies – a job that in the American context is both complex and demanding. In no other comparable political system are legislators so electorally vulnerable as to have to devote themselves wholeheartedly to this task. As table 8.4 shows, in most other systems members of lower houses are relatively secure from immediate electoral pressures. They do not have to fight primary elections, they depend on party identities and financial support rather than personal campaign fundraising at the time of their election, voters tend to use national rather than local cues when voting, and the life of the typical parliamentary session is longer than in the US.

Political scientists have attempted to characterize these efforts in terms of rational choice analysis. David Mayhew, for example, in his stimulating and influential book, *Congress: The Electoral Connection*,[6] argued that members of Congress are mainly motivated by one thing: re-election. Almost all their behaviour inside and outside Congress is shaped by this simple drive. A major *a priori* assumption here is that members can affect their re-election chances. While Mayhew accepts that there are limits to what a representative or senator can do to please his or her constituents – no individual legislator can, after all, banish unemployment or solve the drug abuse problem – he does identify three broad strategies which can improve re-election chances. He or she can, first, advertise by spreading his or her name and reputation and generally creating a favourable image. Exposure on television and in the local press can be important, and unlike the Washington and New York press, local newspapers are generally sympathetic to members of Congress. Sometimes members go to unusual lengths in their efforts at self-promotion. Mayhew reports Charles Diggs Jr (Democrat, Michigan) as running a radio programme with himself as 'combination disc jockey-commentator and minister', and Daniel Flood (Democrat, Pennsylvania) apparently was 'famous for appearing unannounced and often uninvited at wedding anniversaries and other events'.[7]

It used to be the case that credit-claiming, or convincing constituents that the member has 'delivered the goods', was the key motivation of members. Indeed, 'pork-barrel' politics is part of American folklore. (The term derives from the metaphor of spreading the 'pork', or benefits, among constituents.) Pork-barrel politics almost always involves particular rather than collective benefits to constituents. It would be very difficult for an individual member of Congress to claim credit for having balanced the budget, which everyone benefits from. He or she is much more likely to benefit from helping channel direct federal investment (for example, on a military installation or community development project) to his or her constituency. As we shall see in the next chapter, the internal structure of power in Congress, not least the absence of strict party discipline, greatly facilitates just such distributions.

Finally, members benefit from position taking or being identified positively in the minds of constituents with a particular policy position. A predominantly Roman Catholic or Christian right constituency would be gratified by public pronouncements or actual legislative action by their member against abortion; New York's large Jewish community would expect their member of Congress to take a pro-Israeli stance; and so on. Legislators have also formed caucuses, or groups of like-minded members, to promote or defend a particular constituency interest in Congress. Typical examples are the House Auto Caucus and

Table 8.4 Legislators' electoral vulnerability in nine countries

	Maximum legal life of largest house of national legislature (years)	Average actual life of largest house of national legislature 1960–94 (years)	Percentage of years 1960–94 taken up by legislatures that lasted 3.5 years or more[a]	Level of use of primaries for selection of party candidates for national office	Level of candidate-centred, as distinct from party-centred, voting among electorate[b]	Level of member-centred, as distinct from party-centred, voting in national legislature[c]	Level of individual candidate's reliance on own fundraising efforts[d]
Australia	3	2.3	0.0	Non-existent	Low	Low	Low
Britain	5	3.3	94.3	Non-existent	Low	Low	Low
Canada	5	2.9	72.3	Non-existent	Low	Low	Low
France	5	3.5	76.7	Non-existent	Low	Low	Low
Germany	4	3.2	83.3	Non-existent	Low	Low	Low
Italy	5	3.2	85.6	Non-existent	Low	Medium	Low
Japan	4	2.8	31.4	Non-existent	Medium	Low	Medium
New Zealand	3	2.8	0.0	Non-existent	Low	Low	Low
United States	2	2.0	0.0	High	High	High	High

Source: Anthony King, *Running Scared* (New York: Free Press, 1997), table 1. (See original table for explanation of footnotes.) © Anthony King. Reprinted with kind permission of the author.

the Steel Caucus, both of which have striven to counteract economic decline and foreign competition in these industries.

Senators and representatives have always tended their constituencies. But in recent years the pressures to do so have increased considerably. We have already noted the relatively weak political party influence in the US – one potentially major bulwark against an intimate constituency–legislator relationship. Less obvious is the impact of a number of political and technological changes on the information flow between the electorate and members. On the members' side, free mailing (called franking) privileges, together with computerized mailing lists, enable legislators not only to send out a large volume of letters and emails, but also to target mail to particular groups of constituents. So if a legislator wants to publicize his anti-abortion stand to all Roman Catholics and pro-life Christians in his district he can do so. He can even hone down the target group to a particular neighbourhood or block. In recent years the cost of the franking privilege has fallen considerably as both houses have striven to reduce costs by substituting email mailings for conventional postal communications. On the constituents' side, interest groups and political action committees increasingly 'rate' the legislative voting record of individual members. These group ratings enable groups and (via publicity back home) constituents to identify their members as 'liberal', 'conservative', anti-environmental protection, labour, affirmative action, or whatever.[8] In 2008, presidential candidate Senator Barack Obama was branded by the McCain campaign as the 'most liberal member of the Senate' because of his consistently high scores in congressional voting as judged by the liberal interest group, Americans for Democratic Action (ADA), and his low scores from the conservative Americans for Constitutional Action (ACA). While Obama has a liberal record, he had only served three and half years in the Senate by the time of the election campaign.

Predictably, senators are less exposed to such highly focused pressures than are representatives; none the less they are just as instrumental in their quest for re-election as are House members. There is undoubtedly a great deal of validity to the rational-choice approach. Any observer of the Washington scene would have to concede that members are increasingly preoccupied with constituency matters. Richard Fenno, who spent several months with members of Congress as a participant observer, dubbed these activities 'home style'.[9] Fenno also noted another phenomenon, however, which does cast some doubt on the rational-actor thesis. The longer House members remained in Congress, the more concerned they became with Washington affairs and the less diligent they became in their pastoral constituency work. The implication here is that there are forces at work in the lives of members of Congress other than the simple drive to win re-election. It may be, of course, that these other forces complement rather than compete with constituency pressures. Most voters have very little knowledge of what representatives and senators actually do in Washington. And given that the electorate is not so naive as to expect an individual member to transform society, a steady flow of positive messages linked to advertising, credit-claiming and position-taking may be enough to convince voters that 'their' representative or senator is doing a good job.

Undoubtedly there are a number of activities important to the legislators that do not seriously conflict with constituency duties. On some issues – especially technical policy questions on the economy – constituents tend not to have well-formed opinions. Yet if members devote themselves to such issues they are possibly at least indirectly neglecting their re-election chances by not putting their time to the most effective use. The rational-choice theorists' answer here is simple: members devote time to non-constituency questions because the internal dynamics of the House (or Senate) demand it. As separate and individual political actors they can achieve very little for the voters. So in order (say) to ensure that a federal installation is sited in their constituency, they are obliged to form coalitions with other members. Naturally, coalition formation involves give and take. It is necessary for a legislator to spend time on apparently non-relevant legislative activity in order to win support on those issues that are directly relevant. This has come to be known in political slang as 'log-rolling', or the bargaining, vote-trading and exchange of favours that have long been a characteristic of Congress. In recent years this process has led to a rise in 'earmarking' or the insertion of provisions in bills that benefit individual constituencies. As will be developed in the next chapter, this often means attaching money for pork-barrel projects that bear no relationship to the main purpose of the accompanying legislation. So serious had this problem become that the House (and later the Senate) imposed a moratorium on the practice in 2011. As a result, a 98 per cent drop in earmarking occurred – although the pork barrel remained in the form of legislation such as public works that has clear benefits for individual constituencies.

It is principally in any one of the more than 100 workgroups (committees and sub-committees) in the Senate and 150 in the House that dominate day-to-day legislative business that log-rolling takes place. We return to this, and the work of congressional committees, below. For now it is important to stress that, although persuasive, the rational-choice view of the work of Congress has its limitations. It assumes that legislators can know what the interests of their constituencies are. Often this is difficult. Some districts are socially, ethnically and economically diverse. A senator from Washington State may not need any prompting when voting on legislation affecting lumber, aerospace and software – three industries that dominate that state. But it is much more difficult for senators from California, representing diverse and politically volatile populations, to respond in this way. Even the senator from Washington State would today have to think twice about always serving the lumber industry, given the size and the influence of the environmental lobby in that state. More serious is the implication in the rational-choice approach that members of Congress are mere automatons responding to constituency demands. There is no place for ideology, party or individual preferences. Yet a wealth of empirical evidence exists to suggest that at one point or another in a legislator's life all of these can be – and usually are – important. As suggested, until quite recently party influences have historically been weak by European standards, but they have increased perceptibly in the past twenty years. Democrats have many policy positions and perspectives in common, as have Republicans. The next chapter shows, indeed, how party leadership within each House can be crucial in determining the outcome of legislation. Moreover, there is considerable evidence of growing party solidarity –first among Republicans in the House and now among legislators from both parties in both houses. In the 104th Congress, Speaker Newt Gingrich managed to persuade his Republican troops to vote the party line most of the time. Even more dramatic was the almost solid party-line voting in the impeachment trial of President Clinton in 1999. By the 2000s political scientists were referring to the 'shrinking middle' or the decline of ideologically moderate legislators in both houses. We return to this development in the next chapter. And famously not one Republican member of the House voted for Barack Obama's health-care legislation in 2010. Similarly, appeals by a president to his fellow party members in Congress can be effective. Lyndon Johnson used the Democratic majorities in the House and Senate to great effect when passing his Great Society social and civil rights programmes. More recently, George W. Bush relied on an ideologically united Republican House majority to push through his legislative agenda, including sizeable tax cuts in 2002 and 2003. Barack Obama, although less successful with congressional Democrats, none the less managed to win their support on the economic stimulus measures in 2009 and health care in 2010.

The existence of 'conservative' and 'liberal' groupings shows the importance of ideology. In itself this need not be significant – members may after all be simply mirroring their constituents' view – but constituencies are not always easily labelled conservative or liberal, and it is not uncommon for an established conservative or liberal member to represent a constituency which cannot accurately be described as either. Legislators are also influenced by other members and by their staff. In other words, in the context of a legislative process that is both fragmented and complex, they are exposed to a number of pressures and influences. Constituency demands may be important, but this does not mean that we should reduce the role of legislators to the vote-getting machines implied by some political scientists.

In sum, members are exposed to many influences. Given the importance of their constituents' preferences in deciding their electoral survival, it is unlikely that members will do anything directly to antagonize the voters. And, if particularly vulnerable or in a marginal seat, they may indeed devote all their energies to re-election. For some, and particularly members of the Senate, however, political life becomes much more complex, with constituency, party, committee, interest group and ideological pressures competing for the members' favour.

The Work of Members of Congress

The changing pattern of influence on members has had important consequences on the internal structure of power in each House. These changes are analysed in the next chapter. A useful way to link discussion of the activities of members outside and inside the legislature is to examine the typical workload of legislators and the support in staff, offices and other services provided for them.

Clearly representatives and senators are not 'lobby fodder' or bound by party discipline to follow a particular line, as British MPs are often labelled. Members of Congress have little choice but to take note of the needs and demands of their constituents and to act on them. Part of this function involves formulating and monitoring a mass of complex legislation. Given the sheer volume of legislation (about 10,000 bills are introduced every session, but in the 111th Congress (2009–11) less than 1 per cent became law), most members specialize in a particular policy area, often but not always related to their constituents' interests. Senator William Fulbright, for example, was for many years chairman of the Senate Foreign Relations Committee. In this job he took a predominantly liberal stance, especially on the conduct of the Vietnam War – not a strategy that was linked in any obvious way to the

Table 8.5   Activities, actual and ideal, of members of Congress (%)

Activity	Members actually spending time				Members preferring to spend more time
	Great deal	Moderate amount	A little	Almost none	
	Representation				
Meet with citizens in state/district	68	30	1	0	17
Meet in Washington with constituents	45	50	5	0	17
Manage office	6	45	39	10	13
Raise funds for next campaign, for others, for party	6	33	45	16	7
	Law-making				
Attend committee hearings, markups, other meetings	48	46	6	0	43
Meet in Washington on legislative issues	37	56	6	0	43
Study, read, discuss pending legislation	25	56	6	0	31
Work with informal caucuses	8	43	36	13	25
Attend floor debate, follow it on television	7	37	44	12	59
Work with party leaders to build coalitions	6	33	43	18	42
Oversee how agencies are carrying out policies/programmes	5	22	43	29	53
Give speeches about legislation outside state/district	5	23	49	23	16

Source: US Congress, Joint Committee on the Organization of Congress, *Organization of Congress, Final Report*, H. Rept. 103–413 (103rd Congress, 1st sess., Dec. 1993), vol. 2, pp. 231–2, 275–87. Reproduced from Roger H. Davidson and Walter J. Oleszek, *Congress and its Members*, 6th edn (Washington, DC: Congressional Quarterly Press, 1998), table 5.2. Reprinted with permission of SAGE.

Note: A total of 161 members of Congress (136 representatives, 25 senators) responded to this survey, conducted in early 1993 under the auspices of the Joint Committee on the Organization of Congress. This series of questions elicited responses from 152 to 155 members.

interests of his rural and conservative constituency, Arkansas. Most of the crucial legislative work is conducted in the committees and sub-committees, yet as table 8.5 shows, members spend relatively little of their very heavy workloads directly on committee work. The remainder is devoted to a number of tasks, but in particular consulting with interest groups, meeting with constituents and preparing legislation. To help the legislator to perform all these functions, Congress has voted for itself a quite extraordinary number of services.

Office space, furnishings, stationery and postal allowances are generous. All communication with constituents, primarily by mail, is free for senators, and representatives are given generous mailing privileges. All of these benefits pale into insignificance compared with the provisions made for congressional staff. In 2011 a staggering 11,800 people worked for members of the House and around 4,000 for senators. In addition some 8,000 people work in congressional support agencies such as the Library of Congress and the Congressional Research Service. Each representative has approximately 17 people working for him or her, and each senator enjoys the assistance of no fewer than 38 aides. This is vastly more than in comparable legislatures, including the Japanese Diet and the British and Canadian Houses of Commons. Some of these positions are secretarial, but many are professionals, including some (about two for each member in the House and five in the Senate) directly assigned the job of drafting and amending legislation. In addition, over 1,000 staff work for House committees and about 800 for Senate committees. Note how the growth in congressional staff was rapid until the 1980s since when it has levelled off and, under Republican leadership in the House, was reduced sharply after 1995 (figure 8.3).

Between the early 1970s and 1995 there was also a rapid increase in the number of sub-committees, reflecting both an increase in the legislative workload and the increasing independence of members of Congress. Committee staff numbers rose correspondingly. However, as the incoming Republican Speaker in 1994, Newt Gingrich reduced the number of sub-committees and their staffs. We return to this point in chapter 9.

Conclusions

There is no question that the typical member of Congress is a man or woman under pressure. Members are constantly campaigning – raising money, appearing on television, taking very carefully prepared stands on a range of issues. At the same time they are increasingly obliged to seek the lowest-common-denominator issue stance in order to please the largest number of constituents and displease the fewest. It is common to claim that in their scramble for votes members of Congress are widely perceived as self- rather than public-interested, and this is reflected in a growing public disenchantment with the institution (see figure 9.4). To understand the full dynamics of this process and in particular how it interacts with those aspects of the job which are only remotely related to constituency pressures, it is necessary to examine how Congress actually influences the policy process. Are the laws made in a responsible and representative manner? To what extent does it check executive power? In sum, to what extent does Congress defend and promote the public interest?

Summary

The US Congress is the most powerful legislative body in the world, a fact that derives from its wide range of formal powers and from a constituency base separate from the presidency. Control of Congress was firmly in the hands of the Democrats for the 60 years to 1994, when it passed to the Republicans. After a brief period of Democratic control (2007–11), the Republicans regained control of the House and managed to retain control in 2012. They made dramatic gains in the 2014 mid-term elections, capturing the Senate and making significant gains in the House – gains that they largely maintained in 2016. While members of Congress strive to act as direct representatives of their constituents, institutional and other factors mean that they more resemble trustees of the voters' interests. The strong representative–voter link in the US means that members of Congress work hard to please their constituents by claiming credit for constituent benefits and taking sympathetic positions on issues close to voters' hearts. The internal dynamic of Congress means that members can indeed deliver benefits, or 'pork', to constituencies. Members of Congress (most of whom are professional white males) devote much of their time to these tasks, although party and ideology can sometimes trump constituency service.

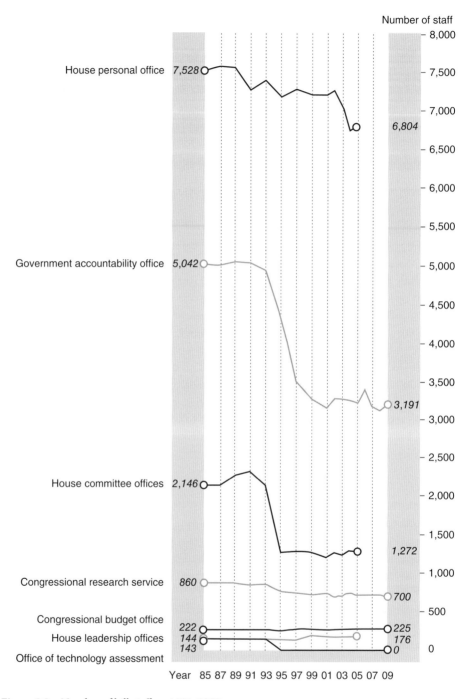

Figure 8.3 Number of hill staffers, 1985–2009
Source: Sunlight Foundation, http://sunlightfoundation.com/policy/documents/keeping_congress_competent/ (CC BY 3.0).

Questions for Discussion

1   What is 'earmarking'? Why did the House impose a moratorium on the practice in 2011 and what have been the consequences?

2   Account for the fluctuating fortunes of the Republicans in congressional elections since 1994.

3   Why is Congress often labelled the most powerful legislature in the world? Is it becoming more or less powerful?

4   Why are so few minorities and women represented in Congress? Answer with reference to the representation of these groups in other national assemblies.

Glossary

bicameralism   Rule by two legislative chambers such as the House and the Senate

direct primaries   Primaries that directly nominate candidates for office

earmarking   Guaranteeing funding for specific constituency projects or benefits as attachments to bills

Electoral Connection (Mayhew)   Servicing constituencies in ways that will maximize the legislator's chance of re-election

first past the post electoral systems   Electoral arrangements based on plurality rather than proportional voting

impeachment   The formal accusation of wrongdoing by an officeholder

party government   Rule based on the dominance of parties in government

political action committees (PACs)   Pressure-group organizations designing to represent interests in the political sphere

pork-barrel politics   Legislation designed to benefit individual constituencies

rational actors   Political actors behaving in ways that maximize power and financial and status benefits

shrinking middle (legislators)   The decline of politically moderate legislators in the House and the Senate

soft money   Political advertising funded not by political parties but by other interests

Notes

1   Only very exceptionally do British MPs survive the removal of party endorsement; they may survive on personal appeal for one election, but rarely longer.

2   There are 435 members of the House of Representatives, 100 senators, three delegates (District of Columbia, Guam and Virgin Islands) and a Resident Commissioner from Puerto Rico. The latter four cannot vote on the floor, but can serve as committee members.

3   Gary C. Jacobson, *The Electoral Origins of Divided Government: Competition in US House Elections, 1946–1988* (Boulder, CO: Westview, 1990).

4   For a discussion of this point, see Gary C. Jacobson, *The Politics of Congressional Elections*, 4th edn (New York: Addison Wesley, 1996).

5   Burdett A. Loomis, *The Contemporary Congress* (New York: St Martin's Press, 2006).

6   David Mayhew, *Congress: The Electoral Connection* (New Haven: Yale University Press, 1986).

7   Both quotes ibid., p. 51.

8   An up-to-date compilation of ratings can be found in Michael Barone and Grant Ujifusa, *The Almanac of American Politics 2008* (Washington, DC: National Journal Group, 2007).

9   Richard E. Fenno, *Home Style: House Members in their Districts* (Boston, MA: Little, Brown, 1978).

Further Reading

David Mayhew's *Congress: The Electoral Connection* (New Haven: Yale University Press, Second edition, 2004) remains the classic statement of the electoral connection. *Home Style* (Boston, MA: Little, Brown, 1978), by Richard E. Fenno Jr, is a book rich in anecdote on the same theme. See also Roger H. Davidson, Walter J. Oleszek and Frances E. Lee, *Congress and its Members*, 15th edn (Washington, DC: Congressional Quarterly Press, 2015). Congressional elections are examined in Gary C. Jacobson, *The Politics of Congressional Elections*, 4th edn (New York: HarperCollins, 1996). A textbook treatment of Congress is provided by Donald Ritchie, *The US Congress: A Very Short Introduction* (Oxford and New York: Oxford University Press, Second Edition, 2016). A good comparative analysis of the electoral connection is Anthony King, *Running Scared: Why America's Politicians Campaign Too Much and Govern Too Little* (New York: Free Press, 1997).

CHAPTER 9
CONGRESS II
FUNCTIONS AND POWERS – THE BROKEN BRANCH?

Let me say this about congress.… A congress is not a president.… A congress should not be a president.… A congress should be nothing more, nothing less than what it is: a reflection of the will of our people and the problems that disturb them and the actions they want taken. The congress ought to improve its ability to serve that function.
– SENATOR EDMUND S. MUSKIE, QUOTED IN STEELE,
THE ROLE OF CONGRESS II

American Politics and Society, Ninth Edition. David McKay.
© 2018 John Wiley & Sons Ltd. Published 2018 by John Wiley & Sons Ltd.

The Broken Branch: How Congress is Failing America
– TITLE OF 2006 BOOK ON CONGRESS BY THOMAS E. MANN AND
NORMAN J. ORNSTEIN

As we stressed in chapter 3, Congress was originally intended to be the key institution in the federal government. It was only through Congress that the people were given a direct control over policy. Members of the House of Representatives were directly elected. Senators, president and vice president were not. Moreover, Congress was meant to formulate and pass laws – the president's main job being merely to implement them. Popular control of government was, of course, limited by the presidential veto and the territorial base of appointed senators. But it was the House of Representatives that controlled the purse strings, and it was Congress as a whole that stood, as legislature, at the apex of the constitutional system.

The actual functioning of the institution never quite worked as intended. During the first 30 years of the nineteenth century, state legislatures voted to adopt what became effectively the direct election of the president, and as the country grew and demands on government increased, presidents took on the major responsibility for formulating legislation. This trend has occurred in almost every country and is an almost inescapable consequence of the vast information and power resources available to modern executive bureaucracies, but not to legislatures. Yet, unlike most national legislatures, Congress retains formidable power. It remains an indisputably important actor in the policy process. It is also an institution whose powers and internal operations are constantly changing. Most recently it has been accused of being too partisan, too intent on serving particular interests rather than the national interest and of failing to oversee the executive. The main purpose of this chapter is to analyse the nature and significance of these changes so that an accurate understanding of the policy-making role of Congress can be achieved.

The Functions of Congress

As indicated in chapter 8, the first and most general function of Congress is one of representation. At its simplest this means that members of Congress are held accountable for their actions through the electoral process. In complex societies the citizen–representative relationship must necessarily be limited, however, so when we talk of the 'representative function of Congress' we are actually referring to a number of different functions, most of which are at least one step removed from the direct influence of the voters. So the business of formulating and passing laws – the legislative function – involves constant interaction between members, and between members and staff, interest groups, executive officials, the courts and the media. Clearly, the individual voter's influence in this process is limited, although, as we have already established, the constant threat of electoral defeat does oblige US legislators to tend to the general pastoral needs of their constituencies. A second major function of legislatures, and especially the Congress, is to oversee the executive branch. Constitutionally and by convention, Congress has a number of established oversight powers. It controls finance, so appropriations bills originate in the House of Representatives and have to be approved by both houses. As we develop below, it is the president who initially produces the annual budget, so the appropriations process is an opportunity for Congress to approve, modify or criticize the executive's spending plans and also to monitor them during implementation. The Senate also approves presidential appointments and treaties, and both houses have the power to investigate inefficiency or wrongdoing in the executive branch, including impeachment of executive officers (the House impeaches and the Senate tries).[1] Finally, Congress has the power to approve all administrative re-organizations in the executive branch. Before we look at these functions in detail, it is necessary to outline the formal structure of power in the two houses.

The Structure of Power in Congress

Two major foci of power exist – committees and party leadership. Table 9.1 lists the standing committees and the more important select committees of Congress. Committees have always been central to the business of legislation in Congress, and if anything their importance has increased over the years. As table 9.1 shows, the permanent committees are distinguished by function, and as government has become more complex, so the number of committees and sub-committees has tended to increase. Consolidation and reorganizations do occur – indeed both the Democrats in the 1980s and 1990s and the Republicans after

Plate 9.1   Speaker of the House Paul Ryan holds his weekly press conference and answers questions about his first meeting with Republican Presidential Candidate Donald Trump at the US Capitol in Washington, USA on 12 May 2016
Source: Anadolu Agency/Getty, www.gettyimages.co.uk/license/530979532.

Table 9.1   House and Senate committees listed by preference motivations of new House members and senators, 110th Congress (2007–9)

House	Senate
Prestige committees	Policy committees
	Homeland Security and Governmental Affairs
Appropriations	Budget
Budget	Foreign Relations
Rules	Governmental Affairs
Ways and Means	Judiciary
	Health, Education, Labor, and Pension
Policy committees	Mixed policy/constituency committees
Financial Services	Armed Services
Foreign Affairs	Appropriations
Education and Labor	Banking, Housing, and Urban Affairs
International Relations	Finance
Government Reform	Small Business and Entrepreneurship
Judiciary	
Homeland Security	
Constituency committees	Constituency committees
Agriculture	Agriculture, Nutrition, and Forestry
Armed Services	Appropriations
Energy and Commerce	
Natural Resources	Commerce, Science and Transportation
Transportation and Infrastructure	Energy and Natural Resources
Science	Environment and Public Works
Small Business	Indian Affairs
Veterans' Affairs	
Other committees	Other committees
Oversight and Governmental Reform	Select Committee on Intelligence
Permanent Select Committee on Intelligence	Select Committee on Ethics
House Administration	Select Committee on Aging
Standards of Official Conduct	Veterans' Affairs

Source: Various including Steven S. Smith and Christopher J. Deering, *Committees in Congress*, 3rd edn (Washington, DC: Congressional Quarterly Press, 1997), updated from House and Senate websites, www.senate. gov and www.house.gov.

1994 managed to reduce the number of sub-committees substantially (figure 9.1 – since 2009 the number of committees has remained roughly constant). It remains the case, however, that both the House and the Senate have a large number of working groups – especially in comparison with other legislatures. Both internal and external pressures are at work to maintain this need. Internally, individual legislators build reputations by specializing in a particular subject. Often this specialization is linked to constituent needs. Moreover, Congress's own bureaucracy has to match developments in the executive branch, and as

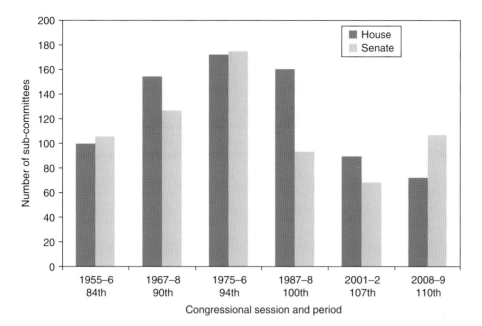

Figure 9.1   Number of House and Senate sub-committees, selected Congresses, 1955–2009
Source: 'Vital statistics 1993–1994: *Congressional Quarterly*'s players, politics and turf of the 104th
Congress', *Congressional Quarterly*, special issue (25 March 1995). Updated from N. Ornstein,
T. E. Mann and M. J. Malbin, *Vital Statistics on Congress, 2001–2002* (Washington, DC: AEI Press,
2002), tables 4.2 and 4.3, and Harold W. Stanley and Richard G. Niemi, *Vital Statistics on American
Politics, 2007–2008* (Washington, DC: Congressional Quarterly Press, 2008). Reprinted with
permission of SAGE.

departments and agencies have increased in number and function, so Congress has been
obliged to respond. For example, the House Select Committee on Homeland Security was
created in direct response to the establishment of the Department of Homeland Security in
2002. Often this is a two-way street. Members' career and constituency needs may benefit
from executive fragmentation, which legislation often encourages.

Note also the distinctions drawn in table 9.1 between policy committees, which are primarily concerned with general policy, and committees that are devoted mainly to servicing constituencies. In addition, the House has what might be called 'prestige' committees,
which are primarily concerned with money – an area where the House has special responsibilities – and with procedural rules.

It is in the committees that the business of framing, amending and rejecting legislation
occurs. Most committees authorize legislation while others provide funds to finance programmes. Hence the House Appropriations, House Ways and Means, House and Senate
Budget, and Senate Finance Committees are concerned with approving income (taxation)
and expenditure bills. We examine the budgetary process in more detail in chapter 18. By
no means are all committees equal in power. The finance committees are particularly prestigious and influential, especially so in the case of the House Appropriations Committee

(which is the source of all appropriations bills), the House Ways and Means and Senate Finance Committees (which are responsible for tax bills), and the two Budget Committees. Of the authorizing committees, the Senate Foreign Relations Committee is of central importance in foreign policy, while the Homeland Security, Banking, and Judiciary Committees are prominent in both Houses. An equivalent hierarchy applies to most sub-committees with, for example, the House Appropriations sub-committee on Defense being markedly more important than the Military Construction sub-committee.

Because the House of Representatives is a larger and, by tradition, more formal body than the Senate, a number of complex rules have been formulated to govern day-by-day business. The Rules Committee is responsible for interpreting these regulations and in particular for helping to decide which bills, and in what form, come before the floor of the House. This power to withhold bills or to allow them to proceed only if certain amendments or provisions are omitted or included gives the Rules Committee considerable political clout. Indeed, during the late nineteenth and early twentieth centuries, the Rules Committee was at the very centre of congressional power. Today, although it continues to perform a gatekeeper function, it is less powerful, in part because the House is less formal than it was (of which more below), and in part because the committee tends to be the voice of the majority party leadership rather than being an independent source of power in Congress.

Clearly, membership of committees is an important determinant of the status and influence of individual representatives and senators, and accordingly the processes whereby members are selected to sit on committees and eventually appointed as chairpersons have long been the subject of debate and controversy. The most basic rule is that the party with a majority in the chamber automatically achieves a majority in the committees, with the minority party represented in rough proportion to its delegation in the chamber as a whole. Committee and sub-committee chairpersons are drawn exclusively from the majority party. In the House members are allowed to sit on a maximum of two standing committees, although House members assigned to the important Rules, Ways and Means, and Appropriations Committees are not normally permitted further assignments. Typically, senators will sit on three standing committees. In both houses party committees selected by party caucuses (meetings of all party members in each House) choose the members of the standing committees. This process is predictably political, with seniority, experience, reputation and connections being the main determinants of assignments. Since the late 1950s the Senate has ensured that all freshmen (new) senators are given at least one major committee assignment (the so-called 'Johnson Rule' introduced under the influence of the then Senate Majority Leader, Lyndon Baines Johnson). By winning prestigious committee jobs, members can enhance their institutional reputations, gain access to legislative programmes of direct interest to their constituents and, occasionally, attract national attention.

During her first term in the Senate, Hillary Rodham Clinton (Democrat, New York) used her position on the prestigious Senate Armed Services Committee to sponsor legislation designed to improve the position of serving members of the forces and their families. For example, in 2004 she introduced a bill designed to provide a small pension ($125 a month) for so-called 'Gold Star' parents or the parents of service personnel killed in combat. In this way she was able to raise her personal profile not so much among her constituents but nationally.

Within individual committees and sub-committees status is no less important, with the chairperson of each workgroup at the very top of the pecking order. Both ranking within committees and the assertion of power by the chairpersons over committee members is largely determined by seniority. Until the early 1970s the seniority rule was condemned by liberals because of the enormous advantage it gave to the solidly Democratic – but conservative and often racist – one-party South. Indeed, the caricature image of elderly, white-haired southerners lording it over all and sundry on Capitol Hill was not far from the truth, as such figures as Richard Russell of Armed Services, Russell Long of Finance and James Eastland of Judiciary in the Senate, and Carl Vinson of Armed Services and Howard Smith of Rules in the House, testified.

Since the 1970s there have been three distinct waves of reform affecting committee power. Until the mid-1970s chairpersons were particularly powerful because of their control of the agenda. They could decide the order in which bills were discussed, the timing of committee meetings, the frequency of public hearings and the management of bills on the floor of the House. They used also to have a major say in the number and composition of sub-committees, together with the selection of sub-committee chairs. During the 1970s the Democrats instituted reforms that removed committee chairs from the very pinnacles of power. Their control of the work and membership of sub-committees was weakened. Moreover, seniority was removed as the only criterion for advancement within committees. In 1975 the House Democratic caucus, caught up in a general atmosphere of reform, removed three of the most powerful committee chairpersons at a stroke (Wight Patman of Texas, Banking and Currency; W. R. Poage of Texas, Agriculture; and F. Edward Hébert of Louisiana, Administration). In fact, seniority remained central to any promotion within committees. From 1975 to 1994 chairpersons were obliged to treat sub-committee chairs (and committee members generally) more as equals than as feudal vassals. This was part of a general democratization and dispersal of power in both the House and (to a lesser extent) the Senate, which we return to below.

This decentralization of power in the House (and to a lesser extent in the Senate) led many commentators to conclude that Congress was incapable of making quick decisions. Worse, decentralized committees were likely to pander to particular (or constituency) rather than general (or public) interest. Republican presidents and congressional opposition spokespersons pointed to the fact that the Democrats' apparently permanent control of the House made it impossible to cut the budget deficit or to pass much-needed reforms in such areas as health care and the economy. Although these criticisms were almost certainly exaggerated, they helped to inspire a second major wave of reforms instituted by the Democratic leadership in the 1980s, which were designed to relocate power away from the committees and return it to the leadership. Although sub-committee powers were reduced (especially in the Senate), the Democrats were less than successful in transforming the system. However, following the Republicans' capture of Congress in the 1994 mid-term elections, Newt Gingrich, the new Speaker, and Dick Armey, the new Majority Leader, were determined to push through the legislative programme outlined in their 'Contract with America'. As a result they persuaded the Republican Conference (the committee representing all the House Republicans) to push through a number of changes in committee operations.

The major objective of these reforms was to strengthen party control over the committees. Judging by the success enjoyed by the Republicans in passing much of the Contract with America legislative programme (although some of it was eventually defeated in the Senate, by presidential veto or invalidated by the Supreme Court), this objective seems to have been achieved. However, as is discussed below, the reforms produced changes in the 'folk-ways' of the House that may have had negative rather than positive consequences. Furthermore, the enthusiasm and determination of the Republican leadership in the 104th Congress began to flag after the Democratic advances in the 1996 and 1998 elections, and by the time the Democrats won back Congress in 2006 much of the steam had gone out of the reform attempts.

In addition to the standing committees in each House, a number of other workgroups exist, including the Conference Committees. These are, simply, ad hoc bodies created to reconcile the differences that occur in the House and Senate versions of the same piece of legislation. Membership is drawn from those members in each House who have been most closely involved with the legislation, usually the relevant committee members – who then vote *en bloc* so as to represent the wishes of their chamber. A great deal of politicking goes on in conference, with bills often amended considerably, and not always in line with the wishes of the House or Senate as a whole.

Conference decisions can, however, be rejected by a subsequent vote on the floor of each chamber, and sent back to the committee (see figure 9.2). In addition, ad hoc committees can be formed by the Speaker of the House to reconcile standing committees with

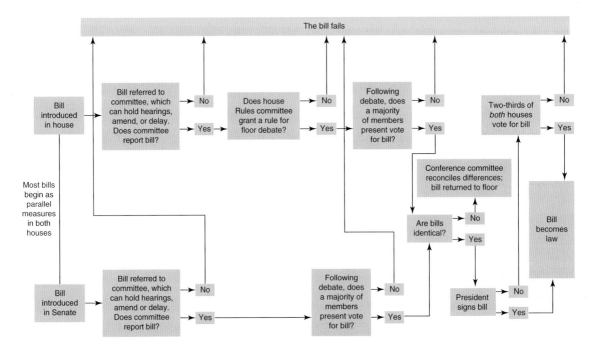

Figure 9.2   How a bill becomes law: the obstacle course for legislation in Congress

overlapping jurisdictions, and select committees appointed by presiding officers can be created in either House to expedite a particular problem, often in association with a congressional investigation. In recent years, for example, select committees on ageing and ethics have been formed in the Senate. Such committees have to be renewed every two years and they cannot report legislation to the floor. In most cases select committees emerge as a forum for airing currently controversial issues. Sometimes, as with the House Select Committee on Intelligence, they are given permanent status.

The second focus of power in Congress is the party leadership. In the House the key figures are the Speaker and Minority Leader, and the key groups are the party caucuses, in particular the majority party caucus (presently the Republican Conference). The Speaker of the House used to have quite substantial formal powers. Until 1911, he was also chair of the Rules Committee and he appointed committee chairpersons. This combination enabled Speakers to control the flow of legislation onto the floor. Concentration of such power in the personage of one particularly assertive Speaker, Joseph Cannon, led to a revolt in 1910–11, which resulted in the removal of the Speaker's control of the Rules Committee and of committee assignments. But the Speaker retains considerable authority. He continues to help to control the flow of legislation, recognizes who is to speak on the floor, can create ad hoc committees, gives advice on assignments to conference and select committees, helps in assigning bills to committees and votes in the event of a tie. While the Speaker has the greatest formal power of any individual in the House, his potential informal power is much greater. As both leading parliamentarian and party leader he can become a crucial link between other centres of power – particularly committee chairpersons – as well as be the person most able to muster often disparate party forces behind a particular bill or the programme of a president. Whether these powers are utilized to the full depends on the personality, capabilities and political skills of the incumbent.

Over the past 70 years, for example, the office has come full circle as incumbents have changed. Between 1940 and 1960 the office was dominated by the forceful and highly political Sam Rayburn (with breaks in 1947–8 and 1953–4 when the Republicans had a majority in the House). Between 1961 and 1978 first John McCormack and then Carl Albert became Speakers, neither of whom had the skills or the charisma of Rayburn. Between 1978 and 1986 the highly partisan and politically astute Thomas (Tip) O'Neill partly returned the office of Speaker to its former glory. O'Neill's personality was ideally suited to the brokerage politics of the House, and he was aided by the 1975 reforms which gave to the Speaker the power to appoint Democratic members to the Rules Committee and to the Democratic Steering Committee, which assigns new committee members within the party. Given the Democratic dominance of the House, these amounted to considerable powers. On his resignation in 1986, O'Neill was replaced by Jim Wright of Texas, a long-time O'Neill supporter and until 1986 Democratic House Majority Leader. In June 1989 Jim Wright was forced to resign after allegations of financial irregularities were brought against him by the House Minority whip, Newt Gingrich. He was replaced by Tom Foley, who had a more accommodating style than the often feisty Wright. Following the 1994 mid-term Republican victory, Speaker Newt Gingrich took on a legislative leadership role unprecedented since the days of Joe Cannon. In addition to the committee reforms (see below), Gingrich's formal powers were enhanced. He was also widely perceived as a major influence on the

Republican victory, so he had built up considerable political capital with House members. His dominance was dented, however, when in 1996 he faced a number of ethics charges and was only narrowly re-elected Speaker in early 1997. As a result, during the 105th Congress (1997–8) his parliamentary position was weakened and some power returned to the committee chairpersons. Gingrich resigned after the Republicans' poor showing in the 1998 mid-term elections. His eventual successor (the first choice, Bob Livingston, was forced to withdraw after he admitted to extramarital affairs) was Dennis Hastert of Illinois, who was elected by the Republican caucus on 6 January 1999. Hastert proved to be a highly partisan Speaker and presided over many of the changes that have brought the House into disrepute. With the Democratic victory in 2006, Hastert was replaced by Nancy Pelosi of California, who became the first female Speaker. (Ironically, Hastert was subsequently convicted of child sex abuse in 2016 and sentenced to 15 months in prison.) With the dramatic defeat of the House Democrats in 2010, the Republicans returned with John Boehner as the new incumbent. Boehner was in many respects a traditional politician willing to strike deals with political friends and foes alike. However, as will be discussed below, he was thwarted in many of these attempts by the Freedom Caucus in his own party and was obliged to resign in October 2015. He was replaced by Paul Ryan of Wisconsin (see biography below).

After the Speaker, the most important offices are the Majority and Minority Floor Leaders, who are elected by the party caucuses and whose main job is to monitor and organize party business on the floor of the House. In fact the Minority Leader is often a more crucial figure than the Majority Leader, largely because the Speaker is the effective majority spokesperson. Finally, both parties appoint whips to help to control floor business. These are in no way equivalent to British parliamentary whips; they have no effective sanctions at their disposal to oblige members to toe the party line. Instead their job is to persuade, negotiate, bargain and cajole members into broad agreement on particular items of legislation. Nancy Pelosi was elected Democratic Minority Leader after the Republican takeover of the House in 2010. The party caucus meets infrequently, and then usually to agree on procedure rather than to discuss substantive policy issues. As important today are the informal caucuses that have emerged over the past 20 years. These are usually organized around a particular interest, such as the Democratic black and Hispanic caucuses, or around an ideological orientation, such as the Democratic Study Group, representing liberal causes, or the conservative Republican Tea Party caucus. In 2016 the typical House member belonged to 16 caucuses and the typical senator to 14.

Leadership in the Senate roughly parallels that in the House, but there are some important differences. Unlike in the House, the presiding officer – formally the vice president of the United States – is an honorific position carrying with it few powers, of which the main one is being able to vote in the event of a tie. Nor does the President Pro Tempore, which position goes by tradition to the longest-serving senator from the majority party, have many powers. On a day-to-day basis, the members of the majority party preside over the chamber in rotation. Real power lies with the Majority and Minority Leaders, although even they can often do little to control the behaviour of just 100 fiercely independent senators. Again, much depends on the personality of the incumbents. Some Majority Leaders, such as Lyndon Johnson (1956–61), built reputations as power brokers, as did Republican Howard Baker, whose management of the Republicans' fragile majority in 1981–5 showed great political skill. Robert Dole of Kansas, who succeeded Baker in 1985, had to use all his political skill to hold together an even narrower Republican majority until the Democrats regained control of the Senate in 1986. In contrast to Johnson and Baker, some recent leaders, such as Mike Mansfield (1961–78), have been either unwilling or less able to assert authority over fellow party members. Following the Republican victory in 1994, Bob Dole became Majority Leader. Although he was a skilled parliamentarian, Dole's energies were diverted by his race for the presidency in 1996. His replacement, Senator Trent Lott of Mississippi, was more in the mould of an old-style party leader. A strong partisan devoted to good organization, Lott was able successfully to exploit the more ideological agenda that came to dominate Congress by the late 1990s. However, like his counterpart in the House, Newt Gingrich, Lott was eventually obliged to resign (in December 2002), although for very different reasons. He made a speech to the effect that he had a liking for the social arrangements of the old segregation South. This made his position untenable. He was replaced by Tennessee Senator Bill Frist, who in turn was replaced by Democrat Harry Reid of Nevada in 2006. Reid was known for his integrity and his knowledge of Senate 'insider' politics. His position became particularly important after 2010 when the Republicans won control of the House of Representatives. With the Democrats continuing to hold the Senate, he became a key player in negotiations over the budget in 2012 and 2013. With the stunning Republican victory in the 2014 mid-term elections, the position passed to Mitch McConnell of Kentucky, an erstwhile centrist, but, like most of his congressional party, more recently a convinced champion of conservative causes. Meanwhile, Chuck Schumer of New York replaced Harry Reid as Minority Leader in November 2016.

So far in our discussion we have concentrated on describing the formal powers of committees and party leaders. This tells us little about the dynamics of the policy-making process, however, and how the institution can be assessed in terms of its performance and effectiveness. One way to examine these questions is first to look at the validity of the criticisms, which have been directed at Congress over recent years, and then to discuss the reform measures adopted in response to these criticisms.

Congress Under Fire

At least since the Second World War, Congress has been the subject of sometimes-intense criticism. Very generally we can divide these criticisms into broad categories: those that are historically specific and those that identify structural features of Congress that persist through time. Of course, the two sets of critiques are related, especially as the institution is constantly changing, but this simple distinction does facilitate a more subtle understanding of how the institution works.

Critique 1: fragmentation and the electoral connection

Perhaps the most common and persistent criticism was that Congress was fragmented and unresponsive; that it was not a 'coherent' policy-making body representing the people, but was instead a forum for the defence and promotion of disparate, unrelated interests. That the policy-making process in Congress is fragmented cannot be disputed. Power is dispersed to committees and sub-committees and the legislative process itself is cumbersome. When a bill is introduced it faces a formidable number of potential veto points before it actually becomes law, and this is true even of those bills which are part of the president's programme, have substantial support in Congress and are recognized as important public questions. Figure 9.2 shows the major obstacles that confront any bill when introduced into Congress. Committee action is the most difficult stumbling block, with less than 10 per cent of bills actually reported out. The presidential veto used to be a much rarer barrier, but since the advent of divided government it is now exercised more frequently on important items of legislation (see chapter 11). Even less common are successful attempts to override a veto. The president can also exercise a pocket veto by failing to sign a bill passed within the last 10 days of a legislative session.

Figure 9.2 also omits reference to the Senate filibuster – a debating device that has ended the life of several controversial bills. Filibustering is the practice, allowed only by Senate rules, of speaking in unlimited debate and eventually forcing the death of a bill through the expiry of parliamentary time. During the 1950s and 1960s many civil rights bills were killed by this method, with segregationist southern senators speaking for many hours against the reform measures. A device does exist for ending a filibuster, known as a cloture (or closure) rule; this can be invoked to end debate if three-fifths of the senators agree. Between 1917 (when the cloture rule was introduced) and about 1970 very few cloture votes were attempted because of the in-built veto power of the southern Democratic senators. However, the decline of this group plus a rule change in 1975 that reduced the percentage needed for successful cloture from 66 per cent to 60 per cent has meant that the measure is now frequently invoked and is often successful. The 60 per cent rule means that if one party wins 60-plus seats in the chamber it can effectively control the agenda (notwithstanding maverick senators who may not vote the party line). This became especially relevant between 2008 and 2010 when the Democrats narrowly failed to reach the magic 60 seats necessary effectively to control parliamentary procedure in the Senate. After 2010 their majority was reduced, thus making it very difficult to pass bills sponsored by Democrats. Indeed in 2013/14, the ideological divide between the parties was so great that 287 cloture votes were invoked of which 187 were successful. During the 114th Congress (2015–16) the position was reversed with the Republican majority of 54 to 46 (including two independents who caucused with the Democrats) – a majority that was reduced to 52 to 48 following the 2016 elections. In 2013, Democrats, frustrated by the use of the filibuster against Obama appointees changed the rules so that a simple majority could approve all executive appointments bar those to the Supreme Court. In 2017 the Republicans extended this to Supreme Court appointments.

In the House, the Rules Committee can constitute a further barrier to the passage of a law. Until 1975, southerners dominated the committee and frequently refused to grant rules to bills they disliked, irrespective of the support the measures may have won in the legislative committees. Again, liberal, and especially civil rights, legislation was the victim. In 1975, however, the Democratic caucus voted to give the Speaker the power to appoint Rules Committee members. As a result, although the committee can still stop bills, it acts more in accordance with the general wishes of the House – and particularly with the relevant legislative committee – than before. Interestingly, debate on the floor used to be one of the least significant aspects of the legislative process, for by the time a bill reached this stage it was already roughly in its final form. Recent reforms, however, have increased floor activity, with individual legislators now more able to attach riders and amendments to bills. Floor votes can also be crucial, of course.

Figure 9.2 gives the slightly misleading impression that bills either proceed past a number of legislative hurdles or are simply killed off. The reality is that most bills are non-starters because they lack the support of key members – although some are initiated simply to attract public attention to an issue – and the remainder embark on a course that is beset with problems and pitfalls. But these do not always involve the possibility of a sudden death. As likely are the possibilities of amendment and delay. Delay can occur at almost any stage of the process, but it is in the committees that bills most often become buried, sometimes never to reappear. Given that Congress has a heavy workload and is constantly under pressure, delaying a bill is often an expedient course to follow. For a bill's supporters, including presidents, this can be highly frustrating.

Few bills emerge from Congress in the precise form in which they entered it. They are amended – sometimes dramatically – from their original form, and this amendment process is the very essence of congressional politics, for it is by changing the detailed provisions of bills that members can indulge in log-rolling, or the exchange of favours which is so crucial to their electoral survival. So items are added to or deleted from bills in accordance with bargains struck between key legislators, usually within or between committees. Committee hearings, open to public scrutiny, also allow organized interests to air their views and generally to advertise particular points of view. And, of course, executive departments and agencies usually have a crucial interest (with positions to defend or promote) in the detail of legislation. Finally, committees may compete one with the other, for, as can be inferred from the list of committees in table 9.1, there are a number of areas where overlapping jurisdictions occur.

When all these influences are at work, as they are in major items of legislation, the potential for delay, obstruction and even confusion can be appreciated. A classic example of what can happen to a vital piece of legislation is provided by President Clinton's health-care reforms introduced in Congress in 1993. Given the enormous complexity of the bill – a fact that resulted from the need to consolidate a large number of existing federal health and welfare programmes – it was assigned to multiple committees. Two of these, the House Education and Labour and the Senate Labour and Human Resources Committees, agreed on a reform package, but only one that was too liberal for the Congress as a whole to accept. In addition, the key finance committee chairs found it difficult to win sufficient committee support for the reforms. As Burdett Loomis has noted, these failures tell us a great deal about congressional power, given that the chairs of the committees involved included some truly formidable legislators – Representatives John Dingell (Energy and Commerce) and Dan Rostenkowski (Ways and Means) and Senator Daniel Patrick Moynihan (Finance). In the end Congress found it impossible to reconcile all the conflicting bureaucratic, health-care and insurance company interests in a way that would produce a coherent legislative package. The bill died a year later during the 1994 mid-term election campaign.[2] A not dissimilar sequence of events characterized President Obama's health-care reforms, although the outcome was successful. The original version included a 'public option' provision or a health programme directly funded by the federal government. This proved unacceptable to all the Republicans and a minority of Democrats in the House. Meanwhile, the Senate passed a more limited version without the public option but including an 'individual mandate' or requirement that the uninsured buy health insurance from a list of government approved providers. Eventually this bill passed both houses – although every Republican member of the Senate voted against it and one Republican representative voted in favour – and then after the bill was already assured passage. In fact, passage came only through the parliamentary device called 'reconciliation' that enables the Senate to vote through a simple majority thus by-passing the filibuster device that allows a 40 per cent minority to block a bill. There have, in fact, been remarkably few occasions when a major legislative package has not been delayed or obstructed by Congress. The early New Deal (1933–5) and Great Society (1965–6) periods are usually mentioned as the notable exceptions (see chapters 15 and 16). In addition, the first two years of the Reagan administration and the 18 months following the 9/11 attacks qualify as periods when Congress was unusually compliant. In the latter case, Congress passed tax cuts in 2002 and 2003, and approved the Patriot Act and the creation of the Department of Homeland Security, in a period when the Bush administration was able successfully to appeal to patriotism and national solidarity.

A further development that demonstrates well the tendency of Congress to serve the particular rather than the public interest is the rapid growth of the pork barrel in the post-1994 period. As Mann and Ornstein point out, 'earmarking', or the allocation of funds for specific constituency projects, increased from $10 billion in 1995 to nearly $23 billion in 2004. So serious had this problem become that the House imposed a moratorium on the practice in 2011. While this dramatically reduced the overt use of the device, the pork barrel remains in other forms. For example, instead of the $533 million earmarked for the Army Corps of Engineers in 2010 bills, the 2012 budget set aside $507 million in 26 slush funds, along with a set of guidelines for making sure the money went to favourite pet projects. A further development since the 1990s has been the rise of partisanship in Congress and especially in the House. As can be seen from figure 9.3, party unity voting increased markedly between 1980 and 2014 reflecting the ideological polarization of the period. Accompanying this, however, came much more blatant use of party to manipulate parliamentary rules and procedures to push through legislation. Hence party leaders have used all means possible, including veiled threats, to ensure legislation was passed (or blocked). So, instead of careful deliberation and the cumulative 'marking up' of bills in committee (allowing committee members of both parties to contribute amendments), partisan legislation has been pushed through with undue haste.

Critique 2: failure of oversight

Congress has failed to perform the oversight function effectively. In addition to passing legislation, Congress is charged with the job of overseeing the executive or holding the president, executive departments and agencies accountable for their actions. The appropriations process in part involves this job and this is dealt with elsewhere (chapter 15). In addition, Congress is responsible for monitoring executive appointments and holding formal investigations into the executive branch, and, as a last resort, it has the authority to impeach executive officers. The Constitution requires the Senate to approve presidential

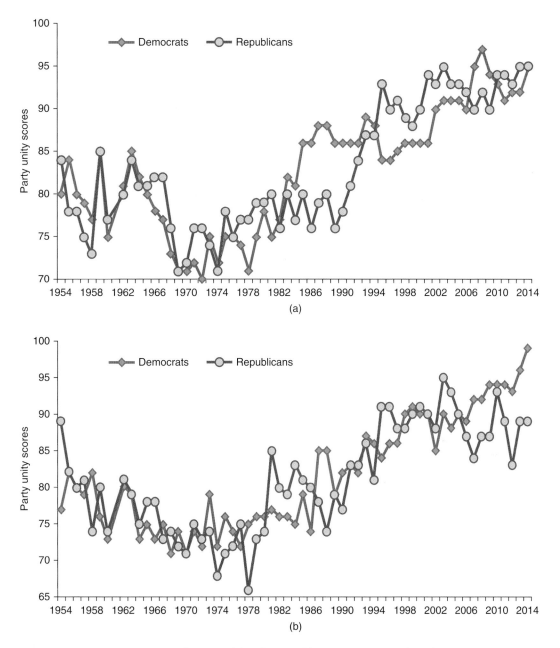

Figure 9.3   Party Unity Scores in the House (a) and Senate (b), 1954–2014. Data show the percentage of all record votes where a majority of Democrats opposed a majority of Republicans
Source: Computed from data provided by the *Congressional Quarterly* magazine at https://library. cqpress.com/cqweekly/toc.php?mode=weekly-date, reprinted with the permission of SAGE.

appointments, but it is not a power that the Senate has used in the strictly ethical sense, i.e. rooting out inefficient, incompetent or corrupt appointees. As often, senators are concerned to ensure that incumbents in the more than 1,500 major posts subject to Senate confirmation are men and women who are sympathetic to the legislators' political or constituency interests, or who are likely to defend an organized interest (such as labour or business) which senators are known to identify with. The appointment process is, in other words, not unlike the legislative process – it is highly politicized and subject to similar constituency interest-group pressures. Only rarely are nominations withdrawn and even more rarely are they rejected. Between 1989 and 2003, for example, only two nominations were rejected out of more than 600,000 submitted – although around 1,200 were withdrawn.[3] One notable exception occurred in 2014 when the Senate rejected Debo Adegbile, President Obama's nominee to head the Civil Rights Division of the Department of Justice because he had once defended the murderer of a police officer.

So Congress is accused of two failings in this area. First, it favours many appointees not because they are likely to serve the public interest, but because they will support particular or special constituency and group interests. And second, independently of this problem, it has failed to root out some of the more obvious and colourful examples of incompetent presidential nominations. The Nixon administration was littered with such cases. But even the Carter presidency was able to produce its Bert Lance (the Budget Director who was eventually obliged to resign following exposure of illegal banking practices). The first Clinton administration also had its share of dishonest or incompetent appointees, with accusations levelled at a number of cabinet secretaries, including Secretary of Housing and Urban Development Henry Cisneros and Commerce Secretary Ron Brown. Most recently, many liberals had deep misgivings about the civil liberties record of John Ashcroft, the George W. Bush administration's Attorney General in his first term, and Bush's first Treasury Secretary, Paul O'Neil, was fired for incompetence and indiscretion. Even more scandalous was the resignation of Attorney General Alberto Gonzales in 2007, following accusations that he had abused his powers in pursuing the 'War on Terror'. By the end of his term, no major Obama nominee of cabinet rank had had to resign because of scandal or incompetence – although Attorney General Eric Holder was censured by the House in that year for allegedly failing to oversee a Justice Department 'sting' operation to apprehend gun running to Mexican drugs barons. This action was politically motivated, however, and Holder continued in office until he voluntarily resigned in 2015.

While all this is true, Congress does now examine the records of the most senior nominees more carefully than in the past. This is particularly true of Supreme Court nominees, who have the potential to shift the ideological complexion of the Court on a range of sensitive issues. Such perceptions certainly applied to Robert H. Bork, Reagan's 1987 nominee to the Court, who was opposed by the wide margin of 58 to 42 senators. Reagan's second nominee for the vacant position, Douglas H. Ginsberg, was obliged to withdraw following an admission that he had smoked marijuana while at law school. Eventually the president nominated a 'safe' candidate, Anthony Kennedy, who was quickly confirmed by the Senate. George Bush Senior had fewer difficulties with his appointees, although his nomination of Supreme Court Justice Clarence Thomas was confirmed by the narrow margin of 52 to 48 following allegations of sexual harassment against the judge. In addition, the Senate, on a 47/53 vote, rejected Bush Senior's first-choice nomination as Defense Secretary, John Tower. George W. Bush also received short shrift from the Senate Judiciary Committee, whose initial enquiries into the nomination of Harriet Miers to the Court in 2005 revealed that she was totally unqualified for the job.

Most commentators agree that, in the context of divided government, presidents have experienced more partisan and ideological objections to their appointees. In particular, President Clinton's efforts to make the US District and Appeals courts look 'more like America' in terms of gender and ethnicity were partly thwarted by the Senate Judiciary Committee's delays on his nominations. Fearing that the Clinton appointments would lead to a more activist (i.e. liberal) judicial branch, the committee tied up many of the Clinton nominations for many months – and sometimes years – during both the president's first and second terms. Even though the Democrats controlled the Senate during Obama's first term, he still encountered problems over his judicial nominees, with Republicans able to use parliamentary manoeuvres to delay confirmations for many months. Perhaps most famously the Republican Senate refused to consider *any* nominee to the Supreme Court until after the 2016 election following the death of conservative justice Antonin Scalia in February of that year.

The investigative power of Congress consists of investigations by the standing committees, the work of special or select committees created for the specific purpose of inquiring into a particular problem, and the work of the General Accounting Office (GAO). GAO auditing of the executive spending is a continuous process, with the office reporting its findings to Congress. Congress can also require the GAO to investigate a particular programme or agency at any time. Standing committee investigations involve public hearings into alleged executive inefficiency or wrongdoing. One of the most famous series of hearings was the army–McCarthy hearings by the Senate Government Operations Permanent Investigations Sub-Committee into communist influence in the army, the Central Intelligence Agency (CIA) and the Department of State. Sub-committee chairman Joseph McCarthy became notorious as a red-baiter in this role, and his unfair and intimidating methods led eventually to his censure by the Senate in 1954.[4]

More typical are the several instances when Congress has created a select committee specifically to investigate a subject of public concern. In recent years, for example, the Senate Select Committee on Campaign Practices – known popularly as the (Sam) Ervin Committee after its chairperson – won great public attention through its inquiries into the Watergate scandal. This in turn spawned further investigations into the security agencies (FBI, CIA and Defense Intelligence), the legality of whose activities had been questioned during the Watergate exposures. In 1987 the Reagan administration was also investigated by congressional select committees set up in each House to investigate the origins and management of the Iran–Contra affair. In this case the House and the Senate decided to conduct joint hearings into the affair. This investigation led directly to a number of indictments and prosecutions, including the prosecution of former Defense Secretary Caspar Weinberger. Weinberger, together with four other former officials, was pardoned by President Bush in late 1992. Later in the 1990s, Congress investigated President Clinton and First Lady Hillary Clinton's involvement in the Whitewater property company, which operated in Arkansas during Bill Clinton's tenure as governor. Other notable congressional investigations include inquiries into racketeering in trade unions, safety in atomic power stations, the conduct of the Vietnam War, and standards in the pharmaceutical industry. More recently Congress has launched a number of investigations into the intelligence failures associated with the 9/11 attacks and the failure to find weapons of mass destruction in Iraq. And in 2016 the Republican Senate launched an investigation into the deal made by the Obama administration over the concessions it granted concluding a nuclear deal with Iran.

Note that it is not only government activities that come under congressional scrutiny – although it is usually investigations into the executive branch that arouse the most feeling, and controversy. The reason for this is simple: investigations (and oversight generally) raise awkward questions about where executive power begins and ends. With the rise of big government and the vast bureaucracy that accompanies it, Congress has found it increasingly difficult to perform the oversight function because it has limited access to exactly what goes on within the executive. Information is a valuable commodity, and one jealously guarded by presidents and their bureaucrats. Even though Congress can subpoena witnesses and documents, presidents have repeatedly refused or been extremely reluctant to hand over information. In recent years they have claimed 'executive privilege' to certain information. Unfortunately, this concept has no clear constitutional status, so the legality of withholding information remains an open question. Since Watergate and Richard Nixon's unprecedented reluctance to furnish evidence to congressional committees (he withheld information at least 19 times on matters unrelated to Watergate), presidents have been more pliant. But as the Iran–Contra affair confirmed, the executive continues to hold the trump card because the sheer volume and technical complexity of documentation often makes it difficult for a hard-pressed committee even to know what to ask for.

This problem has been compounded by institutional changes in Congress. A more confrontational Congress has led to a decline in institutional identity where members have little incentive to act collectively in ways that challenge the executive. The ideological polarization characteristic of the post-1994 period aggravated this problem. Why should members engage in cross-party cooperation against the executive when this may damage party interests? Such allegations were rife during the post-9/11 period, when Congress did little to investigate the abuses at Abu Ghraib (the US military prison in Iraq where torture of prisoners was common), Guantánamo Bay and other abuses relating to the war in Iraq. The response of Congress to the administration's handling of Hurricane Katrina in 2005 was also feeble. Even with Democratic control returning after 2006, relatively few hearings were conducted, although important investigations into waste and corruption in Iraq were held. When the Republicans later assumed control of Congress, they launched two Senate and five House investigations into the causes and administration handling of the attack on the US embassy in Benghazi in 2012 when the US ambassador and other diplomats were killed. By 2016 no clear evidence of wrongdoing had been established and many Democrats considered the hearings to be a politically motivated attack on Hillary Clinton who was Secretary of State at the time.

Finally, Congress has the power to impeach executive officers. Impeachment is a formal accusation of wrongdoing that the House of Representatives carries out, while the Senate actually tries and convicts impeached officials. But on only 13 occasions has the House used this power, and on only four has the Senate convicted. One president, Andrew Johnson, was formally impeached, although the Senate failed to convict (by one vote), and the House Judiciary Committee voted articles of impeachment against Richard Nixon, who resigned before further action could be taken. Most famous of all, of course, was the impeachment of Bill Clinton in 1998 and the subsequent Senate trial in 1999. Clinton's impeachment demonstrated both the advantages and the disadvantages of the impeachment process. On the one hand, the House vote for articles of impeachment (by 258 to 176, with 31 Democrats voting against the president) was widely regarded as a hasty and partisan interpretation of the 'high crimes and misdemeanors' which the Constitution established as grounds for impeachment. On the other hand, the Senate trial, while also partisan, was conducted with great dignity. In the event, the president was acquitted of both charges: perjury, 55 to 45 for acquittal; obstruction of justice, 50 to 50 for acquittal. With a two-thirds vote needed for conviction, neither vote came close to removing the president.

Thus, the Clinton impeachment undermined one of the main criticisms of the impeachment process – that it is so cumbersome and formalized that it is rarely used – while bolstering one of its advantages – that it is very difficult to secure a conviction unless the offences are truly a threat to the integrity of the office and the Constitution.

In addition to these structural criticisms, Congress is at any one time criticized for its specific failure to deal with a contemporary crisis or problem, or observers infer that a structural feature of the institution is permanent when it is only temporary. So in the 10 years following the Second World War it was common to accuse Congress of excessive partisanship, and the red-baiting committees of the late 1940s and early 1950s did in part represent Republican attempts to indict the activities of past or present Democratic administrations. By the late 1950s and early 1960s the charge was somewhat different: Congress was dominated by conservative, segregationist southerners. Following the reforms of the 1970s, the criticism has shifted once again. Now the accusation is that Congress is the creature of increasingly vocal and influential special- and public-interest lobbies – or simply that members serve their own rather than the public interest. Recent events seem to have confirmed this view in the minds of the American public. In 1989 five senators were found to have intervened in favour of Charles Keating of the Lincoln Savings and Loan Association. In 1991 the Senate Ethics Committee found evidence of wrongdoing by Senator Alan Cranston of California, and the other four senators were reprimanded. During the 103rd Congress (1993–4), 267 House members were found to have used an interest-free overdraft facility from a bank set up specifically for use by members of Congress. The public outcry at the extensive use of these 'rubber checks' was considerable. In early 1997, Speaker Newt Gingrich was formally reprimanded and fined by the House for illegally using income from college courses he taught for partisan purposes. Although he was re-elected, this unprecedented action against a sitting Speaker weakened his position as House leader and Gingrich eventually resigned in 1998. In addition the Republican Congress changed the rules on lobbying by launching the 'K Street Project', an insistence that only lobbyists (whose offices are concentrated in K Street in Washington) who sympathized with the Republican agenda would be given full access to the House. The most colourful recent congressional scandal involved the former minority speaker Tom Delay, who in 2011 was sentenced to three years' imprisonment for his part in the Jack Abramoff scandal (see Biography). As can be seen from figure 9.4, public regard for Congress has sunk like a stone in recent years, falling to under 20 per cent in 2016.

■ % Approve

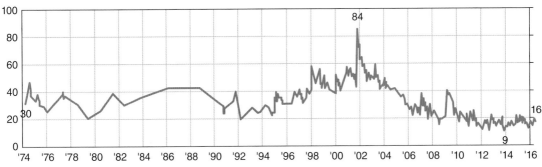

Figure 9.4   Approval rating of Congress, 1974–2016. *Question*: Do you approve or disapprove of the way the US Congress is handling its job?
Source: Congress and the Public, Gallup at www.gallup.com/poll/1600/congress-public.aspx.

Biography   Jack Abramoff – Master Lobbyist and Convicted Felon

Jack Abramoff was a leading Republican supporter and lobbyist, who until his conviction and imprisonment in 2006 led what appeared to be a gilded existence. He had an elite education at Brandeis and Georgetown universities and at one time chaired the College National Republican Committee. After spells as a lawyer and film producer he courted many of the rising right-wing Republican members of Congress during the 1990s, including the future House majority leader Tom Delay. Working through various lobbying firms he offered gifts, campaign donations and other favours including golf trips to Scotland. At one time or another he represented Indian tribes, Russian energy companies and various sporting and gambling interests. Armed with inflated fees he spun a complex web of influence on Capitol Hill that was eventually to lead to the trial, conviction and imprisonment of former representatives Bob Ney and Tom Delay. A number of other officials in the Bush administration and especially those in the Department of the Interior were also convicted.

Abramoff was perhaps the most egregious example of a whole breed of lobbyists who worked on Capitol Hill and in the executive branch during the 1990s and 2000s. A culture of influence peddling pervaded Washington – a culture that was largely tolerated by the Bush administration. On his release from prison Abramoff worked for a year in a pizza parlour and later became a crusader against corruption in government. Casino Jack, a biopic of Abramoff's life starring Kevin Spacey, was released in 2010. In 2012 he was given his own talk radio show devoted to the reform of politics.

CONTROVERSY 9   DIVIDED GOVERNMENT: FOR AND AGAINST

Until 1968 divided government (DG) was very much the exception in the US. Indeed, in the twentieth century there were only 12 years of DG down to 1968. However, from 1969 to 2017 unified government prevailed for just eight years (1977–81, 1993–5 and 2009–2011; although from 1981 to 1987 the Republicans controlled the presidency and the Senate but not the House). Scholarship in this area usually distinguishes between the causes and the consequences of DG. As far as the causes are concerned most attention has been paid to whether DG is purposeful or structural. It could be that voters choose DG (or decide it on purpose). The usual reasoning here is that voters deliberately want to balance presidency and Congress. They may, for example, choose a Republican president because Republicans are traditionally stronger foreign policy leaders, but a Democratic Congress because the Democrats will typically be more generous with constituency benefits than the Republicans. More recently, voters may have chosen a Republican Congress to keep taxes low and eliminate the budget deficit, but opted for a Democratic president who was more liberal on the 'social' issues (health care, abortion, gun control and education). Other scholars have argued that DG is structural or unintended. Much of this work attempted to explain what until 1994 appeared to be the Democrats' permanent residency in the House of Representatives. In particular, they argued that incumbency in itself provided a range of advantages, such as familiarity, ability to raise money and a record of having delivered benefits (the pork barrel) to the constituents.

However, the election of successive Republican Congresses in 1994, a Democratic Congress in 2006 and then a dramatic return to the Republicans in 2010 and 2014 suggests that incumbency is not always a guarantee of success. In fact it may well be that the voters are choosing DG. Of course, this entire debate matters hardly at all if the consequences of DG are benign. Many believe that they are not. On the contrary, they argue that having Congress and the presidency controlled by different parties leads to 'gridlock' – inter-branch conflicts lead to a seizing up of the policy-making process – and also to an adversarial and vindictive politics of the sort that inspired the impeachment of Bill Clinton. While there seems to be some truth to these charges, DG may also have the result of limiting the size and scope of government, and this seems particularly true when the Republicans control Congress. Whatever the case, DG is unlikely to go away. An increasingly fickle electorate, the finely balanced distribution of party seats in Congress and the increasingly competitive nature of presidential elections will ensure this. This pattern was, however, broken in 2016 when the Republicans retained control of Congress and famously won the presidency. However, their majority in the Senate was small and Donald Trump did, of course, win the Electoral College vote but lost the popular vote by a margin of over 2.8 million. All this should lead us to believe that divided government will return sometime in the near future.

Biography   Paul Ryan – Speaker of the House and Republican Unifier?

Paul Ryan (Republican, Wisconsin), who was elected Speaker of the House in October 2015, is typical of a new breed of conservatives elected after 1994 who are committed both to public service and to being loyal to the conservative cause. In fact Ryan who was first elected in 1999 was widely regarded to be on the right of the Republican caucus at the time but because the House Republicans have moved even further to the right since then is now regarded as only 'moderately conservative'. Even so, he is the most conservative Republican speaker in the modern era. He was, of course, Mitt Romney's running mate in 2012 when it was assumed that his rightist views would balance Romney's reputation for pragmatism. He was also chosen as speaker following the resignation of John Boehner, who was unable to accommodate the party's right wing Freedom Caucus on budget and other matters. Ryan has the reputation of being a serious thinker who puts his principles before personal ambition – he accepted the speakership only reluctantly and also resisted the temptation of challenging Donald Trump for the nomination in 2016. While identified as one of the few politicians who have the potential for unifying the diverse constituency that makes up the modern Republican Party, the Trump candidacy posed awkward questions for Ryan. In early June 2016 Ryan effectively endorsed Trump by saying that he would vote for him. However, later he distanced himself from some of Trump's more controversial policy positions and even went so far as to condemn Trump on a number of occasions. However, once Trump was elected Ryan reverted to his earlier position and enthusiastically supported the new president.

Reform and Change in Congress

The major criticisms of Congress prevalent in the late 1960s and early 1970s stressed two failings: legislative business was dominated by a few senior committee chairpersons, and in its dealings with the executive Congress was failing either to provide realistic policy-making alternatives or to check the burgeoning growth of executive power. Commentators had long noted that, if these problems were to be solved, political party organizations in the two houses would have to take the lead. Indeed, if we think in terms of centralizing and decentralizing influences, party and party leadership are clearly centralizing forces, while the committee structure essentially disperses power. Party voting was particularly strong during the 1890–1910 period, when over half the roll calls (votes on the floor) involved 90 per cent of one party voting differently from 90 per cent of the other. As figure 9.4 shows, party unity has increased markedly in the past 20 years so that, as of 2016, most members of each party are voting with their party colleagues the vast majority of the time. These figures apply to the House where party voting has been most pronounced. Since 2008, however, the Senate too has moved further in the direction of party unity.

Part of the increase in party unity in recent years derives from the simple fact that, as a solid conservative voting block, the southern Democrats have declined in number and influence. In fact most of the South is now Republican and conservative.

The role of the southern Democrats as monopolists of almost all the leadership positions in Congress was the major cause of the reform movement in Congress that began in the 1970s. By the early 1970s frustration at this had reached such a point that a number of sweeping reforms were introduced, reaching a crescendo in 1975 following the election of the unusually liberal post-Watergate Congress in 1974. The major changes were:

1   In 1970, the House ended non-recorded teller voting and switched over to electronic voting on all roll calls. As a result, the number of roll calls increased dramatically from 177 in 1969 to 541 in 1978.
2   In 1973, all bill-drafting in committee was opened to public scrutiny, so exposing to organized interests and constituents the precise policy preferences of members.
3   The Democratic caucus in the House voted in 1971 to permit 10 or more members to demand a special vote on a disputed committee chairperson assignment. In 1975 all nominees for chairperson were subject to an automatic secret ballot by caucus members.
4   Also in 1975, the caucus voted to give the Speaker the power to appoint Rules Committee members, subject to caucus approval.
5   Since 1973 all Democratic House members have been guaranteed a major committee assignment, and since 1974 committee assignments have passed from the Ways and Means Committee (traditionally dominated by southerners) to the party's Steering and Policy Committee.
6   Sub-committees were greatly strengthened and increased in number by a series of measures, beginning with the 1970 Legislature Reorganization Act. In 1973, the subcommittees were provided with a 'Bill of Rights' that gave to the full committee caucus the power to set sub-committee jurisdictions and select chairpersons. Subsequently, sub-committees have been allocated extra staff.
7   Although the number of formal changes in the Senate was lower than in the House, reforms were taken in the same general direction and in some cases were quite radical. Committee meetings were opened up to the public, the Democratic caucus's power was strengthened in relation to the nomination of committee chairpersons, and it became much easier to end a filibuster than it was in the early 1970s. Moreover, the committee structure was rationalized, with the number of committees reduced and some overlapping jurisdictions eliminated.

All these reforms were designed to speed up the legislative process and to weaken the entrenched power of committee chairpersons. By so doing, members hoped to make Congress a more effective policy-making body and therefore enhance its position in relation to the executive. In fact, in the wake of the abuse of executive power represented by the conduct of the Vietnam War and Watergate, Congress passed a number of laws specifically designed to curb such excesses and to strengthen the legislative branch. The two most important of these measures were:

• *The 1973 War Powers Act.* Overriding a presidential veto, Congress acted in 1973 to limit the president's ability to conduct war without the prior approval of Congress.

Under this law the commitment of US armed forces could occur only if Congress declared war or authorized the use of forces or if the president acted in a national emergency. During emergency actions, presidents were required to win congressional support after 60 days, and a further 30 days could be granted. After the 90-day period Congress could act to stop the use of troops in a law that is not subject to a presidential veto.

- *The 1974 Budget and Impoundment Control Act.* A perennial complaint of Congress watchers in the post-war period was the failure of the institution to match the executive's budget-making capacity. Presidents presented annual budgets, which had effectively become national policy programmes. Congress, in contrast, seemed unable to see the budget as a coherent whole. Indeed, it dealt with finance in an incremental, piecemeal way, reflecting the fragmentation characteristic of bicameralism and the appropriations process. The 1974 Act attempted to compensate for these problems by creating budget committees in each House and a Congressional Budget Office to provide specialized technical information for both chambers and allow Congress to compete with the president as budget-maker.

The reform movement was fuelled by two main forces – the increasing electoral independence of individual members from party and regional ties which a more rapid turnover of members and other changes had produced, and the already noted disillusionment with the institution's ability to deal with executive power. Chapter 8 showed just how much constituency pressures have increased and how electoral success now depends less on traditional party organization and more on personal resources. In order to 'deliver the goods' to constituents, members needed two things: more control within Congress over legislation and more control over the executive policy-making process. While the reforms went a long way towards the achievement of both objectives, they also had the unintended effect of weakening party leadership in Congress.

During the early 1990s Democratic congressional leaders were only too aware that their control over members was all too limited. The experience of the 103rd Congress (1993–4), when much of President Clinton's programme died in a Democratic Congress, persuaded them of the need for further reform. However, given the entrenched power of large numbers of Democratic congresspersons, this was not possible, and reform had to wait until the arrival of a new cohort of Republican members in early 1995. As mentioned above, the new Speaker, Newt Gingrich, was intent on reform that would strengthen party leadership. His own powers were enhanced and serious efforts were made to weaken committee power in relation to party influence. The main changes were:

1. A one-third reduction in staff.
2. The control of all staff by the chair.
3. A three-term limit for committee and sub-committee chairs.
4. A limit of five sub-committees on most committees, and an overall reduction from 118 in the 103rd Congress to 77 in the 104th.
5. Abolition of the District of Columbia, Merchant Marine and Fisheries, and Post Office and Civil Service Committees.

6   Limiting most members to serving on two committees and a total of four sub-committees.

7   Requiring that all committee votes be published and no proxy voting be allowed.

8   Requiring that almost all committee meetings be open and allowing coverage on television and radio, if requested.

9   The Speaker may no longer, with modest exceptions, refer bills to multiple committees simultaneously.[5]

Although in total these reforms constitute a shift away from committee power, the committees do remain the focal point of activity in Congress. Moreover, any weakness in the party leaders was likely to result in some return of authority to the committees. It should be mentioned that, although parallel moves have occurred in the Senate, reforms were much less radical. As has always been the case, power in the Senate tends to reside in the influence of individual senators, rather than being determined by parliamentary rules and procedures. Although the Gingrich reforms look like a sensible rationalization of decision-making, they were criticized for undermining cross-party civility in the institution and thereby producing a much more combative and abrasive style of decision-making.[6] Moreover, a more partisan Congress works against the sort of bargaining and compromise which, historically, has been necessary for the legislative and executive branches to cooperate effectively.

With the election of George W. Bush in 2000, partisanship increased further as the Democrats felt embattled by an assertively conservative Republican Party. Moreover, politics became notably more ideological, emphasizing a trend that had been ongoing since about 1980 (see figure 9.5). Increased partisanship in Congress can largely be explained by two factors. First, the number of southern Democrats has declined. These members were conservative and often

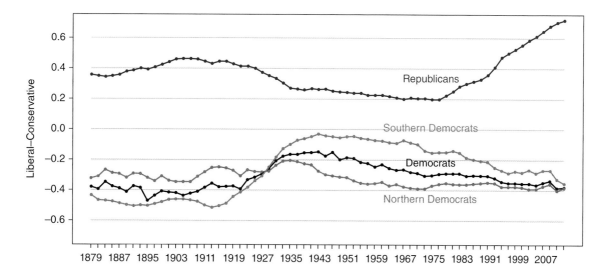

Figure 9.5 House of Representatives, 1879–2014: Chamber and party medians on liberal–conservative dimension
Source: The Polarization of the Congressional Parties, updated 21 March 2015, http://voteview.com/political_polarization_2014.html.

voted with the Republicans rather than their own party. In addition, the southern Democrats that remain have become markedly more liberal (figure 9.5 – the Senate has also polarized but slightly less than the House). Second, the Republicans in both houses have acquired a more cohesive ideology that combines conservatism on economic issues with conservatism on moral, civil liberties and foreign policy issues. As a result, Congress is now more ideologically charged, with personal and political animosities constantly being aired. We develop this point in the next chapters, but a more abrasive legislative environment has undoubtedly increased partisanship across the board in executive and state as well as legislative politics.

With the election of a Democratic Congress in 2006 a further wave of reforms was promised by Speaker Nancy Pelosi and Senate Majority Leader Harry Reid. In 2007 a bill was passed by both houses facilitating the identification of all 'earmarks' in spending bills so that wasteful pork-barrel projects could be identified and eliminated. In addition the bill called for 'unprecedented disclosure of how lobbyists interact with lawmakers', including a flat-out prohibition on lobbyists treating lawmakers to meals and trips; restrictions on the use by members of Congress of corporate jets; and a rule that barred former lawmakers from directly lobbying their old colleagues for two years after retiring, twice the old standard.

In spite of these good intentions, however, earmarking continued almost unabated during 2007 and 2008, with 11,000 earmarks worth more than $15 billon being enacted in 2007. It was not until 2011 that the House declared a moratorium on earmarks that resulted in a significant decline in the practice. However, ever-resourceful members have found ways around this ban, mainly by leaving unallocated amounts in spending bills that can be used for constituency benefits.

In one sense Congress is more efficient, for although no more bills are passed, those that are tend to be more complex and comprehensive. In addition, committees do expedite bills more rapidly than before. But the assignment of bills to several committees cancels out these advantages. In other words, Congress remains an institution where blockages, delays and vetoes can happen at several stages in the legislative process. As a result it retains an inbuilt conservative bias – it is easier to prevent things happening than to pass bills. The increase in the number of 'omnibus' bills represents an attempt to please as many members as possible. But each of these bills is passed only after an enormous amount of members' time and effort has been spent on them. In other words, coalition-building – always a defining characteristic of Congress – has assumed an even greater importance. Partly as a result of this institutional characteristic, although also because of the electoral changes outlined in chapter 6, a conservative coalition continues to exercise considerable influence. Until the early 1970s this consisted of southern Democrats and northern Republicans. During the 1980s it consisted of southern Democrats and Republicans from every region. Since 2006 it has consisted of all Republicans and an ever-dwindling band of Democrats.

Is Congress the 'Broken Branch'?

In some respects, Congress reflects the moods and wishes of the nation more accurately than for many years. This is a direct result of a new, much more intimate congressperson–constituency relationship and the easier access to legislators which organized interests now enjoy. Since the 1980s, public opinion has, at least on same issues, moved to the right, and Congress has accurately mirrored this trend. Indeed surveys repeatedly show that, although members of the public are deeply disillusioned with Congress as an institution, they actually hold their own members in relatively high regard.

However, none of this should blind us to the fact that the essential character of Congress remains. For while the House and Senate can respond to outside pressures or to perceptions that the collective interest must take precedence over particular interests – as was amply shown in the aftermath of 9/11 – collective action of this sort remains rare. The budget battles during 2011 and 2012, when no agreement on spending and tax increases was reached between the warring parties in Congress illustrates this point well. In its everyday business, party and particular interest dominates, for the central dilemma for Congress today is that building coalitions in a highly partisan but fragmented institution involves many trade-offs, with costs in terms of time, coherence and efficiency mounting steadily as the legislative process lumbers on, and, although reforms have to a degree streamlined decision-making, serving party ideology – and thus indirectly constituents – remains the major focus of individual legislators. In other words it is difficult to build a clear *institutional* identity in Congress. This greatly undermines some of the important institutional functions of Congress, including careful deliberation of legislation and oversight of the executive branch. In the late 1990s, amid much fanfare, Congress claimed some responsibility for balancing the national budget. Yet just a few years later the deficit ballooned once more. And while some of the blame for this must lie with a presidency preoccupied with issues of national security, neither Republicans nor Democrats in Congress have done much to hold back federal government spending. Indeed House and Senate Republicans endorsed the Bush administration's tax cuts of the early 2000s that had the effect of reducing government income. And, following the aftermath of the economic dislocation of the 2008–10 period, Congress was once again unable to act decisively. The Obama administration's attempts to build a consensus on how to bring the deficit under control foundered on the rocks of partisan squabbling and an inability of the two parties to agree on even the rudiments of a plan to achieve this objective. Given that Congress had agreed on automatic cuts and tax increases to trigger at the end of the 112th Congress should no agreement be concluded, the economy was in danger of falling off a 'Fiscal Cliff' at the start of the 113th Congress in 2013. In the event a last minute compromise was reached but only at the price of more brinkmanship in 2014 and 2015. Indeed, the resignation of John Boehner in 2015 was in part caused by a battle over spending – on this occasion the federal funding of Planned Parenthood, an organization that the Republicans regard as a champion of women's right to abortion.

Summary

Congress performs a number of vital functions, including representing constituency interests, passing all legislation, confirming nominations to the executive branch and the Supreme Court, approving international treaties, declaring war and overseeing the executive. In both houses power is dispersed to the committees with parties and party leadership provided a countervailing influence. Since the 1960s three main waves of reform have occurred. In the 1970s the main aim was to democratize the House and to reduce the power of the southern Democrats by undermining seniority. After 1994, the aim was to concentrate power in the Republican leadership and reduce the power of the committees. Most recently, after 2006, first the Democrats and then the Republicans tried to control 'earmarking' and the power of outside lobbyists. The chapter concluded with the claim that Congress continues to fail to act as an *institution* that can represent the public interest rather than to serve party ideology and the particular interests of constituents and lobbyists.

Questions for Discussion

1   What are the main powers of Congress? How well does it perform them?
2   What are the advantages and disadvantages of divided government? Answer with reference to the post-2010 period.
3   Why do presidents have such difficulty getting Congress to agree with their proposals? Answer with respect to the period since 2012.
4   What are the main responsibilities of the Speaker of the House of Representatives? Why has the position been so difficult to fill in recent years?

Glossary

Appropriations Committee   The House committee responsible for spending money

cloture (closure rule)   The Senate parliamentary device that allows the overturning of a Senate filibuster (see below). Sixty senators are needed to implement the device

Conference Committees   Cross-house committees designed to reconcile House and Senate versions of a bill

conservative coalition   The combination of southern Democrats and northern Republicans that had a built-in majority in Congress for much of the first two-thirds of the twentieth century

divided government   Party control of Congress and presidency split between the two parties

earmarking   Guaranteeing funding for specific constituency projects or benefits as attachments to bills

Floor Leaders (Majority/Minority)   Party leaders in the House and Senate

impeachment   The formal accusation of wrongdoing by an officeholder

investigative power (Congress)   The power of Congress to investigate the executive branch

Johnson Rule   As Senate Majority Leader Lyndon Johnson established that every freshman senator should have a committee assignment

Log-rolling   The exchange of political favours, or 'I'll scratch your back if you scratch mine'

oversight   The power of Congress to oversee the implementation of policy by the executive branch

pork-barrel politics   Legislation designed to benefit individual constituencies

President Pro Tempore   The honorary position held by the Vice President of the United States, who votes in the Senate in the event of a tie

presidential veto   The ability of presidents to veto legislation that can only be overturned by a two-thirds majority in both houses

purposeful voting   Voting deliberately designed to seat or unseat a candidate based on a rational calculation

Rules Committee   The House committee that decides on important parliamentary procedures, including agendas

select committees   Ad hoc committees established to investigate particular areas of public policy such as ageing or intelligence

Senate filibuster   The parliamentary device that allows a senator to speak without break until the time allotted to the debate is used up

Speaker, House   The leading party spokesperson in the House of Representatives

standing committees   The permanent committees in both houses

subpoena   A legally enforceable requirement that witnesses and evidence be available to congressional committees

War Powers Act 1973   The law that placed formal limits on the president's ability to wage war

Ways and Means Committee   The House committee responsible for taxation matters

Notes

1   Impeachment is a formal act of accusation similar to indictment. The impeachment process involves the gathering of evidence. If sufficient evidence is found, the Senate then tries the impeached person.

2   Burdett A. Loomis, *The Contemporary Congress* (New York: St Martin's Press, 1996), chapter 10.

3   Harold W. Stanley and Richard G. Niemi, *Vital Statistics on American Politics, 2003–2004* (Washington, DC: Congressional Quarterly Press, 2004), table 6.10. See also G. Calvin Mackenzie, *The Politics of Presidential Appointments* (New York: Free Press, 1981), table 8.1.

4   The institution of red-baiting, if not the actual practice, continued with the House Un-American Activities Committee (later the Internal Security Committee) until its abolition in 1975.

5   Loomis, *The Contemporary Congress*, p. 81.

6   Richard F. Fenno Jr, *Learning to Govern: An Institutional View of the 104th Congress* (Washington, DC: Brookings Institution, 1998).

Further Reading

A good textbook treatment of Congress is Burdett A. Loomis and Wendy A. Schiller, *The Contemporary Congress*, 6th edn (New York: Rowman and Littlefield, 2015). A comprehensive treatment is also provided by Roger H. Davidson, Walter J. Oleszek and Frances E. Lee, *Congress and its Members*, 15th edn (Washington, DC: Congressional Quarterly Press, 2015). The reforms of the 1970s and 1980s are covered in James L. Sundquist, *The Decline and Resurgence of Congress* (Washington, DC: Brookings Institution, 1981), and Roger H. Davidson (ed.), *The Post-Reform Congress* (New York: St Martin's Press, 1992). A recent critique of Congress is Thomas E. Mann and Norman J. Ornstein, *The Broken Branch: How Congress is Failing America and How to Get it Back on Track* (New York: Oxford University Press, 2006). Facts and figures on the institution can be found in Norman J. Ornstein, Thomas E. Mann and Michael J. Malbin, Andrew Rugg and Rafaella Wakeman, *Vital Statistics on Congress 2017* (Washington, DC: Brookings Institution, 2017).

CHAPTER 10
THE PRESIDENCY I
POWERS AND SELECTION

> ### Outline
>
> - Formal Sources of Power
> - Briefing: The American Presidency: A Unitary Institution
> - Informal Powers
> - Presidential Selection
> - Controversy 10. Primaries: For and Against
> - Briefing: The Role of Money
> - Presidential Selection: Faults and Foibles
> - Summary
> - Questions for Discussion
> - Glossary
> - Notes
> - Further Reading

There should be no bitterness or hate where the sole thought is the welfare of the United States of America. No man can occupy the office of President without realizing that he is President of all the people.

– FRANKLIN D. ROOSEVELT

In the American political system the president is the only national unifying force. Only the president is elected by a single national constituency, and *all* executive power is vested in the office. He has, therefore, both great responsibilities and great power. Because the chief executive is so centrally placed, public expectations of the office are high.[1] But in recent years few incumbents have possessed the qualities necessary to carry out the job efficiently and responsibly. Every president between the mid-1960s and 2016 was associated

American Politics and Society, Ninth Edition. David McKay.
© 2018 John Wiley & Sons Ltd. Published 2018 by John Wiley & Sons Ltd.

to a greater or lesser extent with failure. Lyndon Johnson was broken by the Vietnam War, and Richard Nixon by Watergate. Gerald Ford was little more than a caretaker president, and Jimmy Carter has been judged indecisive and politically inept. Ronald Reagan – in spite of attempts by many on the right to lionize him – will probably not be deemed one of the great presidents given his involvement in the Iran–Contra affair and the consequences of his economic policies. George Bush lacked the charisma and authority associated with great presidents and, after one term, achieved the dubious distinction of being beaten by a larger margin than any incumbent president since Herbert Hoover in 1932. Bill Clinton's ambitious first-term legislative programme came to little and, at mid-term, the Republicans captured both houses of Congress for the first time since 1952. The Republicans maintained their majority status for the whole of his second term, which was, of course, marked by the only impeachment of a sitting president in the twentieth century. George W. Bush suffered the indignity of losing the popular vote (but not the Electoral College vote) in 2000, and he won the 2004 contest with the lowest public approval rating of any winning president in the modern era. And during his second term these approval ratings sank further, never rising above 35 per cent after 2005 (see figure 11.1). Barack Obama's first term was characterized by constant wrangling with Congress, especially after the Republicans won back control of the House in 2010. Obama's approval ratings were also low – rarely rising above 50 per cent between 2010 and 2012. He none the less won re-election in 2012, faced as he was by a weak opponent in Mitt Romney but he ended his presidency with the re-election of a Republican Congress and a president set on repudiating his whole legislative and diplomatic legacy.

Curiously, this association of the office with mediocrity and the abuse of power is comparatively recent. Most texts on American government written during the 1950s and 1960s saw little wrong either with the nature of the office or with recent incumbents.[2] In retrospect the mid-century presidents – Franklin Roosevelt, Harry Truman, Dwight Eisenhower and John Kennedy – do seem impressive figures. So what has happened since? When trying to answer this question, most commentators point to what might be called the presidential environment, or the pressures that changes in the domestic and foreign policy environment have brought over the past 50 years. We will examine this claim in the next chapter. A second reason why presidents are now more often than not considered failures relates to the process whereby they are recruited, the argument being that changes in the selection process may now pre-select inappropriate presidential candidates. Before we examine this claim in detail, it is necessary briefly to outline the formal and informal sources of presidential power and to trace the growth of the modern presidency.

Formal Sources of Power

To an outside observer, one of the most remarkable features of the American political system is the concentration of governmental functions in one institution, the presidency. The Constitution is partly responsible for this, for it assigns to the presidency the roles of chief executive (Article 2, Section 1), commander-in-chief of the armed forces (Article 2, Section 2), chief diplomat (or the power to make treaties, Article 2, Section 2), chief recruiting officer to the executive and courts (Article 2, Section 2) and legislator (by making recommendations to Congress (Article 2, Section 3) and exercising the veto power under Article 1, Section 7. As was emphasized in chapter 3, the framers did not expect the president also to become *chief* legislator but, over the past 100 years, he has assumed this crucial function. Finally, the president is head of state, so must carry out all those diplomatic and ceremonial duties normally performed by constitutional monarchs (in Britain, the Netherlands) or presidents (in Israel, India and Italy).

Given this panoply of powers, it is not surprising that we automatically think of periods in American history in terms of incumbent presidents. The first years of the republic are inseparable from the personality and influence of George Washington. Andrew Jackson's presidencies are closely associated with the democratization of American politics and the rise of a modern two-party system. Abraham Lincoln's personal conduct of the Civil War effectively shaped a whole era in American history, while Woodrow Wilson was the first president to elevate the United States to the world diplomatic and military stage. Since the New Deal period – itself synonymous with the personage of Franklin D. Roosevelt – every president has made a lasting imprint on American and on world politics. Of course, presidents are constrained, sometimes seriously, by a number of domestic and international forces, but, within the United States, the chief executive is the natural and immediate focus of attention. As we saw in chapters 8 and 9, it would be difficult to consider Congress a natural leader or decision-maker. If anything, the opposite is true. Federalism fragments political power and authority even further, leaving the presidency (and, on rather rare occasions, the Supreme Court) as the sole unifying and centralizing influence in the system.

During the nineteenth and early twentieth centuries, it was the constitutionally assigned powers in military, foreign and diplomatic policy that tended to raise the visibility of the office. Indeed, through exercising these powers, some presidents greatly expanded and even exceeded their constitutional authority. In 1803, Thomas Jefferson authorized the purchase of the Louisiana Territories from France (see map 2.1) without consulting Congress. Abraham Lincoln's conduct of the Civil War was almost authoritarian, involving as it did a blockade of the South, the suspension of *habeas corpus* and unauthorized increases in the size of the army and navy. Much later Woodrow Wilson asked for, and was given, broad powers under the 1917 Lever Act to seize factories and mines and fix prices to help the American role in the First World War. But government, and especially the federal government, played a relatively minor part in economic and social life during this period. An assertive Congress could, and often did, dominate the political agenda. Without the vast bureaucratic and logistical resources of the modern executive, those presidents lacking political skills or unfortunate enough to preside over particularly difficult domestic events, such as the recriminations and confusion characteristic of the post-Civil War period, were truly secondary political figures. From the New Deal period onward, no president has been able to take the back stage because the demands on the office have multiplied so dramatically.

Since the Second World War, commander-in-chief has often meant control over several million men and women under arms and literally the power of life and death over humankind. As chief executives, modern presidents are responsible for numerous programmes and policies affecting every aspect of society. As chief legislator, the president takes to Congress a package of programmes, together with budget requests, which effectively mould the national political agenda. As we catalogued in chapter 4, the rise of federal regulations and grant programmes has meant that even local governments – those bodies so free from central control in the early Republic – now depend in part on the president's policies. Of course, the president is constrained when performing these functions and, of course, every industrial country has been required to centralize power in executives and greatly to expand the role of government. No Western country has acquired such formidable military and strategic power as has the US, however, and in few has the role of state been transformed in quite the way it has in America. The US is, after all, the country where government has traditionally been weak in relation to society, where the market was considered the most appropriate mechanism for distributing resources. Yet by the 2000s, more than 30 per cent of national income was accounted for by government spending, and, in some areas of economic and social life, the federal government had become a major source of income and support for large numbers of individuals, sub-national governments and corporations.

Briefing   The American Presidency – A Unitary Institution

One of the most notable characteristics of the presidency is its unitary nature. In most democratic political institutions chief executives are constrained by parties or by their peers within government. Neither applies in the USA. In almost all European polities and in many others throughout the world, for example, premiers can be removed either by coalition partners within ruling governments or by pressures applied through their own party colleagues. Thus, in the UK Margaret Thatcher was famously ousted by her own cabinet members in 1990, and in Continental Europe and Japan chief executives are frequently replaced when ruling coalitions fail to agree on policy positions. Even in France, where the presidency has most of the features of a unitary institution, the executive role is shared with a prime minister whose power is constrained by the incumbent's parliamentary base. In stark contrast, American presidents cannot be removed either by cabinet members or by party pressures. Indeed, presidents can do as they wish with cabinet members, none of whom have defined constitutional powers. On two occasions in recent history presidents have asked for the resignations of whole cabinets without imperiling their political positions (Richard Nixon in 1972 and Jimmy Carter in 1979). And the loose, decentralized nature of the party system ensures that presidents can usually ignore party pressures with relative impunity. Only impeachment for 'high crimes and misdemeanors' can remove a president, and this sanction has never been implemented to the point where presidents have been forced to stand down.

It could be argued that American institutional arrangements, especially federalism and the separation of powers, are ill suited to the sort of efficient and effective policy-making needed in a modern industrial society. If this is so, it increases the pressures on the executive even more, for, to repeat the point, only the presidency has a truly national constituency and only the presidency is the natural coordinator and organizer of national policy. Put another way, for many Americans, the president is the embodiment of the federal government. It is not surprising, then, that the public's ambivalence about the role of government should often show itself as hostility to the office of the president.

Informal Powers

Given the president's position at the apex of the constitutional system, it is not surprising that the office has also attracted a number of informal powers or influences additional to those constitutionally assigned. These include his position as party leader, agenda-setter, and national leader and world leader. All three can provide presidents with valuable extra resources, but they can also burden the office with extra duties and responsibilities.

Party leader

Once elected, presidents become the de facto leaders of their political party. This position carries with it both advantages and disadvantages. One advantage is that the opposition party has no equivalent position. Even when the party controls Congress (as in the late 1990s and, in the case of the House of Representatives, after 2010) there is no 'natural' leader of the opposition. In the 2008 presidential election year, for example, and before he won the nomination, Barack Obama had a number of competitors for title 'Party Leader'. Speaker Nancy Pelosi could lay claim to it, as could Senate Majority Leader Harry Reid, contender Hillary Clinton or even party chair Howard Dean. In contrast, and in spite of his difficulties, President George W. Bush remained the undisputed Republican leader – a fact that gives incumbent presidents a great advantage over opposition opponents in the race for the second term. This was amply demonstrated in 2012 when Obama enjoyed all the advantages of incumbency. In contrast, in 2016 Republican nominee and eventual president Donald Trump was an 'anti-party' candidate and only assumed (the uncertain) mantle of party leader once he came into office.

Being party leader certainly sounds grandiose and impressive enough – and in the British system, for example, being prime minister and party leader is indeed a great political advantage. But American political parties are often fragmented and weak. Only very rarely in recent history have presidents been *guaranteed* party support in Congress, and lucky is the president who knows he can count on the support of governors, mayors and other party leaders in the federal system. This accepted, weak party ties are almost certainly better than none at all, and presidents do use party connections to rally support (if not always successfully) during elections. Party is also the vital cue available to presidents when they make appointments to the executive branch. Without the myriad party contacts at congressional, state and local events, it would be difficult to fill all the 50,000-plus jobs that are nominated annually. Presidents also use this process to pay off debts for electoral and other services rendered.

Agenda-setter and national leader

Americans expect something more than the efficient execution of policy from their presidents, they also expect them to embody the spirit of the nation or, in Clinton Rossiter's term, to be the 'voice of the people'.[3] It should not be forgotten that the United States has relatively few symbols of national unity, such as the monarchy in Britain or a long-established culture rooted in language and custom as in France. In some respects, the institution of the presidency helps to fill this gap by providing Americans with a sense of national identity. When, at press conferences, an aide announces the entrance of 'The President of the United States', he is presenting a national symbol as well as chief executive, and the simple words of the announcement carry with them a level of respect and gravitas that is notably missing when a British prime minister or German chancellor appears in public.

Related is the expectation that the president will set the national political agenda. This means more than simply sending a legislative programme to Congress in the State of the Union message. The public looks first to the president to shape the terms of debate for national legislation and national action. Presidents are expected to be responsible for the economic and social well-being of the country and are held accountable at the polls should they fail to deliver. In 1992, for example, George Bush was blamed for economic recession and lost the election to Bill Clinton. In addition, during crises and natural disasters, the public looks first to the president for leadership, action and moral support. Hence, following such tragedies as the terrorist attacks on 11 September 2001 or Hurricane Katrina, which struck New Orleans in 2005, it is the president who was expected to respond and to show leadership.

World leader

In recent years, the president's role as a national leader has been reinforced by America's emergence as a world power, a fact amply demonstrated by President Kennedy's famous speech at the time of the Cuban missile crisis:

> Let no one doubt that this is a difficult and dangerous mission on which we have set out. No one can foresee precisely what course it will take or what costs or casualties will be incurred. Many months of sacrifice and self-discipline lie ahead – months in which both our patience and our will will be tested, months in which threats and denunciations will keep us aware of our dangers. But the greatest danger of all would be to do nothing. The path we have chosen for the present is full of hazards, as all paths are; but it is the one most consistent with our character and courage as a nation and our commitments around the world. The cost of freedom is always high – but Americans have always paid it. And one path we shall never choose, and that is the path of surrender or submission.[4]

Such stirring rhetoric may seem inappropriate at the start of a new century, but following the events of 9/11 in 2001 President Bush used very similar language when declaring the 'War on Terror'. In contrast to the fragmentation and particularism of Congress and the federal system, the president alone claims to see foreign policy in terms of what is in the interest of the whole country. In this sense, presidents attempt to elevate themselves above party interests, special interests and even ideology. Of course, they do not always succeed – indeed, few recent presidents have even come close to succeeding – but they are constantly striving for this very special status, and almost certainly the American public expects its presidents to play this part. Indeed, surveys consistently show that the public is dramatically more aware of the presidency (including the vice president) than other public offices, and this consciousness is acquired early in life.

As world leaders, recent presidents have had to adapt their styles and rhetoric in line with the changing nature of American power. But there can be no doubting their very special status in the international system. They can, in extreme circumstances such as those that prevailed after 9/11, even wield great power in the absence of support from much of the international community. Certainly, what presidents say and do is dramatically more important than the speeches and deeds of British and Japanese prime ministers, German chancellors and French presidents. This unique international status adds yet another dimension to presidential power, and also to the pressures of the office.

In sum, because presidents are considered the embodiment of the federal government, they are the focus of myriad public demands. Expectations of the office are, therefore, very high. At the same time public disquiet over the role of government in economy and society is often focused directly on the incumbent in the office of the presidency.

Presidential Selection

Returning to our original questions, it seems reasonable to hypothesize that the crisis of the modern presidency is one of recruitment. It may be simply that the wrong people are being selected for the job. What is the nature of the presidential nomination process? And why is it now the subject of such criticism? We can divide presidential elections into four distinct phases: pre-primary, primary, convention and campaign.

Pre-primary

It is often quipped that no sooner is a president elected than he has to start running for his second term. Although this is an exaggeration, it is not so far from the truth, for any candidate with even the slightest hope of winning nomination must plan his or her campaign several years ahead. In his build-up for the 1976 campaign, Jimmy Carter cultivated newspaper editors and political commentators more than a year before the convention. His strategy was simple: he had to raise his public visibility in order to neutralize the 'Jimmy who?' reaction whenever his name was uttered. Ronald Reagan announced himself more than two years before the 1980 election and by late 1982 former Vice President Walter Mondale was already grooming himself for the 1984 contest. In 1985 Vice President Bush was beginning to build an organization ready for 1988, and Bill Clinton made no secret of his ambition to run for president many years before he formally announced his candidacy in October 1991. By the beginning of Clinton's second term, Vice President Al Gore was carefully positioning himself for the contest in 2000, and Senator John Kerry declared his candidacy in September 2002, some 14 months prior to the election in 2004. In 2008 both Barack Obama and Hillary Clinton made their intentions known over a year before the start of the primary season, as did John McCain and Mitt Romney on the Republican side. Hillary Clinton announced her intention to run in April 2015 more than 18 months before the 2016 election and was quickly followed by Republican Donald Trump in June 2015.

The times are also important. Jimmy Carter's extraordinary journey from obscurity to president between 1972 and 1976 owed much to the prevailing disillusionment with 'Washington' and established party candidates. More typically, candidates must win the support of key political figures if they are to have any chance. In 1980 Ronald Reagan was endorsed by many of the leading Republicans and 'king-makers' of the political right; Gerald Ford notably lacked such support and was well advised to make an early retreat from the race. Edward Kennedy, in contrast, had failed to win the unequivocal endorsement of the Democratic establishment but soldiered on none the less. In 1992 Bill Clinton did win support from established sections of the Democratic Party, which almost certainly helped him to create the image of front-runner early in the campaign. An incumbent president naturally enjoys a huge advantage in winning the party's nomination, and there is no instance in recent years of a president who wants to stand failing to secure nomination.

Curiously, few incumbent vice presidents have been *elected* president in American history. George Bush Senior was to prove an exception, in part because he won the support of many leading Republicans early in Reagan's second term. By way of contrast, in 2000 Al Gore (Bill Clinton's vice president) largely shunned established Democratic figures – a fact that may have contributed to his very narrow Electoral College defeat by George W. Bush. The year 2008 witnessed the unusual spectacle of neither an incumbent president nor vice president standing (the first time this had occurred since 1952). Given the wide-open nature of the contest on both sides, it was not surprising that both parties sported several candidates even before the start of the primary season. The same dynamic applied to the Republicans in 2016 when the party sported more than half a dozen credible candidates early in the campaign.

The primaries

There was a time when a candidate with strong intra-party support could avoid the primary circuit. In 1968, for example, only 49 per cent of the votes cast by delegates at the Democratic convention were decided by primary election; the remainder were in the pocket of party caucuses. By 1976 this figure had risen to 75 per cent, thus making it absolutely essential for candidates to run in the primaries (see figure 5.2). So Hubert Humphrey's strategy of depending on his very considerable Democratic Party connections was successful in 1968, but suicidal just four years later when he entered the primaries late and was effectively beaten before the convention. Following reforms in the Democratic Party, the number of primaries was reduced in 1984 but increased again in the 1990s, so that today no candidate can afford to ignore them.

Today, there are 36 primaries in the Democratic Party and 41 in the Republican Party While the primary season remains lengthy, running from February to June, most of the important primaries are held in April or earlier. Unfortunately, the precise technicalities of primaries defy simple description because each state decides the timing, voter eligibility and general organization of its primary elections. More often than not these technicalities change with every election cycle. An important formal distinction is between *closed primaries*, operative in most states, which are open only to registered party members, and *open primaries*, where voters can vote for either party, but not both, by asking for that party's ballot at the polling station. They do not, in other words, have to be registered as Democrats or Republicans to vote in that party's election. A further distinction is between almost all the Democratic primaries, where delegates are assigned to candidates proportionately, and many Republican primaries, where delegates are, in 10 states in 2012, assigned on a winner-takes-all basis. Hence in 2008 the very close Democratic primary race between Hillary Clinton and Barack Obama was in part a result of a proportional allocation of delegates between two candidates with almost equal popular support. In those states without primaries for presidential nominations (all states have some form of primary for state-wide elections), party caucuses or meetings decide delegate selection. Over the past 30 years, primaries have become more important, not only because they have increased in number, but also because changes in party rules have had the effect of binding delegates more closely to candidates. Moreover, the partial switch back to caucuses in the Democratic Party that has occurred since the 1980s did not signal a return to 'old-style' party politics, for most of the new caucuses are very open (the number of people eligible to attend is very high) and as binding on delegates as primaries. There was a time when bargaining on the convention floor resulted in delegates switching their allegiances, so making the convention a key decision-maker in the nomination process. Today the primaries and caucuses proper play this role. A further important development is the role of the 'superdelegates' in the Democratic Party. As was discussed in chapter 5, superdelegates were created in the late 1970s to ensure that senior party officials (including incumbent members of Congress, and governors) had some say in the nomination of candidates. It was a shift of superdelegates from Hillary Clinton to Barack Obama that helped clinch his nomination in early June 2008. As will be discussed below, these same people are not in any way bound to candidates, however. At the convention they are in theory free to vote for whomever they choose.

Because candidates *must* enter the primaries, they must have the political, financial and even physical resources to endure the long series of campaigns involved. They must also have the *time*, for staging a series of primary campaigns is effectively a full-time job. As is developed below, this fact alone may pre-select certain sorts of candidates. Recent elections have also shown how important it is for candidates to make a good start. There is what might be called a 'media bandwagon effect', where a particular candidate is identified as a potential winner and this itself provides an essential impetus to his or her campaign. Some commentators have even gone as far as to claim that Iowa (an early party caucus state) and New Hampshire (the first primary) hold the key to the fortunes of candidates – and these are hardly representative areas of the United States. Certainly, Jimmy Carter did well in early contests in 1976 and 1980, which helped him to head off opponents with support in larger states. And in 2004 John Kerry, having won both the Iowa caucus and the New Hampshire primary, went on to seal the nomination. Even if candidates do not win all the early primaries, they must at least enter and perform reasonably well. Such was the case with the successful nominees in 1988, George Bush and Michael Dukakis. In 1992 Bill Clinton bucked the trend of winning early primaries. He *lost* the New Hampshire primary to Paul Tsongas,

Table 10.1 Delegate count 2016 primary season (% delegates allocated by date)

	Democrat	Republican
9 February, New Hampshire	1.67	1.8
27 February, South Carolina	3.85	5.15
1 March, Super Tuesday[a]	25.12	30.48
8 March, Michigan[a]	32.93	44.45
15 March, Ohio[a]	50.13	62.25
22 March Utah[a]	53.36	66.46
5 April, Wisconsin	58.89	68.27
19 April, New York[a]	64.44	73.64
3 May, Indiana	76.96	81.16
17 May, Oregon	80.72	85.25
7 June, California	95.5	100.00

Source: Various including reports from the *New York Times.*
[a]indicates more than one state holding a primary.

the South Dakota primary to Bob Kerrey and the Colorado primary to Jerry Brown. Not until 10 March, with the 'Super Tuesday' series of southern primaries, did he establish a lead. Similarly, the early primaries in 2008 see-sawed between the two major contestants, with Hillary Clinton winning New Hampshire and Obama winning Iowa. In 2012 Mitt Romney enjoyed a relatively easy passage to the nomination by winning most of the early primary states. However in 2016 it was not until quite late in the primary season that both Hillary Clinton (Democrat) and Donald Trump (Republican) were assured of victory.

As can be seen from table 10.1, the introduction of Super Tuesday in March when a large number of states hold primaries, means that the two leading candidates in each party – if not the winner – are likely to be known very early in the primary season. This was true even in 2016 when few believed that Donald Trump's early primary successes would be maintained during the rest of the season. In the event, however, his early successes were consolidated after Super Tuesday and he went on to win the nomination by a considerable margin.

CONTROVERSY 10 PRIMARIES: FOR AND AGAINST

Primaries were originally introduced as an anti-party device. By giving to the voters the ability to vote directly for the candidate of their choice, primaries could by-pass party nominations where decisions were often made by a very few party bosses intent on choosing 'their' candidate. The last time this happened at the presidential level was in 1968, where closed caucuses in a number of states chose Democratic Vice President Hubert Humphrey. Robert Kennedy opted for the primary route, but was assassinated before he could face Humphrey at the convention. Primaries also act as 'beauty contests' for candidates, who are able to present both themselves and their policies to the public before the campaign proper. Strengths and weaknesses can be exposed and assessed by the voters. In 2008, for example, Rudy Giuliani, the early Republican front-runner, proved to have little electoral appeal and was soon overtaken by John McCain. Similarly in 2012 all the Republican candidates bar Mitt Romney were well to the right of the typical Republican and Independent voter. Sensing this, many Republicans opted for Romney as the most 'electable' candidate.

It could be argued that in the internet age primaries have the further advantage of giving power to those of limited financial resources both among candidates and among the public. In 2008 Barack Obama had little personal wealth but was able to raise vast amounts from numerous small contributors sending money online. No other candidate was able to use this method so effectively. While primaries appear to democratize the selection of candidates, they also have disadvantages. People who vote in primaries (and even more so in caucuses) tend to be more passionate about politics and candidates. They tend, therefore, to the extremes of both the right and the left. Radical candidates often have an advantage, therefore, as was the case with the leftist candidacy of George McGovern in 1972 and, more notably, Donald Trump in 2016, neither of whom was typical of voters as a whole.

A further criticism is that primaries deny peer group appraisal of candidates. Hence incumbent party officials from governors to presidents and members of Congress have little say in the process. In most countries equivalent politicians are powerful sponsors of candidates for the position of chief executive. This is, of course, the reason why the Democratic Party created superdelegates in the late 1970s – although they have never been decisive in countering the popular vote.

Finally, primaries are expensive and extend over a long period. They sap a lot of energy on the part of the candidates, the media and the public. Because of the need to survive the gruelling schedule, certain personality and even physical types are rewarded (those who are telegenic, extrovert, charismatic) while their opposites are punished. The former may or may not turn out to be good presidents, of course.

Briefing   The Role of Money

Federal election campaigns are expensive, and none more so than presidential campaigns. The Federal Election Commission (FEC) data show that in 2004 more than $1 billion was spent by all candidates on the primaries, the conventions and the federal election campaign. This was significantly greater than in 2000, when $674 million was spent. In 2008 these figures were exceeded again, with just under $1 billion being spent on the pre-convention primaries and caucuses. Barack Obama was the spending champion in 2008, managing to get through almost $300 million in the pre-convention period. These are the official figures; the actual sums are actually significantly greater. For although the 2002 Bipartisan Campaign Finance Reform Act outlawed 'soft money' (non-political party spending in favour or against candidates), it did not outlaw a whole range of activities that do not have to be reported to the FEC. These include voting drives, issue campaigns, door-to-door campaigning on behalf of candidates and other 'unofficial' electoral activities. The year 2008 was notable for another reason – Barack Obama's extraordinary ability to raise large amounts of money from numerous small contributors. By the end of August 2008 he had raised a staggering $427 million in this way. Although the law limits individual contributions to $2,000 per candidate, there is no limit on the total either from individuals or from political action committees (whose limit per candidate is $5,000). This proved a great boon during the campaign, because Obama was able to eschew federal funding, which provides matching funds but only up to strict limits. As a result, both Barack Obama and John McCain rejected federal funding in 2008, thus enabling them to spend as much as they could raise. In the event, Obama raised $742 million and McCain $346 million. From 2010 the money problem was compounded by the Supreme Court decision abolishing the limits on money raised by corporations, unions and other organizations. In the event, the 2012 contest cost a staggering $6 billion, spent on all the primary contests and on the campaign proper. Although the Republicans received donations from big-money contributors, the Obama campaign continued to generate millions from a large number of small contributors. 2016 was unusual because the eventual winner, Donald Trump, actually spent considerably less than his Democratic opponent, Hillary Clinton. Instead he relied on numerous public appearances in the crucial 'battleground states' that were extensively covered by the national media. In addition his frequent – and also well publicized – use of social media and in particular his Twitter account – gave him a much noted (and free) national platform for the expression of his often highly controversial views.

The nominating conventions

To foreign observers, nothing better represents the sheer theatre of American politics than the nominating conventions. During the summer before the election, several thousand party delegates meet to choose their presidential and vice-presidential candidates in an apparently crazy few days of party festival. Although policy is discussed at conventions, they are more of a media event, where candidates and their supporters strive to achieve maximum public exposure. There was a time when the conventions actually chose candidates for the general election, with several ballots required before a majority (until 1936, two-thirds in the Democratic convention) of all the delegates could agree on a candidate. During this period, conventions were an accurate reflection of the vote-trading and coalition formation typical of American politics generally. They were, in other words, highly political, involving deals, bargains and periodic deadlocks as party bosses switched their blocks of delegate votes or opted for a compromise candidate. In recent elections, however, the winning candidate has been identifiable before the convention begins, as the primaries effectively decide the contest – although in 2008 the Democratic race was close enough for there to be much speculation that it might be decided at the convention.

The spread of primaries was part of a general party reform movement prevalent in the late 1960s and 1970s. In the case of the Democrats, calls for reform were greatly aided by the events at the 1968 convention in Chicago, when an old-style party organization nominated Vice President Hubert Humphrey, a candidate associated with organized labour and Lyndon Johnson's conduct of the Vietnam War. But this was the period when the social issue (the war, minority rights, the liberalization of society) was in the ascendant, and traditional Democratic Party organizations were notably unsympathetic to the new movement. Following violent scenes outside the convention hall when the young, radicals and other excluded groups demonstrated against the old-style machine politics, the party was plunged into a turmoil of recriminations.[5] The upshot was the appointment of a commission (the McGovern–Fraser Commission) to recommend changes in delegate selection. Since then the party has never been free of commissions, reforms and debate on how best to organize itself.

McGovern–Fraser resulted in two major changes. From 1972, representation at conventions from minorities and under-represented groups – blacks, women, youth – was greatly increased. Second, a system of proportional representation was recommended for primary elections. Previously, the person winning the primary took all the delegate votes (winner takes all). McGovern–Fraser recommended that the delegates given to a candidate should be in proportion to his share of the vote. Between 1972 and 1984 the rules were modified further following the advice of more commissions, most notably the Hunt Commission, which reported in 1982. From 1980 a minimum 20 per cent cut-off point was established in the primaries to discourage frivolous candidacies (it has since been set at a minimum of 15 per cent). The original McGovern–Fraser idea of quotas for under-represented groups has been replaced with affirmative-action requirements, and, beginning in the early 1970s, the rules governing selection of delegates to party caucuses have been gradually modified to 'open up' meetings and committees to rank-and-file members.

Very generally, these reforms (which were paralleled in an attenuated form in the Republican Party) involved the struggle, which was discussed in chapter 6, between old-style party professionals and a new breed of party activists. As we established, the new party activists generally won out, yet it would be misleading to argue that somehow party influences are stronger as a consequence. In fact the opposite is true. Because delegates are now mainly chosen in primaries and are almost always tied to particular candidates, the voters, not party activists, decide the nomination. And given the rise of candidates' own vote-getting organizations, this effectively relegates political parties to a lesser position in the nominating process.

Not only has the drive for more democratic procedures in party nominations weakened the influence of party, it has also failed to correct the non-representative nature of convention delegates. In 1972 the delegates were certainly younger and more radical than in 1968, but in ideological and programmatic terms they were *not* typical of the average Democratic voter.[6] By 1980 Democratic delegates were markedly more female and black than before, but they were also more middle class, had fewer links with industrial trade unions and traditional Democratic Party organizations, and stronger links with the growing public sector unions. Aware of this, the Hunt Commission also recommended the creation of 'superdelegates' to the convention, or regular party-elected or -appointed officials. It was assumed that state legislators, governors and members of Congress would be more moderate in their views and would inject an element of peer group review into the selection process. In 1984 and again in 1988 about one-seventh of all delegates to the convention were reserved for party and public officials, and, as mentioned, caucuses replaced primaries in several states. Most observers agree that these changes did little to alter the fundamental nature of the nomination process. Although a 'traditional' candidate, Walter Mondale, was nominated, Gary Hart, a 'new-style' candidate, very nearly beat him. And the candidacy of civil rights activist Jesse Jackson, who did well in many primaries, showed how the system was basically unchanged since 1980. In 1988 neither of the two front-runners was an old-style party candidate. Jesse Jackson's impressive showing in the primaries and caucuses came to nothing, not because Michael Dukakis had won the support of the party regulars (which he had), but because Dukakis won more primaries and caucuses than Jackson and therefore came to the convention with enough delegate votes to ensure victory.

By 1992 the number of 'superdelegates' was increased to nearly one-fifth of the total but, again, there is no evidence that their presence made any difference. For one thing, superdelegates are not necessarily more moderate than the typical Democratic voter. For another, it is difficult to imagine how, in a media-infused process, they could make a difference. As Walter Dean Burnham has put it, 'They're little more than window dressing. There's not a lot of room for peer review in the television era … there's just no way superdelegates can exercise a credible veto.'[7] On the other hand, as table 10.2 shows, by the late 1980s almost all important party officeholders were at least attending the Democratic conventions even if their influence was not easy to measure. These figures have remained roughly similar ever since.

Table 10.2   Representation of major elected officials at national conventions, 1968–92 (%)

	1968	1972	1976	1980	1984	1988	1992
Democrats							
Governors	96	57	44	74	91	100	96[a]
US senators	61	28	18	14	56	85	81[a]
US representatives	32	12	14	14	62	87	88[a]
Republicans							
Governors	92	80	69	68	93	82	81
US senators	58	50	59	63	56	62	42
US representatives	31	19	36	40	53	55	30

Source: Figures provided by the Democratic and Republican National Committees, as reproduced in Stephen J. Wayne, *The Road to the White House 1996: The Politics of Presidential Elections* (New York: St Martin's Press, 1996), table 4.6.

Note: Figures represent the percentages of Democratic or Republican officeholders from each group who served as delegates.

[a]Unpledged delegates (i.e. 'superdelegates') only, not including those officeholders who went to the Democratic convention by other means.

The Hunt Commission also recommended that the primary season be shortened and that more primaries be held on the same days. In the event, the primary season was shortened slightly (state laws, not party rules, decide the timing of primaries, although the courts have given the parties the right to decide who is eligible to vote in primaries). Since 1988 some states vote on the same day (the so-called Super Tuesday, 6 March in 2012, when 10 states voted). This last innovation did little to help southerner Al Gore in 1988, but it gave southerner Bill Clinton an essential boost in 1992. Generally the nominees are known by April, although this general rule was broken in 2008 because of the very evenly balanced support enjoyed by the leading Democratic contenders, Barack Obama and Hillary Clinton.

In 2016 Hillary Clinton eventually won the Democratic nomination but only after a bruising battle with the socialist senator from Vermont, Bernie Sanders. By way of contrast Donald Trump had a relatively easy pathway to the nomination having knocked out contenders Jeb Bush and Marco Rubio (both of Florida) quite early in the primary season. He later put paid to the candidacy of John Kasich (Ohio) and eventually beat his nearest opponent, Ted Cruz (Texas) by an impressive 1441 delegates to 551.

The campaign

Before the campaign proper starts, nominated candidates have to choose their vice-presidential running mates. Until recently this decision was taken at the convention. Today, however, nominated candidates choose their running mates some weeks before the convention. Nominees use the opportunity to heal political wounds or to balance the ticket geographically or ideologically. In 1960 John Kennedy's choice of Lyndon Johnson helped to smooth relations between the two main contenders for the nomination; it also balanced the ticket between the urbane Catholic northeasterner and the more populist Protestant southerner. In 2004 the urbane and slightly aloof John Kerry chose the more populist and accessible North Carolina senator, John Edwards. The choice is a crucial one for, although the office of vice president is not in itself very important, no fewer than five of the last 10 vice presidents eventually became presidents themselves (Harry Truman, Lyndon Johnson, Richard Nixon, Gerald Ford and George Bush Senior). Occasionally things go terribly wrong. George McGovern's initial choice of Thomas Eagleton in 1972 had to be changed with indecent haste once it was revealed that Eagleton had once received psychiatric treatment. In 1980 Ronald Reagan's first preference, Gerald Ford, proved politically tactless when Ford, not unsurprisingly, laid down certain conditions for acceptance, including a demand that the vice president should be more an executive partner than a subordinate. In 1984 Democratic vice-presidential candidate Geraldine Ferraro was constantly dogged by revelations of her husband's financial wrongdoings. In 1988 George Bush's choice of Dan Quayle, the junior senator from Indiana, was greeted with surprise and incredulity among Republicans and Democrats alike. Quayle apparently did little to balance the ticket in geographical or ideological terms. In addition he proved an inept and inexperienced campaigner. After a few weeks, the Bush organization was obliged to shunt Quayle off into the political sidings, where any damage he might do would be kept to a minimum. In stark contrast, Bill Clinton chose Tennessee Senator Al Gore as his 1992 running mate. While Gore did not balance the ticket – he was close to being a political clone of Bill Clinton – he did add to Clinton's image of youth, moderation and vigour. In 2000 the politically inexperienced George Bush chose the seasoned Republican stalwart Dick Cheney as his running mate. Cheney had wide experience of government, having been Secretary of Defense in the George Bush 1988–92 administration. In 2008 Barack Obama chose Senator Joe Biden, who had long experience of Washington politics and of foreign policy. John McCain, however, gambled with his choice of Sarah Palin the Governor of Alaska. McCain hoped that an attractive younger woman with right-wing views would strengthen his appeal among the Republican right while broadening it among other groups. But Palin's inexperience and political naivety were to prove a liability rather than an asset – especially as she was constantly lampooned in satirical TV shows such as *The Daily Show* and *Saturday Night Live*. In 2012 Obama stayed with Joe Biden, and Republican candidate Mitt Romney chose Paul Ryan – a fiscally conservative congressman from Wisconsin. It is doubtful that this choice did much to influence the outcome of the election. However in 2016 Donald Trump shrewdly chose Indiana Governor Mike Pence as his running mate. Pence represented 'traditional' Republican conservatism. He was also well connected in Washington having spent 12 years in Congress and served as the Republican Conference Chairman in the House of Representatives (the third highest ranking position in the House party hierarchy). The Pence candidacy helped Trump ingratiate himself with the Washington establishment and also served as an antidote to Trump's unconventional and often unpredictable campaign tactics.

Both the pre-convention and post-convention campaigns are expensive. Advertising, and particularly television advertising, takes the lion's share. Indeed, spending on television has risen almost exponentially since the first major exposure of candidates during the 1960 campaign, when John Kennedy confronted Richard Nixon in live debates. What effect it has on the voters is, however, an open question. Some evidence exists to suggest that general television advertising has little effect; most voters apparently acquire a positive or negative impression of candidates quite early on, and then their perceptions are based on performance rather than image.[8] What advertising and the presidential debates almost certainly do, however, is *reinforce* public perceptions of candidates. In 1988, for example, the Bush campaign's efforts to label Dukakis as a liberal who was soft on law and order almost certainly confirmed in the minds of many voters – Republican, Democratic and Independent – what they had suspected. Similarly, in 1996 Bill Clinton's constant reference to 'building a bridge to the twenty-first century' contrasted with Bob Dole's references to the values of the past and helped to reinforce his appeal as the candidate of youth and of the future. A similar pattern dominated the 2008 campaign when the deepening economic crisis gave Obama the opportunity to emphasize 'change' in contrast to the failed policies of the Republicans. No candidate can afford to drop his or her guard, therefore; television is widely perceived as important even if its effects are difficult to measure.[9] In 1992 Ross Perot used television to quite remarkable effect. By July he was polling approval ratings as high as the party candidates. His subsequent withdrawal and re-entry reduced his support, but he still managed to win 19 per cent of the vote. The 2012 contest was largely devoid of simple rallying slogans, although a clear ideological edge to the contest existed with the president branding Mitt Romney as champion of the rich and privileged. In contrast the

2016 Republican convention acted as a sort of coronation for Donald Trump. Few anti-Trump delegates were present and both during the convention and subsequent campaign Trump loyalists provided vocal support for their candidate. This included constant attacks on their Democratic rival Hillary Clinton including chants of 'lock her up, lock her up!' which referred to allegations that she had used an illegal personal email server to send classified emails during her time as Secretary of State.

For most candidates, a high level of public exposure is maintained by constant travel, usually by air, but still a candidate may hire a train to re-enact the famous whistle-stop tours of an earlier era. Incumbent presidents standing for re-election are usually less eager to engage in constant public image-building. They do, after all, enjoy the advantages of incumbency and can exploit their established position as statesmen. In 1972, for example, Richard Nixon appeared in public infrequently and relied instead on the prestige of the presidential office when appealing to the voters. Whatever the campaign strategy, all candidates continue during the last two or three months before the election to build political bridges, and to strengthen the coalition of support they must already have established to have won the nomination. To non-American observers, the campaigns are remarkably free from reference to specific programmes and policies. Indeed, candidates score points against opponents or make reference to very broad issues and ideological labels. Michael Dukakis was condemned by George Bush as inexperienced and incapable of upholding American power and prestige abroad. Dukakis in turn criticized Bush for his insensitivity to the needs of ordinary citizens. Attacking opponents may not be the only focus. Reagan promised in 1980 to 'get America back to work'. Richard Nixon in 1968 pledged that he would pursue 'peace with honour' in Vietnam. In 1992 Bill Clinton repeatedly made references to the state of the economy and the need for change. George Bush steered away from the issues and emphasized the allegedly weak character of his opponent. In the context of a continuing economic recession this proved an ineffective strategy. In 2000 Al Gore promised to use what was then a budget surplus to cut some taxes but also to increase social spending. By way of contrast George W. Bush promised to reduce taxes across the board, including for richer Americans. This was a pledge he carried out to the letter once elected president. The 2004 contest was, of course, dominated by security concerns, but also by issues relating to family values. On both, incumbent president George W. Bush managed to build an electoral advantage over opponent John Kerry. In contrast, in 2008 the economy dominated the election. In spite of efforts to distance himself from President Bush, John McCain was unable to shake off some association with what were widely regarded as the failed economic policies of the previous eight years. The year 2016 was different again for although the economy had bounced back from recession, real wages for many Americans had continued to stagnate. Donald Trump was able to exploit this by appealing in particular to white working-class voters by promising them jobs and increased income by restricting immigration and offering protection from 'unfair' foreign competition. As we have already noted, the whole of the campaign, pre- and post-convention, has increasingly become an exercise dependent not on traditional party organization but on *personal* party organization and, in some cases, simply on personal followings. Again, this demonstrates the general trend towards personality- rather than party-based politics.

Presidential Selection: Faults and Foibles

Many of the criticisms of the type of person who today is likely to end up as the Democratic or Republican candidate for president relate to party and campaign finance reforms, most of which have weakened candidates' ties with party organizations. Under the 1971 and 1974 Federal Election Campaign Acts, primary candidates receive matching federal funds (financed by a $3 check-off on all income tax returns). In 1992 Clinton and Dole received $23 million between them. In addition, around $11 million was available for each party for the party conventions. During the campaign proper a further subsidy is available provided candidates do not spend more than this from money raised from other sources. In 1996 Clinton and Dole spent a total of $120 million in public money between them. National and state local party committees can also spend a limited amount on the campaign. Crucially, candidates have to raise most of this money from large numbers of individual contributors. Voters can contribute no more than $1,000 to candidates per election (primary and general election) and only $250 of this qualifies for matching funds. Following a 1976 Supreme Court decision (*Buckley* v. *Valeo*), no limit exists on what candidates can themselves spend on their own campaigns. In 1992 Independent Ross Perot spent *only* his own money, and in 1996 Republican candidate Steve Forbes spent a staggering $37 million of his own money. While personal wealth was an important factor in winning the Republican nomination for Mitt Romney in 2012, it played little part in the ensuing campaign against President Obama. For 2012 was the first election fought after the 2010 Supreme Court *Citizens United* decision that effectively removed limits on corporate donations. As a result, Romney could rely on large SuperPAC contributions rather than use his own money.

Ronald Reagan and (in 1976) Jimmy Carter were 'unemployed', middle-aged (or even elderly) men with no experience of Washington and the wider international community. In 1988 and 1992 both Michael Dukakis and Bill Clinton were incumbent governors, but again both lacked any Washington experience. They owed their success to undisputed political acumen devoted to winning their party's nomination. This involved mobilizing a personal party following and exploiting the uniquely open – even populist – nature of the 'new' American nomination process. This tendency was even more extreme in 2016 when 70-year-old Donald Trump a demagogic property developer with no political experience whatsoever became the nominee of the Republican Party. As the critique bluntly asserts, such a system encourages the candidacy of a breed of politicians – the 'unemployed', ambitious and instrumental (and often wealthy) – who are much less likely to make good presidents than those tested by peer group pressures and the rigours of many years' experience in high office.

There is, without doubt, a great deal of truth to these charges. Certainly, few successful European leaders have assumed office with as little experience of the world of high politics as did Ronald Reagan, Bill Clinton or, especially, Donald Trump. But we should be wary of extrapolating from so small a sample; the same accusation would, after all, be difficult to level at the four 'failures' among recent presidents – Lyndon Johnson, ex-Senate Majority Leader and vice president; Richard Nixon, ex-member of Congress, senator and vice president; and Gerald Ford, ex-House Minority Leader and established party man. In 1988 the

American people elected a man of very broad experience, for George Bush had not only been vice president for eight years, he had also been a member of Congress, chief of the CIA and the US ambassador to the United Nations. And while the inexperienced small-state governor Bill Clinton won the Democratic nomination, in 1996 the Republican nomination went to the vastly experienced ex-Senate Majority Leader, Bob Dole. In 2000 both candidates were old-style in the sense that both were members of long-established and highly successful political families. Al Gore comes from a famous Tennessee 'dynasty' that has included major state and national (Senate) figures, and George W. Bush is, of course, the son of a recently incumbent president, although he has remarkably little political experience. However, the eventual winner, Bush, had no experience of Washington and, indeed, very little experience of politics in general. He had served one term as governor of Texas, but his position carried with it relatively little executive power. Perhaps for this reason, Bush gathered around him a number of old Republican hands including Vice President Dick Cheney and Defense Secretary Donald H. Rumsfeld. John Kerry, the 2004 Democratic candidate was an unusually seasoned political campaigner having been in the Senate for 22 years.

The year 2008 also appeared in part to break the mould. Republican candidate John McCain was first elected to the Senate in 1986 and had been a prominent figure in national politics for much of that time. This said, his opponent Barack Obama had been in the Senate for barely four years, although he did have an unusually cosmopolitan upbringing and background. In 2012 Barack Obama faced ex-Massachusetts one-term governor Mitt Romney. While Romney looked inexperienced, he hailed from a family with a long political pedigree, his father having run for the Republican nomination in 1968.

Of course, at least six old-style party candidates (Hubert Humphrey, Gerald Ford, Walter Mondale, Bob Dole, John McCain and Hillary Clinton) did *lose* elections, which may vindicate the charges, but then so did George McGovern in 1972 (very much a non-party candidate). In 1992 an incumbent president was beaten by what at first sight looks like another 'outsider' candidate, the governor of Arkansas – a very small, poor, southern state. But in many respects Bill Clinton was an unusual outsider – he was well connected with the Democratic Party establishment, was widely travelled and had received an elite education at Yale and Oxford. In fact he had all the attributes of the ideal late twentieth-century candidate – his main advantage lay not in long-established party contacts and experience in government, but in the fact that he was a brilliant campaigner.

Old-style candidate Al Gore also lost in 2000 – although only in the Electoral College. And, as noted, in spite of his illustrious family provenance, the inexperienced and sometimes naive George W. Bush looked more like a new-style than an old-style candidate. In 2008 Barack Obama was a new-style candidate – but one with strong backing from the Democratic establishment, including Senator Edward Kennedy. And the defeated 2016 candidate, Hillary Clinton, had almost the ultimate CV to qualify her for the presidency – eight years as First Lady, eight years a US Senator and four years as Secretary of State. Even so she lost the Electoral College, though she did win the popular vote by a margin of nearly 3 million. We can, therefore, conclude that the American presidential selection process is far from ideal and has no doubt contributed to a succession of less than impressive

Plate 10.1   Candidates Hillary Clinton and Donald Trump hold third presidential debate at the University of Nevada. *Source:* Bloomberg/Getty, http://www.gettyimages.co.uk/license/615758800.

presidents. But as the next chapter shows, the very considerable problems associated with the office in recent years also have their origins in forces beyond the technicalities of the selection process.

Summary

Presidents have considerable formal powers – chief executive, commander-in-chief, head of state – and their informal powers – party leader, agenda-setter, world leader – are almost as important. Given the sheer magnitude of what presidents can do both at home and abroad, the way in which they are selected is of great interest. The spread of presidential primaries and changes in campaign finance law have transformed the nomination landscape in the past 30 years. Today candidates have to enter the primaries and win popular support in order to secure the nomination. This undoubtedly limits the pool of candidates able to stand and also gives to poorly qualified candidates the chance of winning the nomination. Party conventions no longer choose candidates. Instead they serve to boost party morale and to publicize the nominees. Campaigns proper are expensive but crucial showcases for the candidates.

Questions for Discussion

1 What are the main informal powers of the president? How important are they in relation to the institution's formal powers?

2 Give an account of the 2016 presidential election campaign. Did the ways in which the candidates conducted the campaign make a difference to the outcome?

3 What are the advantages and disadvantages of the primary system of nominating candidates?

4 How has the role of money in the nomination process changed since the early 1970s?

Glossary

Civil War   The war between the North and the South waged between 1861 and 1865

closed primaries   Primaries where only registered voters of the party holding the primary can cast a ballot

matching federal funds   The device whereby the federal government will match candidate contributions in residential elections up to defined limits

nominating conventions   The party conventions held to formally nominate candidates in the summer of election years

old-style party politics   Party politics based on 'insider' influence and the operation of political machines

open primaries   Primaries where voters of any party can cast a vote

superdelegates   Delegates to the Democratic National Convention chosen on the basis of their position or political service

Watergate   The label attached to attempts by the Nixon administration to spy on and discredit the Democrats in the presidential election of 1972

Notes

1 Because there is no historical example of a female president (or candidate), the presidency is referred to in the masculine throughout this chapter. Things may, of course, well change early in the twenty-first century.

2 For a review of this 'textbook' view of the presidency, see Thomas Cronin, *The State of the Presidency* (Boston, MA: Little, Brown, 1990), chapter 2.

3 In the heady optimism of the late 1950s, Clinton Rossiter's famous essay, *The American Presidency* (New York: Harcourt Brace, 1960), pp. 4–25, listed five informal powers which continue to resonate today: (a) voice of the party; (b) voice of the people; (c) protector of the peace; (d) manager of prosperity; (e) world leader.

4   Quoted in Robert F. Kennedy, *Thirteen Days* (New York: Norton, 1971), p. 37.

5   For a graphic description of these harrowing events and the contrast with the Republican convention of that year, see Norman Mailer, *Miami and the Siege of Chicago* (New York: Donald I. Fine, 1986).

6   See Jeane Kirkpatrick, *The New Presidential Elite* (New York: Russell Sage/Twentieth Century Fund, 1976).

7   Quoted in *Congressional Quarterly*, 4 July 1992, p. 18.

8   Thomas E. Patterson and Robert D. McClure, *The Unseeing Eye: the Myth of Television Power in National Elections* (New York: Putnam, 1976).

9   For an account of how TV encourages personality politics, see Roderick P. Hart, *Seducing America: How Television Charms the Modern Vote* (Sherman Oaks: Sage, 1997).

Further Reading

Presidential elections are covered in Nelson W. Polsby, Steven E. Schier, David A. Hopkins and Aaron Wildavsky, *Presidential Elections: Strategies and Structures of American Politics* (New York: Rowman & Littlefield, 14th Edn 2015), and in Stephen J. Wayne, *The Road to the White House, 2016: The Politics of Presidential Elections* (New York: Wadsworth, 2015). For an amusing analysis of the 2016 contest, see P. J. O'Rourke, *How the Hell Did This Happen?: The Election of 2016* (New York: The Atlantic Monthly Press, 2017).

CHAPTER 11
THE PRESIDENCY II
THE PRESIDENT AS CHIEF EXECUTIVE

The modern Presidency of the United States, as distinct from the traditional concepts of our highest office, is bound up with the survival not only of freedom but of mankind.... The President is the unifying force in our lives.... The President must possess a wide range of abilities: to lead, to persuade, to inspire trust, to attract men of talent, to unite. These abilities must reflect a wide range of characteristics: courage, vision, integrity, intelligence, sense of responsibility, sense of history, sense of humour, warmth, openness, personality, tenacity, energy, determination, drive, perspicacity, idealism, thirst for information, penchant for fact, presence of conscience, comprehension of people and enjoyment of life – plus all the other, nobler virtues ascribed to George Washington under God.

– NELSON A. ROCKEFELLER, UNITY, FREEDOM AND PEACE

American Politics and Society, Ninth Edition. David McKay.
© 2018 John Wiley & Sons Ltd. Published 2018 by John Wiley & Sons Ltd.

The saddest life is that of a political aspirant under democracy. His failure is ignominious and his success is disgraced.

– H. L. MENCKEN

The Presidency in a Changing America

As the last chapter showed, reforms in the selection process reflect deeper changes in the party system and in American society generally. It could well be argued that, almost irrespective of the quality of president, these and other developments have together made the job of chief executive much more difficult than ever before. We can identify three such developments, each of which has added to the burdens of office.

The changing role of parties and the rise of issue and ideological politics

Until recently one of the main reasons why presidents found it increasingly difficult to govern was the weakening of the 'connective tissue' with Congress and the public that political parties provide. Governing in the absence of unifying party forces has clearly been a problem for many presidents. In chapter 5 we listed the functions of political parties, and among the most important were the provision of institutional cohesion and a means to staff the government. Jimmy Carter is usually quoted as the classic case of a president who failed on both counts – largely because he came to Washington with very limited executive experience (as governor of Georgia) and with few connections in the traditional world of the Democratic Party (the unions, urban interests, elite universities, the northeastern establishment). As a result, so the argument runs, his liaison with Congress was poor and his ability to fill key posts with the right men and women wanting. Certainly, Carter had a rough time with Congress and was not personally inclined to create and nurture relationships with congressional leaders. But he was not unique in experiencing difficulties with Congress. As we saw in chapter 8, *all* presidents have had such problems, including John Kennedy and even Franklin Roosevelt, both of whom had strong party contacts and support. In his first two years in office, Clinton enjoyed the advantage of a Democratic Congress and was undoubtedly more politically skilful than Jimmy Carter. None the less, he achieved little in the way of enacting his legislative programme. A similar pattern emerged with Barack Obama after 2008. Even with majorities in both houses of Congress his legislative progamme hardly enjoyed an easy ride, although this was partly because of the obstructive parliamentary tactics of an ideologically united Republican Party.

An additional problem is the rise of 'issue politics', or the mobilization of political resources around particular issues and ideas that may or may not coincide with party alignments. We examine this phenomenon in more detail in chapter 14, but even the most casual observer of the American political scene will be aware of the rise of the minority caucuses, pro- and anti-abortion leagues, women's caucuses, environmental lobbies, the gun lobby,

the Christian Coalition and so on. Each of these movements has its congressional supporters and advocates within administrations and state governments.

Issue politics has had two further subtle effects on the political agenda, however.
First, when policy is defined in terms of discrete issues or one-dimensional ideologies
(such as 'conservatism'), the effect can be to fragment decision-making throughout the
political system. Within the executive departments and agencies, each issue or position has its supporters, so compounding the already problematical business of getting
bureaucrats to implement policy. So a president without a clear ideology (such as Clinton and Bush Senior) will be obliged to balance competing ideological stances within
and outside his administration. George Bush Senior did this with respect to abortion,
as did Bill Clinton with respect to health policy. In sum, in the absence of strong party
linkages, presidents can lack ideological and organizational 'connective tissue' when
performing their duties.

The second consequence of the rise of issue politics may be even more serious, and
this is when the presidency is 'captured' by a single ideological grouping. This happened in part in 1980 with the election of Ronald Reagan. However, Reagan's economic
agenda was broadly in tune with the views of most voters, even if he was clearly to
the right of the electorate on social and moral issues. George W. Bush, however, governed in an even more ideologically charged environment, and his administration was
clearly associated with the right on a range of issues that resonated with many voters,
including abortion and family issues, civil liberties, the status of large corporations and
the environment. With the Bush agenda on these issues reinforced by an ideologically
cohesive Republican Party in Congress, did this represent a return to old-style party
politics? It may have, but the problems experienced by the administration over civil liberties, intelligence-gathering, corporate corruption, Iraq and the economy showed that
its policies were eventually often out of line with the views of the majority of voters. For
although Bush won the 2004 election the Republicans suffered resounding defeats in the
2006 mid-term elections and more famously in the 2008 presidential election. Barack
Obama came into office in the context of an unusually dominant issue – economic
recession – which did help him pass his economic stimulus package in 2009. After that,
however, and especially after 2010 when the Republicans re-captured the House, the
president encountered serious problems with Congress as the failure of the two parties
to reach a compromise on taxing and spending showed (see Briefing, p. 396). Failure
to reach a compromise on the budget showed just how far the two parties had grown
apart on how best to manage the economy, with the Republicans continuing to insist
that economic growth could only come from lower taxes and government spending.
This theme was intensified after 2014 when the Republicans recaptured the House, a
development that rendered presidential–House cooperation effectively dead for the last
two years of the Obama presidency. Perhaps the most unusual election in American
history took place in 2016 when the eventual Electoral College victor, Donald Trump,
became president-elect as an outsider with no direct experience of politics or political
office. He did enjoy Republican support in both houses of Congress, but his radical
agenda was such that he was bound to face difficulties in enacting all his proposals.

He was, in addition, elected by a minority of voters – Hillary Clinton amassed nearly 3 million votes in excess of his total. This alone brought into question the legitimacy of his tenure in the minds of many voters.

The nationalization of politics and society

With improved communications and the spread of governments' responsibilities, the United States has become a much more centralized society over the past 30–40 years. Information is disseminated centrally by the four major television networks (NBC, CBS, ABC and Fox; see chapter 7), by the news services, and by syndicated columns of major newspapers and cable TV networks. Wide internet usage has further facilitated nation-alization trends. Economically, society is more centralized, with giant corporations pro-viding the same goods and services uniformly throughout the country. It follows that the demands on governments have been centralized, with Washington increasingly the focus of political activity. Chapter 4's discussion of intergovernmental relations showed how state and local governments have become more interdependent with the federal gov-ernment in recent years. The same is true of corporations, small businesses and almost all those interests in society affected by federal government spending, regulation and arbitration. Naturally, the president is a major focus of all this attention, for he frames most major laws, draws up the budget and has the responsibility for implementing all laws. As chief executive, the president has to manage the vast bureaucracy responsible for these tasks, a bureaucracy that, in terms of powers and complexity, has grown consider-ably. It also follows that when things go wrong the president is blamed, as was the case with the mishandling of the aftermath of Hurricane Katrina in 2005 and the banking crisis and associated economic downturn after 2008. During his first term, many blamed Barack Obama for failing to preside over a sustainable economic recovery and he won re-election in part because the Republican alternatives looked even less likely to spark rapid economic growth. Economic concerns also dominated in 2016 with the new Republican president Donald Trump promising to curb immigration, increase infrastructure spend-ing, protect American industry from foreign competition and reduce taxes in order to stimulate the economy and create jobs.

The changing nature of American economic and political power

Although not always true, it does seem reasonable to suppose that governing is easier when a country's economy is growing in real terms and its status and power abroad are in the ascendant. Both applied in the case of the United States between 1942 and 1965. Between 1965 and the 1980s American international economic and foreign policy influence experi-enced relative decline. Since the 1980s this trend has continued, although there was some-thing of a respite between the late 1980s and the early 2000s. Perhaps it is not entirely coincidental that the earlier period was associated with the era of 'successful' presidents, while the latter has witnessed the incumbency of executive 'failures'. While it would be foolhardy to accept this argument in full – was Harry Truman, after all, a 'success', and was

Ronald Reagan a 'failure'? – there is no question that the management of the economy and the exercise of military and diplomatic power abroad are *more likely* to be difficult during periods of relative decline or when there is little consensus on management of the economy or on America's role abroad.

The Vietnam War was the first major demonstration of the limits to American military power, and it effectively broke one president (Lyndon Johnson) and led another (Richard Nixon) to commit a series of illegal acts, including the secret bombing of Cambodia and the unauthorized surveillance of opponents of the war. In 1979 and 1980 Jimmy Carter's handling of the Iranian hostage situation dominated the final year of his presidency, and provided a poignant reminder of the limitations of American might. For recent presidents, ventures abroad have been problematical, for nothing increases presidential popularity more instantly than successful – or even unsuccessful but bold – military and diplomatic forays overseas. John Kennedy's popularity soared during the Cuban missile crisis, as did Jimmy Carter's following the signing of the Begin/Sadat and Carter Camp David accords in 1979, and Ronald Reagan's after the US invasion of Grenada and the bombing of Libya. In 1990–1 George Bush Senior's successful execution of the Gulf War led to approval ratings of over 80 per cent, a figure that was matched by his son George W. Bush following the events of 9/11 (figure 11.1). When the USA is apparently 'humiliated', as with the Iran–Contra affair, or when as with the war in Iraq after 2003, it fails to win a clear victory, it puts pressure on presidents to do something about it. Whether the resulting actions are in the public interest or in the interests of world peace are, of course, another matter. Note also how political polarization has resulted in a widening of the public's regard for presidents depending on party identification. So Democrats continued to hold Barack Obama in high regard while Republicans' assessment of his job performance sank to very low levels (figure 11.1).

At home, managing the many distributional questions that are the very essence of the chief executive's job is obviously more difficult when the economy is stagnating or when, even if the economy is growing, there are numerous demands on the government's budget. Even so, no single individual is more centrally placed to make these distributional decisions than is the president. He is responsible for producing an annual budget amounting to over $5 trillion, and for ensuring that this money is properly spent on literally thousands of programmes. Congress is, of course, also involved in this process and, when it comes to contested distributions, the courts become key actors. But neither Congress nor the courts are as politically visible as the president. Only the president is perceived as national leader and defender of the public interest. Small wonder, then, that recent presidents have experienced such difficulties, both in domestic policy and with defence spending, which naturally affects the amount available for domestic programmes. Add to this problem the increasingly strident demands of the single-issue lobbies, and the potential for conflict and failure can be appreciated. So until 1998 no recent president was able to balance the budget (in 1986 Ronald Reagan, a fiscal conservative, presided over a deficit of more than $80 billion, partly because he delivered such large tax cuts), or has come anywhere near to satisfying the demands of social groups. This was amply demonstrated by the experience of the Bush Senior administration. When the economy started to slow down in 1990, the budget deficit began to grow, reaching

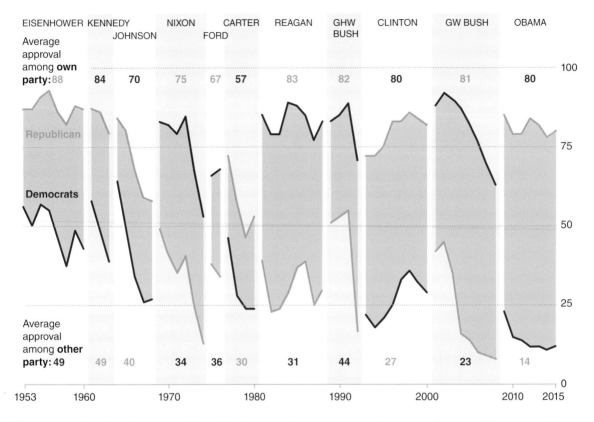

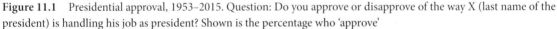

Figure 11.1   Presidential approval, 1953–2015. Question: Do you approve or disapprove of the way X (last name of the president) is handling his job as president? Shown is the percentage who 'approve'
Source: Pew Research Center at www.pewresearch.org/fact-tank/2016/01/12/presidential-job-approval-ratings-from-ike-to-obama/ft_16-01-06_presapproval/.
Note: Data from Eisenhower through George H. W. Bush from Gallup. Because some earlier data did not include partisan leaning, Republicans and Democrats in this graphic do not include leaners. Obama's rating is as of 13 December 2015.

$300 billion by 1992. With the economy in recession, pressure to increase expenditures proved irresistible. At the same time, tax increases were politically as unpopular as ever. In the event George Bush did go along with a tax hike in 1991, which almost certainly contributed to his subsequent defeat in 1992.

During his period in office, Bill Clinton was fortunate to enjoy a growing economy which, combined with controls on federal spending, did result in a meaningful reduction in the federal deficit (see chapter 18). After 1994, however, Republican control of Congress resulted in a serious deadlock over the fiscal 1996 budget and a temporary shutdown of some federal government activities. And even when, as occurred in 1998, the president presented to Congress a balanced budget for the first time since 1969, the distributional questions did not go away. Instead the debate shifted to conflict over how best to spend any surplus. Should it go on lowering taxes (the Republican position) or on improving health and education programmes (the president's position)? Indeed, the achievement of a balanced budget may actually have aggravated distributional problems. For if, as seems likely, politicians from all parties vie with one another to maintain balanced budgets, then satisfying public demands for more and better government services without increasing taxes becomes that much harder. Reagan managed to 'have his cake and eat it' – lower taxes *and* increased spending (mainly on defence) – but at the price of a ballooning deficit. Future presidents are unlikely to enjoy this luxury. Instead they will be obliged to reconcile the apparently irreconcilable – satisfying high public demands and expectations while preaching and practising the merits of limited government. Indeed the much-vaunted budget surplus of the late 1990s and early 2000s soon turned into a substantial deficit, in part because of large increases in military expenditure following the attacks of 9/11. At the same time George W. Bush was obliged to carry through with the large tax cuts that had been a major campaign promise in 2000. By 2004, therefore, the problems of the 1980s and early 1990s had returned with a vengeance, with the budget deficit ballooning to $311 billion in the first half of 2008. These problems were compounded by the collapse in house prices after 2007 and a rapid slow-down in the economy in 2008 that continued through 2009. And even when recovery began in 2010 it was slow and faltering. As a result economic concerns including a ballooning deficit dominated Barack Obama's first term in office. In spite of these continuing problems, Obama won re-election in 2012 in the context of an electorate deeply divided as to how to cure America's economic ills. Republicans saw salvation in lower taxes and spending, while the Democrats favoured higher taxes on the rich and the protection of social programmes. In the event the economy showed slow but steady improvements through 2016 in spite of the continuing and deepening ideological differences between the two parties.

Presidential Abuse of Power and the Congressional Response

In effect, these changes in society and politics have made the country less easy to govern. Public expectations of the central institutions of government have increased, while the ability to respond effectively has been weakened. For the presidency, this unfortunate combination has been particularly serious and helps to explain the waxing and waning of presidential power over the past 50 years. The era of the 'Imperial Presidency' coincided with America's post-war dominance in economic and military affairs, and also, of course, with the incumbency of two especially imperious presidents. By the mid-1960s the office had grown enormously in power, and the pressures imposed by the Vietnam War and a declining economy tested the office to the full. The potential for the abuse of power was considerable. Unfortunately for the American people, Lyndon Johnson and, particularly, Richard Nixon fell to this temptation. The real importance of the Nixon period is not that the president, along with many of his aides and cabinet officers, broke the law, but that the chief executive wielded power in such a way that it raised very serious questions on where, exactly, presidential power began and ended.

Richard Nixon impounded funds appropriated by Congress for programmes he disliked (impoundment is the setting aside by the executive of funds appropriated by Congress).

Towards the end of his presidency, he was exercising the veto power extensively, and few of his vetoes were overridden by Congress. He invoked 'executive privilege' to justify the withholding of information from congressional investigative committees, and he nominated a number of men to official posts who were unqualified or otherwise unsuitable. Even before Watergate, Congress began to fight back, notably by rejecting two of his more outrageous Supreme Court nominees (see chapter 9). In 1972 Congress attempted to control the president's discretion to make executive agreements – effectively treaties with foreign powers which could be concluded, sometimes in secret, without consulting the Senate. Under the Case Act, all such agreements have to be submitted to Congress. More far-reaching was the 1973 War Powers Act passed by Congress over a presidential veto, which put limits on the president's power to commit troops overseas. In 1973 Congress also insisted that the president's director and deputy directors of the vital Office of Management and Budget be subject to Senate confirmation.

Following Watergate, Congress asserted its power even more vigorously – in part because Watergate had precipitated a landslide victory for the Democrats in the 1974 midterm elections. The Budget and Impoundment Control Act of 1974 obliges the president to report 'recission' to Congress when funds appropriated remain unspent. Congress then has to approve recission within 45 days. The same law created the Budget Committees in Congress to enable the legislature to play a more constructive part in the budget process (see chapter 9).

As can be seen from table 11.1, Gerald Ford exercised the veto on major bills frequently and was overridden by Congress on no fewer than seven occasions. Note also the general

Table 11.1 Major bills vetoed, 1933–2016

President	Total	Number involving appropriations	Number involving foreign and foreign economic policy	Major vetoes per year in office	Number overridden
Roosevelt	2	0	0	0.16	2
Truman	6	0	0	0.8	5
Eisenhower	2	2	0	0.25	1
Kennedy	0	0	0	0	0
Johnson	0	0	0	0	0
Nixon	13	10	1	2.4	4
Ford	11	10	1	4.4	7
Carter	5	2	2	1.3	1
Reagan	15	7	5	1.9	5
Bush Senior	15	4	5	3.7	1
Clinton	19	10	4.2	2.5	2
G. W. Bush	7	2	3	1.15	3
Obama	10	2	1	1.25	1

Source: David McKay, 'Presidential strategy and the veto power: a reappraisal', *Political Science Quarterly* (1989), table 5. Updated from *Congressional Quarterly*. For definition of major bills, see original. With permission of SAGE.

tendency for the veto to be applied more frequently and in particular to appropriations and foreign policy bills, which, in the past, almost never attracted the presidential veto. This reflects the much more difficult environment in which today's presidents have to work. Sometimes this means facing a Congress controlled by the opposition party. Equally often it means that there are fundamentally irreconcilable interests represented by a fragmented Congress, on the one hand, and the president on the other. Although, during his first two years in office, Bill Clinton did not use the veto power, he certainly did so thereafter and, by so doing, successfully thwarted the Republicans' attempt to pass much of their ambitious legislative programme during the 1990s. Clinton, was, of course faced with a hostile Republican Congress during his final six years in office.

George W. Bush did not impose one veto on a major bill (or indeed on a minor bill) during the 2001–3 period, thus reflecting both his majority in the House of Representatives – and in the Senate after 2000 – and the spirit of national solidarity that prevailed in the period immediately after the 9/11 attacks. However, with the election of a Democratic Congress in 2006 Bush wielded the veto regularly, imposing it eight times in the 2007/8 period, including bills banning aggressive interrogation techniques (or torture), a children's health-care bill and withdrawal from Iraq. One of his vetoes on a water resources bill was overridden by Congress. The pattern for Barack Obama was similar, although he exercised very few vetoes in his eight years in office. This is partly because he enjoyed a

Plate 11.1 'Nixon Resigns': headline in the *Washington Post*, 1974
Source: Alex Webb/Magnum.

Democratic majority between 2009 and 2011, and partly because the ideological distance between the two branches was so great that it was difficult for any controversial bill to pass. This was so even in the face of Republican control of both houses after 2014 given that the Democrats could always muster the 40 votes (or two-fifths) necessary to block Senate bills by using that chamber's parliamentary procedures. In the event he was overridden only once on his veto of a law that would allow the victims of the 9/11 terrorist attacks the right to sue Saudi Arabia for compensation. Obama's veto was informed by the principle that citizens should not sue foreign governments. But the sympathy in Congress for the victims of the attacks was so great that his veto was easily overridden in both houses.

In 1976 Congress put limits on the president's power to declare emergencies and assume special powers. Under the National Emergencies Act of 1976, Congress can terminate a declaration of emergency, and all declarations must be reported to Congress, together with legal justifications for them.

Finally, in 1978 Congress passed the Ethics in Government Act, which allowed the naming of an independent counsel (sometimes called a special prosecutor) to investigate alleged wrongdoing in the executive branch. Between 1979 and 1998, 18 independent counsels were appointed to investigate a wide range of allegations. In some cases, such as the Iran–Contra affair, indictments and convictions ensued. By the second Clinton term, the independent counsel legislation came under increasing criticism as Independent Counsel Kenneth W. Starr was perceived by many to have exceeded his authority when investigating President Clinton's involvement in the alleged Whitewater real-estate scandal and related matters while he was governor of Arkansas. As is well known, the most serious of the eventual charges related to Clinton's affair with White House intern Monica Lewinsky, and to his untruthful attempts to conceal the affair for an eight-month period from January to August 1998. The ensuing impeachment and trial of the president and the damage done to Clinton and the presidency over what was, at least at first, a private matter, led many to question the scope and methods of the inquiry. Indeed the office was abolished in 1999 and replaced with the US Department of Justice Office of Special Counsel. As an 'in house' investigatory unit the Office of Special Counsel is less likely to be politically hostile to incumbent presidents.

Following the adoption of all these measures and the incumbency of an unusually unassertive president, Jimmy Carter, presidency-watchers began to talk of the *decline* of presidential power and the resurgence of Congress. As we saw in chapters 8 and 9, there can be no doubting that Congress did become more, rather than less, difficult for presidents to deal with in the period down to 2000, and while between 2001 and 2005 an assertive president did appear to exercise greater control over a more compliant Congress, politics returned to 'normal' with the election of a Democratic Congress in 2006. After that time, George W. Bush was increasingly boxed in by the Democratic Congress, hostile public and world opinion.

Whatever the difficulties encountered by presidents they can draw on a number of resources when fighting their political battle. The next section concentrates on those resources not covered in earlier sections and on the ways in which successive presidents have adapted to the pressures and problems associated with the office.

Two main resources can be identified – the public and the presidential bureaucracy – to which a third, conceptually distinct, resource, personality, can be added.

Presidential Resources

The public

It may seem paradoxical in the light of the foregoing discussion to view the public as a resource. Yet under many circumstances it can be just that. As national leaders, presidents can make direct appeals to the public through press conferences and special televised announcements. In some instances, this amounts almost to a limited form of direct democracy. In 1981 and 1982, for example, Ronald Reagan made specific appeals to the public on television that they should write to their members of Congress expressing support for the president's economic policies. Both the tax and spending cuts were passed by narrow margins, and it seems reasonable to assume that Reagan's pleadings had some effect – especially as many members cannot afford to ignore a sudden influx of constituency mail. More recently, George W. Bush made numerous appeals to the American people to support the 'War on Terror' and the invasions of Afghanistan and Iraq, mainly by direct television addresses. As can be seen from figure 11.2, these pleadings appear to have had an effect, with the president's popularity increasing at least in early 2003 during the invasion of Iraq.

Appeals to the public are not always successful, of course, as Richard Nixon's sometimes-painful public attempts to hide his guilt over Watergate demonstrated. But earlier in his presidency, Nixon had made highly effective use of this resource through his carefully constructed public lectures on American disengagement from Vietnam.

Although still a potentially powerful weapon, the public appeal resource is beset with problems and pitfalls. As was established in chapter 6, the American electorate can quickly switch their allegiance and they are always ready to apportion blame for misdeeds and wrongdoings. This has made presidential public appeals more risky than they used to be. During Ronald Reagan's first two years, it seems reasonable to infer that the public was willing to provide support during what was effectively a 'honeymoon' period. Following the mid-term elections when the Democrats made deep inroads into the conservative coalition in the House, such support became more grudging, with the balance of public opinion shifting to Congress rather than to the president. Although he was highly popular during the Gulf War, when he made numerous public appeals, George Bush Senior could do nothing to boost his popularity during the ensuing economic recession. His son experienced a similar, although not as extreme, rise and fall in popularity during his first term in office.

This accepted, no other national institution – Congress, party, the courts – can use the media quite like the president. He is, after all, just one person with a special national status. Given all the problems of governing in the twenty-first century, presidents will continue to make direct appeals to the public, for it is one of the few, if imperfect, means whereby the fragmenting influences in American politics can be overcome. This was demonstrated very well during the impeachment and trial of President Clinton in 1998 and 1999. In spite of all the adverse publicity surrounding the president, not to mention his admission of guilt, he was able to retain a semblance of dignity and authority and he continued to use the public

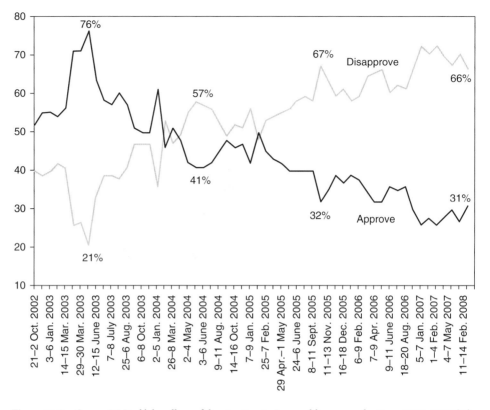

Figure 11.2   George W. Bush's handling of the situation in Iraq, public approval ratings, 2002–2008 (%)
Source: Data from Gallup, Presidential Ratings – Issues Approval, www.gallup.com/poll/1726/
Presidential-Ratings-Issues-Approval.aspx.

as a valuable political resource. Certainly his popularity did not wane significantly during this very difficult period (figure 11.1).[1]

Most commentators agree that the three most important indicators of presidential performance are the state of the economy, the extent of American involvement in foreign wars and the public's approval of the president. As can be seen from table 11.2, these indicators can be closely associated – a weak economy and/or American soldiers dying abroad helped to defeat the incumbent party in 1952, 1968, 1980 and 1992. Table 11.2 emphasizes the president's popularity rather than involvement in foreign wars, but the former is often an indirect measure of long-drawn-out foreign interventions. Curiously, in 2004 George Bush won in spite of high US casualties abroad and a low approval rating. However, accumulating difficulties in Iraq and a weakening economy led to a collapse in his ratings after 2005 (figure 11.1). After an initial surge in popularity Obama suffered a decline with his ratings stuck in the high 40s for most of the remainder of his first term. In spite of this and the poor economy he managed to win re-election, thus confounding the predictions of the model. The model also failed – if only by a small margin – in 2016 when it correctly predicted a Trump win but with a small majority of the popular vote. In the event he lost the popular vote by around 2.1% but won the Electoral College.

Table 11.2 Electoral barometer readings and election results since the Second World War

Barometer reading	Year	Election result margin (%)	Popular vote
82.5	1964	Won	22.6
73.0	1972	Won	23.2
71.0	1956	Won	15.4
51.5	1984	Won	18.2
43.5	1996	Won	8.5
22.0	2000	Won	0.5
13.0	2004	Won	2.5
9.0	1988	Won	7.7
4.5	1948	Won	4.5
2.0	1968	Lost	−0.7
1.5	2016	Lost	2.1
−5.0	1960	Lost	−0.2
−5.0	1976	Lost	−2.1
−21.5	2012	Won	3.1
−22.5	1992	Lost	−5.6
−49.5	1952	Lost	−10.9
−54.0	2008	Lost	−6.1
−66.0	1980	Lost	−9.7

Source: 2008, 2012 and 2016 data compiled by author. Adapted from Alan Abramowitz, in Larry Sabato's Crystal Ball at www.centerforpolitics.org/crystalball/print.php?article=AIA2008052901.

Note: Three indicators of the national political climate have accurately predicted the outcomes of presidential elections since the end of the Second World War: the incumbent president's approval rating at mid-year, the growth rate of the economy during the second quarter of the election year and the length of time the president's party has held the White House. In 2016 the model predicted a Trump win in the popular vote. In the event Trump did win the Electoral College but he lost the popular vote by a margin of 1.6% – more than 2.5 million votes.

The higher the president's approval rating and the stronger the growth rate of the economy, the more likely it is that the president's party will be victorious. However, if the president's party has controlled the White House for two terms or longer it is less likely to be successful. Time-for-change sentiment seems to increase after eight years regardless of the president's popularity or the state of the economy.

These three factors can be combined to produce an electoral barometer score that measures the overall national political climate.

Briefing   Organizing the White House

Most commentators agree that new presidents should follow certain guidelines when staffing the White House. Although there are no hard and fast rules, most presidents are advised to do the following:

1. Get an early start. The model here is Ronald Reagan, who appointed Ed Meese as his Chief Recruiting Officer. By the time of the inauguration all the main jobs were filled, and the president

was able to make an immediate start on his programmes. In contrast both Carter and Clinton delayed filling many key posts and therefore lost out in exploiting the vital first four months or 'honeymoon' period of their presidencies.

2. Appoint a good Chief of Staff. James Baker under Reagan was widely respected by friend and political foes alike. His successor, Donald Regan, was not. Chiefs of Staff should be good political operators rather than gatekeepers to the president. Presidents should not make the mistake of not appointing a chief staffer. Jimmy Carter took this option, which resulted in the impression of a rudderless decision-making process.

3. Use closed discussions when formulating the detail of policy, but be open when 'selling' final programmes to the broader political community. Lyndon Johnson was an exemplar of the former strategy. Bill Clinton was a good example of the latter when his health-care reform plans were widely debated before they were finalized. As a result opponents of reform were able to build support in Congress and elsewhere.

4. Build an *esprit de corps* among staffers and key cabinet secretaries along the lines of Roosevelt, Kennedy, and the first terms of Reagan and George W. Bush. This does not necessarily mean blind conformity to the president's agenda. FDR and Kennedy actually encouraged competing opinions as, to a lesser extent, did the early Reagan. What should be avoided are internal bickering and backbiting (as in the Carter White House) and an organizational structure that isolates the president from political realities (as with Nixon and the later Reagan).

Barack Obama had difficulty building *esprit de corps* until his appointment of Denis McDonagh as Chief of Staff in 2013. McDonagh proved to be very like Obama himself – disciplined, calm, loyal and obsessed with process. This ethos came to dominate the White House during these years. In contrast, Donald Trump gathered around him advisers who shared his combative world view of an administration under siege by hostile forces at home and abroad. In particular, his chief political strategist, Steve Bannon, actively encouraged an atmosphere of perpetual crisis and emergency management (see Biography below).

What is extraordinary is, in spite of the accumulated wisdom on the subject, just how many recent presidents have failed to follow these guidelines. This is almost certainly because many presidents actually do not have clear policy agendas (Carter, Bush Senior, Clinton) or because their personality traits get in the way of a rational and politically savvy White House (Nixon, Carter, Clinton). And Barack Obama managed to get through four Chiefs of Staff before settling on Denis McDonagh in 2013. But Donald Trump provides the most egregious case of a president not following these simple rules. Once in the White House he continued to make frequent and often glib or dishonest comments on Twitter that sometimes contradicted administration policy. He also gathered around him a team of combative advisers who helped create an atmosphere of constant crisis fuelled by a siege mentality. In particular his chief political strategist, Steve Bannon, believed that constant attacks on the media and anyone who dared question administration policy was the most effective way to govern (see Biography below).

Biography   Steve Bannon – Political Strategist and Crisis Junkie

In November 2016 president elect Donald Trump named Steve Bannon as his Chief Strategist in the White House. Later he was also given a seat on the National Security Council. Because he was closely associated with the right-wing Breitbart news and the far right alt-right movement, Bannon's appointment was highly controversial and greeted with dismay by Democrats and the liberal media. Born into a blue-collar Virginia family, Bannon had had a varied career including service with the US Navy, a period with investment bankers Goldman Sachs, as well as numerous journalistic forays in the print, broadcast and documentary film-making media. Bannon's world view was that the United States faces an existential crisis induced by the liberal elite's betrayal of American nationalism, Judeo-Christian values and its weakness in the face of what he called 'Islamic fascism'. Those on the right had a duty, he believed, to reinstate 'true' American values by destroying the liberal elite's grip on power, restricting immigration from countries that hold anti-American values and confronting 'Islamic fascism' through armed conflict. Central to his philosophy was that the US has become morally decadent and only a major catharsis – possibly a major war – could cleanse the nation and restore traditional values of family, religion, community and tradition. He deplored a status quo that, he alleged, had created socialism for the poor (welfare programmes) and privilege for the educated elites. Meanwhile the middle class had become immiserated and ignored. Few doubt Bannon's hand in the many initiatives taken by President Trump in his first year in office, including his attacks on the media, his immigration bans, his demonization of non-Christian foreign powers and his 'America First' strategy in economic and trade policy.

Bureaucracy

As the job of president has become more demanding, so incumbents have adapted their administrative resources accordingly. Every president has had a cabinet composed mainly of departmental heads at his disposal, but as we will see, the cabinet is but one of a number of administrative devices available, most of which have been introduced over the past 100 years to help presidents formulate and execute policy. In 1921 the Bureau of the Budget (now called the Office of Management and Budget) was established to help the president prepare the budget and coordinate spending policies. As can be seen from figure 11.3, since then other agencies have been created which collectively are known as the Executive Office of the President (EOP) (formally established by Congress in 1939). Quite distinct from the cabinet, the Executive Office consists of about 2,000 individuals directly accountable to the president. This figure includes about 500 people who actually work in the White House as personal aides to the president – the White House Office in figure 11.3. How presidents actually use the EOP, and in particular the White House staff, has aroused bitter controversy over the past 30 years. A major criticism, inspired mainly by Watergate, has concerned the extent to which the staff has grown in recent years and has increasingly insulated presidents from public opinion and political reality. A related theme centres on whether any personal

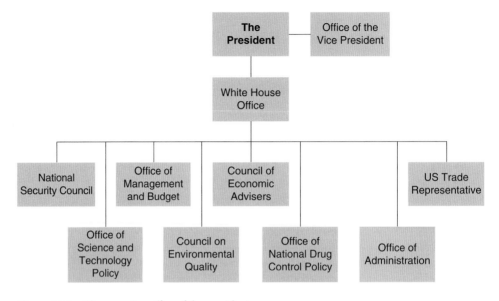

Figure 11.3   The executive office of the president
Source: created from list at https://www.whitehouse.gov/administration/eop.

bureaucracy can be an adequate administrative tool against the vast resources of executive departments and agencies and against a fragmented but powerful Congress.

There can be no disputing that some presidents have used their staffs unwisely. Richard Nixon, in particular, relied heavily on just a handful of personal aides, eschewing most cabinet officers, congressional and party leaders. Three of his closest aides, John Ehrlichman, Bob Haldeman and Ron Zeigler, became so effective in acting as the president's mouthpieces that they earned the sobriquet 'the Berlin Wall'. In the Carter presidency, Stewart Eisenstadt, the domestic policy adviser, almost assumed the status of policy initiator and spokesperson. During the second Reagan administration, Donald Regan guarded his position as Chief of Staff jealously and used it to limit access to the president by other administration officials. Faced with the open hostility of First Lady Nancy Reagan and criticism over his role in the Iran–Contra affair, he was eventually forced to resign. George Bush Senior's first Chief of Staff, John Sununu, was also widely regarded as imperious and insensitive. He, too, was forced to resign following allegations of misuse of government resources, including presidential jets. Bill Clinton's problems with staffers were no less serious, although in his case the criticisms were directed at a group of presidential 'cronies' rather than at the Chiefs of Staff. In the twentieth century there were at least three other instances of staffers assuming national prominence and even notoriety as 'the powers behind the throne'.[2] George W. Bush was also prone to criticism of his running of the White House – especially in the wake of the intelligence failures associated with the invasion of Iraq. Bush was criticized not only for the role played by his personal staff, including Chief of Staff Andrew Card and chief strategist Karl Rove, but also for the crucial role played by cabinet-level officials and the vice president. Hence Vice President Cheney, Defense Secretary Donald Rumsfeld, National Security Adviser Condoleezza Rice and other more junior officials were seen as among the president's closest advisers. Perhaps this development reflects the emergency and almost wartime atmosphere that prevailed during the Bush first term.

Personal staffs – and modern presidents all have domestic, economic and foreign policy advisers, a press secretary, legal counsel and staff responsible for liaison work with Congress – often overlap with members of other agencies within the EOP. Hence presidents' national security advisers are also members of the National Security Council, a body consisting, among others, of the president, vice president and Defense and State Secretaries, set up by Congress in 1947 to help the formulation of foreign policy and aid crisis management. In some instances, the National Security Adviser becomes more important than the Secretary of State, as was clearly the case with Henry Kissinger before he effectively 'deposed' the incumbent, William Rogers, and assumed the office of Secretary of State himself during Nixon's second term. Similarly, the director of the Office of Management and Budget can become a key figure, for the OMB is responsible for monitoring the spending of the various executive departments. In 1980 Ronald Reagan's choice of director, David Stockman, a bright young ex-member of Congress, was designed to ensure that the OMB director would have direct responsibility for handling the budget and the cuts to be imposed on many of the departments and agencies. (Significantly, since 1973 the director of the OMB has been subject to Senate confirmation.) In this sense, the OMB and its director resemble, although they are by no means identical to, finance ministries and ministers in other political systems, such as the British Treasury and Chancellor of the Exchequer.

How presidents use the EOP and especially their personal staff varies greatly from administration to administration. Until Watergate it was common to contrast Franklin Roosevelt's style of creating an atmosphere of constructive competition, with aides deliberately positioned to provide contrasting information and advice, with Eisenhower's tendency to delegate responsibility and Kennedy's emphasis on intelligence and *esprit de corps*.[3]

Since Watergate, however, there is evidence that whatever management strategy is adopted by presidents they will experience serious command problems. Certainly, presidents have felt obliged to innovate and reorganize the executive branch to improve management. As noted, most presidents have adopted 'Chiefs of Staff' specifically to help management of the White House – although four recent incumbents of this position (Bob Haldeman of Watergate fame, Donald Regan in the Reagan White House, John Sununu in the Bush Senior administration and Andrew Card in 2006) were all obliged to resign following allegations of incompetence or wrongdoing. During his first term President Reagan relied on a triumvirate of staffers for policy guidance and political advice – Chief of Staff James Baker, President's Counsel Edwin Meese and Deputy Chief of Staff Michael Deever. All three had left the White House by 1985, however, when ex-Treasury Secretary Donald Regan took over as Chief of Staff.

As mentioned above, Regan was obliged to resign in 1987 and was replaced by the more politically astute ex-Senate Majority Leader Howard Baker. Indeed, Reagan's use of the EOP changed quite dramatically between his first and second terms. In his first term he relied on at least three chief advisers, and in his second just one (apart from his wife, who played an active role throughout). While praised for his management style in the first term, he was condemned for his failure to oversee the detail, and sometimes even the main thrust, of policy in the second. The Iran–Contra debacle resulted in part from this failing. Criticisms of George Bush's management style were of a different order. Although John Sununu was supposed to play the 'bad cop' to Bush's 'good cop' – that is, to be the president's hit man – it soon became obvious that each was not fully aware of the policy position of the other. As a result, an impression of drift and indecision pervaded the Bush presidency. Sununu's replacement, Samuel Skinner, did little to help because he proved to be a grey, almost anonymous figure. Bill Clinton's experience with staffers was also fraught with difficulties. His first choice as Chief of Staff, Mac McClarty, was accused of being an Arkansas crony, and was replaced during the first term with the tougher and more political Budget Director, Leon Panetta, and in his second term with Erskine Bowles. None of these men took on a major executive or gatekeeping role, however. Clinton surrounded himself with numerous confidants, some of whom had little formal authority. Indeed, it could be argued that some of the most influential people in his first term were in this category. They included First Lady Hillary Clinton, staffer Dick Morris and personal confidant Vernon Jordan. Perhaps unsurprisingly, as the 1996 election drew closer, Clinton relied more and more on the advice of political consultant Dick Morris, who urged him to move towards the centre ground of politics and thereby secure victory.

At first few criticisms were directed at George W. Bush's inner circle, but after 2004 disquiet grew at what appeared to be a very closed and partisan style of leadership. Any criticism of the causes and the conduct of the war in Iraq was off the White House agenda. Eventually Chief of Staff Andrew Card, chief strategist Karl Rove and press secretary Scott McClellan all resigned amid criticism both of the war and of the handling of Hurricane Katrina, so that by 2007 almost none of the leading players in the 2004 White House remained.

A more radical ploy has involved attempts to institutionalize the delegation of power through strengthening the cabinet. Although every president has had a cabinet, the Constitution unambiguously assigns executive power to the president, so whether the device is used or not is a matter of great discretion. Its membership consists of the heads of the executive departments plus individuals assigned by the president. Reinvigorating the cabinet is a natural option for presidents to choose, because a major part of executive leadership involves control and management of the vast federal bureaucracy. Much of the work of personal staff involves liaison with this bureaucracy, and the closer the communications and finer the line of command the better. So Presidents Nixon, Carter and Reagan pledged that they would strengthen their cabinets. Nixon patently failed to do this, but Carter did in fact use the cabinet quite frequently, as did Ronald Reagan. Indeed, during his first year in office President Reagan convened his cabinet no fewer than 37 times, a very high figure in historical perspective. It is doubtful that this smoothed relations between the White House and the executive departments. As we will see in chapter 12, a natural antipathy exists between the two, largely because departments and agencies have constituencies and interests of their own. Whatever the promises, presidents generally resort to using their own (usually reliable) staff rather than risk giving real power to departmental secretaries, and recent history is littered with examples of conflict between powerful staffers or EOP members and departmental heads. During his first term, Bill Clinton was no exception to this rule. As already indicated, he acquired an inner circle of advisers. Interestingly, this group contained cabinet secretaries, including Commerce Secretary Ron Brown and the Department of Housing and Urban Development (HUD) Secretary Henry Cisneros. But they were involved as friends and confidants rather than as spokespersons for their departments. (Secretary Brown was subsequently killed in a plane crash over Bosnia. Secretary Cisneros resigned following allegations of sexual and financial misconduct.)

As noted, George W. Bush also experienced resignations during his period in office, including Treasury Secretary Paul O'Neil, who left following accusations of incompetence, and George Tenet, the long-time director of the Central Intelligence Agency (CIA), who resigned just before the Senate delivered its scathing report on the failure of the CIA to provide proper intelligence on Saddam Hussein's alleged weapons of mass destruction. Perhaps the most dramatic resignation was that of Attorney General Alberto Gonzales in 2007, who was accused of incompetence and sanctioning torture in the 'War on Terror'.

The need to reorganize extends to other areas and has included a major reorganization of the EOP by Jimmy Carter, who eliminated seven of the office's administrative units. And Jimmy Carter and Ronald Reagan promised to make greater use of their vice presidents. Traditionally, the position has meant little in itself, or has been 'about as useful as a cow's fifth teat', as Harry Truman colourfully put it. Walter Mondale was, however, accorded a more central position in the Carter administration than many previous vice presidents, and Al Gore was accorded special status in the Clinton White House: he not only assumed the mantle of heir apparent but also became active in a number of policy initiatives. But of all recent vice presidents it was Dick Cheney in the George W. Bush administration who assumed the most visible public profile and the most prominent policy role. For not only was Cheney part of the president's inner circle, but he also took on a major role in the planning and conduct of the war in Iraq. It is also interesting to note that Cheney was almost certainly the most criticized vice president in modern history. In stark contrast Joe Biden was very much in the mould of a 'traditional' vice president, very much playing second fiddle to the president. Crucially, however, he remained an essentially non-controversial figure, whose warm personal style complemented the sometimes aloof and distanced personality style of the president.

All these efforts demonstrate the increasingly difficult political environment in which presidents have to work. Public expectations of the office remain high just as the ability of presidents to meet these expectations has diminished. Together with the nationalization of political life, this has forced presidents to manage numerous centres of political power, each with its own semi-autonomous policy network. As Hugh Heclo has emphasized, staff and other administrative assistants help with, but cannot solve, the central dilemma of the office:

> Whoever the President and whatever his style, the political and policy bureaucracies crowd in on him. They are there in his office to help, but their needs are not necessarily his needs. Delegation is unavoidable; yet no one aide or combination of aides has his responsibilities or takes his oath of office. However much the President trusts personal friends, political loyalties, or technocrats, he is the person that the average citizen and history will hold accountable.[4]

Personality

While no one could deny the importance of changes in the nomination process and the political environment as determinants of change in the nature of the presidency, some observers stress that the most crucial element in the office is the personality of the incumbent. With so much discretion attached to the job and such a premium on leadership skills – judgement, persuasion, manipulation, coercion, insight, charisma – personality is undoubtedly important. Indeed, even the most casual student of American politics has a cognitive picture of certain presidents – Truman as confrontational and combative, Eisenhower as wise and avuncular, Kennedy as inspirational, Clinton as charismatic but erratic, Reagan as reassuring, and above all, perhaps, Richard Nixon as devious and insecure. Borrowing heavily from psychology, one political scientist, James Barber, has attempted to formalize the 'presidential character' by classifying presidents by personality type.[5] Barber's two dimensions are active–passive and positive–negative. Simplifying somewhat, the former describes how much effort presidents put into the job and the latter how much enjoyment or satisfaction they get from it. The key types are active positives, representing individuals who receive enormous satisfaction from being active in the job, and active negatives, who put in intense effort but get little emotional reward for their pains. Beware, says Barber, of the active negatives, who are likely to dig in when under pressure and display a sometimes paranoid inflexibility. Active positives, in contrast, enjoy the cut and thrust of a highly demanding job and are likely to show that spirit of compromise and adaptability that is so essential to the politics of coalition formation.

As with all simple psychological theories, Barber's typology is open to criticism.[6] Events often mould personality rather than the other way round. Who, after all, would have judged Lyndon Johnson 'inflexible' before he became so fatally obsessed with the war in Vietnam? And in many respects Richard Nixon, the epitome of the active negative type according to Barber, was pragmatic and adaptable. Unlike Woodrow Wilson and Lyndon Johnson, Nixon had little moral commitment to causes or higher ideals. Moreover, to put Ronald Reagan in the same category as Warren Harding and William Taft seems misguided, for every modern president has to be 'active'. This may not mean working 18-hour days, but it must at least mean being psychologically active or aware of events and political priorities. While there is no doubt that George Bush Senior was active, some doubt exists as to whether he drew great satisfaction from the job. Certainly, by the end of his term, he displayed an element of weariness and resignation that was not typical of an active positive. In sum, Barber's categories are not very useful guides to presidential quality. Highly successful and 'failed' presidents are put in the same category (Franklin Roosevelt, Barack Obama and George W. Bush as active positives, Dwight Eisenhower and Calvin Coolidge as passive negatives), and the political and historical changes analysed above, especially those associated with presidential selection, appear to bear little or no relationship to Barber's idea of presidential quality.

What the typology does do is force us to think more carefully about the impact of personality on the office. There is no disputing that some men have been more suited to the job than others and that, irrespective of events and of changes in the selection process and in American society, this simple fact continues to hold true. All the evidence suggests, for example, that Ronald Reagan enjoyed being president and had a talent for handling people around him that most other recent presidents have lacked. This does not mean to say that history will judge him a great president or even that his record in dealing with Congress and the public will be deemed successful. His casual style and willingness to delegate undoubtedly helped to lead to the Iran–Contra affair in 1985 and 1986. But having a personality apparently suited to the job must at least help the incumbent to come to terms with what possibly is the most demanding executive position in the modern world.

All the indications are that Bill Clinton, too, enjoyed the business of being president. He is a naturally gregarious and extrovert personality who liked, and was liked by, most of the people who worked with him. During his first term he may have become frustrated at the glacial progress of his legislative programme and his party's subsequent defeat at the mid-term congressional elections, but in response to these events he did not become depressed and introspective. On the contrary, they inspired him to renewed enthusiasm during the last two years of his first term – an enthusiasm devoted not to legislation but to what Clinton does best, campaigning for re-election. During his second term, the trials and tribulations of the myriad accusations of personal wrongdoing levelled at the president only briefly deflected him from the job at hand during the actual impeachment proceedings. But in contrast to Richard Nixon, who resigned before the House of Representatives could vote articles of impeachment, Clinton's popularity actually increased during one period of the scandal.

On his election, George W. Bush found himself with virtually no mandate to govern. He lost the popular vote and the Republicans controlled Congress by the narrowest of margins. Consequently, his public popularity started off at a low level for a newly elected president. But Bush, too, appeared to be a president who received a lot of satisfaction from the job, in part because of the two unusual features that marked his presidency. The first was the emergency environment that prevailed for the first five or six years of his time in office. He was, therefore, obliged to take on the commander-in-chief role in a way that none of his immediate predecessors was able to. This included mobilizing the country behind the 'War on Terror' and waging two air and land wars in Afghanistan and Iraq. The president relished this role, as his dramatic landing on an aircraft carrier in 2003 at the conclusion of the invasion of Iraq demonstrated.

Second, George W. Bush was a president with great Christian faith – a faith that seemed to imbue him with an almost missionary zeal to defeat not only the enemies of America abroad but also to spread Christian values at home. Such religious evangelism is unusual among presidents and added a new dimension to the way in which personality plays a part in moulding presidential performance. Even when his popularity waned as it did dramatically after 2005 (figure 11.1), George W. Bush appeared to continue to enjoy being president. Even Bush's resilience was tested in 2008, however, as the American economy slowed dramatically, and Republican candidates for the presidency worked hard to dissociate themselves from what was widely perceived as a failed president.

Perhaps the most enigmatic of recent presidents is Barack Obama. For in spite of his campaign pledge 'Yes we can!' and the emotive appeal of his autobiography *Dreams From My Father*, Obama proved to be a relatively passionless president. His main mode of operation was rational calculation rather then the sort of high-energy, extrovert and charismatic

Plate 11.2   Barack Obama and Angela Merkel exchange views at the NATO summit in Warsaw, July 2016
Source: Handout/Getty, www.gettyimages.co.uk/license/545633336.

intensity associated with such presidents as Franklin Roosevelt or Bill Clinton. As a result he tended to establish his policy positions but failed always to carry them through with passion and conviction. Generally he surrounded himself with like-minded aides rather than enjoy the hurly burly of competing ideas and options. Obama did not use the classic powers of personal persuasion, such as charm, flattery or browbeating associated with such presidents as FDR and Lyndon Johnson. Instead, he would tend to modify his position in an almost clinical fashion, with little attendant passion or close personal communication with congressional leaders.

Assessing the Presidency: Presidential Power at Home and Abroad

When, in 1960, Richard Neustadt described presidential power as the 'power to persuade', he accurately captured the need for presidents to be successful bargainers, negotiators and manipulators.[7] Coalition-building, in other words, is the very essence of the president's job, and incumbents must have the personal capacity not only to appreciate this fact (as Jimmy Carter constantly said he did) but also to act accordingly (as Jimmy Carter repeatedly failed to do). Coalition-building skills are necessary at every level – within the White House, and in relations with executive departments, Congress, the media, interest groups and the public. Neustadt's famous essay was designed to show that formal command was not enough; that, indeed, it was sometimes quite limited, unless supplemented by the more subtle political skills involved in the art of persuasion.[8] To reduce almost the president's entire job to bargaining skills is, of course, to oversimplify. Constitutionally, the chief executive has immense power of command not least as commander-in-chief – which he can exercise without a finely honed aptitude for bargaining. The presidencies of Lyndon Johnson, Richard Nixon and George W. Bush are proof enough of this. Yet all three presidents have been judged less than successful. Moreover, changes in the selection process, while perhaps not preselecting certain personality types among candidates, have certainly affected the nature of their party and political contacts, and hence their access to major bargaining resources. Add to this the increased expectations of the office on the part of the public and it is easy to appreciate why so many commentators complain of the office being 'overloaded'. While, in such a context, the premium on bargaining and leadership skills is greatly increased, there is also the danger that, under such enormous pressures, presidents will resort to confrontation or to clandestine and possibly illegal acts simply to get things done. Such was the case with the last years of the Nixon administration. Later, in the Iran–Contra affair, it was not the president but his subordinates who initiated illegal acts in order to overcome congressional opposition. And in the case of George W. Bush, most criticism was levelled at the intelligence community and in particular the CIA for its failure to provide reliable intelligence both on terrorists and on weapons of mass destruction in Iraq.

As we saw, in periods of divided government the veto power was used more often than in the past, and presidents are also prone to go over the heads of congressional leaders with appeals direct to the American people. One thing is sure: no matter how difficult the job becomes or how recent presidents are judged by an increasingly fickle and demanding electorate, the position of president of the United States will continue to attract enormous attention both in the US and abroad. For, to repeat the point yet again, alone in a highly fragmented political system, the presidency is the natural coordinating institution of national leadership. The president has at his command, therefore, the vast resources of the American federal government, including by far the largest and most sophisticated military forces in the world. And while all recent presidents have preached the virtues of limited government, none has meaningfully reduced the size of the federal bureaucratic machine. Domestic and foreign demands on the office are such that all presidents are obliged to use the resources of this behemoth – even while they extol the virtues of limited government.

Summary

Changes in the nature of the party system and the rise of issue and ideological politics have made the business of building coalitions more difficult for presidents. Other changes, including major shifts in the nature of American economic and military power, have also had the effect of making the job of president more difficult. Partly as a result of these changes, presidents have often overstepped their powers since the second half of the twentieth century.

Congress and the courts have responded with a number of measures, including the 1973 War Powers Act and major changes in the budget process. Presidents continue, however, to use the varied resources at their disposal to advance their programmes and policies. In addition to constitutional powers these include appeals to the public, and using the White House political machine to good effect. How well presidents use these resources depends in part on their personality and on how personal characteristics interact with what is an increasingly complex political environment.

Questions for Discussion

1   How do presidents use the American public as a political resource? Give examples of the effective use of 'going public' over the past 40 years.
2   Why has the job of the president become more difficult over the past 40 years? Answer with respect to the experience of TWO presidents.
3   Critically assess the presidency of Barack Obama. Answer with respect either to foreign policy *or* to domestic policy.
4   What is the White House Office? How effective have presidents been in organizing the WHO? Answer with reference to Presidents George W. Bush, Barack Obama and Donald Trump.

Glossary

cabinet   The heads of the cabinet departments in an administration

Executive Office of the President (EOP)   The administrative unit under the control of the president that includes agencies such as the Office of Management and Budget as well as the White House Office

executive privilege   The doctrine that certain information in the executive branch should be kept out of the public domain

federal deficit   The gap between income from taxation and other sources and expenditure in the federal budget

impeachment   The formal accusation of wrongdoing by an officeholder

Imperial Presidency   The view popular in the 1960s and 1970s that presidents were unconstrained in foreign policy

impoundment   Funds appropriated by Congress but sequestered by presidents. Impoundment was made illegal by the Impoundment and Budget Control Act 1974

Iran–Contra affair   The attempt by officials in the Reagan administration to sell arms to Iran and use the proceeds to fund the Contra guerrillas fighting the Sandinista regime in Nicaragua

issue politics   Politics based on particular issues such as abortion or taxation

nationalization of politics   The subservience of state and local concerns to national policies and issues

special prosecutor   The position created to investigate wrongdoing by presidents and other executive officials

White House Office   The administrative unit wholly under the president's control in the White House

Notes

1   For a comprehensive account of how presidents use the public resource, see Sam Kernell, *Going Public*, 4th edn (Washington, DC: Congressional Quarterly Press, 2006).

2   Colonel House with Woodrow Wilson, Harry Hopkins with Franklin Roosevelt, and Sherman Adams with Dwight Eisenhower.

3   For an excellent account of how different presidents have used their staffs, see John Hart, *The Presidential Branch*, 2nd edn (Chatham, NJ: Chatham House, 1994).

4   Hugh Heclo, 'The changing presidential office', in Arnold J. Meltsner (ed.), *Politics and the Oval Office* (San Francisco: Institute for Contemporary Studies, 1987), p. 177.

5   James David Barber, *The Presidential Character*, 5th edn (Englewood Cliffs, NJ: Prentice Hall, 2008).

6   For a good critique, see Alexander L. George and Julliete L. George, *Assessing Presidential Personality and Performance* (Boulder, CO: Westview Press, 1998), chapter 5.

7   Richard E. Neustadt, *Presidential Power* (New York: Wiley, 1960).

8   Neustadt showed how the commands of presidents on three occasions – Truman's sacking of General MacArthur, his decision to seize the steel mills in 1953 and Eisenhower's decision to send federal troops to Little Rock, Arkansas, in 1954 – were as much a demonstration of failure as of success, for they represented the failure of persuasion or the bargaining skills so crucial to the office. See *Presidential Power*, chapters 2 and 3.

Further Reading

A textbook treatment of the presidency is provided by James P. Pfiffner and James H. Davidson, *Understanding the Presidency*, 7th edn (New York and London: Pearson, 2012). See also Stanley M. Milkis and Staley C. Nelson, *The American Presidency: Origins and Development 1776–2014* (Washington, DC: Congressional Quarterly Press, 2015). The classic statement on the president's power to persuade is provided by Richard E. Neustadt, *Presidential Power and the Modern Presidents* (New York: Free Press, 1993). For an account of the increasingly public nature of the office, see Samuel Kernell, *Going Public*, 4th edn (Washington, DC: Congressional Quarterly Press, 2006). For an impressive historical sweep through the presidency, see Stephen Skowronek, *The Politics Presidents Make: Leadership from John Adams to George Bush* (Cambridge, MA: Harvard University Press, 1993). A good study of the presidential bureaucracy is by John Hart, *The Presidential Branch* (Chatham, NJ: Chatham House, 1994). See also Lori Cox Han (ed.), *New Directions in the American Presidency* (London: Taylor & Francis, 2011).

CHAPTER 12
BUREAUCRATIC POWER
FEDERAL DEPARTMENTS AND AGENCIES

The fully developed bureaucratic mechanism compares with other organizations exactly as does the machine with the non-mechanical modes of production. Precision, speed, unambiguity, knowledge of the files, continuity, discretion, unity, strict subordination, reduction of friction and of material and personal costs: these are raised to the optimum point in the strictly bureaucratic administration.

– MAX WEBER, *ESSAYS IN SOCIOLOGY*

American Politics and Society, Ninth Edition. David McKay.
© 2018 John Wiley & Sons Ltd. Published 2018 by John Wiley & Sons Ltd.

Our Government has no special power except that granted it by the people. It is time to check and reverse the growth of government which shows signs of having grown beyond the consent of the governed. It is my intention to curb the size and influence of the federal establishment.
– RONALD REAGAN

Few areas of federal government activity come in for as much opprobrium as does the bureaucracy. As the Weber quote suggests, bureaucracies are supposed to work efficiently. Hierarchy, order, responsibility and professionalism are implied by the model of the 'rational' bureaucrat, yet, according to public folklore, typical federal administrators are the very opposite of this. They are overpaid, inefficient and wasteful. Worse, they are often the creatures of special interests, and occasionally they are simply corrupt. Surveys have shown, indeed, that the federal government is considered easily the most inefficient of all the major institutions in American society. And the public's regard for the federal government steadily declined after reaching a peak in the wake of 9/11 (figure 12.1).

While some of the more colourful charges levelled at the federal bureaucracy more closely resemble caricature than accurate portrait, the executive branch does seem unusually inefficient, fragmented and complex. So much so, indeed, that every president has pledged himself to simplify the executive branch and to root out wasteful and unnecessary programmes. Promises of this sort are popular with the electorate, and no doubt presidents genuinely believe that they can actually rationalize the bureaucracy. In spite of some changes, however, the complaints – and frustrated attempts at reform – continue. This issue raises a number

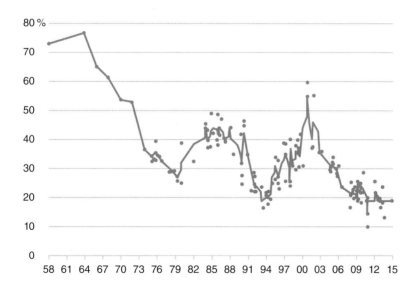

Figure 12.1   Trust in government, 1960–2015. Question: Do you trust the federal government to do what is right just about always/most of the time?
Source: Pew Research Center at www.people-press.org/2015/11/23/1-trust-in-government-1958-2015/.

of questions. Why is it that the executive branch attracts so much criticism? Is the criticism justified? To what extent can the federal bureaucracy be controlled and reformed in ways that make it more responsive to public demands? It may be that the structure and behaviour of the executive departments and agencies reflect other forces in American government that would have to be changed as a prelude to bureaucratic reform. Before we address these questions directly, it is necessary to provide some basic facts about the federal administration in the United States.

The Federal Bureaucracy: Organization and Function

The annual *US Government Manual* produces an organization chart of the government of the United States (figure 12.2). While such charts can be misleading – they imply a hierarchical simplicity and equality between units at the same level that is far from the reality – they do reveal the bare bones of the system.

The most important distinctions are between the 15 executive departments, the independent establishments and the government corporations. Executive or cabinet departments are responsible for the major federal programmes, and their chiefs, the departmental secretaries, are directly answerable to the president or to agencies within the Executive Office of the president, such as the Office of Management and Budget. Given the growth in government over the past 80 years, cabinet departments have not proliferated as might have been expected. In 2016, eight of the 15 departments were creations of the modern era and, of these, one (Defense) grew out of older departments. In fact, successive presidents have worked hard to reduce the number of departments or to rationalize existing ones. In 1949 the Departments of War, Army, Navy and Airforce were combined in one Department of Defense. In 1971 President Nixon set out 'the most far-reaching re-organization of the executive branch that has ever been proposed by a President of the United States'[1] by amalgamating seven cabinet departments into four new ones. His plan was rejected by Congress, but Jimmy Carter and Ronald Reagan continued the campaign to simplify the departments. Ronald Reagan went as far as to label the Departments of Education and Energy unnecessary, and, during 1982, bills were introduced into Congress proposing their abolition. Both were created by Jimmy Carter – the former because the existing Department of Health, Education, and Welfare was so large and cumbersome, and the latter as a direct response to the nation's energy crisis. By 1988 they were still in existence, however, demonstrating Congress's resistance to major rationalizations. In the event, Reagan presided over an expansion of the cabinet departments, with the creation of the Department of Veteran Affairs in 1988. The total was increased to 15 in 2002 with the addition of the Department of Homeland Security. Since then few organizational innovations have occurred.

Most presidents prefer a small, compact cabinet to facilitate smooth policy-making. Yet the number of departments for which they are responsible is but one of a number of management problems they have to face. Another involves the complexity characteristic of each department. This can be formidable, for, with the possible exception of the Department of State (responsible for the foreign service and foreign policy), each department

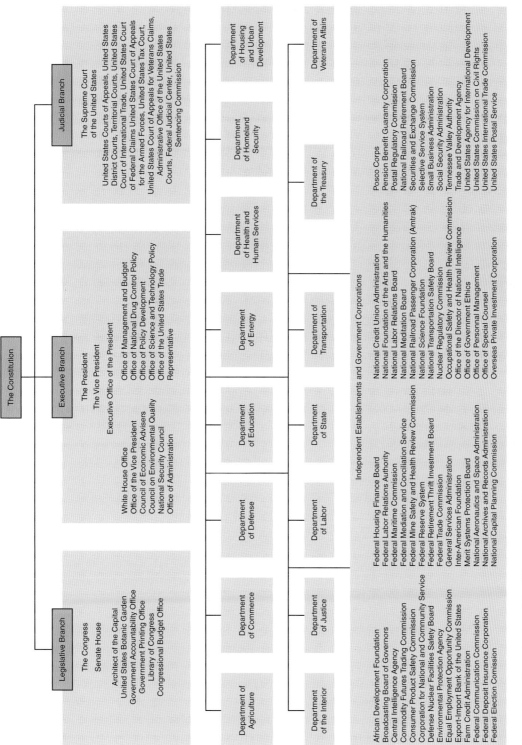

Figure 12.2 Organization of the US government, 2016
Source: US Government Manual (Washington, DC: Government Printing Office).

is itself a collection of different agencies and services, each with its own interests and constituents. So the Department of Health and Human Services (HHS) comprises a whole range of quasi-independent units embracing such areas as the Office for Civil Rights, the Office of Global Health Affairs and the Center for Faith-Based and Neighborhood Partnerships (HHS's present organization is shown in figure 12.3). Again the apparently simple hierarchical structure belies a reality of considerable complexity and competition – although the sheer number of different programmes does give some sense of the complexity of the department. In almost all cabinet departments there is a horizontal division of responsibilities and a vertical division organized geographically. Thus, much of the day-to-day work of HHS and other agencies is carried out at the regional and area levels. There are 10 standard federal regions and, within these, a number of area offices, usually based on large cities. Figure 12.3 also allows us to make some distinction between different sorts of bureaucrats. In the American system, a crucial distinction exists between the *competitive* service, which includes officials recruited by examination or on the basis of technical qualifications determined by the Office of Personnel Management, and the *excepted* service, where appointment is decided, again mainly on merit, directly by such agencies and departments as the Federal Bureau of Investigation (FBI), the Postal Service and the State Department. The excepted service includes the Senior Executive Service (SES) created by the 1978 Civil Service Act. SES appointees are the super-grade grade officials who can, in theory at least, be moved across agencies and given merit pay awards. The excepted service also includes *political* appointees, who make up around 3 per cent of the total. In figure 12.3 the secretary, deputy secretary, assistant secretaries and top officials in each of the sub-units would be political appointees. Other very senior officials would be part of the SES, while the bulk of the remainder would be part of the competitive service. As is developed below, the whole question of the role of political appointees has been highly controversial over the past 30 years.

The independent establishments and government corporations (figure 12.2) include a vast number of agencies performing numerous functions. A very general distinction can be drawn between government corporations (broadly equivalent to state-owned industries in other countries), which include the US Postal Service, and the regulatory agencies. But there are other institutions which fall into neither category, including the General Services Administration and Office of Personnel Management, which deal, respectively, with the provision of buildings, equipment and other services for the whole executive branch, and the recruitment of staff to the cabinet departments. It is a little misleading to label all these institutions 'independent' – the chief administrators (or in a few cases the boards of governors) are appointed by the president, subject to confirmation by the Senate. The president is also a key figure in helping to decide the size of their budgets and in some cases he or the cabinet secretaries take a very direct interest in their activities. This is patently the case with the Central Intelligence Agency (CIA), which is the intelligence arm of the US government abroad and as such is closely monitored by the president and the Defense Secretary.

The regulatory agencies are genuinely more independent, however, because most of them were originally set up by Congress to function as non-partisan organizations responsible for monitoring, controlling or regulating various aspects of economic

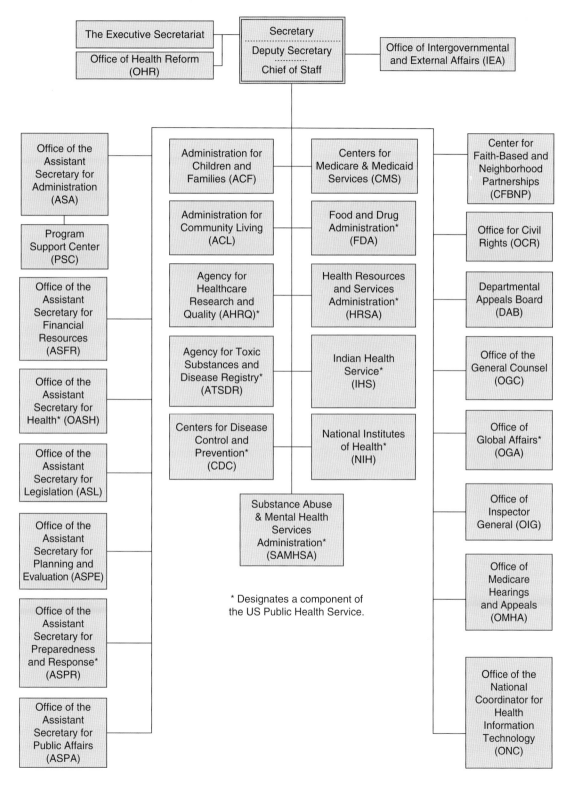

Figure 12.3   Organization of the Department of Health and Human Services, 2016
Source: US Government Manual (Washington, DC: Government Printing Office).

and social life. Three waves of reform in American politics correspond to the three generations of regulatory agencies that exist. Between 1887 and 1915 a rising tide of reform sentiment led to the creation of agencies designed to tame the unacceptable economic and social activities of large corporations and natural monopolies, mainly the railroads. So, during this period, the Interstate Commerce Commission and Federal Trade Commission came into being. During the 1930s, most of the reforms were inspired by the Depression and its consequences. Hence, the Federal Deposit Insurance Corporation underwrites bank deposits to protect the public against bank failures, the Securities and Exchange Commission regulates the stock market and the National Labor Relations Board helps to regulate industrial relations. The final wave of reform, during the 1960s and 1970s, was inspired by, among other things, concern at environmental pollution (leading to the Environmental Protection Agency (EPA), which is, incidentally, not an independent agency but a cabinet-level organization), civil rights (the Equal Employment Opportunity Commission), election malpractice (the Federal Election Commission) and consumer protection (the Consumer Protection Safety Commission). These agencies have sometimes been given formidable powers by Congress to exercise administrative, legislative and judicial powers over corporations, unions and the public at large. Until the 1960s, a common criticism was that they were anything but independent in the use of these powers. Instead the 'regulated controlled the regulators' or, to quote two celebrated cases, the Food and Drugs Administration was in the hands of the drug companies and the Interstate Commerce Commission was deferential to the needs of the truckers and railroads.

Although this is sometimes exaggerated, there is little doubt that many of the regulatory commissions had established a *symbiotic* relationship (each feeds off the other) with what had become their clients. They needed each other – the clients for guidance on how best to operate in (or dominate) the market, and the regulators to ensure political independence[2] and to justify their bureaucratic *raison d'être*.

During the 1960s and 1970s much greater public concern at the abuse of corporate power led to the newer agencies (such as the Environmental Protection Agency) establishing a more *adversarial* relationship with the regulated.[3] This, together with limited reforms in the older agencies and a general increase in the amount of regulation in American life – especially of corporations – has led to a backlash by the corporate world and its political allies, the Republicans.

Contrary to popular belief, the burgeoning responsibilities of the federal government, together with greatly increased expenditure, have not been matched by dramatic increases in the *number* of federal employees responsible for implementing programmes and policies. As can be seen from figure 12.4, the number of federal employees has remained roughly the same over the past 40 years. State and local governments have accounted for the big increases in total government employment. Indeed, starting with the Carter administration and continuing under President Reagan, the absolute number of federal/civilian employees fell – although the decreases were modest and were reversed during the later 1980s and 1990s. Since 2000 the number has remained roughly steady, in spite of increased federal spending. These initial reductions were

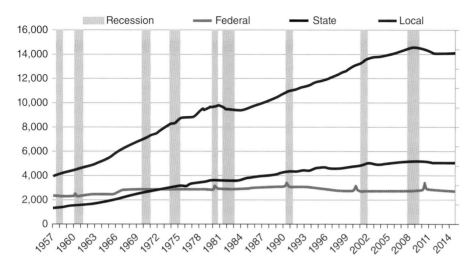

Figure 12.4 Number of government employees: federal, state and local (in thousands), 1957–2014
Source: Wall Street Journal (Dow Jones), http://blogs.wsj.com/economics/2014/11/07/
the-federal-government-now-employs-the-fewest-people-since-1966/, The Federal
Government Now Employs the Fewest People Since 1966, Josh Zumbrun, 7 November
2014 12:03 pm ET.

part of the continuing campaign against big government, but the general failure of
federal employment to rise in the post-war period takes more explaining. Part of the
reason, at least until the early 1980s, was the rapid increase in the number and size of
grant-in-aid programmes to state and local governments. As we saw in chapter 4, a
fair percentage of the general increase in federal spending derives from this source.
Devolved programmes increase employment at the lower, rather than federal, level.
Second, increased expenditure does not necessarily require more federal employees –
although it has almost certainly led to what is a considerable expansion of the number
of professionals in federal employment. Professionals are the middle-grade employees,
often scientists, or the highly trained personnel who have been increasingly recruited
to help run more complex programmes, old and new. In fact (the Post Office excluded)
the federal government employs relatively few less-qualified workers. State and local
governments employ most of the lower grades (transport, hospital, municipal employees) and lower/middle grades (teachers, social workers, police and fire-fighters). A
more professional civil service is harder to control because it can more easily fall back
on technical and highly specialized information when challenged by the public, Congress or the president. Finally, a recent trend in all government bureaucracies, including the federal government, has been to contract out services to the private sector.
Privatization and 'outsourcing' services to private contractors should reduce the number of federal employees and, as discussed below, are likely to become more important
in the future.

CONTROVERSY 11 PRIVATIZATION: FOR AND AGAINST

Privatization takes two main forms: the sale of whole government enterprises to the private sector, and the contracting out of government services to private sector operators. Selling federal government enterprises has been limited in the US mainly because, in comparison with many European countries where everything from railways to car companies has been in public hands, few American corporations have ever been owned by the government. The major exception is the US Postal Service, but political opposition to privatization of the mail has been fierce. Contracting out services, from printing, to canteen meals, to cleaning, to the provision of security in Iraq and Afghanistan, has been prolific, however. In 2002 the Bush administration announced a substantial extension of contracting and promised to shed up to 850,000 jobs over the next several years. In the event, privatization efforts were more limited and most of the privatization in the US has occurred at the state and local levels – in spite of repeated calls from those on the right to privatize the postal service, and such infrastructure assets as ports, airports and roads.

Critics of privatization, who include the labour unions and many Democrats, argue that the device reduces worker security and wages and also leads to less than satisfactory standards in the services provided. Supporters argue that market discipline increases efficiency by lowering costs and reducing waste. They maintain that markets will always be better at working out the most efficient way of providing services. One of the problems with contracting out, however, is that it rarely occurs in perfect market conditions. Some firms may be favoured over others, perhaps for political reasons. Just such accusations were directed at one of the major private reconstruction companies operating in Iraq, Halliburton Oil, whose chief executive officer until 2000 was 2001–9 Vice President Dick Cheney. Another market problem is not favouritism but the possibility that the government will award contracts to the cheapest provider, which may not be the company with the appropriate standards for the job. Whatever the merits and demerits of contracting out, the device is certainly here to stay, for neither Democrats nor Republicans propose a wholesale return of government services to in-house organizations. Indeed on coming into office in 2017 the Trump administration was intent on bringing privatization to a number of federal programmes.

The Bureaucracy: How Uncontrollable?

Students of administrative behaviour are quick to identify certain characteristics of bureaucracy that are present whatever the political system involved or governmental function being performed. Some of these characteristics are labelled 'undesirable' – usually because they greatly reduce the accountability of bureaucrats to elected officials – and, as government becomes larger and more complex, so these undesirable features multiply. There is, of course, no reason to suppose that the United States is exempt from these trends. It is not, and that is problem enough. But critics go much further and argue that US government, and particularly the federal bureaucracy, has a number of additional, and uniquely American, features that make the problem of accountability a particularly serious one. Unfortunately, unravelling cause and effect is difficult in this area, especially in a country where 'federal government' and 'bureaucracy' often hold negative connotations. With so many Americans deeply prejudiced against what they see as big government, it is important to treat with caution some of the more colourful critiques levelled against bureaucracy, regulation, 'Washington' and the civil service. The task of the remainder of this chapter is, therefore, to outline the major criticisms directed at the federal bureaucracy, to assess their validity, and to record the ways in which presidents, Congress, the courts and the public have attempted to increase their control over administrators.

The Inherent Power of Bureaucracy

Simple theories of constitutional government and of administrative behaviour assign little or no independent power or discretion to administrators. Their job is to implement laws. The legislature passes the laws and the chief executive is responsible for managing and directing the administrators in the implementation process. According to classical theories of administration, bureaucrats can do this effectively if they operate in line with certain basic principles – hierarchical command, specialization and delegation of duties. The elected chief executives are at the apex of this system, and they alone give commands; bureaucrats may advise them, but it is not their job actually to give orders. Reality is, of course, very far from this ideal type. In most systems, bureaucrats have two main powers, both of which can give them considerable control over the policy system.

Information

Bureaucrats function as administrative gatekeepers. When laws are being framed, whether by legislatures or executives, it is essential to find out what is achievable and what is not. A new law on lead levels in gasoline, for example, needs to be carefully informed about a host of technical questions, including the efficiency of internal combustion engines, pollution levels, the car industry's ability to compete internationally once its products are adapted and so on. Politicians are obliged to heed the advice of their officials on such technicalities, and the officials themselves can, up to a point, select and organize information according to their own preferences and prejudices, or in favour of one interest rather than another. They may, for example, advise the politicians that certain options are simply not possible for technical reasons. Examples of administrative gatekeeping in highly technical areas may sound understandable, and possibly exceptional. But almost all law making and implementation in modern industrial societies is technical and complex. From housing to transport

Plate 12.1   Aerial view of the Pentagon, Washington, DC
Source: Digital Vision/Getty Images.

to law enforcement to social security and defence, technical questions are paramount. No single president or cabinet secretary can possibly absorb all this information – even with the assistance of professional staffs. They have to rely on their bureaucrats.

Clientelism

Clientelism is the word used to describe the sort of symbiotic relationships between bureaucrats and their customers referred to above. Again, it is not unique to American politics; to a greater or lesser extent it occurs everywhere. It is also an entirely understandable phenomenon. Consider the case of defence agencies and defence contractors. In those Western countries with sizeable defence industries (Britain, Germany, France and the USA) intimate relations exist between contractors and officials in defence departments. Defence officials have, therefore, a continuing interest in particular corporations and defence systems – and also, perhaps, in ensuring that defence spending remains at certain levels. These interests may or may not be the same as those of the administrators' political masters. But there can be no doubting the independent political influence of officials in this context. Information is, again, the crucial resource, but it is not merely technical information; it is this plus all the advantages which daily personal contact and shared values give to the official and which are often denied to the politicians. During periods of national emergency such as prevailed in the years following the 9/11 attacks, this bureaucratic power is enhanced because politicians will fear the consequences of challenging technical advice from bureaucrats.

As government has increased in size and scope, so clientelism has spread. In modern societies all bureaucracies have their customers whose interests and needs must be tended to, whatever the government in power or the values and preferences of elected politicians.

The Bureaucratic Hydra: A Uniquely American Phenomenon?

Scholars of comparative government often refer to the extent to which different political systems are characterized by 'strong' or 'weak' states. Almost invariably, the United States is categorized as a weak state. In other words, rather than government being unified, resolute and separated from the rest of society, it is fragmented, indecisive and infused with social influence. The aforementioned clientelism is a good indicator of the power and autonomy of the state. Although it exists everywhere, clientelism is likely to be more pervasive in weak state systems. In addition, weak states are likely to be characterized by competition between different parts of the administrative process. So sub-units – individual departments and agencies – display a marked degree of *autonomy* from the centre. They serve different interests, and their officials do not all share the same values and policy objectives. We are not referring here to the absolute *size* of government. As noted, in terms of expenditure and function, American government is large by any standards. We are, rather, referring to the extent to which American government is fragmented and simply not amenable to central direction and control.

Much recent criticism centres on this fact. Critics usually do not put the particular American situation in comparative context, but we have good reason to believe that the United States is different from many other countries; that certain institutional relationships make it especially difficult to exercise central control over public policy. Three basic critiques of American bureaucracy have been made over the past 30 years: the 'iron triangle', 'issue network' and public choice/principal–agent critiques.

Iron triangles

Starting with books written by Douglass Cater and Leiper Freeman in the mid-1960s came accusations that sub-governments working as iron triangles – congressional sub-committee, administrative bureau and special interest – were the dominant actors in American politics.[4] The analysis was simple: congressional sub-committees provide the money and monitor regulations, the bureau actually hands over the money or enforces the regulation, and the special interest is the beneficiary. All need one another and the system would break down without equal participation by all – hence the 'iron triangle' metaphor. Empirical confirmation of sub-governments of this sort was readily at hand, especially in public works, defence, agriculture and water policy. Agriculture became a particularly appealing example, with bureaux in the Department of Agriculture handing out subsidies to farmers who, in turn, had established intimate links with members of the several agricultural sub-committees in

Congress. The triangle was 'iron' because it was impenetrable. The combined political clout of the leading sub-government actors was formidable, with no individual president, public interest lobby or congressional leader able to break the pattern of distribution and public expenditure that the triangle had moulded.

While the empirical validity of this case was convincing for certain sorts of public policy, it was clearly inappropriate in other areas. Appreciating this fact, Ripley and Franklin refined the thesis in an important book first published in 1976.[5] They pointed out that, in what they call redistributive domestic policy (where resources are taken from one group or class and given to another, as in social welfare programmes), presidents and top-level (politically appointed) officials, as well as Congress as a whole, play a more important part. And in some regulatory policies, bureaucracy and administration play a relatively small role. Other, more sophisticated refinements were added by the authors to the sub-government theory, all of which demonstrated that the American administrative and political process is indeed unduly complex and often not amenable to simple, single-model characterizations.

Issue networks

A conceptually much simpler, yet almost certainly more accurate, picture of administrative politics in America has been drawn by Hugh Heclo. Heclo argued that, as government programmes have grown in size and scope, so they have generated new lobbies, interests and, simply, a larger number of active participants in the policy process. Moreover, the networks of politicking and lobbying which develop as a consequence are constantly adapting and changing. So it is very difficult accurately to categorize where the policy system begins and ends:

> The notion of iron triangles and sub-governments presumes small circles of participants who have succeeded in becoming largely autonomous. Issue networks, on the other hand, comprise a large number of participants with quite variable degrees of mutual commitment or of dependence on others in their environment; in fact it is almost impossible to say where a network leaves off and its environment begins.[6]

As a result of this much more open and volatile system, no erstwhile secure sub-government can afford to be complacent. The cosy relationships established between corporations and bureaucrats have been challenged by environmentalists, consumer protection advocates and other public interest lobbies (a point developed in chapter 14). The sub-governments continue to exist, of course, but they are increasingly buffeted by competing centres of power. Heclo does not view these developments as entirely negative – indeed, there may be greater scope for executive leadership when the system is more open. But he does view with alarm the increasing complexity of government and the fact that direct democratic accountability is difficult to achieve when the 'real' decisions are taken not by president and members of Congress, but by numerous additional political actors, including bureaucrats, lobbyists, the media and political consultants.

Public choice and the principal–agent problem

Neither the iron triangle nor the issue network approaches offers definitive *solutions* to the problem of bureaucracy. From the 1970s to the 2000s, however, a number of economists and political scientists argued that the central problem of bureaucracy related to the sort of personal incentives available to the bureaucrats themselves. Public choice theory assumes that all actors in the political process (politicians, voters, officials, interest groups) are self-interested and seek to maximize benefits, whether in votes, income or power. Officials will do this by maximizing their budgets so as to accumulate personal benefits (promotion, salary, pension, status). Given this, in the traditionally organized bureaucracy some over-provision will occur and will result in unit costs higher than those that would prevail if the market provided the services. Even in private firms, there remains what some economists have called the principal–agent problem. This assumes that the principal (for example, the owner of a firm) cannot always be sure that his or her managers (the agents) are not shirking or are operating at a level that optimizes profits. This is often because employees will receive the same salary irrespective of effort, so they have little incentive to work hard. In bureaucracies the problem is even more serious because government officials rarely produce anything that can be *measured*. If, for example, an FBI agent makes no arrests, is this because he or she is shirking or because there is little crime? Moreover, what is the equivalent of the private firm owner in a bureaucracy? In a sense, all the managers including those at the very top have little incentive to perform.

Two possible solutions exist to reduce or eliminate this problem. First, services can be privatized so the discipline of the market is imposed (see Controversy 11). Second, if full privatization is not possible the institutional rules and procedures can be changed in ways that alter officials' incentive to maximize spending. Creating quasi-independent agencies run by managers on fixed contracts under instructions to meet predetermined cost and performance targets can facilitate this. As a result, officials will see a common interest between improvements in efficiency and their own career and pay prospects.

What is interesting about these critiques of bureaucratic power is that they are comments not only on administrators and administrative agencies, but also on the whole policy-making system. Many make the *a priori* assumption that more government is by definition a bad thing and that increasing public disenchantment with government derives from the constantly expanding volume of legislation and special regulations. Without commenting on the normative (value) question of whether more government is good or bad, it is obviously the case that government, by whatever definition (number of employees and policies, volume of regulations, amount of public expenditures) has increased in all modern industrial societies over the past 50 years. Though criticism of big government has occurred in other countries, it has been particularly vocal in the USA – a country where, as a percentage of gross national product (GNP), government, though large, is hardly at the top of the international league table. No doubt this can partly be explained in ideological terms. As we have repeatedly noted in this book, the USA has a long-established tradition of antagonism to government. But there are also important institutional differences between the USA and most other countries which may help us to understand both academic and popular critiques of government in general and bureaucracy in particular.

Easily the most important is the independent role of Congress. Iron triangles and issue networks depend at least in part on an autonomous legislature and, within Congress, little legislatures (committees and sub-committees). Although this has long been appreciated – for example, in 1970 Harold Seidman noted that 'meaningful improvements in executive organization and in the management of the Federal system … will depend in the final analysis on re-organization of the congressional committee structure'[7] – it seems to have been partly forgotten amid all the talk of special interest politics, political action committees and the generally more complex and confusing pattern of government typical of the twenty-first century. Although it could be argued that autonomous legislative power increases accountability, it also greatly facilitates the sort of volatile issue network politics where no single actor in the policy process can ever fully understand what is going on, let alone control events. Arguably, this is the very antithesis of accountability. As discussed below, successive governments, including the Clinton, George W. Bush and Obama administrations, have recognized this problem, but few have been able to do much about it.

A second unique feature of the American system is its openness. Access to Congress and members of Congress, as well as to officials at all levels, is remarkably easy compared with most other countries. Exploiting this fact, Washington has become a political consultants' and lobbyists' paradise. No interest, whether economic (corporations, unions), public interest (environment, consumer protection) or governmental (state and local governments), can afford to drop its guard by failing to make full use of the availability of policy-makers. Again, openness is at least partly a function of the proliferation of centres of autonomy or power. With sub-committees, bureaux, agencies and even individual officials competing with one another over particular areas of public policy, they are usually only too ready to make use of any resource that will enhance their autonomy further; in essence this means organized interests (together with their technical advisers, the lobbyists and consultants) and the media. A more open system received fresh impetus from the cathartic effects of the Watergate scandals. Freedom of information became a major public issue during the late 1960s and early 1970s, and the formal legal access of groups and individuals to government files and information was greatly strengthened as a result.[8] But these formal changes were almost certainly not as important in producing greater access as the changes in Congress, the party system and American society generally which earlier chapters have chronicled.

Reform Attempts

Perhaps the most common recent response to the problem of big government and bureaucratic power is simply to propose a reduction in the size and complexity of government. This has been the aim of all four recent presidents.

In his 1982 State of the Union message, Ronald Reagan declared:

> Together, we have cut the growth of new federal regulations in half. In 1981, there were 23,000 fewer pages in the Federal Register, which lists new regulations, than there were in 1980.… Together, we have created an effective federal strike force to combat waste and fraud in government. In just six months it has saved the taxpayers more than two billion dollars – and it's only getting started.

As we noted above, the number of federal employees did decline during the late 1970s and early 1980s, since when the number has steadied through to the mid-1990s then dipped slightly (figure 12.4). Does this mean that presidents are winning the battle against bureaucracy? Not necessarily. Federal employment may not have risen rapidly, but numbers are only loosely related to complexity and autonomy.

Similarly, Ronald Reagan's reductions in new regulations did nothing to alter the fact of already established regulations, together with their policy networks. 'Waste and fraud' in the federal government undoubtedly exist, but this condemnation is more of a populist rallying cry than an attack on the central problems of complexity and autonomy. As we know, several presidents have attempted to reorganize the executive branch, the most dramatic proposal being Richard Nixon's 1971 plan to create four 'super departments' – Natural Resources, Human Resources, Community Development and Economic Affairs. Other, less ambitious reorganizations have been attempted, some successfully, others not. Sometimes these involve the creation of new departments (HUD in 1965, Health, Education and Welfare (HEW) in 1953 (now the Department of Health and Human Services), the Department of Energy in 1977, the Department of Education in 1979, Veteran Affairs in 1988 and Homeland Security in 2002). More common are internal reorganizations, usually aimed at simplifying administration and reducing overlapping jurisdictions. Although well intentioned, reorganization is almost always a less than adequate reform measure. For one thing, Congress is reluctant to approve reorganizations that affect its own internal distribution of power, and accordingly has vetoed the more far-reaching reforms. Committees and, increasingly, sub-committees have vested interests in the continuing autonomy of departments, bureaux and agencies. Second, internal reorganization often involves 'shuffling the same old drones into new hives', as Robert Sherrill has put it, so no real change occurs.

In fact, Ronald Reagan eschewed the reorganization device, opting instead for more direct *political* control of the executive branch. He did this in two ways: through control of agency and departmental rule-making and through the appointment power. In 1980 Congress passed the Paperwork Reduction Act, a law sponsored by the Carter administration and designed to simplify federal regulations. The Act established an Office of Information and Regulatory Affairs (OIRA) within the Office of Management and Budget (OMB). Although it was not in itself very significant, the Reagan administration used this new unit, in combination with two executive orders, to screen new agency regulations. In effect, this required the executive departments and agencies to submit any changes in policy to the OMB. In turn, the OMB rejected any rules considered not in line with administration policy. Not surprisingly, this particularly affected those agencies that, in the past, the administration had considered too progressive in such areas as environmental protection, affirmative action, occupational safety and health, welfare, education, and social security. These centralized gatekeeping efforts provoked a storm of protest in Congress and almost certainly led to a loosening of regulations in a number of areas. As a number of commentators have noted, however, these changes did not amount to a fundamental shift in policy.[9]

The Reagan administration's use of the appointment power attracted a great deal of publicity because it represented a thoroughgoing attempt to politicize the executive branch. As well as placing Reagan supporters in the cabinet departments and regulatory agencies, the administration centralized the appointment, transfer and promotion of members of the

Senior Executive Service. Utilizing the provisions of the 1978 Civil Service Act, the Office of Personnel Management, under direct instructions from Ed Meese in the White House, promoted, rewarded and transferred Reagan loyalists while punishing those considered liberal or disloyal. At the cabinet level, some of the Reagan appointees were so out of tune with their departments and with public opinion that they were forced to resign (Anne Gorsuch at EPA; James Watt at Interior). Lower down, the politicization strategy was also controversial and led to falling morale and frequent resignations among civil servants.

Again, limits exist as to what can be achieved from such a strategy. If Congress establishes an Environmental Protection Agency, its job is to protect the environment. Officials recruited to the EPA will support this basic objective. Changing senior managers can undermine this policy but they cannot transform it. Congress, moreover, is ever vigilant and keen to exercise its oversight function. This extends to the appointment power and, as noted, several Reagan appointees were rejected or obliged to resign (including the director of the Office of Personnel Management, Donald Devine).

Other oversight resources have been utilized by Congress in its attempts to control the bureaucracy. The General Accounting Office has been more rigorous in providing an information base for evaluation, whether the criticism is politicization or not. There has even been some flirtation with 'sunset' legislation. Another symptom of the populist revolt against big government, sunset laws require agencies or programmes to be renewed annually. If they are not fulfilling their purpose, they simply cease to exist. Such measures have not so far been adopted on a significant scale.

George Bush Senior was much more sympathetic to the federal bureaucracy than was Ronald Reagan. He had himself served as an official ambassador to the UN and China and as head of the Central Intelligence Agency, and one of his first acts as president was to invite all the top officials to a reception labelled 'A Salute to Public Service'. His appointments were noticeably less ideological than Reagan's, although, as a Republican, he too favoured the 'core' departments whose values and functions are close to the Republican ethos: State, Defense, Justice, Treasury.

On coming to power, Bill Clinton had two major objectives in terms of administrative reform. First, he wanted to reverse what he saw as the Republican bias towards employing older white males to senior positions in the executive branch. Second, he was intent on a further streamlining of the civil service that would make it more responsive to the public and less enmeshed in red tape and regulations. There is no doubting that he achieved a much greater degree of ethnic, racial and gender diversity than his Republican counterparts. Indeed, in his search for diversity, he was not always able to find appropriate appointees and he was accused of being inordinately slow in his appointment process. Most of the new appointees were what might be called 'New Democrats', or pragmatic rather than ideological reformers. Notably absent were 'Great Society liberals' who believe that the answer to most of society's problems lies in bigger and better federal programmes. The values of these new appointees fitted well with the administration's infatuation with the 'reinventing government' movement. *Reinventing Government* was the title of a book by David Osborne and Ted Gaebler which argued that the public sector could be transformed by applying market principles and the entrepreneurial spirit to it. This involved, among other things, 'empowering' employees by decentralizing decision-making within the civil service, cutting red tape, reducing costs and 'putting customers first'.[10] Note that these reforms, while very much in the public choice tradition of reform, do not, for the most part, involve an *ideological* agenda of the Reagan variety which was designed to meet the objectives of the New Right. Instead, making bureaucracy more *efficient* and responsive was the key objective. In line with these principles, President Clinton commissioned a National Performance Review (NPR) chaired by Vice President Al Gore. The resulting report recommended 384 major changes affecting 27 agencies and departments. Most of these involved reducing the number of rules and regulations and decentralizing power within individual departments and agencies. It should be stressed, however, that it was never Clinton's intention to *weaken* executive power. Rather, the aim was to make the executive branch more *efficient and responsive*. In this sense the president was continuing the trend begun by Jimmy Carter in the 1970s. One final point: as the quotation at the beginning of the chapter suggests, Clinton's NPR initiative is unlikely to succeed without major changes in the way in which Congress deals with the bureaucracy. Reinventing government means making it more autonomous. This means weakening Congress's grip on the executive branch. In fact Congress has produced its own initiative for 'downsizing' government – the Government Performance and Results Act (GPRA) of 1993. By requiring federal agencies to set goals and reach performance targets, this legislation was in much the same mould as the NPR. However, by the end of 1998 the results were highly uneven. Significantly, the one attempt to give the NPR legislative teeth, the creation of Performance-Based Organizations or PBOs, was defeated by Congress in 1996. In sum, while both Congress and the Clinton administration supported administrative reform, they did not act in concert in this crucial area. This is the major reason why, with some exceptions, most of the major moves towards the market in the USA, including most privatizations, have occurred in state and local rather than in federal government. In such countries and Britain and New Zealand, where executive power and party discipline are more unified, moves towards market-like reforms in national bureaucracies have been far more extensive.

The election of the more conservative George W. Bush should, other things being equal, have produced a renewed attack on bureaucracy and government waste. However, the first initiative of the administration was to create by executive order (executive orders do not require congressional approval, but their scope is limited to organizational and other changes within the executive branch) an Office of Faith-Based and Community Initiatives (OFBCI) within the White House. The purpose here was to give official support to church and other charities doing welfare and other good work at the community level. All the relevant government departments were asked to coordinate their programmes in order to further this objective and to direct already appropriated funds towards charity organizations. The sums involved here were small but not trivial. By 2004, $1.16 billion, or 8 per cent of the entire competitive grant programmes distributed by federal agencies (but in reality mainly by the Department of Health and Human Services and Department of Housing and Urban Development), were diverted to faith-based charities. However, this does not really represent a move from the public to the private sector, but more from one part of the private sector to another. This is because most of the competitive grant money in by far the largest programmes involved (housing for the elderly and the poor) already went to private sector and charitable organizations. The Bush administration also proposed further privatizations in the executive branch and far-reaching reform of the civil service to improve efficiency through the introduction of merit-based pay and other performance-related incentives. However, these reforms were rejected by Congress. Generally, the Bush years witnessed a decline in the status of federal civil servants and a return to the politicization of the bureaucracy that was so apparent during the Great Society years and the Reagan years.

If anything, the Obama administration continued this trend by issuing an executive order for a government-wide review of all regulations to reduce costs and inefficiencies. In the event, 26 executive agencies produced efficiency plans involving more than 500 proposals. Among the most effective of the measures were those produced by the Departments of Health and Human Services, Transportation, Homeland Security, Labor, Agriculture and the EPA. Most of the reforms were designed to reduce both waste and costs and to lighten the regulatory burden on users. For example federal requirements on the vapour recovery nozzles used for pumping of gasoline at petrol stations were relaxed because cars themselves had become much less polluting. Whether, in total, these changes reduced the regulatory burden in a meaningful way is doubtful, however. Even more radical proposals for cost reductions including some part privatization of health programmes were proposed by the Trump Administration in 2017. Only time will tell if these will change fundamentally the ways in which the federal bureaucracy operates.

Concluding Remarks

This review confirms that the US bureaucratic system is characterized by numerous and highly volatile issue networks. These are not impenetrable because a more open policy system allows new forces and interests to influence even the most established relationships. These networks remain autonomous, however, not in the sense that they constitute closed policy systems, but because they have proved not to be easily amenable to central control. Even a determined president with great public support like Ronald Reagan, who was intent on imposing radical changes in bureaucratic behaviour, could achieve only limited results. Most recently, public disquiet with the federal bureaucracy has impelled both presidents and Congress to 'downsize' the federal bureaucracy through devolution, the contracting out of services and de-regulation. However, as noted, the two branches have generally failed to act in concert on this issue. And quite apart from executive–legislative difficulties, 'downsizing' does not always have positive results. For example, the number of employees in the Department of Health and Human Services was reduced by almost half in the three years 1993–6, but this was because many medical services were contracted out to the very same personnel removed from that department. Whether this made the agency more 'accountable' and 'responsive' remains in doubt. The experience of other countries suggests that downsizing government sometimes results in less rather than more public confidence in such programmes as health and education.[11] In sum, the currently popular reforms, most of which are influenced by the public choice critique of bureaucratic power, may reduce some waste and costs and make government more accountable. They may not, however, always result in higher-quality service delivery for the public.

Summary

The executive branch of the federal government is a vast bureaucracy consisting of the Executive Office of the President, 15 cabinet departments and numerous independent agencies and commissions. Much of the debate about bureaucracy has centred on its tendency towards complexity and inefficiency. In the American context there has been a particular emphasis on the self-serving nature of federal agencies, with the growth of iron triangles and issue networks being the main targets of critics. Reform attempts have included reorganizations and privatization. In spite of some advances, criticism remains common, although the size of the executive branch has remained roughly constant over the past 20 years.

Questions for Discussion

1   Why do so many Americans believe that federal government bureaucracy is 'out of control'? How successful have attempts to reform the system been since the 1980s?
2   Which are the most powerful cabinet departments? What determines their status? Answer with reference to the period since 2008.
3   How has privatization worked in the US? What are the limits to privatization of the federal government?

Glossary

administrative gatekeeping   The ability of bureaucracies to filter information and access from Congress and the public

Central Intelligence Agency (CIA)   The main intelligence arm for overseas intelligence in the US

clientelism   Bureaucratic links between agencies and the interests they are supposed to fund and regulate

competitive service   Meritocratically appointed civil servants in the US federal government

excepted service   Politically appointed bureaucrats in the US federal service

executive order   A presidential order changing policy within the executive branch

General Services Administration   The agency responsible for buildings and services in the federal government

government corporations   Government-owned enterprises such as the US Postal Service

iron triangles   Intimate links between agencies, congressional committees and organized interests

issue networks   Looser links between bureaucrats, Congress and interests

Office of Faith-Based and Community Initiatives (OFBCI)   George W. Bush initiative to encourage religious funding of public services, later renamed the Center for Faith-Based and Neighborhood Partnerships

Office of Management and Budget (OMB)   The main agency responsible for monitoring government spending and regulatory arrangements

Office of Personnel Management (OPM)   The agency responsible for appointing people to the civil service

outsourcing   Allocating services within government to private contractors

political appointees   Civil servants appointed by presidents on political grounds

principal–agent problem   The problems associated with getting subordinates to comply with managerial or owner directives

privatization   The sale of government assets to private companies

public choice   The branch of social science relating to the problems associated with ensuring public bodies make rational decisions

Notes

1   Quoted in Otis L. Graham, *Toward a Planned Society: From Roosevelt to Nixon* (New York: Oxford University Press, 1976), p. 209.

2   See Murray Edelman, *The Symbolic Uses of Politics* (Urbana: University of Illinois Press, 1964), for a good analysis of this point.

3   For a selection of case studies on regulation, see James Q. Wilson (ed.), *The Politics of Regulation* (New York: Basic Books, 1982).

4   Douglass Cater, *Power in Washington* (New York: Vintage, 1964); J. Leiper Freeman, *The Political Process* (New York: Random House, 1965).

5   Randall B. Ripley and Grace A. Franklin, *Congress, the Bureaucracy and Public Policy*, 5th edn (Homewood, IL: Dorsey Press, 1991).

6   Hugh Heclo, 'Issue networks and the executive establishment', in Anthony King (ed.), *The New American Political System* (Washington, DC: American Enterprise Institute, 1978), p. 102.

7   Harold Seidman, *Politics, Position and Power: the Dynamics of Federal Organization* (New York: Oxford University Press, 1970), p. 285.

8   Under the 1966 and 1974 Freedom of Information Acts, Americans have the right to inspect all federal records. Certain information (for example, relating to criminal investigation, defence or inter-office memos) can be denied, but citizens can appeal against refusals in the courts. The substantive freedom of access in the USA is dramatically greater than in most comparable countries, and especially than in the United Kingdom.

9   For a review, see David McKay, *Domestic Policy and Ideology* (Cambridge: Cambridge University Press, 1989).

10   David Osborne and Ted Gaebler, *Reinventing Government: How the Entrepreneurial Spirit is Transforming the Public Sector* (New York: Penguin, 1993).

11   For a review of the British public's reactions to such reforms, see Ian Budge et al., *The New British Politics* (New York: Addison Wesley Longman, 1998), chapters 10 and 26.

Further Reading

Randall B. Ripley and Grace A. Franklin provide a fascinating insight into the world of sub-governments in their *Congress, the Bureaucracy and Public Policy*, 5th edn (New York: Dorsey Press, 1991). A good textbook treatment of the subject is by Stanley Workman, *The Dynamics of Bureaucracy in the US Government: How Congress and Federal Agencies Process Information and Solve Problems* (Cambridge: Cambridge University Press, 2015).

On reinventing government, see David Osborne and Ted Gaebler, *Reinventing Government: How the Entrepreneurial Spirit Is Transforming the Public Sector* (New York: Penguin, 1996). See also Al Gore, *Common Sense Government Works Better and Costs Less* (Washington, DC: US Government Printing Office, 1995). A good analysis of public disenchantment with bureaucracy is provided by Joseph Nye, Philip Zelikow and David King, *Why People Don't Trust Government* (Cambridge, MA: Harvard University Press, 1998). A more optimistic view is Charles T. Goodsell, *The Case for Bureaucracy* (Washington, DC: CQ Press, 2003). A critique of recent changes is provided by Paul C. Light, *A Government Ill Executed: The Decline of the Federal Service and How to Reverse It* (Cambridge, MA: Harvard University Press, 2009).

CHAPTER 13
THE SECURITY STATE

To those who scare peace loving people with phantoms of lost liberty, my message is this: your tactics aid terrorists for they erode our national unity and diminish our resolve. They give ammunition to America's enemies and pause to America's friends.
                                            – ATTORNEY GENERAL JOHN ASHCROFT, 2001

Just trust us, [Attorney General] John Ashcroft said, as he demanded that Congress pass the Patriot Act, no questions asked. After two and a half years, during which he arrested and secretly detained more than a thousand people, Mr. Ashcroft has yet to convict any actual terrorists.
                                            – PAUL KRUGMAN, *NEW YORK TIMES* COLUMNIST, 2004

American Politics and Society, Ninth Edition. David McKay.
© 2018 John Wiley & Sons Ltd. Published 2018 by John Wiley & Sons Ltd.

In the Middle East, we have people chopping the heads off Christians. We have things that we have never seen before. Not since medieval times have people seen what's going on. I would bring back waterboarding and I'd bring back a hell of a lot worse than waterboarding.
– DONALD TRUMP, 2016

Until 11 September 2001 a foreign force had never directly attacked the continental United States in the modern era. The Japanese attack on Pearl Harbor in 1941 was a strike on a US territory but not (at that time) on a state or on the continent of North America. 9/11 also came at a time when public perceptions of threat to the security of the country were at a historic low. Following the end of the Cold War, the odds of a nuclear confrontation were dramatically reduced, and the 'New World Order' heralded by President George Bush Senior in 1991 seemed to promise a period of relative peace and stability. These hopes were dashed by the events of 9/11, and in response the George W. Bush administration launched a series of initiatives to protect the 'homeland' from international terrorism. The purpose of this chapter is to assess the implications of these initiatives in terms of both American domestic politics and the broader questions of civil liberties and American values.

The Rise of the Security State

Until the twentieth century, the United States was remarkably free from the sort of central government controls over the population that were typical of many European states. No national police force existed, no identity-card system was in place, travel within the country was unrestricted and immigration almost completely unregulated. In addition, the First Amendment, although not strictly enforced at the state and local levels (not least in the segregationist South), was assumed to be an article of faith in supporting freedom of speech, including a free press.

During and following the First World War, however, a number of states passed laws restricting the activities of anarchists, communists and other 'subversives', and in 1917 Congress passed the Espionage Act, which made it an offence to convey false reports or statements with intent to interfere with the operations of the US armed forces. This law was declared constitutional in the famous Schenck case (see chapter 15). Further restrictions were imposed on the freedom of speech by the 1940 Smith Act and the 1952 Internal Security Act (sometimes known as the McCarran Act), both of which were designed to control the activities of 'subversives' – namely fascists and communists whose ideology specifically or implicitly preached the overthrow of the US government. The McCarran Act in particular was much criticized for requiring all communists to register with the Department of Justice, which could then prosecute or even deport them. It also effectively banned people with actual or alleged communist sympathies from government employment. Significantly, President Harry Truman considered the law an affront to the First Amendment and he promptly vetoed it. However, sizeable majorities in both houses of Congress overrode his veto.

Between 1957 and the late 1960s the Supreme Court gradually diluted the effectiveness of the Act, so that by the 1970s it was essentially unworkable. Indeed the Supreme Court gradually strengthened the rights of individuals in relation to the government, so that by the late 1970s allegations of the abuse of individual rights were relatively rare.

Notwithstanding these developments, beginning in the first part of the twentieth century, the federal government acquired a number of new police agencies, and all the existing ones, such as the US Marshals, were expanded in size. The most famous of the federal forces, the Federal Bureau of Investigation (FBI), began as the Bureau of Investigations in the Department of Justice in 1908. It was formally designated as the FBI in 1935, having been built up by its director, J. Edgar Hoover, whose tenure lasted all the way to 1972. By 2016 the FBI had over 35,000 employees, around 14,000 of whom were agents. The Secret Service was created in 1865 following the assassination of Abraham Lincoln, and was specifically briefed to protect the president. Today its duties include the protection of all presidents and vice presidents and their families, past and present. It also investigates counterfeiting and other financial crimes. The Bureau of Alcohol, Tobacco and Firearms (ATF) is the tax-collecting enforcement and regulatory arm of the Treasury. Its origins go all the way back to the beginning of the republic, but it became a full police agency only in 1972. Its brief also includes the use of explosives, which accounts for its involvement in the Waco, Texas, siege in 1999, when 80 followers of cultist David Koresh died in a fire, and in the aftermath of the 1995 Oklahoma bombing of a federal building, when 168 died. The US Marshals Service was created in 1789 to protect the federal courts. Over time, the marshals have been used in a variety of associated roles, including the enforcement of federal court orders to desegregate the South in the 1960s. The US citizenship and Immigration Services (or USCIS, also known as the Immigration and Naturalization Service until 2002) also has a long history, and since 9/11 has taken on a much more active policing role. The Drugs Enforcement Administration (DEA) was created in 1973 to pursue the illegal use of narcotics. The Internal Revenue Service (IRS) also has police enforcement responsibilities with powers of arrest and seizure of property and bank accounts. Finally the US Customs Service (now called US Customs Service and Border Security) dates from 1789 and has extensive police powers relating to customs matters.

Table 13.1 identifies the eight main federal police agencies. Note that while the Customs, Secret Service and USCIS have been transferred to the Department of Homeland Security (DHS), most of the police agencies, including the FBI and ATF, remain with their lead department. (The ATF was transferred from the Treasury to Justice in 2003.) This fragmentation of authority reflects the influence of these departments and the congressional committees that fund them. Table 13.1 only shows some of the *main* federal police agencies. About 60 more exist, covering everything from guarding the Capitol, to the Bureau of Prisons, to the US Park Police, to US Postal Inspectors. For ordinary Americans the most important and familiar of these is the Internal Revenue Service, which is part of the US Department of the Treasury.

Table 13.1   Eight major federal police forces and their lead departments

Lead department				
Justice	DEA (Drugs Enforcement Administration)	FBI (Federal Bureau of Investigation)	ATF (Alcohol, Tobacco and Firearms)	US Marshalls
DHS	USCIS (Citizenship and Immigration)	Customs and Border Security	Secret Service	United States Coast Guard

In addition, there are at least eight intelligence agencies, the most famous of which is the Central Intelligence Agency (CIA). The CIA was created in 1947 as successor to the wartime Office of Strategic Services (OSS). The CIA has the brief of intelligence-gathering on foreign powers and engaging in counter-intelligence. Staff numbers are classified, but thought to be about 15,000–20,000. Finally, at the state and local levels an additional 19,000 police agencies exist, employing about 1 million men and women.

When attempting to assess whether at the federal level the increase in the number of agencies and officials represents a threat to civil liberties, a number of points stand out. First, at around 85,000 (in 2015), the number of federal police officials is actually quite low in relation to a population of over 330 million. Second, the very fragmentation of these forces does lead to overlap, jurisdictional competition and a degree of inefficiency that may at times lead to the abuse of individual rights, but at other times to a failure properly to enforce the law. Third, following the landmark civil liberties cases of the 1960s and 1970s, the courts have been much more vigilant in enforcing the Bill of Rights and the Fourteenth Amendment (which guarantees due process of law). All this accepted, by the end of the twentieth century the US had acquired all the trappings of a 'security state', with extensive powers of surveillance, investigation and arrest. However, it was not until 9/11 that these powers were significantly increased with the passage of the 2001 Patriot Act.

9/11, the Patriot Act and the Department of Homeland Security

Just 45 days after 9/11, the US Congress passed the Patriot Act by overwhelming majorities in both houses (356 to 66 in the House and 98 to 1 in the Senate). Given the common accusation that the legislative process in Congress is slow and cumbersome, the speed at which it went through Congress was remarkable. On 23 October Representative James Sensenbrenner introduced the Act and then sent it to nine major committees where it was voted on and passed. The next day it was sent to the Senate, which promptly passed it, sending it to the president for signature. It was duly signed into law some 72 hours after its introduction! Admittedly other versions had been discussed since earlier in October, but the legislative timetable was astonishingly short. The title of the Act is actually an acronym for 'Uniting and Strengthening America by *Providing Appropriate Tools Required to Intercept and Obstruct Terrorism*'. The aims of the law were to:

- Enhance domestic security against terrorism.
- Enhance surveillance methods on citizens and non-citizens.
- Detain aliens and citizens engaged in terrorist activities.
- Adapt the criminal law and procedures to meet these ends.
- Halt financial support for terrorists.
- Provide for emergency authorizations and appropriations to meet these ends.

In effect the Act gave federal law-enforcement authorities extensive new powers to investigate anyone thought to be engaging in terrorism or associated with those engaging in terrorism. As we will see in the next section, the Patriot Act has been widely viewed as a threat to civil liberties.

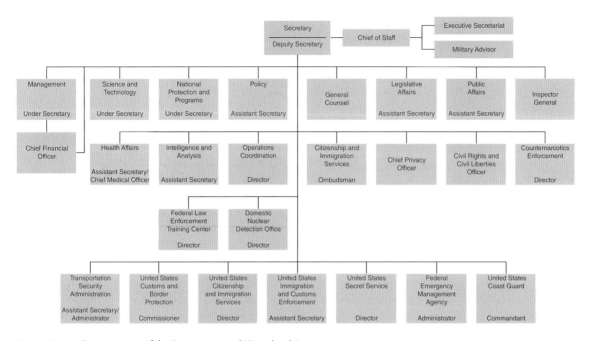

Figure 13.1   Organization of the Department of Homeland Security

The DHS was created in a somewhat less frenzied environment. President Bush announced the proposal in June 2002 and the House voted it into law on 13 November the same year by 299 to 121. The Senate approved it very quickly on 25 November by a 90 to 9 vote. The creation of the DHS was the biggest single administrative reorganization of the federal government since the creation of the Department of Defense after the Second World War. A number of existing agencies were absorbed by it, including the US Coast Guards, the Secret Service, the Immigration Service and the US Customs. With over 170,000 employees and a budget of over $64 billion (by the fiscal year 2016), the DHS became, at once, one of the largest departments in the federal government. As remarkable was the fact that the initial 2003 $37 billion budget was a huge increase on the $19.5 billion current for the equivalent departments in 2002. Thus, the supposedly fiscally conservative Republican administration presided over a massive increase in the size of the federal domestic budget. Apart from civil liberties questions, the main criticism levelled at the agency was that it represented another bureaucratic behemoth that was likely to use resources inefficiently. As can be seen from figure 13.1, the organization of the department is complex – especially so, given that it was created through the amalgamation of a number of existing agencies, each of which retained its own personnel and bureaucratic culture.

One of the most interesting aspects of the DHS is the symbolic importance of its name. 'Homeland' implies a closed community of American citizens, and 'security' implies a community that is under constant threat from outside. Given the events of 9/11 this is hardly surprising, but it did, at least symbolically, imply that the US was no longer a haven for the oppressed and downtrodden, but was, instead, a country besieged by outsiders and aliens, whose values were fundamentally at odds with those of the homeland population. We will return to this point later.

Briefing   The Department of Homeland Security and the Culture of Threat

The DHS has actively encouraged an atmosphere of threat and the prospect of imminent attack on the US. This is reflected in the language of its programmes. The following is a summary of the agency's main objectives as outlined in its fiscal 2017 budget requests:

- *Prevent terrorism and enhance security*. Protecting the American people by leveraging the intelligence, information sharing, technological, operational, and policy-making elements within our purview to facilitate a cohesive and coordinated effort to secure the United States and prevent attacks.
- *Secure and manage our borders*. Employing a layered security approach to reduce the flow of illegal migration and illicit contraband and prevent terrorists from entering the country while fostering legal trade and travel. Investments in critical Border Patrol staffing, equipment, and surveillance technology, and continued recapitalization of Coast Guard assets are imperative to enhancing the capabilities of front-line officers and agents.
- *Enforce and administer our immigration laws*. Focusing on strategies that promote lawful immigration while reducing illegal pathways. The Department has committed resources to unite families entering the country legally while prioritizing the removal of those individuals who fall within the Department's priorities for enforcement, specifically those who pose a threat to public safety, border security, or national security.
- *Safeguard and secure cyberspace*. Developing prevention and mitigation strategies that keep pace in a cyber-security environment with evolving threats. The Budget supports cybersecurity information sharing across the government.
- *Strengthen national preparedness and resilience*. Collaborating with state, local, and tribal governments, the Department will ensure effective response to and recovery from a variety of emergencies and disasters.
- *Countering Violent Extremism (CVE)*. The Budget enhances government-wide efforts to combat violent extremism through better community partnerships. DHS's leadership of the newly formed interagency CVE task force, along with its recently created Office of Community Partnerships will strengthen the interface between the Federal government, community organizations, and local officials. DHS will also work to foster greater cooperation with the technology industry's CVE initiatives, increase philanthropic support for private CVE efforts, and bolster efforts that catalyze and support non-governmental, community-based programs focused on CVE.
- *Chemical, Biological, Radiological, Nuclear, and Explosives (CBRNE) Consolidation*. The Budget supports the consolidation of CBRNE expertise to enhance DHS' Unity of Effort across the components. This will strengthen coordination across the department, streamline organizational structure, and complement other changes to command and control functions.
- *Combating Human Trafficking*. The Budget funds the creation of a new program office managing the Blue Campaign, the

goal of which is to halt human trafficking through law enforcement training, policy coordination across the Department, governmental and private sector partnerships, and a nationwide public awareness campaign to help communities recognize and report human trafficking.

- *Unity of Effort.* Initiatives to strengthen DHS business processes continue with the submission of the Budget in a new Common Appropriations Structure that will improve the Department's planning, programming, budgeting, and execution processes through a common framework of four standardized appropriations.

Source: https://www.dhs.gov/ news/2016/02/09/fact-sheet-dhs-fy-2017-budget.

Threats to Civil Liberties

Both the Patriot Act and the creation of the DHS were the subject of intense criticism from civil liberties groups and interests and, increasingly, from more mainstream political interests, including the Democratic Party. Some critics argued that the laws were too sweeping in scope. One of the main problems derived from the definition of domestic terrorism under the Patriot Act, which was defined as 'acts dangerous to human life that are a violation of the criminal laws of the United States or of any State [and that] appear to be intended … to influence the policy of a government by intimidation or coercion'. It is not difficult to infer that this could be interpreted as simply opposing US foreign policy or showing sympathy with those engaged in acts of protest or terror, even if they were not directly a threat to the US. For example, some suspects were arrested because they had sympathized with Palestinian suicide bombers whose target was the Israeli occupation of Palestine and the Gaza Strip rather than the United States as such.

In addition, the Act permitted the FBI to access information from libraries and bookstores whose employees were forbidden to reveal that the searches had taken place. This, so the critique ran, put librarians and others in the position of 'snoops' for the FBI. It was also, so library associations argued, a fundamental violation of the First Amendment. In fact extensive 'data-mining' of email, telephone, library, employment, credit card and other sources has been legitimated under the Act, and has been the cause of numerous complaints of civil liberties violations.

The Justice Department was also given free access to all educational records that were 'relevant' to domestic terrorism, thus opening up the possibility that foreign students and others with some link, however remote, with terrorist groups might be arrested or deported. This provision also violated the privacy of educational records. Extensive surveillance and wiretapping powers were also granted to federal agencies, and non-citizens, including immigrants, could be certified as 'risks' and subject to indefinite detention. Entry into people's homes for searches without permission or announcement was also sanctioned. Thus, the old search standard of 'knock and announce' was replaced with 'sneak and peek'. Finally, entry to the United States became much more difficult, with the law effectively excluding anyone whose opinions or associations could be interpreted as linked to terrorist organizations. When assessing the experience of the actual implementation of these changes, it is very difficult to find systematic information. However, civil liberties activists have catalogued a number of instances where actual or potential abuse of citizens has occurred and, especially, where immigrants' rights have been violated. One University of Texas professor has listed these as including:

- The arrest of more than 1,200 people, primarily immigrants of Arab descent.
- A refusal to release the names of these people.
- The deportation of around 600 individuals on the Attorney General's assessment that these people had links with terrorist organizations.
- Federal agents have made secret visits to many colleges and universities to gather information about (mainly) foreign students.
- Requiring 6,000 universities to assist the government to carry out surveillance of foreign students and help in the construction of a national databank. Failure to comply could result in a ban on foreign student enrolment at the offending institution.
- Interviewing a large number of American citizens who have been critical of the administration's anti-terrorist and Iraqi policy. Because many of these interviews are secret it is impossible to know how many people the FBI has approached.[1]

Broader criticisms aimed at the administration's general stance on homeland security came from a number of quarters, including the 9/11 Commission report, published in 2004 that stated:

> The burden of proof for retaining a particular governmental power should be on the executive, to explain (a) that the power materially enhances security and (b) that there is adequate supervision of the executive's use of the powers to ensure protection of civil liberties. If the power is granted, there must be adequate guidelines and oversight to properly confine its use.[2]

While the Commission did not propose reduced surveillance, it did recommend the creation of an independent board to oversee government surveillance methods. Moreover the Commission did not recommend the removal of the 'sunset provisions' to the Patriot Act, including the highly controversial power to screen library and other records. In other words, those provisions of the Act that were scheduled to lapse in December 2005 should be allowed to lapse. In the event, however, Congress reauthorized the law in early 2006 without making any substantial changes to its content. Most recently Congress reauthorized the Act in May 2011 for a further four-year period. Again, the law was essentially unchanged from the original version. In the events the Act lapsed in 2015 and was replaced by the Freedom Act which was signed into law by President Obama later that year. Although the Freedom Act was sold as being more protective of civil liberties than the Patriot Act, in effect it merely simplified and codified some of the more sweeping of the surveillance powers given to the federal government by the Patriot Act. As such it has been criticized by civil liberties groups as just as draconian as its predecessor.

This is not to argue that the critics of the federal government wanted to repeal the Freedom Act or abolish the DHS. It is more that they see in the implementation of the law an excessive degree of secrecy and a failure of accountability.

In fact, there has been no direct censorship under the new laws, and very few American citizens have been prosecuted, let alone convicted. The danger to civil liberties came from two rather different sources. There was, first, the status of immigrants and visitors to the US, many of whom were subjected to harassment, internment and deportation. Given the circumstances of 9/11 and the fact that the perpetrators were all immigrants or visitors, this is perhaps not surprising. Second, during the first two years after 9/11, a mood of national unity prevailed that made it difficult for individuals and groups to speak out against the ways in which the administration's war on terror and action in Iraq was conducted. For example, country music group the Dixie Chicks were pulled off numerous radio stations in 2003 after they criticized the president's conduct of the war in Iraq. This and other incidents were not, of course, a direct result of government action. But the Dixie Chicks and others were victims of an element of opinion conformity that made it difficult (or financially risky) to criticize official actions.

Although by the time of the Obama administration the security environment had settled down somewhat, complaints about the operating procedures of the DHS continued. Student visas remained much more difficult to obtain than before 9/11 and Congress even attempted to make the background checks on foreign students even more onerous. In 2011 the DHS invoked the Patriot Act on WikiLeaks' domain register and eventually sought to extradite WikiLeaks founder Julian Assange for sedition. Assange managed to evade extradition by seeking refuge in the Ecuadorian embassy in London, where he remained at least until 2017. The national mood changed once again in 2015/16 following the mass shootings in San Bernardino California and Orlando Florida both of which were perpetrated by American citizens of Pakistani and Afghan origin claiming to be sympathetic to the Islamic State terrorist network. In reaction Republican presidential nominee Donald Trump reiterated his call for bans on all Muslims entering the USA. Later in the campaign he modified this threat saying he would implement 'extreme vetting' of Muslims arriving from countries that harbour terrorists or have a history of terror.

The Security State and American Values

Throughout the history of the republic there have been occasions when, under an external or internal threat, the federal government has acted in ways that have violated civil liberties. Under threat of war with France, the 1798 Alien and Seditions Acts gave the government sweeping powers of arrest and deportation over aliens. At the onset of the Civil War, Abraham Lincoln suspended *habeas corpus*. The 1917 Espionage Act effectively banned opposition to the draft, and more than 900 people were subsequently imprisoned. In 1942 thousands of Japanese Americans, many of them citizens, were stripped of their land and interned in concentration camps. And, as we saw earlier, the 1940 Smith Act and 1952 Internal Security Act had the effect of banning the advocacy of communism. In all of these cases bar the Civil War, the perceived threat came primarily from outside, either in the form of unacceptable ideas such as anarchism or communism, or more palpably from people living in America perceived to be aiding and abetting hostile foreign powers such as Japan and the Soviet Union.

Plate 13.1   Transportation Security Administration (TSA) employees demonstrate a new full-body scanner at Logan Airport in Boston, Massachusetts, USA, 5 March 2010. A total of 150 backscatter imaging technology units were purchased by the TSA with American Recovery and Reinvestment Act (ARRA) funds in the autumn of 2009. The attempted terror bombing on Christmas Day led President Barack Obama to order their purchase
Source: © Matthew Cavanaugh/epa/Corbis.

The Patriot Act was in precisely the same category. Of course the circumstances were very different, and 9/11 represented much more than a mere threat: it was a blatant attack on New York and Washington. But the idea that there were alien forces in the midst of society intent on challenging American institutions and values and that these must be weeded out and eliminated was not new. And as in the past, the Patriot Act and other measures helped to produce a climate of fear and insecurity and not a small degree of conformity. What is interesting about the historical examples is that, following the period of threat, the checks and balances in the US Constitution have come into play in ways that have, eventually, restored civil liberties and provided at least some redress for the aggrieved parties.

Whether and when this will happen once the threat from ISIS (Islamic State), Al-Qaeda and other terror groups has passed cannot, of course, be easily predicted – and as noted the Patriot Act was replaced by the very similar Freedom Act in 2015. However, the nature of information dissemination in modern societies, especially via the internet, is such that it would be impossible for any administration, no matter how determined to stamp out dissent, to succeed in doing so. In addition, the courts are always vigilant and, as the cases involving the detainees in Guantánamo Bay showed, do not always side with the executive branch (see chapter 15). In other words, while not underestimating the ways in which the very hastily drawn-up Patriot Act undermined civil liberties, the United States remained an essentially free country with a free press and freedom of expression. Of course modern communications can also help the federal authorities track down potential terrorists, and in this sense they represent a double-edged sword. Certainly many of the accusations over civil liberties violations concerned the use of electronic surveillance.

Perhaps the most significant aspect of events following 9/11 is that they occurred at a moment when international travel and the movement of people for work and pleasure throughout the world was at an all-time high. Visa restrictions on visits to the United States were relaxed from the 1970s and the foreign student population had increased dramatically. 9/11 put this process into reverse, with visitors from almost all countries now requiring visas (or vetted visa waiver documents) and photographic and fingerprint records, and although the foreign student population has not been seriously reduced, getting access to the United States from Arab and Islamic countries became much more difficult. So the reputation America had built as being a country that welcomed people from all over the world, if only as visitors, was damaged. Some restrictions on movement were no doubt necessary, but the change did represent an important shift in the image that the United States held abroad. As noted above, Donald Trump promised during the campaign to ban *all* Muslims from entering the United States. And although he later modified this threat, together with his tough immigration policies, it did herald in a period when the image of a 'fortress America' was once again projected abroad.

All modern states have extensive security forces, and limits on free expression and movement exist in all. In most a national identity-card system is in place, and in some it is necessary to register with the police every time you move home. By comparison, the United States remains relatively free from an intrusive state role. Yet the sheer scope of the federal police power even before the passage of the Patriot Act was impressive. Since then it has increased even further. It remains to be seen whether in the longer term the civil liberties of Americans, and of immigrants and visitors to the United States, will be permanently compromised. Certainly the US has gone some way down the road to what Clinton Rossiter, writing in the 1950s, once called a 'constitutional dictatorship', referring to the need for even democracies to sometimes take on draconian emergency powers. Perhaps the main lesson to be learned from the post-9/11 period is to warn against the passage of hasty legislation quickly drafted in an atmosphere of national emergency or even panic. History suggests that these laws are eventually discredited – so much so that succeeding generations sometimes marvel that they were passed in the first place.

Summary

The US has gradually built up a range of institutions to ensure domestic security, including the FBI and the ATF. Since 9/11, however, the bureaucratic landscape has been transformed, with the passage of the Patriot Act (and later the Freedom Act) and the creation of the DHS. The former gave the government sweeping new powers to gather evidence on security matters and the latter created a bureaucratic behemoth with a $60 billion budget. Both have been criticized as heavy-handed responses to the terrorist threat, with the Patriot Act attracting particular opprobrium as a threat to civil liberties. However, in spite of protests by civil liberties groups and others, Congress replaced the Patriot Act with an almost equally restrictive Freedom Act in 2015.

Questions for Discussion

1   What was the record of the Obama and Trump administrations in protecting civil liberties in the context of the international terrorist threat?
2   What are the main objectives of the Patriot and Freedom Acts? Why have they still in force more than 15 years after the 9/11 attacks?
3   In what respects is the apparatus of the security state 'un-American'? Answer with reference to the interaction of security legislation with American values.

Glossary

Al-Qaeda   The loose network of terrorists associated with Osama Bin Laden and his followers

Bureau of Alcohol, Tobacco and Firearms (ATF)   The arm of the Treasury responsible for enforcing fiscal law in these areas

constitutional dictatorship   The idea that in emergencies elected governments should act like dictators

Department of Homeland Security (DHS)   The new agency created in the wake of 9/11

Federal Bureau of Investigation (FBI)   The main federal agency responsible for fighting crime in the USA

Freedom Act   The replacement for the Patriot Act passed in 2015

Guantánamo Bay   The base in Cuba under US jurisdiction where terrorist suspects have been detained without charge

habeas corpus   The right to have a criminal case heard in court within a specified period

Internal Revenue Service (IRS)   The tax-collecting and enforcement arm of the federal government

ISIS   The global Islamic State terrorist network based in Syria and Iraq

knock and announce (search procedures)   Open searching of premises for evidence

McCarran Act   The law used after the Second World War to suppress communists and other 'subversives'

Patriot Act   The law that gave the federal government draconian powers after 9/11

sneak and peek (search procedures)   Clandestine searching of premises for evidence

US Customs Service and Border Security   The new agency created to enhance border security after 9/11

Notes

1   This list is adapted from Jim Cornehls, 'The US Patriot Act and censorship', Focus on Faculty Lecture, University of Texas, Arlington, 30 September 2003.

2   National Commission on Terrorist Attacks upon the United States, Report, p. 394; available at www.9-11commission/gov.

Further Reading

Most of the literature on this subject is critical rather than supportive of the security state. A critique of the Patriot Act by an eminent sociologist is provided by Amitai Etzioni in *How Patriotic is the Patriot Act? Freedom versus Security in the Age of Terrorism* (New York: Routledge, 2004). Marcus Ranum's *The Myth of Homeland Security* (New York: Wiley, 2003) exposes weaknesses in the way the DHS operates. Ronald Kessler's *Bureau: The Secret History of the FBI* (New York: St Martin's Press, 2003) is a considered history of the errors made in FBI management structures. An objective analysis of security risks is provided by John Mueller and Mark Stewart, *Error, Security, and Money: Balancing the Risks, Benefits, and Costs of Homeland Security* (New York and Oxford: Oxford University Press, 2011). See also the *National Commission into Terrorist Attacks upon the United States*, which critiques the ways in which successive federal police agencies failed to anticipate 9/11. It is available in full at www.9-11commission/gov. On constitutional dictatorship, see Clinton Rossiter, *Constitutional Dictatorship: Crisis Government in the Modern Democracies* (New York: Transaction Books, 2002). For a critique of homeland security see Donald F. Kettl, *System Under Stress: Homeland Security and American Politics*, 3rd edn (Washington, DC: Congressional Quarterly Press, 2013).

CHAPTER 14
ORGANIZED INTERESTS
THE REAL POWER?

Suppose you go to Washington and try to get at your government. You will always find that while you are politely listened to, the men really consulted are the men with the biggest stake – the big bankers, the big manufacturers, the big masters of commerce.... The government of the United States is the foster child of special interests. It is not allowed to have a will of its own. It is told at every move: 'Don't do that; you will interfere with our prosperity.'

– WOODROW WILSON, *THE NEW FREEDOM*

American Politics and Society, Ninth Edition. David McKay.
© 2018 John Wiley & Sons Ltd. Published 2018 by John Wiley & Sons Ltd.

Concededly, each interest group is biased; but their role ... is not unlike the advocacy of lawyers in court which has proven so successful in resolving judicial controversies. Because our congressional representation is based on geographical boundaries, the lobbyists who speak for the various economic, commercial and other functional interests of this country serve a very useful purpose and have assumed an important role in the legislative process.

– JOHN F. KENNEDY, QUOTED IN CONGRESSIONAL QUARTERLY,
THE WASHINGTON LOBBY

Throughout American history, concern over the power of organized interests has never been far from the surface. Indeed, the growth of the republic can almost be described in terms of successive waves of populist revolt against the undue influence of organized groups, and in particular private corporations. Woodrow Wilson's characterization above came after more than 20 years of public disquiet at the operations of the big companies. During the 1920s, corporate power was regarded more benignly, with capitalism flourishing as never before. The Depression transformed this image, however, and it was not until the 1950s that the benevolent view of private power returned. By the 1970s the critique returned to the centre of the political stage, with popular opprobrium directed at those companies responsible for pollution, consumer exploitation and discrimination against women and minorities. Even during the boom years of the late 1990s and early 2000s, criticism of corporate power was never far from the surface, as public mistrust of some health maintenance organizations (HMOs),[1] oil companies and larger airlines shows. And the collapse of the energy giant Enron in 2001 renewed claims of 'crony capitalism' or the accusation that large, corrupt corporations were buying favours from political leaders. Most recently the critique has centred on irresponsible banks such as Lehman Brothers, which collapsed in 2008, and on the rise of SuperPACs (see below). Criticism of other organized interests – labour, promotional groups – has been more fragmented, although at any particular time a specific group may be the subject of public criticism, as were the labour unions during the 1940s and again during the 1980s.

The critique of corporate power has two related strands. The first is that large private companies are by their very nature ruthless and exploitative. This mainly populist view considers size to be the main problem. Break up large monopolies and oligopolies, and something approaching 'fair' competition will emerge. Second, corporations have been criticized because they exercise power without accountability. They are not, in other words, answerable to democratically elected institutions. They can 'buy' members of Congress, bribe local, state and federal officials, and generally manipulate democratic processes in their favour. We return to these points below, but note that the socialist critique of capitalism that historically has been most influential in most other countries and especially in Europe – that the private accumulation of wealth in business is *by definition* exploitative – has been quite rare in the United States. During the 1990s the criticism shifted away from attacks on large corporations per se to claims that the sheer volume of interest group activity at all levels of government had undermined the capacity of governments to articulate the wishes of the public and to get things done. On every issue lobbies mobilize for and against in ways that make the costs of pursuing a particular policy option very high. Members of Congress, in particular, are electorally vulnerable if they are seen to be taking the 'wrong' position on an issue. As a result, it is increasingly difficult for the public to make a clear connection between their specific electoral demands and the actual policies produced by governments.

The quote by John Kennedy represents the second, quite different, judgement on the role of organized interests in America. According to this view, groups are an essential part of the democratic process; far from undermining representation, they aid it. Advocates of this position point to the multiple access points in the American system and the ways in which myriad organized groups are able to exploit these to their advantage. Crucially, because *all* classes, interests, ideological positions, regions, localities and social groups *can* organize (even if some actually do not) to defend or promote their positions, the potential for fair or just policies is particularly great in the American system.

Much of the comment and discussion in this chapter centres on these contrasting perspectives and how valid they are today. Particular attention is paid to the link between group activity and the increasingly complex nature of what the public expect from political institutions. Before we embark on this exercise, it is necessary to provide some basic information on interest groups in the United States.

Interests, Groups and Lobbyists

In all modern industrial societies, citizens band together to form organizations with social, economic and political aims. American group participation is high in comparative terms, with some 79 per cent of the population being members of a voluntary association (table 14.1). Putting aside inactive memberships more than a third are actively engaged – a figure that remained around the same for the latest data available in 2015 (see https://www.volunteeringinamerica.gov/national). The organizations with the most active membership tend to be 'non-political' charitable and social clubs (youth and sports groups, church-related groups, fraternal organizations – Rotary, the Masons, the Lions – and so on), professional societies (representing doctors, lawyers, etc.), and educational groups (parent–teacher associations, school and college fraternities). About 14 per cent of the adult population is active in political clubs and organizations – a similar figure to that for most social clubs. Note the relatively low figure – and participation rates – for the labour unions. In addition to voluntary associations with individual membership, a number of groups exist representing corporate and governmental interests, such as trade, commerce and manufacturers' associations, and state, local, county and regional government organizations. Finally, a number of single-issue groups exist at any one time, ranging from organizations to outlaw abortion, to proponents of stricter environmental protection, to local groups created to stop the construction of a particular public works project.

All these organizations do have a political dimension; obviously so in the case of corporate, labour and ad hoc groups, but also with most social organizations. Chambers of commerce and professional associations, for example, frequently engage in political activity when laws and regulations affecting their members are introduced or existing laws are changed. As local,

Table 14.1 Types of organizations and nature of affiliation

Organizational type	% of respondents affiliated	Among those affiliated		
		% attend meetings	% give money but no meetings	% say organization takes political stands
Service, fraternal	18	50	35	30
Veterans	16	16	70	59
Religious	12	63	30	27
Nationality, ethnic	4	45	32	61
Senior citizens	12	25	20	61
Women's rights	4	33	52	79
Union	12	52	16	67
Business, professional	23	66	13	59
Political issue	14	20	65	93
Civic, non-partisan	3	60	21	59
Liberal or conservative	1	20	71	95
Candidate, party	5	39	49	94
Youth	17	42	50	18
Literary, art, study	6	72	15	16
Hobby, sports, leisure	21	52	17	18
Neighbourhood, homeowners	12	66	11	50
Charitable social service	44	14	79	16
Educational	25	50	34	43
Cultural	13	14	71	25
Other	4	32	44	30
All organizations	79	65	55	61

Source: Sidney Verba, Kay Lehman Schlozman and Henry E. Brady, *Voice and Equality: Civil Voluntarism in American Politics* (Cambridge, MA: Harvard University Press, 1996), table 3.5. Copyright © 1995 by the President and Fellows of Harvard College. Reprinted by permission of the publisher.

state and federal governments have legislated in almost every conceivable area of economic and social life over the past 30 years, it is not surprising that many erstwhile mainly social groups and associations have found themselves at the very centre of political controversy. The debate on gun control intimately involves the National Rifle Association (NRA); environmental pollution controls involve Friends of the Earth and Sierra Club; and education cuts and school district consolidation involve parent–teacher associations.

Political scientists have long been engaged in the business of trying to classify interest groups, and even now no completely satisfactory taxonomy exists. We have already drawn some distinctions (for example, between voluntary associations with individual members and corporate groups), but as all of these can engage in political activity this distinction is not necessarily that helpful. For our purposes it is more useful to distinguish between three broad categories of organized group – economic, professional and promotional – to which we should add some comments on political action committees and lobbying.

Economic Groups

Business

When discussing business organizations, it is common to distinguish between the activities of individual corporations and those of peak associations (trade-union confederations, employers' and trade associations). In the United States, corporations tend to be both powerful and autonomous, and frequently they exercise political power as independent units. So General Motors, the country's largest vehicle manufacturer, is a political force to be reckoned with in its own right, as are such companies as Microsoft, AT&T, the major oil companies or many of the firms listed in the *Fortune 500*.[2]

In a famous study of business lobbying published in the 1960s, Bauer, Pool and Dexter concluded that the lobbying activities of individual firms were not an important influence on public policy.[3] The authors were, however, primarily concerned with Congress rather than executive departments and agencies, and they did not attempt to measure the effect of lobbying on candidates and elections. Nor was state and local government the subject of their study. Few dispute that corporations do wield enormous influence on lower-level governments. Land-use, taxation, labour and public works policies are often moulded by corporate interests within states. Of course, there is also competition between corporate interests, and between these and other organized groups, but in most locales business is the single most important influence. The precise extent of this power varies from area to area, with some states being effectively dominated by one or two corporations (such as the Du Pont chemical corporation in Delaware or Boeing and Microsoft in Washington State), or by a few interests (until recently, cattle and oil in Texas); while in others (New York, Michigan, California, Massachusetts) individual corporate power is much more diffuse and often ameliorated by union and public interest group activity.

Moreover, since the 1960s there is overwhelming evidence that individual firms have taken a more active part in public policy-making. Most major corporations now have Washington offices and employ professional lobbyists to advance and protect their interests. The size of business lobbying can partly be explained as a response to the increasingly strident and successful efforts of the new public interest lobbies devoted to environmental and consumer protection and to affirmative action in employment.[4] Since the mid-1970s, however, a further important spur to corporate political activity has been the rapidly changing economic environment and increasing vulnerability of US corporations to foreign competition. Business now *needs* to ensure that the federal government provides an amenable climate for investment and growth – although, as Charles Lindblom has pointed out, only business imposes *automatic* sanctions in the form of the threat of recession and unemployment should anti-business policies be pursued.[5]

American business (or trade) associations have been labelled 'weak' in the past. And certainly the influence of the major single-industry associations (representing automobiles, rubber, textiles and so on) as well as the two major cross-industry organizations (the National Association of Manufacturers (NAM) and the US Chamber of Commerce) has historically been weak compared with that of equivalent organizations in such countries as Germany and Japan. Perhaps this should be expected, given the traditional strength of individual corporations in the USA, which we noted in chapter 2. Why, after all, should successful individual firms forfeit some of their independence to a trade association? Indeed, as recently as the 1950s both the NAM and Chamber of Commerce were regarded as a marginal influence in Washington. Both adhered to a sometimes-unthinking anti-regulation philosophy, and were notably less important than the sum of the political efforts of individual corporations. Since then, however, both organizations, plus some new ones (notably the Business Round Table, which represents the chief executives of the 200 leading corporations with a value of $7 trillion and more than 16 million employees), have emerged as more respected spokespersons for corporate interests. This is not to say that American business peak associations have assumed the status of equivalent groups in Germany, Japan or even Britain, but they are now more important than they were. Again, this revival is linked to the general increase in group activity characteristic of the past 20 years. Before we leave our discussion of business interests, a word of caution should be expressed about any comparison between business activity in government during the 1950s and today. As mentioned above, the 1950s were an especially benign period in American politics. For much of the 1950s and 1960s corporations were highly successful and entered the political arena only when necessary. Government policy was favourable towards them, and particularly towards the larger corporations. Iron triangles and cosy relations with executive bureaux do not require lobbying as such, with all that this implies in terms of attention-seeking and publicity. Only when competing or conflicting interests enter the fray is lobbying of the more visible kind necessary.

Briefing   The Enron Collapse and Crony Capitalism

Enron was a power company that grew in the 1990s from virtually nothing through to 2000, when it reported over $100 million in profits on a stock market valuation worth billions. Although primarily an electric power company, Enron's growth was based on trading commodities, including power, plastics and internet connections, on a global scale. Indeed at its peak it had become the largest energy-trading company in the world and the seventh largest US corporation. However, the stock price had been grossly overvalued by illegal accounting practices, and with the stock market crash of 2000 it declared a loss of $638 million in October of that year. It was also forced to admit to overvaluing its stock by $6 billion and it went into bankruptcy soon after, throwing thousands of employees out of work and ruining many small investors, not to mention the pension funds of its workforce. Enron's activities also inflated energy prices and helped contribute to the Californian energy crisis of 2002 and 2003.

The scandal was compounded by the fact that its chief executive officer, Kenneth Lay, sent emails to his employees promising the stock would rise, while at the same time he was selling off his own stock at a healthy profit just before the collapse. Lay was later indicted on fraud charges and brought to trial in 2004.

Lay and other Enron executives had intimate ties with the administration, and Lay was a close friend of the president, to whose campaign he had donated large sums in 2000. The Republicans were further implicated by the fact that House

Majority Leader Tom Delay had acted to coordinate corporate contributions to the party. Among these were Enron contributions and monies spent to help the Republicans redistrict Texas constituencies in their favour. Although by 2004 no direct links between Enron's contributions and Republican favours had been established, deep suspicions about the nature of the relationship remained. Crusading liberals such as Paul Krugman of the *New York Times* kept the debate alive, as did more populist media attacks as represented by radical film-maker and author Michael Moore's hit book *Stupid White Men*.

CONTROVERSY 13   DO THE BANKRUPTCY LAWS DAMAGE WORKERS' RIGHTS?

Since 1979 corporations have been able to file for Chapter 11 under federal bankruptcy law. Chapter 11 allows companies to freeze their debts and reorganize their businesses, usually by selling assets and shedding costs in order to return to profitability. Eventually, and with the approval of creditors, companies can emerge from Chapter 11 and continue to operate as normal. Chapter 11 has been used by a wide variety of companies, and in particular by airlines – in 2011 nearly half of the seating capacity on US airlines was operated by companies in Chapter 11. Unions oppose the law because it is usually the employees and employee rights that suffer during reorganizations. Often workers are laid off, or companies use the law to shed their pension plans – 56 corporations did just this in the 2005–14 period. The critique goes further and argues that, while workers lose their jobs and benefits (often including health care), company executives continue to award themselves large bonuses. A classic case was United Airlines, which saved itself $4 billion by terminating retiree benefits while the top eight company bosses awarded themselves large salary increases and bonuses. Critics claim, therefore, that the system rewards inefficiency and waste. As a result of this and other cases, the AFL-CIO launched a campaign in 2006 and 2007 to persuade Congress to change the law. Opponents of reform argue that but for Chapter 11 many companies would have disappeared along with their employees and company benefits. One possible compromise is to strengthen federal programmes designed to compensate workers for loss of pensions and health-care benefits. In the period after 2008 many more large US corporations entered Chapter 11, including the iconic companies General Motors in 2009, American Airlines in 2011 and Peabody Energy in 2016, thus increasing the insecurity of numerous employees.

Labour unions

American unions have traditionally been considered a relatively weak influence in the policy process. In comparative perspective this is undoubtedly true. In 2015 only 11.1 per cent of wage and salary workers were covered by a union, down from 20.1 per cent as recently as 1983. As table 14.2 shows, however, there are great variations in membership both by state and by occupation. Public sector workers, mainly in local government and education, have high rates of union representation, whereas private sector workers do not. Within the private sector there are great variations ranging from barely 2 per cent in agriculture to over 20 per cent in transport and utilities. The states also show great variations – in the southern states membership is very low but in northern and western states membership is much higher (table 14.2). Indeed there is a trend towards an accelerating decline in most states bar some of the older industrial states such as New York. The unions do not have the unequivocal support of a major political party, and unlike many union movements in Europe they lack ideological cohesion. Almost all the powerful union movements in history have been driven forward by some ideal vision of a new – usually socialist – society. Not so in the case of American unions, which, although by no means un-ideological, are significantly more instrumental than their European counterparts. Interestingly, the period when unions were most ideological in the USA (the 1930s and 1940s) coincided with the years of their most rapid growth and greatest political achievements.

Although relatively weak and divided, trade unions as a whole do constitute one of America's most important organized interests. The US is, after all, a highly industrialized country, and the unions represent around 16 million workers. However, the

Table 14.2   Union membership, selected characteristics, 2015 (%)

All employed workers	11.1
Public sector	35.2
Private sector	6.7
By state	
Lowest	
South Carolina	2.1
North Carolina	3.0
Utah	3.9
Georgia	4.0
Texas	4.5
Highest	
New York	24.7
Hawaii	20.1
Alaska	19.6
Connecticut	17.0
Washington	16.8

Source: Bureau of Labor Statistics, US Government, *Union Members Summary* at www.bls.gov/news.release/union2.t05.htm.

relatively high political visibility of the unions has been achieved only slowly. The first unions in America of any significance were craft- rather than industry-oriented and eschewed any active involvement in politics. Known for their advocacy of 'voluntarism' or 'business unionism', these unions formed the American Federation of Labor (AFL) in 1886 under the leadership of Samuel Gompers. As the name implies, business union- ism involved workers perceiving themselves as part of the capitalist environment. The union's job was, therefore, to bargain with employers in line with what employers could or should afford. If a company was doing well, then the workers would benefit. If it was not, low wages and layoffs were to be expected. With over a million members, the AFL became an important representative of the skilled worker, but its limited approach became very obvious when the economy faced a downturn and in particular after the Great Depression struck. Industry-wide unions (such as the United Steel Workers and United Mine Workers) formed rapidly during the Depression years and banded together in 1935 as the Congress of Industrial Organizations (CIO). In contrast to the AFL, CIO unions saw themselves in an adversarial relationship with employers, and were strongly disposed to use political means to achieve better working conditions and higher wages. Often this was achieved at the cost of lengthy strikes often accompanied by violent confrontations between union members and employers' private police forces often involving multiple deaths.

Since the 1930s the CIO (and, following an amalgamation in 1955, the AFL-CIO) has lobbied hard in Washington over the whole range of public policies which affect workers and working conditions – union rights, social security, job training, voca- tional education, occupational health and safety, overseas trade relations and economic policy generally. Observers generally agree that in terms of organization, staffing and access, the AFL-CIO – mainly through its political organization, the Committee on Political Education (COPE) – has become one of the most coherent and visible of the Washington lobbies. As suggested in earlier chapters, the unions do have links with the Democratic Party, but formal affiliation has always been avoided (although for the first time in 1984, the AFL-CIO endorsed a presidential candidate, Walter Mondale, early in the campaign). Since then all Democratic candidates, including Barack Obama, have received their endorsement. This has almost certainly helped, rather than hindered, the AFL-CIO's public image. In recent years COPE's political interests have widened to include activity on a number of issues not directly related to members' interests; for example, foreign policy and civil liberties. Generally – but by no means always – COPE is identified with a liberal political position.

Although the AFL-CIO's national political activities are important, it would be mis- leading to give the impression that the United States has a centralized and united union movement. In comparison with unions in many countries, the opposite is, if anything, true. Most union structures are highly decentralized, with local and state units often responsible for bargaining over wages and salaries. Moreover, a few of the biggest and most powerful unions are not even members of the AFL-CIO, including the largest teachers' union (the National Educational Association).

Over the past 30 years there has been much talk about the decline of the unions as a political force. Certainly their membership (as a percentage of the labour force) has been falling, and an occupational structure changing in favour of the tertiary sector has generally weakened the unions, whose strength is traditionally rooted in the secondary (manufacturing) sector. In addition, unions suffered from the generally anti-labour policies of the Reagan and two Bush administrations. One indicator of union decline is the extent of strike action. During the 1960s and 1970s the number of major work stoppages fluctuated between 200 and 400 a year. Since then the number has declined dramatically. In 2015 only 12 major work stoppages involving more than 1,000 workers occurred.

Nonetheless, the unions remain highly visible on the Washington political scene. Graham Wilson has noted that this very visibility is a symptom of weakness, for the unions have so much to do in the pursuit of their interests that they are obliged to take a highly active part in politics.[6] While this is probably true, it should also be re-emphasized that almost *all* interests have become more active at the national level in recent years. In effect the nature of the policy process is now such that no one group or sector can afford not to take part in the Washington bargaining and coalition-building game.

It should also be stressed that in some parts of the economy – and notably the public sector – unions remain strong (see table 14.2). Among the most influential of the public sector unions is the Association of Federal, State, County and Municipal Employees (AFSCME), which represents mainly lower-paid, often female, workers in health care, sanitation and other local government jobs.

The farmers

In most modern industrial countries, farmers occupy a special place in society. For strategic and/or electoral reasons they often exercise formidable political power, and in recent history American farmers have proved no exception. They are the recipients of subsidies designed to raise their incomes to a point at or beyond that necessary to keep production up. As in some other countries (notably within the European Union), this has sometimes resulted in over-production and the need to destroy or store produce in order to keep prices buoyant. American farms are also among the most efficient in the world, being highly capital-intensive and mechanized. Given the high rate of innovation and the general trend towards urban and suburban living over the past 60 years, it comes as no surprise to learn that the farm population declined from over 30 million in 1920 to under 10 million in 1970. Indeed, by 2015 less than 1 per cent of the American workforce was employed in agriculture – a remarkably low figure, given the fact that the United States is easily the largest producer (and exporter) of foodstuffs in the world.

Given this, American farming organizations are perhaps rather less cohesive than would be expected. The largest group, the American Farm Bureau Federation (AFBF or Farm Bureau), has, until recently, actually preached the merits of disengagement of the state from the economy, including presumably the removal of farm subsidies. The National Farmers Union (NFU) has taken a pro-subsidy line, but its membership is smaller and more geographically concentrated (in the West and Midwest). Generally, the NFU is more liberal than the Farm Bureau, and it supported Barack Obama's candidacy in 2008 and 2012. While it did not formally support Hillary Clinton in 2016 its position on environmental protection and climate change was much closer to the Democratic stance on these issues than that of the Republicans.

As the farm population has declined, so the electoral influence of farmers has fallen. During the late nineteenth and early twentieth centuries, farmers virtually constituted a separate social class in the United States, a fact that helps explain the emergence of farm-based political movements, including the Populists, the Farmers Alliance and the Grange. However, these parties and organizations failed to establish permanent bases of social support, and most have now passed into history. More recently, farmers' influence in state legislatures has continued, although even here, re-districting and demographic change have produced a steady decline in the family farm agricultural lobby. The same is true of Congress. At one time, many members of Congress were virtually elected by farmers. Not so today, when in most states and districts the farm vote is but one small voice among many.

In spite of the general weakness of the farming organizations, it would be misleading to suggest that farm interests are politically weak. A more accurate way to characterize them would be simply to see the larger farmers (or agribusiness, as it is called) as other corporations. Indeed, general industrial and financial corporations do own a large number of agribusiness farms. No federal government could afford to see these interests seriously damaged. As with defence industries, food is strategically too important for this to happen. However, smaller farmers, and especially those working marginal land or producing products liable to sharp fluctuations in price, are genuinely weak – a fact shown by the occasional public demonstrations to which smaller farmers are sometimes obliged to resort. In 1985, for example, attempts by the Reagan administration to cut agricultural subsidies aroused fierce opposition from midwestern grain farmers. Although the Republicans were 'punished' in the 1988 presidential election in several farming states (Minnesota, Iowa, Wisconsin), this was not sufficient to make any difference to the eventual result.

During the 1990s the Republicans in Congress attempted, as part of their deficit-reduction plan, to replace farm subsidies with 'transition' payments to be phased out after seven years. However, pressures, especially from the corporate farm lobby, led to resumption of large subsidies by the late 1990s, and this trend was continued during the Bush administration elected in 2000. Congress was determined to protect American farmers from foreign competition, and passed a Farm Bill in 2002 that increased farm subsidies to over £190 billion in the ensuing 10 years. During 2007 and 2008 the long decline in agricultural prices was replaced by rapidly increasing prices, especially for corn (maize) and dairy products – a trend that intensified following the decline in all commodity prices after 2015. Even so farm subsidies – mainly to large agribusiness farms – continued at around $20 billion in 2015. This is partly because, whatever the intention of the government, the big farmers and their lawyers are adept at manipulating the subsidy rules to their advantage.

While business and corporate farming remain highly influential they do not account for a high proportion of interest group membership as such. As figure 14.1 shows, the number of trade associations (which includes both business and labour) and farming groups has increased only slightly since 1960, while the growth in other associations has been spectacular. Let us look at these non-trade associations in more detail.

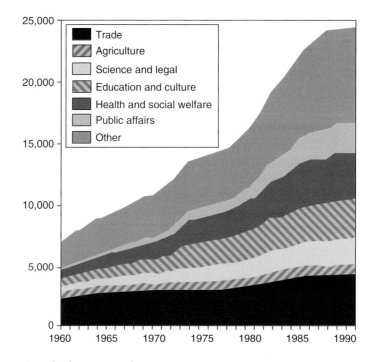

Figure 14.1   Growth of associations by type
Source: Compiled from *Encyclopedia of Associations* (multiple years), as reproduced by F. R.
Baumgartner and J. C. Talbert, 'Interest groups and political change', in B. D. Jones (ed.),
The New American Politics: Reflections on Political Change and the Clinton Administration (Boulder,
CO: Westview Press, 1995), figure 12.1. Copyright © 1995 Perseus Books Group. Reprinted with
permission. All rights reserved.

Professional Groups

Although receiving much less public attention than business or unions, professional
groups have probably grown and improved their political status more rapidly than any
of the other organized interests over the past 40 years. As educational standards have
risen and the premium on expertise in a number of areas – particularly the law, medicine and education – has increased, so the professions have prospered. The role of
the main lawyers' organization, the American Bar Association (ABA), is developed in
chapter 15. The ABA not only acts as gatekeeper for those practising law, it is also a
major source of information on legal standards and procedures. So the nomination of
judges and changes in criminal and civil law depend in part on the opinions and position taken by the ABA. This function came under threat when the Bush administration
announced in March 2004 that it would end the 50-year-old practice of giving the ABA
'preferred status' in screening nominations to the courts, including the Supreme Court.
President Obama did not formally re-instate this status, but was more sympathetic to
ABA advice.

However, with more than 600,000 lawyers in the USA, the central importance of the law in policy-making and the great over-representation of lawyers among state and federal legislators and officials, the ABA's opinions and interpretations must be taken seriously. As with other professional associations, *expert* opinion gives the ABA its special status. It is true that only about half of all lawyers are ABA members, but its members include the more successful lawyers, whose expert, non-partisan opinions are highly respected.

The American Medical Association (AMA) performs a similar function for doctors. Again, not all doctors are members, but those who are tend to be among the most politically active. For many years the AMA was famous for its fight against federal health insurance (or 'socialized' medicine), and from the 1940s to the 1960s it was one of the most vocal and biggest spending of the Washington lobbies. It eventually lost the battle with the enactment of Medicare (medical insurance for the old) and Medicaid (medical aid for the poor) in 1965, but it remains a major influence on all legislation affecting health care. It opposed Bill Clinton's failed health reforms but endorsed Obama's Affordable Care Act in 2009. However, this hardly meant the endorsement of all health professionals for, in recent years, the AMA has been overshadowed somewhat by the rise in importance of groups representing other medical workers and particular medical specialisms. As medicine has become more sophisticated and expensive, so the political strength of the specialists has increased. The same applies to hospitals, health maintenance organizations (HMOs) and the insurance companies responsible for most health-care coverage. Both have become major actors in what is a vast and complex health-care system. The sheer complexity of this policy system helped to contribute to the failure of Clinton's health-care plan in 1993. A large number of medical, insurance and other groups, often with conflicting interests, used their influence with a variety of congressional committees to ensure that no radical change in the health-care system occurred. The total spending by all groups during this campaign came to an estimated $300 million – vastly more than spending in any one presidential election campaign. As will be discussed in chapter 17, the medical profession was split over support for President Obama's Affordable Care Act, with many of the more specialized and highly paid professionals opposing the new law.

Other leading professional groups include some (the American Bankers' Association, the National Association of Home Builders, the National Association of Realtors) whose function is more economic than professional. They are no less important for this, of course. The realtors, for example, contribute large amounts of money mainly to Republican candidates, and generally lobby hard to ensure a growing housing market and low interest rates. At the state and local levels, the realtors are highly active politically, especially in combating what they consider to be any unnecessary regulation of the housing market – whether it be through restrictive zoning laws, building codes, property taxes or fair housing (antidiscrimination) statutes.

In sum, professional associations often represent the rich and the powerful in American society. This can mean the maintenance of professional standards (as in law or medicine), but it can also mean the advancement of particular economic interests (lawyers, doctors, bankers, realtors and so on).

Plate 14.1   Martin Luther King: 'I have a dream'
Source: Bob Adelman/Magnum.

Promotional Groups

By promotional group is meant all those organizations devoted to promoting a particular cause or position. This can include a wide variety of groups, ranging from the NRA, which champions the right of Americans to own firearms, to the National Association for the Advancement of Colored People (NAACP), which represents African Americans, to Common Cause, one of a newer breed of public interest groups, which fights for honesty and efficiency in government. Some of these groups are ad hoc and transitory, as with the several organizations that emerged in opposition to the American presence in Vietnam, but most are at least semi-permanent.

In all democratic societies such groups exist, but in America they are particularly numerous and vocal. Why should this be so? One reason is undoubtedly the openness of the policy system. Promotional groups *know* that with enough organization, public support and media exposure they can influence members of Congress, executive officials and even judges. So in the 1960s Ralph Nader, the consumer advocate and presidential candidate in 2000, 2004 and 2008, went about the business of exposing automobile safety standards with a single-minded determination. Eventually, his methods led to media and later congressional investigations and culminated in stringent new standards imposed by law. Later, other groups mobilized to launch similar campaigns on environmental pollution, occupational safety and women's rights, which led to new, often quite far-reaching, legislation. Common Cause, the 'clean government' public interest group, has supported the reform of the congressional committee system, votes for 18-year-olds, limits on electoral campaign spending, rationalizing government organization and improvements in voter registration.

Although the sudden blossoming of public interest groups since the 1960s has surprised – and even worried – some commentators, it is not so difficult to explain in historical perspective. Middle-class reform movements are, after all, hardly new to the United States. In chapter 4 we saw how reformers attempted to 'clean up' the cities during the nineteenth century, and waves of middle-class moralism have frequently accompanied periods of rapid economic and social change in American history. The 1960s and early 1970s were just such a period, characterized as they were by rapid economic growth, social and political dislocation and, finally, evidence of corruption at the highest level. Moreover, as we chronicled in earlier chapters, this was also a period of party decline, and the increasing atomization of political power. In such a context, coalition-building around such particular issues as environmental protection or clean government became that much easier. This was also a policy context with no parallel in other countries, where, although the same issues have been raised to national prominence, they have tended to be raised via political parties or through the operation of a consensus between political and economic elites.

Although public interest groups claim to represent 'the public interest', in reality they are not value-free and the policies they promote hardly have neutral distributional consequences. New environmental standards may help to produce cleaner air and water, but they can also lead to higher prices. Reforming government sounds admirable enough, but reforms often have unexpected results, as did the nineteenth-century city reforms and the campaign finance reforms of the 1970s.

Today many groups claiming to represent the public interest are as often the champions of special interests. The National Rifle Association fights to prevent federal, state and local governments from passing gun-control laws. In so doing it claims to represent the public interest, but at the same time it also serves the interests of the gun manufacturers and dealers. Even more problematical are those organizations whose cause involves moral absolutes. To a 'pro-lifer' (an anti-abortionist), abortion on demand represents a form of judicial murder that clearly cannot be in the public interest. To pro-choice activists, the free availability of abortion early in a pregnancy represents a basic right of women to exercise control over their own bodies. This too would appear to be in the general or public interest. Clearly, the two positions are irreconcilable. Such issues as capital punishment, the provision of prayers in public schools, the rights of gays and lesbians to marriage, and the identification and treatment of AIDS patients raise similar dilemmas.

In recent years, groups have raised all these issues to the top of the political agenda, but the mere fact that a particular group is well organized and has access to decision-makers does not always equal success. As we develop below, certain groups and interests fail repeatedly. The policy system may be open and complex, but it is not neutral.

Political Action Committees

Political action committees (PACs) are organizations set up by corporations, labour unions and the like specifically to advance a particular political agenda. In the sense that different organized interests have formed Washington committees to fight for or against a particular item of legislation or the electoral success of an individual candidate, PACs are nothing new. We noted above the efforts of the AMA's AMPAC to prevent the passage of Medicare in 1965, for example. Yet since the mid-1970s, PACs have spread to the point where they have spent billions of dollars for and against candidates or supporting/opposing particular policy positions. As of 24 June 2016, 2,310 groups organized as superPACs reported total receipts of $755,031,735 and total independent expenditures of $405,126,326 in the 2016 election cycle.

These figures include sums spent by PACs on individual campaigns and on general efforts to defeat candidates or to support candidates separately from their personal campaign organizations. The rise of the 'electoral' PAC can be explained in the main by changes in campaign finance laws which, by putting restrictions on direct contributions by corporations and unions, have encouraged the big contributors to form committees that in turn can raise money from employees and/or members which is then passed on to (mainly) congressional candidates. (Federal funding of presidential candidates has reduced direct PAC influence in presidential elections.) Fearing that PACs would become simply the 'fat cat' contributors by another name, Congress has amended the 1974 Federal Campaign Act to put further limits on PAC activity. In particular, each PAC cannot contribute more than $5,000 to any one candidate's primary campaign, and a further $5,000 to his or her general election campaign. This limit has not changed since the 1970s, although the 2002 Bipartisan Campaign Reform Act did increase the amount that individuals could contribute to campaigns. The Act also outlawed the use of 'soft money' or contributions from third parties given to campaigns in support of or against candidates. But the law put no limits on PAC 'soft-money' spending which does not go directly into the campaign coffers of candidates, so PACs can still launch their own campaigns against or for particular politicians. For example, it is rare today for any candidate who proposes tighter gun controls not to be attacked in television advertisements paid for by the NRA Political Victory Fund. All was to change following the 2010 *Citizens United* v. *FEC* decision however, when the Supreme Court abolished all limits on political contributions from organizations. While this decision did not approve contributions to *official* election campaigns, it did allow corporations, unions and others to set up 'SuperPACs' that could raise as much money as they liked to support or oppose particular candidates. The upshot has been a rapid rise in the power of SuperPACs. Table 14.3 lists the main SuperPAC operations in 2011 – an off year for federal elections. Most were created for a specific political purpose such as the election of a particular candidate or the defence of the Democratic majority in the House of Representatives. By 2012 both the number and the wealth of SuperPACs rose considerably. During the 2012 election SuperPACs spent $547 million, of which 78 per cent was spent opposing candidates. Significantly, much more was spent opposing Obama's candidacy than was spent opposing Mitt Romney.

The main criticisms of this development are that it makes elections much more expensive and favours those with the deepest pockets. As figure 14.3 shows, however, most

contributions to SuperPACs in 2016 came from private individuals, although the next largest category is for-profit companies. In fact much of the private contributions come from
a few wealthy individuals, so there seems little doubt that SuperPACs privilege those with
money. Worse, the law does not require SuperPACs to disclose their funding sources, thus
compounding the impression that elections are being driven by anonymous rich backers.
While this is true, many on the left have adopted the different – and much less expensive –
strategy of using SuperPAC money to build a permanent infrastructure in society based
on accessing sympathetic voters through social media. The AFL-CIO used this strategy
in 2012 by utilizing an online organization called Workers' Voice. In 2016, however, the
influence of SuperPACs was reduced mainly because some candidates, and in particular
Donald Trump, was able to bypass traditional campaign advertising by winning extensive
(and free) mainstream media coverage of his rallies and by extensive use of social media and
in particular Twitter. So although Hillary Clinton raised vastly more money than Trump
and in particular SuperPAC contributions (Table 14.3), it came to little avail. The same
applied to Jeb Bush, who by early 2016 had raised $127 million in SuperPAC donations but
whose campaign fizzled out early in the election cycle.

Table 14.3 Money raised by Trump and Clinton: 2016
election cycle to 21 July 2016

Hillary Clinton

Campaign raised to date	264.4M
Spent	220.0M
Cash on hand	44.4M
Super PACs raised to date	121.7M
Spent	81.4M
Cash on hand	41.5M
Total raised to date	**386.1M**
Total spent	301.4M
Total cash on hand	85.9M

Donald Trump

Campaign raised to date	89.0M
Spent	68.8M
Cash on hand	20.2M
Super PACs raised to date	5.2M
Spent	4.2M
Cash on hand	2.3M
Total raised to date	**94.2M**
Total spent	73.0M
Total cash on hand	22.5M

Source: Computed from data at Federal Election Commission
www.fec.gov/finance/disclosure/disclosure_data_search.shtml.

Whatever the merits and demerits of PACs and SuperPACs, their rise brought out into the open most of the corporate, labour and association political funding which previously tended to be covert and often illegal. Moreover, by virtue of their ability to make direct appeals to the public on particular issues, PACs have almost certainly aided the rise of single-interest politics and have helped further to weaken traditional political party organizations.

Perhaps not surprisingly, Democrats have been more vocal in their criticisms of PACs than have Republicans. Indeed, in 1983 both Walter Mondale and Gary Hart announced that they would reject all PAC assistance for their 1984 presidential campaigns. Similar pledges were made by Michael Dukakis in 1988, Al Gore in 2000 and John Kerry in 2004. However, in 2008 Barack Obama accepted PAC contributions, although these only amounted to around 1 per cent of his total war chest. In 2012 he also conceded the need for SuperPAC funding, although after some hesitation he did insist that the sources of any SuperPAC money spent on his behalf should be disclosed. Hillary Clinton's warm embrace of SuperPAC money in 2016 may have damaged rather than helped her campaign, for it reinforced the accusation that she was the candidate of 'big money' and Wall Street. Paradoxically the billionaire candidate, Donald Trump, relied more on free coverage by the news networks and social media and was thus able to distance himself from SuperPAC contributors. Until the passage of the 2002 Bipartisan Campaign Reform Act, the most telling criticism of PAC activity used to be not so much that it could influence election outcomes, but that it could change the nature of public debate in the absence of democratic accountability. Indeed, non-connected PAC advertising on such issues as abortion, gun control and capital punishment used to make election campaigns appear much more extreme and adversarial than they actually are. As a result, many moderate voters became disillusioned not only with individual candidates but also with the electoral process itself. The 2002 Reform Act went some way towards correcting this situation by banning soft-money contributions to political parties. However, soft-money issue advertising by PACs of the sort described above remains legal except in the 30-day period before a primary election and 60 days before a general election. In the future, therefore, issue advertising is unlikely to have an immediate effect on election outcomes. However, PACs and SuperPACs are still able to advertise exaggerated positions of candidates and parties outside of these periods. And of course 'hard-money' contributions made direct to official campaign organizations that are subject to the contribution limits described earlier can also be used for negative campaigning.

The Washington Lobby

We have already referred to the 'traditional' interest groups – labour, business, agriculture, the professional associations – to which are added promotional groups and the activities of political action committees. But the Washington lobby consists of much more than this. The executive branch itself lobbies members of Congress for support, as do state and local governments, either individually or through the US Conference of Mayors, Council of State Governments and other umbrella organizations. Finally, foreign governments lobby Congress and executive alike. The *Congressional Quarterly* lists the Israeli, Cuban exile, Arab,

Korean and Taiwan lobbies as the most significant in recent years. Given that American foreign policy decisions affect virtually every country and also the openness of the American policy system, the presence of such interests should perhaps be expected.

All these groups and interests employ consultants and professional lobbyists to collect information and to establish links with the key political actors in the policy system. The result is that Washington is a city alive with political activity, where it is difficult to distinguish between the 'insiders' (elected and appointed officials) and the 'outsiders' (lobbyists, media consultants, interest group leaders). Indeed, the presence of policy networks with fluid memberships and constantly shifting agendas means that there are really only 'insiders'. In 1994 the Republican leadership in Congress launched the K Street project (named after the Washington street that houses the main lobbying firms), which was specifically designed to favour Republican lobbyists and penalize those with Democratic leanings. This overt politicization of the process was condemned by the Democrats, who abolished party preference for lobbyists when they returned to power in 2006. K Street lobbying was damaged by the 2008–11 recession with the revenues of the largest lobbying firms going into decline. However the 2014 Republican takeover of the House resulted in changes to the ways members could amend bills and attach riders favouring particular interests. As a result K Street bounced back in 2015 and 2016 as more corporations sought lobbying help to influence Congress.

These events confirm that openness and accessibility do not always result in neutral policies or in a distribution of public benefits that can be considered fair let alone egalitarian. Let us develop this point further.

Interest Groups: For and Against

Returning to the questions posed at the beginning of this chapter, it is easy to appreciate why, in a society where economic individualism is much admired, a multiplicity of competing interest groups can be regarded as beneficial. In classical economics, equilibrium is reached when demand and supply match each other in a perfectly competitive market. An analogous situation in politics could prevail when groups (analogous to firms) compete with one another in a completely open political environment. The public interest (equilibrium) is hence achieved by the balancing of different interests. No policy, according to this theory, is likely to be completely against any one interest because a group's involvement in the system will ensure it modifies or amends policy at least partly in its favour.

These are, in essence, the theoretical assumptions of the 'traditional' group theorists, notably Arthur Bentley and David Truman.[7] Government's role in such a context is to *arbitrate* between competing interests. By implication, government exercises little independent power; it more resembles a cipher or sorting mechanism and ensures that the rules of the game are abided by.

The group theorists never claimed that in reality there was complete *equality* between groups (although that was the ideal), but they did maintain that if the interests of a particular section of society were seriously damaged, they would mobilize, organize and, through access to representative institutions, manage to do something to redress the balance. The rise of labour union power in the 1930s is often quoted as an example of such mobilization. Neither were the group theorists so naive as to assume that *all* groups had access, even potentially. David Truman, for example, accepted that the position of the American black population (in the 1950s) was exceptional because they patently lacked access to the policy-making process.

Scholars from almost every school of political thought have since criticized classical group theory. Public choice theorists have stressed the tendency in such a system for public expenditure (or the provision of publicly provided goods) to spiral ever upwards. The reasoning here is both simple and familiar. With open access to multiple decision-making centres, the potential for log-rolling is enormous. So if one group, sector, region, state or local government is the recipient of a federal programme, all the others will be too. Anthony Downs has put this nicely, labelling it the 'iron law of political dispersion': 'All benefits distributed by elected officials will be distributed to all parts of the constituency, regardless of the economic virtues of concentrating them upon a few parts of the constituency'.[8] The result is, in fact, the very opposite of equilibrium or the 'optimal' in economics. Governments end up handing out far too much to various interests, which leads to inefficiency and excessive government spending. This particular critique is popular today. The solution is not to abolish groups, but drastically to reduce the role of government in economy and society. Predictably, advocates of this position view with alarm the rise of single-issue and special interest politics. Such changes have fragmented the system further and therefore increased the potential for log-rolling and yet more government programmes and regulations. In essence the critique of the Tea Party movement is based on these sorts of assumptions. They believe that government has grown too large and remote from the interests of the people. But as we have already noted a number of times in earlier chapters, reducing the size and scope of government is easier said than done, especially given that organized groups and interests are now deeply entrenched in the policy system and most have some interest in maintaining the present pattern of expenditure.

Efficiency in resource distribution is the main concern of this essentially conservative critique. Critics on the left have been more interested in the consequences of the classical view for political, social and economic *equality*. They argue that groups are not just unequal, they are grossly unequal, or that there is a bias in the system that some groups are more able to exploit than others. Business or corporate interests, in particular, are advantaged, while labour, the poor and minorities are disadvantaged. This brings us back to the populist condemnation of big business mentioned earlier. How much truth is there to this critique?

First, we should note the obvious fact that in terms of its power to move capital, labour and resources around, business is in a unique position among major organized interests. Only government can exercise anything like an equivalent power; none of the other groups can. Instead they are confined to single issues, or particular geographical areas, or they exercise influence over just one sub-group of the population. Even labour, with its mass membership and finely tuned lobbying machine, has relatively few resources compared with business. It is, perhaps, testimony to the power of the corporations that most of them did not even consider it necessary to engage in overt lobbying until relatively recently, because the policy agenda generally favoured them. While the unions and other interests struggled to get items discussed and legislated, business could often sit back and wait until it perceived its interests to be threatened. Business is privileged in another sense: it has access to large sums of money that can be used to 'lubricate' the policy-making system to its advantage. This is also true of unions and some other groups, but none has access to money in quite the way business has. Revelations of corruption and malpractice in American corporate life (notably the collapse of the energy giant Enron in 2001 – see the Briefing in this chapter – and the banking crisis in the years after 2008) confirm that, quite apart from legal contributions to candidates, the long-established rep-utation of American corporations and business generally for 'crony capitalism' or under-cover financial deals is still very much with us.

Second, if we view society in terms not of discrete groups or organized interests, but of social strata, there is very little evidence that the new politics of openness and accessibil-ity have made very much difference to social and economic mobility. Those groups and classes at the bottom of the social heap 30 or 40 years ago are, generally speaking, still there. Changes in occupational structure have had some impact, but what many have called a 'transformation' of the political system has had little effect. Indeed, it is often the case that the more atomized and complex the decision-making system, the lower the potential for redistributive policies. The two great social reform periods in recent history, which laid the foundations of the welfare state – the New Deal and the Great Society – coincided with what was virtually the antithesis of the new politics – strong presidents, pliant Congresses and a public broadly agreed on the need for reform. To be fair, many redistributive policies (counter-recession economic stimulus programmes, increased social security spending)

Plate 14.2   Anti-abortion protesters outside Culpepper Baptist Church, Virginia, during the Clinton inauguration, January 1993
Source: Martine Franck/Magnum.

have been enacted, and if there is any validity to the public choice critique, greater access should result in more spending, whatever the distributional consequences. This accepted, in a period of fiscal stress, a fragmented political system almost certainly leads to resources being more thinly divided between groups, interests and classes, and those whose need is greatest are likely to find themselves relatively worse off. By the late 1990s it was widely accepted by almost all political interests, including the Clinton administration, that fiscal rectitude (balancing the budget without increasing taxation) was desirable. As such, the potential for redistribution from the haves to the have-nots of society has been seriously reduced. With a short pause in 2008–11 when the federal government injected a massive stimulus into the economy to combat recession, this philosophy has prevailed ever since. No presidential candidate with a hope of success can argue for a major redistribution together with tax rises. Indeed the 2016 victor, Donald Trump, specifically promised tax reforms that would reduce tax rates for everybody, but in particular for corporations and high earners.

Finally, the politics of distribution are now multi-layered, and it is not always adequate to perceive the system only in terms of social classes or strata. Environmental controls, equal opportunities for women and sexual minorities, and improved standards of occupational safety clearly benefit some people more than others, but there is no obvious relationship between the distributional impact of each of these reforms and those that traditional 'class-based' policies (tax reform, welfare, social security) produce. In fact much of the assault on corporate power since the 1970s has involved policies of this sort. Middle-class reformers, outraged at pollution, consumer exploitation and discrimination, launched the new promotional groups that the corporations were then obliged to engage in battle. Meanwhile, the measures by which it is usual to gauge the living conditions of industrial workers, minorities and deprived social groups – income, access to housing and so on – changed very little. Where moral absolutes are concerned – as with abortion, same-sex marriage and capital punishment – the distributional consequences are also difficult to measure. This accepted, critics of the conservative position on these issues would claim that the 'victims' are usually the poor – poor women, African Americans and other minorities.

The proliferation of groups in recent years has led some commentators to argue that they are actually becoming weaker as a political force. The reasoning is that because every issue attracts a range of supporters and detractors in a relatively open policy-making environment, decision-makers are less tied to a particular group or cause. In such a context, the exercise of free choice is easier. Moreover, as constituencies become more complex, so the influence of individual groups in any one constituency is reduced.[9] Of course, another interpretation is that increased group activity actually makes it more difficult for lawmakers to translate individual political demands into public policy. Legislators may not be tied to particular groups as they were to labour or farmers in the past, but now they are bombarded by conflicting opinions and advice from all sides. As a result they often offer constituents broad, lowest-common-denominator benefits such as reduced taxes or reassurances that they will re-establish moral probity through banning abortion or same-sex marriage. Perhaps this helps explain the rise of the Tea Party movement and the Republican right. Whatever the case, organized interests remain a central part of the democratic process. They may be unpopular, or skew political discourse towards the interests of the rich and powerful, but they are very much here to stay.

Summary

Americans have always been ambivalent about the power of organized interests, and waves of populist opposition to groups – and in particular business – have occurred throughout US history. This chapter has summarized the reasons for opposition to interests and catalogued the ways in which the main interests operate today. The activities of labour unions, farmers, business, professional and promotional groups have been covered, as has the work of political action committees and the Washington lobby. The chapter concluded with a discussion on the benefits and costs of interest group activity and assessed their influence in modern American politics.

Questions for Discussion

1   In what ways is business privileged in relation to other groups? Has business become more or less privileged since the economic recession in 2008–11 and its aftermath?
2   What are SuperPACs? How important were they in determining the outcomes of the 2016 presidential and congressional elections?
3   Why is Congress the main focus of interest group activity in the US? Which groups have the most influence on Congress?
4   Discuss the efforts of organized groups to promote or oppose TWO of the following: (a) same sex marriage; (b) gun control; (c) abortion; (d) global warming.

Glossary

AFL-CIO (American Federation of Labor-Congress of Industrial Organizations)   The union 'peak' association representing some of the main unions

American Bar Association (ABA)   The organization representing and defending legal standards

American Farm Bureau Federation (AFBF)   One of the two main unions representing farmers (the other is the National Farmers Union)

American Medical Association (AMA)   One of the main organizations representing doctors and other senior medical professionals

Association of Federal, State, County and Municipal Employees (AFSCME) the main union representing lower-paid municipal and health workers

business unionism   Workers perceiving themselves as part of the capitalist environment

Chapter 11 (federal bankruptcy law)   The ability of companies to freeze debts in order to reorganize and reduce costs

Committee on Political Education (COPE)   The educational and lobbying arm of the AFL-CIO

fat cat contributors   Contributors of large donations to parties and candidates

health maintenance organizations (HMOs)   Organizations designed to provide cost-effective medical care by limiting patient choice of doctors and treatment

K Street project   The plan by congressional Republicans to exclude Democratic lobbyists from access to Congress in the 1990s

lobbyists   Professional interest group employees

National Association for the Advancement of Colored People (NAACP)   A leading interest group defending the rights of African Americans

National Farmers Union (NFU)   One of the two main unions representing farmers (with the American Farm Bureau Federation)

National Rifle Association (NRA)   The organization defending the right of Americans to 'bear arms' by opposing gun-control laws

non-connected PACs   Political action committees supporting causes rather than vested interests

political action committees (PACs)   Pressure-group organizations designed to represent interests in the political sphere

SuperPACs   Political action committees able to spend unlimited amounts in support of or against candidates and issues following the 2010 Supreme Court Citizens United decision

Notes

1   HMOs are (usually private) health companies that pool the resources of hospitals, doctors and other health professionals in order to reduce costs. Many employers provide health benefits only if employees use designated HMOs. This reduces costs, but also limits choice and, many argue, the quality of health care. More than 80 million Americans are HMO users.

2   *Fortune* magazine produces an annual list of the 500 largest corporations in the USA.

3   Raymond Bauer, Ithiel de Sola Pool and Anthony Lewis Dexter, *American Business and Public Policy* (New York: Prentice Hall, 1964).

4   See Graham K. Wilson, *Interest Groups in the United States* (New York: Oxford University Press, 1981).

5   See Charles Lindblom, *Politics and Markets* (New Haven: Yale University Press, 1977).

6   Wilson, *Interest Groups in the United States*, chapter 3.

7   Arthur Bentley, *The Process of Government* (San Antonio: Trinity University Press, 1949); David B. Truman, *The Governmental Process* (New York: Alfred Knopf, 1951).

8   Antony Downs, *An Economic Theory of Democracy* (New York, Harper, 1957).

9   See Robert H. Salisbury, 'The paradox of interest groups in Washington: More groups, less clout', in Anthony King (ed.), *The New American Political System* (Washington, DC: American Enterprise Institute, 1990).

Further Reading

Interest groups and lobbying cover such a wide area of political activity that no one book is a completely adequate guide. For a good account of recent developments see Jeffrey M. Berry and Clyde Wilcox, *The Interest Group Society*, 6th edn (New York and London: Pearson, 2017). More dated but useful is Graham Wilson's *Interest Groups in the United States* (Oxford and New York: Oxford University Press, 1981). Allan J. Cigler, Burdett Loomis and Anthony J Nownes have edited a good collection of readings on the subject, *Interest Group Politics*, 9th edn (Washington, DC: Congressional Quarterly Press, 2015). Matt Grossman's *Not-So-Special Interests: Interest Groups, Public Representation, and American Governance* (Stanford: Stanford University Press, 2012) shows which are the most powerful groups and how they operate. For an analysis of the power of business, see David Vogel, *Fluctuating Fortunes: The Political Power of Business in America* (New York: Bears Books, 2003).

CHAPTER 15
THE SUPREME COURT AND JUDICIAL POLITICS

We are very quiet there but it is the quiet of a storm centre.
– OLIVER WENDELL HOLMES, ASSOCIATE JUSTICE
OF THE SUPREME COURT, 1902–32

In a democracy, politics is a process of popular education – the task of adjusting the conflicting interests of diverse groups … and thereby to the hostility and suspicion and ignorance engendered by group interests … toward mutual understanding.
– FELIX FRANKFURTER, ASSOCIATE JUSTICE
OF THE SUPREME COURT, 1939–62

American Politics and Society, Ninth Edition. David McKay.
© 2018 John Wiley & Sons Ltd. Published 2018 by John Wiley & Sons Ltd.

In all societies, the courts play some political role. In liberal democracies, where the independence of the judiciary is regarded as essential to prevent the exercise of irresponsible executive (and sometimes legislative) power, the political role of the courts as interpreters of the law and as defenders of individual freedoms is well established. In despotic and one-party states, courts are political in the quite different sense that they are the instruments of a dominant executive. However, there are also important distinctions within liberal democratic states, the most crucial being the presence or absence of judicial review. As noted in chapter 4, judicial review is long established in the United States, the Supreme Court being the final arbiter of the meaning of the Constitution. Hence, all laws passed by the state and national legislatures, together with all executive actions, are subject to review by the courts, which judge their compatibility with the Constitution. As the final court of appeal, therefore, the Supreme Court has the legal power to declare any action by any other branch of government as unconstitutional. As we develop below, this apparently formidable power is tempered by a number of factors, but in contrast to many other liberal democracies, there can be no disputing the evidence of what is enormous potential judicial power. In the United Kingdom, for example, the courts can review executive actions – but only by testing them in relation to the content of Acts of Parliament. This can produce sharp rebukes for governments when the courts judge that the government has acted *ultra vires* or beyond its powers, and the British courts are becoming more active in reviewing executive actions. A British parliament controlled by the executive can, however, always reverse a judicial judgment, as sovereignty lies not in a constitution but in parliament (although, at least in 2017, in some matters the European Court of Justice and the European Convention on Human Rights have the final say). In the United States, a decision of the Supreme Court involving the constitutionality of a statute or governmental action can be overturned only by constitutional amendment (or by the Court itself, of course) and, as shown in chapter 3, the amendment procedure is cumbersome and rarely used.

In fact, the Supreme Court uses its power of judicial review quite sparingly, and much of the day-to-day business of the courts is concerned with interpreting the law, rather than making solemn declarations on the constitutionality of legislation. Even in non-constitutional areas, however, American courts are more active than their British equivalents, for the United States is a highly legalistic society. Recourse to the courts for redress of grievances is swift and ubiquitous in American life. Indeed, the country boasts a staggering 650,000 lawyers and judges, and among the occupational backgrounds of American politicians, lawyers constitute the single largest group. A number of reasons could be suggested for this. As we have repeatedly stressed in this book, the USA is a country with a liberal tradition, and the ideology of economic liberalism implies a society made up of individuals rather than social classes, races or other social groups. Distinct and separate individuals acting as self-contained economic units are more likely to defend or promote their interests in the judicial marketplace rather than, as in many other countries, fall back on social class, family, ethnic group or simply custom and tradition for support. There is a danger of making too much of this, but the tendency for individuals to seek legal redress for poor medical care or a faulty consumer product, or for corporations to sue competitors or suppliers for patent violations or breach of contract, is surely related to a pervasive economic liberalism.

In addition, the United States is infused with constitutionalism. With a written constitution granting certain rights and freedoms to citizens, delineating a separation of powers and guaranteeing a federal system of government, disputes between individuals and government, and between branches and levels of government, must be arbitrated. Of course, in every political system disputes of this sort have to be resolved, but in few systems are rather rigidly delineated citizens' rights, separation of powers and federal arrangements married to a strong tradition of legalism and the institution of judicial review. As far as the political role of the courts is concerned, it is the presence of judicial review that marks out the American system as distinctive, and as the Supreme Court is the highest court in the land, it is the Court's judicial review function that has attracted the most attention. The bulk of this chapter is therefore devoted to this subject. Specifically, the chapter examines how the Court has responded to the much more confrontational political environment of the twenty-first century and in particular how judicial decisions affect other actors in the political system, including Congress, the presidency and the states.

The American Legal System

For the vast majority of Americans, state courts are what matter, for of the approximately 10 million cases tried in the United States every year, the federal courts account for fewer than 2 per cent. State, municipal, county and other local courts have jurisdiction over state law – which means that in any one state the vast majority of criminal and civil law cases, from mugging to property disputes, from divorce to homicide, are initiated and concluded within the state system. Almost all of the more sensational criminal and civil cases, such as the trials of O. J. Simpson (the ex-professional footballer accused and acquitted of killing his ex-wife and her boyfriend in 1995, but later in 2008 convicted of armed robbery) and the Menendez brothers (convicted of killing their parents to inherit their estate), start and end in state rather than federal courts. For most of the time, therefore, the two systems operate independently of one another. As can be seen from figure 15.1, however, federal courts can play a crucial part in state law because, if a decision by the highest state courts of appeal is controversial and if the case involves a federal question, then it can be appealed to the US Supreme Court. Effectively, this gives the Supreme Court the power to interpret and judge state law, for 'a federal question' can mean almost anything that is contentious or controversial. In law it means any state court decision which is potentially incompatible with federal law or with the US Constitution. If, for example, a state high court hands down a decision extending the power of state police to search a suspect's house for evidence, this would have to be compatible with the Fourth Amendment of the Constitution, which prohibits unwarranted search and seizure. Only the US Supreme Court can judge whether the state law is unconstitutional or not.

In one sense, the Supreme Court's power of judicial review over state law is its most important function. Without it, the country would cease to be a united nation-state. Instead, a loose confederacy would prevail, with each state going its own way in economic and social affairs.

The power to review state high court decisions is part of the *appellate* jurisdiction of the Supreme Court. In addition, the Court hears cases on appeal from within the federal court system. As shown in figure 15.1, most federal cases originate in the federal district courts

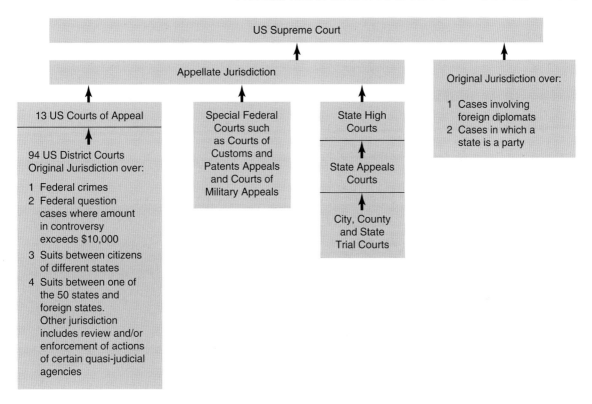

Figure 15.1   Organization of the US court system

(94 in number), whose decisions can be appealed to one of the 13 crucial Courts of Appeal, and thence to the Supreme Court. The Court[1] also has original jurisdiction on a number of minor areas, such as cases involving ambassadors.

Most citizens involved in federal litigation, therefore, have contact with the District Courts that are responsible for cases involving federal criminal and civil law. Compared with state law, federal criminal law is limited to a relatively few – although growing – areas, the most notable being bank robbery, kidnapping, currency forgery, drug trafficking, terrorism and assassination. Most of the work of the District Courts is in the area of civil law, with taxation, regulation, and civil rights and liberty cases dominating. Few of these cases are appealed (about 15 per cent), and those that are, are usually settled in the Appeal Courts, which on a day-to-day basis are the most important judicial policy-makers in the country. They are not, however, the key judicial policy-makers, because their decisions can always be overruled by the Supreme Court.

As can be seen from table 15.1, the District Courts' caseload showed a substantial rise to 1985. A greatly expanded federal role in part accounts for this, and although the precise relationship between spreading federal legislation and litigation is hard to establish, there is no doubt that a more active federal government has greatly increased the caseload of both the District Courts and Appeal Courts. By 1978 the overload of the courts had reached

Table 15.1   Cases filed in US District and Appeals Courts and Supreme Court, 1980–2016

	1975	**1980**	**1985**	**1989**	**1995**	**2001**	**2005**	**2016**
District Courts	117,300	168,800	273,700	233,500	239,013	253,354	282,758	371,507[a]
Appeals Courts	16,668	23,200	33,360	39,734	49,671	46,682	48,907	53,649[a]
Supreme Court	4,764	5,144	5,158	5,746	7,565	9,176	9,608	7,033[b]

Source: For the Appeals and District Courts, www.uscourts.gov/statistics-reports/federal-court-management-statistics-march-2016. For the Supreme Court, www.supremecourt.gov/publicinfo/year-end/2015year-endreport.pdf.
[a]Year to March 2016.
[b]Through 2014.

Plate 15.1   The United States Supreme Court, Washington, DC
Source: Istockphoto/© lillisphotography.

crisis proportions and Congress increased the number of district judges from 281 to 398 and appeal judges from 62 to 97. By 2010 there were over 650 district judges and almost 180 appeal judges. Since the mid-1980s the number of cases filed has continued to increase reaching nearly 400,000 by the year 2016, although the number of these cases successfully appealed to the Courts of Appeal has increased only slightly (table 15.1).

As table 15.1 also shows, the Supreme Court experienced a sharp rise in its caseload until the mid-1980s, followed by a levelling off during the 1990s and a decline in recent years. Increases in the number and use of law clerks (each justice has up to four clerks assigned to him or her), and improved administration of the Court by the then chief justice, Warren

Burger, probably account for the institution's ability to manage. Even so, demands for the creation of a National Court of Appeals to screen cases coming before the Court remain.

As with lower courts, new legislation in civil rights and liberties and in the general area of federal regulation largely account for the new demands on the Supreme Court. So like the Congress and presidency, an ever-expanding federal role has produced new pressures on the Court which have made its operations more complex and difficult and, crucially, more politically visible.

The Supreme Court: Decision-Making

Each year about 150 cases are actually decided by the Supreme Court, and while most of these will be of relatively minor political or constitutional import, some will have profound consequences for the American polity and society. Since 1950, for example, the Court has decided that racially separate educational and other facilities are inherently unequal; that almost exact mathematical equality should be applied to the size of state legislative and congressional districts; that indigent arrested persons should be provided with the services of a lawyer at the government's expense; that tapes of presidential conversations were not so private as to be protected by executive privilege and therefore could be used in court against presidential staff accused of dishonesty; that the bussing of schoolchildren to achieve racial integration is constitutionally required to overcome a historical pattern of legally imposed educational segregation; and that voting procedures in Florida were not inefficient, so as possibly to hand victory in a presidential election to Gore rather than Bush in the 2000 election. More recently the Court decided that the detainees in Guantánamo Bay were entitled to *habeas corpus* rights in the US court system, in 2010 the Court effectively abolished limits on corporate and union campaign contributions and in 2015 it mandated that same-sex marriage should be legal across all 50 states. The very fact that all of these decisions have aroused intense controversy demonstrates their political significance, and the question of how far and in what ways the Court can hand down decisions that are at odds with public opinion or with the other branches of government is a topic we return to below. Clearly, *how* the Court makes decisions is important. How does it decide which cases to hear? What criteria does it employ when deciding a case?

It is misleading to talk of *the* Supreme Court. Rather than being a unified organic body, the Court consists of nine individuals, each with his or her (in 1981 Sandra Day O'Connor was the first woman to be appointed to the Court and in 2016 three women sat on the Court) quite distinctive view of law, politics and society. Justices are appointed by the president with the advice and consent of the Senate. Unlike other executive appointments, they are appointed for life. Once on the Court, then, they are free from the political, financial and other pressures which insecurity of tenure inflicts on most political actors. Of course, only a small percentage of cases coming before the Court are actually heard; most are denied review or, in the language of the Court, are denied *certiorari*. *Certiorari* is, simply, that act whereby the losing party in the lower court appeals the record of the case to the Supreme Court so that details of the case can be made 'more certain'. More than 90 per cent of cases are appealed in this way; in most of the remainder the Court is required to hear cases by a statutory appeals process.[2] The granting or denial of *certiorari* is clearly an important decision and the Court is legally beholden to no one to justify which cases are heard and which are not. From a strictly legal perspective, the criteria for granting *certiorari* are relatively easy to identify. Loren Beth lists seven:

1   How fundamental is the constitutional (or other) issue presented by the case?
2   How many similar cases have been or are being litigated?
3   Is there a conflict of opinion in the lower courts on this particular issue?
4   Does a lower-court decision seem to conflict with an earlier Supreme Court decision?
5   Is there a significant individual right involved?
6   Has the lower court departed significantly from the accepted and usual course of judicial proceedings?
7   Does the case involve the interpretation of a statute never before construed?[3]

At least four of the nine justices have to agree to grant *certiorari* – a fact that strongly implies that the decision is not as clear-cut as the list suggests. Indeed, not one of points 1 to 7 is completely unambiguous or not open to serious disagreement or argument. How many cases in the civil rights and liberties areas – a good proportion of the total – do *not* involve a significant individual right? Almost certainly none. Similarly, many cases claim to involve a 'fundamental constitutional issue', yet few of these are granted *certiorari*. The fact is that while points 1 to 7 may be a legally correct list of criteria, they tell us very little of the political context in which decisions are taken. Why did it take until the 1940s and 1950s before the Court started regularly to hear civil rights cases? Why did it take until the 1960s for criminal defendants' rights cases to come to the fore, and until 1973 for the Court to deliberate on the constitutional status of bans on abortion?

There are two possible answers here. First is that the philosophy and outlook of the justices changes over time, either as a result of turnover or because individual justices change their minds. The second is that the political and social context in which the Court operates has changed over time, thus forcing certain issues onto the judicial policy agenda that were previously excluded. Taking the second point first, it is certain that the Court is influenced by the broader society. In the civil rights area, the Second World War 'nationalized' a number of social issues and brought into sharp focus for both whites and blacks the injustices of segregation in the American South. Publicity on conditions in the South was advanced by a number of interest groups, in particular the National Association for the Advancement of Colored People (NAACP), which also acted as a judicial interest group by providing financial and legal support for litigants involved in civil rights cases.

Although it is impossible to measure the influence on the Supreme Court of the 'social and political environment' or of the work of interest groups intent on promoting a particular cause or defending a special interest, the justices are undoubtedly swayed by such factors, at least in terms of letting them influence the policy agenda, or what sort of cases are actually heard.

But it would be misleading to leave the impression of a court granting *certiorari* only to classes of cases currently subject to public attention. Many cases are heard when the public pressure is minimal or absent. Reapportionment, for example, was not a matter of intense public debate when the Court, in the famous 1962 case, *Baker* v. *Carr*, found that the very unequal Tennessee state legislative districts could be challenged in the federal courts. Later, in *Wesberry* v. *Sanders* (1964), the Court directly invalidated Georgia's grossly unequal congressional districts. Finally, in *Reynolds* v. *Sims* (1964), the Court argued that the equal protection clause of the Fourteenth Amendment should give to all citizens an equal weight in elections. Thereafter, all states reorganized their districts according to the general principle of mathematical equality. The business of getting a case before the Supreme Court is also long and hard. It may be years from the time a case is first filed in the District Court to when it eventually reaches the Supreme Court. Such a process does not always lend itself to instant decision-making in response to public or interest group pressure.

The judicial agenda is also influenced by the philosophies and attitudes of the justices themselves. Generally speaking, a decision not to hear a case which in some way does meet one or more of criteria 1 to 7 and which is currently controversial is a conservative decision. It can reflect a justice's desire to keep the Court out of the 'political thicket' by leaving a lower court's decision or judicial precedent to settle the matter. The fact that the Supreme Court did not hear many civil rights cases in the 1920s and 1930s might be explained in this way, as might the reluctance of the Court to get involved in economic policy during the 1940s and 1950s. We should be wary here, however, for so far discussion has been confined to the influences shaping the Court's policy agenda, i.e. which cases are heard and which are not. Naturally, the crucial question is how the Court decides those cases granted *certiorari*. Even the most conservative justice would have to recommend the issue of a writ of *certiorari* when a Circuit Court of Appeals had decided a case which fundamentally contradicted judicial precedent as represented by an earlier Supreme Court decision. More interesting are those instances when the Court decides to uphold such a radical departure from precedent, or decides that a particular Act of Congress or executive action is unconstitutional.

One basic fact must be appreciated when discussing the Supreme Court as a political actor: it uses its power sparingly. It exercises *judicial self-restraint* (although, as we shall see, some Supreme Courts have been more restrained than others). It follows the doctrine of 'assumption of constitutionality'. In other words, it will use its power of judicial review very selectively, arguing a case on procedural grounds when it can, rather than declaring a law unconstitutional. As can be seen from table 15.2, the Court has, in fact, used its power of judicial review over federal law sparingly – especially down to 1920. Since then it has been more prone to strike down federal law, and this tendency has increased since 1960. As far as state laws are concerned, the Court has been more active (table 15.2). Note that here too the rate increased through to 1990, although it has declined since.

As noted above, the Supreme Court consists of nine individual justices, and the final decision of the Court reflects the interaction of the opinions of these nine people. The formal decision-making process goes like this. Once *certiorari* is granted, the justices first receive written and then hear oral argument from the lawyers on both sides of the case. Later a case conference is convened at which the justices, sitting in private, make a preliminary decision. Five of the justices must agree to constitute a decision and one of these will be assigned to write the majority opinion. If the chief justice is part of the majority, he or another majority member assigned by him will write the opinion. If the chief justice is part of the minority, the most senior member of the majority will make the assignment. Once the assignments have been made, the opinion of the Court is written. This can take many weeks to complete, and once it is published the names of other members of the majority may be added to it. However, some members, while they may agree with the author of the opinion of the Court, may do so for *different* reasons, in which case they will write *concurring* opinions. Finally, those in the minority may choose to write a dissenting opinion, or even a number of dissenting opinions. Usually members will join just the majority or dissenting opinion, but it is quite possible for

Table 15.2   Federal, state and local laws declared unconstitutional by the US Supreme Court, by decade, 1789–2014

Years	Federal	State and local
1789–1799	0	0
1800–1809	1	1
1810–1819	0	7
1820–1829	0	8
1830–1839	0	3
1840–1849	0	10
1850–1859	1	7
1860–1869	4	24
1870–1879	7	36
1880–1889	4	46
1890–1899	5	36
1900–1909	9	40
1910–1919	6	119
1920–1929	15	139
1930–1939	13	92
1940–1949	2	61
1950–1959	5	66
1960–1969	16	151
1970–1979	20	195
1980–1989	16	164
1990–1999	24	62
2000–2009	14	36
2010–2014	13	11
Total	177	1,321

Source: Vital Statistics on American Politics, 2015–16 (Washington, DC: Congressional Quarterly Press, 2015), table 7.12 (p. 291). Reprinted with permission of SAGE.

the Court to publish up to nine separate opinions: an opinion of the Court; four concurring opinions which may support the Court opinion on four different grounds; and four dissenting opinions which dissent on four different grounds. In the celebrated 1978 *Bakke* decision, which limited the use of racial quotas to discriminate positively in favour of minorities when admitting them to university courses, the Court published no fewer than six separate opinions. In this case – and this often applies when the justices are split – the variety of concurring opinions made it difficult to infer the exact meaning of the Court's decision – an outcome possibly preferred by the Court in this politically sensitive and technically complex area.

To the more casual observer of the judicial process, how a justice decides in a particular case may seem obvious. Precedent and a careful interpretation of congressional statutes would be the immediate answer. Naturally, the justices do refer to precedent and they do spend much of their time interpreting legislation. But even reference to precedent can be problematical. What historical precedents were there when the Court first heard cases involving electronic bugging; or genetic engineering; or racial quotas, for that matter? Very few that could be considered even vaguely relevant. And interpreting statute law when it involves overruling executive actions can be politically sensitive, to say the least. In both instances the Court has very considerable discretion not only to follow precedent, but also to create it; not only to interpret statutes, but also to direct the executive branch to change policy. When the formidable power of judicial review is added, the discretion available to the Court widens dramatically. Again, the reflex response to the question 'What guides the Court when it uses judicial review?' is: the Constitution. But, as stressed in chapter 4, there is very little in the Constitution that is unambiguous, and the Supreme Court has reversed itself on a number of occasions when interpreting constitutional provisions.

If the justices cannot rely on precedent or the literal meaning of statutes or constitutional provisions, what does guide their judicial opinions? This is a complex and difficult question. We have already mentioned the political and social environment, and there can be no disputing that the Court has been influenced by pressures from public opinion, presidents and interest groups. Instances of such pressures are recorded below. Partly independently of such forces, however, different Supreme Courts and justices have acquired reputations for being 'conservative' or 'liberal', 'active' or 'passive'. These labels often refer to the jurisprudence or legal philosophy adhered to by different justices. Certainly, no self-respecting Supreme Court justice would rationalize his or her decision in terms of 'political pressures' or 'political expedience' – even if these were truly the main influences. Instead, justices would indeed refer to the Constitution and the ways in which the wording of the Constitution should be interpreted. By so doing they are obliged to look not only at the actual wording of the document but also at the meanings and motives behind the words. If, along with such a 'positivist' approach, the justice also believes that the Court has an unbending duty always to 'discover' the Constitution's true meaning, then an activist Court is implied. For relating the events in a particular case to the true meaning of the Constitution, and then testing whether (say) a law on censorship is reconcilable with the Constitution, invites the Court to declare on the constitutionality of that law. Such was the approach of the two outstanding jurists of the early part of the twentieth century, Oliver Wendell Holmes and Louis Brandeis. In a number of celebrated cases both argued that some federal and state laws on internal subversion were incompatible with the First Amendment's general prohibition of laws abridging freedom of speech – although they accepted that absolute freedom of speech was clearly not intended by the framers of the Constitution. In Justice Holmes's famous example, 'the most stringent protection of free speech would not protect a man in falsely shouting fire in a theatre and causing a panic', they argued that if the First Amendment was to mean anything, some principle inherent in the provision must be detected and invoked. By this reasoning, Holmes elaborated the 'clear and present danger test', or 'the question in every case is whether the words used in such circumstances are of such a nature as to create a clear and present danger that they will bring about the substantive evils that Congress has a right to prevent'. Of course, problems remain here – discovering exactly when the danger is clear and present must in part be a subjective exercise, perhaps especially so when Congress (or a state legislature) has passed a law attempting to prevent subversion in time of war. Indeed, Holmes and Brandeis sometimes believed there was a clear and present danger, as they did in the *Schenck* case from which the above quotation is taken.[4] But the very fact of attempting to find some principle inherent in the Constitution implies a legal philosophy that is largely independent of the vagaries of social and political pressures prevailing at any one time.

In marked contrast, one of the most prominent jurists of the 1940s and 1950s, Felix Frankfurter, believed that the representatives of the American people – Congress and president – should be left to interpret the Constitution, the Court's involvement being confined to mediating disputes between the branches or between federal and state governments. Even then, Frankfurter argued, the Court should attempt to *balance* the various competing interests in society rather than search for some 'inherent principle' or 'higher meaning' behind the wording of the document. Clearly this approach, or one that steers clear of politics, implies a passive Court, letting representative institutions sort out conflict in society. The activism of Holmes and Brandeis and the passivity of Frankfurter represent two of the more coherent of a number of philosophical positions taken by the Court, and the labels 'active' and 'passive', 'liberal' and 'conservative' usually correspond to the perceived philosophy of the Court at a particular time. We should not, however, be deceived into thinking of different Supreme Courts as representing distinct and coherent philosophies. To repeat, nine individuals make the decisions, and each may vary quite dramatically in outlook.

Some Supreme Courts, then, have lacked an identifiable philosophy. More important, it is impossible to separate the decisions of the justices from the political and social environment in which they operate. The 'positivism' of Holmes and Brandeis, with its search for a consistency and justice inherent in the Constitution, irrespective of political and social pressures, failed to dominate even the Court on which they sat, let alone be the main approach of subsequent Supreme Courts. Like any other political institution, the Court has to interact with society and polity. It is subject to a number of pressures and constraints. What makes the institution so interesting, however, is the mix of judicial philosophy and external constraint that has produced an ever-changing political role for the Court in American history. The remainder of this chapter is devoted to studying this role, by analysing the constraints on the Court's power, and in particular by asking whether the institution can perform its role to good effect in the complex and politically charged atmosphere of the twenty-first century.

The Supreme Court and Political Power

There can be no doubting that Supreme Court decisions have political impact. From the momentous *Marbury* v. *Madison* decision in 1803 when, by declaring section 13 of the 1789 Judiciary Act unconstitutional, Chief Justice John Marshall effectively established judicial review, through to the landmark civil rights cases of the past 60 years, the attention of public and polity alike has been concentrated by the political implications of the Court's decisions. But as suggested above, this does not mean that these solemn judicial deliberations take place in isolation from society. On the contrary, many have argued that the Court rarely deviates from the prevailing weight of political or public opinion; that, in fact, its main function has been to legitimize dominant political influences, and when it has gone against these it has soon found itself in trouble of one sort or another. In one rather obvious sense this is always true, for courts depend on their authority rather than naked power. They have no police force or army – or even bureaucrats – to enforce their decisions. For this they have to depend on the other branches of government. Perhaps the most dramatic example of the dangers inherent in fundamentally disagreeing with the other branches of government was the 1857 *Dred Scott* case. In this the Court declared that African Americans had no right to sue under the US Constitution because they were not 'citizens'. In addition, the Court declared unworkable the 1820 Missouri compromise which gave blacks free status in the territories to the north of the Missouri acquired in the Louisiana Purchase. If African Americans were to revert to slave status in these northern and western territories, a forced extension of the culture and values of the South was implied, a change completely unacceptable to Lincoln and the dominant Republican Party. The decision was never enforced because the Civil War soon followed, as did the Thirteenth and Fourteenth Amendments, which specifically granted equal legal status to all citizens. For the other branches of government simply to ignore the Supreme Court is the most serious challenge to its power, for once ignored, its authority and legitimacy are undermined. Without these it loses all influence. After the Civil War the Court did, in fact, reassert its authority, and it has never been seriously undermined since. But there have been ebbs and flows of judicial power, crises of confidence and periods of intense controversy. A useful way to study these is to document the constraints or limitations on the Court's power, or to record those instances when the scope and substance of judicial decisions have, in one way or another, been circumscribed.

Constitutional amendment

Amending the Constitution to overturn the Court is the ultimate legal weapon available to the other branches and to the states. As we know, however, amendments have been few and far between, and just four have been employed to overrule the Court. In one of these – the Twenty-Sixth Amendment ratified in 1971 to extend the vote to 18-year-olds – the Court's *Oregon* v. *Mitchell* (1970) decision was overturned. Another (the Eleventh Amendment, which prohibited a citizen of one state from suing the government of another state) has passed into historical obscurity.[5] Only two amendments stand out as changes crucial to preserve the integrity of the Union and the smooth running of government – the Fourteenth Amendment, which overturned *Dred Scott*, and the Sixteenth Amendment, sanctioning a graduated federal income tax. Ratified in 1913 when increased defence spending was widely perceived as necessary, the Sixteenth Amendment overturned the 1895 *Pollock* v. *Farmers' Loan and Trust* decision, which had declared a graduated or progressive federal income tax unconstitutional. In more recent years calls for constitutional amendments to overturn Supreme Court decisions have been equally rare, although a movement exists to amend the Constitution to overturn the 1973 *Roe* v. *Wade* decision sanctioning abortion. More recently, in a 1989 decision (*Texas* v. *Johnson*) the Court struck down a state law banning the burning of the American flag and a year later struck down a federal law on the same issue (*United States* v. *Eichman*). In response, a movement for a constitutional amendment making it a crime to burn the flag gathered pace. So far, however, Congress and the states have proved reluctant to overturn the Court on what was an issue of entirely emotional and symbolic importance.

Congressional control

The Constitution grants remarkably wide discretion to Congress over the composition and organization of the federal judiciary. Article 3 states, quite simply: 'The judicial power of the

United States shall be vested in one Supreme Court and in such inferior Courts as the Congress may from time to time ordain and establish.' So Congress has the power to determine the size and administration of the federal machinery of justice. Additionally, the Constitution specifically gives to Congress discretion over the Court's appellate jurisdiction and implicitly, at least, over the number of justices and when the Court should actually sit. Only rarely, however, has Congress exercised these very substantial discretionary powers. Easily the most important item of legislation in these areas is the 1789 Judiciary Act, which established the Supreme Court's power to review state court decisions denying federal rights to citizens. Apart from this, Congress has regularly increased the number of federal judges and courts in line with population and caseload increases, and the number of Supreme Court justices fluctuated between six and 10 until 1870, since when it has remained at nine. During the 1930s, President Roosevelt attempted to increase the size of the Court to overcome opposition to his New Deal legislation, but Congress was disinclined to tinker with the Court in this way. By the 1930s the figure of nine justices was regarded as almost a part of the Constitution.

If Congress has been reluctant to alter the Court's composition and jurisdiction, it has shown little hesitation in reversing Court decisions via statutory reversals, or legislating to invalidate a particular judicial interpretation of federal law. Between 1946 and 1968, for example, some 111 roll-call votes in Congress reversed Supreme Court statutory interpretations. Few of these were of great import, however, and of course Congress cannot touch those decisions that are based on *constitutional* interpretation.

Perhaps Congress's most important function in relation to the Supreme Court is as a forum for public opinion. Senators and representatives quite frequently openly attack the Court or even introduce bills designed to curb its power. During the 1950s and 1960s, for example, southerners incensed at the Court's desegregation decisions, and conservatives at its civil liberties and reapportionment decisions, regularly did both. More recently, the 'pro-life' lobby in Congress has attempted to change the law on abortion, following the Court's liberal *Roe* v. *Wade* decision in 1973. Indeed, moral outrage at Court decisions on abortion, obscenity and school prayers inspired no fewer than 30 bills designed to curb the Court's jurisdiction during 1980 and 1981. Most recently a Republican Congress made numerous attempts to repeal the Affordable Care Act (or Obamacare) and in effect reverse the several Supreme Court decisions that have upheld key provisions of the Act. While these attempts have failed, we cannot claim that constant attacks in the national legislature have no effect on the justices. In some contexts they may well influence the Court, especially if the justices are effectively isolated in their policy position, as was the case in 1937, when few sources of power or influence in American society sided with the Court. Finally, the Senate has to confirm all nominations made to the judicial branch by presidents. As discussed below, this is a power the Senate has used with increased vigour in recent years.

Presidential control

Presidents have two main means whereby they can influence the Supreme Court: first, and most important, via the appointment power; second, by appealing to public or congressional opinion to reinforce their opposition to or support for a particular position. All federal judges are political appointees, and the vast majority nominated by a president share his political party label if not his total political and social philosophy. In the case of District

Court and, to a lesser extent, Appeals Court nominations, presidents used to be guided by the advice and influence of the Senate (via the confirmation power) but also by state and local party leaders and dignitaries. Today, however, both lower-court and Supreme Court nominations are very much a matter of presidential preference. Broadly speaking, presidents have appointed justices whose political views are similar to their own. This does not mean to say that presidents deliberately manipulate an appointment in order to change the complexion of the courts – although often they do. Nor does it mean that they are always successful in their attempts to change the courts' outlook and philosophy.

As far as the Supreme Court is concerned, they are circumscribed by chance, for although a vacancy on the Court has on average come up about every two years, some presidents have been denied the privilege of receiving their 'quota' of two nominations. In his four years as president, poor Jimmy Carter made no appointments, while in his first three years in office Richard Nixon made four and in his first two years Bill Clinton made two. Interestingly, it was President Carter who explicitly stated an intention to remove political considerations from the appointment of all federal judges, although as far as the Supreme Court was concerned his pledge went untested.

On three occasions in recent history, presidents have been given and have taken the opportunity to try to change the political complexion of the Court. Roosevelt did so after 1937, Nixon after 1969 and Reagan after 1981. In Roosevelt's case, the Court had repeatedly struck down New Deal legislation on the grounds that it was an unconstitutional exercise of the interstate commerce clause and violated 'substantive' due process under the Fourteenth Amendment. In the face of the possible collapse of his economic recovery programme, Roosevelt attempted to 'pack' the Court by asking Congress to increase the number of justices by one for every existing justice over 70 years old, up to a maximum of 15. His strategy was clear – to tip the ideological balance of the Court away from the so-called 'Four Horsemen of Conservatism' (Justices Butler, McReynolds, Sutherland and Van Devanter) and towards a more liberal stance. He failed in the Court-packing plan largely because by the time it reached the critical stage in a not-too-enthusiastic Congress one of the conservatives, Van Devanter, had retired. Roosevelt then proceeded to fill this and other vacancies, which came thick and fast during the next few years, with 'New Dealers' or justices sympathetic to an enhanced federal role in economy and society. He was remarkably successful. Almost all of his nine appointees toed the New Deal line and the Court kept well out of economic affairs during the 1937–53 period.

The second quite dramatic instance of political use of the appointment power occurred during the first two years of the Nixon administration. One of Richard Nixon's 1968 campaign pledges had been to replace the liberals of the Warren Court with 'strict constructionists', or conservatives less prone to the advancement of civil rights and liberties characteristic of the Warren era. He was given a golden opportunity to do just this, for four vacancies occurred during the 1969–71 period. One of these was for chief justice, and the president lost no time in nominating Warren Burger, chief judge of the District of Columbia Court of Appeals, to the position. Burger, a conservative Republican from Minnesota, remained chief justice until 1986.[6] Nixon's next two nominees ran into serious trouble in the Senate. Only rarely in the twentieth century have Supreme Court nominations been rejected, and it is a remarkable testimony to Nixon's political insensitivity that his second and third nominations, Clement Haynsworth and Harrold Carswell, were voted down in the Upper Chamber. Both were undistinguished as jurists, and Carswell in particular had acquired a dubious record on civil rights in the southern courts from which he hailed. Their rejection illustrates well the simple fact that presidential discretion over appointments is limited. A president may nominate a conservative or a liberal, but not an incompetent or a bigot. A Senate judiciary committee well versed by the American Bar Association, leading jurists and interested groups will see to that. Richard Nixon did, however, succeed with his next three appointments, Harry Blackmun, Lewis Powell and William Rehnquist. Rehnquist was a solid conservative (but a respected jurist), while the others were known as at least moderately conservative.

The Reagan experience was different again. Sandra Day O'Connor, nominated in 1981, was a respected judge who was chosen largely because she was a woman. A conservative, but no ideologue, O'Connor replaced the moderate Potter Stewart, an Eisenhower appointee. In 1986, when Chief Justice Burger retired, Reagan elevated William Rehnquist to the chief justiceship and nominated Judge Antonio Scalia to fill the vacancy. Both moves were highly strategic. Rehnquist was known as a conservative on all major questions. His nomination inspired considerable opposition in the Senate but he was eventually confirmed. Scalia was also known to favour the Reagan agenda, but his nomination met with little resistance.

These controversies pale into insignificance compared with the nomination of Robert Bork following the resignation of Justice Lewis Powell in June 1987. Powell had long held the pivotal vote against the New Right agenda favoured by the administration, involving such issues as affirmative action and abortion. Robert Bork's tenure on the Court of Appeals was marked by a 'strict constructionism' or a consistently conservative interpretation of the Constitution. During the lengthy nomination proceedings Bork worked hard to convince the Senate Judiciary Committee that he was in fact a centrist, rather than an ideologue of the right. It was this inconsistency which helped to produce his eventual defeat by the widest margin ever (58 to 42). Reagan's next nominee, Douglas Ginsburg, was also a conservative but was obliged to withdraw following revelations that he had once smoked marijuana while in law school. Eventually, the Senate confirmed the nomination of Anthony Kennedy, a moderate and pragmatic conservative from California.

At the Appeal Court and District Court level, Ronald Reagan pursued a more overtly political strategy than any previous president. As one commentator put it, 'The striking feature about Reagan's lower-court judges is that they are predominantly young white upper-class males, with prior judicial or prosecuting experience and reputations for legal conservatism established on the bench in law schools, or in politics.'[7] By appointing large numbers of conservatives to the lower courts, President Reagan almost certainly changed the nature of lower-court decisions and therefore the sort of cases which are appealed to the Supreme Court. During his presidency, George Bush Senior was able to make two appointments. In 1990 he nominated David H. Souter to replace William Brennan, almost the last of the Court's liberals and first appointed in 1956. Souter was quickly confirmed by the Senate. In 1991 Bush nominated Clarence Thomas to replace Lyndon Johnson nominee Thurgood Marshall. Thomas was also confirmed in spite of allegations that he had sexually harassed a former employee, Anita Hill. Marshall was the first black member of the Court and Thomas the second. Both Souter and Thomas became identified with the dominant conservative representation on the Court.

On coming to office, Bill Clinton was determined to make his administrative and judicial appointees 'look like America'. As far as gender and ethnicity are concerned the president was true to his word. However, relatively few of his judicial appointments were so liberal as to transform the judiciary from the conservative stance it acquired during the Reagan and Bush years. Indeed, his first two appointments to the Court, Stephen Breyer and Ruth Bader Ginsburg, were widely regarded as moderates. The Senate easily confirmed both nominations. In fact, the justices they replaced (Byron White and Harry Blackmun) were, on the face of it, more liberal than the new appointees. Clinton nominations to the lower courts included a large number of women and African and Hispanic Americans. However, because such nominees are often also liberals, the Republican-controlled Senate Judiciary Committee delayed confirmations for months and even years. As a result, many District and Appeal Court judgeships remained vacant some years into the Clinton presidency.

As was widely expected with eight of the nine justices over 65 years old in 2004, President George W. Bush was given the opportunity to nominate two new justices during 2005. After an unusually long period of stability on the Court (eight years, the longest period without a change in 180 years), the president was thus given an opportunity to change the ideological complexion of the Court. During the summer Justice Sandra Day O'Connor resigned on grounds of ill health and on 20 July the president nominated US circuit judge John Roberts to the bench. Roberts was known as a moderate conservative with a long and honourable pedigree as a lawyer, first as an appellate attorney and more recently as a member of the influential US Court of Appeals for the District of Columbia. Although some Democrats vowed to fight the nomination, opposition was muted and the nomination process was pre-empted by the death of Chief Justice William Rehnquist in September. Bush withdrew the nomination and instead named Roberts as the prospective chief justice. On 29 September the Senate voted 78 to 22 in favour.

As Rehnquist was identified with the conservative wing of the Court, on the face of it his replacement by Roberts changed little. As a result the person nominated to replace O'Connor became pivotal, for O'Connor had often acted as the swing vote on the Court, sometimes taking a liberal position and sometimes a conservative one. His eventual choice of White House Counsel Harriet Miers shocked the whole political establishment, for Miers had no experience as a judge and little experience as a senior lawyer. Conservatives were more outraged than liberals because they had no way of knowing whether she would be loyal to the conservative agenda on such issues such as abortion and same-sex marriage. During preliminary Senate hearings into her nomination she revealed scant knowledge of constitutional law and the nomination was hastily withdrawn on 28 October.

The president acted quickly to nominate Samuel Alito to the vacancy. In stark contrast to Miers, Alito had very extensive judicial experience, having served as a US Appeals Court justice since 1990. He also had clear conservative credentials and immediately won the backing of congressional Republicans and leading conservative interest groups. Democrats, however, vowed to fight the nomination and if necessary to block it through the use of Senate parliamentary rules. With the Senate balanced 55 to 45 in favour of the Republicans, a Democratic filibuster (continual debate to use up time) could have been effective, for it takes 60 Senate votes to end a filibuster. In the event, however, the Democrats decided not to filibuster and Alito's nomination was confirmed on 31 January 2006 by a 58 to 42 majority (only one Republican senator voted against confirmation). In subsequent decisions Alito did indeed join the conservative bloc on the Court, thus giving President Bush an effective 5 to 4 majority on a range of important issues. During his first term Barack Obama successfully nominated Elena Kagan and Sonia Sotomayor to replace David Souter and John Paul Stevens. Both appointees joined the liberal wing on the Court but, because Souter and Stevens had also been on this wing, the ideological complexion of the Court changed little. This said, Sotomayor and Kagan have articulated this position with greater force than their predecessors. The ideological division on the Court thus was intensified rather than reduced. The final twist to the tale came with the sudden death of the conservative justice Antonin Scalia in 2016 and the refusal of the Republican Senate to even consider a replacement until after the 2016 presidential election. For the rest of that year, therefore, the Court consisted of just 8 justices. With 4 committed liberals on the bench this meant that lower court decisions would stand in the event of a 4 to 4 decision. Senate Republicans thus hoped that any liberal judicial activism would be prevented. Their ploy worked, for, on his election, Donald Trump nominated the established conservative Neil Gorsuch to the bench, who was later confirmed by a 54–45 majority.

Clearly, the Burger Court was very different from the openly liberal Warren Court and that the Rehnquist Court and Roberts Courts have in turn proved more conservative than the Burger Court. Personnel changes partly account for these shifts, but presidents can never be sure that, once appointed, a justice will fulfil expectations. Appointed for life to the most respected forum in the land, many justices change their political philosophy once on the Court. Such was the case with Earl Warren, one-time conservative Republican governor of California, and expected by his patron President Eisenhower to continue the self-restraint of the Stone and Vinson Courts. In civil rights and liberties and reapportionment he did just the opposite. And although the Nixon appointees generally moved the Court to the right they did not do so in a coherent and consistent manner. Liberal civil rights and liberties decisions did not suddenly cease in 1971, even if they became infrequent and interspersed with more conservative judgments.

CONTROVERSY 13   THE SUPREME COURT: AN ACTIVE OR A PASSIVE ROLE?

The most enduring debate over the role of the Supreme Court is whether it should play an active political role or be deferential to the elected branches. For most of the Court's history it has been passive rather than active. In part, this reflects the fact that courts rely on the legitimacy of their decisions to ensure compliance. They have no bureaucracy or police force of their own. For enforcement they rely on the other branches, and in particular on the executive. In the worst-case scenario, the courts may be ignored or effectively overruled by the dominant political forces. Just this happened just before the outbreak of the Civil War, when the Lincoln administration in effect ignored the 1857 *Dred Scott* decision on the status of African Americans in the northern and western territories. In the late 1930s, President Roosevelt did his best to bypass conservative Supreme Court decisions with his Court-packing plan during the New Deal period. And during the 1950s and 1960s a highly activist liberal Court handed down decisions in the civil rights and liberties areas that were unacceptable to many southerners and conservatives. In the case of school desegregation, for example, the famous 1954 *Brown v. Board* decision was effectively ignored until Congress acted in 1964 with federal legislation outlawing *de jure* segregation

(segregation sanctioned by law). Does this mean that it is unwise for the Court to become involved in the 'political thicket' and make controversial decisions? There are two reasons usually invoked to argue that the Court cannot and actually should not always be passive. First, and most important, is the fact that the Court is the guardian of the Constitution. If the justices believe that an Act of Congress or of a state or local government is unconstitutional then it has a duty to act and declare that law void. Usually the justices argue cases with sufficient sophistication and sensitivity to the political consequences to ride out the public reaction. This was certainly the case with the civil rights decisions of the 1950s and 1960s. Of course, sensitivity and sophistication are never guaranteed, as the *Dred Scott* and *New Deal* cases showed. This is, in fact, the central dilemma for the whole system of judicial review: how do you ensure high quality and intellectual excellence on the part of the justices? Unfortunately there are no such guarantees. Indeed, the present Court has been much criticized for intellectual incoherence and timidity in establishing broad constitutional principles to guide public policy in such areas as abortion and federalism.

The second reason why the Supreme Court becomes embroiled in the political thicket is that in today's highly litigious society it is simply inevitable that its decisions, no matter how qualified, will have political consequences. This is especially so given that many areas of modern life, such as the internet and genetic engineering, have no historical precedents. Any decision, therefore, makes brand new law and is likely to be controversial. This was amply demonstrated in 2012 when the Court upheld the Obama administration's Affordable Care Act and also in 2016 when it mandated the legitimacy of same-sex marriage throughout the union. By so doing the Court outraged conservative opponents of the law.

Public and political opinion

So the appointment power must by definition be limited because, even when presidents have made appointments, they have no direct control over the justices once they are on the Court. They can, of course, appeal to Congress (as with the Court-packing plan) or to public opinion, but once this happens the independent influence of the president is lost. As noted in earlier chapters, public opinion is hard to define and almost impossible to measure. Scratch the surface and beneath what most commentators mean by public opinion is a particular configuration of political power, expressed either through representative institutions or through the media or organized groups. If we accept this approach, we can confidently state that only very rarely in American history has the Supreme Court challenged a dominant climate of opinion. Between the Civil War and 1937, for example, the Court acquired the reputation for defending the burgeoning capitalist interests of the period by striking down both state and federal legislation designed to regulate industry or protect workers from exploitation. The regulation of interstate commerce did not, the Court argued, extend to such things as federal laws regulating child labour. Or, more importantly, entitlement of 'due process of law' under the Fourteenth Amendment did not extend to *state* attempts to regulate industrial and commercial life. It applied directly only to federal–citizen relationships. As a result, between 1900 and 1937 some 184 decisions invalidated state regulatory provisions. To be fair, a number of state laws were also upheld during these years, but the general stance of the Court was anti-regulation or against government 'interference' in economic affairs. Crucially, however, so generally was public opinion, at least until 1929. Most presidents, Congress and many state legislatures accepted the Supreme Court's judgments with relative equanimity. It was not until the coming of the Great Depression in the early 1930s that the climate of opinion changed dramatically. And when the Court began regularly to strike down federal New Deal legislation it became politically isolated. Within two years, and following intense pressure from unions, Congress and president, the Court had made its 'switch in time that saved nine' and thereafter followed rather than led the other branches in the general area of economic policy. Figure 15.2 shows this transition well.

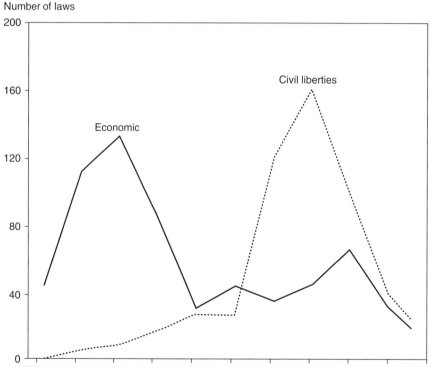

Figure 15.2   Economic and civil liberties laws overturned by the US Supreme Court, by decade, 1900–2009
Source: Harold W. Stanley and Richard G. Niemi, *Vital Statistics on American Politics, 2007–2008,* © 2007 CQ Press, a division of SAGE Publications. Reprinted with permission of SAGE.
Note: Civil liberties category does not include laws supportive of civil liberties. Laws include federal, state and local. During 2000–2, one economic and 14 civil liberties laws were overturned.

From the early 1940s the Supreme Court overturned few laws in the economic policy area, although it has become more active in this area in very recent years.

During the 1940s and up to about 1957, the Court was deferential to Congress and president on questions of 'subversion' and national security. In case after case the Court accepted the restrictions placed on citizens by the 1940 Smith Act, the 1952 McCarran Act and, in the case of the Japanese Americans, by executive fiat.[8] Not until the late 1950s, when public fears about communist subversion began to subside, did the Court begin to relax the restrictions on communists and others perceived to be subversive.

Even in civil rights, it would be difficult to argue that the Court was acting in isolation from broader political and public opinion. *Brown* v. *Board of Education*, the landmark 1954 decision which argued that racially separate facilities in education and other facilities were inherently unequal, may have been highly unpopular in the South, but it was welcomed in the North by many members of Congress, and was not unpopular with the president. What can be claimed for *Brown* is that it helped to push opinion towards the desegregation of the South, although, enforcement problems apart (of which more below), it was not until 1964 that Congress, goaded on by a determined and proselytizing president, passed the first major federal Civil Rights Act.

The apportionment decisions of the early 1960s, extending the principle of representation according to mathematical equality, first to state legislatures and then to congressional districts, were probably more widely unpopular with politicians than the civil rights decisions. But they were not unpopular with the public, most of whom stood to gain from a removal of the bias in representation towards rural areas. And how could state and national politicians justify the gross inequities that had accumulated over time? This is not to deny that the Supreme Court was a genuine innovator in this area, however, as it was in the realm of criminal defendants' rights. Starting with *Mapp* v. *Ohio* in 1961 and continuing through to Earl Warren's resignation in 1969, the Court handed down a remarkable succession of decisions granting defendants the right to state-provided counsel and access to police files, extending the freedom from unlawful search and seizure and generally providing much greater protection to arrested persons. Coming as they did during the disruptions of the 1960s, these changes were welcomed only by what eventually was a diminishing band of liberals. The dramatically increased activism of the Court in the civil rights and liberties area is shown by the number of Acts declared unconstitutional from the late 1950s onwards (figure 15.2).

Undoubtedly, the Warren Court moved well ahead of public opinion in this area. Perhaps predictably, the Burger Court did not continue the crusading spirit of the Warren era. In both civil rights and liberties it was careful to qualify some of the more dramatic decisions of the 1960s. In one sense, the Burger Court was placed in a much more difficult position than the Warren Court, for it had to clarify what were highly complex and difficult questions raised but not settled by Warren. Hence, in school desegregation, the thorny problem of distinguishing between *de jure* or legally sanctioned and *de facto* or naturally evolving segregation emerged as the main civil rights issue. Generally, the Court argued that a past pattern of *de jure* segregation should be reversed via bussing, but not (as generally prevails in the northern US) if the segregation was *de facto* in nature. Similarly, on the use of other affirmative-action measures such as quotas, the Court had to grapple with the problem of choosing between *individual* rights under the Fourteenth Amendment and the *collective* rights of African Americans and other minorities who have sought redress for a pattern of past discrimination. Individual rights generally prevailed. In criminal procedural rights, the Court limited the application of the 'exclusionary rule' or the admissibility of evidence culled during unlawful searches and seizures. And in a number of other areas the protection afforded arrested persons was reduced.

Often the Court cannot predict what the impact of its decisions on public opinion will be. The Burger Court, for example, handed down a decision on abortion in 1973 (*Roe* v. *Wade*) that looked clear enough. The Court effectively established that women had an unrestricted right (following medical advice) to an abortion during the first three months of pregnancy. Hence, state laws banning or restricting abortion in this period were unconstitutional. States could restrict abortion in the next three months, so that it would be legal only if there was a threat to a woman's health. States could ban abortion, unless the woman's life was threatened, in the final three months. This compromise has, however, been seized by the pro-life/anti-abortion interest groups and branded as a further example of the federal courts undermining public morals and the sanctity of family life. Little doubt exists that the decision precipitated debate and political controversy on an issue whose salience increased enormously during the last third of the century and the first part of the twenty-first century. The Court's decisions on capital punishment, which, although laying down pretty strict guidelines, have effectively left to the states the final decision on when (and how) a person should be executed, have also aroused great controversy. In both instances, debates on the issues have passed on to the broader political stage. But they hardly left the judicial policy agenda. Controversy on where individual rights begin and end must by necessity concern the courts, and given governments' intimate involvement in both granting and denying rights to citizens (indeed, in exercising a power over life and death in the two examples cited above), the courts' involvement must also continue.

With the appointment of William Rehnquist by Ronald Reagan and Clarence Thomas by George H. W. Bush, the Supreme Court moved clearly to the right. Indeed, the two most liberal members of the Court in 1993 were Nixon appointees, Harry Blackmun and John Paul Stevens. As noted above, the Clinton appointees, Stephen Breyer and Ruth Bader Ginsburg, did not shift the Court leftwards in ideological terms because they replaced liberals rather than conservatives. Predictably, therefore, the Rehnquist Court advanced the conservative agenda, especially on moral and social issues and in the general area of federalism. As discussed in chapter 4, in a number of areas the Court has revived and enhanced the Tenth Amendment's reserve clause and also the Eleventh Amendment's sovereign immunity clause. By so doing it has promoted administrative and policy diversity among the states. However, it has been very reluctant to strike down any of the landmark liberal decisions of the Warren and early Burger Courts in the moral conscience areas such as *Roe* v. *Wade* or *Miranda* v. *Arizona* (on the rights of accused persons) as unconstitutional. Instead, it argued cases on narrower grounds, often leaving to state and local officials the final decision on how the law should be interpreted. Often this has narrowed the applicability of the landmark cases. In the 1992 case *Planned Parenthood of Southeastern Pennsylvania* v. *Casey*, for example, a divided court upheld the right of states to restrict access to abortions, but it stopped short of invalidating *Roe* v. *Wade*. By avoiding constitutional precedents, the

Court has left open to Congress the opportunity to pass laws reversing its own decisions. Just this has happened. In the 1991 Civil Rights Act Congress overturned the 1989 *Patterson v. McLean Credit Union* decision, which limited an employee's ability to sue for damages if subject to racial harassment on the job. The Court has also been reversed by statutory interpretation over laws involving abortion and affirmative action. The reduced judicial activism of the Court in the civil rights and liberties areas is demonstrated by the data in figure 15.1. Note also the Court's increasing role in economic policy – a fact that reflects the increasingly complex and controversial nature of policy-making in this area.

It should be pointed out that on many of the social issues, the conservatism of the Rehnquist Court was not particularly out of tune with public opinion, partly, it is true, because of its reluctance to set headline-grabbing constitutional precedents, although, as will be discussed below, the increasingly polarized nature of judicial decision-making on the Rehnquist and later the Roberts Court has elevated public interest in the institution.

We can conclude that only rarely has the Court consciously moved against prevailing public and political opinion, and when it has done so, it has not been for long. Two important qualifications have to be applied to this generalization. First, the Court has been reluctant to challenge – or has never for long challenged – a programme or policy supported by the other branches, and which is perceived to be crucial to the integrity of the Union (the status of slavery in the North), to national security in wartime or 'emergency' conditions ('subversion' in the two world wars and afterwards), or to the running of the economy (the New Deal legislation). When, however, there is no consensus on a policy – especially when Congress and/or public opinion and president are in serious disagreement – then the Court plays a central role in arbitrating the conflict. We have several dramatic examples of the Court playing just such a role in recent history. In 1976 the Burger Court showed little reluctance to make deliberations affecting the separation of powers. In *Buckley* v. *Valeo* some key features of the 1974 Campaign Finance Act were struck down. Later, in 1998, the Court struck down the 1995 line item veto, permitting the president to veto part rather than all of a law, as a violation of the separation of powers in the Constitution (*Clinton* v. *New York City*). Finally, in 2008 in *Boumediene* v. *Bush* the Court directly challenged the president by granting *habeas corpus* rights to the Guantánamo Bay detainees (see Briefing below).

Other notable cases include *Printz* v. *United States* (1997), involving federal rules on the enforcement of the Brady Handgun Violation Prevention Act, and of course, the famous *Bush* v. *Gore* case that was to decide the fate of the 2000 election. In this case the majority on the Rehnquist Court (it was decided by a 5 to 4 majority) decided to intervene in what looked like an exclusively state affair (the running of federal elections, which the Constitution assigns to state legislatures) and insist that the ways in which the recounting was proceeding were deeply flawed. At the same time, it declared that, given the constitutionally mandated timetable, there was insufficient time to revise the recounting system. This in effect left in place the original count, thus giving victory to Bush. While this decision was much criticized, the Court was almost obliged to intervene and would certainly have been criticized if it had refused to grant *certiorari* to the case.

Briefing   The Supreme Court and the Guantánamo Bay Detainees

Following the internment of 'enemy combatants' at Guantánamo Bay, Cuba, from 2002, civil liberties groups have challenged the US government's decision to imprison people without charge or trial. The first case was heard by the Supreme Court in 2004 when, in *Hamdi* v. *Rumsfeld*, it decided that Yaser Esam Hamdi, a Saudi and US citizen who was initially held at Guantánamo Bay until transferred to the US, had the right to *habeas corpus* or a hearing before a civilian court. Although the *Hamdi* decision only applied to US citizens, the Court implied that it might be extended to others. Frustrated by the decision, the Bush administration released Hamdi on the condition that he returned to Saudi Arabia and did not return. In *Hamdan* v. *Rumsfeld* (2006) the Court outlawed the use of military commissions or tribunals to try the Guantánamo Bay detainees. Crucially the Court argued the case on the grounds that the president had exceeded his executive authority under the separation of powers, thus leaving open the possibility that Congress could sanction the use of Commissions. Under pressure from the administration, Congress did just this later in 2006 with the passage of the Military Commissions Act. Gradually, in 2007 and 2008, the administration began to try detainees under the new law. However, the whole process was thrown into serious doubt in June 2008 when, in *Boumediene* v. *Bush* the Court decided that the detainees were entitled to the habeas corpus protection of US civilian courts. This was by far the most important of the decisions because it applied to all the detainees irrespective of nationality or legal status. It also cast serious doubt on the viability of the military commissions' process. Significantly, the decision revealed the deep ideological divide in the Court, with the four conservative judges (Roberts, Thomas, Scalia and Alito) aligned against the moderates (Ginsburg, Breyer, Stevens and Souter). The swing vote was cast by Anthony Kennedy, who declared that 'The laws and Constitution are designed to survive and remain in force, in extraordinary times.' Subsequently five detainees were released and travelled abroad, including Boumediene. However in the eight years following this decision the Court has rejected or refused to hear further appeals by Guantánamo detainees by letting lower court decisions favouring the government stand.

The second qualification to the Court's deference to prevailing public and political opinion is that when it does challenge them in areas involving the behaviour of myriad individuals rather than a few institutions or political leaders, it tends to experience serious problems in enforcing its decisions or in predicting their precise impact on public opinion.

Lack of enforcement powers

Without their own police force, army or bureaucracy, the courts cannot enforce their decisions unless their authority is accepted by those who *do* exercise coercive powers. Moreover, the Supreme Court depends on lower courts (federal and state) to implement its decisions, and these may not always interpret or accept the Court's judgments in an unambiguous fashion. The most celebrated examples of judicial recalcitrance and obstruction involved the enforcement of civil rights in the South. Following *Brown* v. *Board*'s 1954 directive that southern schools should desegregate 'with all deliberate speed', southern District Courts were assigned the job of enforcing the order. Appointed by presidents on the advice of local politicians and party faithful, district judges reflect local conditions and interests – and prejudices. Very few of the southern district judges of the 1950s and 1960s were integrationists and most resisted – mainly through delays of one sort or another – the order to desegregate. In fact, not until 1969 in the *Alexander* v. *Holmes County Board of Education* decision – some 15 years after *Brown* – did the Supreme Court finally make it mandatory to desegregate immediately, and by then, of course, the Court was supported by the not inconsiderable weight of the 1964 Civil Rights Act, with its array of compliance and enforcement procedures. The figures on racial segregation demonstrate this point well. In 1963, nine years after *Brown*, only 0.45 per cent of black students in southern schools went to schools where any whites were present. By 1971 this figure had increased to 85.6 per cent.

More rarely, a state or local political actor may openly defy a Court order, as happened in Little Rock, Arkansas, in 1957, when Governor Faubus used the local militia forcibly to prevent black children from entering a high school. Only the eventual use of federal troops on the instruction of President Eisenhower enabled the black children to enter the school. Much more common is evasion of the directives of the Supreme Court, not only by other courts or by outright defiance, but also through ignorance, deception or the simple fact that complete enforcement is technically impossible to achieve. Such has been the case with criminal law decisions like *Miranda* and *Gideon*, which laid down strict procedures for the interrogation of suspects. As research has shown, arrested persons often do not know their rights, and police officers are frequently ignorant of the correct procedures, and even when informed can compromise them. Similarly, the decisions of the early 1960s outlawing special prayers and Bible-reading in public schools (*Engel* v. *Vitale*, *Abington School District* v. *Schempp*) as infringements of the First Amendment's freedom of religion clause have proved very difficult to enforce. Indeed, although the Burger, Rehnquist or Roberts Courts had not (by 2016) seriously compromised the principles laid down in *Engel* and *Schempp*, they remained under pressure from the religious right to do so.

The Polarized Rehnquist and Roberts Courts

From the mid-1990s the Rehnquist Court increasingly displayed two tendencies. The first was an increasing ideological polarization between a moderate or liberal wing and a conservative wing. Justices Stevens, Ginsburg, Souter and Breyer were consistently moderate, while Justices Thomas, Scalia and Rehnquist were consistently conservative. The remaining justices, Kennedy and Sandra Day O'Connor, often held the deciding vote, although Kennedy was more often associated with the conservative than with the moderate camp. The division in the Court on campaign finance, federalism, Miranda rights (the right to remain silent) and religion became obvious during this period.

This illustrates the second interesting feature of the later Rehnquist Court, its judicial activism. In case after case this Court, whether it was the moderate wing, the conservative wing or a coalition of the two, showed little reluctance to overturn state and federal law. In fact it invalidated 24 Acts of Congress in the five years down to 2004 – historically a very high figure and twice that in the 1990–9 period (table 15.2). Sometimes this has meant conservative justices overturning 'conservative' laws, as with its insistence that restricting pornography on the internet is a violation of freedom of speech, or its rulings on state sentencing laws, which contradict the generally pro-state stance of the Court. In sum, the later Rehnquist Court seemed unafraid of challenging the other branches and state governments. In this sense, it has become notably more political in recent years, even if its decisions lack philosophical consistency (see Controversy 13 above). With the appointment of two conservatives in 2005 and 2006 (Alito and Chief Justice Roberts), the division on the Court became even more apparent, with four unambiguous conservatives (Thomas, Scalia, Roberts and Alito) one right-leaning justice (Kennedy), three consistent moderates (Ginsberg, Breyer and Souter) and one liberal (Stevens, ironically appointed by Republican Gerald Ford in 1975). Barack Obama's appointments, Sonia Sotomayor and Elena Kagan, did little to change this pattern given that they were liberal appointments replacing two liberal-leaning justices (Stevens and Sandra Day O'Connor). Polarization is shown well in figure 15.3, which records the ideological leanings of the Justices since the 1930s. Note the convergence of opinion. Between the 1950s and 1980s (Justice Douglas apart) followed by the divergence since. With a 5 to 4 majority conservative decisions have become more common. Among such decisions is *Gonzales* v. *Carhart*, which upheld the congressional ban on so-called 'partial birth', or late-term abortion. Congress passed this law in 2008 with strong support from the president. Critics, including many in the medical profession, argued that the ban made late abortions designed to protect women's lives very hard to justify. Ruth Bader Ginsberg, the only woman on the Court, made an impassioned dissent along these lines. In 2008 Kennedy cast his vote with the liberal bloc in the crucial decision to grant the Guantánamo Bay detainees *habeas corpus* rights (see Briefing). However in a later 2008 case Kennedy sided with the conservatives in a 5 to 4 decision that outlawed Washington, DC's total ban on handguns. Most famously, in 2010 the Court lifted the limits on campaign contributions by corporations, unions and other organizations (*Citizens United* v. *FEC*), thus transforming the campaign finance landscape. However in two 2012 decisions and much to most observers' surprise, the liberal wing of the Court prevailed. In *Arizona* v. *US* much of Arizona's law allowing state police to stop and arrest suspected illegal immigrants was struck down. Later that year Obama's Affordable Care Act was upheld by the Court. In both cases the Court favoured federal over state power, thus perhaps reversing a recent trend in the other direction. Even more surprising was the fact that Chief Justice John Roberts sided with the liberal wing. David Kennedy – usually the swing vote – aligned with the conservatives.

Since then two developments promise to transform the judicial landscape. First, and notwithstanding the above, Justice Kennedy became markedly less conservative after 2012. In 2016 he sided with the liberals in two landmark cases, *Fisher* v. *Texas* and *Whole Woman's Health* v. *Hellerstedt*. In the former, aspects of an affirmative action programme favouring minorities by the University of Texas were upheld and in the latter the Court struck down attempts by the state of Texas to limit women's access to abortions. In both these decisions Kennedy reversed his previously held positions. If this were to continue the Court would have a liberal majority. Second, following the death of Antonin Scalia the Senate refused even to consider President Obama's March 2016 nomination of

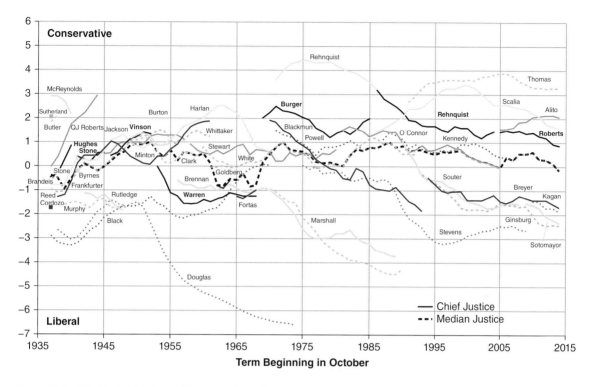

Figure 15.3   Ideological leanings of Supreme Court Justices, 1935–2014

Source: http://mqscores.berkeley.edu/measures.php, Andrew D. Martin and Kevin M. Quinn. 2002. 'Dynamic ideal point estimation via Markov chain Monte Carlo for the U.S. Supreme Court, 1953–1999', *Political Analysis* 10, 134–53. [PDF].

Merrick Garland to the Court. This stonewalling lasted all the way through the election campaign and, in the event, allowed president-elect Donald Trump to replace the nomination with a more conservative choice. These events brought into serious doubt the ability of the president to nominate justices 'with the advice and consent' of the Senate. If the Senate could refuse to review the nomination for nine months, why not for several years? Such is the constitutional import of this matter that it could, eventually, be decided by the Supreme Court itself.

Conclusions: The Court and American Democracy

It is often argued that the greatest limitation on the political power of the Supreme Court is 'judicial self-restraint', or a conscious decision by the justices to avoid the political thicket by deferring to the other branches (or to public opinion), rather than causing great controversy by departing from the dominant opinion. Our discussions above suggest that this is often true, although the later Rehnquist and Roberts Courts have been relatively active in historical perspective. Whether active or restrained, justices have, ultimately, to use their political common sense rather than, as some jurists have argued, make decisions solely on philosophical grounds. Judges may search for a 'higher principle' inherent in the Constitution, or they may be convinced that government 'interference' in the economy is always a bad thing. Sooner or later, however, they have to take cognizance of the political and social environment in which decisions are made. As we noted, the Supreme Court is seriously constrained by this environment; it is not an institution apart from politics, but one that is an organic part of the polity and society.

In spite of these political constraints, from our discussion we can identify three crucial functions performed by the institution of judicial review:

1   The Court arbitrates between federal and state law. In terms of the stability and integrity of the Union this is undoubtedly its most important function.
2   Judicial review provides the Court with an apparently neutral point of reference (the Constitution) for arbitrating between the different branches of government – although historically this has tended to work only when one branch (the executive) is relatively isolated from congressional and public opinion.
3   Judicial review can help defend individual freedoms under the Bill of Rights and Fourteenth Amendment. Of course, there have been numerous occasions when the Court has clearly failed to defend such freedoms, as with the internment of the Japanese Americans in 1942. But – and this is the strongest argument in favour of judicial review under bills of rights – the legislative and executive branches would have denied these freedoms even in the absence of judicial review. Its presence is usually beneficial, therefore, in the sense that when it deviates from the other branches it does so by favouring the individual. As the civil rights and especially civil liberties cases of the mid-twentieth century and the detainee decisions of more recent years demonstrate, this can involve quite radical, if sometimes temporary, departures from prevailing political opinion.

Finally, how has the Court responded to the more polarized polity and society characteristic of the early twenty-first century? In a word, uncertainly. As suggested, recent Courts have had to confront questions involving moral absolutes where *any* compromise would have been unacceptable to some. Issue politics, combined with the increasingly technical nature of cases, can produce a situation where the Court hands down decisions that are highly contentious. Issue politics produces odd, unpredictable political coalitions where it is almost impossible to please everybody. The Court's decisions on abortion and capital punishment, for example, involved issues where the subsequent lines of opposition and support were complex and unpredictable. In some other areas – campaign finance, for instance – the technicalities of the question are so formidable that the Court has produced decisions whose consequences have been unexpected, and perhaps undesirable. Of course when deliberating on contentious moral issues such as capital punishment, same-sex marriage and abortion, where public opinion is deeply divided, the Court is in a no-win situation. Unambiguous decisions on one side or the other would alienate sections of public opinion or the other branches. And when, as was the case from the late 1990s, the balance of opinion on the Court reflects a deep ideological divide that exists in society at large, the potential for unpopular and contentious decisions is greatly enhanced.

In sum, the main function of the Court – the legitimization of the system in the eyes of the citizenry – has become even more difficult in recent years. The comment by noted jurist Felix Frankfurter, written more than 70 years ago, is just as relevant today:

> A gentle and generous philosopher noted the other day a growing 'intuition' on the part of the masses that all judges, in lively controversies, are 'more or less prejudiced.' But between the 'more or less' lies the whole kingdom of the mind, the differences between the 'more or less' are the triumphs of disinterestedness, they are the aspirations we call justice.... The basic consideration in the vitality of any system of law is confidence in this proximate purity of its process. Corruption from venality is hardly more damaging than a widespread belief of corrosion through partisanship. Our judicial system is absolutely dependent upon a popular belief that it is as untainted in its workings as the finite limitations of disciplined human minds and feelings make possible.[9]

Summary

The vast majority of the cases filed in American courts start and are concluded in the 50 state court systems. All cases can potentially be appealed to the Supreme Court, however, which can test cases under state and federal law for their compatibility with the Constitution. The Supreme Court uses a number of criteria when deciding to hear cases, but for the most part practises judicial self-restraint. This said, the Court has handed down a number of decisions with major implications for the broader polity, society and economy on such areas as slavery, the role of government in the economy, civil rights, civil liberties, abortion, capital punishment, same-sex marriage, the status of detainees at Guantánamo Bay, campaign finance and health-care reform. The Court is constrained by a number of factors, including lack of enforcement powers, constitutional amendment, presidential appointments and public opinion. Since the 1990s the Court has been increasingly activist and also ideologically divided, as decisions on the 2000 election result, abortion and campaign finance demonstrate.

Questions for Discussion

1   How much is the Supreme Court influenced by public opinion? Answer with reference to the period since 2000.
2   Outline the effect of Supreme Court decisions since 1990 in TWO of the following areas:
    (a) campaign finance
    (b) separation of powers
    (c) same-sex marriage
    (d) abortion.
3   What have been the consequences for public policy of the ideological polarization characteristic of the Roberts Court?
4   Why did the Senate refuse to consider filling the vacancy left by the death of Antonin Scalia in 2016? What were the consequences?

Glossary

activist Court   A Supreme Court prepared to establish precedents and therefore to make controversial decisions

appellate jurisdiction   Supreme Court jurisdiction involving appeals from lower courts

certiorari   The name given to cases that the Supreme Court decides to hear

concurring opinions   Supreme Court opinions that agree with the majority but on different grounds

de facto **segregation**   Segregation that has emerged through social and economic circumstance

de jure **segregation**   Legally established racial segregation

dissenting opinions   The opinions of the justices in the minority in a Supreme Court decision

habeas corpus   The right to have a criminal case heard in court within a specified period

judicial agenda   The agenda of the Supreme Court in a particular historical period

judicial self-restraint   The practice of the Supreme Court not to make decisions challenging established constitutional norms unless absolutely necessary

New Dealers   The politicians, judges and bureaucrats who supported the New Deal agenda in the 1930s

opinion of the Court   The main opinion of the Supreme Court written by one justice

passive Court   A Supreme Court intent on not making controversial, precedent-setting decisions

political thicket   The problems associated with Supreme Court decisions with serious political implications

positivism   The judicial philosophy that believes that there are specific meanings behind laws and constitutional provisions

substantive due process   The application of due process not just to procedures (i.e. the right to see a lawyer) but also to substantive rights, such as privacy or freedom of speech

ultra vires   Acting beyond one's powers

Notes

1 'Court' and 'Supreme Court' are used interchangeably in the remainder of this chapter.

2 The most important class of cases here are those where *state* high court decisions declare a federal law unconstitutional, or where the constitutionality of state law is in doubt.

3 Loren P. Beth, *Politics, the Constitution, and the Supreme Court: An Introduction to the Study of Constitutional Law* (New York: Harper & Row, 1962), pp. 31–2.

4 *Schenck* v. *United States* (1919).

5 Although the Supreme Court decision which sanctioned such cases, *Chisholm* v. *Georgia* (1793), aroused great controversy at the time.

6 The chief justice position became vacant quite fortuitously for Nixon. President Johnson had nominated Associate Justice Abe Fortas as Warren's successor, but, during the Senate hearings into Fortas's suitability, it was revealed that, among other things, in 1966 he had received a $20,000 fee from a millionaire who at the time was being investigated (and later was convicted) for fraud. Fortas's nomination was withdrawn.

7 David M. O'Brien, 'The Reagan judges: His most enduring legacy?', in Charles O. Jones (ed.), *The Reagan Legacy: Promise and Performance* (Chatham: Chatham House, 1988), p. 75.

8 The Smith Act made it unlawful to advocate the overthrow of the US government, and the McCarran Act required 'subversive organizations' to register with the Subversive Activities Control Board. In 1942 West Coast Americans of Japanese descent (many of them citizens) were arbitrarily interned in concentration camps by the governor of California (ironically, Earl Warren, later the champion of individual freedom on the Court) as a threat to internal security. The Court failed to hear the cases arising from this until 1944, and then argued them on procedural rather than constitutional grounds.

9 Quoted in David F. Forte, *The Supreme Court in American Politics* (Lexington: D. C. Heath, 1972), pp. 93–4.

Further Reading

A good introduction is Lawrence Baum, *The Supreme Court*, 11th edn (Washington, DC: Congressional Quarterly Press, 2016). See also Linda Greenhouse, *The U.S. Supreme Court: A Very Short Introduction* (Oxford and New York: Oxford University Press, 2012). For a comparative analysis see also Henry J. Abraham, *The Judicial Process: An Analysis of the Courts in the United States, England and France*, 7th edn (New York: Oxford University Press, 1998). For a vivid journalists' account of how the court operates, see Bob Woodward and Scott Armstrong, *The Brethren: Inside the Supreme Court* (New York: Simon & Schuster, 1979). An analysis of the Burger Court is Herman Schwartz (ed.), *The Burger Years: Rights and Wrongs in the Supreme Court, 1969–1986* (Harmondsworth: Penguin, 1988). On the Rehnquist Court, see David G. Savage, *Turning Right: The Making of the Rehnquist Supreme Court* (New York: Wiley, 1992). Jan Crawford Greenburg, *Supreme Conflict: The Inside Story of the Struggle for Control of the Supreme Court* (New York: Penguin, 2007) examines recent ideological battles on the court. The classic work on the court and civil rights and liberties is Henry J. Abraham and Barbara A. Perry, *Freedom and the Court*, 8th edn (Oxford: Oxford University Press, 2003). See also David G. Savage, *The Supreme Court and Individual Rights* (Washington, DC: Congressional Quarterly Press, 2004). On the later Roberts Court see Laurence Tribe and Joshua Matz, *Uncertain Justice: The Roberts Court and the Constitution* (Basingstoke: Picador, 2015).

CHAPTER 16
REGULATING MORALITY
CIVIL RIGHTS, LIBERTIES AND
THE CONSCIENCE ISSUES

Outline

- Introduction

- Regulating Public Morality

- Civil Liberties

- Controversy 14. What's So Wrong with Gun Control?

- Briefing: Abortion and American Politics

- Equality and Civil Rights

- Briefing: Federalism and Same-Sex Marriage

- Conclusions

- Summary

- Questions for Discussion

- Glossary

- Note

- Further Reading

What is morality in any time or place? It is what the majority then and there happen to like and immorality is what they dislike.

– ALFRED NORTH WHITEHEAD

American Politics and Society, Ninth Edition. David McKay.
© 2018 John Wiley & Sons Ltd. Published 2018 by John Wiley & Sons Ltd.

Introduction

It would be easy to infer from earlier chapters that decision-making in the American political system is so fragmented and dispersed that the resulting policies are not amenable to simple characterization; that the open and pluralistic nature of the system produces a politics of confusion and unpredictability. While there is no doubt a great deal of truth to this, it would be wrong to leave the analysis without enquiring further into the nature and consequences of policy-making in the United States. The purpose of this and the next four chapters is, therefore, to add perspective and balance to earlier conclusions by examining how policy-making has developed in five important areas – the regulation of morality, social, economic, environmental and foreign policy. Discussion focuses on the following three questions:

1   How does policy develop over time? How do changes in administration and the domestic and international environment affect the ways in which policy is formulated and implemented?
2   Related is the crucial question of the role that political institutions and processes play in the political system. Is it now more difficult to produce effective public policy than in the past? Is the system capable of satisfying myriad public demands while at the same time preserving the ethos of limited government that is at the heart of the American public philosophy?
3   To what extent do policy systems differ in style and substance one from another?

Obviously, we cannot provide definitive answers to these questions, and discussion of each area must, of necessity, be brief. Because we can only touch on the main issues involved, reference to more detailed analysis is provided where appropriate.

Regulating Public Morality

American politics has always been infused with what Samuel Huntington has called a 'creedal passion', or public demands that government should play a role in regulating the public and private behaviour of citizens.[1] In spite of the Civil War and the passage of the Fourteenth and Fifteenth Amendments, between 1870 and the 1950s most of the debate and controversy in this area rarely reached beyond state and local politics. Today, however, the federal government is intimately involved in regulating morality. From civil rights to abortion, gay rights, prayers in public schools and criminal procedural rights, federal, rather than state and local, standards and laws guide public morals. As with so many other areas of policy, the public are deeply ambivalent about (and often deeply divided over) this role. On the one hand, many Americans expect the federal government to be the final authority responsible for outlawing discrimination and protecting individual rights. On the other hand, many people become angry and disillusioned when this role fails to conform to their personal interpretation of what is moral and just.

Plate 16.1   Pro-choice activists stand in front of the US Supreme Court, 27 June 2016
Source: Joel Carillet/Getty Images, www.gettyimages.co.uk/license/576562402.

This tension is, arguably, much greater in the USA than in most comparable countries. As we saw in chapter 2, in comparison with citizens of such countries as Germany and France, Americans are deeply distrustful of government and strongly devoted to the protection of individual freedoms. But quite deep divisions over the meaning of 'individual freedom' exist which have few parallels in western Europe. Nowhere in Europe, for example, are such issues as abortion, gun control or prayers in public schools debated with the intensity and passion that they are in the US.

This chapter addresses the role of the federal government in these and related areas. A special emphasis is laid on the ways in which the role of the federal government has changed over the course of the past 60 years.

Civil Liberties

Civil liberties are usually interpreted as those rights protected under the Bill of Rights (the first 10 amendments to the Constitution) and the due process clause of the Fourteenth Amendment. Typically, therefore, they include freedom of speech, religion and assembly, the right to a fair trial and due process, freedom from unlawful search and seizure and the right to bear arms. In most countries, the terms civil rights and civil liberties are used interchangeably, but in the US civil rights has come to mean the right to be free from discrimination on grounds of race, ethnicity, religion, gender, disability or sexual preference.

Until the twentieth century, protection under the Bill of Rights was, in fact, quite limited. By arguing that the Constitution applied to federal law, and therefore that the Bill of Rights was not applicable to state law, the Supreme Court effectively left the protection of liberties to the various state constitutions. In many parts of the USA, and especially in the South, numerous state laws were passed which today would be considered an affront to the rights of citizens. The most famous of these were, of course, the infamous 'Jim Crow' laws excluding African Americans from full participation in society. But in many other areas, including the treatment of alleged political 'subversives', religious minorities, women and arrested persons, the protection afforded by many states was very limited. How has political action and discourse changed in these areas over the past 100 years?

Freedom of speech

Starting with *Gitlow* v. *New York* (1925), which established that First Amendment freedom of speech rights applied to state law, the Supreme Court gradually began to extend the Bill of Rights to state law. It was not until after 1937 that the Court began consistently to do this, and in particular to argue that the states had an obligation to provide for due process under the Fourteenth Amendment, and that as the Bill of Rights provided for due process, so these rights should be protected by the states. The technical term used was the *incorporation* of the Bill of Rights. After the Second World War and accelerating during the 1960s, all the Bill of Rights protections – from free speech to the right to a counsel for arrested persons – were incorporated into state law.

This period of judicial activism coincided with the incumbency of the liberal Warren Court. In case after case the Court extended the protection afforded to citizens under the Bill of Rights. Initially, the most important cases concerned First Amendment freedom of speech cases. Between 1919 and 1957 the Court had consistently sided with restrictive federal and state laws against the rights of individuals in this area (not withstanding the *Gitlow* case, where the Court upheld New York's right to proscribe speech while incorporating that law under the equal protection clause). Often these decisions translated into action against anarchists, communists and other 'un-American' organizations. In many instances, the Court invoked the 'clear and present danger' test, claiming that communist activity was a clear threat to the Union (see the discussion in chapter 15). In *Yates* v. *United States* (1957), the Court argued that membership of the Communist Party was not in itself a threat, and in *United States* v. *Robel* (1967), the Court effectively established that membership of the Communist Party was protected under the First Amendment.

Until 9/11 it was difficult to imagine Congress passing a law that specifically proscribed the right to join a particular political organization or which banned the publication of a particular political tract. Even the Ku Klux Klan and similar organizations enjoyed First Amendment protection. Generally, federal authorities pursued *acts* of political violence or espionage. With the exception of proscribing those urging others to perform acts of violence, the expression of *beliefs* was broadly protected under the law. However, as we saw in chapter 13, the passage of the Patriot Act signified a return to the days when the mere expression of certain beliefs could under certain circumstances be proscribed and punished.

Freedom of speech extends beyond political freedoms, of course. It also applies to such areas as obscenity and libel. As far as the latter is concerned, the American media have more freedom to publish unsubstantiated facts about groups and individuals than do the media in many other countries, as tabloid stories about movie stars and other public figures show. While this freedom has been challenged in the courts, it continues to be better protected than what is often called the individual's right to privacy. Most jurists argue that while the publication of obscene materials is not protected by the First Amendment, laws proscribing such material are often viewed as infringements of freedom of speech. This is mainly because, apart from child pornography, it is almost impossible to define what is and what is not obscene. In one important area, however, the Supreme Court has been active. In 1997 it struck down the 1996 Communications Decency Act, which sought to restrict internet pornography that might be accessible to those under 18. The Court maintained that the law was too vague and that any attempt by the government to regulate the content of speech was a threat to the free exchange of ideas. This decision was confirmed in with a further case in 2004 when in *Ashcroft* v. *California* the Court declared that a federal law banning online pornography was probably unconstitutional, and that parental filtering devices were preferable to an outright ban.

Criminal procedural rights

It would be fair to say that while rights to freedom of speech are of fundamental importance to democracy, they have generally not aroused as much passion and debate as some other Bill of Rights issues, including criminal procedural rights. As with free speech, the constitutionality of most state laws in this area went untested until the 1960s. During that decade, however, the Warren Court greatly strengthened the rights of accused and arrested persons invoking the Fourth, Fifth and Sixth Amendments. In *Gideon* v. *Wainright* (1963), the right to a counsel irrespective of the ability to pay was established. *Escabedo* v. *Illinois* (1964) prevented the police from carrying out any interrogation until a counsel was available. *Mapp* v. *Ohio* (1961) greatly extended the 'exclusionary rule', or how much evidence the police could use during 'search and seizure'. Only if the police had proper authority to search and what was found was relevant to that search could it be used in court. In other words, if the police legally entered a property looking for weapons, but found drugs, the drugs could not be used as evidence in a subsequent trial. *Miranda* v. *Arizona* (1966) established the precedent that arrested persons should be read their rights (essentially the right to remain silent).

These and other cases represented a transformation in the rights of the accused, but they were hardly without controversy, for they coincided with a rapid increase in crime, especially in the country's inner cities. While cause and effect are difficult to establish in this area, there is little doubt that law-enforcement officials believed that restrictions placed on the power to search and to interrogate were making it difficult to arrest and convict criminals – and especially those with the resources to make full use of the system. The public, too, grew increasingly disenchanted with courts that seemed too 'soft' on crime. As it turned out, both the subsequent Burger Court and the most recent Rehnquist Court gradually narrowed the meaning and application of almost all of these rulings.

As far as the exclusionary rule is concerned, police now have much greater freedom both to enter property and to use evidence found during search and seizure, as long as it was found in 'good faith'. This effectively means they can use anything found during a search as evidence. The Court has also greatly expanded the power of the police to use warrantless searches and has chipped away at the actual effect of the *Miranda* warning. For example, in *Arizona* v. *Fulminante* (1991), the Court argued that evidence culled by undercover police (such as confessions) was permissible even 'though clearly suspects cannot be told of their right to silence in such cases'. In effect, therefore, while none of the famous Burger decisions has been overturned, their application has been progressively narrowed.

A related area of civil liberties concerns the rights of illegal immigrants, an issue that came to a head with the 2012 Supreme Court decision, *Arizona* v. *US*. In 2010 Arizona passed a far-reaching law that allowed state and local police to stop people suspected of being illegal immigrants (or suspected of committing a 'deportable offence'), and demand to see proof of residence. In addition, the law made it a crime for illegal immigrants to seek employment without work permits or to go without their immigration papers at any time. Critics of the law claimed that it provided the police with a *carte blanche* to harass all Hispanics in the state, including citizens and aliens with rights of residence. Although the Court upheld the provision allowing police to stop suspects, it greatly restricted the use of the law by requiring that this happen only in relation to other suspected offences. It also left lower courts free to interpret this remaining provision. The other provisions relating to papers and employment were struck down. In its decision the Court invoked the principle that on immigration matters federal law trumped state law. Those (mainly Republicans) who lauded the Arizona law were disappointed with the ruling, while those championing the rights of illegals (mainly Democrats) considered it a triumph for civil liberties.

In 2014 President Obama signed an executive order extending the Deferred Action for Childhood Arrivals (DACA) policy of protecting the children of illegal immigrants from deportation. In effect this order gave at least temporary relief for around 5 million illegal immigrants. Texas and 24 other states successfully challenged this policy in the courts and in 2016 the Supreme Court, split 4 to 4 following the death of Antonin Scalia, refused to resolve any of the questions raised by the case. While this left the lower court decision standing, it also left unresolved the legitimacy of the president's actions. This whole matter was, therefore, left in legal limbo until the Supreme Court decides the case once the ninth justice is appointed. Given that President-elect Donald Trump nominated the conservative Neil Gorsuch to the Court it is likely that DACA will be reversed.

A further area of controversy concerns the status of the death penalty, and in particular whether it constitutes a 'cruel and unusual punishment' under the Eighth Amendment. Doubts about the constitutionality of the death penalty led all states to postpone executions from the mid-1960s. In the 1971 case *Furman* v. *Georgia*, the Court held that as presently administered there was a random element in deliberations leading to the death penalty that was unacceptable. No executions occurred until after 1976, when the Court upheld the penalty in those cases where juries could consider the unique circumstances of every case. Since then, executions proceeded at an accelerating rate, reaching a peak of 98 in 1999 although they have declined since (figure 16.1). Critics argue that the death penalty remains 'cruel and unusual', both because most of those executed are poor and members of minority

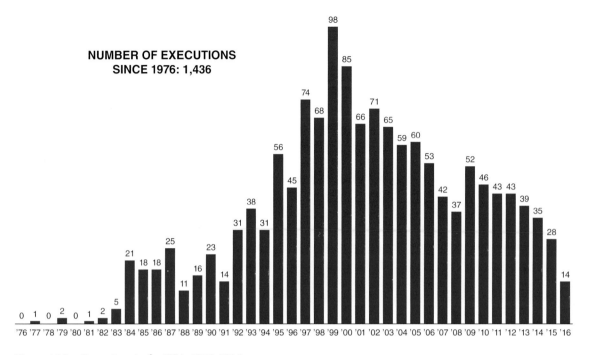

**NUMBER OF EXECUTIONS
SINCE 1976: 1,436**

Figure 16.1   Executions in the USA, 1976–2016
Source: Death Penalty Information Center, www.deathpenaltyinfo.org/executions-year, 2016 data are
for January–June only.

groups, and because convicted persons have to withstand many years of appeals and stays of execution before they are finally put to death.

Although public opinion remains in favour of capital punishment, increasing publicity about hasty and poorly managed trials, mistakes revealed by DNA testing and the enormous variations between state policy in this area have led to a softening of opinion in recent years. The Supreme Court has already deliberated that it is unconstitutional to execute people who are mentally disabled, and further rulings in this area are likely to restrict rather than enhance the powers of the states to execute convicted persons, including juveniles. In 2006 most states put executions on hold following a successful legal challenge to the use of lethal injections as a 'cruel and unusual punishment'. However, in 2007, in *Base* v. *Rees*, the Court finally decided that lethal injections did not qualify as cruel and unusual, thus freeing the states to resume executions, which many of them did. Interestingly, many other countries, and especially those European states that abolished capital punishment many years ago, view American practices in this area with a mixture of horror and contempt. Indeed the US is the only rich industrial country except Japan that continues to practice capital punishment and even there less than one execution a year takes place.

A final area of controversy in the civil liberties area is the Second Amendment's right 'to keep and bear arms'. Supporters of this amendment, and in particular the National Rifle Association (NRA), argue that Congress and the state governments should keep gun-control laws to a minimum. Following the assassination attempt on President Reagan in 1981, Congress passed the Brady Bill, requiring a waiting period for firearms purchase. Later, the 1994 Crime Control Bill banned certain categories of assault rifle. Although most members of the public support stronger gun-control measures, opponents are better organized, well funded and highly focused. Only following gun outrages such as the high-school massacre at Littleton, Colorado, in April 1999 are passions aroused so that the anti-gun movement receives real impetus. Indeed, by 2000 the anti-gun movement had achieved real momentum with the 'million mom march' in Washington, DC, of women campaigning for gun control – although the events of 9/11 seemed to weaken anti-gun sentiment. Again, controversy in this area has uniquely American characteristics. Nowhere else do interest groups organize with such passion and conviction on the issue of the rights of the citizenry to access and bear arms. This said, in a highly controversial 2008 decision the Supreme Court declared Washington, DC's total ban on handguns unconstitutional, thus opening the way for further legal challenges to gun-control laws.

During 2015 and 2016 the salience of the issue increased once again with the massacres in San Bernardino California and Orlando Florida when ISIS inspired assailants killed 14 and 49 people with high-powered assault rifles. In protest a number of Congressional Democrats staged a sit in on the floor of the House in June 2016. However, no reform legislation was forthcoming.

The establishment of religion

Americans have always been ambivalent about the relationship between church and state – a sentiment that stems in part from the status of religion in the early republic. On the one hand, the First Amendment guarantees the 'free exercise' of religion. On the other hand, it prohibits the government from 'establishing' a religion. To the Founding Fathers, the 'free exercise' of religion meant the freedom to set up religious groups and denominations free from government control. But initially, at least, these were always *Christian* groups. From the very beginning of the republic, state and local governments had provided support for Christian organizations, and especially schools.

In recent years debate and controversy over the proper role of government in this area have never been far from the surface. For some, a 'high wall of separation' between church and state should be maintained, while for others an intermediate or accommodationist position is preferred. As with other conscience issues, the Supreme Court has been active in this area, and especially so with regard to the tricky problems of religious aid for schools and religious instruction in schools. In *Engel* v. *Vitale* (1962) the Court declared unconstitutional even the briefest of non-denominational prayers in schools. Later, and following public outcry in many states and communities, it progressively softened its position, until in *Lemon* v. *Kurtzman* (1971) it laid down specific rules on what was permitted and what was not. Most importantly, the 'lemon test', as it came to be known, required that any government aid to schools have a clear secular purpose and that there be no 'excessive governmental entanglement' with religion. What this actually means has been up to the courts to decide, and although the Rehnquist and Roberts Courts have not always been consistent in this area, the Supreme Court has broadly favoured the accommodationist position. Certainly, federal, state and local governments do provide direct and indirect aid for parochial schools, ranging from income-tax deductions to the provision of remedial teachers under the 1965 Elementary and Secondary Education Act. As with capital punishment, the Court has followed rather than led public opinion in this area.

Abortion

As we saw in chapter 15, few areas of public morality have aroused as much passion as the question of abortion. Along with capital punishment, the issue is usually discussed in terms of moral absolutes. For the pro-life opponents of the practice, abortion is tantamount to the murder of the unborn. For pro-choice advocates, the issue is couched in terms of a woman's freedom to exercise control over her own body. Often this argument is expressed in terms of women's right to privacy. Following the landmark *Roe* v. *Wade* decision, which effectively sanctioned abortion in the first three months of pregnancy throughout the USA (see chapter 15), pro-life supporters have used a wide variety of tactics to get the decision reversed, or at least to restrict its application. At the legislative level both Congress and a number of state legislatures have restricted access to abortion by reducing or eliminating government aid, requiring that the parents of minors seeking to terminate be informed, limiting the location of abortion clinics and requiring women to seek counselling before terminating. State courts and ultimately the Supreme Court have generally upheld these laws, although at no point has the Rehnquist Court struck down the principles inherent in *Roe* v. *Wade*. With the replacement of Sandra Day O'Connor by John Roberts, however, the balance of the Court shifted to the right, and in the 2007 decision *Gonzales* v. *Carhart* the congressional ban on so-called 'partial birth', or late-term abortion (see chapter 15). However, in 2016 in a 5 to 3 decision the Court declared a Texas law placing restrictions on women's access to abortion clinics unconstitutional. This was widely seen as the most important Supreme Court decision on the subject for some decades. With the election of a Republican president in 2016 and the prospect of the nomination of at least one more conservative to the Supreme Court, it is likely that this issue will remain on the policy agenda for some years to come.

Pro-life groups have sometimes gone beyond the legislative and judicial process and have taken various forms of direct action against abortion clinics and staff. These range from picketing and demonstrations to, in the most extreme cases, the murder of doctors and abortion proponents.

While public opinion is broadly pro-choice, it is unlikely that the abortion issue will cease to divide both politically and socially. Within the Republican Party, for example, abortion has become a particularly difficult issue, especially at the presidential level. Pro-life supporters look to Republican politicians to support their agenda. At the same time, Republican presidential candidates cannot afford to alienate the broad mass of voters who are pro-choice. As a result, several Republican candidates, including Bob Dole in 1996 and George H. W. Bush in 1992, have attempted to take a middle position, arguing that while they are personally against abortion, it should ultimately be for the individual to choose. Such a position is naturally unacceptable to those who see the issue in terms of moral absolutes. In 2012, however, Republican candidate Mitt Romney came out as a fierce opponent of abortion, thus pleasing the right wing of his party while offending those who saw what was a change of position on the issue as hypocritical. Similarly, in 2016 Republican nominee Donald Trump became a critic of abortion, thus reversing his more liberal stance of some years earlier.

Controversy 14   What's So Wrong with Gun Control?

Foreign observers of the US scene are constantly amazed at the passion with which many Americans defend their right to own firearms. Most opponents of gun control cite the Second Amendment to the Constitution in support of their position. The amendment reads: 'A well regulated militia, being necessary to the security of a free state, the right of the people to keep and bear arms, shall not be infringed.' In recent years the debate over gun control has intensified, not least because of the increasing evidence – much of it publicized by the national media – of the link between violence and the availability of firearms. Periodic assassinations and assassination attempts, as well as mass shootings, have added impetus to gun-control advocates. Some of the first federal laws were introduced following the assassinations of the 1960s (John and Robert Kennedy, Martin Luther King) and further measures were taken in the wake of the attempt on Ronald Reagan's life in 1981. Hence, the so-called Brady Bill (named after James Brady, the president's press secretary, who was disabled in the attack) requires a waiting period and background check for gun purchases. More recently the 1994 Crime Control Bill banned a range of assault rifles.

Tighter controls, including safety locks on all handguns and more stringent checks on purchasers, have so far foundered in Congress – even when (as was shown by the tragic events at Columbine High School in Littleton, Colorado, in 1999, in which two teenage boys murdered 13 students and teachers and then shot themselves) access to deadly weapons remains easy. In 2015 and 2016 further gun outrages, including the slaughter of 49 partygoers at a Florida nightclub, led to calls for a ban on semi-automatic assault rifles. Again, however, these pleas came to nothing.

Opponents of gun control, and especially the lead interest group in this area, the National Rifle Association (NRA), insist that what is needed is not more control but public education. With such slogans as 'Guns don't kill people, people do,' they argue that to restrict access to guns would not only be unconstitutional but would be the thin end of the wedge on the road to the removal of all liberty. Federal legislation is regarded as particularly pernicious because it represents the spread of 'big government' and the advance of a centralized state against individual freedom. The NRA is also opposed to state controls on gun sales (and some states such as Massachusetts have imposed quite draconian restrictions), but knows that in many southern, mountain and western states state legislators will continue to oppose restrictions.

Politically, the issue has taken on new salience in recent years as large numbers of voters – and especially women – have become increasingly angry at the failure of government to protect the innocent against gun outrages. The position taken by the NRA and its president, the conservative movie star the late Charlton Heston, was increasingly viewed as extremist.

Even so, presidential candidates such as Barack Obama and Hillary Clinton still cannot afford to take a strong anti-gun stance. For among many Americans the right to own a gun remains an 'inalienable right' – a right that was confirmed by the 2008 Supreme Court decision striking down controls on handguns in Washington, DC. Republican president Donald Trump has publicly stated that he supports Second Amendment rights, so major changes in the law are unlikely for the foreseeable future.

Briefing   Abortion and American Politics

Between the 1820s and the 1950s all states passed laws restricting access to or totally banning abortion. By the late 1960s, however, a number of states had liberalized their laws, and an increasingly vocal women's rights movement was calling for national standards to guarantee the right to abortion. In the landmark 1973 *Roe* v. *Wade* decision the Supreme Court distinguished between the first trimester, when abortion should be allowed because the state has no interest in what is essentially a women's private business, the second trimester, when the state does have an interest in the health of the mother and the third trimester, when the interest of the foetus is paramount except when the life of the mother is threatened. Although regarded as a victory for pro-choice activists, *Roe* v. *Wade* left open many aspects of the actual implementation of the law. In the subsequent 40 years an increasingly vocal pro-life lobby worked hard both to overturn the decision and to make abortion as restrictive as possible. Although Roe still stands, numerous restrictions have been imposed by the states and the federal government. These include bans on abortion using federal funds and in federal facilities, risk counselling for patients, notification of parents and others for abortions for minors and bans on late-term or 'partial birth' abor-

tions, including a federal ban on such operations. State health coverage for abortion is also very difficult in most states, and indeed 87 per cent of counties have no abortion provider. The effect of these laws – almost all of which have been upheld by the courts – has been to isolate the medical practice of abortion from the rest of the medical world. Hence the US has dedicated 'abortion clinics' often staffed by dedicated medics. This has increased the ability of anti-abortion activists (and sometimes extremists) to target clinics and medical staff, often using violence and intimidation in the process. Abortion has also become a delicate subject for politicians to handle. Given the strength of feeling on both sides, it is risky for candidates for national office to take up unambiguous positions for or against the practice. This is particularly true of Republican candidates, who have been loath to espouse a wholly pro-life stance for fear of alienating moderates. George Bush Senior in 1988 and 1992, Bob Dole in 1996 and George W. Bush in 2000 all stated personal opposition to abortion without endorsing a total ban. However in 2008, and in stark contrast to the pro-choice Barack Obama, John McCain was more clearly aligned with the pro-life position as was Mitt Romney in 2012 and Donald Trump in 2016.

Equality and Civil Rights

'Civil rights' in the USA is usually used as a synonym for the provision of equal rights for racial and ethnic minorities. Discrimination does, of course, affect other social groups, including women and the disabled. This section addresses the evolution of public policy with regard to all these groups.

Racial and ethnic minorities

In the middle part of the twentieth century no area of public policy aroused as much passion and bitterness as the question of the desegregation of the South. Following the notorious 1883 Supreme Court decision in *Plessey* v. *Ferguson*, which declared the 1875 Civil Rights Act unconstitutional, most of the southern states enacted 'Jim Crow' laws that institutionalized segregation and discrimination. As a result, the southern states evolved into dual societies, with African Americans segregated from whites in education, employment, transport and public accommodation. In addition, they were subject to a range of barriers to voting which effectively disenfranchised them.

The civil rights movement began following the Second World War, which had had the dual effect of mobilizing many African American males and inducing a mass migration of blacks to the war factories in the North. Both events helped to reinforce the perception among blacks that conditions in the South were totally unacceptable.

The National Association for the Advancement of Colored People (NAACP) had long been active in fighting discrimination, and by the 1940s was actively supporting lawsuits aimed at discriminatory practices. After some minor victories, the breakthrough came in 1954 with the landmark *Brown* v. *Topeka Board of Education*. The case involved an 8-year-old girl who was required to attend an all-black school five miles away rather than an all-white school a short distance from her home. Invoking the equal protection clause of the Fourteenth Amendment, the Court argued that separate facilities in education were 'inherently unequal'. In a related 1955 decision the Court ordered southern schools to desegregate 'with all deliberate speed'.

Brown v. *Topeka Board* provoked a storm of protest in the South, including clear efforts to obstruct the implementation of the law. Desegregation did eventually begin in earnest, but not until further court action and the passage of the 1964 Civil Rights Act, which added legislative teeth to the judicial decisions (see the chronology of civil rights action in table 16.1). The 1964 Act, together with the 1965 Voting Rights Act, transformed the legal status of southern blacks. Separate public facilities disappeared, and the number of African Americans registered to vote eventually approached white levels. Controversy hardly evaporated, however. Indeed, it increased as many of the issues raised by discrimination became national rather than specifically southern in nature. The first was the distinction between *de facto* or naturally evolving and *de jure* or legally imposed segregation. Clearly, most of the segregation in the South was *de jure* in nature and the Supreme Court consistently argued that it was unconstitutional and should be reversed. Hence, in *Swann* v. *Charlotte Mecklenberg* (1971) the Court sanctioned bussing within a district that had a long history of legally mandated segregation. This and subsequent cases raised the question of the status of *de facto* segregation in the North, where patterns of residential segregation led automatically to separation in schools. Broadly speaking, the Court sanctioned bussing to achieve racial balance within districts where there was a clear pattern of *intent* to separate by race. However, it proved more reluctant to bus children across district lines and to remedy *de facto* discrimination where no intent to separate was evident.

Table 16.1   Chronology of civil rights and political action, 1948–2016

1948	In *Shelley* v. *Kramer* the Supreme Court makes racially restrictive covenants in housing unenforceable.
	President Truman signs an executive order desegregating the armed forces.
1954	In *Brown* v. *Board*, the Court establishes that separate educational facilities are inherently unequal.
1955	The Court orders southern schools to desegregate 'with all deliberate speed'.
1956	Montgomery, Alabama, bus boycott (which followed Rosa Parks' refusal to sit in the 'blacks only' back section of the bus) ends following Supreme Court decision outlawing segregation on buses.
1957	Creation of the Southern Christian Leadership Conference. Martin Luther King Jr. named as first president.
	Troops sent to Little Rock, Arkansas, to enforce desegregation of Central High School.
	Passage of 1957 Civil Rights Act establishes the US Commission on Civil Rights.
1960–5	Continuing civil rights demonstrations in the South, including 'Freedom Rides' to force desegregation of transportation, and other non-violent protests. Many demonstrations are arrested or assaulted by police. The most notable demonstration was the March on Washington for Jobs and Freedom in 1963, during which Martin Luther King delivered his 'I have a dream' speech.
1964	The omnibus 1964 Civil Rights Act outlaws discrimination in education, employment and public facilities.
	Passage of the Twenty-Fourth Amendment prohibits poll taxes in federal elections.
	Martin Luther King Jr. awarded Nobel Peace Prize.
1965	Civil Rights Act bans discrimination in voting and orders the dispatch of federal registrars to southern voting districts.
1968	Martin Luther King Jr. assassinated. Widespread rioting follows, including demonstrations just blocks from the US Capitol.
	Civil Rights Act bans discrimination in housing.
1971	Supreme Court decision in *Swann* v. *Charlotte Mecklenberg* sanctions bussing within a school district that has a long-standing pattern of segregation.
1978	*Regents of the University of California* v. *Bakke*. The Supreme Court ruled that quotas specifically favouring minority groups violated the equal protection clause, but hinted that policies designed to promote diversity that benefited the whole student body were permissible. In a later decision (*Grutter* v. *Bollinger*, 2003) the latter was validated.
2016	In *Fisher* v. *University of Texas* the Supreme Court ruled that the university could take race into account when admitting students. While this was not a reversal of *Bakke* it was a major concession to those supporting affirmative action based on race and ethnicity.

None the less, the issue proved politically explosive in a number of jurisdictions, including Detroit and Boston, and increasingly during the 1970s and 1980s the courts proved reluctant to impose bussing plans on communities. These cases also relate to the second area of controversy – what were the limits of *affirmative action* or attempts to redress a past pattern of discrimination? Affirmative action is inherently problematical because it involves a clash between the liberal notion of what the *individual* is worth and the *collective* interests of a group or race. Following the civil rights revolution of the 1960s, many federal, state and local laws were enacted involving the use of affirmative action devices such as racial preference quotas. However, in *Regents of the University of California* v. *Bakke* (1978) the Supreme Court found that a quota of 16 places reserved for minorities out of 100 available at the Davis Medical School was a violation of a qualified white applicant's rights under the Fourteenth Amendment. In other words, the individual rights of the white applicant were given lower priority than the collective rights of minorities who had suffered discrimination in the past and were, therefore, disadvantaged.

The decline of explicit affirmative action was confirmed when the Supreme Court refused to review California's 1997 Proposition 209 banning 'preferential treatment' for minorities in state programmes. This voter initiative ended effective affirmative action in the University of California and elsewhere in California. As a result, the number of blacks and Hispanics entering some of the more prestigious University of California campuses dropped significantly after 1997. In 1998 voters in Washington State also passed an initiative banning 'preferential treatment for minorities'. In later decisions, the Rhenquist and Roberts Courts have progressively weakened the meaning and application of affirmative action programmes, including the use of quotas.

Not all the decisions have been conservative. In the 2003 case of *Grutter* v. *Bollinger*, the Court held in a 5 to 4 decision that the preferential treatment given to an African American student by the University of Michigan Law School did not violate the Constitution because the law school practised a policy of reviewing every case on its merits rather than applying a blanket quota favouring minorities. Subsequent to this the more conservative Roberts Court consistently restricted the application of affirmative action programmes until the 2016 *Fisher* v. *University of Texas* decision which accepted that race could be taken into account as one of several factors when admitting students to the university.

Gender

The struggle for women's equality has in many ways paralleled the civil rights movement, for although women won the right to vote under the Nineteenth Amendment in 1920, they continued to be subject to extensive discrimination in a wide range of areas, from employment to education to housing. The first major advance was the passage of the Equal Pay Act of 1963 banning wage discrimination in a range of job categories. One year later, all the prohibitions on discrimination in the 1964 Civil Rights Act also applied to gender. Under this law, an Equal Employment Opportunities Commission (EEOC) was created to enforce equal employment conditions for women and minorities. Underfunded and over-burdened with cases, the EEOC made little headway into unequal pay, however; a fact which led many women's organizations to call for an Equal Rights Amendment (ERA) to the Constitution which would guarantee equality of treatment. In spite of a major campaign launched by the National Organization for Women (NOW), passage by Congress in 1972 and the support of presidents Nixon and Carter, the ERA only managed to muster 35 of the 38 state votes necessary for passage. The amendment effort was subject to a seven-year deadline with a three-year extension, and therefore expired in 1982. Thus, women continue not to be specifically mentioned in or protected by the US Constitution.

Notwithstanding this setback, women's groups have been able to advance sexual equality in a number of areas by taking both the legislative and judicial routes. The Equal Credit Act of 1974 (amended 1976) grants equal access to financial credit. In 1993 Congress passed the Family and Medical Leave Act, which provides women (and men) with up to 12 weeks' unpaid leave to tend to a newborn or sick family member. Although considered a significant advance, this law falls far short of the support provided in most other developed nations, most of which allow for *paid* leave for birth and the care of the newborn.

On the judicial front, the Supreme Court has handed down a succession of decisions limiting sexual harassment, reinforcing equal pay and ending discriminatory practices against pregnant women. One of the most celebrated of these cases affected the Virginia Military Academy's ban on female cadets. Along with another all-male school, the Citadel in South Carolina, the Academy was ordered to admit women cadets. By 1999, notwithstanding continuing harassment of females in such schools, women were being admitted in larger numbers. Some of the most far-reaching Court opinions were written by Sandra Day O'Connor and Ruth Bader Ginsberg, thus demonstrating that the incumbency of women in positions of power can make a real difference to how women are treated in society. By 2016 three women sat on the Court (Ginsberg, Sotomayor and Kagan).

Women have, in fact, made major advances in politics, business and other professions. As we saw in chapter 2, however, they still have a long way to go.

Disability

In total, some 20 million Americans suffer from some sort of disability (hearing, speech, sight, mental or mobility impairment). In contrast to legislation related to ethnicity and gender, however, legislative protection for the disabled has been relatively uncontroversial. As early as 1948 discrimination against the disabled in the federal civil service was outlawed. Later, in 1964, the Architectural Barriers Act required all federal buildings to be accessible to the disabled, and the 1988 Civil Rights Restoration Act added disability to the list of categories where federal funds could be withdrawn for discriminatory practices. Most important of all was the 1990 Americans with Disabilities Act (ADA), which provided for comprehensive access for the disabled to all public buildings, transportation and other public facilities. As with other civil rights acts, how the ADA works out in practice has depended on administrative enforcement and judicial interpretation. Since 2005 the Supreme Court has tended to favour rules imposing restrictions on the disabled and in particular disabled prison inmates. This reflects the more conservative

Court that emerged with the appointment of Chief Justice John Roberts and Justice Samuel Alito. While it is easy to be complacent in this area, it is interesting to note that the protection afforded most disabled Americans is considerably greater than in many other countries, including many of the European welfare states. Perhaps this reflects the overarching importance of *equality of opportunity* as a value in American society. Most Americans would balk at the idea that simply because someone is in a wheelchair he or she should be denied access to the social and economic opportunities available to others.

Sexual preference

Until the 1990s the question of discrimination against gays and lesbians was rarely prominent on the national or federal agenda, although at the local level it was often an important issue, as many states and cities had held ballots (initiatives) on gay rights. During the 1990s, however, the Clinton administration advanced the issue, first by attempting to ban discrimination against gays in the military (an attempt that failed in the face of hostile public opinion – instead, a policy of 'don't ask, don't tell' was adopted) and then by issuing an executive order in 1998 banning all federal agencies from discriminating on the grounds of sexual orientation. At the same time much of the social policy and education legislation passed by Congress specifically prohibits the open discussion of homosexuality in a range of federal programmes. In 2011 Barack Obama lifted the ban on gays in the military, a decision that was broadly welcomed by senior officers throughout the US military.

Also in the 1990s a resurgent Republican right was increasingly vocal on the issue of the sanctity of marriage. Homosexual liaisons, they argued, undermined family values, and same-sex marriages should be resisted at all costs. This issue came to a head when Massachusetts became the first state to legalize gay marriages, a decision that was upheld by the state's Supreme Court in 2004. This and other moves in the same direction inspired congressional Republicans to propose a constitutional amendment banning same-sex marriages. Although this proposal was defeated in the Senate in July 2004, conservatives vowed to continue with their campaign – a campaign that was supported by George W. Bush. In 2008 the California Supreme Court held that denying same-sex married couples the same rights as heterosexuals was unconstitutional. However, in the election of the same year California voters rejected the state's same-sex marriage law – a vote that outraged liberals and gay activists. However in a landmark 2015 decision the Supreme Court declared all bans on same-sex marriage unconstitutional (see Briefing).

Gay rights are, in fact, a good illustration of just how polarized the US has become on a range of moral issues. On the two coasts and in many of the large cosmopolitan cities people tend to be relaxed on the issue and generally support anti-discrimination laws. In the southern and mountain states, large parts of the Midwest and in many northern and western suburbs, however, the public are more openly hostile both to anti-discrimination laws and to homosexuality in general – although, as was shown in chapter 2, public attitudes on these questions have become slightly more moderate in recent years.

Briefing   Federalism and Same-Sex Marriage

Over the past 20 years the question of same-sex marriage has become an issue of great controversy. In part this is because feelings on the question run high, but public emotions have been heightened by the often-contradictory positions taken by Congress, the Courts and state governments. As of 2012, nine states and the District of Columbia had recognized same-sex marriage (Connecticut, Iowa, Maine, Maryland, Massachusetts, New Hampshire, New York, Vermont and Washington). A number of other states recognized same-sex marriage validated in other states or had legalized civil partnerships (as in the UK). Thirty-one states had legal bans on the practice insisting that only marriage between men and women was valid. However, in 1996 Congress passed the Defence of Marriage Act (DOMA), which defined marriage under federal law as a union between men and women only. Bill Clinton signed the law only because it changed no practice under federal law and it was left open to the states to decide for themselves how to define marriage. In 2008 California's same-sex marriage law was invalidated by Proposition 8, a popular initiative organized and financed by evangelicals and Republicans. On 9 May 2012 President Obama announced his support for same-sex marriage and called for the repeal of DOMA, and in the landmark 2015 case *Obergefell* v. *Hodges* the Supreme Court declared all laws banning same-sex marriage as unconstitutional. From that point on all states were obliged to recognize the legitimacy of same-sex marriage. This issue illustrates nicely the ways in which federal arrangements feed into the heightened passions that many of the moral issues arouse. Those on the right strongly believe that states should be the final arbiters, while liberals insist that natural justice requires nationwide legal standards.

Conclusions

This chapter has not addressed all the areas that could be included under the general heading of government regulation of public morality. Discrimination against older Americans is also a matter for public debate and government action. Older Americans are represented by the American Association of Retired Persons (AARP), which with 30 million members lobbies hard both to protect social security and other benefits and to fight discrimination against the old in employment, housing and medical care.

With these and all the other issues discussed above, the citizenry look to governments, and increasingly to all three branches of the federal government, for guidance and protection. This activity puts additional pressures on the political system. When, as with abortion and capital punishment, the issues involve moral absolutes, governments are, by definition, unable to please everyone. The nationalization of these issues in recent years thus helps to raise public expectations of what government can do, but also means that in an often-polarized society many will be left disappointed or even angry and frustrated.

One thing is for sure – all these civil rights, liberties and conscience issues will continue to crowd the policy agenda. More open and accessible political institutions, together with increasingly vocal demands for redress among minorities, women and other groups, will ensure this.

A further and obvious conclusion to be drawn from the preceding analysis is that there is no single policy system which can accommodate the very diverse and complex ways in which governments at all levels attempt to regulate public morality. Because this general area involves constitutional rights, the courts are, by definition, intimately involved. But, as we have seen, the courts, and in particular the Supreme Court, have failed to provide consistent and coherent leadership on moral questions. The representative institutions of American government, including the states, presidency and Congress, are also involved, of course. But in contrast to such areas as economic and foreign policy, there is rarely a clear and predetermined policy agenda on civil rights, liberties and the other conscience issues awaiting presidents and members of Congress when they accede to power. Instead, these policy-makers tend to react to outside events such as civil rights demonstrations or a mass-shooting incident, or to the decisions of lower-level governments, rather than take the lead. This reactive rather than proactive stance demonstrates well the perils of making policy in areas where arguments are so often couched in terms of moral and political absolutes.

Summary

This chapter has reviewed the role of the federal government in the regulation of morality over the past 50 years and has thus covered the changes in protection afforded to individuals in the area of civil rights and liberties. Generally the law has favoured the individual over the state in this period, although changes since 9/11 suggest a reversal of this pattern. The chapter has also covered abortion, sexual preference and disability. In abortion, a move towards liberal policy has been followed by a more conservative stance since the 1980s. A generally more liberal position has been adopted in the sexual preference and disability areas, although recent changes in the composition of the Supreme Court may also reverse this trend. The chapter concluded with comments on the contining nationalization of public policy towards questions of morality in the US.

Questions for Discussion

1   Why did civil rights become such an important issue in the mid-twentieth century? How successful were the associated changes in the law?
2   Identify the main milestones in the protection of civil liberties over the past 50 years. Are civil liberties more or less protected today than in 1960?
3   In what ways is the US 'exceptional' in its values and public policies towards one of the following:
    (a) abortion
    (b) same-sex marriage
    (c) gun control
    (d) capital punishment?
4   How important a role have questions of morality played in the last four presidential elections?

Glossary

affirmative action   Policies designed to redress patterns of discrimination based on race, ethnicity, gender, age or disability

Americans with Disabilities Act (ADA)   The main federal law protecting the rights of the disabled

Bill of Rights   The first 10 amendments to the Constitution enumerating basic rights ratified in 1791

civil liberties   Those rights usually associated with criminal procedural rights, freedom of speech, religion and privacy

creedal passion   The idea that Americans are infused with strong feelings on moral issues

criminal procedural rights   The rights of the accused and the convicted in criminal law

de facto segregation   Segregation that has emerged through social and economic circumstance

de jure segregation   Legally established racial segregation

equality of opportunity   The idea that all citizens should be given an equal chance to succeed, irrespective of background

Family and Medical Leave Act 1993   The law providing limited unpaid time off for expectant parents

free exercise of religion   The right to practise the religion of your choice

Jim Crow laws   The segregationist laws passed in the southern states during the 1880s and 1890s.

pro-choice   Those believing that women should have the right to abort a child

pro-life   Those believing that the rights of the foetus should take precedence over those of the mother

right to keep and bear arms   The Second Amendment, which is used by the gun lobby to oppose restrictions on the ownership and use of firearms

same-sex marriage   Extension to all sexual-preference groups of those marital rights given to different-sex marriages

Note

1   Samuel Huntington, *American Politics: The Promise of Disharmony* (Cambridge MA: Harvard University Press, 1981).

Further Reading

The best account of the Supreme Court's role in the civil liberties area is Henry J. Abraham and Barbara A. Perry, *Freedom and the Court: Civil Rights and Liberties in the United States*, 8th edn (New York: Oxford University Press, 2003). Nicholas Lehmann's *The Promised Land: The Great Black Migration and How It Changed America* (New York: Knopf, 1991) provides a vivid account of black migration to the north. Taylor Branch has written two excellent volumes of a planned three-volume biography of Martin Luther King, *Parting the Waters: America in the King Years, 1954–1963* and *Pillar of Fire: America in the King Years, 1963–1965* (New York: Simon & Schuster, 1988 and 1998). Jane J. Mansbridge, *Why We Lost the ERA* (Chicago: University of Chicago Press, 1986), examines the reasons for the failure of the Equal Rights Amendment. A good discussion of the politics of abortion in Congress is provided by Scott H. Ainsworth, *Abortion Politics in Congress: Strategic Incrementalism and Policy Change* (Cambridge: Cambridge University Press, 2011). On disability, see Robert A. Katzman, Richard Scotch, Kay Schriner and Brenda McCoy, *Americans with Disabilities and Political Participation: A Reference Handbook* (New York: ABC-CLIO, 2002). For an account on federal policies regarding morality under George W. Bush, see Edward Ashbee, *The Bush Administration, Sex and the Moral Agenda* (Manchester: Manchester University Press, 2007).

CHAPTER 17
SOCIAL POLICY IN AMERICA
SELF-RELIANCE AND STATE DEPENDENCE

Sooner or later cuts in Social Security and Medicare which provide benefits for older Americans are unavoidable, because the alternatives – huge tax increases or peacetime budget deficits – are worse and probably politically unacceptable.

– ROBERT J. SAMUELSON

This is not the end of welfare reform; it is the beginning.
– PRESIDENT CLINTON, ON SIGNING WELFARE REFORM, 22 AUGUST 1996

American Politics and Society, Ninth Edition. David McKay.
© 2018 John Wiley & Sons Ltd. Published 2018 by John Wiley & Sons Ltd.

The Federal Government and Social Welfare in America:
The Reluctant Provider

Governments have always been more reluctant to intervene in the general area of social policy in the USA than they have in western Europe. Indeed, it was not until the 1930s that the federal government laid down a framework of law providing for welfare and social security benefits for the poor and the old. Even then, the extent and level of welfare coverage were limited. Contributory earnings-related pensions applied only to certain kinds of workers. Welfare was restricted to families with dependent children (effectively mothers and children) and was distributed through the states on a matching federal–state basis. As a result, great disparities in the provision of welfare from state to state developed – disparities that remain to this day. Housing and health, moreover, were not considered legitimate parts of federal social policy until the 1960s, and since then housing subsidies have been subject to periodic cuts, to the point where, during the Reagan years, subsidies for the construction of new housing all but disappeared – if only temporarily. Only education has been universally accepted as a legitimate part of the social policy agenda. But, until very recently, it was always local and state governments, rather than the federal government, which provided for elementary, secondary and higher education.

The roots of the American antipathy to anything but limited and selective social benefits are not difficult to identify. They lie in the strongly held notions of self-reliance which have been discussed a number of times in earlier chapters. By the 1970s, however, some areas of social policy had become established as proper and legitimate roles for the federal government. Almost all of these involved earnings-related social security benefits for widows, widowers, the disabled, the blind and, above all, veterans of foreign wars and the old. Most Americans now consider these benefits as rights, not handouts by the government. There is, in fact, a sizeable 'handout' element in the social security programme, as benefits are not strictly related to what has been paid in. In addition, Medicare, the programme providing medical aid for the old, is also now considered a right, even though the redistributive element in the programme is very considerable (benefits rarely relate precisely to what recipients have paid in). Finally, many Americans, even those on the right, look more benignly on the welfare programmes for the old and disabled, such as Supplementary Security Income (SSI), than they do on other welfare programmes. Clearly, the elderly are given a special status as a group who cannot be expected to help themselves.

The same sympathy is not, paradoxically, extended to children in poor families who, though provided with a range of welfare benefits, do not fare as well as the old. One reason for this is the problem of ensuring that the benefits received by parents do actually reach needy children. Because of this and the belief among many politicians that many of those on welfare can and should be capable of supporting a family through work, what used to be the two main welfare programmes – food stamps and Aid for Families with Dependent Children (AFDC) – were always politically vulnerable. Similarly, medical care for the poor (Medicaid) is less well protected than Medicare.

As can be seen from table 17.1, most of the major social policy bills were enacted during the New Deal and in the Great Society period of the 1960s. Since then, there have been numerous amendments to the original legislation but until 1996, no wholesale reform. In fact, reform attempts have come from left and right, with the most recent assault on the system from the right being led by the Republican 104th Congress. In 1996 Congress did

Table 17.1   Major federal social policy legislation, 1935–2010

1935	Social Security Act – established the basic old-age, survivors and disabled insurance programme, as well as unemployment insurance and the main welfare programme, Aid to Families with Dependent Children (AFDC).
1937	Public Housing Act – provided limited grants for the construction of municipal housing.
1964	Food stamps – the provision of stamps that the poor can exchange for food – renamed Supplementary Nutrition Assistance Program (SNAP) in 2008.
1965	Creation of Medicare (medical care for the old) and Medicaid (medical care for the poor). Elementary and Secondary Education Act – federal aid for local school authorities in disadvantaged areas.
1968	Housing Act – the provision of housing subsidies for the owners and renters of low- and moderate-income housing.
1971	Supplementary Security Income (SSI) – the provision of welfare benefits for older citizens.
1988	Family Support Act – requires states to provide work or training programmes for welfare recipients.
1996	Personal Responsibility and Work Opportunity Reconciliation Act (PRWORA) – limits recipients to five years of benefits (with some exceptions). Consolidates federal programmes as block grants for the states. Limits welfare benefits for young mothers.
2001	No Child Left Behind Act introduces universal testing in elementary and secondary education.
2003	Medicare Modernization Act – greatly increased prescription drug benefits for the old and those with disabilities.
2010	Affordable Care Act – provided health insurance for most of the uninsured and reformed insurance-provided health care.

pass a Welfare Reform Bill, which President Clinton eventually signed. The grandly titled Personal Responsibility and Work Opportunity Reconciliation Act abolished AFDC and instead provided the states with block grants to fund their own programmes. A new programme, TANF (Temporary Assistance for Needy Families), was introduced that required all welfare recipients to work or to undergo work training. Recipients could receive welfare for only five years and the states were required to monitor their programmes to ensure compliance with federal rules.

What accounts for the particular shape of social policy programmes in the USA? We can identify both institutional and ideological answers to this question.

Federalism

Federalism has always had an important influence on welfare provision in the USA. AFDC was originally organized on a matching basis with the states, with the result that benefits varied greatly from state to state. In 1996, for example, the maximum monthly benefit payable to a one-parent family of three in Alaska was $923, compared with just $120 in Mississippi. Cost-of-living differences between the states compensate for part, but by no means all, of this difference. Supplementary Assistance Nutrition Program (food stamp) benefits also vary from state to state, but were partly designed to make up for the AFDC inequities. Federalist sentiment was also an important influence on the 1996 welfare reforms. Following the passage of the law, it is up to the states to draw up welfare plans designed to reduce the number of recipients to a minimum. How, precisely, the states have replaced welfare with 'workfare' varies with the political culture of the individual states. Some states, such as Wisconsin and Minnesota, implemented plans very quickly and reduced their welfare rolls accordingly, while others, such as California, were slower to implement the law. Once elected, the George W. Bush administration took on the philosophy of the new law with great enthusiasm and increased the pressure on the states to reduce the number of people on welfare and to reduce costs. Indeed when TANF has come up for reauthorization, as it did between 2002 and 2006, the administration has taken the opportunity to tighten the rules further, mainly by requiring the states to increase the proportion of recipients who actually work as opposed to those in training or not at work. And while Congress has renewed the federal block grant programme, the assumption is that for the first time since before the New Deal the states will remain the main providers of income support for families. As can be seen from figure 17.1, the welfare participation rate has fallen dramatically in recent years, although the rate of slowdown declined with rising unemployment after 2008. Moreover there is evidence that the new system works least well where it is needed most – among African American families in the inner cities. Moreover, with the coming of recession in 2008 the TANF block grant from Washington to the states did not increase. And while some states did boost their contributions in 2009 and 2010, continuing fiscal pressures obliged many of them to cut their programmes thereafter. Overall, TANF funds lost more than 30 per cent of their real value between 1996 and 2015.

Social Security, Medicare and the Electoral Connection

As suggested above, social security has a special status as a protected set of measures in the United States. In 1982 President Reagan attempted to cut benefits, but was unable to do so

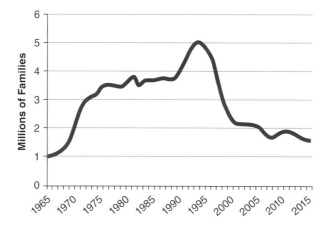

Figure 17.1   AFDC/TANF caseloads 1965–2015
Source: Federal Safety Net, http://federalsafetynet.com/tanf.html.

because of fierce opposition from Congress and public opinion generally. More recently, Newt Gingrich and the Republican 104th Congress made a serious attempt to cut back on the increase projected in the cost of Medicare over the next several years. This threat provoked a storm of anger from older Americans and their organizations. Most Americans, regardless of their economic position, expect to receive Medicare benefits at some time during their lives. By attacking the burgeoning cost of the programme, Newt Gingrich was taking a considerable political risk. And even though he was not planning to cut social security, there was a widespread impression that this would be next on the list. Meanwhile, during the 1996 election campaign President Clinton could project himself as the guardian of these programmes and accuse Gingrich and the Republicans of being mean spirited and insensitive to the needs of the old. It seems likely that these events helped Clinton to victory in the 1996 presidential elections.

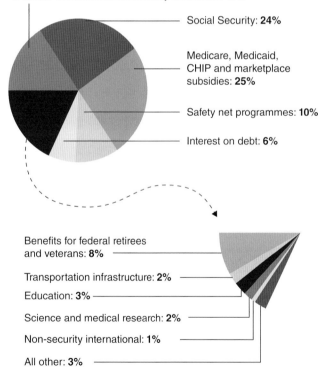

Most of Budget Goes Toward Defence, Social Security and Major Health Programmes

Defence and international security assistance: **16%**

Social Security: **24%**

Medicare, Medicaid, CHIP and marketplace subsidies: **25%**

Safety net programmes: **10%**

Interest on debt: **6%**

Benefits for federal retirees and veterans: **8%**

Transportation infrastructure: **2%**

Education: **3%**

Science and medical research: **2%**

Non-security international: **1%**

All other: **3%**

Figure 17.2   Federal outlays by function, fiscal year 2015 (CHIP – Children's Health Insurance Program)
Source: Policy Basics: Where Do Our Federal Tax Dollars Go? 4 March 2016, Center on Budget and Policy Priorities, www.cbpp.org/research/federal-budget/policy-basics-where-do-our-federal-tax-dollars-go.

Social Security (mainly old-age pensions, but also unemployment benefits) is one of the largest items in the federal budget (figure 17.2), and, as an entitlement programme, it is effectively uncontrollable. Increasingly, however, benefits for the old, which have little or no contributory element (SSI, Medicare and Supplementary Medicare), are also electorally protected (figure 17.3). Health benefits are also increasing very rapidly in cost, and it was this very rapid growth that inspired Gingrich to propose what were in effect modest cuts. While the Republicans may have been politically foolish to propose such measures, there is no doubt that, in the longer run, they are needed. The fundamental problem with social security and with Medicare is that the numbers of contributors to the programmes through payroll taxes gradually decreases after about 2017, while the number of beneficiaries increases. To put it another way, with the 'baby-boom' generation (those born between about 1945 and 1965) retiring, there will be fewer workers in the labour force to replace them.

This is an actuarial problem facing all welfare states at the century's beginning, and in fact it is not as serious in the USA as in some countries, and especially Italy, France and Russia, given that the American birth rate is one of the highest among richer countries. Nonetheless, something will have to be done about the problem over the next decade. This is amply demonstrated by figure 17.4, which shows what will happen to the Social Security

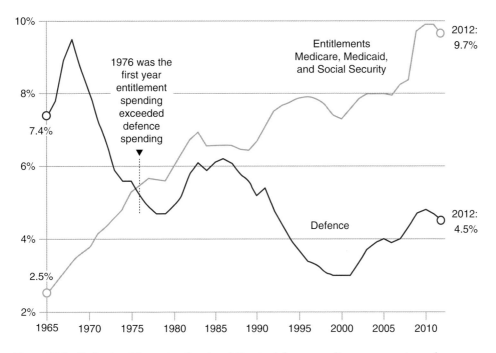

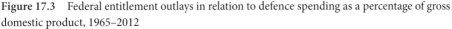

Figure 17.3   Federal entitlement outlays in relation to defence spending as a percentage of gross domestic product, 1965–2012

Source: Office of Management and Budget, US Government, www.whitehouse.gov.

Note: 2012 figures are estimated.

Trust Fund by 2040 if no reforms are instituted. Congress originally created a trust fund to ensure that the programme was self-financing and immune to 'raids' by the federal government. A large surplus will build up as the baby-boom generation pays in more and more as their incomes increase. After about 2025, however, the programme slides inexorably towards insolvency. Aware that a good part of his constituency consisted of older Americans, George W. Bush pledged in 2000 that he would increase Medicare benefits, mainly by cutting the cost of prescription drugs. This he duly did with the passage in 2003 of the Medicare Modernization Act, which extended free and limited-cost prescription drugs under Medicare. Interestingly, Bush did this even although the new programme was very expensive and in the face of a burgeoning budget deficit. During his second term Bush launched a politically risky reform of social security that involved a part-privatization of the whole system. Predictably, these reforms ran into opposition from organized interests and quickly died in Congress in 2005. By 2016 the salience of the issue was raised when Bernie Sanders the socialist contender for the Democratic nomination proposed raising the 'cap' on contributions past the $118,500 income maximum. In other words he proposed raising benefits by abolishing the limit on salary contributions. There is little chance, however that Congress would accept such a reform and of course Sanders was beaten by Hillary Clinton to win the nomination. Clinton remained largely silent on the issue and was narrowly defeated by Donald Trump, whose policies on welfare stress self-reliance rather than enhanced federal aid.

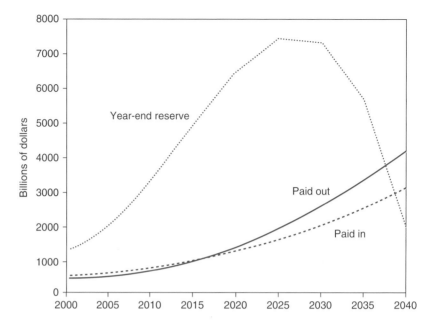

Figure 17.4   Social security receipts, spending and reserve estimates, 2001–2040
Source: Office of Management and Budget, US Government, www.whitehouse.gov.
Note: Amounts are in current dollars.

The Continuing Importance of Self-Reliance

While the old and disabled are largely protected, younger, able-bodied citizens are under increasing pressure to take jobs and support themselves. The 1988 Family Support Act required the states to provide work or training programmes for all welfare recipients, but it was not until the passage of the 1996 Personal Responsibility and Work Opportunity Reconciliation Act that the federal government fully embraced a philosophy of self-reliance. Under the Act, welfare recipients cannot receive benefits for more than five years. In addition, the eligibility criteria for the receipt of SSI, food stamps and other benefits were narrowed to include only the very needy. Indeed, both Democrats and Republicans are now committed to 'workfare', or the linking of benefits to training and jobs. This new consensus reinforces the ideology of self-reliance that has been the main characteristic of American social policy for more than 100 years. By the 2008 presidential election, the issue was effectively off the political agenda, for neither John McCain nor Barack Obama proposed any substantive change in welfare provision. Instead, the main difference between the candidates was on the subject of health-care reform with Republican candidate Mitt Romney pledged to make the repeal of Obama's Affordable Care Act a first priority if elected. With the re-election of Barack Obama in 2012 the Affordable Care Act looked secure for the foreseeable future – in spite of numerous attempts by the congressional Republicans during 2013–2017 to get the law repealed.

One of the most interesting aspects of the widespread public concern at the growth in welfare expenditure and the related belief that most welfare recipients are scroungers rather than the deserving poor is that, in relation to the size of other federal programmes, public assistance spending is relatively low. As can be seen from figure 17.2, the major welfare programmes in 2015 (marked 'social safety net') accounted for just 10 per cent of federal spending. The welfare category consists mainly of TANF, food stamps (now called SNAP – Supplementary Assistance Nutritional Program) and also a number of other programmes for the poor, but the major item here is SSI, which provides welfare for older Americans and the disabled. This programme has not been the main butt of public criticism. Whatever the objective situation, Democrats and Republicans have shown a determination to cut the welfare rolls and, as noted (figure 17.1), they have so far been remarkably successful in doing so.

Briefing   Why Was Health Care So Hard to Reform?

The main reason why reform was so difficult was that, by the end of the twentieth century, with more than 16 per cent of GDP devoted to health care, powerful vested interests with a stake in maintaining the status quo had been established. These included the large health insurance companies and drug suppliers, as well as a host of health-care providers and employees. With healthy profits and high medical salaries, few of these actors would have benefited from wholesale health-care reform. Major reform would have to extend health coverage to the 40 million plus non-insured. This could only be done by providing cost-limited health care or services with a strict cap on costs. Clearly the vested interests did not support lower drug prices, 'cheaper' doctors and nurses or caps on insurance premiums, and extending the present system through federal subsidies to the uninsured would have been expensive and therefore unpopular among the mass of taxpayers. For this reason presidential candidates had to tread carefully when promising reform. In 2008 John McCain offered simply to tweak the present system by allowing people to buy health insurance nationwide instead of limiting them to in-state companies, and by providing tax credits of $2,500 to individuals and $5,000 to families as an incentive to help them buy insurance. Barack Obama proposed a national insurance programme to allow individuals and small businesses to buy affordable health care

similar to that available to federal employees, funded by a tax on employers who didn't provide coverage. Individuals would not lose coverage when they switched jobs and insurance companies could not refuse reasonable cover for those with pre-existing conditions. In the event the 2010 Affordable Care Act (Obamacare) passed through Congress as a compromise measure fiercely opposed by the Republicans (not one Republican senator voted for the final version of the bill). Even when passed, the act aroused fierce opposition, especially to the individual mandate or the requirement that the uninsured buy insurance. The matter was not finally settled until 2012 when the Supreme Court declared most of the reforms constitutional. Even after the defeat of Mitt Romney in 2012, many Republicans continued to work for the repeal of the law and numerous legal challenges to the detail of the law's implementation were filed in state and federal courts. Finally, in the 2015 case *King* v. *Burwell*, the Supreme Court held that the law's federal subsidies to help individuals pay for health insurance should be available in all states, not just in those that have set up state special exchanges for that purpose. Donald Trump vowed to repeal the Affordable Care Act during the 2016 campaign, but with about 15–20 million Americans covered by the new law, replacing it proved to be very hard without reducing or removing coverage for this large number of new beneficiaries.

Health-Care Reforms

When he came to office, Bill Clinton was determined to reform America's health-care system. His motives were twofold. First, as a reforming Democrat, he wanted to extend medical coverage to the 15 per cent of Americans who were totally without medical insurance. Second, he wanted to stem the spiralling cost of medical care. He delegated the job of producing a health-care plan to his wife Hillary and to Ira Magaziner, an old confidant and author of books on industrial policy in the USA. It took them 15 months to produce an outline Health Security Act, which, among other things, required employers to provide health-care coverage, extended coverage to the whole population, created an internal market device called alliances to purchase coverage and services, and placed price controls on insurance policies.

The plan was submitted to Congress in October 1993. Twelve months later it was still in Congress, never to emerge as legislation. What went wrong? Most commentators agree that some of the blame must be attributed to the plan itself. It proposed the creation of a new bureaucracy; it was unpopular with business and especially with smaller companies; and it was not at all obvious that it would cut costs. As a result, it was heavily criticized in Congress, where it was referred to a number of committees, each with different priorities. Congressional Democrats and Republicans eventually drew up alternative plans, but these proved unacceptable to the White House. Indeed, the president and his team proved less than adept at guiding the legislation through Congress – although, to be fair, any major reform of the health-care system, however well steered through Congress, would have encountered difficulties. The

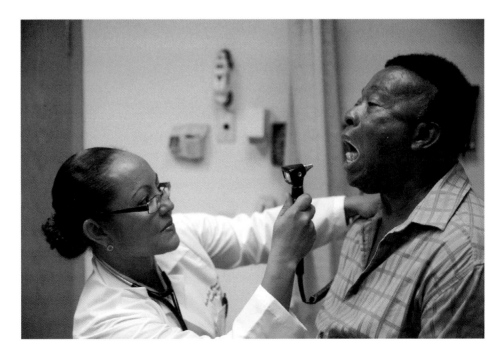

Plate 17.1   Patient receiving care under Affordable Care Act (Obamacare)
Source: Joe Raedle/Getty, www.gettyimages.co.uk/license/484931475.

major problem with the policy area is that American health care has developed into a three-tier system – those with private insurance cover, those in health maintenance organizations (HMOs) and the uninsured. The emergence of HMOs, which use market criteria to cost (and limit) health care provided by doctors and hospitals, already constitutes a major change in the system. Around 140 million Americans are in HMOs, and there is widespread disquiet at the way they operate. Providing health care for the approximately 40 million who have no health insurance would, unless taxes were to be increased, imply a further squeeze on what has become the most important part of the health-care system. In sum, an effective low-cost reform to provide for the uninsured could only be achieved at the expense of the majority. Such a situation is not amenable to easy solutions – and especially not when the major priority of government is to maintain a balanced budget without increasing taxation.

George W. Bush showed little interest in comprehensive health-care reform, although he did favour tinkering with the system, including providing tax breaks through the creation of health savings accounts. The 2004 Democratic opponent John Kerry did promise reform, however, including the provision of cover for catastrophic health costs in excess of $50,000. In other words, should any American not be able to pay costs for care beyond $50,000 a federal insurance scheme would cover the costs. By 2008 health care had developed into a major political issue and one that sharply divided the two contenders (see Briefing). Given the strength of feeling among voters, it is not surprising that both candidates in that year promised major health-care reforms. In the event Barack Obama made an affordable health-care act the centrepiece of his first term in office. After much horse-trading, the bill that eventually emerged from Congress was very much a compromise. It did, however, include an individual mandate or requirement that the uninsured buy coverage from a list of providers approved by the government. Those who refused to do so would be 'fined' through the tax system. Uniquely for a major piece of social policy legislation, opposition to the law continued unabated even after passage. Republicans were particularly outraged by the individual mandate and took their case to the Supreme Court. Eventually the Court held that the mandate was constitutional, although it limited the requirement by the states that they greatly expand Medicaid coverage (*National Federation of Independent Business et al. v. Sebelius Secretary of Health and Human Services et al.*, 2012).

As a result of the law the percentage of adults who were uninsured dropped from 18 per cent in the third quarter of 2013 to 11 per cent in the first quarter of 2016. While this represents a considerable achievement, the programme has been plagued with problems ranging from accusations of burdensome bureaucracy, to increased premiums for many recipients, to claims that while it helps many access health care it fails to help the very poor. One thing is sure: with the Republicans controlling presidency and Congress from January 2017, Obamacare will be challenged and probably replaced during the ensuing two years.

The Federal Government and Education

Education has always been considered 'different' in the United States. In contrast to other areas of social policy, few have questioned the need for free universal provision of elementary and secondary education by local governments, and indeed American states and communities were among the first countries to introduce such a system in the nineteenth century. The philosophy of equality of opportunity (see chapter 2) assumes that every American should be given an equal start in life through access to free education. Except in higher education, it was long established that local governments would be the main education providers. Later, states became involved, and by the twentieth century the federal government acquired a limited role in the funding of higher education. It was not until 1965, however, with the passage of the Elementary and Secondary Education Act, that the federal government directly funded school education. Initially funding was limited to the provision of buildings and teaching materials, but over the next 40 years the scope of federal provision increased to include school lunches, special aid for deprived areas and teacher training. In 2001, however, the federal role was transformed with the passage of the No Child Left Behind Act (NCLB). This bipartisan law required all schools to introduce standard tests in literacy and numeracy. The carrot was extra federal funding; the stick was the threat of denial of that funding; the result was universal testing. NCLB was designed to improve standards, but has been criticized for giving schools an incentive to 'teach to the test' rather than provide a broad and rounded education. Funding for education increased significantly, from $42.2 billion in 2001 to $68.3 billion in 2011, of which NCLB received some $21.5 billion. However, with the Republicans back in control of Congress after 2012 and 2014, federal education spending was slowly reduced – in spite of President Obama's protestations. NCLB was also greatly modified and continuing accusations that the law was too inflexible led to the passage of the Every Student Succeeds Act in 2015. While endorsing the need to test performance this law gave to the states much greater flexibility as to how this was to be implemented on a state-by-state basis. With the election of Donald Trump in 2016 it is likely that the states will be given further freedom from federal control including a renewed emphasis on parental choice via the issue of vouchers and the expansion of the charter school movement. Indeed, on coming to power Donald Trump appointed Betsy DeVos as Secretary of Education. DeVos was known as a champion of charter schools (schools that are free from local government control and instead operate independently, but usually with the continuation of public funding).

Conclusions

Perhaps the most remarkable development in American social policy over the past 30 years is the attempt to reduce the status of the sort of redistributive measures associated with the New Deal and the Great Society. For, while social security and Medicare remain politically sacrosanct, welfare and a number of other income support programmes are now viewed with increasing hostility. For Republicans and those on the right, it was always thus. Today, many Democrats have joined them – although substantial ideological differences between the two parties remain.

In this sense, the status of a major aspect of American social policy is now highly contested. Income support should be provided for the 'truly needy', who are unable to work. Any adult who is able to work must do so, or forfeit the support of the state. There is, however, a major difference between the New Deal era and today. Put simply, as far as social security and health care are concerned, most Americans do expect the federal government to play an important role. Indeed, their expectations in both areas have, if anything, been increasing over recent years. At the same time, the political system has found it hard to institute major reforms because reform must entail either increased taxation or reduced benefits. In this sense social security and health care remain very much at the centre of the political stage, and in neither area have public demands been satisfied – only in the welfare area have they partly been met. But, as indicated, welfare provision has always been viewed with suspicion in the USA, and reform has been achieved largely because the traditional supporters of welfare – the Democrats – now see welfare cuts as both possible and politically expedient. State and local governments remain the key providers in elementary, secondary and college-level education, but the federal government's role has increased in recent years.

Summary

Nothing illustrates the importance of self-reliance in the US as well as the contrasting status of welfare and social security. Welfare – or non-contributory benefits for the poor – is unpopular, and following the 1996 reforms has been widely regarded as a temporary 'relief' programme. In contrast, social security – or contributory benefits mainly for old-age pensions and benefits for the disabled – enjoys wide public support, and attempts to reform it have repeatedly failed. Health care lies somewhere between the two. Medicare, which provides benefits for the old, is popular, while Medicaid, providing for the poor, is more vulnerable. But these programmes only cover a minority of the population. Comprehensive health-care reform extending coverage for everyone is difficult because it would be both expensive and would challenge vested interests, including insurance companies and many medical professionals. After an almighty political battle, a limited form of health-care reform was enacted in 2010, but the Republicans are committed to repealing this legislation should they be given the chance.

Generally, the federal government has been called on to play an ever-greater role in social policy – even in the context of continuing hostility to that role among many Americans.

Questions for Discussion

1   Outline the attempts to reform the health-care system from 1993 to 2017. Why was 'Obamacare' so contentious? Discuss with reference made to the changes made by the Trump administration after 2016.
2   What are the main features of the American social security system? Why is the programme popular compared with federal welfare programmes?
3   What is the federal government's involvement in education? How has it changed since 1965?
4   To what extent has US social policy been influenced by notions of self-reliance? Answer by comparing US social policy with that of ONE other country.

Glossary

Aid for Families with Dependent Children (AFDC)   The main welfare programme in operation between 1935 and 1996

baby-boom generation   The 1945–60 generation of larger families now reaching retirement age

Elementary and Secondary Education Act 1965   The first major federal programme for funding schools

Every Student Succeeds Act 2015   Modifies the No Child Left Behind Act to allow states more flexibility in the testing of children

health maintenance organizations (HMOs)   Organizations designed to provide cost-effective medical care by limiting patient choice of doctors and treatment

Medicaid   The main federal medical programme for the poor

Medicare   The main federal medical programme for the old

No Child Left Behind Act (NCLB)   The institution of universal testing of schoolchildren's performance by the federal government

Social Security Trust Fund   The monies collected via social security taxes and specifically allocated to social security (mainly pension) payments

SNAP – Supplementary Nutritional Assistance Program or food stamps   Tokens introduced in 1964 that the poor could exchange for food. They remain in use in a modified form today

Supplementary Security Income (SSI)   A welfare programme to provide benefits for the old and the sick whose social security payments are inadequate

TANF (Temporary Assistance for Needy Families)   The 'workfare' programme introduced in 1996 and designed to get people off welfare and into work

Further Reading

On the origins of social policy, see Theda Skocpol, *Protecting Soldiers and Mothers: The Political Origins of Social Policy in the United States* (Cambridge, MA: Harvard University Press, 1995). On welfare see Anne Marie Cammisa, *From Rhetoric to Reform: Welfare Policy in American Politics* (Boulder: Westview Press, 1998). On health care, see Daniel Beland, Philip Rocco and Alex Wadden, *Obamacare Wars: Federalism, State Politics, and the Affordable Care Act* (Lawrence: University of Kansas Press, 2016). On poverty see Sasha Abramsky, *The American Way of Poverty: How the Other Half Still Lives* (New York: Nation Books, 2014).

CHAPTER 18
MANAGING ECONOMIC CHANGE

Sometimes magic works, sometimes it doesn't. For a generation after World War II, America had (as Tom Wolfe put it) a 'magic economy.' … In less than thirty years everything doubled. That is the real earnings of the typical worker, the real income of the typical family, consumption per capita. 'In 1973 the magic went away.'
— PAUL KRUGMAN, *PEDDLING PROSPERITY*

American Politics and Society, Ninth Edition. David McKay.
© 2018 John Wiley & Sons Ltd. Published 2018 by John Wiley & Sons Ltd.

As recently as 40 years ago, a section on economic policy in a textbook on American politics would not have been considered necessary. Today it is essential. Not since the 1930s have economic issues dominated the policy agenda as they do now. Abroad, America's standing has changed in a new and often hostile international economic order. At home, maintaining steady growth with low inflation and balanced budgets has become the number one domestic policy priority. It hardly needs stressing that the state of the economy is vitally important, not only for the economic role of governments in society and the ways in which they tax citizens and allocate expenditure, but also for the health of the polity. Small wonder, then, that economic policy has come to dominate the agenda since the 1970s. Governments, moreover, are now irrevocably involved in economic affairs. Some 42.2 per cent of gross domestic product is accounted for by government expenditure at all levels – a very high figure in historical perspective and not seriously out of line with the European welfare states (table 18.1); federal regulation of industrial and commercial affairs, from environmental protection to anti-monopoly law, is widespread; and, by manipulating aggregate levels of expenditure and taxation and altering the supply of money in the economy, all federal governments now accept the need to 'manage' the economy. Regulation has been discussed elsewhere (chapter 14), and this chapter's aim is to study economic management policies, and in particular to identify those forces that shape the economic policy-making agenda. As with social policy, particular attention will be paid to the relationship between public expectations and the objective performance of the government in the economic policy area.

State and Economy in the United States

As chapter 2 emphasized, the traditional view of the United States is of a country where the state plays a relatively minor role. In contrast to the burgeoning welfare states and mixed economies of Europe, convention has it that Americans prefer market to public mechanisms to distribute goods and services in society. By most simple quantitative measures this view used to have some validity. However by 2014 the United States had crept up the table of government spending and in that year scored just slightly lower than its neighbour Canada (table 18.1).

Much of the recent growth is a direct result of the economic dislocation experienced after 2008 – although spending in most countries was reduced by 2015. In effect, a combination of a faltering private sector together with an increase in entitlement and economic stimulus programmes greatly increased the relative size of governments. These data apply to *all* government spending, federal, state and local. Of course, if a longer time-span is taken, then the growth of public expenditure has been even more dramatic. In 1930 the percentage of gross national product (GNP) accounted for by public expenditure was less than 10 per cent. Much of the increase since then is a result of massively enhanced defence spending and, since the early 1960s, of the partial replacement of defence expenditure with spending on a range of domestic entitlement programmes. If we examine *federal* government expenditures alone, what stands out is the rapid growth in spending precipitated by the two world wars and by the New Deal. Until the early 1930s, less than 5 per cent of GNP was accounted for by federal spending. Since 1945 it has been rising slowly and erratically until

Table 18.1   General government expenditures as percentage of GDP, 1997 and 2014, selected OECD countries

Country	1997	2014	% Change
Australia	35.4	35.3	−0.1
Canada	44.3	41.9	−2.4
France	54.1	56.1	2.0
Germany	48.3	45.4	−2.9
Italy	50.2	49.8	−0.4
Japan	35.7	42.0	6.3
Spain	41.6	45.2	3.6
Switzerland	35.5	33.8	−1.7
UK	40.6	48.5	7.9
USA	**35.4**	**41.6**	**6.2**
Average	42.1	44.0	1.9

Source: OECD National Reports; World Bank.

falling through 2000, and today it is around 21 per cent of GNP. Since 9/11 and especially after 2008 it has started to increase once more before falling as the economic recovery set in after 2011 (figure 18.1).

Whatever the relative position of the USA, the sheer size of the government budgets should not be underestimated. In 2016 the federal government alone spent around $3,800 billion, and total expenditures of all governments came to around $6,000 billion. As figure 18.1 shows, the gap between this expenditure and income – the federal debt – increased rapidly until 1992, so that, by the mid-1990s, the size of the deficit had become the number one economic issue. After a rapid recovery in the 1990s the deficit reappeared in the early 2000s and ballooned to over 10 per cent of gross domestic product (GDP) by 2011. With economic recovery after 2012 it had declined to around 3.2 per cent of GDP in 2016. Like those of every other developed economy, American governments – and particularly the federal government – have enormous potential power over economic activity. By increasing spending and lowering taxation the economy can be stimulated. Conversely, lower spending and higher taxes can lower the level of economic activity. Used in this way, fiscal policy is a major tool of macro-economic policy. Other tools include control over credit and the money supply, both of which are currently in fashion as means of fighting inflation.

American government affects the economy in a number of other ways, most of which can be contained under the general description of micro-economic policy. Micro-economic policy is concerned not with pulling fiscal and monetary levers to affect the general direction in which the economy moves, but with a range of policy instruments that affect the specific behaviour of individuals, firms, sectors and regions. Hence, industrial policy, labour relations, education, training and regional and urban policy are typical micro-economic tools. Regulatory policy can also be a micro-economic device, although as we saw in chapter 16

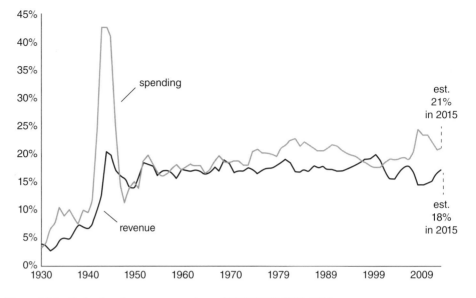

Figure 18.1   Federal outlays as a percentage of GNP/GDP, 1930–2015
Source: National Priorities Budget, https://www.nationalpriorities.org/analysis/2014/presidents-2015-budget-in-pictures/.

it is often motivated by non-economic considerations such as the promotion of equality or the protection of the environment. It hardly needs mentioning that policy-makers do not perceive this range of macro- and micro-policies as a coherent set of interrelated instruments. Neither do the policies always complement one another according to some coherent economic rationale. If anything, the very opposite applies. Politicians and bureaucrats are not in agreement as to which policy should be applied at any particular time, and the policies themselves often compete with, rather than complement, one another; or, as the economists would put it, *trade-offs* exist between (say) education and training policy and taxation, or between inflation and unemployment.

When one is attempting to identify the scope and limitations of economic policy in any society, institutional and ideological factors are important. How do these constrain economic policy-making in the United States?

Ideology and Economic Policy

As our discussion in earlier chapters showed, ideology plays an important part in shaping the policy agenda or in influencing which issues or alternative policies are available for debate and discussion at any one time. In most Western countries economic policy has been influenced by three distinct philosophies, each of which has its defenders among economists, as well as its political champions. On the right, economic liberals look to the market for salvation. In the centre, Keynesians believe that, when the market fails to provide full employment and steady growth, governments should step in and, via increased spending and borrowing, stimulate demand. On the left, socialists place the market in a subordinate position in relation to a public sector that would plan the allocation of resources in society. Socialist solutions are effectively excluded from the policy agenda in the United States, and by the end of the twentieth century were discredited almost everywhere else. They carry connotations of collectivism unacceptable in a society so infused with economic individualism. Until the 1980s, most debate involved clashes between economic liberals and Keynesians. Much of the politics of economic policy, then, centred on levels of taxation and spending, and on the extent to which credit and the money supply should be controlled. Prior to 1933, liberal economics dominated; it was not until the New Deal and the Second World War that federal governments began to 'borrow and spend their way out of trouble', either to stimulate a depressed economy or to produce war *matériel* on a massive scale. To the economic liberal, high levels of government expenditures are bad enough, even if they are covered by taxation. But deficit spending and loose money-supply policies are even worse, for these lead directly to inflation and, so the argument runs, eventually to disaster. Economic liberals' antipathy even to higher levels of government expenditure adequately financed by taxation derives from their conviction that the market is the only efficient and acceptable allocator of resources. When governments allocate they do so wastefully and inefficiently. Of course, the free marketeers accept that governments have to play some role, especially in defence. But the essence of their philosophy is to reduce what has become a very intrusive role in society and always to ensure that what expenditure remains is recovered by taxation.

During the late 1930s and the 1940s Keynesian thinking dominated, and successive federal governments ran up large deficits, the peak being reached in the admittedly unusual conditions of wartime in 1943 when, in one year, a $54.8 billion deficit amounted to some 35 per cent of GNP. Interestingly, though most of the post-war period is usually labelled 'Keynesian', total federal debt as a percentage of GNP declined steadily until 1970, although it rose sharply thereafter until levelling off in the early 1990s, building to a surplus in 2000 only to sink substantially into the red by the mid/late-2000s. As debt increased, spending rose, and in recent years there has been a tendency towards increased domestic, rather than defence, spending. To the economic liberal (a supporter of the free market) the latter may be justifiable; the former rarely is. The liberal position was given further stimulus by the events of the early and mid-1970s. During the 1971–3 period, loose money-supply policies were accompanied by steep rises in commodity prices, culminating in the 1973–4 fourfold increase in oil prices. These fuelled inflation and wrought serious damage on the supply side of the economy. Producers, in other words, found their costs increasing rapidly. Their incentive to produce and invest was greatly undermined, resulting in a drop in output and rising unemployment. The ensuing recession convinced many in the Ford and Carter administrations that the way back to economic health lay in recreating the right production and investment environment – low taxes, inflation and interest rates. This, they argued, could be achieved only if governments avoided over-stimulating demand through expenditure and borrowing. But neither president was very successful in keeping government spending down, and, when elected in 1980, President Reagan made a much stronger pledge to cut expenditure, borrowing and taxes, and therefore provide an amenable investment environment. We will examine how Ronald Reagan's new economic programme fared later.

Although, by the new millennium, we can conclude that a near-consensus on the need for liberal, free-market economics existed, conflicts over the consequences of liberal policies remain. Many in the Democratic Party and in the labour unions continued to advocate Keynesian solutions, and most commentators remained wary of the *political* feasibility of exclusively free-market solutions, whatever their economic merits. In addition, many political leaders are concerned about the social consequences of expenditure cuts. As established in earlier chapters, federal, state and local governments are now irrevocably involved in the business of providing a wide range of economic and social services whether they like it or not. The public *expects* a wide range of services from the federal government, and the tension between this plain fact and the prevailing liberal economic philosophy is considerable and unlikely to disappear in the immediate future.

The liberal–Keynesian conflict in economic policy is essentially about macro-economic management. What then of the relationship between ideology and micro-economic policy? In some respects, adopting interventionist micro-strategies to solve economic problems is more of a challenge to liberal ideology than is Keynesian demand management. For industrial or regional policy assumes that governments can and should interfere with individual economic actors or sectors by providing incentives, subsidies, loans or guidance. Perhaps for this reason, the United States has less consciously planned and developed industrial, regional and labour market policies than any comparable country. Indeed, there is *no* federal industrial or regional strategy worth the name, and training and labour force policies are more ameliorative ad hoc measures than true labour market strategies. Japan and France, by way of contrast, have had, at least in the past, highly developed industrial policies involving centrally coordinated resource and investment planning. In Japan's case, industrial planning by sector involved close linkages between government, corporations and unions. Such corporatist arrangements were, until recently, quite alien to the American way of doing things.

None the less, during the 1970s, a number of commentators, noting the relatively poor economic performance of the United States, called for a federal industrial policy. These calls went unheeded and all but faded away amidst the freewheeling economic boom of the middle and later Reagan years. By the early 1990s, however, industrial policy had returned to the centre of the economic stage. Slow or even negative economic growth continued for several years, and increasingly invidious comparisons were made between the performance of American as opposed to Japanese and German industry. By 1993 the incoming Clinton administration was committed to an economic strategy that could be interpreted as industrial policy, including an economic stimulus package: infrastructure investment, a federal training programme and special help to facilitate innovation in high-growth industries such as microchips and genetics. Very early in the first Clinton term, however, the advocates of industrial policy, and especially Labor

Secretary Robert Reich, were eclipsed by economic and political events. The economy recovered rapidly from 1993, thus partly removing the need for an economic stimulus package. This recovery was, moreover, steady and non-inflationary. Further government expenditure may have resulted in 'overheating' and renewed inflation. As important for the fate of the package were dissenting voices from within the administration. Deputy Director of the Office of Management and Budget, Alice Rivlin, had written a book, *Reviving the American Dream*, which argued that what the economy needed was less, not more, federal government expenditure and regulation. Although her perspective was at first unpopular, by the middle of 1993 it was her views, rather than those of Robert Reich, which were in the ascendant within the White House. Finally, there was deep disquiet among Republicans in Congress that the stimulus package represented a giant pork-barrel give-away. This combination of factors killed the stimulus package in Congress. Indeed, by the end of 1993, the whole industrial policy question had slipped from the policy agenda. And even during the economic dislocation induced by the sub-prime crisis (see Briefing) and high fuel costs in 2008 and 2009, most politicians called for economic stimulation in the form of lower taxes and tax credits rather than economic packages targeted at particular economic sectors or regions. In the event, the Bush and Obama administrations were obliged to enact two massive rescue/stimulus programmes in 2008 and 2009. The first of these, the Troubled Asset Relief Program (TARP), pumped over $430 billion into financial institutions to prevent a 'melt down' of banks. Even larger was the economic stimulus package, the American Recovery and Re-investment Act passed in 2009. By pumping more than $800 billion into the economy the stimulus programme alleviated some of the worst effects of the recession by creating jobs and tax revenue.

Of course, the US has had a range of industrial policies for many years, from loans provided by the Small Business Administration to aid for urban transport and interstate highway schemes, from employment-creation programmes for poor cities and rural areas to investment incentives for commercial and industrial development. At the state and local levels, similar programmes and schemes exist. Crucially, however, these have in the main been ad hoc and uncoordinated, and have emerged as a result of the lobbying and bargaining processes outlined in earlier chapters. They cannot, therefore, be considered as part of an economic or industrial *strategy*.

A final but crucial point to be noted about the US economy is the overwhelming importance of the growth imperative. No national politician can afford not to emphasize the importance of growth and job creation. While this is now true in all countries, it has a special force in the US, where low taxes, population growth and territorial expansion have always been part of the national ethos. However, in an increasingly globalized world, this growth ethos can clash with other values, and in particular environmental protection. As the world's greatest producer of greenhouse gases, the US is constantly being criticized by other states and by environmental interests for its failure to take a lead in this and other environmental issues. Presidents and other politicians may pay lip-service to the need for reforms in this area, but all too often the growth imperative overwhelms the environmental case (see chapter 19).

CONTROVERSY 15   FOREIGN ECONOMIC POLICY: IS
                  FREE TRADE ALWAYS BENEFICIAL
                  FOR US INDUSTRY?

Since the Second World War, the United States has been a consistent pro-
ponent of free trade. During the successive rounds of tariff reductions
required by the General Agreement on Tariffs and Trade (GATT) through to
the creation of the World Trade Organization (WTO), the USA has always
adopted an official pro-trade line. Until the 1970s the issue was essentially
non-controversial. However, the dislocation caused by successive oil crises and an increasing perception that US industry was falling behind such
competitors as Japan and Germany led to ever more urgent calls for protection for domestic producers. This movement reached a peak in the late
1970s and early 1980s, when controls were placed on the import of Japanese cars and other goods. Even so, the USA operated within the GATT
rules and always retained an official pro-free trade line.

When recession hit during the early 1990s the anti-free trade movement
received fresh impetus, with such figures as Representative Richard Geph-
art (later to be Minority Leader in the House) and right-wing populist Pat
Buchanan taking up the banner against open and free trade. Support for
their positions came not only from workers in the manufacturing industry,
but also increasingly from farmers whose incomes were being hit by falling world prices and lower federal subsidies. During the next economic
downturn in 2008, protectionist sentiment grew again. This time the target was cheap goods imported from the emerging industrial giants, and
in particular China. In his 2016 election campaign Donald Trump took up
the protectionist banner with renewed enthusiasm, arguing that China,
Japan, Mexico and other countries were trading 'unfairly' and therefore
stealing Americans' jobs. Supporters of free trade generally subscribe to
the theory of comparative advantage. This holds that free trade is always
beneficial because in any one country the market will sort out which producer is least bad at producing a particular product in relation to another.
Hence, Country A may produce coffee beans more efficiently than anything
else even if Country B is a more efficient coffee producer. The difference
will be reflected in the lower price charged by Country A. By this logic, it
pays for Country A to continue coffee production. So free trade tends to
reduce prices and increase efficiency. American farmers have to tolerate
lower world prices – even if they are being driven down by less efficient
producers. The answer is for American agriculture to become even more
efficient through capital investment and the elimination of small, inefficient
producers. This is precisely what has happened over the past 30 years. Tens
of thousands of small farms have disappeared.

Another tactic is for American industry to 'outsource' components to
poorer countries, such as Mexico and China, where the price of labour
is low. In some cases it might even be worthwhile to shift production

abroad completely. Again, American companies have employed both tactics over the past several decades. Following the boom years of the late 1990s and early 2000s, when the debate on free trade almost seemed an irrelevance, the debate returned with a vengeance after 2008 in the context of a serious economic downturn and rising unemployment. Particular concern was expressed at the ways in which China allegedly flouted WTO rules and manipulated its currency to enhance its exports. In 2012 the administration formally brought a WTO case against China over its restrictive trade practices. Once elected in 2016 Donald Trump reiterated his intention to 'punish' China and other 'trade cheats' by favouring US companies that invest in the US and making it more difficult for them to outsource jobs abroad.

Institutions and Economic Policy

The relationship between ideology and political and social institutions has inspired debate within social science for many years. In American politics, for example, whether federalism is a cause of a limited federal planning and coordinating role in society or whether it has been maintained as a result of the power of liberal ideology has never been resolved. Whatever the causal directions, there can be no doubting that institutional arrangements continue to have a profound effect on economic policy-making. Indeed, some would argue that the institutional constraints are such that no administration can effectively manage the American economy. What are the constraints?

Federalism and localism

Chapter 4 referred to competitive interdependence in US intergovernmental relations and showed how the federal government is now locked in a symbiotic relationship with lower-level governments. So, although federal governments continue to hand out large sums of money to states and localities, it is no easy thing to withdraw this largesse in line with economic imperatives. State and local governments have multiple channels of access to officials in Washington and, notwithstanding recent cutbacks in federal aid, formidable political resources can be harnessed to defend federally funded programmes. Of course, to a greater or lesser extent, this goes on everywhere, but the institution of federalism gives to individual states added legal weight in their efforts to maintain federal funding. Federalism also encourages 'highest common denominator' options when funds are being allocated. In other words, federal governments find it very difficult to discriminate between states according to some rational economic principle. When regional economic or research and development aid is being provided, for example, who gets what depends more on lobbying, criteria of equity, or mere chance than on the needs of economy. The failure to develop a coherent micro-economic strategy must in part be related to this phenomenon.

State and local governments also have independent revenue sources, which can weaken the scope and substance of federal fiscal policy. Federal revenues account for only about 60 per cent of all government income in the USA, the remainder deriving from state and local sales, property and income taxes. Constitutionally, and in marked contrast to the situation in a country like Britain, the federal government cannot *directly* affect these revenues. It is easy to make too much of this point, however. Runaway spending by sub-national governments is uncommon. Many state constitutions prohibit deficit spending – although as we saw in chapter 4 that has not stopped some states building up sizeable deficits in the medium term – and the bulk of government debt in the US has been incurred at the federal level. But, in a rather indirect sense, the fiscal goings on of state and local governments do affect federal budgets, for their fiscal problems, together with opposition by publics to increased state and local taxes, can lead to calls for federal revenues to fill the gaps left by tax-limitation measures. Some commentators have, indeed, pointed to the paradoxical possibility that antipathy towards impersonal government and high taxes will lead to greater centralization at the state and federal levels.

Separation of powers

When studying economic policy-making in the US, foreign observers usually look first to the budgetary process and in particular to the conflicts between Congress and president that the spending power produces. Given the American concern with macro-policy and with controlling spending, this is perhaps not surprising. Indeed, as chapters 9–14 showed, battles over spending are the very essence of presidential and of congressional politics. Much of the conflict derives from a simple constitutional fact: Congress, and in particular the House of Representatives, was given the power to raise taxes and appropriate monies for the executive branch to spend. As the role of the government has expanded, so the need for institutional mechanisms to coordinate and control spending has also increased. So president and Congress have improved and streamlined their budgetary bureaucracies, each intent on providing the other branch with a coherent spending and taxing policy.

On the executive side, the first important item of legislation was the 1921 Budget and Accounting Act, which created the Bureau of the Budget, a bureaucracy designed to provide improved budget advice and review for the president. At first, the Bureau of the Budget was intended to help control spending – an objective in line with the prevailing laissez-faire or liberal philosophy that spending was essentially a bad thing. All changed with the coming of the New Deal, when, under the leadership of Franklin Roosevelt, the Bureau became a partisan for increased spending in opposition to a sometimes hostile Congress. The Bureau was also formally incorporated into the Executive Office of the President during this period, and its staff increased from 40 to over 600. The next significant law was the Full Employment Act 1946, a piece of legislation that effectively endorsed Keynesian demand management by pledging the federal government to full-employment policies. Among other measures, the Act created the Council of Economic Advisers, a further White House innovation, but this time designed to encourage presidents to pursue 'rational economic policies to foster and promote free competition, to avoid economic fluctuations or to diminish the effects thereof, and to maintain employment, production, and purchasing power'. The 1946 Act also mandated the president to produce an annual Economic Report to document economic performance over the past year and to provide Congress with a programme for the coming year. Since 1946, successive presidents have experimented further with the budget machinery, usually to inject rationality into burgeoning federal budgets. Lyndon Johnson ordered the adoption of planning programming-budgeting systems, effectively a technique to link spending with preconceived planning priorities. Jimmy Carter, in turn, adopted zero-base budgeting, or budget plans organized from the bottom up according to spending limits rather than according to specific programme objectives. The latter adapts spending to (say) the construction of so many miles of interstate highway or to a particular objective in the space programme, and thus tends towards expenditure rising incrementally. The point about these and other innovations is that they reflect presidents' growing concern with the sheer size of the budget and the need to present Congress with a coherent spending plan.

Congress has responded with its own innovations. The 1946 Act, for example, created a joint Economic Committee consisting of seven senators and seven members of Congress to provide Congress with a total view of the economy and aid the legislature's response to presidential initiatives. More recently, the 1974 Budget Reform Act created a Congressional Budget Office, together with budget committees, to provide each House with a coherent view of budget-making and instil a sense of spending priority, rather than proceed, as had been the case in the past, on an incremental basis. Although, in the first few years of this innovation, congressional control appeared to improve, fundamental problems of budget-making soon reappeared. These are simply that Congress's role is negative rather than positive. Or, as we discovered in chapter 11, 'the president proposes and Congress disposes'. Economic management is first and foremost an executive responsibility. Until the reforms, the role of Congress was confined to trimming, tinkering with or otherwise modifying the president's budget on an ad hoc basis. After the reforms, the congressional budget committees played a more prominent role that almost certainly made the budget process more cumbersome. The budget timetable remained effectively the same. In the spring of Year One the departments and agencies submit their expenditure estimates to the Office of Management and Budget (OMB). The OMB then spends several months reviewing – and often cutting – these estimates until the president formally submits the budget to Congress in early February of Year Two. During the ensuing months, the budget committees work with the legislative and appropriations committees to reconcile competing interests and objectives, until a budget resolution or reconciliation is passed in April. Further modifications, both from the appropriations committees and the president, follow until the beginning of the financial year on 1 October. During the first years of the Carter presidency the system seemed to work moderately well, but then the economy was growing rapidly and deficits actually ended up quite close to the president's projections. Between 1980 and 1995 the situation was transformed, first by deepening recession, and later by deficits far exceeding expectations (figure 18.1). This period also saw the most radical and frenzied activity in the politics and procedures of congressional budget-making ever experienced.

Briefing   Institutional Sclerosis and the Budget, 2011–2013

In 2011 it was necessary for the US government to increase the national debt ceiling by $400 billion in order to meet its obligations. Congress, however, refused to sanction this in the absence of a longer-term budget deficit reduction of $900 billion over 10 years. Following the failure of the two houses of Congress to agree on how this was to be achieved, Congress took the unusual step of setting up a Joint Selective Committee on Deficit Reduction made up of six House and six Senate members with both parties equally represented. Any recommendations would be verified by a simple vote in both houses with no opportunity for amendment or filibuster. The Committee was due to report in the autumn of 2011, but failed to reach an agreement. In essence, the Democrats wanted a combination of tax increases and expenditure cuts, while the Republicans wanted mainly spending reductions. In the event of failure, tax and spending changes would, unless Congress acted to the contrary, begin automatically in January 2013.

The automatic triggers would have included the expiry of the Bush-era tax cuts as well as some unemployment benefits. In addition some $1.2 trillion of across-the-board spending cuts equally divided between defence and domestic programmes would have been imposed over 10 years. Some economists estimate that this would have resulted in a new recession as tax revenues fall and unemployment increases. This scenario came to be known as the 'Fiscal Cliff'. In the event this was avoided when in January 2013 Congress accepted that the spending cuts could be accompanied by some tax increases on the wealthy. Since then, further mandatory cuts have been imposed on a range of domestic and defence programmes thus helping to bring the deficit down to around 3 per cent of GDP.

At the heart of this policy mess is the highly partisan nature of Congress and the refusal of the two sides to reach an agreement through bargaining and compromise. While the reemergence of unified government after 2017 may alleviate this problem, it is highly unlikely that it will herald in a period of smooth cooperation between president and cooperation between president and Congress.

This started in the first few weeks of the Reagan administration, when the president submitted major changes for spending in 1982, 1983 and 1984. Large increases in defence spending and cuts in domestic programmes were proposed. Parallel, quite radical, cuts in taxation were also introduced into Congress. On the budget side, a new resolution, known as Gramm–Latta I (after Phil Gramm, a leading Democratic conservative on the House Budget Committee, and Delbert L. Latta, the ranking Republican on the committee), actually instructed 15 House committees and 14 Senate committees on how their budgets would be slashed over the next three years. The amounts involved – $36 billion, $47 billion and $56 billion in each of these years – were huge. Finally, the resolution was framed in such a way that any subsequent supplementary appropriations would be very difficult to achieve. In reaction to these draconian measures, congressional committees submitted a mass of new legislation designed to reassert traditional congressional power. The administration, fearing a sudden increase in spending, accepted a modified resolution (Gramm–Latta II) that was finally passed, very speedily, in August.

Plate 18.1   Protesters at Zuccaro Park for Occupy Wall Street on 1 October 2011 in New York City
Source: Jeff Kravitz/Getty, www.gettyimages.co.uk/license/127944135.

Although the final bill imposed less extensive cuts than those originally planned, this particular budget experience was almost the antithesis of the slow, incremental, deliberative process for which Congress is famous. In retrospect, we can conclude that President Reagan was fortunate to have the support of three key groups in Congress – the conservative Republicans, conservative southern Democrats (the 'Boll Weevils') and, crucially, moderate Republicans (the 'Gypsy Moths'). It was this coalition that also helped the administration to achieve quite startling tax cuts in the same session. This was always a fragile arrangement: signs of collapse were evident even by late 1981, and after 1982 the administration was much less successful in handling Congress.

Within Congress, the 'traditional' centres of budgetary power, the appropriations committees and sub-committees, reasserted their influence. During his last few years in office, Reagan found it easier to deal directly with these committees rather than work through the budget committees that were prone to tinker endlessly with the details of the budget. The events of 1981 were, in other words, exceptional.

What the 1981 experience does show is that Congress was at least capable of rapid response to presidential economic initiative. It also demonstrated the growing influence of the OMB, which, under the leadership of David Stockman, assumed a very central position as designer and as manager of government spending priorities. The problem of dealing with the deficit was sufficiently serious to inspire Congress, under pressure from the administration, to pass the Gramm–Rudman–Hollings Deficit Reduction Act in 1985. By imposing on Congress a timetable for mandatory spending cuts, the law would indeed have solved the budget deficit, with major cuts falling on defence and the discretionary programmes. In 1986, however, the Supreme Court declared the mandatory provisions of the law unconstitutional violations of the separation of powers. As a result, that which is now an advisory law has produced much smaller cuts than originally anticipated.

George Bush Senior faced a Democratic Congress intent on defending a range of entitlement and other domestic programmes. In each of Bush's four years in office, Congress and president were at loggerheads on the budget, which, together with a weakening economy, resulted in the ballooning of the deficit during 1989–92 (figure 18.2).

Budget drama continued with the first Clinton administration. During his first two years in office, things went relatively smoothly. Congress was still in the hands of the Democrats, the economy was growing steadily and, during 1993, the president's budget included expenditure cuts that helped reduce the budget deficit (figure 18.2). All changed with the election of a Republican Congress in 1994, however. Under the leadership of House Speaker Newt Gingrich, the Republicans were intent on extensive cuts in federal social spending for fiscal year 1996. President and Congress failed to agree on a budget by the October 1995 deadline and this resulted in a much-publicized partial closedown of the federal government. 'Non-essential' workers were laid off, national parks closed, and the crisis was not resolved until early 1996. These events were not repeated in 1996, mainly because of the political costs to all parties of being seen as uncooperative during an election year. During 1997 and 1998 a buoyant economy helped to reduce the annual deficit to zero and budget crises took second place to other aspects of presidential–congressional relations – not least the president's serious personal and political problems.

On coming to power George W. Bush inherited a sizeable budget surplus and all the projections at the time were that this would remain for some years. However, three factors came together very quickly to return the US to a position of budget deficit – in numerical terms the biggest ever. First, the economy slowed down perceptibly in 2001 and 2002, thus reducing tax receipts. Second, 9/11 resulted in greatly increased expenditure on

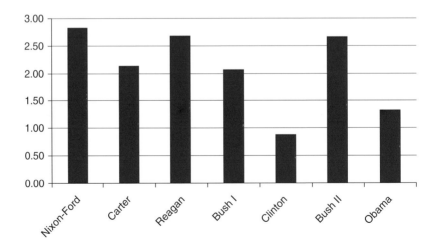

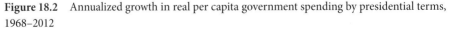

Figure 18.2   Annualized growth in real per capita government spending by presidential terms, 1968–2012
Source: Friday, 16 March 16 2012, Per Capita Government Spending by President, http://economistsview.typepad.com/economistsview/2012/03/per-capita-government-spending-by-president.html. Reprinted with permission. Mark Thoma on Friday, 16 March 2012.
Note: Starting quarter of inauguration to last (partial) quarter (Q1/Q2).

homeland security and, to a lesser extent, on defence. Third, the administration, together with a sympathetic Congress, proved eager to please its core constituencies and thus to expand agricultural subsidy, Medicare and other programmes. The result was that a Republican administration increased spending by 25.3 per cent from 2001 to 2005 – the greatest increase in 30 years (figure 18.2). Unified government and a Congress that was just as given to political expediency as the president no doubt aided this expansion. With the election of a Democratic Congress in 2006, cross-party budget battles re-emerged with George Bush wielding his veto pen on two major spending bills in 2007 and 2008.

In the context of serious economic dislocation, the budget system was sorely tested in the 2009–13 period. With the Republicans recapturing the House in 2010 but with the Democrats controlling the presidency and the Senate, the stage was set for partisan conflict. This duly transpired in 2011 when Congress could not agree on the longer-term spending cuts that it insisted went hand in hand with a $400 billion jump in federal lending. As explained in the Briefing above, the upshot was the creation of a congressional 'supercommittee' whose brief was to reach a bipartisan agreement by the autumn of 2011. Failing this, automatic tax increases and spending cuts would kick in from January 2013. Failure duly ensued, and in the absence of further congressional action, the cuts and tax increases were set to trigger on 1 January 2013. Known as the 'Fiscal Cliff', this episode demonstrates just how wide the ideological gap between the Republicans and Democrats had become. With the stunning Republican victory at the 2014 mid-term elections relations between the president and Congress deteriorated further and budget crises were only averted because of the automatic cuts mandated (or sequestered in the language of the legislation) in 2013 and set to continue all the way through to 2021.

The economic problems of the 1980s through 2016 highlighted another important institutional relationship that is peculiarly American: the unique political position of the American central bank, the Federal Reserve System. Created in 1913, the Federal Reserve is a 'decentralized' central bank consisting of 12 Federal Reserve districts governed by a board in Washington. Congress deliberately gave the board some autonomy from the president and, in recent years, the chairmen of the board have asserted their independence to some effect. This is important because the Federal Reserve has special responsibility for implementing monetary policy and in particular for setting interest rate levels. With budget deficits increasing, one recent chairman, Paul Volcker, insisted on controlling the money supply through a policy of high interest rates. Although at first the Reagan administration accepted the Federal Reserve's policy in this area, by late 1982 serious disagreement had emerged between Volcker and Donald Regan, the Treasury Secretary. Volcker continued to insist on a tight money policy, while some members of the administration wanted some relaxation to help lift the economy out of recession. Later, Volcker became a vocal critic of the rapidly appreciating dollar, while the administration generally viewed this as a problem for other countries. In these countries, central banks, if not the creatures of executives, are often significantly less autonomous than the Federal Reserve System.

George Bush Senior had an easier time with a Federal Reserve under the chairmanship of Alan Greenspan – although the president did call for a more rapid reduction in interest rates during the recession of 1991/2 than the Federal Reserve eventually sanctioned. Greenspan continued as chairman during the Clinton administrations. Bill Clinton was fortunate, however, that, during the whole of his first term, the economy grew steadily without threatening inflation. As a result, interest rates were kept relatively low, and the Federal Reserve's

Plate 18.2   New York Stock Exchange traders look anxiously at stock prices following the recent, October 2008 market crash
Source: Spencer Platt/Getty, www.gettyimages.co.uk/license/83245179.

fine-tuning of the economy remained essentially non-controversial. During Clinton's second term, however, deepening crisis in the world economy again raised the political salience of the Federal Reserve and eventually culminated in calls for coordinated interest rate cuts among all the richer countries, led by the United States, to alleviate the problem. By 1999 and 2000, overheating in the US economy (by early 2000 the economy was growing at a rate of more than 5 per cent per annum) led to interest rate hikes. The stock market crash of 2001 changed the situation further, and fears of deflation led to all-time low interest rates in the modern era by 2003. Again the economy overheated, leading to rapid rate hikes in 2005 and 2006. With the emergence of the sub-prime crisis, however, which led to a collapse in house prices and of many leading banks, the Federal Reserve, now under the leadership of Ben Bernanke (replaced by Janet Yellen in 2013), had reduced rates to 1 per cent by 2008 and eventually to close to zero by 2011. This time, however, the remedy failed to work because problems in the banking sector led to a serious shortage of credit. Even with low official rates, banks and other lenders continued to charge high rates to borrowers (see Briefing).

Briefing   The Great Housing Crash, 2007–2012

Following a period of very rapid house price appreciation between 2000 and 2006, the housing market collapsed in many parts of the country after 2007. As figure 18.3 shows, the decline was precipitous, reaching nearly 15 per cent in the year to March 2008. This cycle of boom and bust was fuelled in part by very low interest rates after 2001, but in the main by unregulated and often corrupt mortgage-lending practices. In the upper Midwest and other parts of the country, poorer homeowners were duped into apparently cheap remortgage deals with low initial payments that ballooned after a few years. The result was a rapid rise in bank repossessions after 2007. In California, Arizona, Nevada and Florida the problem was rather different. Here rapid price increases spurred massive building programmes. New buyers took out 'jumbo' loans, again at initially low cost, only for the interest rate to rise rapidly later. When the crash came, a large oversupply of homes existed, together with many homebuyers sitting in houses with negative equity. Spiralling foreclosures followed. The sub-prime crisis became an international problem because banks had sold on billions of dollars' worth of 'bad' mortgages to banks across the world. As a result, the housing crisis spread to a number of other countries, including Spain, the UK and Ireland. The effect of the crisis on American politics was profound. First it helped plunge the economy into recession – a recession that in turn helped Barack Obama secure the presidency in 2008. Second, it spurred presidents and Congress into a variety of rescue policies including a massive $800 billion rescue package for banks and other financial institutions, and a major fiscal stimulus for the economy. Similar rescues were launched in other countries, including Britain. Third, it revealed the weaknesses in federal regulation of the banking sector. As a result Congress passed a wave of regulations including the 2010 Dodd–Frank Wall Street Reform and Consumer Protection Act that gave to federal agencies sweeping new powers to regulate banking and consumer credit.

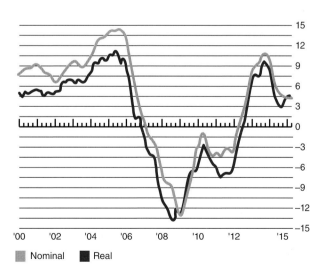

Figure 18.3   Changes in US house prices, 2001–2015

Source: Global Property Guide at www.globalpropertyguide.com/North-America/United-States/Price-History, 26 July 2016, How much longer can the U.S. housing market grow at this amazing rate? Lalaine C. Delmendo.

Conclusions: Economic Policy in an Age of Uncertainty

In many respects, the economic policy-making system resembles the social policy system. In both, the chief executive has the major responsibility for policy formulation and implementation, and in both he faces competition from other centres of power – notably Congress, executive departments and agencies, state and local governments, and organized interests. There are, however, some important qualitative differences between the two policy areas. Economic policy is obviously more important in the sense that most other domestic and foreign policies depend on it. All parties and politicians have an interest in economic performance and all believe that the federal government has to play a key role in economic management. They may disagree – sometimes radically – on what that role should be, but no one disputes the need for economic policy. Social policy, in contrast, is considered by many on the right not to be a legitimate concern of the federal government. The great paradox of social policy is the incontrovertible fact that dozens of federal programmes exist in the absence of central coordination and control. Control problems apply to economic policy, too, of course, but not in quite the same way. Measures of performance – inflation, growth, interest rate levels, the deficit, unemployment – exist to provide a focus of activity for policy-makers, as does the budgetary process itself. None the less, macro-economic management is shared between at least three major institutions (the presidency, Congress and the Federal Reserve), which is highly unusual in comparative context. And micro-economic policy-making is as confused and incoherent as social policy. What the two policy systems do share in common is that both are attempting to solve apparently intractable problems. Most other countries are experiencing similar difficulties of economic and social management, but in few are institutional arrangements organized in such an apparently inconvenient manner.

Before we end our discussion of economic policy, some reference to the growing consensus on economic management during the late 1990s and early 2000s should be made. Much of this consensus revolved around two themes. First was the almost universal perception that the budget must be kept in surplus without increasing taxation. Holding this consensus together proved relatively easy while the economy was growing. Once it faltered after 2008, however, the institutional conflicts inherent in the American system received fresh impetus and the budget deficit returned. The second and related dimension to the consensus was the wide acceptance that free markets at home and abroad are the only mechanism that can produce lasting prosperity. This meant less government interference at home and the achievement of open markets in international trade. While every recent administration has been committed to free trade, it is clear that the 2000–2009 Bush administrations were less committed to the idea than was Clinton or Bush Senior. This established agenda changed again, however, with the housing crash and 'credit crunch' starting in 2008. By early 2009 the resulting economic dislocation was global in nature, leading President Obama to launch a massive stimulus to the economy through big spending increases and tax reductions. While there was general agreement that these drastic measures had to be taken, the period of consensus was brief. With the Republican re-capture of the House of Representatives in 2010 and the Senate in 2014 the institutional conflict over economic policy returned with a vengeance. Agreement within Congress on how to reduce the deficit and increase economic growth proved elusive, leading to the possibility of automatic spending cuts and tax increases from 2013. Both parties agree that the deficit should be reduced but they fundamentally disagree on how this should be achieved. The Republicans insist that much lower social spending is the answer, while the Democrats want higher taxes for the rich combined with moderate cuts in social spending and defence. Although the election of Donald Trump in 2016 is likely to attenuate these problems, they are highly unlikely to go away for Congress will always serve a different constituency from that of the president, and institutional checks and balances will always guarantee some degree of conflict over economic policy.

Summary

Economic policy is the 'key' public policy because it helps determine the resources available to fund other policy areas. As such, it has more direct effect on politics than other policies. Although traditionally the federal government has played a smaller role in guiding the economy than have governments in other countries, periodic economic crises ensure that the federal role has increased in salience over the past 60 years. Presidents and the executive branch are the main actors in the area, although Congress is also central to budgeting and tax policy, as is the Federal Reserve in interest rate policy. The chapter concluded with a review of economic management from Nixon through Obama, paying special attention to tensions in economic management in the trade and budget areas.

Questions for Discussion

1   Why is economic policy the key policy area? How does it affect the substance of other major policy areas?
2   What accounts for fluctuations in the budget deficit since the 1980s? What has been the impact of the deficit on American politics?
3   Assess the economic policies of the 2009–17 Obama administrations. Answer with special reference to federal spending.
4   What is the role of Congress in economic policy? How has this changed in the past 40 years?

Glossary

Boll Weevils   The conservative Democrats in Congress during the 1970s and 1980s

comparative advantage   The international trade theory that assumes all countries benefit from open international trade

economic liberal   Those adhering to free-market principles

federal debt   The national debt of the United States

Federal Reserve System   The US central banking system that sets interest rates

Frank–Dodd Wall Street Reform and Consumer Protection Act 2010   strengthening of federal controls over credit and bank lending

Full Employment Act 1946   The Keynesian law that established the principle that the government was responsible for maintaining full employment

General Agreement on Tariffs and Trade (GATT)   The international agreement establishing successive rounds of tariff reduction

Gypsy Moths   The moderate northern Republicans active in Congress in the 1970s and 1980s

industrial policy   Guided government help to rescue declining industries and establish new ones

Keynesians   Those adhering to the idea that government spending and deficit finance should be used to maintain high employment during periods of economic distress

laissez-faire   Economic liberalism, or the idea that economies are at their most efficient if freed from government controls

macro-economic policy   Policy designed to guide the whole economy, such as interest rate policy

micro-economic policy   Policy designed to guide sectors or regions of the economy, such as regional aid and labour policies

New Deal   The collection of measures designed to rescue the economy from depression during the 1930s

outsourcing   Allocating aspects of government operations to private companies

TARP   Temporary Asset Relief Program to help the bail out of financial institutions in 2008

World Trade Organization (WTO)   The tariff-reduction organization that replaced GATT

Further Reading

A general critique of recent economic policies is provided by Paul Krugman, *End This Depression Now!* (New York: Norton, 2012). On recent changes in economic growth, see Robert J. Gordon, *The Rise and Fall of American Growth: The US Standard of Living Since the Civil War* (Princeton: Princeton University Press, 2016). On economic ideas, see Peter Hall, *The Political Power of Economic Ideas* (Princeton: Princeton University Press, 1998). The annual *Economic Report of the President* (Washington, DC: US Government Printing Office) provides a clear account of recent and predicted US economic performance.

CHAPTER 19
ENVIRONMENTAL POLITICS

The concept of global warming was created by and for the Chinese in order to make U.S. manufacturing non-competitive.

– DONALD TRUMP TWEET, 2012

All across the world, in every kind of environment and region known to man, increasingly dangerous weather patterns and devastating storms are abruptly putting an end to the long-running debate over whether or not climate change is real. Not only is it real, it's here, and its effects are giving rise to a frighteningly new global phenomenon: the man-made natural disaster.

– BARACK OBAMA, 2010

American Politics and Society, Ninth Edition. David McKay.
© 2018 John Wiley & Sons Ltd. Published 2018 by John Wiley & Sons Ltd.

Background

Americans have always had an ambivalent attitude to the natural environment. In contrast to most European countries, from the very beginning of the republic part of the rationale of being American was the exploitation of the natural environment through an ever-westward territorial expansion. The aim was to 'tame' or 'civilize' the great expanses through mining and agriculture and eventually to create the good transportation and utility facilities necessary for urbanization. Quite early in this process, however, many Americans became aware of the costs to the environment of this expansion. After 1851 writer and philosopher Henry Thoreau became a leading exponent of the merits of the wilderness, and in 1890 the first national parks were created in Yosemite and Sequoia, California. In 1892 the first environmental interest group, the Sierra Club, was created to help preserve the American wilderness. The first organized farmers' movement, the Grange, dating from 1873, was created to fight the big banking and railroad monopolies. For all of its history the Grange has championed the small farmer and careful husbandry of the land. As such it is an unusual amalgam of farm group and environmental organization.

During the twentieth century this tension between exploitation and protection of the natural environment not only continued but also intensified. A National Parks Service was created in 1908, and during the New Deal a number of federal laws were passed, including the 1934 Wildlife Coordination Act and the 1935 Soil Conservation and Domestic Allotment Act. After the Second World War federal environmental laws came thick and fast, in particular during the 1964–80 period (see Chronology below). The late twentieth century also witnessed what might be called the internationalization of the issue, with recognition that environmental problems increasingly spilt over national and continental boundaries.

The Emerging Environmental Agenda

It was not until the 1970s and after, however, that the environment became a major political issue, and it did so on a number of fronts, namely:

- *Nuclear power safety.* Following the 1979 accident at Three Mile Island nuclear plant in Pennsylvania, opposition to further nuclear power stations increased to the point where no new plants were commissioned or ordered without later being cancelled for more than 20 years. However, rising energy costs and global warming have led to renewed interest in nuclear power and, as of 2016, a number of new plants were in the process of being planned or built to be commissioned by 2020. Around 20 per cent of US energy needs are met by nuclear power.
- *Toxic waste.* In 1972 a large number of homes were polluted by toxic waste seeping from a facility in Love Canal, New York. This event raised consciousness of the dangers of toxic poisoning, including by the asbestos that was widely used in construction until the 1960s. As a result more stringent laws on the storage and disposal of toxic waste were introduced after the early 1970s.

- *Suburban sprawl.* By the 1960s increasing concern at what looked like unconstrained urban sprawl led many states to legislate to protect areas of natural beauty and importance – for example, the California shoreline – and in some cases to restrict sprawl. However, while some states, such as Oregon and Hawaii, became leaders in the land use planning area, others, such as Arizona and Texas, did little to check development. Apart from federal land, which is extensive in the West and in Alaska and for the most part is well protected, the federal government has played no role in this area. By 2010, this issue had become more salient, as rapidly rising energy costs led many to question the viability of ever-expanding cities and low-density single-housing developments.

- *Offshore and environmentally sensitive onshore oil exploitation and spillage.* In the wake of a serious oil spillage from a well-off Santa Barbara in 1969, Congress banned offshore oil leases except in the western Gulf of Mexico and Alaska. In addition, drilling has been banned in sensitive areas such as the Arctic National Wildlife Refuge adjacent to the Alaskan North Slope oil wells. By 2008, easing restrictions on offshore drilling had become a major election issue, with John McCain and the Republicans arguing for a relaxation of the policy and Barack Obama and the Democrats supporting the status quo. Following the Deepwater Horizon disaster in April 2010 when a British Petroleum (BP) rig in the Gulf of Mexico blew out causing 11 deaths and widespread pollution, President Obama announced no more new drilling in the Gulf until 2017. However in his 2012 State of the Union address he announced that, in order to reduce dependency on foreign oil, 75 per cent of potential offshore sites would be open to drilling.

- *Fracking (hydraulic fracturing of rock to produce oil and gas).* The US has pioneered this method of extraction and by 2016 fracking provided one half of US oil and two thirds of natural gas production. It has not been without controversy, with local, state and organized group opposition focused on claims of pollution and higher instances of earthquakes. In Oklahoma for example, the frequency of 3.0 plus magnitude quakes increased to more than 300 every year after 2010 compared with just 21 per year in the preceding decades. In spite of some successes, however, the oil and gas industry has prevailed as the production figures testify.

- *Carbon and other emissions from vehicles and industrial processes.* During the 1960s, California was the first state to enact emissions controls to combat urban smog; since then a vast array of measures have been enacted both at the state and the federal levels. Starting in 1970 Congress enacted a series of Clean Air Acts that required vehicle manufacturers and power and other industries to meet national air standard targets for the reduction of carbon monoxide, nitrogen oxide, sulphur dioxide, particulate and lead emissions. In 2009 the Environmental Protection Agency (EPA) classified carbon dioxide as a 'public danger' and has interpreted existing laws in ways that require much more stringent emissions controls on carbon dioxide. Generally, these measures have been successful at reducing emissions, although the United States remains the largest source of 'greenhouse gases' in the world. As such it has been subject to considerable international pressure to agree to international standards of carbon reduction. However, to a greater or lesser extent these have been resisted by successive administrations (see Briefing).

- *Wildlife protection.* In 1973 Congress passed the Endangered Species Act, which places the protection of rare and endangered animals above economic considerations. This law has been targeted by the political right as inappropriate when, for example, thousands of logging jobs in the Pacific Northwest were threatened by measures to protect the spotted owl.

- *Genetically modified (GM) foods.* By the 1990s scientists had developed means to genetically modify certain foods, such as cereals, to make them resistant to disease. By 1994 the first GM foods were released in the US market. By 2011 the vast majority of some basic crops were genetically engineered (figure 19.1). Opponents of the use of genetics in this way argue that the process may eventually be harmful both to humans and to the natural ecological balance in the countryside. Although this process has not faced the intensity of opposition in the US that has been witnessed in some other countries, it is a controversial matter. Part of the opposition comes from small farmers who cannot afford the capital investment in such crops and fear that their livelihoods are threatened by corporate interests or 'agribusiness'. Generally crop production in the US is increasingly divided between these small (often organic) farmers and big corporate interests. In the defence of small growers, in 2011 the US Department of Agriculture proposed banning new GM alfalfa crops within five miles of non-GM production, with fines imposed on violators. Whether this will be implemented is in doubt, however, and will likely eventually be decided in the courts.

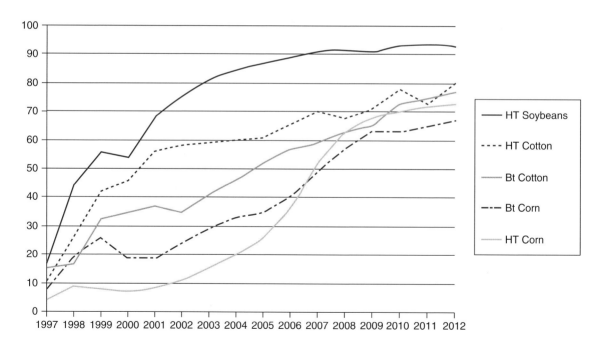

Figure 19.1   Growth of genetically engineered soybean, cotton and corn crop, 1997–2012
Source: US Department of Agriculture at www.ers.usda.gov/data-products/adoption-of-genetically-engineered-crops-in-the-us/recent-trends-in-ge-adoption.aspx.
Note: Data for each crop category include varieties with both HT and Bt (stacked) traits.

What is interesting about this environmental protection agenda is that, with the exception of land-use planning and genetically modified foods, the USA has often been the leader rather then follower among richer industrial nations. This is particularly true with regard to vehicle emissions, with the US legislating for lower emissions many years before European and other richer nations. In one sense this is surprising because, as with many other aspects of policy-making in the US, the policy environment is highly complex and pluralistic involving as it does numerous actors and agencies. As a result, achieving meaningful change is a long and politically hazardous exercise.

CONTROVERSY 16   CLINTON, BUSH AND OBAMA:
THE KYOTO CONVENTION AND
ECONOMIC GROWTH

In 1992 the Bush administration signed the United Nations Framework Convention on Climate Change (UNFCCC), which was subsequently ratified by the Senate. As part of the progress towards this end, the 1997 Kyoto Protocol set targets for the reduction of greenhouse gas emissions, including a 7 per cent reduction (on 1990 levels) to be achieved between 2008 and 2012. Never happy with the precise terms of the agreement, the Clinton administration, while officially a signatory, kept negotiating amendments that would satisfy the 'gas-guzzling' US economy. The fundamental problem for the US was the fact that it was by far the largest producer of greenhouse gases, and the agreed 7 per cent reduction was greater than the 5 per cent required of the more energy-efficient European countries, and substantially higher than the percentage required of the high-growth emerging economies of India and China. Moreover, for Kyoto to be effective at least 55 per cent of the total pollution would have to be subject to the agreement. Without participation by the US there was some doubt that this would be achieved.

In 2001 George W. Bush announced that the US would be withdrawing from the agreement, claiming that the new technologies implied in the 7 per cent reduction would cost the country 4.9 million jobs. In the event, the US unilaterally agreed to a 4.5 per cent reduction by 2020 – a target that most experts agreed was hopelessly inadequate. The US was subsequently condemned by the world community as an 'environmental rogue state'.

Kyoto captures nicely the problems associated with the low energy costs that characterize the US economy. Uniquely among the richer industrial nations, the US does not tax fuel and energy highly, and Americans expect cheap petrol and heating fuel. Some economists argue that the whole economy is geared around low-cost energy, and any rapid adjustment would cause a serious economic downturn. Incumbent presidents have, therefore, no incentive to bring about a rapid reduction in emissions. On the other hand, without US participation, reductions in emissions and a serious effort to reduce global warming will come to little. By 2008, in the context of rapidly increasing energy costs, President Bush had come to accept that global warming was a serious issue, and at the 2008 G8 summit (the regular meeting of the world's leading rich industrial nations) the US agreed that the problem would have to be solved through technological change and the pursuit of alternative energy sources. However, the administration continued to resist signing up to Kyoto-type emissions targets. Although Bush's association with the oil industry is often cited as the main reason for opposing Kyoto, signing the agreement would incur political costs for any president. This was amply demonstrated by President Obama's decision to let Kyoto expire in 2009 by deferring to Congress in this area. For while the rhetoric of the administration is much more sympathetic to the perils of global warming than was that of the Bush government, little in the form of binding action has been taken, with the US position at the 2009 climate change summit in Copenhagen and at the 2012 Rio summit broadly resistant to mandatory international emissions reductions. Part of the problem is, of course, the clash between binding emissions controls and economic efficiency. When, as with diesel emissions, the two are seen to be compatible, laws ensue. Just this happened in 2009 when Congress passed a law requiring sweeping reductions in US diesel emissions by 2020. However, if the trade-offs fall the wrong way, the US resists emissions controls. In late 2015 the US was a signatory to a UN Treaty on climate change (the Paris Treaty) that required countries to act to limit average global warming to 2°C above pre-industrial temperatures and a limit of 1.5°C if possible. However the policies required to implement these targets were not spelt out. As a result most commentators agreed that the accord meant little in terms of actual policy change. Moreover, President-elect Trump declared in 2016 that he intended to pull the US out of the Paris accord.

Policy Actors and Institutions

The Environmental Protection Agency (EPA), created in 1970, is the lead agency for the environment. Although not a cabinet-rank department, it was established to bring together diverse federal agencies into one administrative unit. Its main job is to establish and implement national standards for air, water and soil quality, and to supervise other areas such as the disposal of toxic waste. It also has the major responsibility for enforcing federal law. The EPA is led by an administrator, who, as is discussed below, can be a highly controversial figure. Above all, the job of the EPA is to *coordinate* the policies of numerous other federal, state and local agencies to ensure that they comply with federal law. At the federal level this would include coordinating with the Departments of Energy, Agriculture, the Interior and Transportation. In addition since 1970 the National Environment Policy Act (NEPA) requires all federal departments and agencies to produce Environmental Impact Statements in any area affecting human activity. Other lead actors in this policy area include the presidency, Congress, the courts and organized interests. Let us deal with each of these in turn.

Presidents

Presidents are important because they can help set the national agenda in this as in other policy areas. They can do this both in terms of presidential rhetoric and style and in terms of the substance of policy. For example, two recent Republican presidents, Ronald Reagan and George W. Bush, gained reputations as being hostile to strict environmental protection and friendly towards industrial and development interests. Presidents have two main tools available to them in this policy area. First, they can hold back on new legislation or international treaties (such as the Kyoto Protocol). Second, and in terms of domestic politics more importantly, they can appoint EPA directors and other officials with values similar to their own. As a result regulations under existing legislation can be interpreted in ways that favour looser or tighter environmental controls. Just this happened in the first Reagan administration when EPA director Anne Gorsuch and Interior Secretary James Watt both eventually had to resign because of their anti-environmental bias. With Gorsuch, Congress had subpoenaed many thousands of pages of EPA documents on the disposal of asbestos waste that Gorsuch refused to provide. Presidents can be less blatant than this, however, by judicious manipulation of the Office of Information and Regulatory Affairs (OIRA) within the Office of Management and Budget. OIRA is responsible for monitoring all those federal regulations that guide policy implementation within the cabinet departments and other agencies. By changing the regulatory brief, policy can be altered in subtle but important ways.[1] In 2008, EPA administrator Stephen L. Johnson and the president himself were castigated by Congress for changing the rules on the implementation of Clean Air Acts (see below).

Congress

Apart from its obvious role in passing legislation, Congress can hold hearings and investigate what it considers inappropriate executive policy decisions and implementation. We have already noted the hearings into the EPA and the Department of the Interior during the Reagan years. More recently, EPA administrator Stephen L. Johnson was attacked by a Democratic Congress for his alleged failure to implement EPA regulations. YubaNet. com, an environmentally friendly California website, listed his alleged transgressions in the 2005–8 period:

- 'In 2005, Johnson's EPA issued an air pollution rule on mercury emissions that failed to protect the public. This rule would have allowed concentrated levels of mercury, known as hot spots that would pose a threat to children's health. That Johnson policy was harmful to the American people and was overturned by the federal courts.'
- 'In 2006, Johnson's EPA weakened the toxic chemical release reporting requirements, undermining the public's Right to Know about pollution released in their communities. That Johnson policy was harmful to the American people and is in place now.'
- 'In 2006, Johnson's EPA decided there would be no further testing for the toxic chemical perchlorate in drinking water. Despite scientific evidence of a threat to pregnant women, infants and children, EPA has failed to set a standard for perchlorate in drinking water. This policy is harmful to the American people.'

- 'In 2007, Johnson denied a waiver that would have allowed California to address global warming pollution from automobiles. This decision blocks as many as 18 additional states. Johnson ignored the conclusion by his legal and technical staff that the Clean Air Act requires that the waiver be granted. This decision is not supported by the law. This decision is harmful to the American people.'
- 'In 2008, Johnson's EPA issued a final air pollution standard for ozone or smog that disregarded the recommendations of scientists. Ozone has dangerous health effects and can cause premature death. This policy is harmful to the American people.'
- 'In 2008, Johnson's EPA proposed an air-quality standard for lead that does not reflect the science. Lead is a dangerous toxin, especially to the health of children. This policy is harmful to the American people.'
- 'In 2008, Administrator Johnson's EPA finalized a program that undermines the Agency's ability to establish the risk to humans from toxic chemicals. The public would also no longer have access to scientific information that impacts the health of our families. With this decision, polluting agencies and associated industries were placed in the driver's seat. This policy is harmful to the American people.'

Following these allegations and Johnson's repeated refusal to appear before congressional committees, California Senator Barbara Boxer, chair of the Committee on the Environment and Public Works, called for his resignation in 2008.[2]

Plate 19.1   Floodwaters in the Gentilly neighbourhood of New Orleans. Hurricane Katrina devastated large parts of New Orleans and the Mississippi Gulf Coast, 29 August 2005
Source: Jerry Grayson/Helifilms Australia PTY Ltd/Getty Images.

What is interesting about these events is how they contrast with the efforts of a Republican Congress to hold back the Clinton administration's environmental agenda from 1995 to 2001. During that period the political dynamics were quite different, with Congress using its appropriations power to cut the EPA budget and pass legislation qualifying and restricting existing laws. In response Clinton exercised his veto on attempts to cut the EPA budget by a third. In other words, when a liberal president faces a Republican Congress in this policy area the resulting politics are much more 'open' and 'traditional', involving as they do legislation, appropriations and the veto. When a conservative president faces a liberal Congress, however, as was the case during most of the 1980s and the 2007 to 2009 period, the politics that result are more indirect and less obvious. One consequence of this is that the public is less likely to be alerted to policy changes. Obscure agencies such as OIRA changing regulations may inspire a congressional backlash, but it is different, for example, from attempts by Congress to change the law and remove certain species from the endangered list, as happened during the 1990s.

This dynamic was once again reversed after 2010 when the Republican House of Representatives waged a campaign against EPA Director Lisa Jackson. At the heart of this dispute was the EPA's interpretation of the Clean Air Acts, which required much more stringent carbon dioxide emission controls from industry over a 15-year period. Claiming that this interpretation of the law was 'killing jobs and growth', the House Energy and Commerce Committee's Subcommittee on Energy and Power has held hearings to investigate the EPA, and several bills have been introduced designed to curb the agency's powers. As of 2013, however, the courts have validated the EPA's stance.

A final point about Congress is, of course, that as we saw in chapter 8, members do have an incentive to serve their constituents by bringing home the 'pork' in the form of public works and employment opportunities. Often these conflict with environmental concerns in such areas as power stations, dams, transportation links and the like. Even liberal Democrats are exposed to these pressures, so it would be wrong to leave the impression that all congressional Democrats have impeccable green credentials and Republicans have none. As so often in American politics, much depends on the values of individual politicians and on the economic and political context.

The courts

Almost by definition, given the disputes over the precise meaning of federal regulations, the courts are active in environmental policy, so it is common for interested parties to challenge administrative and congressional rulings in the area. For example, in April 2007 the Supreme Court upheld an EPA ruling dating from the Clinton years that required older coal-fired power stations to meet new emissions controls. This case was brought by an environmental group, Environmental Defense, against a power company, Duke Energy Corp. A more contentious ruling was made in the same month when the Supreme Court, in a 5 to 4 decision, established that the EPA was required to interpret the Clean Air Act in ways that applied to carbon dioxide and other greenhouse gases from automobile emissions. This was a particularly important decision because the EPA, the automobile industry and a number of 'conservative' states (including Alaska, Texas and Utah) were aligned on one side but 12 liberal states (including California, Massachusetts and New York) were aligned on the other side. Interestingly, Michigan, a major car-producing state, argued against extending the law to car emissions. What in effect this decision meant was that California's strict emission controls on cars, which were in part designed to combat global warming, would have to be extended to all other states.

Given the changing political complexion of the Supreme Court, there is, of course, no guarantee that it will favour one side or another. Also in 2007, the Court ruled that the federal Clean Water Act took precedence over the Endangered Species Act when builders draw up development plans. The case involved an EPA decision to hand over to Arizona the authority to approve water-treatment regulations for new developments. Environmental groups argued that this would lead to water standards that threatened endangered species. The Court effectively argued that as long as water quality reached acceptable standards this took precedence over the interests of wildlife. The decision was widely interpreted as a victory for developers and builders. Justice Samuel Alito wrote the opinion of the Court in an ideologically split 5 to 4 decision.

A further conservative decision was taken in *Michigan* v. *EPA* (2015) when in a 5 to 4 ruling the conservative majority on the Court ruled that the EPA's strict limits on mercury pollution from coal and gas power stations would be too costly to implement. By focusing on the costs the Court did however leave open the possibility of compliance procedures that the EPA may be able to implement at a lower cost.

Organized interests

Few areas of public policy are so infused with group activity as is the general area of environmental policy. Almost all economic activity impacts the environment, so almost every industry and economic enterprise is involved. In addition, environmental groups, from the Sierra Club to Greenpeace, are not only numerous but are also well funded and attract supporters whose commitment to environmental protection is often fierce. In addition, the states and localities often act as lobbyists for or against particular laws and, as indicated above, they are frequently litigants in the courts. Whatever the political make-up of Congress, the executive branch and the courts, therefore, group activity will always ensure that environmental issues receive a high level of publicity and political exposure.

Chronology

1849   Department of the Interior created

1854   Henry David Thoreau publishes *Walden; or, A Life in the Woods*

1890   First US national parks created in California

1916   National Parks Service created

1932–7 Heavy rain and over-farming create dust bowl in the plains, causing widespread distress

1934   Fish and Wildlife Conservation Act

1944   Flood Control Act provides federal funds for flood control

1956   Fish and Wildlife Act

1964   Wilderness Act

1969   National Environmental Policy Act (NEPA) requires all federal agencies to produce Environmental Impact Assessments

1970   Environmental Protection Agency (EPA) created to coordinate federal policy across agencies and departments

1970   Clean Air Act

1972   Congress enacts a series of laws, including the Marine Mammal Protection Act, Noise Control Act, Clean Water Act and Coastal Zone Management Act

1972   Love Canal toxic waste leak in New York State

1975   Energy Policy and Conservation Act

1976   Resource Conservation and Recovery Act

1977   Surface Mining Control and Reclamation Act; Soil and Water Resources Conservation Act

1979   Three Mile Island nuclear accident, the worst in US history

1980   Mount Helen volcanic eruption devastates a vast area of Washington state

1987   Ocean Dumping Act

1989   Exxon Valdez tanker oil spill in Alaska

1990   National Environment Education Act

1990   Clean Air Act initiates new standards for emissions

1992   Earth Summit, held in Rio de Janeiro under the auspices of the UN, establishes the principle of sustainable development – economic and industrial development has to be balanced with environmental factors

1997   Kyoto Protocol on Climate Change negotiated in Japan, setting targets for reductions in greenhouse gases

2001   US rejects ratification of the Kyoto Protocol

2004   Tsunami in the Indian Ocean kills up to 250,000 people

2005   Hurricane Katrina devastates Mississippi and New Orleans, killing nearly 2,000 people

2006   Former Vice President Al Gore releases *An Inconvenient Truth*, on the dangers of global warming

2008   Bush administration acknowledges the need to reduce greenhouse gases, but refuses to agree to international reduction targets

2010   BP's Deepwater Horizon oil spill in the Gulf sparks universal outrage and encourages the Obama administration to take legal action against BP.

2015   Paris Conference. Along with 194 other countries President Obama agrees to targets on limitation of rise in global temperatures but implementation to achieve targets is vague.

2016   President-elect Trump says he will withdraw the US from the Paris agreement.

Plate 19.2   Fire-boat response crews battle the blazing remnants of the off-shore oil rig Deepwater Horizon in the Gulf of Mexico on 21 April 2010 near New Orleans, Louisiana. An estimated 1,000 barrels of oil a day leaked into the Gulf. Multiple Coast Guard helicopters, planes and cutters responded to rescue the Deepwater Horizon's 126-person crew
Source: US Coast Guard/Getty Images.

Political Parties and the Environment

Just as the US is considered exceptional because of the absence of a socialist party in government or the national legislature, so it is also exceptional in not producing a green party of any significance. For although in 2000 consumer activist Ralph Nader ran on the Green Party ticket and won 2.7 per cent of the vote, many of these ballots were cast for Nader rather than the Green Party as such. In 2004, when Nader ran separately from the Green candidate David Cobb, the two together managed less than 1 per cent of the vote. Undoubtedly one of the main reasons for this failure is the ability of the two main political parties to absorb interests and values across a wide ideological and issue spectrum. So, most of those sympathetic to environmental questions are accommodated within the Democratic Party. Indeed the most effective advocate of strong measures to counter global warming over recent years has been ex-senator and vice president, Al Gore, a man who has devoted his whole career to the Democratic Party.

As earlier established, since 2000 the party divide in this issue area has widened as the Republicans became increasingly identified with business interests and the Democratic

Party with environmental interests. However, it would be misleading to characterize the two parties as being consistently aligned on either side of the ideological divide. Many in the Democratic Party remain sympathetic to developers and business interests. In some cases, the strength of the 'electoral connection' (see chapter 8) leaves them little choice. Similarly, some Republicans are more sensitive to environmental considerations than others. In 2008, for example, Republican presidential candidate John McCain was markedly more supportive of measures to combat global warming than was the incumbent president George W. Bush. In 2012, Republican candidate Mitt Romney 'flip flopped' on the issue, shifting from moderate support for environmental protection to a more mainstream and sceptical Republican position. Meanwhile Obama has been broadly supportive of a more interventionist environmental stance, although until the 2015 Paris Accord he failed to endorse far-reaching international agreements on climate change.

In 2016 Republican candidate Donald Trump made his position on climate change very clear. Among other things Trump promised to repeal Obama's measures to reduce emissions, cancel the Paris climate agreement and revitalize the coal industry. He is also on record as claiming that climate change is a 'hoax'.

Conclusions: The Future of Environmental Politics

By the early years of the twenty-first century environmental questions had been elevated right to the top of the political agenda. With global warming established as a real threat, the continued use of carbon-based fuel was being questioned by important political actors in the United States. For Americans this and other environmental issues pose a particularly difficult political dilemma, because the American economy has been built on cheap, carbon-based fuel. In addition, for most of their history Americans have assumed that the unlimited human exploitation of the environment is the natural route to economic success. While over the past several decades this philosophy has been challenged by both environmental activists and many mainstream politicians, the needs of the economy and job creation still continue to take precedence over environmental protection. This was amply demonstrated by America's refusal to sign up to the Kyoto Protocol, and by the continuing insistence by those on the political right that global warming and the shortage of oil and gas is greatly exaggerated.

More than in any other issue area, environmental questions represent a fundamental challenge to America's long love affair with cheap fuel and unbridled economic development. Serious constraints on either in the name of environmental protection are bound to inspire conflict.

Summary

Since the 1970s environmental issues, including nuclear safety, disposal of toxic waste, land-use planning, emissions controls, protection of wildlife, oil exploration and GM foods, have gradually been elevated to the top of the political agenda. However, as with other policy areas in the US, the process whereby policy is made is highly complex and pluralistic, involving as it does Congress, the presidency, the courts, state and local governments and organized interests. Since the 1980s clear political battle lines have been drawn between the more environmentally conscious Democrats and most Republicans, who tend to favour business and development interests over the environment. However, the complex trade-offs between economic growth and job creation, on the one hand, and environmental protection on the other, are such that few politicians of whatever party can ignore constituency needs for both jobs and a cleaner and safer environment. As a result, this issue is likely to remain at the top of the agenda for many years to come.

Questions for Discussion

1   Assess the policies of the Obama administration in the general area of environmental protection.
2   Why are Republicans so hostile to greater controls on carbon emissions? How have inter-party differences changed over the past 20 years?
3   What is the role of Congress and the president in environmental policy? Which branch is most influential in making policy?

Glossary

Clean Air Acts   The series of Acts, the first dating from 1970, that set targets or emissions

Environmental Protection Agency   The main agency for enforcing environmental/ protection established in 1970

genetically modified or engineered (GM or GE) foods   Foods cultured to resist disease and increase yields

global warming   The effects on the climate of emissions from vehicles and industrial processes

greenhouse gases   The mix of carbon-based gases that lead to global warming

Kyoto Protocol (Convention)   The 1997 international convention setting targets for reducing emissions that the USA refused to ratify

Paris Climate Conference 2015   195 countries agree on targets to reduce global warming

Public Right to Know   The open government laws that establish the right to public information

sustainable development   The idea adapted by the 1992 Earth Summit that economic development should be balanced by environmental considerations

Three Mile Island   The site of the worst nuclear accident in US history, which effectively stopped new nuclear power developments

Notes

1   For a review, see David McKay, *Domestic Policy and Ideology* (Cambridge: Cambridge University Press, 1989), chapter 7.

2   YubaNet: http://yubanet.com/usa/Senator-Barbara-Boxer-Calls-for-Resignation-of-EPAAdministrator-Johnson.php.

Further Reading

In *This Changes Everything: Capitalism v The Climate* (New York: Penguin, 2015), Naomi Klein argues that the economic system needs radical changes if climate change is to be addressed. Anthony Giddens, *The Politics of Climate Change*, 2nd edn (Oxford: Polity Press, 2011) provides an excellent perspective on the international politics of the subject. David W. Orr, *The Last Refuge: Patriotism, Politics, and the Environment in an Age of Terror* (Washington, DC: Island Press, 2005), provides a critique of the Bush administration's policies in this area. Rick Adair (ed.), *Critical Perspectives on Politics and the Environment*, Scientific American Critical Anthologies on Environment and Climate (New York: Rosen Press, 2006), brings together articles from the *Scientific American* on the subject. For a dispassionate account of policy-making, see Christopher McGrory Klyza and David Sousa, *American Environmental Policy, 1990–2006: Beyond Gridlock* (Boston: MIT Press, 2008). A polemic against US policy is provided by John Wills, *US Environmental History: Inviting Doomsday* (Edinburgh: Edinburgh University Press, 2012).

CHAPTER 20
THE AMERICAN WORLD ROLE

We will not hesitate to act alone, if necessary to exercise our right of self-defense by acting preemptively … our best defense is a good offence.… We must adapt the concept of imminent threat to the capabilities and objectives of today's adversaries.… To forestall or prevent hostile acts by our adversaries, the United States will, if necessary, act preemptively.

– GEORGE W. BUSH, SEPTEMBER 2002

America is back, anyone who tells you otherwise, anyone who tells you that America is in decline or that our influence has waned, doesn't know what they're talking about. That's not the message we get from leaders around the world, all of whom are eager to work with us; where opinions of America are higher than they've been in years. Yes, the world

American Politics and Society, Ninth Edition. David McKay.
© 2018 John Wiley & Sons Ltd. Published 2018 by John Wiley & Sons Ltd.

is changing; no, we can't control every event. But America remains the one indispensable nation in world affairs – and as long as I'm president, I intend to keep it that way.
                                                                    – BARACK OBAMA, 2012

Over the past 80 years the United States has been transformed from one of six or seven world powers with a standing army of under 200,000 and few foreign alliances or military bases into a country with a military machine of 1.5 million men and women under arms (nearly a quarter of a million of whom are stationed overseas), alliances with nearly 50 countries, and unrivalled military and diplomatic status and capacity. From being isolationist and contemptuous of the 'corruption' and imperialism of the old European powers, the United States is itself, in spite of recent uncertainties, now in a position to exploit and occupy other countries and, unlike the pre-war powers, literally to determine the fate of all humankind.

The country's political processes and institutions have not always handled these new responsibilities well. Indeed, one school of thought argues that a country infused with a past characterized by a combination of isolationism and idealism is ill suited to playing the role of world police officer. Certainly, there have been many foreign and military policy mistakes in the post-war era, including the Vietnam War, which caused serious domestic conflict and terrible suffering and instability throughout Indochina, and the 2003 invasion of Iraq, which led to the US becoming embroiled in a prolonged and inconclusive policing action. This chapter does not, however, concentrate on normative questions of fortune and folly in American foreign policy. Instead, our discussion focuses on the policy-making process and on the constraints imposed on foreign policy by institutional arrangements and public opinion.

Plate 20.1   US drone carrying a hellfire missile over the Persian Gulf on its way to operations over Syria, January 2016
Source: John Moore/Getty, www.gettyimages.co.uk/license/503832796.

The Institutional Context

As with social and economic affairs, it is somewhat misleading to refer to an American foreign *policy*, for there are at least three distinct types of foreign and defence policies. There is, first, strategic foreign policy, or the general stance of the United States in relation to other countries over time. Scholars have been quick to identify two competing themes in the post-war period – realist and idealist. Realism is, simply, the pursuit of 'national self-interest', and is associated with international power politics and the implementation of policies that have clear military, diplomatic or economic benefits.[1] Idealism, in contrast, injects a moral or normative element into policy, as such presidential rhetoric as 'making the world safe for democracy' or achieving 'peace with honour' in Vietnam implies. We return to these two characterizations of strategic policy later. Although strategic policy is influenced by the broader society and polity, its main institutional context comprises the presidency, the National Security Council (NSC) and the State Department.

Second, crisis management is a crucial part of foreign policy. Since the Second World War, the Berlin airlift, the Cuban missile crisis, numerous military actions in Indochina, the Iranian hostage crisis, American reactions to military activity in the Middle East, including the first Gulf War, intervention in Bosnia and Kosovo, and the terror attacks of 9/11 have all involved the United States in quick crisis-management decisions. Generally, the presidency and NSC are the institutional foci of these decisions, although the longer a crisis drags on, the more likely are Congress and the public to become involved. Just this happened with the year-long Iranian hostage crisis in 1980–1.

Third, logistical or structural defence policy involves the deployment of billions of dollars' worth of material and over a quarter of a million personnel around the globe. As we established in earlier chapters, this process entails voters, organized interests (defence contractors), state and local governments and congressional committees, as well as the more obvious institutions of the Department of Defense and the presidency. While this policy system is much more open and accessible than strategic and crisis-management policy, it is almost certainly less fragmented and pluralistic than the processes associated with social or economic policy. Oligopolistic defence industries are often protected by government contracts,[2] and the defence budget has a powerful base of support in Congress.

These three contrasting institutional settings for foreign and defence policy do impinge on one another. Logistics and weapons systems can influence strategic thinking (the Cruise missile) and crisis management (the Iranian hostage crisis, the bombing of Libya, the Gulf War), while strategic considerations are obviously important determinants of logistical policy. Similarly, crisis management is profoundly affected by the strategic context. During the Cuban missile crisis, for example, President Kennedy referred constantly to the infringement of an American sphere of influence (the western hemisphere), which was a long-established part of American foreign policy.

How has decision-making in each of these policy areas changed over time? Perhaps obviously, crisis management has always primarily been the prerogative of the president and his closest aides in the NSC. Quick response requires tightly knit decision-making structures, and, as commander-in-chief, the president has the constitutional as well as political position to assume the leadership of such structures. Not that this means that the president and his aides are completely insulated from the outside world during a crisis and make their choices according to strictly rational criteria. As Graham Allison has shown in his brilliant study of the Cuban missile crisis, at least three competing models of decision-making can be used to explain the events of the crisis, two of which put great premium on outside information and political and bureau-cratic procedures and pressures.[3] But crisis management is, compared with other policy-making processes in American government, relatively free from political and societal pressures.

The main development in strategic foreign policy-making in the post-war period has been the gradual centralization of power in the president and NSC, at the cost of State Department influence. This showed itself most graphically in the eclipse of some recent Secretaries of State in the shadow of National Security Advisors – most notably Henry Kissinger under Nixon (although he eventually became Secretary of State) and Zbigniew Brzezinski under Carter. More recently, in George W. Bush's first term, Secretary of State Colin Powell often took a back seat in relation to National Security Advisor Condoleezza Rice and, more often, to Defense Secretary Donald Rumsfeld and Vice President Dick Cheney. Presidents have increasingly eschewed State Departments and their secretaries because they can represent independent sources of authority and control over particular issues and areas. Certain countries or policy options are championed within the department, and it is simply not convenient for presi-dents to have to join battle with the professional bureaucrats when foreign policy is formu-lated. White House–departmental antagonism occurs in other areas, of course, but, within foreign policy, presidents do at least have the option of, if not ignoring the State Department, at least bypassing it. For the State Department effectively has no domestic constituency, and its officials are unusually neutral and apolitical, versed as they are in the arts of diplomacy and moderation. So while presidents may find it almost impossible to disregard the Departments of Defense, Agriculture or Commerce, they can almost do this in the case of the State Depart-ment. Foreign policy is also more insulated from the other 'traditional' centres of power in American government. House and, particularly, Senate foreign relations committees are important forums for discussion and criticism, but their function is qualitatively different from (say) those of the armed services and agriculture committees, with their entrenched relationships with big-spending bureaux and powerful corporate clients.

In other words, foreign policy decision-making is different. Within the White House the NSC is uniquely important and, in theory at least, consistency and coherence are almost certainly more achievable in foreign affairs than in many domestic areas. It may be, of course, that clarity and coherence can lead to greater errors of judgement and strategy, and that more pluralistic arrangements would lead to greater moderation. But it should be noted that, in a *cross-national* context, American presidents are not particularly free from institutional and political constraints in foreign policy-making. Public and congres-sional opinion has been exerted on presidents with increasing intensity since the events of Vietnam and Watergate. Earlier chapters have catalogued some of these constraints, including the 1973 War Powers Act. President Reagan's 1983 remark, when he heard of British Prime Minister Margaret Thatcher's carefully disguised visit to the Falklands, that he 'couldn't even go to church in secret', reveals a great deal. Presidents and their policy-makers are constantly exposed to public scrutiny. They may be able to secrete themselves away in the NSC and plan general strategy. They may also be relatively free from direct and imme-diate congressional or bureaucratic pressure. But they still have to operate in the context of the American political system, with all that this implies in terms of openness and accessibility. So, individual ethnic groups, such as Americans of Cuban or Jewish origin, constantly monitor the administration's policy towards Cuba or Israel. Right-wing congressional caucuses campaign strongly in favour of a hard line towards Cuba. Between the Vietnam War and 9/11, the involvement of American troops in counter-insurgency wars abroad became especially difficult because of the ever-present potential for serious domestic political opposition. This was graphically illustrated in the case of the American-led North Atlantic Treaty Organization (NATO) bombing of Kosovo in 1999. Using air power alone to solve the problem was directly a result of the domestic political costs of the alternative – American casualties resulting from the use of ground troops. In addition, the openness of the American system can lead to the conflation of domestic and foreign policy in ways that are unusual in some other countries. Presidents have been accused of using foreign interventions to divert attention from their domestic troubles. Such allegations were levelled at President Reagan following the US invasion of Grenada in 1983; at Bill Clinton following his decision to attack terrorist installations in Sudan and Afghanistan in 1998; and at George W. Bush in his conduct of the Iraq War both before and after the 2004 presidential election. Most recently, Barack Obama's flagging public popularity received a sudden (if temporary) boost with the capture and slaying of Osama Bin Laden in 2011.

The openness of the official system has led to the evolution of an 'unofficial' foreign policy system on at least two occasions. Such was the case during 1969–73, when illegal acts were committed in Southeast Asia. More dramatic were the events of the Iran–Contra affair, which involved the creation of alternative foreign policy machinery in the White House under the guidance of NSC Advisor John Poindexter, Central Intelligence Agency (CIA) chief William Casey and Colonel Oliver North. By agreeing to secure the release of American hostages in the Lebanon by selling arms to the Iranians, the proceeds from which would go to help the Contras fighting for the overthrow of the Sandinista regime in Nicaragua, these officials were acting contrary to both the spirit and the letter of the law. President Reagan and Secretary of State George Schultz either did not know of these events or were only vaguely aware of them, thus demonstrating the extent to which the president had lost control of this particular policy system during his second term. But the culprits in the Iran–Contra affair were discovered, thus perhaps demonstrating how much more public and press opinion can do to expose the errors of foreign policy compared with the situation in (say) Britain and France.

It was, of course the media (notably the *60 Minutes* CBS news magazine programme) that first exposed the abuse of Iraqi prisoners by Americans at the Abu Ghraib prison in Iraq. This and other events associated with the Iraq and Afghan wars, although often very serious, were, however, conducted in an atmosphere where public support for official action was relatively high.

American Foreign Policy in the Post-9/11 World

Until recently, the most striking feature of American foreign policy was the overwhelming influence of the realist, as opposed to idealist, school. In the context of the Cold War, American policy was couched in terms of self-interest; indeed, in terms of national survival. The ideological struggle between East and West centred on territory (in Europe and in the Third World) and on economic interest (was capitalism or communism to be the model for world development?). During the early and mid-1980s, the Reagan administrations elevated this competitive struggle to the top of the policy agenda. Increased defence spending and military action in the Middle East, Grenada, Libya and Central America were all justified in terms of the national interest. By the late 1980s, signs that this particular perspective on international relations was becoming obsolete were clearly evident, and by 1991 conditions had changed to the point where presidents were making reference to what was called 'the New World Order'.

The crucial change was, of course, the demise of the Soviet Union, and more generally of communism as a viable alternative to capitalism. Even in China, the last major redoubt of political communism, a rejection of the centralized resource allocation of economic communism had occurred. Communism's collapse did not transform the realist focus of American foreign policy. The Gulf War, for example, was fought at least in part to protect the West's oil supplies. But it did greatly complicate the business of identifying where, exactly, America's national interest lay. When there was an identifiable enemy whose economic and political system was so obviously alien to the American one, justifying high defence spending and the deployment of US troops abroad was relatively easy. Today, such justification is harder. Instead of appealing only to self-interest, the New World Order sometimes appeals to humanitarian motives. In Somalia, Bosnia and, most dramatically, in Kosovo, no American interests were directly threatened, yet American troops, aircraft and ships were deployed under the auspices of a NATO- or UN-sponsored humanitarian mission.

Idealism in foreign policy and the idea of a world community of nations were rudely shattered by the events of 9/11. At once, the US adopted an unusual hybrid of realist and idealist foreign policy designed to make both the 'homeland' and American interests abroad safe from terrorist attacks. Part and parcel of the new philosophy was pre-emptive attacks on allegedly rogue states such as Afghanistan and Iraq, as well as a substantially increased effort devoted to weeding out terrorist activity at home and abroad (see chapter 13). Given that the action in Iraq went ahead in the absence of a UN mandate for invasion (although the US did enjoy the support of the UK and some other countries) this policy represented something quite new in the history of foreign relations. Never in the modern era had the US taken pre-emptive action without the support of a broad alliance of countries usually acting under NATO or the UN. Even the Korean War was officially a UN-sanctioned action, and Vietnam was, arguably, a defensive war fought at the behest of the South Vietnamese government. For the most part these actions were justified not only in terms of US national interest but also as part of the broader objective of spreading democracy and political freedom to other countries and in particular Middle Eastern autocracies. The idea that under the right conditions any country could adopt democracy was part of the neoconservative philosophy that was so influential during the first Bush administration (see Briefing).

The wide perception outside the US that that unilateral action was both immoral and illegal led to a dramatic reduction in respect for America that extended across a wide range of countries. America's reputation in poorer countries, and especially in the Middle East, was particularly badly damaged – although it could be argued that the US was always poorly thought of in these parts of the world. As worrying was the low esteem in which the US was held in the European Union (EU), including the expanding 27-member EU.

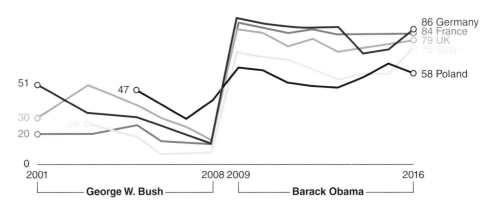

Confidence in the US president to do the right thing regarding world affairs

Figure 20.1 European views on reputation of US presidents in foreign affairs
Source: Pew Research Center, www.pewglobal.org/2016/06/29/as-obama-years-draw-to-close-president-and-u-s-seen-favorably-in-europe-and-asia/.

Aware of these problems, Barack Obama attempted to restore America's reputation abroad by pursuing a more multilateral foreign policy through consultation with allies and the UN. In the main, this policy was successful. As can be seen from figure 20.1, America's reputation in Europe did recover after 2009, having fallen to historic lows during the Bush administration. As noted, the new unilateralism of the Bush administration had a further unique characteristic: the realist objective of securing America from terrorism was conflated with the idealist objective of imposing 'democracy' and 'freedom' on the invaded states. The dominant neo-conservative thinking in the Department of Defense (although not in the State Department) argued that any society could, with enough coercion, education and aid, become a functioning democracy. Although the progress towards such an ideal in Afghanistan and Iraq was halting, to say the least, the belief that democracy was exportable to almost every part of the world remained the dominant view of the administration (see Briefing).

Interestingly, the CIA and other intelligence sources were less convinced – a fact that contributed towards the resignation of CIA director George Tenet and his deputy in 2004. On the other hand, it was the CIA that produced highly misleading intelligence on Iraq's supposed weapons of mass destruction – intelligence that helped precipitate the invasion of 2003. As is well known the consequences of this invasion were tragic, leading among other things to tens of thousands of civilian casualties and continuing instability. By 2016 it was clear that the US strategy in Iraq had totally failed – the country continued to be plagued by insurrectionist movements and had become host to a number of terrorist organizations including the so-called Islamic State (ISIS).

As can be seen from figure 20.2, defence expenditure has risen and fallen in line with changes in world events. When, in the late 1980s and the early 1990s, communism collapsed in eastern Europe, a steep rise in public regard for the Soviet Union (or Russia) and a sharp decline in the perceived need for defence spending occurred. Defence spending did indeed decrease following these events: expressed as a percentage of gross domestic product (GDP),

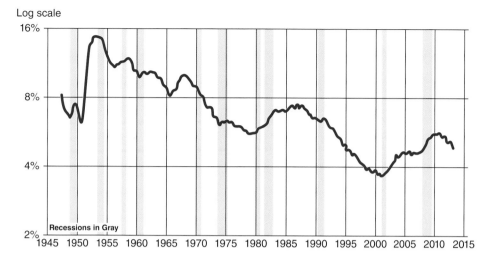

Log scale

Figure 20.2   US defence spending as a percentage of GDP, 1945–2014
Source: Advisor Perspectives, www.advisorperspectives.com/dshort/commentaries/Sequestration-
National-Defense-130211.php, Sequestration and National Defense: Some Historical Background by
Doug Short, 2 November 2013.

from well over 6 per cent in the mid-1980s to an estimated 3.5 per cent in 1999. However, the
fall was temporary as the demands of the post-9/11 period kicked in. By 2012 defence spending stood at 4.8 per cent – still a relatively low figure by historical standards.

In 2012 the Obama administration announced a major defence review to be implemented over the ensuing decade. Entitled *Sustaining US Global Leadership: Priorities for
21st Century Defense*, the review proposed major reductions in active duty forces and a
switch from a 'two ground war' to a 'one ground war' strategy. In future the US should be
prepared to conduct one major war and two minor wars, rather than two major wars as in
the past. In addition there would be a shift of strategic resources from Europe to the Pacific
and from conventional forces to anti-terrorist special forces. Republican opponents considered the cuts unacceptable. Indeed Mitt Romney proposed an alternative strategy involving
a substantial increase in the size of the defence budget – thus demonstrating that the ideological divide between the parties in 2012 extended to foreign affairs. With Obama's victory,
however, the new strategy began to be adopted in 2013.

Even with these cuts, the United States easily remained the world's most powerful military force (figure 20.3). In terms of rapid deployment, it has no peer. Only American forces
can be moved rapidly around the world to meet a crisis or emergency. No other country has
this capacity. This fact alone puts pressure on American politicians to play the role of global
police and to take on the role of international regulator of relations between countries – a
role that became highly controversial in the wake of the actions taken after 9/11.

In spite of recent setbacks to US foreign policy, the US will almost certainly continue
to broker peace, whether it is in Israel, Iraq, Afghanistan, Syria, the Korean peninsula or
Sudan. The danger comes when the costs of intervention, whether measured in terms of
expenditure or of American lives, become too great for public opinion to tolerate. When

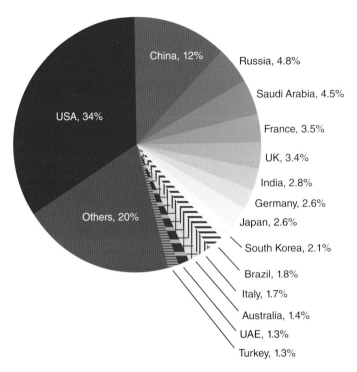

Figure 20.3   World shares of world military expenditure, 2014
Source: Perlo-Freeman, S. et al., 'Trends in world military expenditure, 2014', SIPRI Fact Sheet, April 2015, SIPRI, https://www.sipri.org/publications/2015/sipri-fact-sheets/trends-world-military-expenditure-2014.

this happens, there is always the possibility that America will revert to the isolationist stance typical of the pre-1941 period. So far, however, interventionism has prevailed, even if it has been of the unilateralist rather then multilateralist variety. Supporters of genuine isolationism in both the Democratic Party (usually on foreign economic policy issues) and the Republican Party (a diminishing group) certainly exist, but no president of any party has espoused the cause. Even in the post-2006 Democratic Congress none of the new congressional leaders supported an isolationist position. Instead, by 2008 Speaker Nancy Pelosi and Senate Majority Leader Harry Byrd, along with Democratic candidate Barack Obama, favoured an orderly withdrawal from Iraq but a continuing engagement with other states and international institutions in order to solve world problems. In the event this was precisely the policy pursued by the Obama administration, and this position was more rather than less multilateral than that of the outgoing Bush administration. However during the 2016 election campaign Donald Trump condemned this policy as leaving a political vacuum in Iraq that has bred extremism and encouraged the rise of ISIS.

Indeed, unlike the Cold War period achieving international consensus on how to fight terrorism and insurrection in countries like Syria and Iraq has proved elusive. Massive intervention on the 2001–3 scale has become all but politically impossible, so Obama and Secretary of State Kerry relied on persuasion, admonitions and, more rarely, threats to support US policy objectives. Rarely were these backed up by military action and where they were – as in the case of air power in Syria – they have had but limited results. And while this approach has not undermined foreign perceptions of the US role (see figure 20.3), it did lead many Americans to believe that the Obama administration was weak and irresolute – a sentiment that was ruthlessly exploited by Donald Trump during the 2016 election campaign.

Briefing   The Rise and Fall of Neoconservatism

By the late 1990s a group of right-wing intellectuals, prominent among whom were Irving Kristol, Robert Kagan and Paul Wolfowitz, had concluded that the United States could use its massive power to extend a 'benevolent hegemony' over the world by intervening to snuff out terrorism, weapons of mass destruction and other threats to US interests. The idealist (even naive) assumption in this strategy was that the US would face limited resistance because 'It is precisely because American foreign policy is infused with an unusually high degree of morality that other nations find they have less to fear from its otherwise daunting power'.[4] Such thinking also assumed that all countries would not only benefit from democracy and freedom, but would welcome it once the barriers to its creation (usually dictators) were removed. This philosophy greatly affected foreign policy in the Bush administration through the influence of such figures as Deputy Secretary of Defense Paul Wolfowitz, Vice President Richard Cheney and Chief of Staff to Cheney, Lewis 'Scooter' Libby (who was also assistant to the president), and led directly to the invasion of Iraq. Events proved the neoconservatives wrong. Americans were not greeted as saviours by the Iraqi people but as hostile occupiers. Part of the misconception was an underestimation of the threat of radical Islam, and of the resources needed to build not only democracy but also the infrastructure in a country riven with sectarian conflict and greatly weakened by decades of underinvestment. Critics claim that, rather than reducing the threat to the US, the invasion of Iraq actually increased it by radicalizing not only many of Iraq's population but people throughout the Muslim world including Syria. By 2007 all of the main proponents of neoconservatism except Vice President Cheney had passed from political influence, and during the second Bush term the administration adopted a more accommodating stance towards foreign dictatorships. Barack Obama's foreign policy team – Hillary Clinton as Secretary of State, Robert Gates continuing as Defense Secretary and ex-Marine Commander Jim Jones as National Security Advisor – looked like a traditional realist line-up that pursued a cautious, multilateralist approach in foreign affairs. If anything, this was reinforced by Gates and Jones's successors in 2011 and 2010, Leon Panetta and Tom Donilon, and Clinton's successor in 2012, John Kerry. The election of Donald Trump in 2016 led to a major shift in this policy, but not in the direction of neoconservatism. Instead Trump and his team of foreign policy hardliners proposed a strengthening of American resolve against China, Iran, Syria and Russia based more on realism and deterrence than on any intention to transform the domestic situations in foreign states.

Conclusions: Bound to Lead or Bound to Fail?

It should be obvious from this discussion that US foreign policy remains essentially informed by realist thinking. Militarily, the US is as privileged is as ever and who would have remotely guessed that the United States would, by 1997, be negotiating with Russia over the eastward expansion of NATO? Where the USA is more circumscribed is in terms of defining its new mission and in building domestic support for an active role abroad. This applies to 'traditional' foreign policy and to foreign *economic* policy. As indicated above, the US now lives in a much more interdependent world. It is in relations with the EU, negotiations in the World Trade Organization (WTO), the North American Free Trade Area (NAFTA) and American contributions to the International Monetary Fund and the

Plate 20.2   President Barack Obama and Vice President Joe Biden, along with members of the national security team, receive an update on the mission against Osama Bin Laden in the Situation Room of the White House, 1 May 2011. Seated, from left, are: Brigadier General Marshall B. 'Brad' Webb, Assistant Commanding General, Joint Special Operations Command; Deputy National Security Advisor Denis McDonough; Secretary of State Hillary Rodham Clinton; and Secretary of Defense Robert Gates. Standing, from left, are: Admiral Mike Mullen, Chairman of the Joint Chiefs of Staff; National Security Advisor Tom Donilon; Chief of Staff Bill Daley; Tony Blinken, National Security Advisor to the Vice President; Audrey Tomason, Director for Counterterrorism; John Brennan, Assistant to the President for Homeland Security and Counterterrorism; and Director of National Intelligence James Clapper
Source: Official White House photo by Pete Souza.
Note: A classified document seen in this photograph has been obscured.

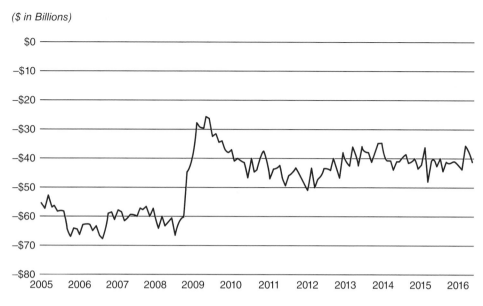

($ in Billions)

Figure 20.4   US trade deficit in $billions, 2005–2016
Source: US Bureau of Economic Analysis at www.bea.gov/newsreleases/international/trade/trade_
glance.htm.

World Bank that some of the more important foreign policy questions are raised. Clearly, these have a much greater input from domestic politics than do most 'traditional' foreign policy areas – especially as the US has had a continuing high trade deficit in recent years (figure 20.4).

This interdependence often makes it difficult to distinguish clearly between different policy systems, and there is no doubt that it makes the business of government more burdensome. Given the external constraints imposed by interdependence and the internal pressures resulting from a fragmented and open political system, it is not surprising that presidents have sought to centralize decision-making in the White House. 9/11 made this imperative even more necessary. As a result, a number of serious policy mistakes were made, including the botched invasion of Iraq, the abuse of Iraqi prisoners, the internment without trial of detainees in Guantánamo Bay, Cuba, and the alienation of most other members of the world community, including many EU countries. And, although Barack Obama helped to restore the status of the US abroad, he inherited a complex and demanding foreign policy agenda including unresolved wars in Iraq and Afghanistan, dangerously fragile relations with Iran and North Korea and a continuing threat of terrorist attacks both at home and abroad. To compound his difficulties, he also faced unprecedented fiscal problems that have forced the US to make difficult choices on defence spending. These difficult problems will require presidential leadership of the highest quality if the US is to resume its traditional role as global defender of freedom and democracy.

Summary

With military and foreign policy obligations across the globe, foreign policy has assumed a prominent position in American politics. While the main actors in the policy process remain the president and the executive branch, Congress, the media and public opinion are also closely involved. Major changes in the direction of US foreign policy have occurred since 9/11, including the adoption of a more unilateral stance. The invasion of Iraq and its subsequent occupation resulted in serious operational problems for US forces and greatly damaged the reputation of the United States abroad. These and other problems relating to interdependence mean that even though the US is the only world power it is increasingly obliged to cooperate with the broader international community when designing and implementing foreign policy.

Questions for Discussion

1   What was the US response to the Syrian insurrection after 2012? What accounts for the nature of this response?
2   What are idealism and realism in foreign policy? Answer with reference to the experience of presidents Clinton, George W. Bush, Obama and Trump.
3   Contrast Republican foreign policy with that of Barack Obama. Answer with reference to the 2008–17 period.

Glossary

benevolent hegemony   The idea that American world dominance can be used for good purposes

communism   The system of beliefs that assumes that the collective ownership of the means of production, control and exchange was the most beneficial for humankind. Communism as an alternative to capitalism has now been largely discredited

crisis management   The process whereby presidents handle international crises such as the Cuban missile crisis or 9/11

idealism   The theory of international relations that assumes countries have benevolent intentions towards one another

SIS   Name given to Islamic State, the international terrorist organization based in the Middle East

isolationism   The assumption, prevalent in the 1930s, that the US could isolate itself from the rest of the world in international relations

logistical/structural defence policy   The detailed content of defence policy involving such things as weapons systems and the movement of resources

National Security Council (NSC)   The White House-based organization responsible for national security

Neoconservatism   A system of beliefs supporting the view that US military intervention abroad can encourage democracy and freedom

North American Free Trade Area (NAFTA)   The free-trade agreement between Mexico, Canada and the USA

realism   The theory of international relations that assumes countries have selfish and hostile intentions towards one another

strategic foreign policy   Policy involving the broad objectives relating to American interests, such as the Truman and the Reagan doctrines

Notes

1   The classic account of the realist position is Hans J. Morgenthau, *In Defense of the National Interest* (New York: Knopf, 1951).

2   Among the leading contractors in terms of defence contracts in 2008 were Lockheed Martin, Boeing, Carlyle Group, BAE Systems, General Dynamics, AAI Corporation, United Technologies, General Electric and Northrop Grumman.

3   Graham T. Allison, *Essence of Decision: Explaining the Cuban Missile Crisis* (Boston: Little, Brown, 1971).

4   *New York Times*, 19 February 2006.

Further Reading

On recent developments see Stephen W. *Hook US Foreign Policy: The Paradox of World* (Washington, DC: CQ Press, 2016). For a general review, see Michael Cox and Doug Stokes (eds), *US Foreign Policy* (Oxford and New York: Oxford University Press, 2012). For a critique of the 'War on Terror' see Stephen Holmes, *The Matador's Cape: America's Reckless Response to Terror* (Cambridge: Cambridge University Press, 2007). For an analysis of the problems facing American foreign policy in the post-9/11 era, see Chalmers Johnson, *The Sorrow of Empire: Militarism, Secrecy and the End of the Republic* (London: Verso, 2004), and also Ivo Daalder and James M. Lindsay, *America Unbound: The Bush Revolution in Foreign Policy* (Washington, DC: Brookings Institution, 2004); John Lewis Gaddis, *Surprise Security and the American Experience* (Cambridge, MA: Harvard University Press, 2004). See also Joseph S. Nye Jr., *Soft Power: The Means to Success in World Politics* (New York: Public Affairs, 2004), and also his *The Paradox of American Power: Why the World's Only Superpower Can't Go It Alone* (New York: Oxford University Press, 2003). On recent changes in defence priorities, see Michael O'Hanlon, *The Wounded Giant: America's Armed Forces in an Age of Austerity* (London and New York: Penguin, 2011).

CHAPTER 21

THE AMERICAN POLITICAL SYSTEM IN AN UNCERTAIN WORLD

With people whom we distrust, it is as difficult to do business as to search for scientific truth, arrive at religious harmony, or attain justice. When one must first question words and intentions, and start from the premise that everything said and written is meant to offer us an illusion in place of truth, life becomes strangely complicated.

– CHARLES WAGNER, THE SIMPLE LIFE

American Politics and Society, Ninth Edition. David McKay.
© 2018 John Wiley & Sons Ltd. Published 2018 by John Wiley & Sons Ltd.

Assessing the American Polity

No political system is perfect. Most regimes are fragile in the extreme, lasting no more than a few years or decades. Others may be longer-lived but fail the tests of equality, justice and democracy. Some simply fail to provide citizens with basic protection against violence and disorder, or with the minimum of food and shelter necessary for human survival. By these very elemental measures the American system has been very successful. The basic constitutional structure has remained unchanged for more than 230 years. Few regimes are as stable and none has been more successful at generating wealth. Violence has always been a feature of American society, but only very rarely has it translated into politically motivated civil disorder. Inequalities of wealth and income are considerable – and certainly greater than in comparable developed countries. While this problem should not be underestimated, wealth and income inequalities have never threatened the stability of the system. Measuring justice and democracy is notoriously difficult, of course, but the United States probably scores highly on both counts compared with other most countries. No one questions the availability of institutional mechanisms for democracy in America or the opportunity for participation in politics. In the sense that public discourse is essentially free from government controls and basic rights are protected by the courts, the USA also does more to promote justice and equity under law than most comparable countries. This said, recent events point to some erosion of these freedoms in the guise of the Patriot Act and other measures adopted at home and abroad as part of the 'War on Terror'. Economically, few doubt the success of the American system, but here too recent successes have been followed a period of great economic uncertainty engendered by recession, weaknesses in the banking sector and foreign competition. As a result, disenchantment with the American political system has increased both at home and abroad. And, quite apart from these specific problems, the American public does seem increasingly disillusioned with their political institutions.

Earlier chapters have pointed to the crucial link between the institutional structure of American government, on the one hand, and the unique American political culture, on the other, which provides pointers both to the causes of disenchantment and to the ways in which it might be reduced. Let us examine this relationship in more detail.

Institutional fragmentation

The Founding Fathers deliberately created an institutionally fragmented political system in order to limit the possibility of power being usurped either by a single person or by a particular group or faction. While they were brilliantly successful in achieving just this, the resulting fragmentation has made the business of governing problematical in the USA. Earlier chapters have shown how federalism and the separation of powers have combined to make it inordinately difficult to create clear and unambiguous public policies. Comparison with those countries that lack these institutional checks makes the point. In New Zealand and the United Kingdom, for example, governments intent on transforming the public sector by privatization and the application of market principles to government programmes have achieved almost all their objectives. The progress of similar reforms in the USA, even with the support of both Republican and Democratic presidents, has been much slower. Congress and president have found it difficult to agree on how, exactly, the reforms should be implemented. Progress at the state and local levels has depended on the policies of individual states and localities and has thus varied from area to area.

More serious have been failures associated with substantive areas of public policy, such as health care, immigration and environmental protection. In these and other policy areas, the separate constituencies of president and Congress have worked against each other to such an extent that little has been achieved – even though a broad consensus exists that reform is urgently needed in all of these areas. Divided government has served to aggravate rather than soothe the effects of jurisdictional fragmentation by making compromise and bargaining between president and Congress more fractious and conflictual than it used to be. Conflict between the two branches reached an embarrassing climax with the impeachment of President Clinton in 1998. In spite of the weak constitutional case against the president and low levels of public support for congressional action, a partisan House of Representatives persisted and eventually voted for articles of impeachment in late 1998. Trial in the Senate, although conducted with some dignity, produced the outcome that all expected – acquittal. Many foreign commentators were puzzled by this series of events. How could a great nation such as the United States embroil itself in such a damaging confrontation between the two major branches of government, for what looked like such irrelevant offences? And even when, following 9/11, something approaching a consensus on the need for a unified national response to terrorism emerged, it did not last long, as the conflicts between Congress and the president in the second Bush administration and the Obama administrations showed. By 2012 the two branches had reached an impasse on how to tackle the budget and debt crisis, with the Republicans refusing to accept any deal that involved raising taxes on the very richest Americans. This legislative/executive impasse had reached a point that was arguably quite new in the long history of the constitution. For up until the later part of the last century the essential features of American politics were bargaining and compromise. In a sense this was necessary to overcome a separation of powers that gave to each branch a potential veto power. Today, however the emergence of what Thomas Mann and Norman Ornstein have called 'asymmetric polarization' has rendered the USA almost ungovernable. Their claim is that the Republican Party has moved much further to the right than the Democratic Party has to the left resulting in a toxic mix of extreme rhetoric and political impasse. As they put it: 'The Republican Party has become an insurgent outlier – ideologically extreme; contemptuous of the inherited social and economic regime; scornful of compromise; unpersuaded by conventional understanding of facts, evidence and science; and dismissive of the legitimacy of its political opposition.'[1]

As shown in chapter 14, the Supreme Court has not been able to resolve these differences by brokering conflict between the two branches. This is mainly because the Court only has negative powers. It is meant to resolve differences between the branches when a matter of great constitutional interest is raised, such as the refusal by the Nixon White House to release the Watergate tapes to Congress. When the differences are *political* the Court can do little. In addition, in those areas such as federalism and the conscience issues where Court decisions may have made public policy less ambiguous, the Roberts Court, in spite of its openly conservative stance, has, for the most part, kept out of the 'political thicket' by arguing cases on narrow rather than broad constitutional grounds. This may reflect the fact that the public is itself deeply divided on such issues as abortion, immigration and affirmative action. None the less it has sometimes found itself very much in the middle of the 'political thicket' with the *Bush* v. *Gore* case on the outcome of the 2000 election (chapter 15) and *Citizens United* v. *FEC* on campaign finance (chapter 15).

Open government and pluralistic politics

There is no doubt that many of the problems associated with jurisdictional fragmentation have been aggravated by what has become a much more accessible and pluralistic political system. As earlier chapters have shown, Americans can voice their interests and grievances more effectively than ever before. This applies both to public opinion broadly defined and to the activities of organized interests. Public opinion makes itself felt in a number of ways, whether it be through the ballot box, social media, members of Congress reading their email or watching the polls, or presidents following their approval ratings.

In addition, organized interests are active at every level of politics. Corporations, labour unions and promotional groups all work hard to protect and promote their interests. As we have seen, through the use of advertising some groups have added to such issues as abortion and affirmative action an adversarial tone that may project opinions which are more extreme than those held by the public at large.

In addition, the extensive and highly commercial public media are constantly hungry for news and political happenings. Their influence permeates almost all public discourse and they now play a key role in election campaigns at every level. While no one disputes the value of the freedom to disseminate information, the particular way in which the media operate in the US (and indeed how they are used by well-financed political campaigns) can have the effect of distorting and misleading, rather than educating, the public. While openness is increasingly a characteristic of public affairs in comparable political systems, nowhere has it developed to the degree prevalent in the United States. A good illustration of this is the attention paid to US service personnel involved in foreign wars. When they are injured, captured or lost, TV crews rush to the affected families for national coverage, and although, during the Iraq conflict beginning in 2003, the Bush administration went to some effort to stifle camera shots of returning coffins and graveside scenes, it was largely unsuccessful. Such publicity increased greatly in line with the mounting death toll in Iraq and later in Afghanistan, so that by the end of the first decade of the twenty-first century both wars had become deeply unpopular with most Americans.

Limited government and public expectations

Open government and a pluralistic, polarized politics (some even call it hyper-pluralism) thrive when it is possible to access a range of political institutions operating at several levels. In other words, this combination seems almost designed to raise the expectations of mass publics and organized interests alike. The great paradox is, of course, that institutional fragmentation was deliberately instituted by the Founding Fathers to *limit* government, not to increase public expectations of what it can do. Yet the philosophy of limited government continues to this day. Surveys repeatedly show that Americans distrust the state and are more imbued with notions of self-reliance than are the citizens of comparable countries. This shows itself in Americans' distrust of big government and in a general aversion to taxing and spending. When it comes to the federal governments' provision of *specific* benefits, however, Americans expect a great deal. Indeed, a wide range of services and programmes provided by the federal government have now achieved the status of citizens' *rights*, rather than benefits which may be withdrawn should the conditions warrant it. This certainly applies to social security, Medicare and many other social programmes. In addition, few seriously expect the federal government's role in protecting the environment, the consumer and the employee in the workplace suddenly to end in the near future. During national emergencies, such as Hurricane Katrina in 2005 or the banking and 'sub-prime' mortgage crisis after 2008, citizens look to an activist *federal* government for help. When the government fails to act it is punished by the voters at the polls, as happened so dramatically in the 2006, 2010 and 2014 mid-term elections.

Disputes over the exact extent of this role and how it should be shared with the states will continue, but most Americans expect a leadership role from the federal government in these areas. Similar disputes surround the conscience issues, such as abortion, same-sex marriage, penal standards and affirmative action. Many also look to the federal government to address the growing income and wealth inequality that has become a prominent feature of American society. While few would argue that such inequality is in the public interest, correcting it through government action, such as significant increases in the minimum wage or taxing the wealthy, is clearly incompatible with a limited government philosophy. A striking illustration of this was the Bush tax reductions of 2001–3. By reducing taxes for almost all American families – but especially for the very rich – Bush espoused a limited government philosophy while at the same time refusing to reduce expenditure, and thus encouraged the growth of big government (and the budget deficit). Big government received an additional boost after 2008 when recession and rapidly rising unemployment led the Obama administration to use deficit spending to stimulate the economy and reduce taxation. These policies sowed the seeds of intensely partisan conflict between Democrats and Republicans over the proper role for government in a society that is so ambivalent about the nature of federal power. While political polarization was nothing new – witness the impeachment of Bill Clinton in 1998 – it reached new heights during the Obama years. Some commentators have argued that polarization is essentially an elite phenomenon, rather then something that permeates through the whole of society.[2] In other words it is the *political parties* that are polarized rather than the voters at large. While this may have been true of the early 2000s there is accumulating evidence that voters too are becoming more polarized into conservative and liberal factions – a phenomenon that was confirmed by the contentious 2016 election campaign.[3] The result confirmed this polarization, with Hillary Clinton winning nearly 3 million more votes than Donald Trump, but with Trump winning the Electoral College and thus the presidency. His tenure in office is unlikely to attenuate the ideological divide. On the contrary, confrontation and conflict are almost the hallmarks of his leadership style. This new era of confrontational politics has made the business of coalition building much more difficult. Historically, American politics has always been defined in terms of coalition building, bargaining and compromise. Without compromise there is the danger that the system will become dysfunctional or able to produce only perverse outcomes that are not in the public interest. This seemed to be the case with the failure of Congress to reach agreement on longer-term budget and tax changes after 2011. House Republicans refused to accept any deal that allowed the tax cuts first implemented during the Bush years to expire, while President Obama insisted that raising taxes on the very rich was the most efficient and fairest way to get the deficit under control. More inaction was caused by the refusal of the Senate Republicans even to consider a replacement on the Supreme Court for the conservative justice Antonin Scalia, who died in early 2016, until after the November election. As a result the Court remained at just eight justices for the remainder of the 2016 term. In the event, the election of Donald Trump left open the opportunity to nominate a conservative justice to the bench.

Contradictions also surround America's world role, and especially so since 9/11. Most Americans expect the USA to play a key role both in protecting democracy and freedom and in maintaining a stable and healthy international trading environment. At the same time many are deeply ambivalent about the costs of such actions, including the price that may be paid in American lives and in the economic costs of supporting such international bodies as the United Nations.

Military actions in Afghanistan and Iraq cost more American lives than in any encounter since Vietnam. Military spending on these interventions and generally on the fighting the terrorist threat increased substantially. And while the Obama administration promised a rationalization of defence commitments in the 2011 defence review, no one expected a substantial cutback in America's overseas commitments. As with domestic policy, Democratic and Republican politicians are deeply divided on this question. During the 2016 election campaign, Republican Donald Trump promised to increase defence spending in real terms but paradoxically also called for a scaling back of American Treaty obligations, implying a withdrawal into a fortress America policy.

Reform and Renewal

As the quote at the beginning of this chapter indicates, distrust can be damaging. In political systems, disillusionment with political processes and institutions can undermine the legitimacy of the system. In many countries it is just such sentiments that lead to a breakdown of the regime. In the American case, while regime change seems a very distant prospect, most observers view declining faith in the polity and in the veracity of political leaders as a serious development. As table 21.1 shows, of all the institutions of public life in the US, the military scores the highest in terms of public regard, with churches scoring higher than the presidency and substantially higher than Congress and the media. Note also the decline in regard for Congress, the media, bank and even organized religion in the 10 years to 2016. Interestingly the reputation of the presidency was enhanced during the Obama years.

Cynicism with public institutions makes it more difficult to institute and legitimize much-needed reforms. In the worst-case scenario it may help the political fortunes of extremists and demagogues. No sensible commentator believes that 'solutions' to this problem exist in

Table 21.1   Americans' confidence in institutions, 2006–2016

	June 2006 (%)	June 2016 (%)	Difference, 2006 to 2016 (percentage points)
Military	73	73	0
Police	58	56	−2
Church or organized religion	52	41	−11
Medical system	38	39	+1
Presidency	33	36	+3
US Supreme Court	40	36	−4
Public schools	37	30	−7
Banks	49	27	−22
Organized labour	24	23	−1
Criminal justice system	25	23	−2
Television news	31	21	−10
Newspapers	30	20	−10
Big business	18	18	0
Congress	19	9	−10

Source: Gallup at 13 June 2016, Americans' Confidence in Institutions Stays Low by Jim Norman, www.gallup.com/poll/192581/americans-confidence-institutions-stays-low.aspx.

the sense that public demands will suddenly be lowered or that Americans' attitudes towards government will miraculously be transformed. There is, however, no shortage of suggested reforms, most of which offer at least partial solutions.

One thing is for sure – there is no constituency of support for fundamental constitutional change. Calls for the abolition of the separation of powers and the introduction of a parliamentary system have always fallen on deaf ears, and will almost certainly continue to do so in the future.Instead, most commentators today call for changes in the way in which Americans think about politics. Quick-fix and gimmicky solutions should be replaced by solutions based on longer-term thinking. Hence public officials and public discourse should be educating the public on the nature of policy commitments (such as the funding of social security) and on the need for individuals to take on more personal responsibility for their future (such as saving for retirement or educating their children). In effect these pleas ask for a rethinking of what citizens should expect from government. In most instances they think the public should be educated to expect less, but to do more in the context of families and local communities to help each other. George W. Bush constantly made appeals along these lines and even launched a 'faith-based initiative' designed to enhance the role of organized religion in solving community problems.

The snag is, of course, that many of the problems that affect modern America are not amenable to family- or community-based solutions. Such objectives as affordable health care, reducing income and wealth inequalities, immigration reform, full employment and effective protection from terrorism can only be achieved through government. And when the economy falters or terrorists threaten American interests, the electorate is quick to call for firm and decisive action from the federal government. Hence the rapid increase in public expenditure during the 2002–13 period and the return of the budget deficit. Calls for firm government also led to the passage of the Patriot Act and the creation of the Department of Homeland Security, and to claims that an emerging 'security state' was threatening civil liberties. With the election of Barack Obama in the context of the worst economic crisis since the 1930s, the demands for federal government action reached new heights. By 2013 the federal government was playing a more intrusive role in the economy than any government since the Second World War. Yet Americans remain deeply suspicious of Washington's ability to solve economic problems – even as they demand more action to reduce unemployment and economic inequalities. Donald Trump's avowed policies declared in 2017 seemed to confirm these contradictions. For although he proposed increased intervention to protect American jobs from foreign competition, he also advocated reduced taxes and deregulation. Reconciling these conflicting demands and policies constitutes the most serious challenge for any new administration – a challenge that will only be met through the exercise of great political and leadership skills.

Questions for Discussion

1   To what extent is the separation of powers the root of the 'governance' problems in the United States?
2   Why are American politics so polarized? What have been the policy consequences of polarization?

Glossary

asymmetric polarization   Term to describe the move of the Republican Party far to the right that is not matched by an equivalent move by the Democratic Party to the left

demagoguery   Speech and rhetoric that panders to the fears of an audience

faith-based initiative   George W. Bush's idea that religious organizations could replace governments in some contexts

institutional fragmentation   When political power is divided among many institutions both horizontally (separation of powers) and vertically (federalism)

jurisdictional fragmentation   When political power is divided among many jurisdictions and constituencies

limited government   The philosophy that limited government is the best government

sub-prime mortgage crisis   The crisis resulting from over-generous lending policies by banks that led directly to the housing crash of 2007–9

Notes

1   Thomas E Mann and Norman J. Ornstein, *Its Even Worse than it Was*: *How the American Constitutional System Collided with the New Politics of Extremism* (New York: Basic Books, 2016), p. xv.

2   Morris P. Fiorina and Samuel J. Abrams, *Disconnect: The Breakdown of Representation in American Politics* (Norman: University of Oklahoma Press, 2011).

3   See the surveys from the Pew Organization, including www.people-press.org/2016/06/22/partisanship-and-political-animosity-in-2016/.

Further Reading

For up-to-date critiques of recent developments in politics, Thomas E Mann and Norman J. Ornstein, *Its Even Worse than it Was: How the American Constitutional System Collided with the New Politics of Extremism*, updated paperback edn (New York: Basic Books, 2016. See also Alan Abramowitz, *The Disappearing Center: Engaged Citizens, Polarization, and American Democracy* (New Haven: Yale University Press, 2011) and Morris P. Fiorina and Samuel J. Abrams, *Disconnect: The Breakdown of Representation in American Politics* (Norman: University of Oklahoma Press, 2011).

WEBSITES

Chapter 2

Comprehensive demographic and other data are available from the US Census Bureau at www.census.gov. Historical data on immigration are available from www.migrationpolicy.org/programs/data-hub/us-immigration-trends. Information on immigration (and how to achieve US citizenship) is available from the US Citizenship and Immigration Service at https://www.uscis.gov.

Chapter 3

The Constitution Center (http://constitutioncenter.org) provides documents and background information on the Constitution. The Congressional Research Service also provides good information and links at www.opencrs.com. A good search engine is at www.constitutioncenter.org.

Chapter 4

The Council of State Governments has a good site and provides links to all state governments (www.csg.org). For information on cities, access the US Conference of Mayors at www.usmayors.org. The Forum of Federations is also good at www.forumfed.org.

American Politics and Society, Ninth Edition. David McKay.
© 2018 John Wiley & Sons Ltd. Published 2018 by John Wiley & Sons Ltd.

Chapter 5

The official site of the Democratic National Committee is www.democrats.org and of the Republicans www.gop.com. A useful site for accessing many aspects of American politics is www.realclearpolitics.com. It also lists all registered political parties. See also Fivethirtyeight at https://fivethirtyeight.com, which provides statistical analysis of all aspects of US politics with an emphasis on polling.

Chapter 6

The Federal Election Commission is at www.fec.gov. The Institute for Social Research at the University of Michigan has good voting data at www.isr.umich.edu/cps. Further poll data are at www.gallup.com and at www.PollingReport.com. See also Larry Sabato's Center for the Study of Politics at www.centerforpolitics.org/crystalball. For public opinion on all aspects of politics, see http://pollingreport.com and also https://fivethirtyeight.com.

Chapters 8 and 9

The House of Representatives site is www.house.gov and the Senate www.senate.gov. The National Republican Congressional Committee is at www.nrcc.org and the Democratic caucus is at www.dems.gov. The Library of Congress is at www.lcweb.loc.gov. For data on how members of Congress vote, see https://ssl.capwiz.com/aclu/keyvotes.xc/?lvl=C (a liberal perspective), and http://all4cra.tripod.com/ACAindex.html for a conservative perspective.

Chapters 10 and 11

The official site for the White House is www.whitehouse.gov. The Center for the Study of the presidency is also useful at www.thepresidency.org. An excellent teaching resource is the presidency project at the University of California, Santa Barbara, at www.presidency.ucsb.edu.

Chapter 12

The Library of Congress lists the websites for all departments and agencies at www.lcweb.loc.gov. The Department of Justice is at www.usdoj.gov. State is at www.state.gov.

Chapter 13

The Department of Homeland Security is at www.dhs.gov. A critique of the Patriot Act and its threat to civil liberties is at the American Civil Liberties Union website at www.aclu.org. See also https://epic.org/privacy/terrorism/usapatriot for information on the Act and generally on electronic surveillance.

Chapter 14

The AFL-CIO is at www.afl.cio.org. The National Association of Manufacturers is at www.nam.org. The Business Round Table can be found at www.businessroundtable.org. Information on all the leading political action committees is provided at www.opensecrets.org/pacs. Another good source on interest groups is the public interest organization Common Cause (www.commoncause.org).

Chapter 15

The official Supreme Court site is www.supremecourtus.gov. Summaries of all the leading cases decided since 1937 are given at http://litigation.findlaw.com/legal-system/the-u-s-supreme-court-overview.html.

Chapter 16

On civil liberties see the ACLU site at www.aclu.org. The NAACP is at www.naacp.org. Emily's List supports female candidates and favours pro-choice candidacies (www.emilyslist.org). The American with Disabilities Act has a website listing resources for the disabled at https://www.ada.gov/ada_intro.htm. A site promoting same-sex marriage is at www.marriageequality.org.

Chapter 17

The American Medical Association is at www.ama-assn.org and the Medicare site is at www.medicare.org. The homepage of the Department of Health and Human Services is at https://www.hhs.gov

Chapter 18

The Council of Economic Advisers is at www.whitehouse.gov/cea. The Office of Management and Budget is at https://www.usa.gov/federal-agencies/office-of-management-and-budget. The Federal Reserve is at https://www.federalreserve.gov. A website devoted to the economy and markets is at www.realclearmarkets.com.

Chapter 19

The Environmental Protection Agency is at www.epa.gov. Friends of the Earth USA is at www.foe.org. The Sierra Club is at www.sierraclub.org. A site devoted to gathering data on global warming is at www.globalwarming.org.

Chapter 20

The State Department is at www.state.gov and Defense is at https://www.defense.gov. A site devoted to critiquing all aspects of US foreign policy is www.alternet.org. See also Real Clear Defense at realcleardefense.com.

Other

Most of the US media have very good sites, including:

www.nytimes.com
www.washingtonpost.com
www.usatoday.com
www.time.com
www.abcnews.com
www.nbc.com
www.cbs.com
www.cnn.com
www.c-span.org
www.huffingtonpost.com
www.thedailybeast.com
www.commentarymagazine.com

Some of these sites are on a subscription-only basis. In addition Real Clear Politics provides daily summaries of editorial and other opinion from all the US media (www.realclearpolitics.com) and https://fivethirtyeight.com provides statistical analysis of polling and all aspects of politics (and US sports!).

GLOSSARY

activist Court   A Supreme Court prepared to establish precedents and therefore to make controversial decisions

administrative gate-keeping   The ability of bureaucracies to filter information and access from Congress and the public

affirmative action   Policies designed to redress patterns of discrimination based on race, ethnicity, gender, age or disability

AFL-CIO (American Federation of Labor-Congress of Industrial Organizations)   The union 'peak' association representing some of the main unions

African American   Americans of African (usually of slave) descent

Aid for Families with Dependent Children (AFDC)   The main welfare programme in operation between 1935 and 1996

Al-Qaeda   The loose network of terrorists associated with Osama Bin Laden and his followers

alienation   The concept that citizens are alienated from, hostile to or distant from values in society

American Bar Association (ABA)   The organization representing and defending legal standards

American Farm Bureau Federation (AFBF)   One of the two main unions representing farmers (the other is the National Farmers Union)

American Medical Association (AMA)   One of the main organizations representing doctors and other senior medical professionals

'American Voter' model   The model of voting behaviour based on party identification

Americanism   A unique mix of characteristics that constitutes the American 'ideology'

American Politics and Society, Ninth Edition. David McKay.
© 2018 John Wiley & Sons Ltd. Published 2018 by John Wiley & Sons Ltd.

Americans with Disabilities Act (ADA)   The main federal law protecting the rights of the disabled

appellate jurisdiction   Supreme Court jurisdiction involving appeals from lower courts

Appropriations Committee   The House committee responsible for spending money

Articles of Confederation   The first US Constitution drawn up after the War of Independence

Association of Federal, State, County and Municipal Employees (AFSCME)   the main union representing lower-paid municipal and health workers

asymmetric polarization   Term to describe the move of the Republican Party far to the right that is not matched by an equivalent move by the Democratic Party to the left

baby-boom generation   The 1945–60 generation of larger families now reaching retirement age

Balanced Budget Amendment   The (failed) amendment introduced in the 1980s banning the federal government from running a deficit

benevolent hegemony   The idea that American world dominance can be used for good purposes

bicameralism   Rule by two legislative chambers such as the House and the Senate

Bill of Rights   The first 10 amendments to the Constitution enumerating basic rights ratified in 1791

birthers   Those who believe that Barack Obama was not born on the United States

block grants   Grants from the federal government to the states not allocated to specific purposes

Boll Weevils   The conservative Democrats in Congress during the 1970s and 1980s

Bureau of Alcohol, Tobacco and Firearms (ATF)   The arm of the Treasury responsible for enforcing fiscal law in these areas

business unionism   Workers perceiving themselves as part of the capitalist environment

cabinet   The heads of the cabinet departments in an administration

candidates at large   Two or more party candidates elected across constituencies rather than on the basis of exclusive constituencies

categorical grants   Grants from the federal government to the states allocated to specific purposes

Central Intelligence Agency (CIA)   The main intelligence arm for overseas intelligence in the US

centralization   The act of centralizing authority and power

certiorari   The name given to cases that the Supreme Court decides to hear

Chapter 11 (federal bankruptcy law)   The ability of companies to freeze debts in order to reorganize and reduce costs

Christian right   Those holding fundamentalist Christian views on the political right

civil liberties   Those rights usually associated with criminal procedural rights, freedom of speech, religion and privacy

Civil War   The war between the North and the South waged between 1861 and 1865

classical federalism   Federal arrangements where the division of power between the centre and the states is clear and unambiguous

Clean Air Acts   The series of Acts, the first dating from 1970, that set targets or emissions

clientelism   Bureaucratic links between agencies and the interests they are supposed to fund and regulate

closed primaries   Primaries where only registered voters of the party holding the primary can cast a ballot

cloture (closure rule)   The Senate parliamentary device that allows the overturning of a Senate filibuster. Sixty senators are needed to implement the device

coattails   The secondary political effects of victory in a presidential election that spills over into victory for the president's party in Congress

Cold War   The ideological conflict between the West and the Soviet Union and China between 1949 and 1991

collectivist   The notion that society is made of collective units such as class, religion or ethnicity

Commerce Clause   The power in the US Constitution giving the federal government the power to regulate interstate commerce

Committee on Political Education (COPE)   The educational and lobbying arm of the AFL-CIO

communism   The system of beliefs that assumes that the collective ownership of the means of production, control and exchange was the most beneficial for humankind. Communism as an alternative to capitalism has now been largely discredited

comparative advantage   The international trade theory that assumes all countries benefit from open international trade

competitive interdependence   The modern condition of US federalism where the states and the federal government are competitive and interdependent

competitive service   Meritocratically appointed civil servants in the US federal government

Compound Republic   The Madisonian notion that the US was made of numerous interests and factions that could be accommodated by federalism and the separation of powers

concurring opinions   Supreme Court opinions that agree with the majority but on different grounds

Conference Committees   Cross-house committees designed to reconcile House and Senate versions of a bill

conflictual federalism   The condition where conflict between the states and federal government exists

Connecticut Compromise   The constitutional compromise that established the House of Representatives elected on a population basis and the Senate on a territorial basis

conservative coalition   The combination of southern Democrats and northern Republicans that had a built-in majority in Congress for much of the first two-thirds of the twentieth century

conservative editorial style   The staid and traditional presentational style of most American newspapers

constitutional dictatorship   The idea that in emergencies elected governments should act like dictators

cooperative federalism   The condition where the relationship between the states and the federal government is essentially cooperative

creedal passion   The idea that Americans are infused with strong feelings on moral issues

criminal procedural rights   The rights of the accused and the convicted in criminal law

crisis management   The process whereby presidents handle international crises such as the Cuban missile crisis or 9/11

cross-cutting cleavages   Issues that elicit support patterns across ideological, class, ethnic, gender or territorial lines

de facto **segregation**   Segregation that has emerged through social and economic circumstance

de jure **segregation**   Legally established racial segregation

dealignment   The weakening of party identification in elections to the point where voters abandon traditional voting cues

deindustrialization   The process of moving from an industrial or manufacturing economy to a knowledge-based service economy

demagoguery   Speech and rhetoric that panders to the fears of an audience

Department of Homeland Security   The new agency created in the wake of 9/11

developmental policies   Those policies that involve economic and social development, such as transportation and urban renewal

deviating elections   Elections, such as those of 1952 and 1956, where voters temporarily vote out of line with their party identification

direct primaries   Primaries that directly nominate candidates for office

dissenting opinions   The opinions of the justices in the minority in a Supreme Court decision

divided government   Party control of Congress and presidency split between the two parties

dual sovereignty   The division of power and sovereignty between different levels of government

due process   The idea that all citizens should be subject to clear and fair processes under law

earmarking   Guaranteeing funding for specific constituency projects or benefits as attachments to bills

economic liberal   Those adhering to free-market principles

editorial and opinion distinction   The distinction in US papers and television between reporting facts and opinions

Electoral College   Election of the chief executive by a college of electors rather than directly by the people

Electoral Connection (Mayhew)   Servicing constituencies in ways that will maximize the legislator's chance of re-election

Elementary and Secondary Education Act 1965   The first major federal programme for funding schools

Environmental Protection Agency   The main agency for enforcing environmental protection established in 1970

Equal Rights Amendment (ERA)   The failed amendment guaranteeing rights to women proposed in the 1970s

equality of opportunity   The idea that all citizens should be given an equal chance to succeed, irrespective of background

excepted service   Politically appointed bureaucrats in the US federal service

Executive Office of the President (EOP)   The administrative unit under the control of the president that includes agencies such as the Office of Management and Budget as well as the White House Office

executive order   A presidential order changing policy within the executive branch

executive privilege   The doctrine that certain information in the executive branch should be kept out of the public domain

faith-based initiative   George W. Bush's idea that religious organizations could replace governments in some contexts

Family and Medical Leave Act 1993   The law providing limited unpaid time off for expectant parents

fat cat contributors   Contributors of large donations to parties and candidates

Federal Bureau of Investigation (FBI)   The main federal agency responsible for fighting crime in the USA

Federal Communications Commission (FCC)   The authority responsible for regulating the electronic media

federal debt   The national debt of the United States

federal deficit   The gap between income from taxation and other sources and expenditure in the federal budget

Federal Reserve System   The US central banking system that sets interest rates

federalism   The division of sovereignty between national state governments

first past the post electoral systems   Electoral arrangements based on plurality rather than proportional voting

fiscal federalism   Those aspects of federalism involving taxing and spending

Floor Leaders (Majority/Minority)   Party leaders in the House and Senate

food stamps   Tokens introduced in 1964 which the poor could exchange for food. They remain in use

Freedom Caucus   A grouping of 30 plus House Republicans devoted to the advance of far right public policies

free exercise of religion   The right to practise the religion of your choice

Full Employment Act 1946   The Keynesian law that established the principle that the government was responsible for maintaining full employment

General Agreement on Tariffs and Trade (GATT)   The international agreement establishing successive rounds of tariff reduction

General Services Administration   The agency responsible for buildings and services in the federal government

genetically modified or engineered (GM or GE) foods   Foods cultured to resist disease and increase yields

gerrymandering   The manipulation of electoral boundaries for political advantage

global warming   The effects on the climate of emissions from vehicles and industrial processes

government corporations   Government-owned enterprises such as the US Postal Service

governmental stability   Continuity of government incumbency over time

Great Depression   The economic dislocation during the 1929–38 period

greenhouse gases   The mix of carbon-based gases that lead to global warming

gross domestic product (GDP)   The financial total of all activity in the economy

Guantánamo Bay   The base in Cuba under US jurisdiction where terrorist suspects have been detained without charge

Gypsy Moths   The moderate northern Republicans active in Congress in the 1970s and 1980s

habeas corpus   The right to have a criminal case heard in court within a specified period

health maintenance organizations (HMOs)   Medical organizations designed to provide cost-effective medical care by limiting patient choice of doctors and treatment

hegemony   The idea that one country is powerful enough to dictate economic and military terms to other nations

Hispanic American   Americans with Spanish second names, mainly of Mexican origin but also from other parts of the Americas, the Caribbean and the Iberian peninsula

idealism   The theory of international relations that assumes countries have benevolent intentions towards one another

ideology   A coherently interrelated set of ideas guiding the organization of society

impeachment   The formal accusation of wrongdoing by an officeholder

Imperial Presidency   The view popular in the 1960s and 1970s that presidents were unconstrained in foreign policy

impoundment   Funds appropriated by Congress but sequestered by presidents. Impoundment was made illegal by the Impoundment and Budget Control Act 1974

industrial policy   Guided government help to rescue declining industries and establish new ones

initiative   Voters placing an item on the ballot sheet through the presentation of a minimum number of signatures

institutional fragmentation   When political power is divided among many institutions both horizontally (separation of powers) and vertically (federalism)

intergovernmental relations   The political relationship between federal state and local government

Internal Revenue Service (IRS)   The tax-collecting and enforcement arm of the federal government

investigative power (Congress)   The power of Congress to investigate the executive branch

Iran–Contra affair   The attempt by officials in the Reagan administration to sell arms to Iran and use the proceeds to fund the Contra guerrillas fighting the Sandinista regime in Nicaragua

iron triangles   Intimate links between agencies, congressional committees and organized interests

isolationism   The assumption, prevalent in the 1930s, that the US could isolate itself from the rest of the world in international relations

ISIS   Name given to the global terrorist movement self-described as Islamic State

issue networks   Looser links between bureaucrats, Congress and interests

issue politics   Politics based on particular issues such as abortion or taxation

Jim Crow laws   The segregationist laws passed in the southern states during the 1880s and 1890s

Johnson Rule   As Senate Majority Leader Lyndon Johnson established that every freshman senator should have a committee assignment

judicial agenda   The agenda of the Supreme Court in a particular historical period

judicial review   Review of legislation and executive actions by the Supreme Court to determine compatibility with the constitution

judicial self-restraint   The practice of the Supreme Court not to make decisions challenging established constitutional norms unless absolutely necessary

jurisdictional fragmentation   When political power is divided among many jurisdictions and constituencies

K Street project   The plan by congressional Republicans to exclude Democratic lobbyists from access to Congress in the 1990s

Keynesians   Those adhering to the idea that government spending and deficit finance should be used to maintain high employment during periods of economic distress

knock and announce (search procedures)   Open searching of premises for evidence

Kyoto Protocol (Convention)   The 1997 international convention setting targets for reducing emissions that the USA refused to ratify

laissez-faire   Economic liberalism, or the idea that economies are at their most efficient if freed from government controls

legitimacy   Moral acceptance of political or constitutional arrangements among voters

limited government   The philosophy that limited government is the best government

lobbyists   Professional interest group employees

localism   The devotion of citizens to a local territory or jurisdiction

logistical/structural defence policy   The detailed content of defence policy involving such things as weapons systems and the movement of resources

log-rolling   The exchange of political favours, or 'I'll scratch your back if you scratch mine'

macro-economic policy   Policy designed to guide the whole economy, such as interest rate policy

maintaining elections   Elections, such as those of 1960 and 1964, that maintain the majority party in power

majoritarianism   The idea that what the majority wants has value in itself

majority rule   Rule by a plurality of the voters

market-driven journalism   News, programmes or editorial content designed to maximize commercial revenue

mass media   The general term governing mass communication via television, radio the press and the internet

matching federal funds   The device whereby the federal government will match candidate contributions in residential elections up to defined limits

McCarran Act   The law used after the Second World War to suppress communists and other 'subversives'

median voter   The typical voter, or that which approximates to the statistical median

Medicaid   The main federal medical programme for the poor

Medicare   The main federal medical programme for the old

micro-economic policy   Policy designed to guide sectors or regions of the economy, such as regional aid and labour policies

'motor voter' law   Voter registration laws that allow voters to register to vote when renewing their driving licences

National Association for the Advancement of Colored People (NAACP) A leading interest group defending the rights of African Americans

National Farmers Union (NFU) One of the two main unions representing farmers (with the American Farm Bureau Federation)

national networks The three main television and radio networks – CBS, NBC and ABC – that sell programmes to franchised local stations

National Rifle Association (NRA) The organization defending the right of Americans to 'bear arms' by opposing gun-control laws

National Security Council (NSC) The White House-based organization responsible for national security

nationalization of politics The subservience of state and local concerns to national policies and issues

neoconservatism A system of beliefs supporting the view that US military intervention abroad can encourage democracy and freedom

New Deal The collection of measures designed to rescue the economy from depression during the 1930s

New Deal coalition The coalition of industrial workers, farmers, intellectuals and the South that underpinned Democratic Party success from 1933 to 1969

New Dealers The politicians, judges and bureaucrats who supported the New Deal agenda in the 1930s

New Federalism The label attached to Ronald Reagan's attempts to devolve power to the states

New Jersey Plan The defeated constitutional proposal that the US should be governed by a single house based on equal votes for each state

No Child Left Behind Act (NCLB) The institution of universal testing of schoolchildren's performance by the federal government

nominating conventions The party conventions held to formally nominate candidates in the summer of election years

non-connected PACs Political action committees supporting causes rather than vested interests

North American Free Trade Area (NAFTA) The free-trade agreement between Mexico, Canada and the USA

Obamacare The pejorative name attached to the Obama administration's Affordable Care Act passed in 2010

objective/subjective social class The difference between the actual economic/social condition of individuals and perceptions of their condition by themselves or others

Office of Faith-Based and Community Initiatives (OFBCI) George W. Bush initiative to encourage religious funding of public services, later renamed the Center for Faith-Based and Neighborhood Partnerships

Office of Management and Budget (OMB) The main agency responsible for monitoring government spending and regulatory arrangements

Office of Personnel Management (OPM) The agency responsible for appointing people to the civil service

old-style party politics Party politics based on 'insider' influence and the operation of political machines

open primaries   Primaries where voters of any party can cast a vote

opinion of the Court   The main opinion of the Supreme Court written by one justice

outsourcing   Allocating services within government to private contractors

overload thesis   The idea that excessive demands on governments undermine their ability to govern

oversight   The power of Congress to oversee the implementation of policy by the executive branch

party government   Rule based on the dominance of parties in government

party identification   The psychological attachment to parties held by voters over time

passive Court   A Supreme Court intent on not making controversial, precedent-setting decisions

Patriot Act   The law which gave the federal government draconian powers after 9/11

plurality   The party or political unit that wins the most votes in an election, which may not be a majority

political action committees (PACs)   Pressure-group organizations designing to represent interests in the political sphere

political appointees   Civil servants appointed by presidents on political grounds

political culture   The beliefs and values that make up society

political machine   A structured political party organization that monopolizes power in a jurisdiction

political thicket   The problems associated with Supreme Court decisions with serious political implications

pork-barrel politics   Legislation designed to benefit individual constituencies

positivism   The judicial philosophy that believes that there are specific meanings behind laws and constitutional provisions

President Pro Tempore   The honorary position held by the Vice President of the United States, who votes in the Senate in the event of a tie

presidential veto   The ability of presidents to veto legislation that can only be overturned by a two thirds majority in both houses

primaries   Intra-party elections to decide nominated candidates for the general election

principal–agent problem   The problems associated with getting subordinates to comply with managerial or owner directives

privatization   The sale of government assets to private companies

pro-choice   Those believing that women should have the right to abort a child

programmatic parties   Parties presenting clear programmes for change to the electorate

prohibition   The constitutional amendment banning the production, sale and consumption of alcohol in the USA between 1919 and 1933

pro-life   Those believing that the rights of the foetus should take precedence over those of the mother

public choice   The branch of social science relating to the problems associated with ensuring public bodies make rational decisions

Public Right to Know   The open government laws that establish the right to public information

purposeful voting   Voting deliberately designed to seat or unseat a candidate based on a rational calculation

ratings   Viewing, listening and readership figures widely used to inform programme content and design

rational actors   Political actors behaving in ways that maximize power and financial and status benefits

realignment   A major shift in party identification from one party to another, as happened in 1932

realism   The theory of international relations that assumes countries have selfish and hostile intentions towards one another

recall (elections)   Citizen-inspired elections to recall an official from office. Used at the state level only

redistributive policies   Policies designed to redistribute resources across social classes, age cohorts or jurisdictions

referendums   Votes directly on state ballot sheets on a particular aspect of public policy

regime stability   Constitutional systems that persist through time

regulatory powers   Powers designed to regulate economic, social or political activity

retrospective voting   Voting in support of or against candidates based on their record in office

right to keep and bear arms   The Second Amendment, which is used by the gun lobby to oppose restrictions on the ownership and use of firearms

Rules Committee   The House committee that decides on important parliamentary procedures, including agendas

same-sex marriage   Extension to gays of all those marital rights given to different-sex marriages

segregationist   Social systems based on the segregation of society on racial or ethnic grounds

select committees   Ad hoc committees established to investigate particular areas of public policy such as ageing or intelligence

Senate filibuster   The parliamentary device that allows a senator to speak without break until the time allotted to the debate is used up

separation of powers   The separation of governmental powers into legislative, executive and judicial

shock jocks   Radio journalists with sensationalist and/or extreme political views

shrinking middle (legislators)   The decline of politically moderate legislators in the House and the Senate

sneak and peek (search procedures)   Clandestine searching of premises for evidence

social capital   The accumulated networks of social interaction based on trust and community identity

social contract theory   The idea that the people enter into a contract with the government with both sides accountable for their actions

Social Security Trust Fund   The monies collected via social security taxes and specifically allocated to social security (mainly pension) payments

soft money   Political advertising funded not by political parties but by other interests

solidaristic communities   Homogeneous communities that share values and political views

soundbite   A brief extract from a television or radio interview designed to attract viewers' or listeners' attention

South, the   The 12 southern states of the Union made up of the 'Deep South' and the border states

Speaker, House   The leading party spokesperson in the House of Representatives

special prosecutor   The position created to investigate wrongdoing by presidents and other executive officials

standing committees   The permanent committees in both houses

strategic foreign policy   Policy involving the broad objectives relating to American interests, such as the Truman and the Reagan doctrines

subpoena   A legally enforceable requirement that witnesses and evidence be available to congressional committees

sub-prime mortgage crisis   The crisis resulting from over-generous lending policies by banks that led directly to the housing crash of 2007–9

substantive due process   The application of due process not just to procedures (i.e. the right to see a lawyer) but also to substantive rights, such as privacy or freedom of speech

Sunbelt–Snowbelt   The distinction between the high growth states of the South and Southwest and the slower growth states of the upper Midwest and the Northeast

superdelegates   Delegates to the Democratic National Convention chosen on the basis of their position or political service

SuperPACs   Political action committees able to spend unlimited amounts in support of or against candidates and issues following the 2010 Supreme Court *Citizens United* decision

Supplementary Security Income (SSI)   A welfare programme to provide benefits for the old and the sick whose social security payments are inadequate

survivalist movement   Extremist militia groups who prepare for complete social breakdown and possible violent conflict with the federal government

sustainable development   The idea adapted by the 1992 Earth Summit that economic development should be balanced by environmental considerations

talk radio   The label given to non-music radio stations

Tammany Hall   A general term to describe big-city political machines

TANF (Temporary Assistance for Needy Families)   The 'workfare' programme introduced in 1996 and designed to get people off welfare and into work

TARP   Temporary Asset Relief Program to help the bail out of financial institutions in 2008

Tea Party   A movement within the Republican Party started in 2009 to promote candidates adhering to a right-wing minimal federal government agenda

Three Mile Island   The site of the worst nuclear accident in US history, which effectively stopped new nuclear power developments

ultra vires   Acting beyond one's powers

unfunded mandates   Federal policies requiring states to implement policies but not funded by the federal government

unitary system   A system of government where the central government is sovereign and local units subordinate to the centre

US Customs Service and Border Security   The new agency created to enhance border security after 9/11

Virginia Plan   The defeated constitutional proposal involving an elected lower house and an upper house elected by the lower house with nominees from the states

voter registration laws   Laws governing the conditions under which citizens can register to vote

Warmists   Name given by right-wing politicians to those who believe in the scientific basis of climate change

War Powers Act 1973   The law that placed formal limits on the president's ability to wage war

Watergate   The label attached to attempts by the Nixon administration to spy on and discredit the Democrats in the presidential election of 1972

Ways and Means Committee   The House committee responsible for taxation matters

White House Office   The administrative unit wholly under the president's control in the White House

winner-take-all   The arrangement whereby a majority or plurality in a constituency wins all the representation

workable programme   Policies with provisions designed to assess the social and economic impact of programmes

World Trade Organization (WTO)   The tariff-reduction organization that replaced GATT

APPENDIX
THE CONSTITUTION OF THE UNITED STATES

[PREAMBLE]

We the people of the United States, in order to form a more perfect union, establish justice, insure domestic tranquility, provide for the common defense, promote the general welfare, and secure the blessings of liberty to ourselves and our posterity, do ordain and establish this Constitution for the United States of America.

ARTICLE 1 [THE LEGISLATURE]

Section 1

All legislative powers herein granted shall be vested in a Congress of the United States, which shall consist of a Senate and House of Representatives.

Section 2

1   The House of Representatives shall be composed of members chosen every second year by the people of the several States, and the electors in each State shall have the qualifications requisite for elections of the most numerous branch of the State legislature.
2   No person shall be a representative who shall not have attained to the age of twenty-five years, and been seven years a citizen of the United States, and who shall not, when elected, be an inhabitant of that State in which he shall be chosen.
3   Representatives and direct taxes[1] shall be apportioned among the several States which may be included within this Union, according to their respective members, which shall be determined by adding to the whole number of free persons, including those

American Politics and Society, Ninth Edition. David McKay.
© 2018 John Wiley & Sons Ltd. Published 2018 by John Wiley & Sons Ltd.

bound to service for a term of years, and excluding Indians not taxed, three-fifths of all other persons.[2] The actual enumeration shall be made within three years after the first meeting of the Congress of the United States, and within every subsequent term of ten years, in such manner as they shall by law direct. The number of representatives shall not exceed one for every thirty thousand, but each State shall have at least one representative; and until such enumeration shall be made, the State of New Hampshire shall be entitled to choose three, Massachusetts eight, Rhode Island and Providence Plantations one, Connecticut five, New York six, New Jersey four, Pennsylvania eight, Delaware one, Maryland six, Virginia ten, North Carolina five, South Carolina five, and Georgia three.

4   When vacancies happen in the representation from any State, the executive authority thereof shall issue writs of election to fill such vacancies.

5   The House of Representatives shall choose their speaker and other officers; and shall have the sole power of impeachment.

Section 3

1   The Senate of the United States shall be composed of two senators from each state, chosen by the legislature thereof,[3] for six years; and each senator shall have one vote.

2   Immediately after they shall be assembled in consequence of the first election, they shall be divided as equally as may be into three classes. The seats of the senators of the first class shall be vacated at the expiration of the second year, of the second class at the expiration of the fourth year, and of the third class at the expiration of the sixth year, so that one-third may be chosen every second year; and if vacancies happen by resignation, or otherwise, during the recess of the legislature of any State, the executive thereof may make temporary appointments until the next meeting of the legislature, which shall then fill such vacancies.[4]

3   No person shall be a senator who shall not have attained to the age of thirty years, and been nine years a citizen of the United States, and who shall not when elected, be an inhabitant of that State for which he shall be chosen.

4   The Vice-President of the United States shall be President of the Senate, but shall have no vote, unless they be equally divided.

5   The Senate shall choose their other officers, and also a President pro tempore, in the absence of the Vice President, or when he shall exercise the office of President of the United States.

6   The Senate shall have the sole power to try all impeachments. When sitting for that purpose, they shall be on oath or affirmation. When the President of the United States is tried, the chief justice shall preside: and no person shall be convicted without the concurrence of two-thirds of the members present.

7   Judgement in cases of impeachment shall not extend further than to removal from office, and disqualifications to hold and enjoy any office of honor, trust or profit under the United States: but the party convicted shall nevertheless be liable and subject to indictment, trial, judgement and punishment, according to law.

Section 4

1   The times, places, and manner of holding elections for senators and representatives, shall be prescribed in each State by the legislature thereof; but the Congress may at any time by law make or alter such regulations, except as to the places of choosing senators.
2   The Congress shall assemble at least once in every year, and such meeting shall be on the first Monday in December, unless they shall by law appoint a different day.

Section 5

1   Each House shall be the judge of the elections, returns and qualifications of its own members and the majority of each shall constitute a quorum to do business; but a smaller number may adjourn from day to day, and may be authorized to compel the attendance of absent members, in such manner and under such penalties as each House may provide.
2   Each House may determine the rule of its proceedings, punish its members for disorderly behavior, and, with the concurrence of two-thirds, expel a member.
3   Each House shall keep a journal of its proceedings, and from time to time publish the same, excepting such parts as may in their judgment require secrecy; and the yeas and nays of the numbers of either House on any question shall, at the desire of one fifth of those present, be entered on the journal.
4   Neither House, during the session of Congress, shall, without the consent of the other, adjourn for more than three days, nor to any other place than that in which the two Houses shall be sitting.

Section 6

1   The senators and representatives shall receive a compensation for their services, to be ascertained by law and paid out of the Treasure of the United States. They shall in all cases, except treason, felony and breach of the peace, be privileged from arrest during their attendance at the session of their respective Houses, and in going to and returning from the same; and for any speech or debate in either House, they shall not be questioned in any other place.
2   No senator or representative shall, during the time for which he was elected, be appointed to any civil office under the authority of the United States, which shall have been created, or the emoluments whereof shall have been increased during such time, and no person holding any office under the United States shall be a member of either House during his continuance in office.

Section 7

1   All bills for raising revenue shall originate in the House of Representatives; but the Senate may propose or concur with amendments as on other bills.

2   Every bill shall have passed the House of Representatives and the Senate, shall, before it become a law, be presented to the President of the United States; if he approve he shall sign it, but if not he shall return it with his objections to that House in which it shall have originated, who shall enter the objections at large on their journal, and proceed to reconsider it. If after such reconsideration two-thirds of that House shall agree to pass the bill, it shall be sent, together with the objections, to the other House, by which it shall likewise be reconsidered, and if approved by two-thirds of that House, it shall become a law. But in all such cases the votes of both Houses shall be determined by yeas and nays, and the names of the persons voting for and against the bill shall be entered on the journal of each House respectively. If any bill shall not be returned by the President within ten days (Sundays excepted) after it shall have been presented to him, the same shall be a law, in like manner as if he had signed it, unless the Congress by their adjournment prevent its return, in which case it shall not be a law.

3   Every order, resolution, or vote to which the concurrence of the Senate and House of Representatives may be necessary (except on a question of adjournment) shall be presented to the President of the United States; and before the same shall take effect, shall be approved by him, or being disapproved by him, shall be repassed by two-thirds of the Senate and House of Representatives, according to the rules and limitations prescribed in the case of a bill.

Section 8

1   The Congress shall have the power to lay and collect taxes, duties, imposts, and excises, to pay the debts and provide for the common defense and general welfare of the United States; but all duties, imposts, and excises shall be uniform through the United States;

2   To borrow money on the credit of the United States;

3   To regulate commerce with foreign nations, and among the several States, and with the Indian tribes;

4   To establish an uniform rule of naturalization, and uniform laws on the subject of bankruptcies through the United States;

5   To coin money, regulate the value thereof, and of foreign coin, and fix the standard of weights and measures;

6   To provide for the punishment of counterfeiting the securities and current coin of the United States;

7   To establish post offices and post roads;

8   To promote the progress of science and useful arts, by securing for limited times to authors and inventors the exclusive right to their respective writings and discoveries;

9   To constitute tribunals inferior to the Supreme Court;

10 To define and punish piracies and felonies committed on the high seas, and offenses against the laws of nations;

11 To declare war, grant letters of marque and reprisal, and make rules concerning captures on land and water;

12 To raise and support armies, but no appropriation of money to that use shall be for a longer term than two years;

13 To provide and maintain a navy;

14 To make rules for the government and regulation of the land and naval forces;

15 To provide for calling forth the militia to execute the laws of the Union, suppress insurrections and repel invasions;

16 To provide for organizing, arming, and disciplining the militia, and for governing such part of them as may be employed in the service of the United States, reserving to the States respectively the appointment of the officers, and the authority of training the militia according to the discipline prescribed by Congress;

17 To exercise exclusive legislation in all cases whatsoever, over such district (not exceeding ten miles square) as may, by cession of particular States, and the acceptance of Congress, become the seat of the government of the United States, and to exercise like authority over all places purchased by the consent of the legislature of the State in which the same shall be, for the erection of forts, magazines, dockyards, and other needful buildings; and

18 To make all laws which shall be necessary and proper for carrying into execution the foregoing powers, and all other powers vested by this Constitution in the government of the United States or in any department or officer thereof.

Section 9

1 The migration or importation of such persons as any of the States now existing shall think proper to admit, shall not be prohibited by the Congress prior to the year one thousand eight hundred and eight, but a tax or duty may be imposed on such importation, not exceeding ten dollars for each person.

2 The privilege of the writ of *habeas corpus* shall not be suspended, unless when in cases of rebellion or invasion the public safety may require it.

3 No bill of attainder or *ex post facto* law shall be passed.

4 No capitation, or other direct, tax shall be laid, unless in proportion to the census or enumeration hereinbefore directed to be taken.[5]

5 No tax or duty shall be laid on articles exported from any State.

6 No preference shall be given by any regulation of commerce or revenue to the ports of one State over those of another: nor shall vessels bound to, or from, one State be obliged to enter, clear, or pay duties in another.

7 No money shall be drawn from the treasury, but in consequence of appropriations, made by law; and a regular statement and account of the receipts and expenditures of all public money shall be published from time to time.

8 No title of nobility shall be granted by the United States: and no person holding any office or profit or trust under them, shall, without the consent of the Congress, accept of any present, emolument, office, or title, of any kind whatever, from any king, prince or foreign State.

Section 10

1 No State shall enter into any treaty, alliance, or confederation; grant letters of marque and reprisal; coin money, emit bills of credit; make anything but gold and silver coin a tender in payment of debts; pass any bill of attainder, *ex post facto* law, or law impairing the obligation of contracts, or grant any title of nobility.

2 No State shall, without the consent of the Congress, lay any imposts, or duties on imports or exports, except what may be absolutely necessary for executing its inspection laws: and the net produce of all duties and imposts laid by any State on imports or exports, shall be of the use of the treasury of the United States; and all such laws shall be subject to the revision and Control of the Congress.

3 No State shall, without the consent of Congress, lay any duty of tonnage, keep troops, or ships of war in time of peace, enter into any agreement or compact with another State, or with a foreign power, or engage in war, unless actually invaded, or in such imminent danger as will not admit of delay.

ARTICLE 2 [THE EXECUTIVE]

Section 1

1 The executive power shall be vested in a President of the United States of America. He shall hold his office during the term of four years, and, together with the Vice-President, chosen for the same term, be elected as follows.[6]

2 Each State shall appoint, in such manner as the legislature thereof may direct, a number of electors, equal to the whole number of senators and representatives to which the State may be entitled in the Congress: but no senator or representative, or person holding an office of trust or profit under the United States, shall be appointed an elector.

   The electors shall meet in their respective States, and vote by ballot for two persons, of whom one at least shall not be an inhabitant of the same State with themselves. And they shall make a list of all the persons voted for, and of the number of votes for each; which list they shall sign and certify, and transmit sealed to the seat of the government of the United States, directed to the president of the Senate. The president of the Senate shall, in the presence of the Senate and House of Representatives, open all certificates, and the votes shall then be counted. The person having the greatest number of votes shall be the President, if such a number be a majority of the whole number of electors appointed; and if there be more than one who have such majority, and have an equal number of votes, then the House of Representatives shall immediately choose by ballot one of them for President; and if no person have a majority, then from the five highest on the list the said House shall in like manner choose the President. But in choosing the President, the votes shall be taken by States, the representation from each State having one vote; a quorum for this purpose shall consist of a member or members from two-thirds of the States, and a majority of all the States shall be necessary to a choice. In every case, after the choice of the President, the person having the greatest number of votes of the electors shall be the Vice-President. But if there should remain two or more who have equal votes, the Senate shall choose from them by ballot the Vice-President.[7]

3   The Congress may determine the time of choosing the electors, and the day on which they shall give their votes; which day shall be the same throughout the United States.

4   No person except a natural born citizen, or a citizen of the United States, at the time of the adoption of this Constitution, shall be eligible to the office of President; neither shall any person be eligible to that office who shall not have attained to the age of thirty-five years, and been fourteen years a resident within the United States.

5   In case of the removal of the President from office, or of his death, resignation, or inability to discharge the powers and duties of the said office, the same shall devolve on the Vice-President, and the Congress may by law provide for the case of removal, death, resignation, or inability, both of the President and Vice-President, declaring what officer shall then act as President, and such officer shall act accordingly, until the disability be removed, or a President shall be elected.[8]

6   The President shall, at stated times, receive for his services a compensation, which shall neither be increased nor diminished during the period for which he shall have been elected, and he shall not receive within that period any other emolument from the United States, or any of them.

7   Before he enter on the execution of his office, he shall take the following oath or affirmation: 'I do solemnly swear (or affirm) that I will faithfully execute the office of the President of the United States, and will to the best of my ability, preserve, protect and defend the Constitution of the United States.'

Section 2

1   The President shall be commander in chief of the army and navy of the United States, and of the militia of the several States, when called into the actual service of the United States; he may require the opinion, in writing, of the principal officer in each of the executive departments, upon any subject relating to the duties of their respective offices, and he shall have power to grant reprieves and pardons for offences against the United States, except in cases of impeachment.

2   He shall have power, by and with the advice and consent of the Senate, to make treaties, provided two-thirds of the senators present concur; and he shall nominate, and by and with the advice and consent of the Senate, shall appoint ambassadors, other public ministers and consuls, judges of the Supreme Court, and all other officers of the United States, whose appointments are not herein otherwise provided for, and which shall be established by law; but the Congress may by law vest the appointment of such inferior officers, as they think proper, in the President alone, in the courts of law, or in the heads of departments.

3   The President shall have power to fill up all vacancies that may happen during the recess of the Senate, by granting commissions which shall expire at the end of their next session.

Section 3

1   He shall from time to time give to the Congress information of the state of the Union, and recommend to their consideration such measures as he shall judge necessary and expedient; he may, on extraordinary occasions, convene both Houses, or either of them, and in case of disagreement between them with respect to the time of adjournment, he may adjourn them to such time as he shall think proper; he shall receive ambassadors and other public ministers; he shall take care that the laws be faithfully executed, and shall commission all the officers of the United States.

Section 4

The President, Vice-President, and all civil officers of the United States, shall be removed from office on impeachment for, and conviction of, treason, bribery, or other high crimes and misdemeanors.

ARTICLE 3 [THE JUDICIARY]

Section 1

1   The Judicial power of the United States shall be vested in one Supreme Court, and in such inferior courts as the Congress may from time to time ordain and establish. The judges, both of the Supreme and inferior courts, shall hold their offices during good behavior, and shall, at stated times, receive for their services, a compensation, which shall not be diminished during their continuance in office.

Section 2

1   The Judicial power shall extend to all cases, in law and equity, arising under this Constitution, the laws of the United States, and treaties made, or which shall be made, under their authority; to all cases affecting ambassadors, other public ministers and consuls; to all cases of admiralty and maritime jurisdiction; to controversies to which the United States shall be a party; to controversies between two or more States; between a state and citizens of another State,[9] between citizens of different States, between citizens of the same State claiming lands under grants of different States, and between a State, or the citizens thereof, and foreign States, citizens or subjects.
2   In all cases affecting ambassadors, other public ministers and consuls, and those in which a State shall be party, the Supreme Court shall have original jurisdiction. In all the other cases before mentioned, the Supreme Court shall have appellate jurisdiction, both as to law and to fact, with such exceptions, and under such regulations as the Congress shall make.

3   The trial of all crimes, except in cases of impeachment, shall be by jury; and such trial shall be held in the State where the said crimes shall have been committed; but when not committed within any State, the trial shall be held at such place or places as the Congress may by law have directed.

Section 3

1   Treason against the United States shall consist only in levying war against them, or in adhering to their enemies, giving them aid and comfort. No person shall be convicted of treason unless on the testimony of two witnesses to the same overt act, or on confession in open court.
2   The Congress shall have power to declare the punishment of treason, but no attainder of treason shall work corruption of blood, or forfeiture except during the life of the person attained.

ARTICLE 4 [INTERSTATE RELATIONS]

Section 1

Full faith and credit shall be given in each State to the public acts, records, and judicial proceedings of every other State. And the Congress may by general laws prescribe the manner in which acts, records and proceedings shall be proved, and the effect thereof.

Section 2

1   The citizens of each State shall be entitled to all privileges and immunities of citizens in the several States.
2   A person charged in any State with treason, felony, or other crime, who shall flee from justice, and be found in another State, shall on demand of the executive authority of the State from which he fled, be delivered up, to be removed to the State having jurisdiction of the crime.
3   No person held to service or labor in one State under the laws thereof, escaping into another, shall, in consequence of any law or regulation therein, be discharged from such service or labor, but shall be delivered up on claim of the party to whom such service or labor may be due.

Section 3

1   New States may be admitted by the Congress into this Union; but no new State shall be formed or erected within the jurisdiction of any other State; nor any State be formed by the junction of two or more States, or parts of States, without the consent of the legislatures of the States concerned as well as of the Congress.

2   The Congress shall have power to dispose of and make all needful rules and regulations respecting the territory or other property belonging to the United States; and nothing in this Constitution shall be so construed as to prejudice any claims of the United States, or of any particular State.

Section 4

The United States shall guarantee to every State in this Union a republican form of government, and shall protect each of them against invasion; and on application of the legislature, or of the executive (when the legislature cannot be convened) against domestic violence.

ARTICLE 5 [AMENDMENT PROCESS]

The Congress, whenever two-thirds of both Houses shall deem it necessary, shall propose amendments to this Constitution, or, on the application of the legislature of two-thirds of the several States, shall call a convention for proposing amendments, which, in either case, shall be valid to all intents and purposes, as part of this Constitution when ratified by the legislatures of three-fourths of the several States, or by conventions in three-fourths thereof, as the one or the other mode of ratification may be proposed by the Congress; Provided that no amendment which may be made prior to the year one thousand eight hundred and eight shall in any manner affect the first and fourth clauses in the ninth section of the first article; and that no State, without its consent, shall be deprived of its equal suffrage in the Senate.

ARTICLE 6 [DEBTS, SUPREMACY]

1   All debts contracted, and engagements entered into, before the adoption of this Constitution, shall be as valid against the United States under this Constitution, as under the Confederation.
2   This Constitution, and the laws of the United States which shall be made in pursuance thereof; and all treaties made, or which shall be made, under the authority of the United States, shall be the supreme law of the land; and the Judges in every State shall be bound thereby, anything in the Constitution or laws of any State to the contrary notwithstanding.
3   The senators and representatives before mentioned, and the members of the several State legislatures, and all executive and judicial officers, both of the United States and of the several States, shall be bound by oath or affirmation to support this Constitution; but no religious test shall ever be required as a qualification to any office or public trust under the United States.

ARTICLE 7 [RATIFICATION]

The ratification of the conventions of nine States shall be sufficient for the establishment of this Constitution between the States so ratifying the same.

Done in Convention by the unanimous consent of the States present the seventeenth day of September in the year of our Lord one thousand seven hundred and eighty-seven, and of the independence of the United States of America the twelfth. In witness whereof we have hereunto subscribed our names.

[Names omitted] ARTICLES IN ADDITION TO, AND AMENDMENT OF, THE CONSTITUTION OF THE UNITED STATES OF AMERICA, PROPOSED BY CONGRESS, AND RATIFIED BY THE LEGISLATURES OF THE SEVERAL STATES, PURSUANT TO THE FIFTH ARTICLE OF THE ORIGINAL CONSTITUTION.˙

[The first 10 Amendments were ratified 15 December 1791, and form what is known as the 'Bill of Rights']

AMENDMENT 1 [FREEDOM OF RELIGION, SPEECH, ASSEMBLY, PETITION]

Congress shall make no law respecting an establishment of religion, or prohibiting the free exercise thereof; or abridging the freedom of speech, or of the press; or the right of the people peaceably to assemble, and to petition the Government for a redress of grievances.

AMENDMENT 2 [RIGHT TO BEAR ARMS]

A well regulated Militia, being necessary to the security of a free State, the right of the people to keep and bear Arms, shall not be infringed.

AMENDMENT 3 [QUARTERING OF SOLDIERS]

No Soldier shall, in time of peace be quartered in any house, without the consent of the Owner, nor in time of war, but in a manner to be prescribed by law.

AMENDMENT 4 [SEARCH AND SEIZURE]

The right of the people to be secure in their persons, houses, papers, and effects, against unreasonable searches and seizures, shall not be violated, and no warrants shall issue, but upon probable cause, supported by Oath or affirmation, and particularly describing the place to be searched, and the persons or things to be seized.

AMENDMENT 5 [CRIMINAL PROCEDURAL RIGHTS]

No person shall be held to answer for a capital, or otherwise infamous crime, unless on a presentment or indictment of a Grand Jury, except in cases arising in the land or naval forces, or in the Militia, when in actual service in time of War or public danger; nor shall

---

* Amendment 21 was not ratified by state legislatures, but by state conventions summoned by Congress.

any person be subject for the same offence to be twice put in jeopardy of life or limb; nor shall be compelled in any criminal case to be a witness against himself, nor be deprived of life, liberty, or property, without due process of law, nor shall private property be taken for public use, without just compensation.

AMENDMENT 6 [CRIMINAL COURT PROCEDURES]

In all criminal prosecutions, the accused shall enjoy the right to a speedy and public trial, by an impartial jury of the State and district wherein the crime shall have been committed, which district shall have been previously ascertained by law, and to be informed of the nature and cause of the accusation; to be confronted with the witness against him; to have compulsory process for obtaining witnesses in his favor, and to have the Assistance of Counsel for his defence.

AMENDMENT 7 [TRIAL BY JURY IN COMMON LAW CASES]

In suits at common law, where the value in controversy shall exceed twenty dollars, the right of trial by jury shall be preserved, and no fact tried by a jury, shall be otherwise re-examined in any Court of the United States, than according to the rules of the common law.

AMENDMENT 8 [BAILS, FINES AND PUNISHMENT]

Excessive bail shall not be required, nor excessive fines imposed, nor cruel and unusual punishments inflicted.

AMENDMENT 9 [RIGHTS RETAINED BY THE PEOPLE]

The enumeration in the Constitution of certain rights, shall not be construed to deny or disparage others retained by the people.

AMENDMENT 10 [RIGHTS RESERVED TO THE STATES]

The powers not delegated to the United States by the Constitution, nor prohibited by it to the States, are reserved to the States respectively, or to the people.

AMENDMENT 11 [SUITS AGAINST THE STATES]

[Ratified 7 February 1795]

The judicial power of the United States shall not be construed to extend to any suit in law or equity, commenced or prosecuted against one of the United States by Citizens of another State, or by Citizens or Subjects of any Foreign State.

AMENDMENT 12 [ELECTION OF PRESIDENT AND VICE-PRESIDENT]

[Ratified 27 July 1804]

The Electors shall meet in their respective states and vote by ballot for President and Vice-President, one of whom at least, shall not be an inhabitant of the same State with themselves; they shall name in their ballots the person voted for a President, and in distinct ballots the person voted for as Vice-President, and they shall make distinct lists of all persons voted for as President, and of all persons voted for as Vice-President, and of the number of votes for each, which lists they shall sign and certify, and transmit sealed to the seat of the government of the United States, directed to the President of the Senate; The President of the Senate shall, in presence of the Senate and House of Representatives, open all the certificates and the votes shall then be counted; The person having the greatest number of votes for President, shall be the President if such number be a majority of the whole number of Electors, appointed; and if no person having such majority, then from the persons having the highest numbers not exceeding three of the list of those voted for as President, the House of Representatives shall choose immediately, by ballot, the President. But in choosing the President, the votes shall be taken by States, the representation from each state having one vote; a quorum for this purpose shall consist of a member or members from two-thirds of the States, and a majority of all the States shall be necessary to a choice. (And if the House of Representatives shall not choose a President whenever the right of choice shall devolve upon them, before the fourth day of March next following, then the Vice-President shall act as President, as in the case of the death or other constitutional disability of the President.)* The person having the greatest number of votes as Vice-President, shall be the Vice-President, if such number be a majority of the whole number of Electors appointed, and if no person have a majority, then from the two highest numbers on the list, the Senate shall choose the Vice-President; a quorum for the purpose shall consist of two-thirds of the whole number of Senators, and a majority of the whole number shall be necessary to a choice. But no person constitutionally ineligible to the office of President shall be eligible to that of Vice-President of the United States.

AMENDMENT 13 [ABOLITION OF SLAVERY]

[Ratified 6 December 1865]

Section 1

Neither slavery nor involuntary servitude, except as a punishment for crime whereof the party shall have been duly convicted, shall exist within the United States, or any place subject to their jurisdiction.

Section 2

Congress shall have power to enforce this article by appropriate legislation.

* Superseded by Section 3 of the Twentieth Amendment.

AMENDMENT 14 [CITIZENSHIP, DUE PROCESS, EQUAL PROTECTION]

[Ratified 9 July 1868]

Section 1

All persons born or naturalized in the United States, and subject to the jurisdiction thereof, are citizens of the United States and of the State wherein they reside. No State shall make or enforce any law which shall abridge the privileges or immunities of citizens of the United States; nor shall any State deprive any person of life, liberty, or property, without due process of law; nor deny to any person within its jurisdiction the equal protection of the laws.

Section 2

Representatives shall be apportioned among the several States according to their respective numbers, counting the whole number of persons in each State, excluding Indians not taxed. But when the right to vote at any election for the choice of electors for President and Vice-President of the United States, Representatives in Congress, the Executive and Judicial officers of the State, or the members of the Legislature thereof, is denied to any of the male inhabitants of such State, being twenty-one years of age,* and citizens of the United States, or in any way abridged, except for participation in rebellion, or other crime, the basis of representation therein shall be reduced in the proportion which the number of such male citizens shall bear to the whole number of male citizens twenty-one years of age in such State.

Section 3

No person shall be a Senator or Representative in Congress, or elector of President and Vice-President, or hold any office, civil or military, under the United States, or under any State, who, having previously taken an oath, as a member of Congress, or as an officer of the United States, or as a member of any State legislature, or as an executive or judicial officer of any State, to support the Constitution of the United States shall have engaged in insurrection or rebellion against the same, or given aid or comfort to the enemies thereof. But Congress may by a vote of two-thirds of each House, remove such disability.

Section 4

The validity of the public debt of the United States, authorized by law, including debts incurred for payment of pensions and bounties for services in suppressing insurrection or

* Changed by Section 1 of the Twenty-sixth Amendment.

rebellion against the United States, or any claim for the loss or emancipation of any slave; but all such debts, obligations and claims shall be held illegal and void.

Section 5

The Congress shall have power to enforce, by appropriate legislation, the provisions of this article.

AMENDMENT 15 [THE RIGHT TO VOTE]

[Ratified 3 February 1870]

Section 1

The right of citizens of the United States to vote shall not be denied or abridged by the United States or by any State on account of race, color, or previous condition of servitude.

Section 2

The Congress shall have power to enforce this article by appropriate legislation.

AMENDMENT 16 [INCOME TAX]

[Ratified 3 February 1913]

The Congress shall have power to lay and collect taxes on incomes, from whatever source derived, without apportionment among the several States, and without regard to any census or enumeration.

AMENDMENT 17 [DIRECT ELECTION OF SENATORS]

[Ratified 8 April 1913]

The Senate of the United States shall be composed of two Senators from each State, elected by the people thereof, for six years; and each Senator shall have one vote. The electors in each State shall have the qualifications requisite for electors of the most numerous branch of the State legislatures.

When vacancies happen in the representation of any State in the Senate, the executive authority of such State shall issue writs of election to fill such vacancies: Provided, That the legislature of any State may empower the executive thereof to make temporary appointments until the people fill the vacancies by election as the legislature may direct.

This amendment shall not be so construed as to affect the election or term of any Senator chosen before it becomes valid as part of the Constitution.

AMENDMENT 18 [INTRODUCTION OF PROHIBITION]

[Ratified 16 January 1919]

Section 1

After one year from the ratification of this article the manufacture, sale, or transportation of intoxicating liquors within, the importation thereof into, or the exportation thereof from the United States and all territory subject to the jurisdiction thereof for beverage purposes is hereby prohibited.

Section 2

The Congress and the several States shall have concurrent power to enforce this article by appropriate legislation.

Section 3

This article shall be inoperative unless it shall have been ratified as an amendment to the Constitution by the legislatures of the several States as provided in the Constitution, within seven years from the date of the submission hereof to the States by the Congress.*

AMENDMENT 19 [WOMEN'S RIGHT TO VOTE]

[Ratified 18 August 1920]
    The right of citizens of the United States to vote shall not be denied or abridged by the United States or by any State on account of sex.
    Congress shall have power to enforce this article by appropriate legislation.

AMENDMENT 20 [TERMS OF OFFICE, CONVENING OF CONGRESS AND SUCCESSION]

[Ratified 23 January 1933]

Section 1

The terms of the President and Vice-President shall end at noon on the 20th day of January, and the terms of Senators and Representatives at noon on the 3rd day of January, of the

* Repealed by Section 1 of the Twenty-first Amendment.

years in which such terms would have ended if this article had not been ratified; and the terms of their successors shall then begin.

Section 2

The Congress shall assemble at least once in every year, and such meeting shall begin at noon on the 3rd day of January, unless they shall by law appoint a different day.

Section 3

If, at the time fixed for the beginning of the term of the President, the President elect shall have died, the Vice-President elect shall become President. If a President shall not have been chosen before the time fixed for the beginning of his term, or if the President elect shall have failed to qualify, then the Vice-President elect shall act as President until a President shall have qualified; and the Congress may by law provide for the case wherein neither a President elect nor a Vice-President elect shall have qualified, declaring who shall then act as President, or the manner in which one who is to act shall be selected, and such person shall act accordingly until a President or Vice-President shall have qualified.

Section 4

The Congress may by law provide for the case of the death of any of the persons from whom the House of Representatives may choose a President whenever the right of choice shall have devolved upon them, and for the case of the death of any of the persons from whom the Senate may choose a Vice-President whenever the right of choice shall have devolved upon them.

Section 5

Sections 1 and 2 shall take effect on the 15th day of October following the ratification of this article.

Section 6

This article shall be inoperative unless it shall have been ratified as an amendment to the Constitution by the legislatures of three-fourths of the several States within seven years from the date of its submission.

AMENDMENT 21 [REPEAL OF PROHIBITION]

[Ratified 5 December 1933]

Section 1

The Eighteenth Article of Amendment to the Constitution of the United States is hereby repealed.

Section 2

The transportation or importation into any State, Territory, or possession of the United States for delivery or use therein of intoxicating liquors, in violation of the laws thereof, is hereby prohibited.

Section 3

This article shall be inoperative unless it shall have been ratified as an amendment to the Constitution by conventions in the several States, as provided in the Constitution, within seven years from the date of the submission hereof to the States by the Congress.

AMENDMENT 22 [LIMITATION OF PRESIDENTIAL TERMS]

[Ratified 27 February 1951]

Section 1

No person shall be elected to the office of the President more than twice, and no person who has held the office of President, or acted as President, for more than two years of a term to which some other person was elected President shall be elected to the office of the President more than once. But this Article shall not apply to any person holding the office of President when this Article was proposed by the Congress, and shall not prevent any person who may be holding the office of President, or acting as President, during the term within which this Article becomes operative from holding the office of President or acting as President during the remainder of such term.

Section 2

This article shall be inoperative unless it shall have been ratified as an amendment to the Constitution by the legislatures of three-fourths of the several States within seven years from the date of its submission to the States by the Congress.

AMENDMENT 23 [PRESIDENTIAL ELECTIONS FOR THE DISTRICT OF COLUMBIA]

[Ratified 29 March 1961]

Section 1

The District constituting the seat of Government of the United States shall appoint in such manner as the Congress may direct:

A number of electors of President and Vice-President equal to the whole number of Senators and Representatives in Congress to which the District would be entitled if it were a State, but in no event more than the least populous State; they shall be in addition to those appointed by the States, but they shall be considered, for the purposes of the election of President and Vice-President, to be electors appointed by a State; and they shall meet in the District and perform such duties as provided by the Twelfth Article of Amendment.

Section 2

The Congress shall have power to enforce this article by appropriate legislation.

AMENDMENT 24 [POLL TAX ABOLISHED]

[Ratified 23 January 1964]

Section 1

The right of citizens of the United States to vote in any primary or other election for President or Vice-President, for electors for President or Vice-President, for Senator or Representative in Congress, shall not be denied or abridged by the United States or any State by reason of failure to pay any poll tax or other tax.

Section 2

The Congress shall have power to enforce this article by appropriate legislation.

AMENDMENT 25 [PRESIDENTIAL DISABILITY AND VICE-PRESIDENTIAL VACANCIES]

[Ratified 10 February 1967]

Section 1

In case of the removal of the President from office or of his death or resignation, the Vice-President shall become President.

Section 2

Whenever there is a vacancy in the office of the Vice-President, the President shall nominate a Vice-President who shall take office upon confirmation by a majority of both Houses of Congress.

Section 3

Whenever the President transmits to the President *pro tempore* of the Senate and the Speaker of the House of Representatives his written declaration that he is unable to discharge the powers and duties of his office, and until he transmits to them a written declaration to the contrary, such powers and duties shall be discharged by the Vice-President as Acting President.

Section 4

Whenever the Vice-President and a majority of either the principal officers of the executive departments or of such other body as Congress may by law provide, transmit to the President *pro tempore* of the Senate and the Speaker of the House of Representatives their written declaration the President is unable to discharge the powers and duties of his office, the Vice-President shall immediately assume the powers and duties of the office as Acting President.

Thereafter, when the President transmits to the Present *pro tempore* of the Senate and the Speaker of the House of Representatives his written declaration that no inability exists, he shall resume the powers and duties of his office unless the Vice-President and the majority of either the principal officers of the executive department or of such other body as Congress may by law provide, transmit within four days to the President *pro tempore* of the Senate and the Speaker of the House of Representatives their written declaration that the President is unable to discharge the powers and duties of his office. Thereupon Congress shall decide the issue, assembling within forty-eight hours for that purpose if not in session. If the Congress, within twenty-one days after receipt of the latter written declaration, or, if Congress is not in session, within twenty-one days after Congress is required to assemble, determines by two-thirds vote of both Houses that the President is unable to discharge the powers and duties of his office, the Vice-President shall continue to discharge the same as Acting President; otherwise, the President shall resume the powers and duties of his office.

AMENDMENT 26 [VOTE FOR 18-YEAR-OLDS]

[Ratified 1 July 1971]

Section 1

The right of citizens of the United States, who are eighteen years of age or older, to vote shall not be denied or abridged by the United States or by any State on account of age.

Section 2

The Congress shall have power to enforce this article by appropriate legislation.

AMENDMENT 27

[Ratified 18 May 1992]
No law varying the compensation for the services of the Senators and Representatives shall take effect, until an election of Representatives shall have intervened.

Notes

1   See the Sixteenth Amendment.
2   Partly superseded by the Fourteenth Amendment.
3   See the Seventeenth Amendment.
4   See the Seventeenth Amendment.
5   See the Sixteenth Amendment.
6   See the Twenty-second Amendment.
7   Superseded by the Twelfth Amendment.
8   See the Twentieth Amendment and the Twenty-fifth Amendment.
9   See the Eleventh Amendment.

INDEX

American Politics and Society, Ninth Edition. David McKay.
© 2018 John Wiley & Sons Ltd. Published 2018 by John Wiley & Sons Ltd.